THE NEW
AMERICAN
COMMENTARY

An Exegetical and Theological
Exposition of Holy Scripture

THE NEW AMERICAN COMMENTARY

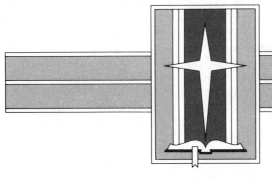

Volume
7

1, 2 SAMUEL

Robert D. Bergen

BROADMAN
&HOLMAN
PUBLISHERS

© Copyright 1996 • Broadman & Holman Publishers
All rights reserved
ISBN: 978-08054-0107-3
Dewey Decimal Classification: 222.4
Subject Heading: BIBLE. O.T. 1, 2 SAMUEL
Library of Congress Catalog Number: 96–41891
Printed in the United States of America
15 14 13 12 11 10 09   15 14 13 12 11 10 9

Library of Congress Cataloging-in-Publication Data

Bergen, Robert D.
    1, 2 Samuel / Robert D. Bergen.
      p. cm. — (The new American commentary ; v. 7)
    Includes bibliographical references and indexes.
    ISBN 0–8054–0107–5 (hardback)
    1. Bible. O.T. Samuel—Commentaries.   I. Title. II. Series.
BS1325.3.B47   1996
222'.4077—dc20

To Martha and Wesley

God's Gift of Family in My Life

Editors' Preface

God's Word does not change. God's world, however, changes in every generation. These changes, in addition to new findings by scholars and a new variety of challenges to the gospel message, call for the church in each generation to interpret and apply God's Word for God's people. Thus, THE NEW AMERICAN COMMENTARY is introduced to bridge the twentieth and twenty-first centuries. This new series has been designed primarily to enable pastors, teachers, and students to read the Bible with clarity and proclaim it with power.

In one sense THE NEW AMERICAN COMMENTARY is not new, for it represents the continuation of a heritage rich in biblical and theological exposition. The title of this forty-volume set points to the continuity of this series with an important commentary project published at the end of the nineteenth century called AN AMERICAN COMMENTARY, edited by Alvah Hovey. The older series included, among other significant contributions, the outstanding volume on Matthew by John A. Broadus, from whom the publisher of the new series, Broadman Press, partly derives its name. The former series was authored and edited by scholars committed to the infallibility of Scripture, making it a solid foundation for the present project. In line with this heritage, all NAC authors affirm the divine inspiration, inerrancy, complete truthfulness, and full authority of the Bible. The perspective of the NAC is unapologetically confessional and rooted in the evangelical tradition.

Since a commentary is a fundamental tool for the expositor or teacher who seeks to interpret and apply Scripture in the church or classroom, the NAC focuses on communicating the theological structure and content of each biblical book. The writers seek to illuminate both the historical meaning and contemporary significance of Holy Scripture.

In its attempt to make a unique contribution to the Christian community, the NAC focuses on two concerns. First, the commentary emphasizes how each section of a book fits together so that the reader becomes aware of the theological unity of each book and of Scripture as a whole. The writers, however, remain aware of the Bible's inherently rich variety. Second, the NAC is produced with the conviction that the Bible primarily belongs to the church. We believe that scholarship and the academy provide an indispensable foundation for biblical understanding and the service of Christ, but the editors and authors of this series have attempted to communicate the findings of their research in a manner that will build up the whole body of Christ. Thus, the commentary concentrates on theological exegesis while providing practical, applicable exposition.

THE NEW AMERICAN COMMENTARY's theological focus enables the reader to see the parts as well as the whole of Scripture. The biblical books vary in content, context, literary type, and style. In addition to this rich variety, the editors and authors recognize that the doctrinal emphasis and use of the biblical books differs in various places, contexts, and cultures among God's people. These factors, as well as other concerns, have led the editors to give freedom to the writers to wrestle with the issues raised by the scholarly community surrounding each book and to determine the appropriate shape and length of the introductory materials. Moreover, each writer has developed the structure of the commentary in a way best suited for expounding the basic structure and the meaning of the biblical books for our day. Generally, discussions relating to contemporary scholarship and technical points of grammar and syntax appear in the footnotes and not in the text of the commentary. This format allows pastors and interested laypersons, scholars and teachers, and serious college and seminary students to profit from the commentary at various levels. This approach has been employed because we believe that all Christians have the privilege and responsibility to read and seek to understand the Bible for themselves.

Consistent with the desire to produce a readable, up-to-date commentary, the editors selected the *New International Version* as the standard translation for the commentary series. The selection was made primarily because of the NIV's faithfulness to the original languages and its beautiful and readable style. The authors, however, have been given the liberty to differ at places from the NIV as they develop their own translations from the Greek and Hebrew texts.

The NAC reflects the vision and leadership of those who provide oversight for Broadman Press, who in 1987 called for a new commentary series that would evidence a commitment to the inerrancy of Scripture and a faithfulness to the classic Christian tradition. While the commentary adopts an "American" name, it should be noted some writers represent countries outside the United States, giving the commentary an international perspective. The diverse group of writers includes scholars, teachers, and administrators from almost twenty different colleges and seminaries, as well as pastors, missionaries, and a layperson.

The editors and writers hope that THE NEW AMERICAN COMMEN-

TARY will be helpful and instructive for pastors and teachers, scholars and students, for men and women in the churches who study and teach God's Word in various settings. We trust that for editors, authors, and readers alike, the commentary will be used to build up the church, encourage obedience, and bring renewal to God's people. Above all, we pray that the NAC will bring glory and honor to our Lord who has graciously redeemed us and faithfully revealed himself to us in his Holy Word.

SOLI DEO GLORIA
The Editors

Author's Preface

Having been raised in a Christian home in which Bible reading and biblical discussions were an integral part of family life, I consider myself blessed to have been called of God into a ministry that builds on this precious part of my heritage. When in 1987 Broadman Press (now Broadman & Holman) presented me with the opportunity to extend my ministry through the writing of a commentary on one of the most significant portions of Old Testament narrative, I made the decision to accept without hesitation. Fulfilling the commitment, however, was harder than making it.

Many people provided encouragement to move forward with the task. Certainly the most meaningful and consistent help came from my wife, Martha. She prayed for me without ceasing and uncomplainingly gave me the hundreds of late-night blocks of time necessary to do the research and writing. This commentary exists today because of her unfailing, good-natured support.

If this commentary proves to be valuable to others, a significant measure of credit must go to the editorial staff of the New American Commentary. Their extensive and thoughtful interaction with my original draft provided invaluable suggestions that measurably improved the final product. I am also grateful for the competent assistance of Dr. Alan Buescher, who carefully checked the manuscript's many scriptural cross-references for accuracy.

My hope is that those who use this commentary will come away with a greater appreciation of 1, 2 Samuel as the accurate, trustworthy, and relevant Word of God—a Word that both builds upon the sturdy foundation of the Torah and itself is a foundation for understanding the work and significance of Jesus Christ the Messiah.

—Bob Bergen
Hannibal-LaGrange College
Hannibal, MO

Abbreviations

Bible Books

Gen	Isa	Luke
Exod	Jer	John
Lev	Lam	Acts
Num	Ezek	Rom
Deut	Dan	1, 2 Cor
Josh	Hos	Gal
Judg	Joel	Eph
Ruth	Amos	Phil
1, 2 Sam	Obad	Col
1, 2 Kgs	Jonah	1, 2 Thess
1, 2 Chr	Mic	1, 2 Tim
Ezra	Nah	Titus
Neh	Hab	Phlm
Esth	Zeph	Heb
Job	Hag	Jas
Ps (pl. Pss)	Zech	1, 2 Pet
Prov	Mal	1, 2, 3 John
Eccl	Matt	Jude
Song	Mark	Rev

Apocrypha

Add Esth	The Additions to the Book of Esther
Bar	Baruch
Bel	Bel and the Dragon
1,2 Esdr	1, 2 Esdras
4 Ezra	4 Ezra
Jdt	Judith
Ep Jer	Epistle of Jeremiah
1,2,3,4 Mac	1, 2, 3, 4 Maccabees
Pr Azar	Prayer of Azariah and the Song of the Three Jews
Pr Man	Prayer of Manasseh
Sir	Sirach, Ecclesiasticus
Sus	Susanna
Tob	Tobit
Wis	The Wisdom of Solomon

Commonly Used Sources

AB	Anchor Bible
ABD	*Anchor Bible Dictionary,* ed. D. N Freedman
AEL	M. Lichtheim, *Ancient Egyptian Literature*
Ag.Ap.	*Against Apion,* Josephus
AJSL	*American Journal of Semitic Languages and Literature*
Akk.	Akkadian
AnBib	Analecta Biblica
ANET	*Ancient Near Eastern Texts,* ed. J. B. Pritchard
Ant.	*Antiquities of the Jews, Josephus*
AOAT	Alter Orient und Altes Testament
AOS	American Oriental Society
AS	Assyriological Studies
AUSS	*Andrews University Seminary Studies*
AV	Authorized Version
BA	*Biblical Archaeologist*
BAGD	W. Bauer, W. F. Arndt, F. W. Gingrich, and F. W. Danker, *Greek-English Lexicon of the New Testament*
BARev	*Biblical Archaeology Review*
BASOR	*Bulletin of the American Schools of Oriental Research*
BDB	F. Brown, S. R. Driver, and C. A. Briggs, *Hebrew and English Lexicon of the Old Testament*
BHS	*Biblia hebraica stuttgartensia*
Bib	*Biblica*
BibOr	Biblica et orientalia
BibRev	*Bible Review*
BJRL	*Bulletin of the Johns Rylands University Library*
BJS	Brown Judaic Studies
BSac	*Bibliotheca Sacra*
b. Sanh.	Babylonian Talmud, *Sanhedrin*
b. Hag.	Babylonian Talmud, *Hagiga*
BSC	Bible Student Commentary
BST	Bible Speaks Today
BT	*The Bible Translator*
BZ	*Biblische Zeitschrift*
BZAW	Beihefte zur ZAW
CBC	Cambridge Bible Commentary
CBQ	*Catholic Biblical Quarterly*
CBQMS	Catholic Biblical Quarterly Monograph Series
CD	Cairo *Damascus Document*
CGTC	Cambridge Greek Testament Commentaries
CHAL	*Concise Hebrew and Aramaic Lexicon,* ed. W. L. Holladay
Comm.	J. Calvin, *Commentary on the First Book of Moses Called Genesis,* trans., rev. J. King
CSR	*Christian Scholar's Review*
CT	*Christianity Today*
CurTM	*Currents in Theology and Mission*
DSS	Dead Sea Scrolls
EBC	Expositor's Bible Commentary

Ebib	Etudes bibliques
EE	*Enuma Elish*
EGT	*The Expositor's Greek Testament*
EV(s)	English Version(s)
EvQ	*Evangelical Quarterly*
EvT	*Evangelische Theologie*
ExpTim	*Expository Times*
FOTL	Forms of Old Testament Literature
Gen. Rab.	*Genesis Rabbah,* ed. J. Neusner
Gk.	Greek
GKC	*Gesenius's Hebrew Grammar,* ed. E. Kautzsch, trans. A. E. Cowley
GNB	Good News Bible
GTJ	*Grace Theological Journal*
HAR	*Hebrew Annual Review*
Hb.	Hebrew
HBD	*Harper's Bible Dictionary,* ed. P. Achtemeier
HBT	*Horizons in Biblical Theology*
HS	*Hebrew Studies*
HSM	Harvard Semitic Monographs
HTR	*Harvard Theological Review*
HUCA	*Hebrew Union College Annual*
IBC	Interpretation: A Bible Commentary for Teaching and Preaching
IBD	*Illustrated Bible Dictionary*
IBS	*Irish Biblical Studies*
ICC	International Critical Commentary
IDB	*Interpreter's Dictionary of the Bible,* ed. G. A. Buttrick, et al.
IDBSup	Supplementary volume to *IDB*
IBHS	B. K. Waltke and M. O'Connor, *Introduction to Biblical Hebrew Syntax*
IEJ	*Israel Exploration Journal*
Int	*Interpretation*
IOS	*Israel Oriental Society*
ISBE	*International Standard Bible Encyclopedia,* rev. ed., G. W. Bromiley
ITC	International Theological Commentary
ITQ	*Irish Theological Quarterly*
JAAR	*Journal of the American Academy of Religion*
JAARSup	*Journal of the American Academy of Religion,* Supplement
JANES	*Journal of Ancient Near Eastern Society*
JAOS	*Journal of the American Oriental Society*
JBL	*Journal of Biblical Literature*
JBR	*Journal of Bible and Religion*
JCS	*Journal of Cuneiform Studies*
JETS	*Journal of the Evangelical Theological Society*
JJS	*Journal of Jewish Studies*
JNES	*Journal of Near Eastern Studies*
JNSL	*Journal of Northwest Semitic Languages*

JPOS	*Journal of Palestine Oriental Society*
JRT	*Journal of Religious Thought*
JSOR	*Journal of the Society for Oriental Research*
JSOT	*Journal for the Study of the Old Testament*
JSOTSup	JSOT—Supplement Series
JSS	*Journal of Semitic Studies*
JTS	*Journal of Theological Studies*
JTT	*Journal of Translation and Textlinguistics*
Jub.	*Jubilees*
KB	L. Koehler and W. Baumgartner, *Lexicon in Veteris Testamenti libros*
KB^3	L. Koehler and W. Baumgartner *Hebräisches und Aramäisches Lexikon zum Alten Testament*
KB^3 (Eng.)	L. Koehler and W. Baumgartner, *The Hebrew and Aramaic Lexicon of the Old Testament*, trans. M. E. J. Richardson
KD	*Kerygma und Dogma*
LSJ	Liddell-Scott-Jones, *Greek-English Lexicon*
LW	*Luther's Works. Lectures on Genesis*, ed. J. Pelikan and D. Poellot, trans. G. Schick
LXX	Septuagint
MT	Masoretic Text
NAB	New American Bible
NASB	New American Standard Bible
NAC	New American Commentary
NB	*Nebuchadrezzar and Babylon*, D. J. Wiseman
NBD	*New Bible Dictionary*, ed. J. D. Douglas
NEB	New English Bible
NIB	The New Interpreter's Bible
NICNT	New International Commentary on the New Testament
NICOT	New International Commentary on the Old Testament
NIVBC	NIV Bible Commentary, ed. K. L. Barker and J. Kohlenberger III
NIVSB	NIV Study Bible
NJB	New Jerusalem Bible
NJPS	New Jewish Publication Society Version
NovT	*Novum Testamentum*
NRSV	New Revised Standard Version
NRT	*La nouvelle revue théologique*
NTT	Norsk Teologisk Tidsskrift
OBO	Orbis biblicus et orientalis
Or	*Orientalia*
OTL	Old Testament Library
OTP	*The Old Testament Pseudepigrapha*, ed. J. H. Charlesworth
OTS	*Oudtestamentische Studiën*
PEQ	*Palestine Exploration Quarterly*
POTT	*Peoples of Old Testament Times*, ed. D. J. Wiseman
PTMS	Pittsburgh Theological Monograph Series
PTR	*Princeton Theological Review*
Pss. Sol.	*Psalms of Solomon*

RA	*Revue d'assyriologie et d'archéologie orientale*
RB	*Revue biblique*
REB	Revised English Bible
ResQ	*Restoration Quarterly*
RevExp	*Review and Expositor*
RTR	*Reformed Theological Review*
SANE	Sources from the Ancient Near East
SBLDS	Society of Biblical Literature Dissertation Series
SBLMS	Society of Biblical Literature Monograph Series
SBLSP	Society of Biblical Literature Seminar Papers
SBT	Studies in Biblical Theology
Sib. Or.	*Sibylline Oracles*
SJT	*Scottish Journal of Theology*
SJLA	Studies in Judaism in Late Antiquity
SLJT	*Saint Luke's Journal of Theology*
SOTI	*A Survey of Old Testament Introduction,* G. L. Archer
SP	Samaritan Pentateuch
ST	*Studia theologica*
Syr.	Syriac
TD	*Theology Digest*
TDNT	*Theological Dictionary of the New Testament,* ed. G. Kittel and G. Friedrich
TDOT	*Theological Dictionary of the Old Testament,* ed. G. J. Botterweck and H. Ringgren
Tg(s).	Targum(s)
Tg. Onq.	*Targum Onkelos,* ed. B. Grossfield
Tg. Neof	*Targum Neofiti 1,* ed. M. McNamara
Tg. Ps.-J.	*Targum Pseudo-Jonathan,* ed. M. Mahler
T.Levi	*Testament of Levi*
TNTC	Tyndale New Testament Commentaries
TOTC	Tyndale Old Testament Commentaries
T.Rub	*Testament of Reuben*
TS	*Theological Studies*
TWOT	*Theological Wordbook of the Old Testament*
TynBul	*Tyndale Bulletin*
UF	*Ugarit-Forschungen*
Ug.	Ugaritic
UT	C. H. Gordon, *Ugaritic Textbook*
Vg	Vulgate
VT	*Vetus Testamentum*
VTSup	Vetus Testamentum, Supplements
WBC	Word Biblical Commentaries
WTJ	*Westminster Theological Journal*
YES	Yale Egyptian Studies
ZAW	*Zeitschrift für die alttestamentliche Wissenschaft*

Contents

1, 2 Samuel

──────── **INTRODUCTION** ────────

1. Name, Extent, and Location in Scripture

The pair of books known in the Protestant and more recent Jewish traditions as First and Second Samuel have carried three other titles in Judeo-Christian tradition. In the LXX and Greek Orthodox traditions these books have been known as First and Second Kingdoms. In the Vulgate and Catholic traditions they are termed First and Second Kings.[1] Hebrew Bibles recognized no division between the books prior to the publication of the Bomberg edition in 1516/17, which called the longer book simply Samuel.

The earliest indication that Judaism treated 1, 2 Samuel as a single literary entity is found in the Qumran manuscript 4QSam^a, dateable to the first half of

---

[1] In both the Greek Orthodox and Catholic traditions, the books of Samuel and Kings are treated together; in the former these books are split into four smaller books named 1–4 Kingdoms; and in the latter, 1–4 Kings.

the first century B.C.[2] The custom of dividing the book into two separate entities apparently was instituted by the Greek-speaking Jewish community, which preferred to divide longer books into units that would fit on standard-sized scrolls.[3]

Two different traditions exist in the Greek versions of Samuel concerning the point at which the book concludes. In most of the surviving Greek manuscripts of Samuel, the text terminates after 2 Sam 24:25; however in a few, Samuel extends through 1 Kgs 2:11.[4] Though this tradition has no ancient witness in extant Hebrew manuscripts, the practice is quite understandable; 1 Kings' opening chapters provide details of David's latter days and death and assume the readers are aware of facts presented in 1, 2 Samuel.

Following the LXX's practice of arranging the narrative books chronologically, Christian Bibles have placed 1, 2 Samuel immediately after the book of Ruth. In the Hebrew Bible these books stand as the third and fourth books in the Former Prophets, being positioned immediately after Judges.

First and Second Samuel are part of the section of the Hebrew Bible known as the Former Prophets. This section, which includes the books from Joshua to 2 Kings (excluding Ruth), presents a theological narrative of the history of Israel from the time of Israel's entrance into Palestine under Joshua through its departure from the land in the time of Zedekiah. Its overarching purpose is to affirm and explain the teachings of the Torah. Particularly prominent in the Former Prophets are narratives that demonstrate the influence of the Lord's prophets in Israel's history. At times their influence eclipsed that of the kings, perhaps explaining why this section title includes the word "prophets."

2. Origins of the Canonical Text and the Question of Authorship

The books of 1, 2 Samuel are anonymous. Jewish tradition associates the levitical prophet-judge Samuel, as well as the prophets Gad and Nathan, with the writing of the books.[5] Although many modern scholars believe Samuel

---

[2] E. C. Ulrich, Jr., *The Qumran Text of Samuel and Josephus* (Missoula: Scholars Press, 1978), 10. Fragments from forty-three of the fifty-five chapters of 1, 2 Samuel, including portions of 1 Samuel 1 and 2 Samuel 24, have been recovered from the 4QSam[a] manuscript. Cf. Ulrich for a complete listing of fragments (p. 271).

[3] The splitting of Samuel into two books apparently became necessary as a direct result of the translation process. The Greek's use of vowel letters, a practice absent from Hebrew, effectively forced the translated manuscript to be approximately twice the length of the original document.

[4] Five extant Greek manuscripts, all of which were used to reconstruct the so-called "Lucianic" version of the LXX, make the division at this point. Cf. H. St. J. Thackeray, Jr., "The Greek Translators of the Four Books of Kings," *JTS* 8 (1907): 264–66. Diodorus and Theodoret are claimed to have recognized this division as well (ibid., 264). Josephus, who seems to have made use of the LXX, also begins a new section of his history of the Jews at the same point (*Ant.* 8.1). These witnesses provide evidence of the original literary unity of Samuel-Kings.

[5] T. *Baba Bathra* 14b, 15a.

played an important role in recording some of the materials that now comprise the work, the consensus view is that the development of the original canonical (= autographic) form of the book was relatively complex. It is generally conceded that several intermediary steps took place over a considerable period of time leading up to the production of the final form of the book. One especially important aspect of 1, 2 Samuel's prehistory would have been the production of several source documents that were used by the person who produced the canonical work. A discussion of both biblical evidence for the existence of such documents as well as scholarly proposals for a different set of sources follows.

(1) Precanonical Sources Mentioned in the Bible

Explicit textual evidence (cf. 2 Sam 1:18) suggests that at least one preexistent written source, the Book of Jashar, was used in creating the autographic text of 1, 2 Samuel.[6] First Chronicles indicates that at least four other documents from the early monarchical period were available for later generations to study and use: the Court Records of King David (1 Chr 27:24), the Records of Samuel the Seer (29:29), the Records of Nathan the Prophet (29:29), and the Records of Gad the Seer (29:29). Although it cannot be proven that the writer of 1, 2 Samuel used or even had access to any or all of these other documents, it is reasonable to consider them as possible or even probable sources for the information presented in the canonical book. The relatively heavy emphasis on the roles played by prophets in 1, 2 Samuel, as well as the inclusion of many technical details concerning events within David's reign—for example, lists of David's administrative personnel and key military officers (cf. 2 Sam 8:15–18; 20:23–25; 23:8–39)—provide additional evidence that these sources were indeed utilized.

(2) Proposed Precanonical Sources

Many nineteenth- and twentieth-century scholars have suggested that written and unwritten sources other than those mentioned in the Bible were utilized in creating the canonical form of 1, 2 Samuel. These proposed sources were identified on the basis of several text-based criteria: (1) seeming or actual duplications of materials, (2) seeming or actual contradictions, (3) sharply contrasting theological perspectives, and (4) seeming anachronis-

---

[6] Nothing is known of the exact nature of the Book of Jashar. It is mentioned elsewhere in the Bible only in Josh 10:13, where an abbreviated poetic account of an important victory over the Amorites is recorded.

tic references to different offices and geopolitical entities.[7] Although it is impossible to discuss or even mention all of the proposals that have been made, a short explanation of the most prominent ones is appropriate.

ELI AND SAMUEL TRADITIONS (1 SAMUEL 1–3). M. Noth has suggested that three different traditions were brought together to produce 1 Samuel 1–3: (1) an account, originating in Shiloh, of Samuel's birth and childhood (1:1–2:11), (2) a special tradition, arising from Jerusalem, dealing with problems and judgments against the house of Eli (2:12–17,22–36), and (3) a tradition, written later than the other two, relating Samuel's entrance into the prophetic movement (3:1–21).[8]

ARK TRADITIONS (1 SAMUEL 4–6; 2 SAMUEL 6). A theory crystallized by Rost in 1926 suggests that 1 Sam 4:1b–7:1 and 2 Samuel 6 were originally part of a larger document made up of stories about the ark of the covenant.[9] According to Rost, this composition came from a member of the priesthood living in Jerusalem during the reign of either David or Solomon. Its purpose was to outline the previous history of the ark for the benefit of festival pilgrims visiting Jerusalem.[10] The absence of any reference to Samuel in this section, even though he is mentioned in the chapters before and after 1 Sam 4–6, is often

---

[7] Apparent or actual duplications mentioned by scholars include Eli's dual warnings of God's judgment (1 Sam 2:27–36; 3:11–14); dual origins of the Saul proverb (1 Sam 10:11; 19:24); Saul's dual acclamation as king (1 Sam 10:17–24; 11:15); Saul's dual rejection by God (1 Sam 13:14; 15:23); David's dual introductions to Saul (1 Sam 16:14–23; 17:1–18:2); David's triple (!) establishment of a covenant with Jonathan (1 Sam 18:3; 20:16–42; 23:18); David's triple (!) offer to marry a daughter of Saul (1 Sam 18:17–19,20–21a,22b–29a); David's dual escapes from Saul's court (1 Sam 19:12; 20:42); the Ziphites' dual betrayal of David (1 Sam 23:19–28; 26:1–5); David's dual escape to the Philistines (21:11–16; 27:1–3); David's dual sparing of Saul's life (1 Sam 24:1–22; 26:6–25); and dual accounts of Saul's death (1 Sam 31; 2 Sam 1). Cf. A. Bentzen, *Introduction to the Old Testament,* 2d ed. (Cogenhagen: G. E. C. Gad, 1952), II:93; and R. L. Cate, *An Introduction to the Old Testament and Its Study* (Nashville: Broadman, 1987), 238–39.

Contradictions—seeming or real—that are often noted include: Philistine activity during Samuel's day (1 Sam 7:3–14 versus 13:10); differing attitudes toward Israelite kingship (1 Sam 7:1–8:22 versus 1 Sam 9–11); differing accounts regarding David's introduction to Saul (1 Sam 16:14–23 versus 17:1–18:2); discrepancies in Saul's awareness that David had left the royal household (1 Sam 19:17; 20:25–29); discrepancies concerning the death of Goliath (1 Sam 17 versus 2 Sam 21:19); differing accounts of the cause of Saul's death (1 Sam 31 versus 2 Sam 1); differing information regarding Absalom's children (2 Sam 14:27 versus 18:18).

The primary theological tension is that of differing attitudes toward Israelite kingship (1 Sam 7:1–8:22 versus 1 Sam 9–11). Especially noted is the use of the term "king" in Hannah's song (1 Sam 2:10) at a time when there was no king in Israel and the repeated references to Judah and Israel as though they were distinct national entities (1 Sam 11:8; 18:16; 2 Sam 11:11; 19:11,40–43; 21:2; 24:1,9).

[8] M. Noth, "Samuel und Silo," *VT* 3 (1963): 390–400.

[9] Cf. L. Rost, *Succession to the Throne of David,* trans. M. D. Rutter and D. M. Gunn (Sheffield: Almond, 1982).

given as a primary reason for accepting these chapters as coming from a separate source. On the other hand, the close linkage between the events and characters of chaps. 4–6 and those of chaps. 1–3 raises questions about any neat cleavage between these two units of material.

PRO- AND ANTI-MONARCHICAL STORIES (1 SAMUEL 7–15). A theory that goes back at least as far as the late nineteenth century[11] suggests that two irreconcilable viewpoints regarding the value of kingship for ancient Israel are set forth in 1 Samuel 7–15. One perspective, supposedly coming from an early written source, favors the idea of a king at the crest of the Israelite social and political structure. Sections of 1 Samuel that are believed to come from this hypothetical source include 9:1–10:16; 11:1–11,15. Excerpts from a second nonextant source, this one attributed to a later period in Israelite history when the shortcomings of kingship were well-known, are purportedly found in 7:2–8:22; 10:17–27; 12:1–25. More recent scholarship has tended to reject the theory of juxtaposed, contradictory documents in this section.[12]

RISE-OF-DAVID STORIES (1 SAMUEL 16–2 SAMUEL 5). Since the time of Rost's writings on 1, 2 Samuel, many scholars have accepted the assertion that these twenty-one chapters were originally an independent document written to defend David's right to rule following the death of King Saul.[13] The sympathetic portrayal of David in these chapters, showing him to be a zealous worshiper of the Lord who used his great abilities in unswervingly loyal service to the king, demonstrates that David was uniquely qualified to lead Israel following Saul's tragic death. Proponents of an originally independent document note numerous instances in the text of these chapters to suggest that they were essentially an apology and thus in "a special category of ancient Near Eastern literature in which the accession of a ruler whose right to the throne is somehow suspect is shown to have been in accordance with the will of the gods and therefore lawful."[14] Difficulties with this position are seen in the inability of schol-

---

[10] J. Willis, McCarter, and others have disagreed with the boundaries of this supposed document. McCarter suggests that the ark narratives include 1 Sam 2:12–17,22–25; 4:1b–7:1. Cf. P. K. McCarter, Jr., *I Samuel*, AB (Garden City: Doubleday, 1980), 23–26. J. T. Willis, "An Anti-Elide Narrative Tradition from a Prophetic Circle at the Ramah Sanctuary," *JBL* 90 (1971): 288–308. Scholars from various points on the theological spectrum accept the possibility of a collection of originally independent ark traditions being incorporated into 1, 2 Samuel. For an evangelical scholar who accepts this position, cf. R. P. Gordon, who suggests that "that chs. 4–6 form at least the nucleus of a tradition which once enjoyed a separate literary existence" (*I and II Samuel: A Commentary* [Grand Rapids: Zondervan, 1986], 24).

[11] Cf. J. Wellhausen, *Prolegomena to the History of Ancient Israel* (1878; reprint and trans., New York: Meridian, 1957).

[12] Cf. L. Eslinger, "Viewpoints and Points of View in 1 Samuel 8–12," *JSOT* 26 (1983): 61–76.

[13] Among contemporary scholars who accept the basic validity of Rost's proposal of a Rise-of-David document are: McCarter (*I Samuel*, 27–30); R. W. Klein, (*I Samuel*, WBC [Waco: Word, 1983], xxxi–xxxii); A. A. Anderson, (*2 Samuel*, WBC [Waco: Word, 1989], xxvi–xxxiii).

[14] McCarter, *I Samuel*, 29. McCarter compares this section with the thirteenth century B.C. Hittite "Apology of Hattušiliš."

ars to agree on the beginning (1 Sam 15:1 or 16:1 or 16:14) and ending points (2 Sam 5:10; 6:23; 7:29) of such a document and in the fact that an apologetic dimension to the presentation of David's story is observable beyond the bounds of this supposed document (cf. 2 Sam 9; 19:9a; 21:1–14; 22:1).

SUCCESSION STORIES (2 SAM 9–20). The possibility of this section together with 1 Kings 1–2 being a separate document also was expressed by Rost in 1926. His proposal, followed by many other twentieth-century scholars, was that the document was composed "to show how it was that Solomon, and not one of David's other sons, followed his father on the throne."[15] Noting that the narratives in these chapters only rarely explicitly affirm God's involvement in the events being described (cf. 2 Sam 11:27; 12:24; 17:14), G. von Rad has suggested that this supposed document demonstrates "a wholly new conception of the nature of God's activity in history."[16] Here the presence of God is more hidden, and thus the resulting historical account appears more secular.

Even so, there is no unanimity among scholars regarding the writer's purpose in creating this section of 2 Samuel. W. Brueggemann (following Carlson) understands this section to be more concerned with "the demise and failure of David's career" than with the rise of Solomon's.[17]

OTHER SOURCES. Attempts to identify the putative pentateuchal sources J and E—two of the sources hypothesized to have been used in the production of the Torah—in 1, 2 Samuel[18] have been fraught with difficulties. Today this attempt has been abandoned.

(3) Production of the Canonical Text

First and Second Samuel were not written to bring recognition to any human author—the text makes no claims concerning its authorship. Like so many other works of God, a community of individuals apparently was utilized. What is more, the individuals may have lived at different periods in Israel's history, perhaps stretching from the eleventh century B.C. down to the sixth century B.C. Accounts of events at Shiloh (1 Sam 1–3), movements of the ark of the covenant (1 Sam 4–6), Samuel's activities as a prophet and judge over Israel (1 Sam 7–10), events associated with Saul's tenure as king of Israel (1 Sam 11–31), and events in the earlier portion of David's career (2 Sam 1–6) may have been recorded by Samuel or some other contemporary

---

[15] Gordon, I and II Samuel, 41.

[16] G. von Rad, "The Beginning of Historical Writing in Ancient Israel," in The Problem of the Hexateuch and Other Essays, trans. E. W. T. Dicken (New York: McGraw-Hill, 1966), 204.

[17] W. Brueggemann, First and Second Samuel (Louisville: John Knox, 1990), 265. Cf. also R. A. Carlson, David: The Chosen King (Uppsala: Almqvist & Wiksell, 1964).

[18] Cf. the efforts of G. Hölscher, Geschichtsschreibung in Israel (Lund: C. W. K. Gleerup, 1952); and O. Eissfeldt, The Old Testament, An Introduction, trans. P. R. Ackroyd (New York: Harper & Row, 1965), 270–71.

during the eleventh century B.C. Since David's career is often understood to have stretched from about 1010 B.C. until about 971 B.C., many of the events that occurred during David's reign would have been recorded during the early part of the tenth century B.C. The mention of the length of David's reign suggests that at least portions of the book were written after David's death (2 Sam 5:4). The narrator's efforts to separate the activities of Judah and Israel suggests that some portions of the text were worded after the dissolution of the united monarchy following the death of King Solomon (ca. 931 B.C.), a conclusion that is strengthened by a mention of the "kings of Judah" (1 Sam 27:6) and the use of the phrase "to this day" (1 Sam 5:5; 6:18; 27:6; 30:25; 2 Sam 4:3; 6:8; 18:18). The inclusion of a textual note explaining an obscure term (1 Sam 9:9) that was used at least as late as the eighth century B.C. (cf. Amos 7:12) suggests that some modifications occurred to the precanonical text no earlier than 750 B.C. Finally, the strong literary connections between 1, 2 Kings and 2 Samuel, especially in the matters of Solomon's rise to power, as well as the fates of Joab, Shimei, and Zadok—to say nothing of the apparent attempt to parallel the story of David with the history of Israel—suggest that 1 Samuel and 2 Samuel achieved their final canonical form no earlier than the last events recorded in 2 Kings.

Thus, a fair assessment of the textual data leads to the conclusion that the canonical form of 1, 2 Samuel was produced anonymously no earlier than the middle of the sixth century B.C. It was based on written documents produced contemporaneously with Eli, Samuel, Saul, and David but contains reflective theological insights that were not present in the original source documents. As such, it is possible for 1, 2 Samuel to be simultaneously an accurate historical record of key events in the political and religious history of Israel, as well as a highly theological document relevant to the exilic Israelite community.[19]

Though the identity of the author of the canonical version of 1, 2 Samuel probably will never be known, several observations can be made about him. First, the author was aware of and accepted the absolute authority of the Torah's teachings (cf. discussion under "1, 2 Samuel as Scripture," p. 45).

Second, the writer had a high estimation of the value of genuine prophetic activity. Individual prophets of the Lord were always portrayed in "power" roles, as presenters of supremely authoritative pronouncements that defined the destinies of all about whom they spoke—judges, kings, and commoners alike. Five different true prophets were mentioned in the text. In addition, Saul was described as one who made prophetic utterances, though it is perhaps better to

---

[19] This conclusion matches that of D. M. Howard, Jr.: "It appears reasonable enough to assume composition of [1, 2 Samuel's] major portions in the days of David and Solomon themselves and to postulate final compilation and editing some time near or during the Exile" (*An Introduction to the Historical Books of the Old Testament* [Grand Rapids: Baker, 1993], 145).

describe him as one who behaved more as a false prophet than a true one.

The five prophets performed many significant tasks in the course of 1, 2 Samuel. The unnamed "man of God" (1 Sam 2:27) spoke accurate and fateful words of judgment against Eli's house. Samuel, the greatest of the prophets, was termed both a "man of God" (1 Sam 9:7–8) and a "seer" (1 Sam 9:9–11,18–19). He spoke accurately concerning the tragic outcomes of having a king (1 Sam 8:11–18); anointed Saul as king and announced it as God's will (1 Sam 10:1); prophesied about lost donkeys, Kish's thoughts, and Saul's future (1 Sam 9:20); and spoke words of decisive judgment against Saul and Saul's kingship (1 Sam 15:26). Nathan revealed God's covenant with David (2 Sam 7:2–17), revealed God's judgment on David for his sinful acts against Bathsheba and Uriah (2 Sam 12:1–15), and also revealed God's love for Solomon; thus, in essence, he functioned as a kingmaker (2 Sam 12:25). Gad gave David lifesaving directions for hiding from Saul (1 Sam 22:5) and announced God's judgment on David for taking the census (2 Sam 24:11–14). David himself acted as a prophet as he pronounced an oracle under the influence of the Holy Spirit (2 Sam 23:1–7).

Third, the author recognized the importance of Levites in the history of Israel and was supportive of the Zadokite priesthood. The books of Samuel gave narrative prominence to representatives of at least four different levitical families, three of which were associated with the high priesthood: the Elides (1 Sam 1–6), the Ahimelechites/Abiatharites (1 Sam 21–22), the Zadokites (2 Sam 15:24–36; 17:15–21), and Samuel. In addition, narrative accounts of the actions of the citizens of the levitical cities of Beth Shemesh (1 Sam 6:19–21) and Kiriath Jearim (7:1) are recorded.

Finally, the author believed in the divine right of the descendants of David to rule over Israel (cf. 2 Sam 7:11–16). David was given more narrative space than any other human being in the biblical account of Israel's history, and the account is sympathetically told. In addition, the promises accorded David regarding rulership are shown to remain intact in spite of challenges mounted against it by reluctant Israelites and Sheba.

(4) Integration of the Text into a Larger Literary Unity

In recent years scholarly works about 1, 2 Samuel—as well as the rest of the Former Prophets—have commonly viewed Deuteronomy–2 Kings as a literary unity having been produced by an individual or group of individuals collectively known as the Deuteronomistic editors. The so-called Deuteronomistic (or Deuteronomic) school of writers was believed by many scholars to have produced a connected history of Israel that interpreted the course of events in the nation's history in light of the teachings found in the Book of Deuteronomy. Their writings "stressed centralization of worship in Jerusalem, obedience to Deuteronomic law, and the avoidance of any kind of apostasy, all according to a rigid system of reward and punishment."[20] This work, which is believed by some to have gone through two editions (one Josianic, the other exilic),[21] would have been produced no earlier than the reign of Josiah and perhaps as late as the exile.[22]

Those who approach the Bible from the perspective of modern literary criticism are open to the possibility of viewing 1, 2 Samuel as part of a much larger literary unity. Such a text may be understood to stretch from Genesis to 2 Kings[23] or perhaps even from Genesis to Revelation.[24]

3. Transmission of the Canonical Text

One of the more challenging issues facing the serious student of 1, 2 Samuel regards the wording of the book's original canonical (= autographic) text.[25] Although there is overwhelming agreement on the semantic level between the MT, LXX, and the three fragmentary remains of the book that have come from

[20] McCarter, *1 Samuel,* 15.

[21] Cf. F. M. Cross, *Canaanite Myth and Hebrew Epic* (Cambridge: Harvard University, 1973); and McCarter, *1 Samuel,* 15.

[22] For a critique of Noth's work as well as Cross's subsequent revision of it from the standpoint of one who studies 1, 2 Samuel as a literary critic, cf. R. Polzin, *Samuel and the Deuteronomist* (San Francisco: Harper & Row, 1989), 9–13. Polzin concludes Noth's work is characterized by a "discrepancy between his evaluation of Dtr's compositional techniques ('this is great work,' 'Dtr's very lucid method of composition,' 'a work of art that merits our respect') and his accompanying description of this author at work (Dtr mostly arranged a collage of traditions, very rarely changing them to remove inconsistencies but often unintentionally altering their meaning. He wrote in a dully repetitive style, making the same point over and over again)." Additionally, Polzin notes that Noth "mostly fails to account for [Deuteronomy–2 King's] artful construction because it unduly concentrates on superficial aspects of the composition, . . . and therefore completely neglects the many artful features of the text" (pp. 10–11).

[23] Cf. J. Rosenberg, who asks the question regarding 1, 2 Samuel, "What role do the books thus construed play in the larger narrative corpus extending from Genesis through 2 Kings?" ("1 and 2 Samuel," in *The Literary Guide to the Bible,* ed. R. Alter and F. Kermode [Cambridge: Belknap, 1987], 122). He then goes on to criticize Rost's and Noth's proposals because "they tended to obscure the literary character of the Samuel books by depriving them both of their autonomy as books and of the commonality of texture and perspective that unites them with most of the other books of the Hebrew Bible" (pp. 122–23). Also see the useful chart in J. G. Baldwin, *1 and 2 Samuel,* TOTC (Leicester: InterVarsity, 1988), 30.

[24] Cf. T. S. Warshaw, "Some Methodological Considerations," in *Literary Interpretations of Biblical Narratives,* II:25–34, ed. K. R. R. Gros Louis (Nashville: Abingdon, 1982), 27: "If both testaments constitute one book written under the influence of the same holy spirit [sic], then many of the events of the OT must be read as instances of the writer's use of foreshadowing, a perfectly normal literary device."

[25] Key works relating to this subject include J. Wellhausen, *Der Text der Bücher Samuelis untersucht* (Göttingen: Vandenhoeck & Ruprecht, 1871); A. E. Brooke et al. eds., *The Old Testament in Greek,* vol. II, pt. I, *I and II Samuel* (London: Cambridge, 1927); and E. C. Ulrich, Jr., *The Qumran Text of Samuel and Josephus* (Missoula: Scholars Press, 1978). Of value to one initially investigating this issue is J. A. Martin's article, "The Text of Samuel," *BibSac* 141 (1984): 209–22.

cave four at Qumran (4QSam[a,b,c]),[26] there are also a few sizeable differences.[27] What is more, divergences exist between the MT, LXX, and Qumran manuscripts, so that there is no overall agreement between two of these ancient texts against the third—even though there are considerably more similarities between the LXX and the Qumran texts than with any other combination.[28] Thus serious concerns—and, frequently, highly negative evaluations—have arisen concerning the quality of text transmitted to us in the MT.[29]

The majority of modern researchers who have studied this issue conclude that in most cases where there is disagreement in the wording of a passage, the LXX's reading is superior to that of the MT—especially in shorter passages and when the reading is corroborated by Josephus and/or the Qumran materials.[30] S. Pisano's studied conclusions are worthy of note in this instance: "It is undeniable that in the long history of the transmission of the Hebrew text of the Old Testament corruptions have crept into the text and that the texts of LXX and 4QSam[a] are helpful for their restoration."[31] How-

---

[26] The largest Qumran fragment, 4QSam[a], contains somewhat less than 10 percent of the total text of 1, 2 Samuel. Cf. Ulrich, *The Qumran Text of Samuel and Josephus*, 257.

[27] The following comparisons present fairly typical examples of the divergences: 1 Sam 4:1, MT: "And the word of Samuel came to all Israel. And Israel went out to meet the Philistines for war"; 1 Sam 4:1, LXX: "And the word of Samuel came to all Israel. And in those days the Philistines gathered themselves for war against Israel, and Israel went out to meet them for war"; 1 Sam 14:41, MT: "Then Saul prayed to the LORD, the God of Israel, 'Give me the right answer'"; 1 Sam 14:41, LXX: "Then Saul prayed to the LORD, the God of Israel, 'Give me the right answer. Why have you not answered your servant today? If the fault is in me or my son Jonathan, respond with Urim, but if the men of Israel are at fault respond with Thummim." Cf. Martin, *The Text of Samuel*, 216–17, and R. W. Klein, *Textual Criticism of the Old Testament* (Philadelphia: Fortress, 1974).

[28] Cf. E. Tov, "The Textual Affiliations of 4QSam[a]," *JSOT* 14 (1979): 37–53.

[29] Note Howard's opinion: "The present Masoretic Hebrew text of the books of Samuel has suffered greatly in transmission, more so than almost any other OT book. Many passages are almost unintelligible on their own" (*Introduction to the Historical Books of the Old Testament*, 145). In my opinion Howard is exaggerating when he states that "many" MT passages are essentially incomprehensible. Gordon shares Howard's general thought: "For some reason the books of Samuel have suffered more in the process of transmission than perhaps any other part of the Old Testament" (*I and II Samuel*, 57); as does S. R. Driver: "The Books of Samuel are not so suitable as a reading book for a beginner in Hebrew as some of the other historical books: for though they contain classical examples of a chaste and beautiful Hebrew prose style, they have suffered unusually from transcriptional corruption" (*Notes on the Hebrew Text of Samuel*, 2d ed. [1912; reprint, Winona Lake: Alpha, 1983], preface to the First Edition). G. L. Archer, Jr., hypothesizes that the reason for the poor condition of the MT is that "the official temple text drawn up in the intertestamental period relied upon a very ancient Vorlage . . . which contained occasional lacunae (perhaps due to a worm-eaten or frayed condition resulting from overuse)" (*A Survey of Old Testament Introduction*, rev. ed. [Chicago: Moody, 1974], 291).

[30] One exception is D. Barthélemy, "La qualité du Texte Massorétique de Samuel," in *The Hebrew and Greek Texts of Samuel*, 1980 Proceedings of IOSCS, ed. E. Tov (Jerusalem, 1980), 1–44.

[31] S. Pisano, *Additions or Omissions in the Books of Samuel* (Göttingen: Vandenhoeck & Ruprecht, 1984), 284.

ever, scholars investigating the text of Samuel are careful to note that whole-
sale acceptance of readings at variance with the MT is unwarranted. As
Gordon notes: "4QSam[a] has its own crop of errors—errors often enough
shared with the LXX—whether it is a double rendering at 1 Samuel 2:24, a
question of congruence at 1 Samuel 8:16, or transposed letters and confused
sense at 2 Samuel 7:23."[32]

The two most celebrated discrepancies between the MT and the others are
found at 1 Sam 11:1; 17:1–18:16. In the first instance, evidence from
4QSam[a] and Josephus[33] suggests that the MT had accidentally omitted about
a paragraph of material from the text.[34] Though many tend to accept the
Qumranic addition as part of the autograph (e.g., NRSV), others point out
that the materials contained in the paragraph supply only background material and therefore may represent a supplemental note supplied later by a well-
meaning scribe.[35]

The LXX version of 1 Sam 17:1–18:16 is considerably shorter than that of
the MT, consisting of 17:1–11,32–40,42–48a,49,51–54; 18:6–8a,9,12a,13–16.
This omission of more than thirty-three verses is taken by some to demonstrate
that the MT version is actually an awkward conflation of two separate
accounts, with the LXX providing an unadulterated version of the single original account. However, detailed study of the MT and LXX versions has led
more than one scholar to conclude that the Greek is a late editorial abridgment
of the original.[36]

The position taken in this commentary is that generally the MT is to be
accepted as the most probable original reading, except in cases where insuperable problems are created by holding to it.

4. Functions and Purposes of 1, 2 Samuel

Over the years researchers have proposed various answers to the question,
Why were 1, 2 Samuel written? Scholars have reached various conclusions
concerning the books' functions and purposes. Like an intricately cut dia-
mond, the functions are understood to be multifaceted. Samuel was simultaneously a historical work, literary art, apologetic literature, a theological
treatise, and Holy Scripture used especially in the Jewish and Christian

---

[32] Gordon, *I and II Samuel*, 59.

[33] Josephus, *Ant.*, 6.5.1.

[34] Cf. discussion at 1 Sam 11:1 for the supposedly omitted material.

[35] Cf. Gordon, *I and II Samuel*, 64.

[36] Ibid., 65–66. Note also Pisano's cautionary statement (*Additions or Omissions in the Books
of Samuel*, 284–85): "Where it is a question of these long pluses and minuses, however, especially
those which facilitate the reading of the less carefully elaborated text which MT seems often to witness to, perhaps more caution must be used before emending MT too quickly on the basis of
another text."

faiths. In the present section each of these five different functions and purposes will be presented.

(1) 1, 2 Samuel as History

Since 1, 2 Samuel are commonly classified as Historical Books, it is perhaps not surprising that many scholars state that the main purpose for this pair of books is that of conveying history.[37]

HISTORICAL FUNCTIONS OF THE NARRATIVES IN 1, 2 SAMUEL. Several different significant threads within the mosaic of Israelite history are traced in the books of Samuel. At least the following eight different tasks apropos to a historian are discernible: (1) chronicling crucial events in the downfall of the Aaronic priestly line of Ithamar; (2) relating significant and characteristic events from the lives of the post-Mosaic levitical judges; (3) providing historical details relevant to Israel's transition from judgeship to kingship; (4) detailing events from the reigns of Israel's first two kings; (5) documenting the establishment of Jerusalem as Israel's capital; (6) documenting the establishment of the Davidic dynasty as Israel's sole legitimate dynasty; (7) providing details of the life and faith of David, Israel's most famous king; and (8) documenting events associated with the growing rift between Judah and Israel.

SCHOLARLY ASSESSMENT OF SAMUEL'S VALUE AS HISTORICAL REPORTAGE. Disagreement exists among scholars regarding the historical accuracy of the narrative accounts in 1, 2 Samuel. Evaluations range from complete confidence in the reliability of the accounts[38] to the conclusion that there is essentially no historical value.[39] Most scholars are somewhere in

---

[37] The following quotes are reflective of scholarly comment regarding the historical function of 1, 2 Samuel. B. F. Philbeck, Jr.: "The narratives in Samuel may legitimately be considered Israel's history of the establishment and development of a united monarchy over Israel and Judah" ("1–2 Samuel," BBC [Nashville: Broadman, 1970], 1); H. W. Hertzberg: "The books of Samuel contain that part of the history of Israel which describes the foundation of the State, running from the close of the period of the Judges to the establishment of the united kingdom" (*I and II Samuel,* trans. J. S. Bowden, OTL [Philadelphia: Westminster, 1964], 17); and E. J. Young: "The purpose of the books of Samuel is to relate the account of the establishment of the monarchy, and of Samuel's part therein" (*An Introduction to the Old Testament,* rev. ed. [Grand Rapids: Eerdmans, 1960], 179).

[38] E.g., Archer: "These, then, are the only alternatives available to us as we confront the Scriptures: either they are inerrant, or else we are" (*Survey of Old Testament Introduction,* 29).

[39] E.g., G. W. Ahlström on the biblical record of Samuel's life: "Can the historical Samuel be recovered? This question cannot be answered in the affirmative. His political importance eludes us. To describe his life and career is impossible. There is, in fact, very little reliable information about him" (*The History of Ancient Palestine* [Minneapolis: Fortress, 1993], 425). Of Saul, Ahlström writes (p. 429): "The biblical presentation of the rise of Saul's kingship has utilized an old folktale (or the literary structure of a folktale) and a well-known enthronement pattern (1 Sam 9–11)."

between these two poles, expressing doubt about certain numeric claims,[40] details of reported conversations,[41] and some geopolitical details but accepting the general portrayal of the events as accurate to a greater or lesser extent.

Archaeological discoveries, though sparse for this time period and by their nature incapable of verifying much of the narrative material in 1, 2 Samuel (e.g., conversations, family relations, minor armed conflicts between tribes and peoples), does not contradict the overall picture of events outlined in 1, 2 Samuel.[42] The Philistines did possess a cultural presence in Palestine during the eleventh century B.C., many armed conflicts occurred in the cities of Palestine at this time, and sites showing evidences of Israelite culture increased in number in the region during the tenth century B.C.

CHRONOLOGICAL ISSUES IN 1, 2 SAMUEL. A relevant task for those who assume that the writer of 1, 2 Samuel intended to convey accurate historical data is producing a chronology consistent with the narratives. This process

---

[40] Invariably, modern scholars are inclined to revise numbers downward rather than upward or to dismiss the numbers as fanciful fabrications without any historical value. Scholars of the more evangelical persuasion who make downward revision of numbers in the text generally do so through textual emendation (e.g., 50,070 Beth Shemeshite casualties being emended to 70 casualties [1 Sam 6:19; cf. NIV's rendering]; 30,000 Philistine chariots emended to 3,000 chariots [1 Sam 13:5; cf. NIV]); or redefinition of terms (e.g., 330,000 Israelite soldiers becoming 330 clan-based military units [= אֶלֶף; 1 Sam 11:8]). Among evangelicals, the comments of R. F. Youngblood concerning 1 Sam 11:8 are typical: "As in 1 Samuel 4:2,10, so also here in v. 8, we cannot be sure whether *ʾelep* means 'thousand' or is used in a more general sense to refer to a military 'unit' (as in 17:18; 29:2; 2 Sam 18:4 . . .). Nor can the possibility of hyperbole be discounted (cf. 18:7; 21:11)" ("1, 2 Samuel," EBC 3:553–1104 [Grand Rapids: Zondervan, 1992], 638).

[41] The basic assumption of nonevangelical biblical scholars is that the biblical writers exercised the right to create narrative dialogue—and perhaps to create much more than that. Cf. Ahlström: "The religious historiography does not per se need to build upon any reality because religion makes its own reality" (*History of Ancient Palestine*, 44). Evangelical scholars may not admit that the biblical writers invented any details, including dialogue. Cf. Howard: "If, in the last analysis, God is the 'author' of Scripture, then He who knows all things would have written an accurate record of those things. Thus, what the Scriptures claim to be true is indeed true" (*Introduction to the Historical Books of the Old Testament*, 35). V. P. Long (*The Art of Biblical History* [Grand Rapids: Zondervan, 1994], 73) suggests that three elements—"simplicity, selectivity, suggestive detail"—are hallmarks of historiography that accurately interprets history. Applied to biblical narrative accounts, Long's assertion implies that the reported dialogue in Scripture may be a simplified, selective representation of the actual words of the biblical personages.

[42] Cf. the evaluation of A. Mazar: "Can archaeology throw light on the transition from tribal life in the period of the Judges to the centralized rule of a monarchy? Do the discoveries reflect the existence of a mighty kingdom as that described in the biblical sources? To what extent are the elaborate international commercial and political relations evidenced in the remains? Do the material finds reflect the internal development of the kingdom from Saul until the time of Solomon? Unfortunately, the archaeological evidence for the period of the United Monarchy is sparse, often controversial, and it does not provide unequivocal answers to these questions" (*Archaeology of the Land of the Bible: 10,000–586 B.C.E.* [New York: Doubleday, 1990], 371).

proves to be rather complex since the text provides few specific chronological relationships between events.

The primary references in the text that might be used to compile a general chronology include the following: Eli's age at the time of his death (ninety-eight years; 1 Sam 4:15); Eli's length of service as judge over Israel (forty years; 1 Sam 4:18); the amount of time the ark spent at Kiriath Jearim (twenty years; 1 Sam 7:2); the number of years Saul reigned as king (forty years; 1 Sam 13:1; Acts 13:21);[43] the length of time David spent among the Philistines (sixteen months; 1 Sam 27:7); Ish-Bosheth's age at the time of his accession (forty years; 2 Sam 2:10); the length of Ish-Bosheth's reign over Israel (two years; 2 Sam 2:10); the amount of time David served as king over Judah while at Hebron (seven years and six months; 2 Sam 2:11); Mephibosheth's age at the time of Jonathan's death (five years; 2 Sam 4:4); David's age when he became king (thirty years; 2 Sam 5:4); the length of David's reign over Israel (forty years; 2 Sam 5:4); the length of time David ruled over all Israel (thirty-three years; 2 Sam 5:5); the number of years between Tamar's rape and Amnon's death (two years; 2 Sam 13:23); the number of years Absalom lived in Geshur (three years; 2 Sam 13:38); the number of years Absalom lived in Jerusalem without seeing David (two years; 2 Sam 14:28); the number of years Absalom was reconciled with David in Jerusalem (four years; 2 Sam 15:7); the number of consecutive years of famine (three years; 2 Sam 21:1); the length of time needed for David's census (nine months, twenty days; 2 Sam 24:8).

Additional references that indicate shorter spans of time—usually seven days or less—or specific points in time are also present in the text.[44] However, these references are of value for producing chronologies of episodes rather than for the narrative framework.

Unfortunately, the information provided in the text is of such a nature that it precludes the establishment of a coherent chronology that assigns a date to every event or series of events. Such potentially useful details as David's age at the turning points in his life (e.g., his anointing by Samuel, his killing of Goliath, his sin with Bathsheba and the onset of Absalom's rebellion, as well as the duration of that rebellion) have been denied us. Furthermore, some events seem to have been chronologically displaced, being presented out of their chronological order. This displacement occurred, of course, because the writer exercised his right to arrange the material so as to achieve his larger thematic and artistic purposes. Consequently, most of the events portrayed in 1, 2 Samuel can with integrity only be assigned to general time frames. The follow-

---

[43] For more information on this temporal reference, cf. the comments at 1 Sam 13:1.

[44] Cf. 1 Sam 4:12; 5:3; 6:15–16; 7:6; 9:15,20,24; 10:9; 11:3; 12:18; 13:8; 14:23–24,31,37,45; 15:28; 17:16; 18:2; 19:24; 20:26–27,34; 21:7,10; 22:18; 25:32–33,38; 26:21,24; 27:6; 28:18; 30:1,12–13,17; 31:6,13; 2 Sam 1:1–2,17; 3:38–39; 4:8; 5:8; 6:9; 11:12; 12:18; 17:22; 18:7–8,31; 19:2–3; 19:20; 20:4; 21:9–10,12; 23:10,20; 24:8,18.

ing two sections list those events that seem to permit the assignment of a date as well as the events that seem to be out of order.

DATABLE EVENTS IN 1, 2 SAMUEL.   In the following chronology, the interlocking events of 1, 2 Samuel are coordinated with a reasonable date for the beginning of David's reign as king, 1010 B.C.[45] At its best, this work is somewhat subjective and is certainly subject to revision. This having been stated, the following years are suggested for dateable events:

Table 1: Datable Events in 1, 2 Samuel

1050	Saul publicly anointed king after defeat of Nahash (cf. 1 Sam 11:1–11; 13:1; Acts 13:21)[a]
1045	Ish-Bosheth born (cf. 2 Sam 2:10)
1040	David born (cf. 2 Sam 5:4)
1015	Mephibosheth born (cf. 2 Sam 4:4)
1012	David flees to Ziklag near Gath (cf. 1 Sam 27:7)
1010	David defeats the Amalekites (cf. 1 Sam 30:9–19); Saul and three sons killed on Mount Gilboa during Philistine battle (cf. 1 Sam 31:6); David becomes king at Hebron (cf. 2 Sam 2:1–4a)
1005	Ish-Bosheth becomes king over northern tribes in Mahanaim (cf. 2 Sam 2:8–9)
1003	Abner murdered by Joab (cf. 2 Sam 3:27–39); Ish-Bosheth murdered by Recab and Baanah (cf. 2 Sam 4:1–12); David anointed king over northern tribes (cf. 2 Sam 5:1–3); David conquers Jebusites, moves capital to Jerusalem (cf. 2 Sam 5:6–9)

a. Although the length of Saul's reign is disputed, the apostle Paul says he reigned forty years.

In addition to the dates mentioned in the previous chart, certain, less specific, ones can also be proposed. Since Eli judged Israel forty years, Samuel judged Israel all his life (cf. 1 Sam 7:15), and was "old" at the time of Saul's

---

[45] Cf. J. H. Walton (*Chronological and Background Charts of the Old Testament*, rev. ed. [Grand Rapids: Zondervan,1994], 40) and Howard (*Introduction to the Historical Books of the Old Testament*, 148). J. F. Walvoord and R. B. Zuck (Bible Knowledge Commentary [n.p.: Victor, 1985], 13) accept 1011 B.C. as the beginning point of David's reign. R. L. Cate (*An Introduction to the Old Testament and Its Study* [Nashville: Broadman, 1987], Appendix) and J. Bright (*A History of Israel,* 3d ed. [Philadelphia: Westminster, 1981], 195) place the beginning of David's reign at around 1000 B.C.

anointing in 1050 B.C. (cf. 1 Sam 8:1), it seems reasonable to assume that Eli's years of service as judge could have begun prior to the end of the twelfth century B.C. Additionally, Samuel's service as a judge must have incorporated all of the second quarter of the eleventh century B.C., and at least part of the first quarter as well.

CHRONOLOGICAL DISPLACEMENTS IN 1, 2 SAMUEL. The books of Samuel usually report the events of the period extending from Eli through David in chronological order, in keeping with the writer's concern to preserve a useful historical record of the era. However, the writer was not bound to a strict chronological presentation: summary sections interspersed in the narrative (1 Sam 7:14b–16; 14:47; 2 Sam 3:2–6; 5:14–16; 8:2,13–14) set certain events in indefinite, extended time frames that clearly overlap with events presented later in the narrative. In addition, the author sometimes presents extended narratives that relate simultaneous events. This is most clearly seen in 1 Sam 28:1–31:13, a section of narrative that contrasts the actions of David and his militia with those of Saul and the army of Israel.

Beyond these, scholars often have concluded that some events are more subtly reported out of chronological sequence. The two most obvious examples are the destruction of the house of Saul by the Gibeonites (2 Sam 21), which is often understood to have occurred sometime prior to Absalom's rebellion (2 Sam 15:7ff.), and the sinful census (2 Sam 24), which occurred at an unknown time. Some scholars also see chronological displacement in 2 Sam 5:9b–11. E. H. Merrill, for example believes that David may have built his palace twenty five years after his conquest of Jerusalem,[46] an observation not immediately discernible from the narrative context.

The presence of these features in the books of Samuel does not detract from the historical value of the books. However, they do serve as reminders that the canonical writer had a larger agenda than mere historical reportage; theological and literary considerations were certainly also at play.

(2) 1, 2 Samuel as Literary Art

The books of Samuel are masterful examples of ancient Hebrew narrative art. They possess all the characteristics of a timeless literary classic: a magnificent central plot involving kings, international wars, ambition, murder, deception, and sexual intrigue; complex character portrayals; skillful use of varied settings ranging from mountains to deserts; and masterful use of wordplays and allusions.

This has led some modern biblical scholars to treat the books of Samuel as

---

[46] E. H. Merrill, *Kingdom of Priests* (Grand Rapids: Baker, 1987), 244. Youngblood ("1, 2 Samuel," 862) agrees with Merrill's conclusion that some displacement has occurred in these verses.

though they were only a literary creation, to be judged by all the criteria that would be applied to a piece of secular literature. As K. R. R. Gros Louis notes:

> The text to us is not sacred and whether the events it describes are historical is not relevant to our purposes. . . . Our approach is essentially ahistorical; the text is taken as received, and the truth of an action or an idea or a motive, for literary criticism, depends on its rightness or appropriateness in context. Is it true, we ask, not in the real world but within the fictive world that has been created by the narrative?[47]

In analytic treatments generated from this perspective such issues as theological relevance, historical accuracy, and biblical authority are considered irrelevant. The modern literary critic's de-emphasis of the biblical text's historical dimension is considered a virtue of the discipline by those who practice it. As L. Eslinger notes:

> Literary explanations of the narrative are inherently stronger [than historical-critical readings] because they are primarily descriptive and so subject to refutation; a holistic literary approach eliminates the undesirable muliplication of historical assumptions, and its conclusions can be accepted or rejected as they agree with the text. . . . The literary approach is a way out of the proliferation of studies whose conclusions cannot be compared because they depend on varying, nonverifiable hypotheses and assumptions.[48]

Evangelical scholars, while expressing "justifiable concern for the inspired truth and moral excellence of Scripture,"[49] have noted the literary assets of the text of the books of Samuel. Youngblood, for example, praises 1, 2 Samuel for their "consummate beauty," "exquisite literary structure," "architectonic structure that is impressive indeed," and "memorable and striking" use of poetry.[50] Howard, who affirms the complete accuracy of the text, also lists "large portions of the stories about David" as among "the sections of the historical books that pay the most attention to the artistic forms of communication."[51]

Brief consideration will be given below to three aspects of the literary dimensions of the text: plot, characterization, and wordplays.

PLOT.   The primary story line in the books of Samuel presents the life of David son of Jesse in his transformation from an unappreciated rural shepherd boy to his status as the most celebrated king in the history of Israel, followed by his virtual loss of it all because of a tragic sin. The amplitude of this story line is exceeded in biblical literature only by the New Testament's collective

---

[47] K. R. R. Gros Louis, ed., *Literary Interpretations of Biblical Narratives*, vol. II (Nashville: Abingdon, 1982), 14.
[48] L. Eslinger, *Kingship of God in Crisis* (Sheffield: Almond, 1985), 427–28.
[49] Youngblood, "1, 2 Samuel," 558.
[50] Ibid., 558–59.
[51] Howard, *Introduction to the Historical Books of the Old Testament*, 45.

presentation of the story of Jesus, who experienced the transformation from Creator and Sustainer of the universe (Col 1:16–17), to that of a baby lying in a feeding trough (Luke 2:7), to that of Savior of humanity (John 3:16–17).

David's story, already possessing intrinsic interest because of the magnitude of the reversals in his life, is made all the more interesting through the other roles played by David in the narrative. David is consecutively a youthful giant killer, Israel's most famous military commander, son-in-law of the king, the most feared outlaw in Israel, a marauding soldier under the protection of a hostile nation, a rival Israelite king, king of all Israel, an adulterer, a murderer, a refugee living in exile, and leader of an armed military force that killed his primary heir. So complex and varied is the story of David that it is difficult to imagine the successful presentation of the material in any single drama or film today.

The literary success story of David is heightened by the use of subplots. The tragic subplot involving the downfall of Israel's most famous—and corrupt—high priestly family is artfully woven into David's own story: David plays the role of a naive accomplice in the murder of eighty-five priests and their families. Though he attempts to compensate for his role in the tragedy by making the lone survivor of the massacre his primary priest (cf. 1 Kgs 2:35), he is actually only setting up the priest and his descendants for their permanent removal from sacerdotal service (1 Kgs 2:27).

Likewise the subplot centering around the prophet/judge Samuel also ties in with the life of David. Though the greatest of Israel's judges, Samuel also is Israel's last. It is he, acting as the Lord's agent, who defrocks Israel's first king, thus opening the way for David to assume the position of supremacy in Israel. It also is he who anoints David as king and provides supernatural protection when Israel's rejected king tries to kill him. Lastly, it is the dead Samuel who speaks the final prophetic words of doom against David's predecessor on Israel's throne, thereby preparing the audience to experience David's kingship.

The subplot revolving around the person of Saul also supports and enhances the story of David. His primary function is that of a foil, providing a vivid contrast between his own life and that of David. Saul is first portrayed as a bad shepherd; David, as a faithful shepherd; Saul is a king such as the nations have; David is a king after Yahweh's heart; Saul disobeys the Lord repeatedly throughout his career; David, only once. When confronted, Saul confesses his sin only begrudgingly; David, without hesitation.

The subplot involving the ark of the covenant also interlocks with the story of David. Whereas the ark brought judgment in every Philistine city into which it was taken, it resided in David's Jerusalem without incident.

CHARACTERIZATION. Perhaps the most effective literary dimension of the books of Samuel is that of characterization. With unmatched skill the author succeeds in creating three major characters—Samuel, Saul, and David—who simultaneously become real people and larger-than-life entities that cement the books of Samuel into their scriptural matrix.

Samuel. The writer's portrayal of this prophet/judge functions as a bridge between the text of 1, 2 Samuel and the Torah. Through the careful and highly selective use of historical detail, the author succeeds in portraying Samuel as the long-foreseen prophet who would be like Moses (cf. Deut 18:15–18).[52] Both Samuel and Moses were raised in environments outside their own homes. Both received their initial revelations from God in solitude, in the presence of a burning object, with their name being mentioned twice by God at the beginning of the encounter. During that first encounter with the Lord both were told of divine judgments that would come against the authority structures in which they were reared. Both were called prophets, and unlike any others in the Torah and Former Prophets, both were called "faithful." Both spoke words of judgment against leaders who had abused the Israelites. Both personally killed one oppressor of Israelites and then went into a season of self-imposed exile. Both wrote down regulations that were deposited before the Lord. Both performed some priestly duties, yet neither was ever termed a priest. Both acted as judges and were responsible for major transitions in Israelite history. Both had two named sons, none of whom played significant roles in later history. At the Lord's direction, both anointed individuals who led Israel to fight against—and defeat—the inhabitants of Jerusalem, act in behalf of the Gibeonites, and conquer the Promised Land.

The deliberateness and precision with which the writer demonstrated the parallels between Moses and Samuel betray his consummate skill and a sophisticated, nuanced understanding of Israelite history and religion.

Saul. To create a foil to David, the writer carefully chose details from the life of Saul that emphasized his identity as a king "such as all the other nations have"—that is, a king unfit to lead the Israelites. From the opening image through the depiction of his death, Saul is shown to be one who was alien to the practices and values of proper Israelite culture.

Being noted genealogically as a member of the most spiritually degraded tribe in Israel (1 Sam 9:1), Saul is first presented as being tall, a trait used elsewhere in the Bible only to describe noncovenant people. The first Saul narrative depicts him as an incompetent shepherd—symbolic in Israelite culture of an unfit ruler—one so inept that over a period of days he cannot find a pack of donkeys that temporarily strayed from home (1 Sam 9:3ff.). Immediately thereafter the writer demonstrates Saul to be spiritually dark: he has to be told that Samuel, the most famous spiritual leader since Moses, lives nearby and can help him with his problems; he does not recognize the prophet/judge when he sees him, and then believes he must pay to receive insight from a Yahwistic prophet

---

[52] For a more detailed description of the comparison, cf. the discussion prior to 1 Sam 1:1.

(1 Sam 9:6–19); later he will seek insight through the forbidden practice of necromancy (1 Sam 28:7–15). Even though he knows God has selected him to be Israel's first king, Saul initially refuses to attend his anointing ceremony, hiding instead among the baggage (1 Sam 10:17–24). He alone among all the kings of Israel and Judah is described as being periodically under the influence of an evil spirit (1 Sam 16:14,23; 18:10; 19:9). Though he was made king in order to bring Israel military victories against their foes (1 Sam 8:20; 12:12), Saul showed repeated evidence of incompetence and abuse as commander-in-chief: he crippled his troops' abilities by ordering them to fast on the day of battle (1 Sam 14:28), foolishly gave orders to kill two of Israel's finest soldiers (1 Sam 14:43–44; 19:1), spared the life of one of Israel's most hated enemies (1 Sam 15:8–9), and diverted the use of national military resources to pursue a personal enemy (1 Sam 23:7ff.). He was depicted as an unjust judge who wrongfully ordered the death of eighty-five Aaronic priests and their families (1 Sam 22:6–19). On two occasions he attempted to kill his own son (1 Sam 14:43–44; 20:33); on sixteen occasions (!) he attempted to kill David, the Lord's anointed (cf. note in "1, 2 Samuel as Apology"). When mortally wounded on the battlefield, Saul attempted to end his own life through suicide (1 Sam 31:4); however, so incompetent was he even in this disgusting matter that he had to order an enemy to finish the job (2 Sam 1:8–10).

To be fair, the writer also notes certain virtuous and heroic aspects of Saul's career—his deliverance of the Jabeshites (1 Sam 11:1–11); victories against Moab, Ammon, Edom, Zobah, Amalek, and the Philistines (1 Sam 14:47–48); enforcement of certain Torah regulations throughout society (1 Sam 28:9); and bringing of increased economic prosperity to Israel (2 Sam 1:24). These more complimentary facts regarding Saul's career can be gleaned from the text, but they are deliberately minimized in order to achieve the writer's desired literary and thematic effects. As such, this is not a fault but a freedom unapologetically exercised by a writer pursuing a purpose higher than the reporting of materialistic, geopolitical history.

David. David's life is a literary hologram of the history and destiny of Israel. Through the discreet selection and arrangement of events included in the telling of David's life, the writer has given a sophisticated theological shape to the David narratives—one that would have communicated hope to a people who doubted the status of Israel's covenant promises, especially that of return to the Promised Land (cf. Deut 30:3–5). The parallels between David's life and key aspects of the history of Israel are numerous and deliberate: like Abraham and Isaac, Israel's founding patriarchs, David was a shepherd (1 Sam 16:11); like Joseph he received a divine promise during his youth that he would be leader of his people (1 Sam 16:12); like Joseph also he faithfully served in a king's court (1 Sam 16:19–22); like Moses and Israel in Egypt, youthful David defeated a seemingly invincible opponent (1 Sam 17:32ff.); like Israel, David had an extended experience in the wilderness that involved moving from place to place (1 Sam 22:1ff.); like Israel he fought and defeated the Amalekites during his time in the wilderness (1 Sam 30:1ff.); like Israel, David received prophetic blessings from an opponent during his wilderness experience (1 Sam 26:25); like Israel, David reentered the land but took control of it only gradually over a period of time (2 Sam 2:1ff.); like Israel, David conquered Jerusalem and established it as the nation's capital (2 Sam 5:6ff.); like Israel, David possessed the Promised Land and defeated enemies on every side (2 Sam 8:1ff.); like Israel, David committed grievous violations of the Torah that resulted in divine judgment and escalating internal problems (2 Sam 11:1ff.); like Israel, David was forced to go into exile east of the Jordan River (2 Sam 15:13ff.) and resided, like a later Davidic king, in a capital city previously considered hostile (2 Sam 17:24); like Israel, David went into exile without the ark (2 Sam 15:25); like Israel, David ultimately returned from exile to Jerusalem (2 Sam 19:11ff.); like Israel, David experienced opposition from people in the land following his return from exile (2 Sam 20:1ff.).

Once again the writer's careful selection, arrangement, and presentation of biographical data achieves effects that go far beyond those of uninspired, secular history. The author's craftsmanship has produced a vision of David that is as big as the nation of Israel, as grand as the covenantal promises of God.

WORDPLAYS. The writer of 1, 2 Samuel displayed great ability as a wordsmith. Two of the best examples of his artistry involve the use of the Hebrew roots *ngd* and *nbl*. The writer plays upon two widely disparate meanings of the first of these roots in 1 Samuel 9: in v. 6 Saul's servant suggests that Samuel "will tell" (lit., "will cause to *ngd* [make known]") Saul where to find the missing donkeys. In v. 16 the Lord tells Samuel to make a man from the land of Benjamin a *ngd*, and in 10:1 Samuel does indeed act as an agent *ngd*-ing Saul.

The root *nbl* ("fool") is used throughout 1 Samuel to draw comparisons between Saul and Nabal (1 Sam 13:13; 25:3–5,9–10,14,19,25–26,34,36,38; 26:21). Both are described as kings or kinglike, and both behave wrongly toward David. The death of Nabal vindicates David and foreshadows the death of Saul. The use of the term *nbl* reinforces this theme.

(3) 1, 2 Samuel as Apology

Another possible approach in reading 1, 2 Samuel is to view them as literature written to defend certain leading figures in the Israelite monarchy from accusations made against them and to provide an accounting for some of their controversial actions and policies. Although scholars do not understand the entire composition to have been written solely for this purpose, many twentieth-century scholars have assumed that major portions of this work— especially the so-called "Rise of David" and "Succession Narrative" sections (approx. 1 Samuel 16–2 Samuel 5 and 2 Samuel 9–20, respectively) were written to strengthen David's and Solomon's claims to the throne of Israel.[53]

Three politically and religiously sensitive events are accounted for in the 1, 2 Samuel narratives. In their order of significance they are the following: David's displacement of Saul and his male heirs on the throne of Israel, Solomon's rise to kingship, and the Abiatharites' disqualification from priestly service. The text's treatment of each of these matters will be examined below.

DAVID'S DISPLACEMENT OF SAUL AND HIS MALE HEIRS ON THE THRONE OF ISRAEL. This issue receives the majority of the narrator's attention in 1, 2 Samuel. A careful reading of the stories involving Saul and David suggests that a number of serious accusations were made against David by Israelites who had supported Saul and resented David's kingship. Some of the most damaging accusations against David would be the following: he usurped the throne of Saul;[54] he coerced Israel's religious establishment into conspiring against Saul's kingship; he organized and led a rebel military force for the purpose of overthrowing the Saulide dynasty; after being banished from Israel, he conducted plundering raids against Israelite territories; he fought against Israel alongside the Philistines in the battle in which Saul died; he was responsible for the execution of Saul's surviving male relatives; he was responsible for the murder of Abner.

These charges are understandable in light of the some of the facts presented in 1, 2 Samuel. Consider the following details concerning David: he did indeed become king after Saul, even though at one time the Lord had indicated that the kingdom would be passed on to Saul's descendants (cf. 1 Sam 13:13–14); he himself spread reports that he was plundering Israelite territory (1 Sam 27:10); David was so thoroughly admired and trusted by the Philistine king Achish that he was appointed his chief bodyguard (1 Sam 28:2); Saul and his three primary heirs died in a battle against the Philistines at the very time the Philistines were protecting David from Saul; shortly after Saul's death, David took possession of Saul's royal jewelry (2 Sam 1:10); David took possession of Saul's harem (2 Sam 12:8); at least eight of Saul's male descendants were killed while David was king (2 Sam 4:6; 21:8–9); half of Saul's family estate was taken away from his heirs at David's command (2 Sam 19:29); Abner, Saul's relative and com-

---

[53] Cf. Rost, *Succession to the Throne of David*. Rost's main thesis is that this section of Scripture was written originally to justify the claim of Solomon to the throne of David.

[54] Note the statement by J. M. Miller and J. H. Hayes: "I Samuel 16–II Samuel 7 serves as an apology for David's usurpation of the throne and functions as authenticating tradition to legitimate both the Davidic dynasty and the preeminence of Jerusalem in the life of the people and the plan of Yahweh" (*A History of Ancient Israel and Judah* [Philadelphia: Westminster, 1986], 154). Cf. also N. P. Lemche, "David's Rise," *JSOT* 10 (1978): 2–25; L. Rost, *Succession to the Throne of David,* trans. M. D. Rutter and D. M. Gunn (Sheffield: Almond, 1982); P. K. McCarter, Jr., "The Apology of David," *JBL* 99 (1980): 489–504; J. C. Vanderkam, "Davidic Complicity in the Deaths of Abner and Eshbaal: A Historical and Redactional Study," *JBL* 99 (1980): 521–39; and Klein, *1 Samuel,* xxxi.

manding officer, died in David's capital city at the hands of David's commanding officer. If supporters of Saulide dynastic hopes were hostile toward David,
it is no wonder!

Nevertheless, the books of Samuel make it abundantly clear that David at
no time acted improperly toward Saul or any member of Saul's household,
even though Saul made at least sixteen different efforts to murder David.[55] The
narrative portrays David as absolutely loyal to Saul and his household, even
long after the first king's death.

The following events can be presented as evidence of the profound effort
made by the narrator to present David as Saul's most loyal and devoted citizen:
David regularly delivered Saul from the torment of a troubling spirit (1 Sam
16:23; 18:10–11); David delivered Saul and his army from the humiliation of
Goliath's challenge (1 Sam 17:26,36); David successfully performed every
military task given him by Saul (1 Sam 18:5); David wept more than Jonathan
did when they were forced to be separated from one another (1 Sam 20:41);
David served as captain of Saul's bodyguard (1 Sam 22:14); Ahimelech indicated that David was Saul's most loyal servant and highly respected in Saul's
household (1 Sam 22:14); when presented with the opportunity, David refused
to take Saul's life at En Gedi (1 Sam 24:4–6); David refused to let his men take
Saul's life at En Gedi (1 Sam 24:7); David bowed down and prostrated himself
before Saul (1 Sam 24:8); even after David was sentenced to death by Saul, he
called him "my master," "the LORD's anointed" (1 Sam 24:10), "father," and
"king" (1 Sam 24:10–11,14; 26:20); David swore an oath to Saul that he would
not cut off Saul's family line (1 Sam 24:21–22); when given the opportunity,
David refused to kill Saul in his camp at night (1 Sam 26:11); David carried out
the death penalty against the man who helped Saul die (2 Sam 1:14–15); David
publicly lamented both Saul's and Jonathan's deaths (2 Sam 1:17–27); David
called Saul and Jonathan "[Israel's] glory" (2 Sam 1:19), "the mighty" (2 Sam
1:19,21–22,25,27), "loved and gracious" (2 Sam 1:23); David called Saul one
who "clothed [the daughters of Israel] in scarlet and finery" and "adorned
[their] garments with ornaments of gold" (2 Sam 1:24); David publicly
lamented Abner's murder and called him a "prince and a great man" (2 Sam
3:31–38); David pronounced an eternal curse on the family line of Abner's
murderer (2 Sam 3:28–37); David called Ishbosheth "an innocent man" (2 Sam
4:11); David executed Ishbosheth's murderers (2 Sam 4:12); David treated Ish-

---

[55] Saul made three attempts to kill David using a spear (1 Sam 18:11; 19:10); Saul twice tried
to use the Philistines to kill David (1 Sam 18:17,25); Saul told his son Jonathan to kill David
(1 Sam 19:1); Saul twice told his slaves to kill David (1 Sam 19:1,11); Saul ordered his servants to
fetch David from Michal's house so he could kill David himself (1 Sam 19:15); Saul sent three
groups of men to murder David while he was with Samuel (1 Sam 19:20–21); Saul himself tried to
murder David at Naioth (1 Sam 19:23–24); Saul led at least three military expeditions into Judah
to kill David (1 Sam 23:8; 24:2; 26:2).

bosheth with respect after his death (2 Sam 4:12); David initiated the efforts to honor his covenants with Jonathan and Saul by instituting a search for an heir to Jonathan (2 Sam 9:1–5); David restored all of the family lands to Mephibosheth (2 Sam 9:7); David permitted Mephibosheth to live in Jerusalem and eat at the royal table for the rest of his life (2 Sam 9:13); in spite of Mephibosheth's possible treachery, David permitted him to retain his life and half of the family estate (2 Sam 19:29); David provided Saul, Jonathan, and the victims of the Gibeonite execution with a dignified burial in the family tomb at Zela in Benjamin (2 Sam 21:12–14).

What is more, key members of Saul's family, administration, and kingdom respected David and recognized him as Saul's rightful successor. Saul, Jonathan, Michal, Abner, the elders of Israel, and Saul's military officers are all represented in 1, 2 Samuel as responding positively to some aspect of David and his career. Consider the following details from Saul's life presented in 1 Samuel: it was Saul himself who brought David to his court (16:19–20); Saul at one time loved David (16:21); Saul chose to keep David at his court (18:2); Saul elevated David to a high rank in his army (18:5); Saul twice invited David to become his son-in-law (18:17–27); Saul personally gave his daughter Michal to David in marriage (18:27); Saul called David "my son" (24:16); Saul confessed to David that David would be king (24:20); Saul blessed David and confessed that David would do great things and triumph (26:25).

Jonathan, the heir-apparent to Saul's throne, likewise is portrayed in 1 Samuel as one who had extremely high regard for David: Jonathan loved David and sensed a oneness in spirit with him (18:1); Jonathan initiated and later affirmed a loyalty covenant with David (18:3–4; 20:42); Jonathan informed David of Saul's intention to kill him (19:1); Jonathan served as an advocate for David before Saul (19:4–5); when David asked Jonathan to kill him if he judged him worthy of death, Jonathan refused (20:8–9); Jonathan served as David's informant, helping him find out Saul's true intentions for David (20:4–40); when David was fleeing from Saul, Jonathan went to David to help him find strength in God (23:16); Jonathan confessed to David that David would be king (23:17).

In addition, 1, 2 Samuel note the following details concerning Michal, Abner, Saul's officers, Israel's elders, and the general population of the kingdom: Michal loved David (1 Sam 18:28); Michal warned David of Saul's intention to kill him (1 Sam 19:11); Michal helped David escape from Saul's men (1 Sam 19:12–13); Abner stated that the Lord promised that David would rescue Israel (2 Sam 3:18); Saul's military officers were pleased when Saul elevated David's rank (1 Sam 18:6); Israel's elders confessed publicly the Lord had commissioned David to lead Israel (2 Sam 5:2); Saul's constituents were pleased with his decision to elevate David's rank in the military (1 Sam 18:6); all Israel loved David (1 Sam 18:15); and all Judah loved David (1 Sam 18:15).

Though Saul's family experienced a series of profound tragedies, David was shown to be completely free of any responsibility for any of them. Instead, it was the Philistines, Amalekites, and Saul himself who were represented in the text as sharing culpability for Saul's death (1 Sam 31:3,5; 2 Sam 1:10). Jonathan, Malkishua, and Abinadab were killed by the Philistines (1 Sam 31:2). Ishbosheth was murdered by two of his own military personnel, Recab and Baanah (2 Sam 4:7). Seven of Saul's other male descendants were slain "before the LORD" by the Gibeonites as a recompense for Saul's unwarranted actions against this Amorite group (2 Sam 21:2,9). If the biblical explanations are accepted, then David is not only vindicated but exemplary in his conduct.

SOLOMON'S RISE TO KINGSHIP. Since Rost's publication of *Die Überlieferung von der Thronnachfolge Davids* in 1926, Samuel scholars have regularly assumed that 2 Samuel 9–20 and 1 Kings 1–2 were originally part of a connected, independent narrative written to describe the process by which a successor to David was chosen. This presumed work usually is termed the Succession Narrative.[56] More recently, scholarly opinion has interpreted these chapters as a sympathetic presentation of the process by which Solomon rose to power and secured his position as Israel's third king.[57]

The existence of an originally independent Solomonic apology, however, is highly questionable. It generally is fruitless to speculate on hypothetical documents that may underlie the canonical text. Nevertheless, it seems clear that 1, 2 Samuel—not just 2 Samuel 9–20—was written in part to provide a defense to charges that Solomon acted improperly in challenging Adonijah's right to kingship and in carrying out certain activities during the earliest period of his administration. There were aspects of Solomon's reign that must have been troubling to many Israelites of his day. Solomon rose to power in a disturbing way—he made a public claim to the throne only after his brother Adonijah had already been anointed as king (1 Kgs 1:5–39). Not only did Solomon's claim come later than Adonijah's, but it also was weaker, since Adonijah was David's oldest living son and Solomon apparently was only David's tenth-born son (2 Sam 3:2–5; 5:14). Soon after toppling Adonijah from power, Solomon had him killed (1 Kgs 2:25). Abiathar, the Aaronic priest who had anointed Adonijah as king, was banished from Jerusalem by Solomon and stripped of his right to perform priestly functions (1 Kgs 2:26–27). Solomon also had Joab, David's most capable military commander, put

---

[56] Reflective of the tendency to view these chapters as an originally separate document are Philbeck, "1–2 Samuel," 3:5–7, 107; and Hertzberg, *I and II Samuel,* 299.

[57] McCarter's perspective differs from many others in that he assumes that no Solomonic apology exists in 1, 2 Samuel. It is confined instead to 1 Kgs 1–2 (*II Samuel,* 13–16). His analysis, however, fails to account adequately for the fact that Solomon's actions against Joab and Abiathar find much of their historical justification in 1, 2 Samuel, and the description of Adonijah and his actions plays off parallels contained in the Absalom account.

to death (1 Kgs 2:28–34). Finally, he continued the bloodbath among Saul's relatives, ordering the execution of Shimei (1 Kgs 2:36–46).

Nevertheless, readers of 1, 2 Samuel are prepared to react positively to these events in Solomon's life. Significant indications are given in 2 Samuel that the Lord had long desired Solomon to be Israel's next king. Of David's fifteen sons mentioned by name in 2 Samuel, only of Solomon is it stated that "the LORD loved him" (2 Sam 12:24–25). Solomon is also the only child who was given the rare privilege of being renamed by the Lord—an event not seen since the days of the Torah patriarchs.

Because 1 Samuel has informed the reader that Abiathar is a direct descendant of Eli (22:20; 14:3) and therefore under a generations-old divine curse (1 Sam 2:36), Solomon's actions toward Abiathar are viewed as a divinely mandated inevitability (cf. Exod 20:5), essentially the performance of a drama scripted by the Lord himself. Because of two unjustified killings committed by Joab and recorded in 2 Samuel, Joab's execution can be seen as the fulfillment of the Torah-mandated penalty for murder (cf. 2 Sam 3:29; 20:10; Gen 9:6). Shimei's death likewise was warranted because he violated an especially serious aspect of the Torah's code of conduct (cf. 2 Sam 5–13; Exod 22:28; 1 Kgs 21:10–13). Thus Solomon, like his father David before him, can justifiably be perceived as Israel's rightful monarch, innocent of any wrongdoing in the disputable matters arising in the earliest period of his kingship.

THE ABIATHARITES' DISQUALIFICATION FROM PRIESTLY SERVICE. As suggested above, it is probable that Solomon's expulsion of Abiathar (and presumably his family as well) from Jerusalem and his removal from the priesthood created an uproar. After all, Abiathar had been of inestimable help to David's family for many years. As the priest entrusted with the reve-latory ephod, he had disclosed the Lord's will to David at critical points in his career (1 Sam 22:10,15; 23:1–6; cf. also 30:8; 2 Sam 2:1; 5:19,23). Abi-athar also had risked his life and the life of his son Jonathan to provide intelligence reports to David during Absalom's rebellion (2 Sam 17:15). Ahimelech, another of his sons, had served as one of David's chief priests (2 Sam 8:17).

Solomon's immediate reason for defrocking Abiathar was the priest's role in placing Adonijah on Israel's throne. Ostensibly, Solomon was punishing Abiathar for participating in a second filial rebellion against David (cf. 1 Kgs 1:17–18). Yet the biblical writer de-emphasizes this aspect, directing the reader instead to interpret Solomon's actions in light of the Lord's judgment on the house of Eli (1 Kgs 2:27; cf. 1 Sam 2:35–36). Solomon, like the Philistines and Saul before him, acted as God's agent in removing all priestly authority from a rejected Aaronic family; 1 Samuel provides the context necessary for under-standing the deeper meaning of Solomon's activities.[58]

(4) 1, 2 Samuel as Theology

Certainly a central purpose for writing 1, 2 Samuel was to communicate and reinforce religious beliefs of profound importance to the writer and his community. This "overarching theological perspective"[59] served as the framework into which historical and literary data were woven. The primary theological purpose was to support the teachings of the Torah and thus (cf. also the discussion under "1, 2 Samuel as Scripture," p. 45) to provide guidance and hope for Israel's exilic community.

Samuel's narrative tapestry is woven around the theological threads of the Torah. Accordingly, the themes of covenant, land, divine presence, and demand for wholehearted obedience to the Lord's revelation can all be discerned in these books.

COVENANT. Yahweh, the God who spoke gracious covenantal words to Noah (Gen 9:1–17), Abraham (Gen 15:18–21; 17:4–14), Isaac (Gen 17:19,21), Jacob (Exod 2:24), Eleazar (Num 25:12–13), and the people of Israel (Exod 24:8), is shown establishing a covenant with David in the books of Samuel (2 Sam 7:8–16). In the covenantal promise with David the Lord bestowed eternal, unmerited blessings, while at the same time promising stern judgment for sin. The Lord's covenant with David and his descendants was unconditional and eternal (cf. 2 Sam 7:16; 1 Chr 7:14; Pss 45:6; 89:36–37; Heb 1:8); however, as Walton has pointed out, "the covenant was subject to periodic renewal" and was subject to modification because of sins committed by David's son Solomon (cf. 1 Kgs 11:31–39).[60]

---

[58] Readers familiar with the Torah will be able to see an even wider context for understanding the actions against Abiathar and his family. Israel's first high priest, Aaron, had four sons—Nadab, Abihu, Eleazar, and Ithamar—all of whom were originally consecrated for the purpose of performing priestly service. However, over the years three of the four family lines were disqualified by Yahweh from service at the central altar (cf. Lev 10:1–2; 1 Sam 3:35–36). The family lines of Nadab and Abihu were eliminated early in Israel's history (cf. Lev 10:1–2). The two remaining family lines, those of Eleazar and Ithamar, served side by side in the priesthood for hundreds of years. Yet in the Torah Yahweh promised only the family of Eleazar that they would continually possess the right to provide priestly leadership for Israel (Num 25:12–13). Abiathar was from the family line of Ithamar; Zadok was a descendant of Eleazar (cf. 1 Chr 24:3). Consequently Solomon's actions in 1 Kings 2 can be seen as a double fulfillment of Yahweh's declarations. Zadok's rise to the position of sole high priest was the climactic outcome of a divine promise found in the Torah, even as Abiathar's downfall was the result of the divine curse presented in 1 Samuel 2.

[59] B. S. Childs, *Introduction to the Old Testament as Scripture* (Philadelphia: Fortress, 1979), 278.

[60] A. E. Hill and J. H. Walton, *A Survey of the Old Testament* (Grand Rapids: Zondervan, 1991), 198. According to Walton (p. 199), "the New Testament came to recognize Jesus as the one who would bring the renewal of the David covenant" after its Solomonically induced modification. Thus, Davidic messianism after the time of Solomon was based on "the promise of a continued 'lamp' [cf. 1 Kgs 11:36] and the understanding that reduced control [i.e., kingship over Judah only] was only temporary" (cf. 1 Kgs 11:39).

LAND. Likewise, a major emphasis in the Torah is possession of the Promised Land.[61] In the Torah Israel's retention of the land promised to Abraham
was dependent on Israel's obedience to the Lord. So it was also in 1, 2 Samuel.
Israel's grip on the Promised Land was especially related to the spiritual obedience of its leadership, for pious rulers naturally led the nation to follow
divinely mandated ways. Thus, under obedient and faithful leaders Israel
retained and even expanded its control over the Promised Land. Samuel (cf.
1 Sam 7:14) helped Israel regain territories taken by the Philistines. David—
prior to his sin against Uriah and Bathsheba—led Israel to even greater degrees
of possession, perhaps even helping Israel gain control of the full extent of the
lands first promised to Abraham (cf. 1 Sam 27:8–9 [the southern boundary];
2 Sam 8:3–9 [the northern boundary]). On the other hand, the sins of Israel's
leaders inevitably resulted in military defeat, loss of territory (1 Sam 4:10
[Elides]; 31:7 [Saul]), and even exile from the land (2 Sam 15:14; 17:22
[David]).

THE PRESENCE OF GOD. Consistent with Torah theology is an emphasis
on the presence of God among his chosen and faithful followers. The two most
well-defined servants of the Lord in 1, 2 Samuel are also those of whom it was
said, "The LORD was with" him—Samuel (once: 1 Sam 3:19) and David (seven
times: 1 Sam 16:13,18; 18:12,14,28; 2 Sam 5:10; 7:3).

The theme of God's presence among his people is not limited to the examples of Samuel and David; the various ark narratives in 1, 2 Samuel reinforce
the teaching that the Lord possessed an abiding presence with the ark (cf. Lev
16:2). The Lord's presence with the ark meant that where the ark went, the Lord
went (1 Sam 4:4); where the ark went, the Lord's hand of judgment (1 Sam 5:6;
6:19–20; 2 Sam 6:6–7) and blessing (2 Sam 6:11–12) was also present; where
the ark was, revelation was to be found (1 Sam 3:3–14). Because the Lord's
presence in the earthly order is real and dynamic, the ultimate Source of all
blessing and judgment is equally at hand, ready to dispense either according to
human choices and divine grace.

THE DEMAND FOR WHOLEHEARTED OBEDIENCE TO THE LORD. First
and Second Samuel resonate with the central theological thesis of the Torah,
namely that obedience to Yahweh brings about blessing while disobedience to
him—even in the least detail—brings about judgment (cf. Gen 22:15–18; Lev
26; Deut 28). Appropriately, the most-remembered theological statement in

---

[61] Cf. Gen 12:7; 13:15–17; 15:7,18–21; 17:8; 24:7; 26:3; 28:4,13; 35:12; 48:4,21; 50:24; Exod
3:8,17; 6:4,8; 12:25; 13:5,11; 20:12; 23:31; 32:13; 33:1–3; Lev 14:34; 20:22–24; 23:10; 25:2,38;
26:42; Num 11:12; 13:2; 14:8,16,23–24,30–31; 15:2,18; 20:12; 27:12; 32:11; 33:51–54; 32:2–14;
35:10; 36:2; Deut 1:8,21,25,35–36; 2:12; 3:18–20; 3:28; 4:1,5,14,21–22,26,38,40; 5:16,31,33;
6:1,10,18,23; 7:1,13; 8:1,7,10; 9:5–6,23,28; 10:11; 11:8–12,17,21,29; 12:1,10,29; 15:4,7; 16:20;
17:14; 18:9; 19:1,8,10,14; 23:20; 24:4; 25:15,19; 26:1–3,9; 27:2–3; 28:8,11,52,63; 30:5,16,18,20;
31:7,13,21,23; 32:47,49,52; 34:4.

1, 2 Samuel is found on the lips of Samuel, the levitical prophet whose life story was deliberately shaped to be like that of Moses (cf. discussion at section heading preceding 1:1): "Does the LORD delight in burnt offerings and sacrifices as much as in obeying the voice of the LORD? To obey is better than sacrifice, and to heed is better than the fat of rams" (1 Sam 15:22). Yet this theological affirmation is by no means monolithic. Similarly Mosaic in tone are the following admonitions from Samuel: "If you are returning to the LORD with all your hearts, then rid yourselves of the foreign gods and Ashtaroths, and commit yourselves to the LORD and serve him only, and he will deliver you" (1 Sam 7:3); "Do not turn away from the LORD, but serve the LORD with all your heart. . . . Be sure to fear the LORD and serve him faithfully with all your heart. . . . Yet if you persist in doing evil, both you and your king will be swept away" (1 Sam 12:20b,24a,25).

This most significant of theological themes, stated eloquently in the quotational sections of Samuel, is underlined through the events of the books of Samuel. It was the sinful acts of Hophni, Phinehas, and Eli (cf. 1 Sam 2:17,29) that eventuated their judgment and death, just as it was Samuel's pious and obedient service (cf. 1 Sam 2:26; 3:18) that caused him to rise to the status of an esteemed national leader (cf. 1 Sam 3:20). It was Saul's repeated sins (cf. 1 Sam 13:8–13; 15:9,23–24; 28:7–16) that led to his disqualification as dynastic founder and king, as well as his death. It was the actions issuing from David's obedient heart (cf. 1 Sam 13:14) that led the Lord to give him "victory wherever he went" (2 Sam 8:14), just as it was David's disobedience (cf. 2 Sam 11:2–17; 12:9) that brought about the curses that devastated his family (cf. 2 Sam 12:10–12,14–15; 13:14,28–29; 16:22; 18:15).

(5) 1, 2 Samuel as Scripture

The primary function of the books of Samuel throughout history within Judaism and Christianity has been and continues to be that of Holy Scripture, that is, as the Word of God written. As Scripture they have historically functioned as a supremely trusted source of guidance and hope for individuals and communities of faith. As holy Scripture they have been and continue to be confidently utilized as a source of accurate, authoritative insight into the past, present, and future. They are part of the Bibles of both Judaism and Christianity, a situation that accounts for the fact that they, along with the remainder of the corpus of Judeo-Christian Scriptures, have been reprinted more than any other document in the history of humanity.

The primary functions of 1, 2 Samuel as Scripture in both Judaism and Christianity are discussed below.

1, 2 SAMUEL AS JEWISH SCRIPTURE.   Judaism has historically understood 1, 2 Samuel to be the totally authoritative, accurate, and trustworthy Word of God. For historic Judaism these holy books contained both backward and for-

ward looks. They looked backward to Moses and the Torah, yet they also
looked to the future, giving definition and focus to the messianic tradition.

1, 2 Samuel as a Witness to the Torah.   Jewish tradition originating prior to
the first century A.D. recognized the books of Samuel as the very word of God
conveyed through prophets; they were thus appropriately included among the
Former Prophets in the Hebrew canon. Their primary function, like that of all
the other prophetic books, was to reiterate and clarify the message of the Torah,
not to nuance, extend, or contest it. As the Talmud notes: "Our rabbis learned:
48 prophets and 7 prophetesses prophesied for Israel and they did not detract
from or add to that which is written in the Torah except for the reading of the
Megillah."[62] The books of Samuel would never have been included in the
Hebrew canon of Scripture or used in worship if they were perceived to contradict the Torah in any way.[63] Thus 1, 2 Samuel, like other portions of the
Former and Latter Prophets, play a supportive role in Scripture. They are

> transmitters of a continuous tradition beginning with Moses; the Prophets and
> the Hagiographa explain the Pentateuch. Thus all the rest of the sacred books,
> with no detraction from their divine inspiration and authority, are an authority
> of the second rank; they repeat, reinforce, amplify, and explain the Law, but are
> never independent of it. Proof-texts are often quoted in threes, a verse from the
> Pentateuch, another from the Prophets, and a third from the Hagiographa, not
> as though the word of the Law needed confirmation, but to show how the
> Scripture emphasizes the lesson by iteration.[64]

Evidences of 1, 2 Samuel's interconnections with the Torah are wide-rang-
ing and abundant. They include explicit references and inferences to historical
details found in the Torah, awareness of Torah legal materials, theology, prophecies, and even literary motifs. Historical and legal connections are reflected in
the following charts.

---

[62] Tractate *Megillah* 14a. Cf. A. Cohen, *Everyman's Talmud* (New York: Schocken, 1975), 123.
My thanks to S. Klammer for providing me with this quotation.

[63] Reflective of the extreme concern Judaism has had for all portions of the Prophets to agree
with the Torah is the Talmudic notation that Hananiah ben Hezekiah burned three hundred jars of
oil in his efforts to harmonize Ezekiel with the Torah. Furthermore, chap. 1 was banned from use
in synagogue worship during the first century A.D. Cf. W. S. LaSor et al., *Old Testament Survey*
(Grand Rapids: Eerdmans, 1982), 464, who referred to *t. Šabb.* 13b. For the talmudic passage
itself, cf. Cohen, *Everyman's Talmud*, 145.

[64] G. F. Moore, *Judaism in the First Centuries of the Christian Era: The Age of the Tannaim,*
Vol. I (Cambridge: Harvard University Press), 239–40.

Table 2: Historical Interconnections

	Samuel	Torah
Jacob	2 Sam 23:1	
Jacob goes to Egypt	1 Sam 12:8	
Rachel	1 Sam 10:2	cf. Gen 35:19; 48:7
Aaron and Moses	1 Sam 12:6,8	
Israel's cries for deliverance	1 Sam 12:8	cf. Exod 2:23
exodus	1 Sam 12:6,8	
Gad's land in Transjordan	1 Sam 13:7	cf. Num 34:14
house of Joseph leader in Israel	2 Sam 19:20	cf. Gen 49:26; Deut 33:16
Tribes of Israel: Levi Judah Dan Gad Ephraim Benjamin	1 Sam 6:15; 2 Sam 15:24 1 Sam 11:8; 15:4, etc. 1 Sam 3:20, etc. 1 Sam 13:7 1 Sam 1:1 1 Sam 4:12, etc.	
tribal land allotments	1 Sam 1:1; 3:20; 9:4; 13:7; 17:1	
Israel's eleven tribal allotments[a]	2 Sam 19:43	
Levi's sacerdotal duties	1 Sam 6:15; 2 Sam 15:24	
Calebites' inheritance	1 Sam 30:14	cf. Num 14:24: Deut 1:36

a. The number eleven—the "ten" of 2 Sam 19:43 plus the tribe of Judah—implies that
the reckoning included the assumptions that the house of Joseph was ultimately
one tribe and that the Levites were not allotted any land.

One historical reference in Samuel seems at variance with the Torah: the mention of gods who struck the Egyptians in the desert (1 Sam 4:8). However, this allusion is found in a Philistine quotation and probably is meant to portray the foreign soldiers' ignorance of even the most well-known aspects of Torah history.

Table 3: Legal Interconnections

	Samuel	Torah
Nazirite vow	1 Sam 1:11	cf. Num 6:1–21
annual pilgrimages	1 Sam 1:3,7,21	cf. Deut 12:5–7
husband's approval of vow	1 Sam 1:21–23	cf. Num 30:10–15
bull, flour, wine offerings	1 Sam 1:24	cf. Num 15:9–10
freewill offerings	1 Sam 2:17,29; 3:14; 26:19	
three-pronged offering fork	1 Sam 2:13	cf. Exod 27:3; 38:3
order of sacrificial actions	1 Sam 2:15	cf. Lev 3:1–16; 7:28–34
Tent of Meeting	1 Sam 2:22	Exod 26:7–37
use of incense	1 Sam 2:28	cf. Exod 30:1–9
inherited priesthood	1 Sam 2:30	cf. Exod 29:4–9,46
perpetual lamp	1 Sam 3:3	cf. Exod 27:20–21; Lev 24:2–4
ark of God	1 Sam 3:3; 4:3–22; 5:1–11; 6:2–21; 7:1–2; 14:18; 2 Sam 6:2–17; 7:2; 11:11; 15:24–29	cf. Exod 25:10–22
ark kept at worship center	1 Sam 3:3	cf. Exod 26:34
ark as protection in battle	1 Sam 4:3–11	cf. Num 10:33–36
priestly presence in battle	1 Sam 4:4; 13:7–10	cf. Deut 20:2–4
guilt offering	1 Sam 6:3–4,8,17	cf. Lev 5:6–6:7

Table 3: Legal Interconnections

	Samuel	Torah
burnt offering	1 Sam 6:15; 7:9–10; 10:8; 15:22; 2 Sam 6:17–18; 24:24–25	cf. Lev 1:3ff.
death for touching ark	1 Sam 6:19; 2 Sam 6:7	cf. Num 4:15
local judges	1 Sam 8:1–2	cf. Deut 16:18
bribes prohibited	1 Sam 8:3	cf. Deut 16:19–20
offering portion set aside	1 Sam 9:23–24	cf. Lev 7:32–34
king's copy of Torah	1 Sam 10:25	cf. Deut 17:18
circumcision as covenant sign	1 Sam 14:6; 17:26,36; 31:4; 2 Sam 1:20	cf. Gen 17:10–27; Exod 12:48–49; Lev 12:3
blood prohibition	1 Sam 14:33–34	cf. Gen 9:4; Lev 3:17; 7:26; 17:10–14; 19:26
Urim and Thummim	1 Sam 14:41; 28:6	cf. Exod 28:30
fat of rams	1 Sam 15:22	cf. Exod 29:22; Lev 9:19
stoning blasphemer	1 Sam 17:49	cf. Lev 24:16
exclusion from meal for uncleanness	1 Sam 20:26	cf. Lev 11; 15
New Moon sacrifice	1 Sam 20:24–29	cf. Num 29:6
holy bread only for Levites	1 Sam 21:4	cf. Lev 6:16; 24:8–9; Num 18:8–10
military cleanness	1 Sam 21:5	cf. Lev 15:18; Deut 23:9–11
Bread of the Presence	1 Sam 21:6	cf. Exod 25:30
linen ephod for priests	1 Sam 22:18	cf. Exod 28:1–14
bloodguilt retribution rules	1 Sam 25:26; 2 Sam 3:27; 21:1	cf. Num 35:18–19

Table 3: Legal Interconnections

	Samuel	Torah
spiritists banished	1 Sam 28:3,9	cf. Exod 22:18; Lev 19:26,31; 20:6; 20:27
hand carry ark	2 Sam 6:3,13	cf. Exod 25:14
ark in tent	2 Sam 7:2; 11:11	cf. Exod 26:34
women and uncleanness	2 Sam 11:4	cf. Lev 15:19–30
compensation for sheepstealing	2 Sam 12:6	cf. Exod 22:1
death penalty for adultery	2 Sam 12:13	cf. Exod 20:14; Lev 20:10; Deut 22:22
sin bringing curse on offspring	2 Sam 12:14,18	cf. Deut 28:18
no death penalty for rape	2 Sam 13:12–14,29,32	cf. Deut 22:28–29
cities of refuge	2 Sam 14:14	cf. Num 35:15,22–25
removal of corpse before night	2 Sam 18:15–17	cf. Deut 21:23
stoning rebellious son	2 Sam 18:17	cf. Deut 21:21
cursing a ruler	2 Sam 19:21	cf. Exod 22:28
lex talionis	2 Sam 21:4–6	cf. Exod 21:24; Lev 24:20; Deut 19:21
census causing plague	2 Sam 24:15	cf. Exod 30:11–16

Regarding legal interconnections, the writer seems to describe some situations that do not agree with the stipulations of the Sinai covenant—for example, how the Elide priests received their portion of the offerings. The narrator may have described the irregularities in order to show the informed reader that curse-invoking aberrations were present in the sacrificial rituals performed at the Shiloh sanctuary. These deficiencies in the sacrificial ritual could have been used to help later Israelites understand why God allowed the Philistines to destroy the Shiloh worship site. In the same way, the description of Philistine guilt offerings deemed detestable in the Torah (cf. 1 Sam 6:4–5) was probably designed to demonstrate the spiritual darkness of those non-covenantal peoples.

Theological Framework.   As noted in "1, 2 Samuel as Theology" (p. 43), the books of Samuel resonate with the basic theological themes of the Torah: covenant, land, divine presence, and the demand for obedience to the Lord.

Prophetic Statements.   The Torah has served as a sourcebook of prophetic promises for both Judaism (cf. Isa 51:2–3; Mic 7:20) and Christianity (cf. Luke 24:44; John 5:46; Gal 3:8). A comparison of the Torah with the events recorded in 1, 2 Samuel suggests that one of the conscious intentions of the canonical writer was to document the fulfillment of prophetic promises found in the Torah. At least five such promise/fulfillment combinations may be identified through a comparative study.

One of the most obvious of these is the rise of kingship in Israel. First hinted at in Gen 36:31, then stated explicitly in Deut 17:14, the Torah predicted that Israel would someday ask for a king "like all the nations around us have." In 1 Sam 8:5—exactly as foreseen—Israel asked for a king "such as all the other nations have."

The rise of a Judahite dynasty that would hold the "scepter" and "ruler's staff" in Israel also was foreseen in the Torah (cf. Gen 49:10). The covenant established between the Lord and David recorded in 2 Sam 7:8–16 narrated the confirmation of this promise. In fulfillment of the patriarchal prophecy, David's house, kingdom, and "throne will be established forever" (v. 16).

In Balaam's "star-and-scepter" prophecy, the Torah promised the coming of a ruler who would crush Moab and conquer Edom (Num 24:17–19), just as it had been foretold by Moses (Exod 14:14). In the same context the destruction of the Amalekites also was foretold (Num 24:20). Only two kings in Scripture are recorded as having brought defeat to all three of these enemies: Saul (1 Sam 14:47–48; 15:7–8) and David (1 Sam 30:17; 2 Sam 8:2,12–13). Though Saul is faulted for disobeying a divine mandate regarding the destruction of the Amalekites (1 Sam 15:9–10), David avoided such a criticism. David probably was intended to be portrayed as the one who fulfilled the Balaam prophecies.

The unfolding of the Torah's declaration of "a covenant of lasting priesthood" for the Eleazarite family (Num 25:13) is chronicled in 1, 2 Samuel. The Elides—a non-Eleazarite clan (cf. 1 Chr 24:3) that included Abiathar among its members (cf. 1 Kgs 2:27)—was the leading priestly family of Israel during the last days of the Judges and the beginning of the united monarchy. Yet the narratives of 1, 2 Samuel document the decimation of this prestigious family and provide a rationale for the ultimate fulfillment of the promise to Eleazar in the days of Solomon (cf. 1 Kgs 2:35).

Literary Motifs.   One of the most well-known literary motifs in the Torah is that of the barren wife who, with God's help, overcomes her barrenness and bears a child of great significance in the history of Israel (cf. Gen 11:30 [Sarah]; 25:21 [Rebekah]; 29:31 [Rachel]). The historical narrative of Hannah's experience is cast as a re-presentation of this motif, and the effect is profound. Without having to stoop to the level of the explicit, the author implicitly provides the prophet-judge Samuel with the stature of Israel's great patriarchs.

A second significant literary motif traceable throughout the Torah is that of the shepherd as a noble leader: righteous men and great patriarchs in the Torah were consistently portrayed as shepherds (Abel [Gen 4:2], Abraham [Gen 12:6], Isaac [Gen 26:14], Jacob [Gen 30:29–31], Judah [Gen 38:13], Moses [Exod 3:1]). Thus in 1 Samuel when the opening image of Saul is that of an incompetent shepherd who cannot even find large animals who stray from the family home—ones that later return home without Saul's assistance—the audience is prepared to evaluate Saul as an unrighteous and tragic character in the history of Israel. On the other hand, the expectation that David will be a righteous and great man is produced through the initial depiction of David as a shepherd who faithfully abides with the sheep when all others have abandoned him.

The Torah motif of a shepherd's implement as instrument of salvation was also reemployed with great effect in 1 Samuel. In the Torah, Moses' staff functioned as the appliance that brought judgment against an enemy of God's people (cf. Exod 4:17; 7:12,20; 8:17; 9:23; 10:13); in Samuel it was David's sling (1 Sam 17:40,50). Both pastoral tools in the hands of righteous shepherds were used to bring about the downfall of powerful opponents.

The Torah image of an outwitted Philistine king—in fact, of one outwitted by a protection-seeking member of the covenant community—is also reused in 1 Samuel. Like Abraham (Gen 20:1–18) and Isaac (Gen 26:1–11) before him, David sought protection from a Philistine (1 Sam 27:1ff.). Likewise, the "Philistine phase" of the lives of Abraham, Isaac, and David resulted in a dramatic increase in wealth (Gen 20:16; 26:12–14; 1 Sam 27:6,9) for these Israelites.

Dramatic echoes of the sibling-murdering-sibling motif present in the Cain/ Abel story (Gen 4:8–15) are present in the fiction composed by Joab and presented to David by the woman of Tekoa (2 Sam 14:3,6–7). In both stories a brother killed his brother in a field; both murderers were in danger of being killed by others, yet both were permitted to live because of the intervention of a sovereign being. In the Samuel story it seems plausible that Joab deliberately created parallels with the Torah history so that David would recognize them and be compelled to make a judgment that followed the divine precedent.

The sinner-going-eastward-into-exile motif presented in the Torah (cf. Adam and Eve [Gen 3:23–24]; Cain [4:16]) resurfaces in the life of David. Like Adam and Cain before him, following willful disobedience and divine judgment, David left God's presence (focused in the ark) to go eastward into exile (2 Sam 17:22,24).

The younger-sibling-who-surpasses-the-elders motif, repeatedly expressed in the Torah (Seth [Gen 4:26], Isaac [Gen 17:18–21], Jacob [Gen 25:23], Joseph [Gen 37:3–9], Perez [Gen 38:29], Ephraim [Gen 48:14–20], and Moses [Exod 6:20]), is repeated in the presentations of Samuel (1 Sam 1:4–5,20), David (1 Sam 16:11–12), and Solomon (2 Sam 12:24–25).

A careful study of the biographical materials presenting the life of the prophet-judge Samuel indicates that they were selected and worded so as to create parallels with the Torah's presentation of Moses. As noted elsewhere (cf. introductory remarks preceding 1 Sam 1:1), similarities exist in their childhoods, callings, careers, legacies, and offspring. Similarly, the life of David is deliberately patterned after the Torah's presentation of the history of Israel (cf. "1, 2 Samuel as Literary Art," p. 32).

1, 2 Samuel as Major Link in the Messianic Tradition.[65] As books that portray the fulfillment of Torah prophecies regarding the Judahite "scepter" and "ruler's staff" (Gen 49:10), as well as the "star" and "scepter" that would crush Moab and Edom while helping Israel increase in strength (Num 24:17–19), 1, 2 Samuel resonate with messianic themes. It is important to note, however, that the books of Samuel are not the origin and basis of the messianic tradition in the Hebrew Bible—the Torah alone claims that privilege. Instead, 1, 2 Samuel function as the historical record and theological clarification associated with the rise of the prophetically announced, divinely ordained family of leaders and deliverers coming from the tribe of Judah.

The accuracy and validity of the messianic record in 1, 2 Samuel, especially as presented in 1 Sam 25:28; 2 Sam 7:8–16,18–20,25–29; 22:51; 23:5, is uncontested elsewhere in the Prophets and Writings. In the remainder of the Former Prophets David's descendants are assumed without question to have the right to rule Israel, even though sin might reduce their hold on the nation.[66] In the Latter Prophets, likewise, the promises given to David and recorded in 2 Samuel are accepted as valid—the Lord works uniquely through the Davidic dynasty to lead Israel and will continue to work through them to bring about even more glorious days for his people.[67] Likewise in the Writings there is both explicitly and implicitly an acceptance of the privileged position of David and the Davidic line, as presented in 1, 2 Samuel.[68]

1, 2 SAMUEL AS CHRISTIAN SCRIPTURE. Beginning with the New Testament writers, Christians have used 1, 2 Samuel in private and public worship as the accurate and trustworthy Word of God. Paul's words to Felix reflect Christianity's historically dominant position: "I believe in everything that agrees with the Law and that is written in the Prophets" (Acts 24:15)—the

---

[65] A good introductory study of messianic prophecy in the OT is found in LaSor, et al., *Old Testament Survey,* 396–402. Cf. also H. Ringgren, *The Messiah in the Old Testament* (London: 1956), and J. Klausner, *The Messianic Idea in Israel,* trans. W. F. Stinespring (New York: 1955).

[66] Cf. 1 Kgs 2:33,45; 3:6; 8:16,20,25–26; 9:4–5; 11:11–13,31–39; 15:4; 2 Kgs 8:19; 19:34; 20:6.

[67] Cf. Isa 7:2,13; 9:1–7; 11:1,10; 16:5; 22:22; 55:3; Jer 13:13; 17:25; 21:2; 22:2,4,30; 23:5; 29:16; 30:8–9; 33:15–17,20–21,26; Ezek 34:23–24; 37:24–25; Hos 3:5; Amos 9:11; Zech 12:7–8,10,12; 13:1.

[68] Cf. Pss 18:50 [Hb. v. 51]; 78:70; 89:3–4,20–37 [Hb. 4–5,21–38]; 132:10–12,17–18; Ruth 4:17,22; 1 Chr 17:7–14,16–17,19,23–27; 28:4–7; 2 Chr 6:6,16; 7:18; 13:5; 21:7; 23:3.

books of Samuel being reckoned, of course, among the Former Prophets. The Gospel writers indicate that Jesus likewise accorded 1, 2 Samuel full scriptural status: he affirmed (cf. Luke 24:25), interpreted (cf. Matt 7:12; 22:40; Luke 24:27), and fulfilled (Matt 5:17; 26:56; Luke 18:31; 24:44) that portion of the Hebrew Bible known as the Prophets, without making distinction between individual books within that section.

The New Testament provides evidence that the books of Samuel were used in the first-century Christian community in at least four different ways:

1. Background for understanding Christian doctrine and preaching. The New Testament writers assumed their audience had an accurate, and even detailed, knowledge of the persons and events chronicled in 1, 2 Samuel. Casual references and sophisticated allusions to events that occurred during the pre-Solomonic period of Israel's united monarchy are present throughout the New Testament: in recorded statements of Jesus during both his earthly ministry (Mark 2:26) and after his ascension (Rev 3:7; 22:16), in comments attributed to Jews (Mark 11:10; John 7:42), in narrator comments in the Gospels (Matt 1:1), in apostolic preaching (Acts 2:30; 13:34; 2 Tim 2:8), in epistles (Rom 1:3; 2 Tim 2:8; Heb 11:32), and in apocalyptic writings (Rev 5:5).

"David" son of Jesse is mentioned fifty-four times in the Greek New Testament; "Samuel," three times; "Saul son of Kish," once; "Uriah," once; and "Abiathar," once. The phrase "son of David" is employed sixteen times in the New Testament, mostly in reference to Jesus;[69] it has meaning, however, only in light of 2 Samuel 7.

2. An accurate historical record. In a dispute with Pharisees, Jesus used historical materials from Samuel to clarify a theological principle (Mark 2:26). In doing so he implicitly accepted the full scriptural authority—and, accordingly, the accuracy—of the books of Samuel.

While preaching in Pisidian Antioch, Paul provided his audience with a thumbnail sketch of the history of Israel. As part of the sermon he alluded to several events and descriptions recorded in 1, 2 Samuel: the life of "Samuel the prophet"; Israel's demand for a king; God's selection of "Saul son of Kish of the tribe of Benjamin" to be Israel's king; God's removal of Saul from the office of kingship; and God's selection of "David son of Jesse," a pious and God-pleasing individual, as Israel's next king (Acts 13:21–22; cf. 1 Sam 8:5,19; 9:1–2; 10:1; 13:14). His inclusion of these materials in a communication situation requiring strong credibility is understandable only if Paul believed the materials to be historically accurate.

The genealogical records of Jesus, to avoid rooting the New Testament presentation of Jesus in error or myth, must be historically accurate. Matthew's

---

[69] Matt 1:1,20; 9:27; 12:23; 15:22; 20:30–31; 21:9,15; 22:42; Mark 10:47–48; 12:35; Luke 18:38–39; 20:41.

presentation of Jesus' genealogy, which mentions "King David" and "Solomon, whose mother was Uriah's wife" (Matt 1:6), and Luke's, which speaks of "Nathan the son of David" (cf. 2 Sam 5:14), relied on materials gleaned from 1, 2 Samuel.

3. Prophetic word regarding the life, work, and significance of Jesus. In the New Testament Jesus' identity was first established and developed in terms of his relationship to David (Matt 1:1); he was both genealogically and functionally the ultimate Son of David. Only as the son of David could Jesus be the Messiah. Thus for Paul, an essential part of the *kerygma* was the proclamation of Jesus as the descendant of David (2 Tim 2:8). Peter affirmed that "all the prophets from Samuel on" foretold the coming of Jesus (Acts 3:24) and revealed "that everyone who believes in him receives forgiveness of sins through his name" (Acts 10:43). Consistent with this position, Paul understood the books of Samuel to foretell the salvation of the Gentiles (Rom 15:9; cf. 2 Sam 22:50; see also Acts 26:22–23). Samuel was thus understood in the New Testament to function as a harmonious and—because of its presentation of the life of David—particularly significant witness to Jesus.

4. A source of instruction, encouragement, and hope. True to their nature as holy Scripture, the books of Samuel were "written to teach us, so that through endurance and the encouragement of the Scriptures we might have hope" (Rom 15:4). As a source of instruction the writer of Hebrews used 1, 2 Samuel, citing David and the prophet Samuel as heroic examples of faith in action (cf. Heb 11:32–34). James urged his readers to take "as an example of patience in the face of suffering . . . the prophets who spoke in the name of the Lord" (Jas 5:10); presumably he was in part referring to Samuel (cf. 1 Sam 19:18–24). Along with the rest of Scripture, the New Testament writers urged Christians to keep the words of 1, 2 Samuel in remembrance (2 Pet 3:2) and to implement their teachings (Jas 1:22).

OUTLINE OF THE BOOKS

I. The Lord Raises up Samuel and Deposes the House of Eli (1:1–7:17)
   1. The Lord Rewards Hannah's Faith (1:1–2:11)
   2. The Lord Blesses Hannah's Family, Judges Eli's Family (2:12–36)
   3. The Lord Makes Samuel Israel's Prophet (3:1–22)
   4. The House of Eli Is Devastated as the Ark of God Is Captured (4:1b–22)
   5. The Lord Triumphs during Samuel's Career (5:1–7:17)
II. The Lord Gives Israel a King "Such As All Other Nations Have" (8:1–14:51)
   1. Samuel's Sons Are Rejected as Judges (8:1–3)

I. THE LORD RAISES UP SAMUEL AND DEPOSES THE HOUSE
   OF ELI (1:1–7:17)
   1. The Lord Rewards Hannah's Faith (1:1–2:11)
      (1) The Lord Opens Hannah's Womb (1:1–20)
      (2) Hannah Dedicates Samuel to the Lord's Service (1:21–28)
      (3) Hannah Rejoices in the Lord (2:1–10)
      (4) Young Samuel Ministers before the Lord (2:11)
   2. The Lord Blesses Hannah's Family, Judges Eli's Family (2:12–36)
      (1) Eli's Sons Treat the Lord's Offerings with Contempt (2:12–17)
      (2) Samuel Ministers before the Lord as His Family Receives the
          Lord's Blessing (2:18–21)
      (3) The Lord Determines to Kill Eli's Sons for Their Sins
          (2:22–25)
      (4) Samuel Grows in Favor before the Lord (2:26)
      (5) Judgment Is Pronounced against the House of Eli (2:27–36)
   3. The Lord Makes Samuel Israel's Prophet (3:1–22)
      (1) The Lord Reveals to Samuel His Judgment against the House
          of Eli (3:1–18)
      (2) The Lord Makes Samuel a Prophet to All Israel (3:19–4:1a)
   4. The House of Eli Is Devastated as the Ark of God Is Captured
      (4:1b–22)
      (1) The Philistines Kill Eli's Sons and Capture the Ark (4:1b–11)
      (2) Eli Dies; Ichabod Is Born (4:12–22)
   5. The Lord Triumphs during Samuel's Career (5:1–7:17)
      (1) The Lord Overwhelms the Philistine's God (5:1–6:12)
      (2) The Lord Judges Irreverent Israelites (6:13–7:1)
      (3) The Lord Routs the Philistines' Army (7:2–17)

I. THE LORD RAISES UP SAMUEL
AND DEPOSES THE HOUSE OF ELI (1:1–7:17)

This introductory section of Samuel forms a semantically seamless narrative link with the conclusion of the Book of Judges, the book that immediately
precedes 1 Samuel in the Hebrew Bible.[1] Judges ends with stories of spiritual

---

[1] In the Hebrew Bible the Book of Ruth occurs in the Writings section, after the Book of Prov-
erbs and before Song of Songs.

ineptitude among the Levites (cf. Judg 17:1–18:31), sexual misconduct in Shiloh (Judg 21:15–24), and Levitical involvement in tragic military encounters (Judg 19:29–20:48); 1 Samuel opens with all three: spiritually dull Eli and his corrupt sons operate the Shiloh sanctuary contrary to the Torah guidelines (2:12–17); Hophni and Phinehas abuse the women serving at the Tent of Meeting (2:22); and ultimately, Eli's sons die in a catastrophic battle with the Philistines (4:10–11). The Book of Judges concludes with a collection of stories that portray Levites guiding the tribes of Israel into sin—idolatry and fratricide. Samuel opens with sinful Levitical activity—forcing Israelite worshipers to offer unacceptable sacrificial portions to the Lord and playing a role in Israel's disastrous loss to the Philistines.

The opening seven chapters of 1 Samuel trace the rise of Samuel and the downfall of the house of Eli. In portraying the life of Samuel, the narrator—surprisingly—begins by focusing on Hannah, a married woman who was struggling with a divinely ordained condition of barrenness. The woman's struggle ends when, in response to a faith-filled vow, the Lord enables her to give birth to Samuel, a child who is given to God for a lifetime of service as a Nazirite. Samuel's youth and adulthood prove to be as marvelous as his birth; while still a child he becomes Israel's greatest judge, providing justice and deliverance from the Philistines, Israel's most strident enemy at this juncture in history.

The second narrative prong of this section provides details of the tragic downfall of Israel's most powerful priestly family in that day, the house of Eli. Their destruction comes from the Lord, the result of sinful conduct while administrating over Israel's holiest shrine. As portrayed by the biblical writer, God used the occasion of a military encounter with the Philistines to bring deadly judgment on the Elides. As a result of the priests' sin, Israel was bereft of its leading priests and temporarily lost possession of the ark, the visible throne of God. Yet all was not lost; the Lord used this circumstance to humiliate the Philistine god Dagon and thus reaffirm to Israel and the world that his greatness could not be diminished either by a decadent priesthood or a menacing foreign power.

Two vital offices in Israel are highlighted in the opening section of Samuel, those of priest and prophet. On the one hand, the priesthood is portrayed as being in decline. Neglectful Eli, himself too old to participate actively in the priestly activities (cf. Num 8:23–26), allows the sanctuary ritual to run amok and his sons' abuses to go unchecked. On the other hand, the office of prophet is elevated to a height not reached since the days of Moses,[2] as Samuel boldly declares the counsel of God from his youth onward.

---

[2] As portrayed by the biblical writers, the prophetic word of the Lord was indeed rare following Moses' death. Only two individuals after Moses and before Samuel—and both of these are unnamed—are identified using terms customarily referring to a prophet (cf. Judg 6:8; 1 Sam 2:27).

Key events related to the fulfillment of three Torah prophecies are presented in this section of Samuel. Narrative incidents in this passage relate to the elevation of the Eleazarite line to priestly preeminence (cf. Num 25:6–13), the selection of the site where the Lord would cause his name to dwell (cf. Deut 12:5,11,21; 14:23–24; 16:2,6,11; 26:2), and the appearance of the prophet who would be like Moses (cf. Deut 18:15).

The Eli stories bring to the surface a narrative thread stretching from Exodus through 2 Kings that portrays the emergence of the Zadokites from the family line of Eleazar ben Aaron to priestly preeminence in Israel.[3] In anticipation of the Zadokites' selection as the sole legitimate priestly line in Jerusalem (cf. 1 Kgs 2:26–27,35), the house of Eli (primary representative of the family line of Ithamar ben Aaron) is prophetically disqualified from continuing service.

The theme of the divine selection of Jerusalem as the site where the Lord's name would dwell is intertwined with the theme of the ascent of the Eleazarite line. Just as the fall of the House of Eli was a necessary precursor to the emergence of the Zadokites, so Shiloh's loss of status (cf. Ps 78:60; Jer 7:13–14) was an essential precursor to the rise of Jerusalem. Jerusalem's selection as the site for the Lord's central sanctuary later will be interpreted by the narrator as the Lord's will (1 Kgs 11:13,32,36), even as the selection of the Zadokites was (1 Sam 2:35–36).

The Samuel stories portray him as the long-anticipated prophet who would be like Moses (Deut 18:15).[4] Fascinating similarities exist between the portrayal of Samuel and Moses in the narrative accounts. Both had remarkable childhoods, being nurtured in their earliest years by mothers of faith (cf. Exod 2:1–2,9; 1 Sam 1:20,28) but raised during their formative years in environments other than their own homes (cf. Exod 2:10; 1 Sam 1:24–25). Both disavowed the corrupt elements of the environments in which

---

[3] Viewed from the perspective of the narrative unity of Genesis to 2 Kings, the Zadokite family's ascension to priestly preeminence is portrayed as the fulfillment of a Torah mandate given by Yahweh during Israel's Sinai experience (cf. Num 25:6–13). That ordinance declared that Eleazar ben Aaron and his descendants were to be Yahweh's authorized priests. Zadok is elsewhere portrayed in Scripture as a direct descendant of Eleazar ben Aaron (cf. 1 Chr 6:3–10) and thus the rightful heir of the promise, whereas Eli is understood to be a descendant of Ithamar ben Aaron (cf. 1 Chr 24:3 [5:29–36]). The culturally literate exilic or postexilic audience to whom the author was writing would doubtless have been aware of this genealogical distinction and the Torah teaching, even though explicit genealogical information is not supplied in the Samuel narratives.

[4] This observation is in no way intended to negate the NT understanding that Jesus is the ultimate prophet who was "like Moses" (cf. Acts 3:22; 7:37). First Samuel deliberately portrays Samuel as one who in many ways was "like Moses" and thus intentionally sets Samuel up as a fulfillment of the Torah promise. Samuel's initial fulfillment of a prophecy that was later fulfilled ultimately by Jesus Christ is paralleled by Jesus' fulfillment of Isa 7, a prophecy initially fulfilled during Ahaz's time (second half of 8th cent. B.C.) but later surpassed by Jesus' fulfillment (cf. Matt 1:22–23).

they were raised (cf. Exod 2:11–12; Heb 11:25; 1 Sam 2:22–26). Both received their initial revelations from the Lord in the presence of an object that was burning but not consumed (Exod 3:3–10; 1 Sam 3:3–14). In both cases, the Lord's revelatory message was preceded by a double mention of the prophet's name (cf. Exod 3:4; 1 Sam 3:10). The two share the distinction of being the only prophets in Genesis–2 Kings to be called "faithful" (Hb. ne°ĕmān; Num 12:7; 1 Sam 3:20). Both were commanded by the Lord to pronounce judgment against the leaders of the sinful regimes that oppressed Israel during the initial phase of their prophetic careers (cf. Exod 7:14–18; 1 Sam 3:11–18). Both killed an enemy of Israel with their own hands and immediately thereafter went into a period of self-imposed exile (cf. Exod 3:12–15; 1 Sam 15:33). Both wrote down regulations (mišpāṭîm) that were deposited before the Lord and used to guide the nation (Lev 26:46; 31:9; 1 Sam 10:25). Both functioned as judges (cf. Exod 18:13; 1 Sam 7:6,15–16), and both were prophets (cf. Deut 18:15; 34:10; 1 Sam 3:20). Both built altars to the Lord (cf. Exod 17:15; 24:4; 1 Sam 7:17). Neither was ever called a priest, yet both were recorded as performing activities associated with the priesthood (cf. Lev 8:14–29; 1 Sam 7:9). Both functioned as transition figures, being responsible for major course changes in Israelite history. Though both had two sons (cf. Exod 18:2–3; 1 Sam 8:2; 1 Chr 6:28; 23:15), neither had offspring who were remembered as playing a significant role in later Israel. Instead, at the Lord's behest both set apart nonfamily members who led Israel to possess through conquest land the Lord promised to Abraham's descendants (cf. Deut 34:9; 1 Sam 16:13).[5]

The sharp contrast between the decadence and incompetence of the genealogically designated spiritual leaders and the capable service of the Lord's true prophet in this section mirrors the experiences of Israel throughout its history and recorded in passages found elsewhere in Scripture (Jer 20:1–6; Amos 7:10–17). The events portrayed in these chapters are reminiscent of the Torah contrast between a decadent priesthood and a strong prophet—exemplified in Aaron and his sons (cf. Exod 32:1–5,25; Lev 10:1–2) and Moses (cf. Deut 34:10–12).

Theologically, one of the central truths discernible in this passage is that everyone—even Levitical judges—must be subject to the requirements of the Torah. Judges, like kings of later generations who failed to follow the dictates of the Torah, would be judged and condemned, and their work would be destroyed. The judgment on the house of Eli is the judgment on all Israelite leadership that would fail in its commitment to obey the Lord's revealed will.

---

[5] In addition to the information about Samuel conveyed in 1 Samuel, 1 Chronicles permits us to understand that both Moses and Samuel were from the Levitical subtribe of Kohath (1 Chr 6:2[3 Hb.]–3[5:29 Hb.],22–25 [6:7–10 Hb.]).

A second key theological insight discernible in these chapters is that the Lord uses socially powerless individuals possessing profound faith in him (in this case a barren woman) to overturn and transform the social order. The Lord uses that which is not to negate that which is (cf. 1 Cor 1:28).

A third major theological affirmation is that Yahweh's kingship is absolute and extends to all lands and peoples. His power is not limited by national boundaries, nor is it diminished by Israel's failures. As exemplified in his dealings with the Philistines and their god Dagon, Yahweh exercises unchallenged dominion over all peoples and all gods.

Consistent with his role as sovereign, the Lord is portrayed as the stern enforcer of the Sinai covenant. When Israel fails to live up to divinely mandated obligations, the Lord brings judgment to bear. Furthermore, he reserves the right to carry out personally the Torah commands that Israel fails to execute. Within these chapters he shatters a detestable idol in the Promised Land (cf. Exod 23:24; 34:13; Deut 12:3).

Obedience to the Lord in fulfilling vows brings blessing both for the individual who fulfills them as well as for society as a whole. Hannah made a vow to God. By obediently fulfilling her vow, she built a family for herself and gave birth to a servant of giant proportions in the history of Israel.

1. The Lord Rewards Hannah's Faith (1:1–2:11)

In this section the Lord demonstrates his absolute power over all human institutions by changing the course of Israel's history through one of Israel's weakest and least significant individuals—a rural, barren woman named Hannah. God's action is triggered by Hannah's remarkable faith in the very One who engineered the circumstances of her humiliation. Her trust in the Lord brings rewards that surpass the pain she experienced earlier in life and makes her an object lesson demonstrating the Lord's awesome power to bless anyone who possesses tenacious, risk-taking faith in him.

(1) The Lord Opens Hannah's Womb (1:1–20)

[1]There was a certain man from Ramathaim, a Zuphite from the hill country of Ephraim, whose name was Elkanah son of Jeroham, the son of Elihu, the son of Tohu, the son of Zuph, an Ephraimite. [2]He had two wives; one was called Hannah and the other Peninnah. Peninnah had children, but Hannah had none.

[3]Year after year this man went up from his town to worship and sacrifice to the LORD Almighty at Shiloh, where Hophni and Phinehas, the two sons of Eli, were priests of the LORD. [4]Whenever the day came for Elkanah to sacrifice, he would give portions of the meat to his wife Peninnah and to all her sons and daughters. [5]But to Hannah he gave a double portion because he loved her, and the LORD had closed her womb. [6]And because the LORD had closed her womb, her rival kept pro-

voking her in order to irritate her. [7]This went on year after year. Whenever Hannah went up to the house of the LORD, her rival provoked her till she wept and would not eat. [8]Elkanah her husband would say to her, "Hannah, why are you weeping? Why don't you eat? Why are you downhearted? Don't I mean more to you than ten sons?"

[9]Once when they had finished eating and drinking in Shiloh, Hannah stood up. Now Eli the priest was sitting on a chair by the doorpost of the LORD's temple. [10]In bitterness of soul Hannah wept much and prayed to the LORD. [11]And she made a vow, saying, "O LORD Almighty, if you will only look upon your servant's misery and remember me, and not forget your servant but give her a son, then I will give him to the LORD for all the days of his life, and no razor will ever be used on his head."

[12]As she kept on praying to the LORD, Eli observed her mouth. [13]Hannah was praying in her heart, and her lips were moving but her voice was not heard. Eli thought she was drunk [14]and said to her, "How long will you keep on getting drunk? Get rid of your wine."

[15]"Not so, my lord," Hannah replied, "I am a woman who is deeply troubled. I have not been drinking wine or beer; I was pouring out my soul to the LORD. [16]Do not take your servant for a wicked woman; I have been praying here out of my great anguish and grief."

[17]Eli answered, "Go in peace, and may the God of Israel grant you what you have asked of him."

[18]She said, "May your servant find favor in your eyes." Then she went her way and ate something, and her face was no longer downcast.

[19]Early the next morning they arose and worshiped before the LORD and then went back to their home at Ramah. Elkanah lay with Hannah his wife, and the LORD remembered her. [20]So in the course of time Hannah conceived and gave birth to a son. She named him Samuel, saying, "Because I asked the LORD for him."

Here the Lord gives barren and humiliated Hannah a son in answer to her prayer. The story of Hannah presents a sharp contrast with that of Deborah, another significant woman of Ephraim from the period of the Judges. Deborah's career impacted Israelite society through political clout, judicial leadership, and prophetic activity; Hannah's effect on Israelite society came through the gentle forces of faith and motherhood. Through Hannah the point is made that women of faith played a legitimate and even formative role in shaping Israel's history. Hannah's faith turned the tide of the period of the Judges by producing the transitional figure Samuel.

In this passage Israelite faith expresses its supreme paradox and boldest affirmation—the Lord may create social and natural tragedies in order to accomplish his purposes that far outweigh the calamity. The Lord sometimes engineers social tragedies, yet he carries them out "that the work of God might be displayed" (John 9:3). Accordingly, human tragedy can be properly evaluated and appreciated only when viewed with a consideration of the end results and ultimate purposes brought about by God.[6]

This passage also teaches that true power is to be found not in one's position in society but in one's posture before God. Accordingly, the motif of appearance versus reality is prominent in this passage. Eli, who possessed "spiritual competence" because of his office, was in fact a spiritual bumbler; the spiritual powerhouse in this narrative was a socially impotent woman from the rural regions of Ephraim. Hannah alone understood the true power of undivided faith in the Lord.

Furthermore, this passage suggests that spiritual power triumphs over social power. Socially powerless individuals can transform social institutions through faith in the Lord and in the process can triumph over their own circumstances.

1:1 The location of "Ramathaim" (lit., "Two Heights") is disputed. Earlier suggestions included Beit Rima (thirteen miles northeast of Lydda), Ram Allah (nine miles north of Jerusalem), Er-Ram (five miles north of Jerusalem), and Neby-Samwil (four miles northwest of Jerusalem).[7] More recent commentators equate it with New Testament Arimathea (cf. Mark 15:43 and parallels) and, following an early Christian tradition, suggest Rentis (sixteen miles east of Tel Aviv) as the site.[8] It is almost certainly the same as Ramah (cf. 1:19, etc.).

"Zuphite" (lit., "Zophim"), taken as part of a compound place name in some translational traditions (e.g., KJV), probably refers to the region settled by Elkanah's ancestor Zuph (cf. 1 Sam 9:5) and not to Elkanah's tribal identity.[9]

Following in the tradition of others who reject the historical veracity of this section of narrative, McCarter suggests that key aspects of this story in its original form related to the birth of Saul, not Samuel.[10] Miller and Hayes present two reasons for their acceptance of this skeptical interpretation: "(1) The explanation of the child's name in v. 20 corresponds to the name 'Saul' rather than 'Samuel.' (2) Saul is said to have been supported by the Elide priests of Shiloh in his later career (1 Sam 14:3,18). Samuel, on the other hand, while he is connected with Shiloh in this story and its continuation in 1 Samuel 2–3, is never

---

[6] Israelite faith is at its core teleological. It insists that Yahweh will ultimately straighten out every crookedness and judge every sin. While consistently taking a pessimistic view of the human condition, it nevertheless insists that the present order must be viewed with the awareness that God will ultimately transform the prevailing conditions. Though human beings are capable of much good, the corruptions of human nature assure that much evil will be done; however, the injustices of this present age are not permanent. In his day Yahweh will sweep them aside and bring about an era when justice will prevail.

[7] H. P. Smith, *Samuel* (Edinburgh: T & T Clark, 1899), 5.

[8] P. K. McCarter, Jr., *I Samuel*, AB (Garden City: Doubleday, 1980), 58; R. W. Klein, *I Samuel*, WBC (Waco: Word, 1983), 5.

[9] Cf. S. R. Driver, *Notes on the Hebrew Text of Samuel*, 2d ed. (1912; reprint, Winona Lake: Alpha, 1983), 1.

[10] McCarter, *I Samuel*, 65.

associated with Shiloh in other narratives."[11] Miller and Hayes's suggestion is unconvincing for three reasons. First, it is rooted in an overzealous skepticism regarding the narrator's concern for historical accuracy; second, it apparently is based on a misunderstanding of the etiological section of this chapter (cf. comment on v. 20). Third, it fails to give adequate regard to Old Testament passages suggesting that Shiloh was destroyed in the Philistine onslaught (cf. Ps 78:60; Jer 7:12,14; 26:6).

Different explanations have been put forward in an attempt to harmonize biblical statements relating to Elkanah's/Samuel's family background. According to 1 Chr 6:22–28,33–38, Samuel was born into the family line of Kohath in the tribe of Levi. Here Samuel's father is said to be from Ephraim. It is possible that Elkanah was an Ephraimite who married Hannah, ostensibly a woman from the tribe of Levi. It also is possible that Samuel was adopted into the Levitical tribe after coming to Shiloh, and therefore his genealogical record was altered. However, both of these explanations are fraught with difficulties. An explanation that reduces tensions between portions of the biblical record suggests that Samuel was geographically an Ephraimite but genealogically a Levite. In support of this, Josh 24:33 affirms that Levites lived in a hilly region of Ephraim. Thus, in the case of Samuel's family both tribal relationships can be compatible. Samuel, like his Ephraimite Levitical predecessor Phinehas, would play a significant role in wars (cf. Num 31:6; Josh 22:13–32; Judg 20:28). Eli's willingness to have Samuel perform a task reserved in the Torah for Levites[12] also makes this solution more likely.

Elkanah's heritage is traced back four generations.[13] The genealogical list found here differs in some details from its counterpart in 1 Chr 6:25–26. Differences between the two may be accounted for in several ways: (1) existence of alternate spellings for individuals' names (Zuph in 1 Sam 1:1 = Zophai in 1 Chr 6:26); (2) existence of alternate names for the same individual (Elihu in 1 Sam 1:1 = Eliab in 1 Chr 6:26 = Eliel in 1 Chr 6:34; Tohu in 1 Sam 1:1 = Nahath in 1 Chr 6:26 = Toah in 1 Chr 6:34); and (3) "gapped genealogies" that skip generations.

1:2 Elkanah is introduced as having two wives, Hannah ("Gracious Woman") and Peninnah ("Pearl"[?]). The order in which the wives are named suggests that Hannah was Elkanah's first wife. Elkanah's possession of two

---

[11] J. M. Miller and J. H. Hayes, *A History of Ancient Israel and Judah* (Philadelphia: Westminster, 1986), 125.

[12] Cf. discussion and footnote at 3:1–3.

[13] Note that genealogical lists in the Torah precede the Noah, Abraham, and Joseph cycles as well as the central stories relating to Moses and Aaron (Gen 5:1–32; 11:10–32; 35:23–26; Exod 6:13–25). The Ezra cycle is likewise introduced by an extended genealogy (Ezra 7:2–6). Narrative accounts of significant rebels in the history of Israel may also be marked by extended genealogical introductions, e.g., Korah and Achan (Num 16:1; Josh 7:1).

wives should not be taken as a disparagement of his character, even though his actions appear to violate the spirit of Gen 2:24 and would be untenable for Christians (cf. 1 Tim 3:2,12). Though a king's taking of "many wives" was prohibited (Deut 17:17), bigamy was not condemned in Hebrew Scriptures and on one occasion was even encouraged by a pious priest (2 Chr 24:3). Elkanah is likely another example in Scripture of an individual whose first wife was (initially) infertile and who thus, perhaps lacking faith, took a second wife in order to produce an heir (cf. Gen 16:2–3; 30:3–4,9).[14] The circumstance of having a beloved wife who was incapable of bearing children links Elkanah with the Torah patriarchs Abraham, Isaac, and Jacob. To the reader familiar with the Torah the connection is a favorable one, for it suggests the possibility—later realized—that a child of great significance to God's kingdom may ultimately result.

1:3,21 Far from being yet another decadent Israelite in the period of the Judges, Elkanah is consistently portrayed as one who is devoted to the Lord. His piety is suggested first by the fact that "year after year" he "went up from his town to worship and sacrifice to the LORD Almighty." According to the Torah, every Israelite family was to make the journey to Israel's central Yahwistic worship center (Deut 12:5–7). By leading his family in annual trips to Shiloh, Elkanah is shown to be a man both submissive to the Torah and strong in his domestic leadership. His example contrasts sharply with Eli, another member of the tribe of Levi, who failed to provide proper leadership in either religious or family matters (cf. 2:29).

Shiloh (modern Seilun, nine miles north of Bethel) had functioned as the early center of the Israelite worship of Yahweh since the days of Joshua. It was there that the Tent of Meeting (ʾōhel môʿēd) was set up (Josh 18:1), and covenant-related activities—for example, the determination of tribal allotments within the Promised Land, celebration of annual festivals, and calls to holy war—were carried out (cf. Josh 18:8; 19:51; 21:1–2; 22:9,12; Judg 18:31; 21:12,19,21). Even in Eli's day the Tent of Meeting was still in use at Shiloh (cf. 2:22), but it had been augmented by a more permanent architectural structure (cf. 1:7,9; 3:15) that served as the center of Yahwistic activity.

Verse 3 includes the first Old Testament use of the phrase "the LORD Almighty" (lit., "Yahweh of Armies/Hosts"). This phrase, which acclaims Yahweh's dominion over spiritual entities and thus his unmatched authority, is used elsewhere in the Old Testament primarily in the writings of the prophets, espe-

---

[14] The Code of Hammurabi (nos. 145–48) includes four laws dealing with the taking of a second sexual partner in the event of a first wife's inability to produce an heir (*ANET*, 154). This fact, in combination with the biblical record, suggests that a major concern of all ancient Near Eastern societies was the provision of social mechanisms—including bigamy—to assure genealogical continuity and the preservation of estates within tribes and clans. The Torah's provision for the preservation of a family line was levirate marriage (cf. Deut 25:5–10).

cially Isaiah (62x), Jeremiah (79x), Zechariah (53x), and Malachi (24x). Hophni and Phinehas, Eli's two sons, were the priests of the Lord at Shiloh. Eli is not here called the priest, probably because he was too old to serve actively in that capacity (cf. 4:15; Num 8:23–26).

1:4–6 A climactic event in Israel's religious celebrations was the slaying of sacrificial animals, followed by the consumption of a lavish meal. At religious festivals individuals were expected to present burnt offerings, grain offerings, drink offerings, and fellowship offerings (Num 29:39), though other offerings (e.g., sin, guilt, and vow) might also be given. Portions of the animals slain for fellowship offerings *(šĕlāmîm)* and other voluntary offerings would have been consumed in the sanctuary area by one who presented the animal.

In this section Elkanah is shown equitably sharing with family members his portion of the meat from one of his offerings. Meat, a rarity in the typical Israelite diet of that day, was apportioned to each wife in proportion to the number of children she had produced so that she could share it with her children. The NIV's translation of the oblique Hebrew phrase "a portion of one pair of nostrils" *(mānâ ʾaḥat ʾappāyîm)* as "a double portion" (v. 5) is a charitable attempt to portray Elkanah's sensitivity to Hannah. More likely it should be translated as "[only] one portion" in light of the cold reality—prominently highlighted in other ways elsewhere in the passage—that Hannah had no offspring.[15] Thus, the rest of the verse should be translated, "For although[16] Elkanah loved her, God had closed her womb."[17]

The Lord had closed Hannah's womb.[18] This surprising affirmation—without parallel in Hebrew narrative regarding the Lord's people (but see Gen 18:20)—appears twice in these verses (vv. 5–6). Hannah's infertility was no accident of nature; it was the deliberate work of the Lord. There is an inescapable irony in these statements. The same God who in the Torah commanded

---

[15] After some discussion, F. Deist ultimately recommends that *Tg. Ps.-J*'s translation of the phrase be followed: "a selected portion" ("*APPAYIM* [1 Sam I 5] אפים *VT* 27 [1977]: 205–9).

[16] This is a well-known way to translate the Hb. preposition כִּי, and the NIV itself opts for "though" or "although" on sixty-eight occasions. Cf. E. W. Goodrick and J. R. Kohlenberger III, *The NIV Exhaustive Concordance* (Grand Rapids: Zondervan, 1990), 1486.

[17] The biblical statement that comes closest to paralleling the omniscient narrator's affirmation is Gen 16:2, where Sarah (not the narrator) states that Yahweh kept her from having children. The fact that this statement is found only on Sarah's lips leaves open the possibility that the narrator does not agree with it. Certainly there are other occasions in the biblical text where people are quoted as saying things with which the narrator disagreed (cf. Job 42:7).

[18] Thus the Scriptures of Israelite faith abound with examples of Yahweh administrating over calamities in the human experience that ultimately he transformed into blessing. Job's end far exceeded his beginnings; from the barren wombs of Sarah, Rebekah, and Rachel came Isaac, Jacob, and Joseph; Joseph's sufferings brought salvation for the family of Jacob, as well as all of Egypt; from the furnace of Egyptian oppression came the nation of free Israel; from Naomi's tragic losses in Moab came Israel's greatest king. Now from the social tragedy of Hannah's sterility sprang forth Samuel, the long-prophesied prophet like Moses.

humanity, and specifically Israel, to be fruitful and multiply (Gen 1:28; 9:1; 35:11) had made Hannah the Israelite incapable of fulfilling the divine command. The text's statement that it was God who closed Hannah's womb is significant here, for biblical narratives usually use God's personal name when they describe activities that are significant in Israel's covenantal relationship with God. Yet in this pair of statements lies a mystery: What good covenantal purposes can be accomplished through a woman's sterility?

Hannah's sterility made her vulnerable to ridicule. Her rival provoked her in order to *(ba'ăbûr)* irritate her. Was this what the Lord had in mind when he closed Hannah's womb? The thoughtful reader recalls that in the Torah the people of Israel were forced to endure much torment before the Lord delivered them. Perhaps the portrayal of Hannah's affliction was meant to draw this parallel to mind, thus preparing them for an act of divine deliverance in Hannah's behalf.

1:7 In spite of—or perhaps because of—her infertility, Hannah was a woman of faith. In fact, Hannah is portrayed as the most pious woman in the Old Testament. Here she is shown going up to the Lord's house; no other woman in the Old Testament is mentioned doing this. In addition, Hannah is the only woman shown making and fulfilling a vow to the Lord; she is also the only woman who is specifically said to pray (Hb. *pll*; 1:10,12,26–27; 2:1); her prayer is also among the longest recorded in the Old Testament. Furthermore, her prayer includes the most recorded utterances of Yahweh's name by a woman (eighteen). She is shown avoiding the faults of the first infertile covenant woman by seeking help from Yahweh rather than pursuing crafty schemes (cf. Gen 16:2). She also avoided the fault of Jephthah, who likewise made a vow that separated him from his child; whereas Jephthah gave his daughter as a burnt offering, Hannah gave her child as a living sacrifice (cf. Rom 12:1).

Peninnah is called Hannah's "rival." The Hebrew term *(ṣārâ)* suggests a woman who is a "troubler." The term is an apt one, considering her effect on Hannah; Hannah "wept" as a result of Peninnah's taunts. These insults appear to have been particularly poignant during the annual festival times at Shiloh because the family sacrificial meal that rewarded Peninnah's maternal blessings also insulted Hannah's unproductive womb. As a result, Hannah lost her desire to participate in the meal "and would not eat."

1:8 Hannah's good-hearted but insensitive husband Elkanah attempted to console her, suggesting to her that he was better to her than "ten sons." The reference to "ten sons" suggests the ten sons born to Jacob during Rachel's period of barrenness (cf. Gen 29:31–30:22). The patriarchal allusion also suggests a parallel between Jacob's love for Rachel and Elkanah's for Hannah. At the same time it foreshadows a happy outcome from Hannah's plight.

1:9 When Hannah left the family celebration, Eli was sitting on a chair—

a sign of authority[19]—at the doorposts of the sanctuary. Though too old to participate in the active leadership of the worship center (cf. Num 8:23–26), Eli was still able to sit at the entrance to the "holy place" *(hēkal),* much as elders would sit at the city gate in ancient Israel (Deut 21:19; 22:15; 25:7; Josh 20:4; Ruth 4:2,11; Lam 5:14). This position may have permitted him to act simultaneously as a judge (cf. 1 Sam 4:18) and a protector of worship (Deut 16:18).

According to the text, Eli's exact location was at the "doorpost of Yahweh's Holy Place" *(mĕzûzat hēkal yhwh).* This phrase suggests that the Shiloh worship center was a structure of some architectural permanence built in a traditional tripartite Semitic temple design (cf. also Judg 18:31; 1 Sam 1:24). Other Scriptures suggest that a tent was a central part of the worship site there (Josh 18:1; 19:51; 2 Sam 7:2,6; Ps 78:60). Perhaps the earlier tabernacle set up at Shiloh in Joshua's day had been supplemented by a building during the days of the Judges; alternatively, a smaller ceremonial tent may have housed the ark within the holy of holies (e.g., Hb. *dĕbîr,* "inner sanctuary," in 1 Kgs 6:19–21).

1:10 Hannah wept and prayed to the Lord "in bitterness of soul," a phrase used elsewhere to characterize the psychological pain experienced by one who has been deprived of a child through death (cf. Ruth 1:13,20; 2 Kgs 4:27; Zech 12:10) or who is experiencing great personal physical suffering (cf. Job 3:20; 7:11; 10:1; Isa 38:15). Relief from this sort of pain is never pictured in the Hebrew Bible as coming from a human being; in each case divine intervention was the only remedy. Wisely, Hannah also went to the Lord for help.

1:11 Hannah's prayer was specifically addressed to the omnipotent deliverer of those in distress, "the LORD Almighty" (cf. comment on 1:3). Her pain had made her a theologian—no character in Scripture prior to Hannah had ever used this term to address the Lord. In her prayer she implicitly recognized that the Lord alone is the giver of life. She also understood that the proper position of a believer in relation to the Lord is that of absolute subjection; three times she referred to herself as "your servant" (Hb. *ʾămātekā),* a term used elsewhere to describe a female household slave. Furthermore, she recognized that a relationship with the Lord involves giving, not just taking. She made a vow—an act without parallel for women elsewhere in Hebrew narrative but conditionally permissible for a married woman (cf. Num 30:6–8)—to "give [him] to the LORD for all the days of his life."

Hannah was certainly portrayed as more intimate in her relationship with the Lord than Eli, the spiritual icon of his generation. Within her prayers in chap. 1 Hannah seven times used Yahweh's name (1:11,15,17,26–28), whereas Eli never used the term in this episode; he used the more distant

---

[19] The term "seat" (כִּסֵּא) occurs 135 times in the Hebrew Bible and is translated in the NIV as "throne(s)" or "seat of honor" or "authority" on 122 occasions. Apparently it was more usual for people to sit on mats or on the earth itself; sitting above ground level implied the possession of social authority.

phrase "God of Israel" instead.

As part of her vow, Hannah seems to have promised to give her son to the Lord as a lifelong Nazirite (cf. Num 6:1–21).[20] The assumption is based on Hannah's declaration that "no razor will ever be used on his head" (cf. Num 6:5), a general parallel to the prebirth circumstances of Samson (cf. Judg 13:5–7) and the support of at least one ancient textual tradition.[21]

1:12–18 Hannah's lengthy silent prayer caught the watchful Eli's attention and led him to an incorrect conclusion. On the one hand, Eli appeared to be doing his job, vigilantly guarding the sanctuary from possible desecration by Hannah (lit., "keeping watch over [Hannah's] mouth"; cf. also Ps 39:1; Prov 21:23); on the other hand, he was actually demonstrating his incompetence. Here, as elsewhere, Eli is portrayed as a man unable to distinguish appearance from reality, as a man who himself lacked substance. Though Eli was the high priest of Shiloh—and ostensibly a man of exceptional spiritual maturity, he is consistently depicted by the narrator as spiritually blind and inert. He was a man who watched lips instead of perceiving hearts, who judged profound spirituality to be profligate indulgence in spirits,[22] who heard nothing when the Lord spoke (1 Sam 3:4,6), and who criticized his sons for abusing the sacrificial system yet grew fat from their take (2:22–24; 4:18). Fittingly, in the end his powerful career was surpassed by those who were "nothing"—a socially powerless rural woman and a child.

The fact that Hannah was portrayed as conversing with Yahweh suggests that Yahwism was not as "sexist" as some may portray it to be. A woman was not so unimportant in Israel as to be considered incapable of communicating with Israel's God. Significantly, Yahweh was also portrayed as a deity who listened to a woman and answered her prayer.

Drinks made from fermented grain ("beer"; v. 15) or fruit ("wine") were an important part of the worship of the Lord since, as products issuing from the Lord's bounty, they were used in the sacrificial ritual (cf. Exod 29:40;

---

[20] It should be noted, however, that the Torah's conditions for entry into a Nazirite vow assume self-admission rather than the decision of a parent or other authority. The fact that Samuel's—as well as Samson's—status as a Nazirite apparently remained in force from the moment of his birth and throughout his lifetime is undoubtedly a reflection of the degree of parental authority that existed in ANE cultures; parents were permitted to make significant decisions regarding a child's future as long as that child was under the parents' care; e.g., Abraham deciding to make Isaac a burnt offering (Gen 22), Samson being made a Nazirite by his parents (Judg 16:17), and Jesse sending David to serve King Saul (1 Sam 16:20–21).

[21] The LXX[B] and probably 4QSam[a]. Cf. E. Ulrich, *The Qumran Text of Samuel and Josephus* (Missoula, Mont.: Scholars Press, 1978), 39; and McCarter, *I Samuel*, 53. Cf. also Josephus, *Ant.* 5.10.3, and the *t. Nazir* 9.5. D. F. Payne suggests that "very possibly a contrast is intended with Samson, a Nazirite who did not fully maintain his consecrated state" (*I and II Samuel*, DSB [Philadelphia: Westminster, 1982], 10).

[22] The LXX records that Hannah was rebuked by Eli's servant, not Eli himself.

Lev 23:13; Num 15:5–10; 28:14; Deut 14:26; 32:38). However, Eli's rebuke of Hannah suggests that personal consumption resulting in alcohol abuse was a problem at the religious festivals held in Shiloh. Biblical evidence elsewhere suggests that drunkenness and immorality were not uncommon at Israelite religious centers (cf. 2:22; Judg 9:27; 21:21–23; Isa 28:7; perhaps also Lev 10:1–11).

Hannah asked that Eli not take her for a "wicked woman" (Hb. *bat bĕlîyāʿal* = "daughter of Belial"). The phrase suggests one who failed to give due respect to God or others and who therefore represented a threat to proper religious and societal order.[23] Rather than showing disrespect for God, she was praying to him in a state of "great anguish and grief" (v. 16) inflicted by Peninnah's affronts. Hannah's deep respect for authority is affirmed by her self-deprecating use of "your servant" in her response to Eli.

Eli proved quite capable of fulfilling his priestly role, even if he was spiritually dull. Learning the true nature of Hannah's actions, he validated her prayer with a wish and a blessing. Hannah responded to Eli's blessing with a winsome and gracious pun—the "Woman of Grace" (the Hb. meaning of Hannah's name) expressed hope of finding grace (Hb. *hēn*) in Eli's eyes.

Hannah's departure from the sanctuary area was an example of faith triumphant. Though she had approached the Lord in the depths of despondency, she left the sanctuary elevated and transformed. Hannah's spiritual victory, won through the labor of tearful prayers, enabled her to eat the festival meal in peace and hope.

1:19–20 At the time of the daily morning sacrifice the next day, Elkanah and his family worshiped at the Lord's house and then began their journey home (v. 19). "Ramah," previously identified by the alternate name Ramathaim (cf. 1:1), is the more common name for the hometown of Elkanah's clan.

In the context of the marital union between Elkanah and Hannah, "the LORD remembered" (*zākar*) Hannah. "Remembered" is a soteriological verb when used with the Lord as the subject and suggests the initiation of a major new activity by the covenant-making God (cf. Gen 8:1; Exod 2:24; cf. also Gen 19:29; 30:22). In most miracles touching human lives, the Lord chooses to achieve his desired ends with the assistance of people. Certainly this was true in Hannah's case.

Not long afterward Hannah was found to be pregnant and in the course of time gave birth to a son. The child was given a name intended to memorialize

[23] "Belial" (בְּלִיַּעַל), a word of uncertain origin, is a characteristic term in 1, 2 Samuel, with ten of its fifteen OT occurrences being found in these books. Hophni and Phinehas (2:12), opponents of the newly anointed king Saul (10:27), Nabal (25:17,25), troublemakers in David's militia (30:22), and Sheba (2 Sam 20:1) were all evaluated as "Sons of Belial" by the narrator. All demonstrated a threatening lack of respect for God or others. In Prov 6:12 אָדָם בְּלִיַּעַל is paired with אִישׁ אָוֶן, "man of trouble."

Hannah's bold faith and the Lord's gracious response. That name—Samuel—has also created an etymological and interpretive puzzle for generations of European and American scholars. The majority of interpreters have rejected the etymological link suggested in the text (vv. 17,20,27–28; 2:20) between the name *šĕmûʾēl* and the verb "ask" *(šāʾal)*.[24] However, consonantal and acrostic links do exist. Metathesizing (i.e., reversing) the first two letters of Samuel's name *(= mĕšûʾal)* creates a word meaning "He who was asked for"; acrostically, the name may be derived from the Hebrew phrase meaning "asked from God" *(= šāʾûl min ʾel)*.

(2) Hannah Dedicates Samuel to the Lord's Service (1:21–28)

[21]When the man Elkanah went up with all his family to offer the annual sacrifice to the LORD and to fulfill his vow, [22]Hannah did not go. She said to her husband, "After the boy is weaned, I will take him and present him before the LORD, and he will live there always."

[23]"Do what seems best to you," Elkanah her husband told her. "Stay here until you have weaned him; only may the LORD make good his word." So the woman stayed at home and nursed her son until she had weaned him.

[24]After he was weaned, she took the boy with her, young as he was, along with a three-year-old bull, an ephah of flour and a skin of wine, and brought him to the house of the LORD at Shiloh. [25]When they had slaughtered the bull, they brought the boy to Eli, [26]and she said to him, "As surely as you live, my lord, I am the woman who stood here beside you praying to the LORD. [27]I prayed for this child, and the LORD has granted me what I asked of him. [28]So now I give him to the LORD. For his whole life he will be given over to the LORD." And he worshiped the LORD there.

In this section Hannah and Elkanah fulfill a vow and entrust Samuel to Eli's care at Shiloh for lifelong Nazirite service. As preparation for this event, Hannah devotedly nurtures the child at Ramah, then presents him before the Lord, accompanied by a lavish sacrifice.

The best model of vow fulfillment in the Old Testament is presented here, as both Elkanah and Hannah make commitments to the Lord and then fulfill them diligently (cf. Eccl 5:4–5). Elkanah is particularly exemplary, in that he not only voluntarily made vows and then fulfilled them annually, but he also affirmed his wife's right to make commitments to God as well. Furthermore, the family's extreme generosity in their giving to God sets an example that is challenging for any person of faith.

1:21–23 The passage stresses Elkanah's exemplary piety. He faithfully

---

[24] Suggested meanings for Samuel's name include "His Name Is El," "Name of El/God," "Heard of God," "Asked of God," "He Who Is from God," "Offspring of God," and "El Is Exalted." Cf. Klein, *1 Samuel,* 9–10; R. Gordon, *I and II Samuel* (Grand Rapids: Zondervan, 1988), 76; McCarter, *I Samuel,* 62; and Driver, *Notes,* 19.

led his family to participate in annual Torah-prescribed pilgrimage festivals (Deut 12:5–7) and voluntarily made vows and then fulfilled them (Num 30:2; Deut 23:21). Although the Torah explicitly gave him the right to nullify Hannah's vow regarding Samuel's service in the Shiloh sanctuary (cf. Num 30:10–15), he chose instead to confirm her vow to the Lord, even though it meant losing the firstborn son from his beloved wife's womb. This latter act places him in a category with Abraham, who gave over his son Isaac (Gen 22; cf. also Gen 37:34–35; 42:4,36–38; 44:22–34).

Though Elkanah and the remainder of the family made their annual pilgrimage to Shiloh, Hannah chose to remain at Ramah to care for the infant Samuel. She maintained this practice each year until the boy was weaned, perhaps a total of three years.[25]

Hannah indicated that when the child appeared (literally) "before the face of Yahweh," he would "live there always" (v. 22). The phrase "appear before the face of Yahweh" is found elsewhere only in the Torah (Exod 34:24; Deut 16:16; 31:11) and refers there to annual sacrifice pilgrimage or solemn assembly meetings. Thus Hannah apparently was saying, "When he finally does go on the annual pilgrimage, he will never return home; he will stay at the pilgrimage site as long as he lives."

Perhaps the most prominent catchphrase in the story of Samuel is "before the Lord." Samuel was to live "before the Lord" always (cf. also 2:11,18,21), and this he actually did (cf. 7:6; 10:19; 11:15; 12:3,7; 15:33). This presents a stark contrast with the life of Saul, who was "before the Lord" only during his anointing by Samuel. At the same time, this phrase strengthens the comparison of Samuel with Moses, of whom it was said that he spoke "face to face" with the Lord (Exod 33:11; Deut 34:10). The "word" Elkanah prayerfully asked the Lord to "make good" (v. 23) cannot be discerned from the text; perhaps it was an otherwise unknown divine promise made to Elkanah and Hannah when they made their vows. Going a different direction, the LXX and Dead Sea Scrolls indicate that Elkanah was asking the Lord to establish Hannah's words.

1:24–28 In this passage Hannah is shown actively fulfilling her preconception promise to the Lord. According to the Torah, every firstborn male child belonged to the Lord (cf. Exod 13:2,13; Num 3:47; 8:16–17; 18:15–16) yet was to be redeemed at one month of age for the price of five shekels. As part of a vow, a male child could be given over to the Lord for a period of years, then presumably redeemed later (cf. Lev 27:1–8).[26] However, Hannah chose instead

---

[25] According to 2 Macc 7:27, a child might not be weaned until three or more years of age. While this might sound excessive to American mothers, it should be pointed out that no Israelite homes had running water, and most villages did not have access to a reliable supply of safe drinking water. While alcohol might be added to water as a bactericide, parents might wish to delay children's consumption of alcohol during the earliest years of life.

[26] Cf. R. L. Harris, "Leviticus," NIVBC (Grand Rapids: Zondervan, 1994), 167.

to give Samuel to the Lord in permanent Nazirite service.

Though the entire family was involved in the journey to bring Samuel to Shiloh, only Hannah was the subject of the key verbs in the passage: she "took" (v. 24) Samuel and a generous offering with her and "brought" him to the sanctuary complex; finally, she "said" the words that committed Samuel to Eli's care. Significantly, however, Hannah was not the subject of the verbs describing the sacrificial event accompanying Samuel's entrance into permanent service. Undoubtedly this is because females were not permitted to perform these actions.

The size of the offering that accompanied Hannah's vow fulfillment is a point of scholarly debate. The NIV's mention of "a three-year old bull" is based on readings found in the LXX, Dead Sea Scrolls, and Peshitta. However, the MT's reading, "three bulls," is to be preferred.[27] According to the Torah (Num 15:8–10), when a bull was given as part of a vow offering, only three tenths of an ephah of flour and half a hin of wine were to accompany the offering. But Hannah brought one ephah and a whole skin of wine—just over three times the amount needed for one bull. These amounts would have been appropriate only if three animals were being sacrificed. Clearly, the writer expected the audience to be impressed with the extreme generosity represented by the gift and thus with the heart of faith that conceived it.

Hannah's explanation of her acts were simple yet profound: "I prayed for this child, and the LORD has granted me what I asked of him" (v. 27). Interwoven into her confession in vv. 27–28 is an artful wordplay involving four different forms of the Hebrew root *šʾl*.[28] Samuel's name is an extension of the wordplay, combining the concept of "asking from" *(šāʾaltî mēʿim)* God and being "given over" *(šāʾûl)*. More than that, it is an expression of Hannah's faith. As Payne notes: "God had given him; Hannah gave him back; and Samuel's very name was a reminder of these things. We should not overlook the sacrifice made by Hannah; but her loss was to be Israel's gain, and she felt amply compensated."[29]

The final statement that "he worshiped the LORD" is problematic and is dealt with differently by interpreters; 4QSam[a] indicates that Hannah is the one who worshiped Yahweh.[30] Modern versions generally leave the verb with a masculine subject, though the referent is ambiguous, either Eli or Samuel. The sentence is found in 2:11 in the LXX. If Samuel is the referent, then this statement

---

[27] For further evidence buttressing this suggestion, cf. R. Ratner, "Three Bulls or One?: A Reappraisal of 1 Samuel 1,24," *Bib* 68 (1987): 98–102.

[28] A noun שְׁאֵלָתִי, "my request" (NIV leaves it untranslated); a *qal* perfect verb שָׁאַלְתִּי, "I asked"; a *hiphil* perfect verb, הִשְׁאִלְתִּהוּ, "I lend him" (NRSV "I have lent him"; NIV "I give him"); and a *qal* passive participle שָׁאוּל, "asked, borrowed?" (NIV "will be given over").

[29] Payne, *I and II Samuel*, 12.

[30] This reading probably results from a scribal attempt to clarify the text and is not original.

is a proleptic summary of the result of Hannah's actions. In such a case, this notation, along with the one in 2:11, would serve as an inclusio (bracketing device) framing Hannah's theologically rich prayer.

(3) Hannah Rejoices in the Lord (2:1–10)

[1]Then Hannah prayed and said:

"My heart rejoices in the LORD;
   in the LORD my horn is lifted high.
My mouth boasts over my enemies,
   for I delight in your deliverance.

[2]"There is no one holy like the LORD;
   there is no one besides you;
   there is no Rock like our God.

[3]"Do not keep talking so proudly
   or let your mouth speak such arrogance,
for the LORD is a God who knows,
   and by him deeds are weighed.

[4]"The bows of the warriors are broken,
   but those who stumbled are armed with strength.
[5]Those who were full hire themselves out for food,
   but those who were hungry hunger no more.
She who was barren has borne seven children,
   but she who has had many sons pines away.

[6]"The LORD brings death and makes alive;
   he brings down to the grave and raises up.
[7]The LORD sends poverty and wealth;
   he humbles and he exalts.
[8]He raises the poor from the dust
   and lifts the needy from the ash heap;
he seats them with princes
   and has them inherit a throne of honor.

"For the foundations of the earth are the LORD's;
   upon them he has set the world.
[9]He will guard the feet of his saints,
   but the wicked will be silenced in darkness.

"It is not by strength that one prevails;
[10]those who oppose the LORD will be shattered.
He will thunder against them from heaven;
   the LORD will judge the ends of the earth.

"He will give strength to his king
   and exalt the horn of his anointed."

This section, which contains Hannah's last recorded words and her longest quotation (112 words), provides a triumphant climax to the narrator's portrayal of the humble woman's faith. It is often considered to be a deliberate literary complement to 2 Samuel 22.[31] Hannah's monologue is described as a prayer; it is cast as a poetic hymn or Psalm of Thanksgiving[32] and is considered by many scholars to be among the earliest extant examples of Israelite poetry.[33]

Hannah's prayerful song eloquently affirms core concepts of Israelite faith: the Lord is the great judge and overseer of human destinies and a rewarder of those who earnestly seek him (cf. Heb 11:6). He is the source of empowerment and victory for those who fear him, but for all others he is the overpowering authority who dispenses fearful judgment.

The prayer's emphasis on the Lord's exaltation of those devalued by others serves not only as a testimony of God's action in Hannah's own life. It also foreshadows the Lord's ways in the lives of Samuel, David, and the nation of Israel. Negatively, it also presages what the Lord would do in judgment against the house of Eli.

2:1–2 Hannah's prayer begins on an exuberant and highly personal note, employing four first-person references that express unbridled delight in the Lord. Even as Peninnah had taunted Hannah, so now Hannah "boasts" (v. 1; lit., "my mouth is enlarged"; cf. also Ps 35:21; Isa 57:4) over her enemies because of the Lord's "deliverance" (Hb. *yĕšûʿâ,* "salvation"). The object of Hannah's delight is neither herself—that she has overcome the disgrace of barrenness—nor her son; instead it is the Lord, who is the source of both her son and her happy circumstance.

Borrowing images and confessions from the Torah, Hannah affirms the Lord's supreme holiness (cf. Lev 10:3; 11:44; 19:2; 20:26) and uniqueness (cf. Exod 15:11), and calls him the "Rock" (v. 2; Hb. *ṣûr,* "bedrock"; cf. Deut 32:4,15,18,30,31).

2:3–5 In her prayer, which apparently was uttered in a public forum where others could give consideration to her words (contrast with 1:13), Hannah

---

[31] Cf. W. Brueggemann, "I Samuel 1: A Sense of Beginning," *ZAW* 102 (1990): 33–48.

[32] Form criticism recognizes that psalms of thanksgiving characteristically contain (1) proclamation of love and praise (2:1), (2) introductory summary, (3) poetic recollection of the time of need, (4) report of the petition and rescue (2:5?), (5) renewal of the vow of praise, and (6) expression of praise (2:8–10). The fact that many of these elements cannot clearly be identified in Hannah's prayer does not deter scholars from categorizing this passage as a thanksgiving psalm. Cf. W. S. LaSor et al., *Old Testament Survey* (Grand Rapids: Eerdmans, 1982), 519–20.

[33] For discussions related to the dating of Hannah's poem, cf. J. Willis, "The Song of Hannah and Psalm 113" *CBQ* 35 (1973): 139–54 (eleventh cent. B.C.); J. Baldwin, *1 and 2 Samuel,* TOTC (Leicester: InterVarsity, 1988), 55–56 (eleventh cent. B.C.); McCarter, *I Samuel,* 75–76 (late tenth or early ninth cent. B.C.); Klein, *1 Samuel,* 15 (preexilic, monarchical period). For a serious treatment of the poem from a text-critical perspective, including a series of proposed emendations, cf. T. J. Lewis, "The Textual History of the Song of Hannah: 1 Samuel ii 1–10," *VT* 44 (1994): 18–46.

admonished all who would foolishly brag about or exalt themselves. Over them stands the Lord, who is aware of their thoughts and constantly evaluating their "deeds" (Hb. ʿălilâ, "wanton conduct"). When warranted, the Lord will act as the great reverser of fortunes in matters of military force, food, and fertility. He can bring low, and he can exalt. Mighty soldiers can be rendered defenseless, while the weak may perform valiantly; those who once had a surplus may be reduced to destitute servitude, while the hungry may cease (Hb. hādal) to be so. Most relevantly for Hannah, a barren woman may, with the Lord's help, bear "seven children"—a number suggestive of completeness—while others who once had large families may end life bereft and mournful.[34]

2:6–10 This section, which is linguistically marked as the most important component of the prayer,[35] contains an extended list of contrastive actions the Lord performs in his dealings with humans. The Lord's actions can be extremely positive: he "makes alive" (v. 6), "raises . . . from the dust" (v. 8), lifts . . . from the ash heap" (v. 8), "exalts" (v. 7), causes people to "inherit a throne" (v. 8), "seats" people "with princes" (v. 8), "sends . . . wealth" (v. 7), "will guard" (v. 9), "will give strength" (v. 10), and "raises up" from "the grave" (v. 6). In contrast, the Lord also "sends poverty" (v. 7), "humbles" (v. 7), "will thunder" (v. 10), "will judge" (v. 10), "brings death" (v. 6), and "brings down to the grave" (v. 6).

Yet the Lord does not perform these actions indiscriminately. As judge of "the ends of the earth" (v. 10), he brings the worst against "those who oppose" him (v. 10), while bestowing protection, strength, and exaltation to "his saints" (v. 9; Hb. hăsîdîm, "pious/godly") and "his king"/"his anointed" (v. 10).

Much scholarly discussion has centered around Hannah's use of the terms "king" and "anointed" (Hb. melek and měšîaḥ) in her prayer. Many scholars judge these words to be anachronistic, since Israel obviously had no king at the time.[36] However, it is possible that the words are (1) allusions to the office of kingship mentioned in the Torah (cf. Deut 17:15), (2) references to local Isra-

---

[34] This phrase is sometimes used as evidence that this prayer was not originally spoken by Hannah, since she is recorded as giving birth to only six children (see 2:21). Cf. Klein, *1 Samuel,* 14. However, if this number is recognized to be used here poetically or rhetorically, this argument loses its strength. Cf. Payne, *I and II Samuel,* 14.

[35] Linguistic marking is seen in the employment of a divine figure, in this case Yahweh, as the subject of eighteen different verbs in a section containing only fifty-eight words. Though comparative statistics presently are unavailable, it is accurate to say that these verses contain one of the Hebrew Bible's highest concentrations of verbs with Yahweh as the subject. Linguistic peak-marking is seen also in the employment of five mentions of Yahweh's name, as well as the mention of the highest-ranking social position in Israelite society, that of "king"/"messiah." The mention of nouns (to say nothing of verbs) of extreme semantic amplitude—sheol/heaven, ash heap/throne, saints/wicked ones, the poor/princes—also adds to the highlighting present within this section.

[36] Cf. Klein, *1 Samuel,* 15; B. F. Philbeck, "1–2 Samuel," BBC, ed. C. J. Allen (Nashville: Broadman, 1970), 16.

elite rulers (cf. Judg 9:6), (3) prophetic of the Davidic dynasty (cf. Gen 49:10–12), or (4) references to an anticipated, eschatological figure. The close parallels between Hannah's Prayer and Mary's Song (Luke 1:46–55) suggest that the first-century Christian community considered the entire passage, and especially the phrases "his king" and "his anointed," to be prophetic references to Jesus Christ and his ministry.

(4) Young Samuel Ministers before the Lord (2:11)

¹¹Then Elkanah went home to Ramah, but the boy ministered before the LORD under Eli the priest.

This verse provides a transition between the story of Elkanah's family and the story of Eli's family. Responsibility for Samuel's upbringing was now transferred from Elkanah to Eli as the youth was set apart as a lifelong attendant (Hb. mĕšārēt) to the Lord. Samuel's connections with Eli and the Lord would serve as both a link to and a contrast with Eli's own sons.

2. The Lord Blesses Hannah's Family, Judges Eli's Family (2:12–36)

This section contrasts the destinies of two families. The tragic story of Hophni and Phinehas, which is to be read in light of Lev 10:1–11, demonstrates the seriousness with which God takes priestly misconduct. It affirms that relatedness to a high priest is no substitute for a relationship with God, that pedigree or social power is not an alternative to purity.

At the same time, the section demonstrates the Lord's faithfulness in fulfilling Torah promises to bestow bounty on those who live lives of pious faith. Elkanah and Hannah received a priestly blessing from Eli (2:20) and abundant life from the Lord (2:21; cf. Lev 26:9; Deut 28:4) because of their righteous lives. By contrast, Hophni and Phinehas received a priestly rebuke (2:23–25) and a death sentence from the Lord (2:25).

(1) Eli's Sons Treat the Lord's Offerings with Contempt (2:12–17)

¹²Eli's sons were wicked men; they had no regard for the LORD. ¹³Now it was the practice of the priests with the people that whenever anyone offered a sacrifice and while the meat was being boiled, the servant of the priest would come with a three-pronged fork in his hand. ¹⁴He would plunge it into the pan or kettle or caldron or pot, and the priest would take for himself whatever the fork brought up. This is how they treated all the Israelites who came to Shiloh. ¹⁵But even before the fat was burned, the servant of the priest would come and say to the man who was sacrificing, "Give the priest some meat to roast; he won't accept boiled meat from you, but only raw."

¹⁶If the man said to him, "Let the fat be burned up first, and then take whatever you want," the servant would then answer, "No, hand it over now; if you don't, I'll

take it by force."

17This sin of the young men was very great in the LORD's sight, for they were treating the LORD's offering with contempt.

2:12 This verse consists of two complementary evaluative comments: Eli's sons were "wicked" (lit., "sons of Belial"); they had "no regard for" (lit., "they did not know") the Lord. The words cast an ominous pall over the passage and prepare the reader for the sequence of disasters that unfold in chap. 4.

The verbless clause in v. 12—literally, "the sons of Eli, the sons of Belial"— serves as a sort of double entendre: besides indicating the perverse character of Eli's sons, the construction has the effect of equating Eli with Belial. Indeed, Eli was a Belial because he failed to give due respect to God and therefore threatened the sanctity of the Lord's name in the community of faith. This subtle indictment of Eli will become more apparent in v. 29.

Hophni, Phinehas, and Samuel were skillfully portrayed by the writer as being similar in the sense that at the beginning of the story none of them knew the Lord (cf. 2:12; 3:7). Yet at the same time, differences and contrasts were also being established. While Hophni and Phinehas were despising the Lord, Samuel was serving him.

The evaluative comments in vv. 12 and 17 form an inclusio (i.e., an envelope structure); they have the effect of setting off and highlighting the disgusting actions of the priestly pair.

2:13–14 The priestly practices customary at Shiloh in matters of sacrifice are unlike those mentioned anywhere else in the Old Testament and clearly differ from those prescribed in the Torah (cf. Lev 10:14–15; Num 18:18). The writer described the strange traditions of the Shiloh priests in detail to clarify the need to destroy the Elide line and remove the central Israelite worship site from Shiloh.[37]

2:15–17 These verses focus on the climactic flaw in the priestly practices at Shiloh: Hophni and Phinehas were taking the priestly share of the fellowship offerings "before the fat was burned"—that is, before the Lord had been given his portion (cf. Lev 3:3–5; 7:30). Furthermore, the priests were consuming fat

---

[37] Shiloh is a symbol of what was wrong with the period of the Judges. Clearly idolatry was a part of Israelite society at that time (cf. Judg 2:12–13; 3:7; 6:25–32; 8:33; 9:4; 10:6–13); but in the events and descriptions of Shiloh provided here it becomes clear that even the worship of Yahweh at his holiest central sanctuary had become corrupt. Consequently, it is best to view Eli's function as high priest at the major cultic center as a desecration of Yahweh's intentions as expressed in the Torah. In that sense Eli the Levite's actions can be placed in the same general category as the Levite who led the Danites in idolatry (Judg 17:7–8:31). That an unhappy parallel is intended between the worship centers in Dan and Shiloh is suggested by Judg 18:30–31, where it is noted that Moses' grandson Jonathan (following the implication of the נ *suspensum,* as well as the reading of some LXX manuscripts) established an idolatrous cultic site in Dan that lasted as long as the religious center at Shiloh, officiated over by Aaron's descendant Eli. Cf. E. Tov, *Textual Criticism of the Hebrew Bible* (Minneapolis/Assen/Maastricht: Fortress/Van Gorcum, 1992), 57.

from the sacrificial animals, an act explicitly prohibited in the Torah (cf. Lev 7:22–26). In addition, they used the threat of violence to get their way. This blasphemous expression of self-interest and disregard for the law was a sin that "was very great in the LORD's sight" (v. 17; cf. Lev 7:25). Even the laypersons, who acceded to the wrongful demands placed on them, were more pious than the priests and their servants in that they tried to get the priests to give the Lord his portion first. The MT suggests that the priestly actions were causing the worshipers (Hb. *hāʾănāšîm*, "the men") to look disrespectfully upon the free-will offerings made to the Lord. Priestly abuse was giving religion a bad name in Israel.

(2) Samuel Ministers before the Lord as His Family Receives the Lord's Blessing (2:18–21)

[18]**But Samuel was ministering before the LORD—a boy wearing a linen ephod. [19]Each year his mother made him a little robe and took it to him when she went up with her husband to offer the annual sacrifice. [20]Eli would bless Elkanah and his wife, saying, "May the LORD give you children by this woman to take the place of the one she prayed for and gave to the LORD." Then they would go home. [21]And the LORD was gracious to Hannah; she conceived and gave birth to three sons and two daughters. Meanwhile, the boy Samuel grew up in the presence of the LORD.**

Samuel's precocious childhood, one marked inwardly by his unique relationship with the Lord and outwardly by his priestly attire and his presence at Shiloh, contrasted sharply with that of Hophni and Phinehas. The final portrait of Elkanah's family, which is also presented in this section, contrasted just as vividly with the destiny of Eli's family. Elkanah's family was depicted in acts of exemplary piety; Eli's family will be depicted in acts of disgusting sacrilege. Elkanah's family received a blessing and fruitful multiplication; Eli's would receive a curse and desolation. The family portraits are studies in Torah blessings and curses (cf. Lev 26; Deut 28).

2:18 Samuel's service before the Lord is rhetorically underlined through the repetition of the phrase "was ministering" (Hb. *hāyâ měšārēt*) in vv. 11,18. The verbal construction suggests an ongoing activity, something ingrained in Samuel's lifestyle. The placement of this phrase in v. 18 is doubly emphatic because of its juxtaposition with the description of Hophni and Phinehas.

In his service at Shiloh, Samuel wore the ephod, a sleeveless, hip-length garment that only members of the Levitical tribe were authorized to wear. The clear implication is that Samuel was a member of this tribe (cf. 1 Chr 6:22–28). Samuel's youthful opportunity to wear garments of privilege and position are reminiscent of both Joseph (Gen 37:3) and David (1 Sam 17:38–39).

2:19 Samuel's mother annually brought Samuel a robe *(měʿîl),* a longer outer garment worn by members of the Levitical tribe involved in priestly service (cf. Lev 8:7). This thoughtful gift from Hannah suggests that although

Samuel was gone from the household in Ramah, he was still very much in Hannah's heart (cf. Prov 31:19–21). Through the use of the clothing motif in portraying Samuel's career (cf. also 15:27), the writer suggests that Samuel's life was the outcome of a splendid mother of faith.

2:20–21 Eli annually pronounced over Elkanah and Hannah a blessing calling for the Lord to compensate the couple for relinquishing Samuel.

Verse 21 answers the seemingly incongruous statements of 1:5–6. The Lord's harshness is only apparent. The Lord, who had commanded human fertility (Gen 1:26–28), had withheld it from a faithful servant. Yet in this case, the denial of offspring was only temporary and had the effect of multiplying blessings in Hannah's life. Ultimately God's gracious (Hb. *ḥēn*) nature (cf. Exod 34:6) was demonstrated as the Lord provided Hannah, the Woman of Grace, with five additional children—three sons and two daughters.

Samuel grew up "in the presence of the LORD," literally, "with Yahweh." This Hebrew phrase is used in the Torah to describe Moses' position when he received the Decalogue (Exod 34:28). In Psalms (130:7) "with Yahweh" is said to be a place of "unfailing love" and "full redemption." In the present context it seems to suggest that Samuel enjoyed a childhood marked by divine favor and a lifestyle evidencing a Moses-like relationship with the Lord.

(3) The Lord Determines to Kill Eli's Sons for Their Sin (2:22–25)

[22]**Now Eli, who was very old, heard about everything his sons were doing to all Israel and how they slept with the women who served at the entrance to the Tent of Meeting.** [23]**So he said to them, "Why do you do such things? I hear from all the people about these wicked deeds of yours.** [24]**No, my sons; it is not a good report that I hear spreading among the LORD's people.** [25]**If a man sins against another man, God may mediate for him; but if a man sins against the LORD, who will intercede for him?" His sons, however, did not listen to their father's rebuke, for it was the LORD's will to put them to death.**

The elderly priest Eli is shown chiding his sons for their professional misconduct and threatening them with dire consequences for their sins. The warning was unheeded by Hophni and Phinehas, however.

In fact, the writer indicates that this was consistent with the Lord's desire "to put them to death." In keeping with his righteous and unchanging nature, the Lord takes pleasure in upholding the Torah. Here the Lord had already determined to destroy Hophni and Phinehas for their sin. During an earlier portion of the period of the Judges, God had previously sent an evil spirit against Abimelech, the wicked son of a good judge, for the purpose of bringing death to sinners (Judg 9:23,56–57).

2:22–25 Eli's first recorded rebuke of his sons' misconduct came when he was "very old." The writer may be implying that Eli neglected his parental responsibilities earlier in life (cf. Deut 6:7; 21:18–21). Eli reprimanded them because he "heard about everything his sons were doing to all Israel." To the previously reported offenses (cf. vv. 12–17) a new charge was added—they were having sexual relations with "the women who served at the entrance to the Tent of Meeting."[38] Perhaps these women were Nazirites involved in volunteer service at the worship site (cf. Num 6:2; Exod 38:8); alternatively they may have been cultic prostitutes.[39] However, they were being treated as though they were pagan shrine prostitutes (cf. Hos 4:14).

Eli the judge used the imagery of a legal dispute in warning his sons. In a case pitting two people against each other, God[40] could work either through his revealed law or through circumstances to exonerate the person charged with wrongdoing. However, if a person were pitted against the Lord in court, the human could expect only condemnation. Hophni and Phinehas, having committed capital offenses (cf. Lev 7:25; 22:9), could expect the Lord to bring the death penalty upon them.

The phrase "it was the LORD's will" (v. 25) also can be translated "the LORD was pleased." Although it would be misleading to say that the Lord takes pleasure in killing people (cf. Ezek 18:32; 33:11; 2 Pet 3:9), it is certainly true that he delights in bringing justice to the world order. Justice is a central trait in God's character (cf. Exod 34:7; 2 Chr 12:6), and the implementation of divine justice always brings satisfaction.

(4) Samuel Grows in Favor before the Lord (2:26)

26And the boy Samuel continued to grow in stature and in favor with the LORD and with men.

2:26 The subject-first word order in the Hebrew text suggests that this verse was intended to present a contrast to v. 25. Samuel's life certainly contrasted sharply with Eli's sons. While the sins of Hophni and Phinehas were increasing in magnitude (2:17), Samuel's stature and good standing were increasing. As God and society were condemning Hophni and Phinehas, Samuel was being commended. In Samuel God had preserved a remnant of faithful servanthood at Shiloh. The New Testament recognized in the precocious spirituality of the boy Samuel a foreshadowing of Jesus' own boyhood development (cf. Luke 2:52).

---

[38] The LXX[B] and 4QSam[a] omit this sentence. McCarter (*I Samuel*, 81), following F. M. Cross, suggests this may be a late interpolation designed to link this passage with Num 25:6–15. Without denying a possible link with the Torah passage, I consider this statement part of the original composition.

[39] R. F. Youngblood, "1, 2 Samuel," EBC (Grand Rapids: Zondervan, 1992), 585.

[40] The term rendered "God" (אֱלֹהִים) here may mean either God himself or God's appointed human representative (thus a "judge"; cf. Exod 22:8–9; Ps 89:). In my estimation the NIV correctly prefers the translation "God." McCarter chooses to translate it as "gods" (*I Samuel*, 77). C. Houtman also concludes the term does not refer to God ("Zu I Samuel 2:25," ZAW 89 [1977]: 412–17).

(5) Judgment Is Pronounced against the House of Eli (2:27–36)

²⁷Now a man of God came to Eli and said to him, "This is what the LORD says: 'Did I not clearly reveal myself to your father's house when they were in Egypt under Pharaoh? ²⁸I chose your father out of all the tribes of Israel to be my priest, to go up to my altar, to burn incense, and to wear an ephod in my presence. I also gave your father's house all the offerings made with fire by the Israelites. ²⁹Why do you scorn my sacrifice and offering that I prescribed for my dwelling? Why do you honor your sons more than me by fattening yourselves on the choice parts of every offering made by my people Israel?'

³⁰"Therefore the LORD, the God of Israel, declares: 'I promised that your house and your father's house would minister before me forever.' But now the LORD declares: 'Far be it from me! Those who honor me I will honor, but those who despise me will be disdained. ³¹The time is coming when I will cut short your strength and the strength of your father's house, so that there will not be an old man in your family line ³²and you will see distress in my dwelling. Although good will be done to Israel, in your family line there will never be an old man. ³³Every one of you that I do not cut off from my altar will be spared only to blind your eyes with tears and to grieve your heart, and all your descendants will die in the prime of life.

³⁴"'And what happens to your two sons, Hophni and Phinehas, will be a sign to you—they will both die on the same day. ³⁵I will raise up for myself a faithful priest, who will do according to what is in my heart and mind. I will firmly establish his house, and he will minister before my anointed one always. ³⁶Then everyone left in your family line will come and bow down before him for a piece of silver and a crust of bread and plead, "Appoint me to some priestly office so I can have food to eat."'"

An unnamed prophet came to Eli and pronounced terrifying words of judgment against the priest and his descendants. After reciting the historical background of God's dealings with Eli's ancestors, the man of God presented a litany of crimes against the Lord committed by the house of Eli. In a climactic conclusion the prophet then announced the Lord's punishment (vv. 30–36).

The pronouncement of judgment simultaneously had the effect of promising an end to the dominance of the house of Eli in priestly matters in Israel and opening the way for Torah promises relating to the descendants of Eleazar (cf. Num 25:12–13) to be fulfilled.

2:27–29 The unnamed individual who spoke in the Lord's name to Eli is termed a "man of God" (v. 27), the second most common designation for a prophet in the Old Testament (used seventy-one times). The man of God's statement opened with the classic introduction to the body of a prophetic speech, "This is what the LORD says" (lit., "Thus said Yahweh").⁴¹ "Your

---

⁴¹ "Thus said Yahweh" (כֹּה אָמַר יהוה) is used 293 times in the Hebrew Bible. According to H. V. D. Parunak, this phrase "validates the message that it introduces as a word from Yahweh." Cf. Parunak, "Some Discourse Functions of Prophetic Quotation Formulas in Jeremiah," in *Biblical Hebrew and Discourse Linguistics,* ed. R. Bergen (Dallas: SIL Press, 1994), 505.

father's house" and "your father" were references to Eli's forebear Aaron (cf. 14:3; 1 Chr 24:3), whom Yahweh "chose out of all the tribes of Israel" to perform the priestly functions (cf. Exod 28:1). These functions included going up to the altar in the tabernacle courtyard (cf. Exod 20:24) and burning incense in the holy place (cf. Exod 30:7–9; 40:5), as well as all other official priestly activities performed while wearing "an ephod" (cf. Exod 28:1–6).

As noted in v. 28, the Lord ordained that the sacrificial meat portions given to him by offerers were to be eaten by the priests (cf. Lev 7:34; 10:14). However, the priests were "fattening" themselves by eating the "choice parts of every offering" (lit., "the first of every freewill offering"), that is, the fatty portion that was to be burned in the fire (cf. Lev 7:25). The use of plural pronouns in the Hebrew of "you scorn" and "fattening yourselves" in v. 29 indicates that Eli was implicated in some sense in the sin, even if it was only in the sense that as the eldest priest at the sanctuary he bore ultimate responsibility for what occurred there. However, while condemning their sin, he may have been participating in it. This interpretation is reinforced by the narrator's comment in 4:18, where it is noted that Eli was "heavy"—a condition that could have resulted from eating the forbidden food.

Though Eli's sons committed grave sins, Eli did not bear responsibility for their misconduct. He was condemned for his own sin—honoring his sons more than the Lord. This sin amounted to a violation of the First Commandment (Exod 20:2–3).

2:30–36 The sins of Eli and his sons represented a breach of contract with the Lord. Thus, the Lord was no longer bound by the terms of the agreement. God expressed the conditional nature of his dealings with humanity with the epigram, "Those who honor me I will honor, but those who despise me will be disdained" (v. 30).

As a result of the house of Eli's sins, the Lord would "cut short" (v. 31; lit., "shatter the arms of") their "strength."[42] The practical outworking of this judgment was twofold. First, the current generations of Eli's family would suffer penalties: Eli himself would witness distress in the Lord's dwelling (cf. 4:13), and Eli's sons Hophni and Phinehas would die on the same day (cf. 4:11), a sign confirming the reality of God's judgment.

Second, future generations of Eli's family would suffer penalties. They would persistently experience untimely deaths (cf. 22:18–19), so that males

---

[42] The figure of speech "to shatter the arms" is without parallel elsewhere in OT literature and prefigures what happened literally to the statue of Dagon in chap. 5. As such it draws a subtle yet significant parallel between the judgment against the house of Eli and that of the house of Dagon. Both involved Yahweh bringing about the downfall of central figures related to their respective sanctuaries following a time when Yahweh's reputation was in doubt. By literarily paralleling the judgments, the narrator was in effect equating Shiloh's condition under Eli with that of a pagan house of worship, reinforcing the image of life in Israel presented in the Book of Judges.

who lived to old age would not be found among Eli's descendants. By being denied elders, the most socially powerful age group of individuals in clan-based societies, the line of Eli would be denied a significant form of power and influence in society. Eli's descendants would be disqualified from cultic service as well. The Lord would raise up another family to perform the most weighty duties associated with Israelite sanctuary worship. This promise appears to have been fulfilled with the rise of Zadok, who displaced Abiathar as the high priest in Israel (cf. 1 Kgs 2:35; 1 Chr 29:22). The priestly line of Eli would become so unimportant in the religious power structure of future generations that they would not even be eligible to receive payment for the services they rendered (v. 36).[43]

The story of the downfall of the house of Eli plays an important role in Hebrew narrative because it is the last non-Zadokite priestly family with an active role in Old Testament narrative. When the Lord cursed Eli's line, the way was cleared for Eleazar's descendants, the promised heirs to the high priest-hood, to assume their proper position.[44] The details would be worked out in good time.

3. The Lord Makes Samuel Israel's Prophet (3:1–22)

This section depicts Samuel's transformation from *na'ar* ("boy," 3:1) to *nābî'* ("prophet," 3:20), from being a juvenile ignorant of the Lord to one who functioned as the Lord's impeccable and revered spokesman. With this event the child Samuel, the first named male prophet since Moses, begins his career as a prophet who will be like Moses (cf. Deut 18:15–19). In it all the Lord once again demonstrated his propensity for confounding human systems, bypassing the exalted in favor of the humble.

---

[43] Critical scholarship has suggested a complex literary prehistory to the prophetic message of 2:27–36. Generally it has been proposed that the passage represents either a conflation of prophe-cies once related to the rise of Samuel and Zadok or a *vaticinia post eventum* concocted to support Zadokite claims to the priesthood over Levitical ones, and that in any event it has been infused with Josianic/Deuteronomistic theology. Cf. H. W. Hertzberg, *I and II Samuel*, OTL (Philadelphia: Westminster, 1964), 37–39; Klein, *1 Samuel*, 26–28; McCarter, *I Samuel*, 92–93. Such interpreta-tions are mere conjectures; they ignore the narrative dynamic of Genesis to 2 Kings and are unnec-essarily skeptical of prophetic activity depicted in the OT.

[44] The rise of the Zadokites is chronicled throughout the history of Israel from Sinai through the period of Israel's monarchy in Exodus to 2 Kings. The first expression is seen in Exod 6:23–25, where Zadok's forebear Eleazar is given special genealogical prominence by being the only son of Aaron whose wife and offspring are mentioned. It is carried forward in Num 25:6–13 when Phinehas ben Eleazar zealously defends God's glory and is rewarded by Yahweh with "a covenant of a lasting priesthood." The Eleazarite motif reaches its climax in 1 Kgs 2:35, where Solomon "replaced Abiathar with Zadok the priest."

*(1) The Lord Reveals to Samuel His Judgment against the House of Eli
     (3:1–18)*

[1]The boy Samuel ministered before the LORD under Eli. In those days the word
of the LORD was rare; there were not many visions.

[2]One night Eli, whose eyes were becoming so weak that he could barely see, was
lying down in his usual place. [3]The lamp of God had not yet gone out, and Samuel
was lying down in the temple of the LORD, where the ark of God was. [4]Then the
LORD called Samuel.

Samuel answered, "Here I am." [5]And he ran to Eli and said, "Here I am; you
called me."

But Eli said, "I did not call; go back and lie down." So he went and lay down.

[6]Again the LORD called, "Samuel!" And Samuel got up and went to Eli and
said, "Here I am; you called me."

"My son," Eli said, "I did not call; go back and lie down."

[7]Now Samuel did not yet know the LORD: The word of the LORD had not yet
been revealed to him.

[8]The LORD called Samuel a third time, and Samuel got up and went to Eli and
said, "Here I am; you called me."

Then Eli realized that the LORD was calling the boy. [9]So Eli told Samuel, "Go
and lie down, and if he calls you, say, 'Speak, LORD, for your servant is listening.'"
So Samuel went and lay down in his place.

[10]The LORD came and stood there, calling as at the other times, "Samuel! Samuel!"

Then Samuel said, "Speak, for your servant is listening."

[11]And the LORD said to Samuel: "See, I am about to do something in Israel that
will make the ears of everyone who hears of it tingle. [12]At that time I will carry out
against Eli everything I spoke against his family—from beginning to end. [13]For I
told him that I would judge his family forever because of the sin he knew about; his
sons made themselves contemptible, and he failed to restrain them. [14]Therefore, I
swore to the house of Eli, 'The guilt of Eli's house will never be atoned for by sacrifice or offering.'"

[15]Samuel lay down until morning and then opened the doors of the house of the
LORD. He was afraid to tell Eli the vision, [16]but Eli called him and said, "Samuel,
my son."

Samuel answered, "Here I am."

[17]"What was it he said to you?" Eli asked. "Do not hide it from me. May God
deal with you, be it ever so severely, if you hide from me anything he told you."
[18]So Samuel told him everything, hiding nothing from him. Then Eli said, "He is
the LORD; let him do what is good in his eyes."

Samuel's first act as prophet was perhaps his most difficult; though only a
child, he had to announce the Lord's fatal judgment against Israel's most powerful family. Samuel's message came on the heels of the unnamed prophet's
condemnation of the house of Eli and confirmed the certainty and severity of
the Lord's judgment (cf. Gen 41:32).

3:1–3 Samuel, as a youthful Levite,[45] was providing service to the Lord under Eli's tutelage. In the days of Eli, prophetic revelations in the form of visions and divine words had been "rare" (v. 1; lit., "precious"), a circumstance that can be linked to divine displeasure (cf. 14:37; 28:6) and helps explain why society was so degenerate at that time (cf. Prov 29:18; Amos 8:11).

Background details provided here are laden with symbolism relevant to the events that follow; Eli's eyes—and by extension his spiritual insight—were "so weak that he could barely see" (v. 2). The mention of "the lamp of God" (v. 3) still burning in the midst of Shiloh's darkness provided not only a temporal setting—the predawn hours (cf. Exod 27:21)—but also a symbol of Samuel's presence in that spiritually benighted worship center. Samuel lying down in the Lord's temple, "where the ark of God was," positions the youth not only spatially but also spiritually; he was of all Israelites closest to the Lord's throne (cf. 4:4; Num 7:89).[46]

3:4–14 While Samuel was fulfilling the Torah obligations to tend the lamp of God (cf. Lev 24:3; Num 18:23), the Lord called the youth and delivered a message of judgment to him. In a form paralleling Abraham, Jacob, and Moses' obedient responses to divine calls (Gen 22:1,11; 31:11; Exod 3:4), Samuel responded, "Here I am" (v. 4). Because he did not initially know the Lord, however, Samuel at first went to Eli for further instructions (vv. 5–6,8).

Eli twice turned Samuel away (vv. 5–6), perhaps because Eli essentially was blind to the possibility of the Lord's revealing himself in a personal manner.[47] Eventually, however, the elderly priest came to understand that the Lord was calling the youth and advised him to respond submissively.

On the climactic fourth approach to Samuel, the Lord called the boy's name twice and also "stood." The repetition of the personal name is reminiscent of the divine call to Abraham at Mount Moriah (Gen 22:1,11) and the one to Moses at the burning bush (Exod 3:4). The similarity suggests that this moment was as important in Samuel's life and for all Israel as the parallel moments were in the lives of the earlier heroes of the faith. Samuel obedi-

---

[45] Josephus, apparently reflecting a popular first-century Jewish understanding, indicated that Samuel was twelve at the time of the events (*Ant.* 5.10.4).

[46] Some commentators understand Samuel's presence in the temple as an example of "incubation." Cf. Hertzberg, *I and II Samuel*, 41. However, it is more probable that the writer included this note to demonstrate Samuel's diligence in fulfilling Torah mandates. As a son of Aaron, Eli was required "to keep the lamps burning before the LORD from evening till morning" (Exod 27:21; cf. Lev 24:3; also Num 18:23). However, since Eli apparently was too old for active service before Yahweh as a priest (cf. Num 8:23–26), the Levite Samuel was permitted to act as his surrogate in this matter (cf. Num 18:23).

[47] The narrator's portrayal of Israel's high priest as a man who required three tries to perceive Yahweh's work in a child's life probably is intended to confirm the correctness of God's judgment on Eli's house. It reinforces the image cast in 1:12–16 of Eli as a spiritual dolt. The venerable patriarch was scarcely more spiritually enlightened than his spiritually benighted sons.

ently identified himself as the Lord's "servant" (v. 10; cf. 1:11) and urged the Lord to speak.

The Lord's terrifying revelation was in fact a confirmatory repetition of the judgment against the house of Eli given by the unnamed prophet (2:30–36). Though prophetic messages could be conditional—warnings of possible consequences resulting from continued disobedience (e.g., Jonah 3:4)—in the case of the words spoken against the house of Eli they were certain. Every promised outcome—"from beginning to end" (v. 12)—would become reality. And Eli, as the family patriarch, would bear the brunt of the blame because "he knew about" (v. 13) his sons' "contemptible"[48] sins but "failed to restrain them" (cf. Deut 21:18–21). Eli's conscious failure to enforce divine law in his own family amounted to a high-handed (i.e., deliberate) sin; as such it could "never be atoned for by sacrifice or offering" (v. 14; cf. Num 15:30–31). Furthermore, the magnitude and form of God's judgment would be so shocking that it would cause "the ears of everyone who hears it to tingle"—that is, to give rise to great fear and dismay (cf. 2 Kgs 21:12; Jer 19:3).

3:15–18   With the coming of morning, Samuel "opened the doors of the house of the LORD."[49] The description of a dawn marked by the prophet's reopening the way into the Lord's presence is an obvious double entendre: on the one hand, Samuel was merely performing his daily duty as a temple servant; on the other hand, he was ushering in a new era of spiritual consciousness in Israel.[50]

But Samuel did not enter into his role as the Lord's spokesman without hesitation: "He was afraid to tell Eli the vision" (v. 15). Eli's fatherly reassurances and stern admonition provided the encouragement the lad needed to perform his duty. Eli's threat in v. 17 is reminiscent of the Lord's words to Ezekiel: "When I say to a wicked man, 'You will surely die, and you do not warn him or speak out to dissuade him from his evil ways . . ., that wicked man will die for his sin, and I will hold you accountable for his blood" (cf. Ezek 3:17–21).

The interaction between Eli and Samuel in vv. 17–18 conveys an idealized model of prophetic activity in society: the addressee encourages the prophet to speak the full revelation, the prophet does so, and the addressee accepts it will-

---

[48] The word "contemptible" (מְקַלְלִים) literally means "making light" and stands as the semantic antonym of "honoring"/"giving weight" (כָּבֵד). The term indicates an action that detracts from the prestige or esteem of authority. For other uses of the word קלל, cf. Exod 21:17; Lev 24:14; 2 Sam 16:5; Prov 20:20.

[49] The tabernacle described in the Torah did not have doors. Since the Shiloh worship center did, it is possible that the tabernacle was housed within a more permanent structure. This verse compares favorably with the notation in 1:9. Cf. Baldwin's useful discussion of Shiloh (*1 and 2 Samuel*, 65–68).

[50] For more comment concerning the symbolic nature of this narrative note, cf. J. G. Janzen, "'Samuel Opened the Doors of the House of Yahweh' (1 Samuel 3:15)," *JSOT* 26 (1983): 89–96.

ingly.[51] In these verses both the seriousness of the prophetic responsibility and a model of its proper discharge are presented. Samuel's alert, expectant reception of the divine message (v. 10b) and his full disclosure of the Lord's revelation (vv. 17–18a) in spite of personal misgivings (v. 15) are the proper responses of a prophet to a revelatory divine visitation.

(2) The Lord Makes Samuel a Prophet to All Israel (3:19–4:1a)

[19]The LORD was with Samuel as he grew up, and he let none of his words fall to the ground. [20]And all Israel from Dan to Beersheba recognized that Samuel was attested as a prophet of the LORD. [21]The LORD continued to appear at Shiloh, and there he revealed himself to Samuel through his word.
[1]And Samuel's word came to all Israel.

3:19–4:1a "The LORD was with Samuel" (v. 19). The drumbeat of the writer is that the Lord was at work in Samuel's life—from the moment of his conception (1:19–20), through his early development (2:21,26), into his entrance into the prophetic ministry (3:4,6,8,10), and now in the maturation of that ministry. The Lord did not let Samuel's prophetic pronouncements "fall to the ground"; the young man's words, like those of any authentic prophet, were authoritative and trustworthy because they were the Lord's words. Samuel's success was in fact the Lord's success.

Most Israelite leaders during the period of the Judges exercised authority in only small areas of the country,[52] but not Samuel. Though his role as a judge was almost certainly limited to the central region of Israel,[53] his prophetic ministry was not so restricted. Because of his service at Israel's central sanctuary during the earlier years of his ministry, pilgrims visiting Shiloh spread his reputation as a prophet throughout "all Israel from Dan to Beersheba" (v. 20). Like Moses the prophet before him (cf. Num 12:7), Samuel was "attested" (Hb. ne'ĕmān, "established," "confirmed," "faithful");[54] his words had passed the

---

[51] Contrast Eli's words with the reactions of Israelites presented elsewhere in both the Former and Latter Prophets: e.g., 1 Kgs 22:4–8; Jer 5:31; 11:21; Amos 7:16; Mic 2:6,11.

[52] The essentially unanimous opinion of modern biblical scholarship is that Israelite judgeships were regional. Among the conservative commentators, cf. A. E. Hill and J. H. Walton, *A Survey of the Old Testament* (Grand Rapids: Zondervan, 1991), 178: "It is very possible that many of the judges exercised only local jurisdiction." Also F. D. Lindsey: "Many (if not all) of the judges probably ruled in geographically limited portions of Israel" ("Judges," in *Bible Knowledge Commentary of the Old Testament,* ed. J. F. Walvoord and R. B. Zuck [n.p.: Victor, 1985], 374).

[53] Samuel's only recorded locations for holding court were Bethel, Gilgal, Mizpah (cf. 7:16), and his hometown of Ramah. All of these sites were clustered together in a fifteen-mile-wide ellipse in central Israel, within the tribal regions of Benjamin, Ephraim, and southern Manasseh. Cf. Y. Aharoni et al., *The Macmillan Bible Atlas,* 3rd ed. (New York: Macmillan, 1993), 69.

[54] In this verse yet another link is forged between Moses and Samuel, this time on the lexical level. Moses is the only person in the Torah or to this point in the Former Prophets to whom the virtuous adjectival participle נֶאֱמָן is applied.

Torah's test for authenticity (cf. Deut 18:22). For the first time since Moses, Israel had a national prophet.

"The LORD continued to appear [lit., "was seen"] at Shiloh" (v. 21). These appearances took the form of prophetic words given through Samuel rather than through any physical manifestation.

4. The House of Eli Is Devastated as the Ark of God Is Captured (4:1b–22)

This section[55] provides narrative confirmation of the destruction of Eli's family line, just as Samuel's words to Eli in the previous section provided its verbal confirmation. As at other times in Israelite history and in accordance with Torah promises (cf. Lev 26:17; Deut 28:25), here the Lord would bring judgment to bear on the sins of his people through the medium of a troublesome foreign army (cf. 2 Sam 24:1,13), in this case the Philistines.[56] In so doing the Lord demonstrates his sovereignty over all peoples, even those outside the covenant tent.

(1) The Philistines Kill Eli's Sons and Capture the Ark (4:1b–11)

Now the Israelites went out to fight against the Philistines. The Israelites camped at Ebenezer, and the Philistines at Aphek. [2]The Philistines deployed their forces to meet Israel, and as the battle spread, Israel was defeated by the Philistines, who killed about four thousand of them on the battlefield. [3]When the soldiers returned to camp, the elders of Israel asked, "Why did the LORD bring defeat upon

---

[55] Modern scholars usually treat chaps. 4–6 as a separate literary entity that has been inserted by an editor into their present position in the text. Cf. esp. L. Rost, *Die Überlieferung von der Thronnachfolge Davids,* BWANT III, 6 (Stuttgart: W. Kohlhammer, 1926); Eng. trans.: *The Succession to the Throne of David* (Sheffield: Almond, 1982); and A. F. Campbell, *The Ark Narrative (1 Sam 4–6; 2 Sam 6)* (Missoula: Scholars Press, 1975). Scholars see in this narrative an Israelite example of "an account by a vanquished army of its defeat and the capture of its 'gods' (of which the ark was the Israelite equivalent" (McCarter, *I Samuel,* 25). However, strong reasons exist for questioning this literary hypothesis: (1) the tight semantic linkage between this section and the anti-Elide judgment passages in the previous chapters (cf. 2:25,27–34; 3:12–14); (2) deliberate use of parallel images between 2:31 and 5:4; and (3) the fact that Samuel is never mentioned in connection with Shiloh after chap. 6, even though he had been set apart for service at that sanctuary and would have no explicit motive for leaving Shiloh if Eli had not died and the site been overrun by the Philistines. If these chapters did in fact originally comprise a separate document, they have been integrated so thoroughly into the present text as to make any reconstruction of the original impossible. Among those who doubt its existence, cf. K. A. D. Smelik, "The Ark Narrative Reconsidered," *OTS* 25 (1989): 128–44; and Y. Gitay, "Reflection on the Poetics of the Samuel Narrative: The Question of the Ark Narrative," *CBQ* 54 (1992): 221–30.

[56] This perspective is consistently reflected in the Latter Prophets as well, e.g., Israel's destruction at the hands of the Assyrians and Judah's destruction by the Babylonians as Yahweh's use of foreigners for the purpose of judgment. Cf. Isa 10:5; Hab 1:6.

us today before the Philistines? Let us bring the ark of the LORD's covenant from Shiloh, so that it may go with us and save us from the hand of our enemies."

⁴So the people sent men to Shiloh, and they brought back the ark of the covenant of the LORD Almighty, who is enthroned between the cherubim. And Eli's two sons, Hophni and Phinehas, were there with the ark of the covenant of God.

⁵When the ark of the LORD's covenant came into the camp, all Israel raised such a great shout that the ground shook. ⁶Hearing the uproar, the Philistines asked, "What's all this shouting in the Hebrew camp?"

When they learned that the ark of the LORD had come into the camp, ⁷the Philistines were afraid. "A god has come into the camp," they said. "We're in trouble! Nothing like this has happened before. ⁸Woe to us! Who will deliver us from the hand of these mighty gods? They are the gods who struck the Egyptians with all kinds of plagues in the desert. ⁹Be strong, Philistines! Be men, or you will be subject to the Hebrews, as they have been to you. Be men, and fight!"

¹⁰So the Philistines fought, and the Israelites were defeated and every man fled to his tent. The slaughter was very great; Israel lost thirty thousand foot soldiers. ¹¹The ark of God was captured, and Eli's two sons, Hophni and Phinehas, died.

4:1–4 An undisclosed period of time after Samuel's conversation with Eli, the Israelites became involved in a "fight against the Philistines" (v. 1). The Philistines, who are understood to have migrated to the coastal regions of southwest Israel in large numbers during the first half of the twelfth century B.C., had become a serious threat to the Israelites during the period of the Judges.[57] The Philistine army established a base camp along the banks of the Yarkon River at Aphek (NT Antipatris, modern Ras el-Ain/Tel Aphek), some twenty miles northeast of Ekron (modern Khirbet el-Muqanna?); the Israelites encamped two miles to the east at Ebenezer (modern Izbet Sartah). Taking the initiative in battle, the Philistines attacked and slew "about four thousand" Israelites (v. 2).

Consistent with the biblical perspective presented elsewhere in the Former Prophets, the elders interpreted Israel's defeat at the hands of the Philistines as a judgment from the Lord (cf. Judg 2:14; 3:8; 4:2; 1 Sam 12:9). Their solution, bringing the ark of the Lord's covenant into the battle arena, suggests that they were attempting to demonstrate in a tangible way their commitment to the covenant. Alternatively, it might have been an attempt by the elders to twist God's arm into helping them instead of trying to find out the reason for

---

[57] Although the biblical text indicates that Philistines had lived in Palestine since the time of Abraham (cf. Gen 21:32; 26:1; Exod 23:31), they were not mentioned as an active military or territorial threat until early in the period of the Judges (cf. Judg 3:31). Three of the pre-Elide judges were mentioned as having led Israel during times of Philistine oppression: Shamgar (Judg 3:31), Jephthah (10:6–8), and Samson (13:1–16:30). For further information on the history of the Philistines, cf. D. J. Wiseman, *Peoples of Old Testament Times* (Oxford: Clarendon Press, 1973); T. Dothan, *The Philistines and Their Material Culture* (New Haven/London: Yale University Press, 1982).

God's displeasure. First Samuel 8:4f. doesn't speak well for the elders' spiritual wisdom.[58]

The NIV's translation of 4:3 assumes the second possibility—that the elders believed the ark's presence among them would save them. This rendering misses the sense of the original. The Hebrew syntax in 4:3 suggests instead that the elders believed that the Lord, not the ark, would go with them and save them from their enemies. In fact, the ark was present among Israel's forces for leadership and protection at various times in Israel's history (cf. Num 10:33–36; Josh 3:3–7; 4:1–18; 6:6–21). The problem with Israel was not the bad theology of the elders—faith in things rather than faith in God—but the sins of "Eli's two sons, Hophni and Phinehas," who "were there with the ark of the covenant of God." As in the case of Achan (cf. Josh 7), all Israel would have to suffer because of the sins of a very few.

4:5–9 The arrival of the "ark of the LORD's covenant" was greeted with wild shouts of exhilaration that caused "the ground" (v. 5) to shake. So great was the commotion in the Israelite camp that the Philistines heard it two miles away.

The Philistines expressed two significant reactions to the ark's presence among the Israelites: fear and vigorous determination to defeat Israel and its God. Fear arose in the Philistine camp because of their knowledge—however imperfect it may have been—of Israelite religion and history. They apparently understood that the ark was the visible throne of Israel's invisible deity (cf. 4:4; Exod 25:20–22; Num 7:89).[59] They also believed the Israelites to be polytheistic, an assumption that was justified during much of the period of the Judges (cf. Judg 2:12,17,19; 3:6; 6:10; 10:6,13–14; 18:14–24). Finally, the Philistines understood that Israel had experienced a supernatural deliverance from the Egyptians, though the details were muddled (*"gods"* had "struck the Egyptians with all kinds of plagues in the desert"! [v. 8]).[60] Knowledge of these details, compounded by a fear of the consequences of losing to "the Hebrews" (v. 9)—

---

[58] The Torah teaches that divine curses come against Yahweh's people when they abandon the Sinai covenant (cf. Deut 29:24–25 [Hb. 29:23–24]). The writer apparently assumes that the elders were thoroughly familiar with the terms of the Sinai covenant. Consequently, it seems deliberate that they specifically requested that the "ark of Yahweh's covenant"—the most highly visible sign of Israel's covenant relationship with Yahweh—be brought forward into a central position among the troops. The threefold repetition of the phrase "ark of Yahweh's covenant" (אֲרוֹן בְּרִית יהוה) in vv. 3–5 is the greatest number of repetitions of this phrase within a three-verse span in the MT. S. R. Driver suggests the phrase "was introduced here into MT at a time when the expression was in more general use than it always had been" (*Notes on the Hebrew Text of Samuel*, 2d ed. [Winona Lake: Alpha, 1912], 46; reprint 1983).

[59] Biblical evidence suggests that bringing deity images and/or thrones of deities onto the battlefield was a common practice in ANE societies (cf. Josh 6:7–8; 2 Sam 5:21; Ezek 21:21).

[60] That the Philistines assumed more than one god had assisted the Israelites in Egypt is implicit in the use of plural adjectives, pronouns, and verbs.

a term used mainly by non-Israelites[61]—energized the Philistines to battlefield bravery.

4:10–11 Israel's earlier joyful shouts welcoming the Lord's arrival among them proved premature. The presence of Yahweh, God of the Sinai covenant, in the camp of Israel meant that the covenant's Supreme Enforcer had now been forced into a direct confrontation with the two most egregious violators of the covenant. Though the Israelites expected God to be an ally against the Philistines, the Lord had his own agenda. Judgment would begin at home; sons of the covenant who violated the covenant would experience God's wrath first. The Israelites were routed, and "the slaughter was very great"—some "thirty thousand" (v. 10) casualties. As staggering as the loss of human life was, it was dwarfed by the losses dealt to Israelite culture. For the first time in history Israel's most sacred material possession was now in the hands of pagans, and its two most powerful active priests had died at the hands of infidels.

The sanctuary at Shiloh seems to have been destroyed by the Philistines shortly after this time. Four textual reasons can be cited in support of this conclusion: (1) never again in 1, 2 Samuel is the city mentioned as a worship center for Israel; (2) the ark was not returned to Shiloh following its reacquisition by Israel (cf. 7:1–2); (3) Samuel moved the center of his activities back to his hometown of Ramah (cf. 7:17); and (4) references in the Books of Psalms (78:60) and Jeremiah (7:12–14; 26:6,9) explicitly mention its destruction. Taken together, these facts suggest the possibility that the city—or at least its sanctuary—was violently ransacked during this period of hostility. Archaeological excavations conducted by I. Finkelstein at the site confirm that Shiloh was destroyed by fire in the mid-eleventh century B.C.[62]

(2) Eli Dies; Ichabod Is Born (4:12–22)

12That same day a Benjamite ran from the battle line and went to Shiloh, his clothes torn and dust on his head. 13When he arrived, there was Eli sitting on his chair by the side of the road, watching, because his heart feared for the ark of God. When the man entered the town and told what had happened, the whole town sent up a cry.

14Eli heard the outcry and asked, "What is the meaning of this uproar?"

---

[61] The term "Hebrew" (עִבְרִי) in its variant forms occurs thirty-six times in the OT. In the overwhelming majority of occurrences it is employed in a context that includes non-Israelites either as speakers (e.g., Gen 39:14; Exod 2:11; 1 Sam 13:19) or auditors (e.g., Gen 40:15; Exod 10:3; Jonah 1:9). The term may be derived from the early patriarch Eber (cf. Gen 10:21); or it may be a derivative of the noun עֵבֶר, "the region beyond," or a pan-Semitic term for a nomadic alien living on the fringes of settled areas. For a fuller treatment of this subject cf. R. L. Harris, "עָבַר," *TWOT;* and N. Na'aman, "Habiru and Hebrews: The Transfer of a Social Term to the Literary Sphere," *JNES* 45 (1986): 271–88.

[62] Cf. I. Finkelstein, "Shiloh Yields Some, But Not All, of Its Secrets," *BAR* 12 (1986): 22–41.

The man hurried over to Eli, [15]who was ninety-eight years old and whose eyes were set so that he could not see. [16]He told Eli, "I have just come from the battle line; I fled from it this very day."

Eli asked, "What happened, my son?"

[17]The man who brought the news replied, "Israel fled before the Philistines, and the army has suffered heavy losses. Also your two sons, Hophni and Phinehas, are dead, and the ark of God has been captured."

[18]When he mentioned the ark of God, Eli fell backward off his chair by the side of the gate. His neck was broken and he died, for he was an old man and heavy. He had led Israel forty years.

[19]His daughter-in-law, the wife of Phinehas, was pregnant and near the time of delivery. When she heard the news that the ark of God had been captured and that her father-in-law and her husband were dead, she went into labor and gave birth, but was overcome by her labor pains. [20]As she was dying, the women attending her said, "Don't despair; you have given birth to a son." But she did not respond or pay any attention.

[21]She named the boy Ichabod, saying, "The glory has departed from Israel"— because of the capture of the ark of God and the deaths of her father-in-law and her husband. [22]She said, "The glory has departed from Israel, for the ark of God has been captured."

The prophetically announced curse against the house of Eli proceeds here, as two additional generations are now touched by it. Not only does the elderly Eli die in this tragic section, but Eli's grandson Ichabod is made an orphan, deprived not only of his father but now his mother as well.

4:12–18 News of the battlefield catastrophe soon found its way some twenty miles back to Shiloh. A Benjamite fleeing the conflict ran past a waiting Eli into the heart of the city to inform the inhabitants of the day's events. The messenger's appearance revealed the conflict's outcome as eloquently as his words; symbolically torn clothing and the heaping of dust on the head were expressions of grief and mourning in ancient Israel (cf. Gen 37:29,34; 44:13; 2 Sam 1:2).

Blind Eli, however, could see none of these portents; he could only hear the sound of all Shiloh's inhabitants crying out in anguish. The elderly priest had been sitting beside the main road to Shiloh awaiting news from the front. The sound of a city in mourning enabled him to formulate a general understanding of the battle's outcome; however, specific details were lacking. How many had died? Who had died? What of the ark? Eli's main concern was not for the safe return of his two sons; rather, "his heart feared for the ark of God" because it was his responsibility (v. 13).

The writer heightens the drama of the key narrative moment by allowing the audience to listen in on the dialogue between the blind priest and the dust-laden Benjamite. Methodically the increasingly awful details were revealed: "Israel fled"; "the army has suffered heavy losses"; "your two sons . . . are dead"; "the ark of God has been captured" (v. 17). The messenger's climactic disclosure so stunned Eli that he fell off his chair (Hb. *kissēʾ* = "chair"/"throne"), broke his neck, and died.

With great artistic skill the writer captured this fateful moment with words that convey at least two messages simultaneously. First, it signifies the end of the Elide dynasty. Eli's fall from his chair literally dethroned the Elide dynasty in Israel. Second, Eli's death ended an abomination in Israel that rivaled that of pagan idolatry.[63] The Lord would soon bring an end to an unseeing Philistine abomination by causing an image of Dagon to fall and its neck to break, but first he would bring about the same fate to a blind Hebrew abomination. The parallel between the events of the present section and those of the next chapter are striking and deliberate.

The writer notes that at the time of Eli's death he was "heavy" (v. 18). The Hebrew word employed here *(kbd)* is aptly chosen, for its spectrum of meaning—"honored," "heavy," "burdensome"—applies broadly to the man (perhaps a play on words). As high priest at Shiloh, Eli was a man with much social "weight"/"significance"; because of his practice of eating unauthorized sacrificial portions (cf. comments at 2:29), he was also "heavy"; finally, as a result of the sins he permitted in his own life and household, Eli was a burden that weighed down and ultimately brought disaster upon Israel.

4:19–22 The shredding of the Elide dynasty occurred quickly and violently. On the same day that Eli, Hophni, and Phinehas died, Phinehas' wife went into premature labor and "was overcome by her labor pains" (v. 19). Fatal complications in the birthing process caused the woman to die shortly after giving birth to a son. Instead of rejoicing in the most honorable achievement a woman in the ancient Near East could attain—the birthing of a son— she was listless and distracted because of her anxiety over the ark. With her dying gasps she named the child "Ichabod" (Hb. *ʾî-kābôd*, lit., "Where [is] glory?" or "Nothing of glory"). The name, a derivative of *kbd* (cf. discussion of v. 18), was appropriate, for with the deaths of the patriarch and his two sons the *kbd*—honor, weight, burden—of the Elide dynasty was gone. More than that, the glorious "ark of God" (v. 21), the Lord's throne, had "been captured" (v. 22). For Israel on that day the *kbd* was gone. Not until the glory departed from the temple in the days of Ezekiel would an event of similar magnitude occur again (cf. Ezek 10:18).

---

[63] R. Polzin suggests a different significance to the death of Eli: "Eli falling backward off his throne to his death is this overture's central event, the Deuteronomist's view of kingship in a nutshell. Eli represents all the burden and doom that kingship brought Israel. He had 'judged' Israel for forty years; that is to say, in the fullness of time kingship in Israel would disappear" (*Samuel and the Deuteronomist* [New York: Harper & Row, 1989], 64).

5. The Lord Triumphs during Samuel's Career (5:1–7:17)

In this section the Lord continues his fearful judgments against both non-Israelites and Israelites who display a lack of respect for him (cf. 2:30). The Lord acts without regard to geographical boundaries, with equal competence on foreign soil and in Israel's heartland. His actions confirm the Torah's teaching that he is indeed "the Judge of the whole earth" (cf. Gen 18:25; 1 Sam 2:10).

In the previous section the Lord acted in judgment against a religious establishment in Israel that had displayed its contempt for him; here he acts triumphantly against a Philistine religious establishment that held him up to ridicule. In both cases the Lord brought the central religious figure tumbling to the ground.

But the Lord's fierce judgment against Israel's religious establishment centered in Shiloh did not conclude with the destruction of the house of Eli. Citizens of a Levitical city in Israel, Beth Shemesh, who acted contemptuously toward God's holiness are taught in this section that the Lord is a far more fearsome and deadly adversary than any earthly foe. Philistine armies, too, are taught this lesson. When they disrupt a holy convocation to honor the Lord, they become targets of divine wrath.

A common thread binds together the three acts of the Lord's judgment found in 5:1–7:17. At the heart of each of the stories is a terrifying and deadly action carried out without a human intermediary. The Lord acts as a divine warrior (cf. Exod 15:3; Isa 42:13; Jer 20:11) as he breaks out in judgment against all who violate his holiness; he enforces the Sinai covenant even—or perhaps especially—when the objects of his judgment are his own earthly representatives.

(1) The Lord Overwhelms the Philistines' God (5:1–6:12)

¹After the Philistines had captured the ark of God, they took it from Ebenezer to Ashdod. ²Then they carried the ark into Dagon's temple and set it beside Dagon. ³When the people of Ashdod rose early the next day, there was Dagon, fallen on his face on the ground before the ark of the LORD! They took Dagon and put him back in his place. ⁴But the following morning when they rose, there was Dagon, fallen on his face on the ground before the ark of the LORD! His head and hands had been broken off and were lying on the threshold; only his body remained. ⁵That is why to this day neither the priests of Dagon nor any others who enter Dagon's temple at Ashdod step on the threshold.

⁶The LORD's hand was heavy upon the people of Ashdod and its vicinity; he brought devastation upon them and afflicted them with tumors. ⁷When the men of Ashdod saw what was happening, they said, "The ark of the god of Israel must not stay here with us, because his hand is heavy upon us and upon Dagon our god." ⁸So they called together all the rulers of the Philistines and asked them, "What shall we do with the ark of the god of Israel?"

They answered, "Have the ark of the god of Israel moved to Gath." So they moved the ark of the God of Israel.

[9]But after they had moved it, the LORD's hand was against that city, throwing it into a great panic. He afflicted the people of the city, both young and old, with an outbreak of tumors. [10]So they sent the ark of God to Ekron.

As the ark of God was entering Ekron, the people of Ekron cried out, "They have brought the ark of the god of Israel around to us to kill us and our people." [11]So they called together all the rulers of the Philistines and said, "Send the ark of the god of Israel away; let it go back to its own place, or it will kill us and our people." For death had filled the city with panic; God's hand was very heavy upon it. [12]Those who did not die were afflicted with tumors, and the outcry of the city went up to heaven.

[1]When the ark of the LORD had been in Philistine territory seven months, [2]the Philistines called for the priests and the diviners and said, "What shall we do with the ark of the LORD? Tell us how we should send it back to its place."

[3]They answered, "If you return the ark of the god of Israel, do not send it away empty, but by all means send a guilt offering to him. Then you will be healed, and you will know why his hand has not been lifted from you."

[4]The Philistines asked, "What guilt offering should we send to him?"

They replied, "Five gold tumors and five gold rats, according to the number of the Philistine rulers, because the same plague has struck both you and your rulers. [5]Make models of the tumors and of the rats that are destroying the country, and pay honor to Israel's god. Perhaps he will lift his hand from you and your gods and your land. [6]Why do you harden your hearts as the Egyptians and Pharaoh did? When he treated them harshly, did they not send the Israelites out so they could go on their way?

[7]"Now then, get a new cart ready, with two cows that have calved and have never been yoked. Hitch the cows to the cart, but take their calves away and pen them up. [8]Take the ark of the LORD and put it on the cart, and in a chest beside it put the gold objects you are sending back to him as a guilt offering. Send it on its way, [9]but keep watching it. If it goes up to its own territory, toward Beth Shemesh, then the LORD has brought this great disaster on us. But if it does not, then we will know that it was not his hand that struck us and that it happened to us by chance."

[10]So they did this. They took two such cows and hitched them to the cart and penned up their calves. [11]They placed the ark of the LORD on the cart and along with it the chest containing the gold rats and the models of the tumors. [12]Then the cows went straight up toward Beth Shemesh, keeping on the road and lowing all the way; they did not turn to the right or to the left. The rulers of the Philistines followed them as far as the border of Beth Shemesh.

In this section Yahweh demonstrates his awesome power against Israel's most feared adversary. Initially he performs a ritual execution of Dagon, the deity who was thought to have given the Philistines victory over both Israel's greatest human champion Samson (cf. Judg 16:23) and over Israel's God. After slaying their god, Yahweh then directs his judgments against the people who worshiped that god. In so doing Yahweh demonstrates his unconquerable nature and his superiority over all foes.

Yahweh shows that the battlefield capture of the ark is only an apparent conquest of Israel's God. In truth, it is a divine ruse used to gain even greater
opportunities to display his unparalleled majesty.

5:1–12 The Philistines, flush with victory over the Israelites, removed
"the ark of God" (v. 1) from the abandoned Israelite campsite at "Ebenezer"
and brought it some nineteen miles south "to Ashdod." Ashdod was one of the
five major Philistine cities located in the Promised Land at this time (cf. 6:17)
and apparently was the site of the most important worship center for the god
credited with the Philistines' recent battlefield success. The ark was placed
there "beside Dagon" (v. 2) within "Dagon's temple." Though Dagon was a
well-known Semitic deity worshiped for centuries throughout western Asia as
a meteorological and military deity,[64] the non-Semitic Philistines had incorporated this god into their pantheon as well, assigning it a central role in their cult.

Placing the captured symbol of Israel's God in the stronghold of Dagon
reflected the Philistines' understanding of the theological dimension of their
recent military conquest. The Philistine soldiers had prevailed over Israelite
forces, they believed, because Dagon had proven superior to Yahweh on the
divine battlefield. Thus it was fitting that Yahweh should exist as an attendant
in the household of Dagon, just as Israel would serve Philistia.

However, the Lord defied the Ashdodites' theological understanding of the
recent turn of events. Early the next morning, at the time of day prescribed in
the Torah for the first daily act of worship toward the Lord (cf. Exod 24:14;
29:39,41; 30:7; Lev 6:12,20; 9:17; Num 28:4,23), Dagon was found in a posture of reverence and submission before "the ark of the LORD" (v. 3); "his face"
was "on the ground" (cf. Gen 19:1; 24:52; Neh 8:6). The writer, subtly suggesting the futility of the Philistine's idolatrous practices (cf. Isa 44:9–20; Jer 10:5;
Hab 2:18; Acts 19:26; 1 Cor 8:4), noted that the people of Ashdod had to "put"
Dagon "back in his place." Their god, thought to be so virile on the battlefield,
in the confines of his own dwelling did not even have the strength to lift his face
out of the dust!

Dagon's humiliating act of self-abasement was repeated the following
morning, a sure sign that the previous day's events had not been accidental.
Once again Dagon was lying prostrate "before the ark of the LORD" (v. 4), but
this time there was a difference. Dagon's head and hands had been "broken off"
(Hb. *krt*; "cut off") in a manner reminiscent of grisly military executions (cf.
17:51; 31:9; 2 Sam 4:12).[65] The Philistines' conquering divine hero had been

---

[64] Cf. F. J. Montalbano, "Canaanite Dagon: Origin, Nature," *CBQ* 13 (1951): 381–97. Cf. also
ABD, s.v. "Dagon."

[65] W. Zwickel compares the text's description of the statue's broken form with archaeological
data and concludes the story has been modified during the postexilic period to conform to later
iconoclastic customs ("Dagons abgeschlagener Kopf [1 Samuel v 3–4]," *VT* 44 [1994]: 239–49).
This suggestion misses the parallels noted in the other Scriptures that suggest that Yahweh was
"executing" Dagon using a technique of military execution.

humbled and then mercilessly executed in his own stronghold. Though "in exile," the Lord had proven his superiority to the regional supreme deity.

Dagon's bodily extremities had first been discovered "lying on the threshold" of his temple. Out of respect for their deity, therefore, worshipers entering the temple instituted a policy of refusing to "step on the threshold" (v. 5). Though the practice of recognizing the special character of an entrance into sacred space by means of some ritual was common in ancient Palestine (cf. Exod 3:5; Zeph 1:9), this particular expression apparently was adopted in Ashdod only after the Lord desecrated Dagon.[66]

The Philistines were aware that the Lord had brought plagues against Egypt in a previous generation (cf. 4:8). Now they themselves would experience a foreshortened version of that scourge. Like the plagues of Egypt, the Lord's plagues in Philistia brought judgment to the foreign gods (cf. 6:5; Exod 12:12) and disease and death to oppressors of the Hebrews. The people of "Ashdod and its vicinity" (1 Sam 5:6) were afflicted "with tumors." The tumors, often understood to be buboes—not anal tumors or hemorrhoids (= KJV's "emerods")—caused by a rodent-borne disease (cf. 6:4),[67] were one of the maladies the Lord promised to send against those who violated his covenant expectations (cf. Deut 28:27). Perhaps learning a lesson from history, the Ashdodites decided that "the ark of the god of Israel must not stay" (v. 7) among them. Calling together a pan-Philistine council of "rulers" (Hb. *sĕrānîm*, "tyrants"), the group decided to "have the ark of the God of Israel moved to Gath" (v. 8). The reasons for Gath's selection are not supplied in the text; perhaps Gath possessed an Israelite populational element or at least had favorable relations with Israel that were believed to make the city immune from the Lord's attack (cf. 7:14; 21:10; 27:3; 2 Sam 15:18; 1 Kgs 2:39).

Whatever their reasons for moving the ark to Gath, the logic proved defec-

---

[66] Perhaps the Ashdodites believed their failure to treat his temple with proper respect had been the cause for their deity's problems. Better to blame themselves than admit their god's inferiority!

[67] The MT's *kethiv* reading is עפלים, a term that apparently meant "tumors" (so McCarter, *I Samuel*, 123) or "boils, abscesses (at the anus), or buboes (so W. L. Holladay, CHAL, 123). The qere טחרים may be a euphemism (so Driver, *Notes on the Hebrew Text of Samuel*, 51). Among those favoring the affliction as a disorder related to the bubonic plague are R. F. Youngblood (*1, 2 Samuel*, EBC, ed F. E. Gaebelein [Grand Rapids: Zondervan, 1992], 3.388), R. P. Gordon (*I and II Samuel: A Commentary* [Grand Rapids: Zondervan, 1986], 99), D. F. Payne, *I and II Samuel*, DSB (Philadelphia: Westminster, 1982), 32, and J. Wilkinson ("The Philistine Epidemic of I Samuel 5 and 6," *ExpTim* 88 [1977]: 137–41). A. F. Kirkpatrick prefers the translation "boils" (*The First Book of Samuel*, CBSC [Cambridge: University Press, 1891], 77). Josephus (*Ant.*, vi.1.1) suggested dysentery was the plague. Those favoring the interpretation of either a hemorrhoidal problem or anal tumors include W. L. Holladay, *CHAL*, 123; and E. Merrill ("1 Samuel," in *Bible Knowledge Commentary of the Old Testament*, ed. J. Walvoord and R. Zuck [Wheaton: Victor, 1985], 436. L. I. Conrad takes the untenable position that no actual disease can be discerned from the text since the text was not intended to portray accurate history ("The Biblical Tradition for the Plague of the Philistines," *JAOS* 104 [1984]: 281–87).

tive. The Lord only increased the magnitude of his judgments, breaking forth in onslaughts against both the emotional and physical well-being of the citizens of Gath. In keeping with a Torah threat directed against Israel's enemies in the Promised Land, the city was thrown "into a great panic" (v. 9; cf. Deut 7:23). Additionally, all age groups in the city were afflicted "with an outbreak of tumors."

In an effort to end the reign of terror in Gath, the ark was "sent" (or "exodused," v. 10; a form of *šlḥ*, "send") to Ekron. The language describing the Gathites' action in removing the ark from their city suggests the writer was consciously alluding to the Egyptian exodus event (cf. Exod 12:33).

The ark was "sent" north "to Ekron," where its arrival created even more distress than it had in Gath. "God's hand was very heavy upon" (v. 11) that city as the Lord once again increased the intensity of his judgmental actions. In addition to the "panic" (lit., "panic of death") and "tumors," the Lord also slew many individuals. The entire city joined in an anguished cry "to heaven" (v. 12) for deliverance.

6:1–12 After a period of seven months—a number to be understood literally but probably included because of its symbolic overtones[68]—the Philistines made the decision to "send" the ark "back to its place" in Israel. Following the MT, the NIV states two reasons for the decision to return the ark: so "you will be healed, and you will know why his hand has not been lifted from you" (6:3). The LXX and 4QSam[a] read differently and suggest it was for the purpose of removing the Lord's hand of judgment from the land. Whatever the reason, sending away an offended and powerful deity was not a task to be undertaken lightly; if done improperly, Yahweh might become even more provoked, with dire consequences for all Philistia. Thus "the priests and diviners" (v. 2) were called upon to determine the most efficacious means of removing the ark from their region. "Diviners" were a class of religious leaders that Israelites were forbidden to consult (cf. Deut 18:10,14).

With remarkable concern for detail the writer chronicles the ensuing conversational exchange between the Philistines and their religious experts. The present section contains the longest recorded speech given by Philistines in the Old Testament (120 words in the Hebrew), as well as the Old Testament's longest stretch of dialogue between Philistines (four consecutive statements). Such

---

[68] The number *seven* was understood in ancient Israel to suggest "completeness, perfection, consummation" (M. H. Pope, *IDBSup*, s.v. "Seven, Seventh, Seventy"). Cf. also G. Archer, who indicated this number suggested "the perfect work of God" (*A Survey of Old Testament Introduction*, rev. ed. [Chicago: Moody, 1974], 247). In addition to stating the number of months the ark was in Philistine hands for the purpose of making a more complete historical record, the writer was apparently making a symbolic statement such as, "When the time of exile allotted by God had been fulfilled . . ." Such a secondary message would have been particularly relevant to readers/auditors in an Israelite exilic community.

extraordinary detail by the writer suggests that he may have had access to an eyewitness source but also that he was guided in formulating the present composition by motives beyond those of mere historical reportage.

The writer used the Philistine dialogue—particularly the statements by Philistia's religious authorities—to demonstrate a theological point: the spiritual darkness of Philistia's leaders—the diviners and those who consulted them—was in fact the true source for their present problems. The Torah (Deut 18:9–19) warned that although surrounding nations consulted diviners, Israel must not; for such individuals were "detestable to the LORD" and a cause for the Lord driving inhabitants from the Promised Land. Instead, Israel must listen to a prophet like Moses, whom the Lord would raise up. Of course, such a prophet already had been provided in the person of Samuel (cf. 3:20). Thus, this passage implicitly buttresses the theological foundation laid elsewhere for two prominent ideas: holy war against the Philistines and the divine authority of Samuel.

Interestingly, the diviners' statements express a knowledge of certain details of the Torah's narrative (6:6), theology (6:5), and ritual (6:3). The diviners understood, for example, that the Philistines needed to "pay honor to Israel's god" and that one way to do that was by presenting "a guilt offering" (ʾāšām; cf. Lev 5:14–6:7; 7:1–6). However, the means they recommended was totally wrongheaded.

In addition to missing the Torah requirement of the slaying of a ram as part of the guilt offering (cf. Lev 5:15), the detestable diviners recommended appeasing Yahweh with ten fashioned images of gold, a violation of the Decalogue's prohibition against all likenesses of animals and humans (cf. Exod 20:4; Deut 5:8). Incredibly, the recommended statues were to be of ritually detestable animals (cf. Lev 11:29)—"rats"![69] As if that were not enough, Yahweh was also to be given a gift of five golden images of unclean portions of the human anatomy—"tumors"! This advice apparently represents a syncretistic blend of pagan imitative magic[70] and perverted Torah ritual.

Lastly, the priests and diviners directed the Philistines to transport the ark on a cart, a means of transportation for the ark expressly forbidden in the Torah (Num 7:7–9; cf. 2 Sam 6:3–13). Their recommendations were framed in a historical lesson from the Torah suggesting the need for immediate action: "Why harden your hearts as the Egyptians and Pharaoh did?" (v. 6).

---

[69] O. Margalith ("The Meaning of ʿplym in 1 Samuel v–vi," *VT* 33 [1983]: 339–41) ingeniously suggests that the Philistines actually fashioned images of Apollo Smintheus, a mouse god. J. B. Geyer prefers to connect these objects with the Hittite ritual of Ambazzi, in which a mouse carries off a portion of a bowstring ("Mice and Rites in I Samuel v–vi," *VT* 31 [1981]: 293–304).

[70] The fashioning of five mice and five tumors, followed by their subsequent removal from the territory, was no doubt meant to bring about the removal of the troublesome rodent and disease from the region of the five cities.

The diviners and priests directed the Philistines to send the ark back to Israel for two purposes: first, to remove the deadly object—and thereby Israel's deity—from their territory; and second, to determine the true origin of the Philistines' recent societal upheavals. To accomplish both ends simultaneously, the ark along with a chest containing the Lord's guilt offering were to be placed on "a new cart" (v. 7) pulled by "two cows" that had calved and had "never been yoked" and who had been forcefully separated from their unweaned calves. If a team of cows that had never been trained or yoked could work together to pull the cart straight for a stretch of several miles, all the while ignoring their maternal instincts to respond to the cries of their unweaned calves, then Yahweh would indeed be accepted as the source of "this great disaster." However, if the cows failed to pull the cart "as far as the border of Beth Shemesh," then the whole series of recent Philistine catastrophes would be understood to have happened "by chance" (v. 9).

Having set up the test according to the diviners' guidelines, the Philistines observed that "the cows went straight up toward Beth Shemesh, keeping on the road and lowing all the way" (v. 12). Not once did the untrained cows "turn to the right or to the left." In convincing fashion Yahweh had demonstrated that the Philistines' troubles were no accident of nature. To the Philistines their troubles were thus interpreted as the deliberate actions of an angry foreign deity; however, to the informed Israelite audience they were the triumphant execution of Torah-promised judgments against a nation who had desecrated the Promised Land through abominable practices.

(2) The Lord Judges Irreverent Israelites (6:13–7:1)

[13]Now the people of Beth Shemesh were harvesting their wheat in the valley, and when they looked up and saw the ark, they rejoiced at the sight. [14]The cart came to the field of Joshua of Beth Shemesh, and there it stopped beside a large rock. The people chopped up the wood of the cart and sacrificed the cows as a burnt offering to the LORD. [15]The Levites took down the ark of the LORD, together with the chest containing the gold objects, and placed them on the large rock. On that day the people of Beth Shemesh offered burnt offerings and made sacrifices to the LORD. [16]The five rulers of the Philistines saw all this and then returned that same day to Ekron.

[17]These are the gold tumors the Philistines sent as a guilt offering to the LORD—one each for Ashdod, Gaza, Ashkelon, Gath and Ekron. [18]And the number of the gold rats was according to the number of Philistine towns belonging to the five rulers—the fortified towns with their country villages. The large rock, on which they set the ark of the LORD, is a witness to this day in the field of Joshua of Beth Shemesh.

[19]But God struck down some of the men of Beth Shemesh, putting seventy of them to death because they had looked into the ark of the LORD. The people mourned because of the heavy blow the LORD had dealt them, [20]and the men of

Beth Shemesh asked, "Who can stand in the presence of the LORD, this holy God? To whom will the ark go up from here?"

²¹Then they sent messengers to the people of Kiriath Jearim, saying, "The Philistines have returned the ark of the LORD. Come down and take it up to your place."

¹So the men of Kiriath Jearim came and took up the ark of the LORD. They took it to Abinadab's house on the hill and consecrated Eleazar his son to guard the ark of the LORD.

The Lord's stern judgment of sin was not limited to actions against the house of Eli or the Philistines. When the citizens of the Levitical city of Beth Shemesh—people who should have been especially cognizant of Torah guidelines regarding the proper treatment of the ark—failed to obey divine law (cf. Num 4:15), they too were judged. This section details the tragic results of Israelites trifling with the holy throne of Yahweh's presence. The magnitude of the divine judgment against them suggests that Israel was to fear the Lord far more than Philistia or any other earthly foe.

The present narrative appears to be yet one more indictment against the Levites during the period of the Judges. It thus takes its place alongside the story of the Levite who served as priest for the Danites (cf. Judg 17:7–18:31), of the Levite who cut up his wife's corpse and mobilized Israel in fratricidal warfare (cf. Judg 19:1–20:10), and of Eli and his sons.

6:13–18 The citizens of Beth Shemesh were working in the fields harvesting wheat "when they looked up and saw the ark" (v. 13). Beth Shemesh was a Levitical city set aside for the clan of Kohath, the Levitical family charged with responsibility of caring for the ark of the covenant (Num 4:4,15) and was also a designated home for the descendants of Aaron (cf. Josh 21:13–16). It is reasonable to assume that many if not most of the Israelites in this city were from the tribe of Levi and that they, more than most Israelites, would have had cause to celebrate the ark's return.

Acting in priestly fashion, the people prepared a great sacrifice to the Lord in celebration of the ark's return. "The field of Joshua of Beth Shemesh" (v. 14) was turned into a temporary worship site as the cows that had pulled the cart were ritually slaughtered and presented "as a burnt offering [ᶜōlâ] to the LORD" in a fire made from the chopped up remains of the wooden cart. Though this act was seemingly one of great reverence for Yahweh, it was actually a reckless one: the Torah taught that only male animals were to be used in burnt offerings (cf. Lev 1:3). The author's description of this forbidden act of offering up heifers as burnt offerings thus serves as an early indication of impending divine judgment against the Beth Shemeshites.

With the ark and the golden gifts from the Philistines displayed prominently atop a "large rock" in Joshua's field, one that would be celebrated in subsequent Israelite history (v. 18), the Israelites continued their revelry with a festive event that included additional offerings of food gifts. The Philistine tyrants observed the Israelites' joyous activities and then returned to Ekron "that same day" (v. 16), no doubt with a sense of relief. They left behind not only the Israelite ark but five gold tumors and five gold rats "according to the number of the Philistine towns belonging to the five rulers" (v. 18), the fortified cities of "Ashdod, Gaza, Ashkelon, Gath and Ekron" (v. 17). Ironically, their foolish strategy for ridding themselves of the ark had worked!

6:19–20 According to the Torah (Num 4:5–6), no Israelites outside the Aaronic priesthood were permitted to see even the exterior of the ark, much less its interior. Even the Kohathites, whose God-given duty it was to transport the ark, were forbidden either to touch or view the sacred box. Thus, the first duty of the Israelites—especially the Kohathites, whose charge it was to care for the holy things of Israelite worship (cf. Num 4:2)—would have been to hide the ark from view while avoiding any physical or visual contact with it.[71]

However, during the festivities associated with the ark's return, "some of the men of Beth Shemesh" did just the opposite. Far from concealing the ark, they displayed it on a "large rock" and then "looked into the ark of the LORD," touching it in the process. This shameless disregard for the ark's sanctity and the violation of its sacred space brought swift and direct judgment from Yahweh. According to both the MT and LXX, God "struck down" (Hb. *nkh*; cf. 5:6,9) fifty thousand and seventy men from Beth Shemesh. The number, so large as to defy reason, has been reduced in the NIV and other modern versions, which choose to follow Josephus (*Ant.* 6.1.4) to a more rational "seventy."

Though there are obvious difficulties associated with the extremely large number preserved in ancient versions—for example, the unlikelihood that fifty thousand people ever lived in ancient Beth Shemesh at one time—the MT's reading apparently is the original.[72] Accepting the larger number results in a theological truth consonant with the teachings of the book retained: Israel must respect the Lord more than the might of the Philistines. Although the Philistines with their military prowess could kill thirty thousand Israelites (4:10), God in his holiness could kill more than fifty thousand. For Israel, life could be found only in a fear of Yahweh that issued forth in obedience to his Torah and his prophet.

In responding to the judgments inflicted on them by the Lord, the Beth Shemeshites behaved like the Philistines: instead of mourning penitently for their sins, they "mourned because of the heavy blow the LORD had dealt them"

---

[71] The task required of the Kohathites would have been parallel to the one performed by Shem and Japheth when they were called upon to cover their father's nakedness. Cf. Gen 9:23. Instead, the Beth Shemeshites behaved like Ham (Gen 9:22), a fact that probably would not have been lost on the original audience.

[72] For further discussion—and a contrary conclusion—cf. D. M. Fouts, "Added Support for Reading '70 men' in 1 Samuel vi 19," *VT* 42 (1992): 394.

(v. 19; cf. 5:12) and then came up with a plan to remove the ark from their territory (cf. 5:8–9; 6:2). Thus they demonstrated the magnitude of their spiritual darkness and so confirmed the Lord's righteous judgments against them.

The Beth Shemeshites summoned the citizens of Kiriath Jearim (also called Baalah [Josh 15:9] and Kiriath Baal [Josh 15:60]; modern Abu Ghosh), a Gibeonite city some fifteen miles to the east, to "come down and take" the ark "up to your place" (1 Sam 6:21).

7:1 Accepting the offer, "the men of Kiriath Jearim came and took up the ark of the LORD."[73] There is not a little irony in the fact that the ark of the Lord, which had so recently executed the Philistines' most powerful god, scourged Philistia with deadly plagues, and slain more than fifty thousand Israelites was provided such protection.

No genealogical information regarding Abinadab of Kiriath Jearim or Eleazar his son is provided in the Bible; however, Eleazar is a common priestly name in the Old Testament (cf. Exod 6:23; 1 Chr 9:20; 23:21; Ezra 8:33) and it is possible both men were members of the Levitical tribe.

The fact that the ark was taken to Kiriath Jearim and not back to Shiloh suggests strongly that the Shiloh worship center had been destroyed by the Philistines the previous fall.[74] No explanation is given for the choice of Kiriath Jearim as the new abode for the ark, but it may be attributable to the city's prominence as a traditional religious center (cf. its former name, "Kiriath Baal" = "Baalville"). Some scholars, citing differences in vocabulary and noting that Samuel played a key role in the narratives of chaps. 1–3 but is completely absent from the following three chapters, have concluded that 4:1b–7:1 was from an originally independent source later inserted into 1 Samuel.[75] However, vocabulary changes are to be expected with a change in topic, and Samuel's absence from this section of text can best be explained as the writer's attempt to demonstrate that Israel—with the exception of Samuel—from high priest to Kohathite to ordinary citizen, was spiritually more culpable than the Philistines. Though the Philistines would suffer for their ignorance of the Lord and

[73] For further information regarding the role of Kiriath Jearim in the history of the ark, cf. J. Blenkinsopp, "Kiriath-Jearim and the Ark," *JBL* 88 (1969): 143–56.

[74] Further evidence is found in the fact that, though Samuel was given to the Lord at Shiloh to serve as a lifelong Nazirite, he is never associated with Shiloh after 4:1. Instead, his residence in subsequent chapters is in Ramah. Both the Books of Psalms (78:60) and Jeremiah (7:12,14; 26:6,9) express a tradition suggesting that Shiloh was ransacked earlier in Israelite history. It is important to note that archaeological evidence coming from the site of Shiloh seems to confirm an eleventh century B.C. destruction of the site. Cf. I. Finkelstein, "Shiloh Yields Some, But Not All, of Its Secrets," 22–41.

[75] Cf. L. Rost, *Die Überlieferung von der Thronnachfolge Davids,* BWANT III, 6 (Stuttgart: W. Kohlammer, 1926; Eng. trans.—*The Succession to the Throne of David* (Sheffield: Almond, 1982). More recent commentators have affirmed the original independence of 4:1–7:1a from the remainder of 1 Samuel. Cf. R. P. Gordon, *I and II Samuel,* 24; Klein, *1 Samuel,* 39.

his Torah, the Israelites would suffer worse for their failure to act in accordance
with the spiritual enlightenment that was theirs.

(3) The Lord Routes the Philistines' Army (7:2–17)

[2]It was a long time, twenty years in all, that the ark remained at Kiriath Jearim,
and all the people of Israel mourned and sought after the LORD. [3]And Samuel said
to the whole house of Israel, "If you are returning to the LORD with all your hearts,
then rid yourselves of the foreign gods and the Ashtoreths and commit yourselves
to the LORD and serve him only, and he will deliver you out of the hand of the Philistines." [4]So the Israelites put away their Baals and Ashtoreths, and served the
LORD only.

[5]Then Samuel said, "Assemble all Israel at Mizpah and I will intercede with the
LORD for you." [6]When they had assembled at Mizpah, they drew water and
poured it out before the LORD. On that day they fasted and there they confessed,
"We have sinned against the LORD." And Samuel was leader of Israel at Mizpah.

[7]When the Philistines heard that Israel had assembled at Mizpah, the rulers of
the Philistines came up to attack them. And when the Israelites heard of it, they
were afraid because of the Philistines. [8]They said to Samuel, "Do not stop crying
out to the LORD our God for us, that he may rescue us from the hand of the Philistines." [9]Then Samuel took a suckling lamb and offered it up as a whole burnt offering to the LORD. He cried out to the LORD on Israel's behalf, and the LORD
answered him.

[10]While Samuel was sacrificing the burnt offering, the Philistines drew near to
engage Israel in battle. But that day the LORD thundered with loud thunder
against the Philistines and threw them into such a panic that they were routed
before the Israelites. [11]The men of Israel rushed out of Mizpah and pursued the
Philistines, slaughtering them along the way to a point below Beth Car.

[12]Then Samuel took a stone and set it up between Mizpah and Shen. He named
it Ebenezer, saying, "Thus far has the LORD helped us." [13]So the Philistines were
subdued and did not invade Israelite territory again.

Throughout Samuel's lifetime, the hand of the LORD was against the Philistines.
[14]The towns from Ekron to Gath that the Philistines had captured from Israel
were restored to her, and Israel delivered the neighboring territory from the power
of the Philistines. And there was peace between Israel and the Amorites.

[15]Samuel continued as judge over Israel all the days of his life. [16]From year to
year he went on a circuit from Bethel to Gilgal to Mizpah, judging Israel in all
those places. [17]But he always went back to Ramah, where his home was, and
there he also judged Israel. And he built an altar there to the LORD.

This section contrasts the juridical ministry of Samuel with that of the house
of Eli. Hophni and Phinehas had sought to bring victory to Israel by bringing
the Lord's ark against the Philistines. Samuel brought victory to Israel by
bringing Israel back to the Lord.

In chronicling the events of this section, the narrator is careful to indicate that mighty deliverance from the Philistines came about only after Israel repented and turned wholeheartedly back to God. The movement of Israel's heart, not Yahweh's ark, brought about true freedom from Israel's oppressors.

7:2–4 Twenty silent years separate 7:1 from 7:2.[76] During that time the Israelites experienced a change of heart. Instead of mourning "because of the heavy blow the LORD had dealt them" (6:19), they now "mourned and sought after the LORD" (v. 2). Noting Israel's godly sorrow (cf. 2 Cor 7:10), Samuel seized the opportunity to lead Israel in a spiritual cleansing reminiscent of those instituted by great leaders in the past. He used language recalling that of Jacob (cf. Gen 35:2) and Joshua (Josh 24:14,23) to summon the people to "rid yourselves of the foreign gods and the Ashtoreths" (v. 3). Samuel's separation of Ashtoreths from "foreign gods" may have been for either of two purposes: (1) to indicate that Israel was to rid itself entirely of all the gods, male and female alike, of the fertility religions or (2) to suggest that Israel had two separate tasks to perform in its spiritual purgation. In the second case these two tasks would have been to get rid of all pagan forms of idolatry and to purify the worship of Yahweh by ending the practice of giving Yahweh a divine consort.[77]

But purging the land of the foreign gods and religious practices was only the negative side of Israel's spiritual renewal. A positive action also was needed. The Israelites had to "commit" themselves (lit., "establish your hearts") "to the LORD and serve him only." As they got rid of their idols and embraced the Lord wholeheartedly, they could expect the Torah-promised benefits of a right relationship with the Lord, one of which was victory over enemies (cf. Lev 26:7–8; Deut 28:7).

The Israelites accepted Samuel's spiritual challenge: they "put away their Baals and Ashtoreths, the Canaanite male and female deities, and served the LORD only" (v. 4). To formalize Israel's renewed relationship with Yahweh, Samuel called all the people to assemble "at Mizpah" (v. 5; modern Tell en-Nasbeh [?], five miles north of Jerusalem), a center for tribal convocations dur-

---

[76] Disagreement exists about the significance of the phrase "twenty years." Hertzberg and Klein understand this phrase to be symbolic, a Deuteronomistic addition to the text, "apparently meant to represent half of Samuel's period of office (the first)" (Hertzberg, *I and II Samuel*, 66; cf. also Klein, *I and II Samuel*, 65–66). Others understand this phrase literally, to refer to the period extending from the Beth Shemesh incident until David's removal of the ark to Jerusalem (Philbeck, *1–2 Samuel*, 27; Baldwin, *I and 2 Samuel*, 77–78). I prefer to understand the twenty years literally, as referring to "the time that elapsed before the reformation now to be recorded" (Kirkpatrick, *The First Book of Samuel*, 87). The position of Baldwin and Philbeck produces insoluble chronological problems, considering that all of Saul's rise to power and his reign, as well as David's rise to power, including his conquest of Jerusalem, would have had to occur in those twenty years.

[77] Archaeological evidence suggests that in some locations a heterodoxical Yahwism was practiced that included the recognition of a female divine companion for Yahweh. Cf. A. Lemaire, "Les Inscriptions de Khirbet el-qom et l'asherah de YHWH," *RB* 84 (1977): 595–608; and W. G. Dever, "Asherah Consort of Yahweh? New Evidence from Kuntillet Ajrud," *BASOR* 255 (1984): 21–37.

ing the period of the Judges (cf. Judg 20:1), for a time of intercessory prayer, fasting, and confession of sin. When Israel "drew water and poured it out before the LORD" (v. 6), an action unparalleled in the Old Testament in an Israelite religious convocation, they evidently were denying themselves liquids as a symbolic confession that the Lord's favor was more important to them than life-sustaining water (cf. Jonah 3:7; 2 Sam 23:16).

For the first time in the Book of 1 Samuel, Samuel is portrayed acting as a "leader" (Hb. *špṭ*; trad. to act as a judge). Thus at Mizpah began the ministry of Israel's most venerable judge/prophet since Moses. In his role as judge, Samuel's task was to bring Israelite society into conformity with the Lord's judgments and to mobilize the covenant people in the task of bringing God's judgments to bear on his enemies. Gordon draws parallels between Samuel's activities at Mizpah and those of Moses in Exodus 17–18.[78]

7:7–8 When "Israel had assembled at Mizpah" (v. 7) for national recommitment to the Lord, word reached the Philistines. In all likelihood the Philistines had forbidden the Israelites to hold public assemblies since such meetings could easily be used to mobilize the tribes for war. Thus "the rulers of the Philistines" dispatched a large military force to Mizpah "to attack them." Fear gripped the Israelites when they learned that an attack by their adversaries was imminent.

In language reflecting descriptions of Israel's previous revivals during the days of the Judges, the Israelites urged Samuel to continue "crying out" (v. 8; cf. Judg 3:9,15; 6:6–7; 10:10) to the Lord so that he would "rescue" (cf. Judg 2:16,18, etc.) them.[79] The people's appeal to Samuel to intercede before the Lord on their behalf probably was motivated by their knowledge that he was a prophet in addition to being a judge. Previously in Israelite history only Moses the prophet-judge was asked by the Israelites during a time of national emergency (cf. Num 21:7).

7:9–11 This section stands as the actional peak of the deliverance narrative. It is marked as such through its restatement of the key events, with narrative expansion.[80] Samuel's appeal to the Lord included a blood sacrifice of a "suckling lamb" as a "whole burnt offering to the LORD" (v. 9, restatement in v. 10)—an undertaking usually carried out by an Aaronic priest—and a wholehearted prayer "to the LORD on Israel's behalf." In response to Samuel's prayer,

---

[78] Cf. Gordon, *I and II Samuel*, 106.

[79] Prophets were attested as individuals who had a special relationship with Yahweh. Thus, during times of distress prophets were regularly sought out to deliver up efficacious prayers in behalf of individuals and nations. Cf. Gen 20:7; Num 11:2; 21:7; Jer 37:3; 42:2–4.

[80] This restatement of key events within narrative is practiced widely in Biblical Hebrew narrative. Examples include Gen 1:27; 7:6–16; Josh 3:17–4:18. For a contextualization of this practice within the realm of languages around the world, cf. R. Longacre, *An Anatomy of Speech Notions* (Lisse: Peter De Ridder, 1976), 217–18.

"the LORD answered him" audibly, responding "with loud thunder against the Philistines" (restatement in v. 10; cf. John 12:29). In so doing Yahweh was acting in accordance with Hannah's prophetic prayer (2:10).

Because the peoples of the ancient Near East believed that every military combat involved a conflict being played out on two planes, the human (terrestrial) and the divine (atmospheric), any unusual meteorological phenomenon during a military operation would naturally be interpreted as evidence of a deity at work (cf. Josh 10:11; Judg 5:4,20–21). The loud, unexpected thunder was immediately understood by the Philistines as a bad omen, and it "threw them into such a panic that they were routed before the Israelites." Emboldened by their enemies' flight, the newly rededicated soldiers of the Lord "rushed out of Mizpah and pursued the Philistines, slaughtering them along the way to Beth Car" (v. 11), a village of unknown location probably west of Mizpah.

7:12 The victory was a significant one for Israel, and Samuel helped to memorialize it by erecting a stone monument "between Mizpah and Shen," apparently at the point to which the Philistines had been driven back. The phrase "Thus far" can be taken either spatially (= "as far as this spot") or temporally (= "all along"). The location of Shen (Hb. *haššēn* = "The Tooth"; LXX, Syriac "Jeshanah") is unknown, but the Hebrew name implies that it was a jagged rock outcropping rather than a settlement.

Samuel named the newly erected stone monument "Ebenezer" (Hb. *ʾeben hāʿāzer*, "The Stone of [the] Help" or "The Help[er] Is a Stone") because "the LORD helped us." The name given the memorial undoubtedly is a confession of faith and trust in the Lord. In the Torah the Lord is poetically referred as the "Stone of Israel" (Gen 49:24), an obvious reference to his strength exercised in Israel's behalf; in the Psalms the Lord is frequently praised as a Helper (cf. Pss 10:14; 33:20; 40:17; 46:1; 63:7; 115:9–11; 118:7; 146:5). Thus whether Samuel was confessing that Israel's strong God is also a source of help for his people or that Israel's assistance-giving God is strong, the name affirms two of the Lord's virtues. The phrase "Here I raise mine Ebenezer," found in the popular hymn "Come Thou Fount of Every Blessing," alludes to this passage.

Uncertainty exists whether the Ebenezer mentioned in 4:1b is an anachronistic reference to the site where Samuel's monument was erected or whether there are two different geographic locations named "Ebenezer." In either case, the writer seems to be drawing deliberate contrasts between the narratives of chaps. 4–6 and 7:3–13. All that was lost through sin in the first Ebenezer event was restored through repentance in the second.

7:13–17 Verse 13 summarizes Samuel's career as leader/judge, characterizing it as one that effectively brought the Lord's judgments to bear against the Philistines. Furthermore, under Samuel's administration portions of the Promised Land "from Ekron to Gath" (v. 14) were brought back under Israelite control, an area whose control was contested by the Philistines earlier in the history of Israel (cf. Josh 13:1–2). Israel's success against the Philistines during the days of Samuel's leadership was a demonstration of their conformity to the Torah (cf. Judg 3:3–4), even as their losses to the Philistines under Eli (cf. 1 Sam 4:10) and Saul (cf. 31:1) were the result of breaches of divine law. Since Ekron and Gath were the two easternmost cities of the Philistine pentapolis and thus the ones closest to Israel's border, it is to be expected that these cities would be hit hardest by an Israelite resurgence.

One of the dividends resulting from Israel's successes against the Philistines was "peace between Israel and the Amorites." Having defeated the dominant regional power, Israel had for now become the force to be reckoned with. Rather than challenging the Israelites militarily, Canaanite remnants in the area (cf. Judg 1:18,34–35) apparently found it preferable to pursue peace.

Samuel continued faithfully in his role as leader/judge over Israel "all the days of his life" (v. 15), apparently even after Saul had become king. Samuel, who is described by the narrator as one who acted as "judge" (Hb. *špṭ*) more times than anyone else in the Bible (four times: 7:6,15,16,17), is portrayed as the ideal leader who faithfully dispensed justice among the Lord's people. His career was an itinerant one, as he annually traveled to four cities in the tribal areas of Benjamin, Ephraim, and Manasseh to dispense justice. These cities were Ramah (cf. 1:1), his home now that his ties with Shiloh were broken; Bethel (modern Tell Beitin, six miles north of Ramah); Gilgal, a city in the vicinity of Jericho (cf. Josh 5:9); and Mizpah (modern Tell en-Nasbeh [?], three miles north of Ramah). Both Mizpah and Bethel were cities that had functioned as gathering places for the entire nation during the period of the Judges (cf. Judg 20:1,18,26; 21:1–2); Gilgal had been a national religious shrine since the days of Joshua (cf. Josh 5:2–10) and perhaps an early administrative center as well (cf. Josh 14:6). The LXX suggests that Samuel conducted his tasks in "sanctuaries" within these cities.

Samuel enhanced the religious significance of his hometown Ramah by building "an altar there to the LORD" (v. 17). Since the Torah prohibited the offering of sacrifices at local sites (cf. Deut 12:13–14), Samuel's construction of such a site implies strongly that Shiloh had been destroyed.

The limited geographic scope of Samuel's activities implies that his primary area of influence was in the tribal domains of Benjamin, Ephraim, and Manasseh. However, Samuel also had a national reputation and sphere of influence. For "all Israel" he (1) was a prophet (3:20; 4:1); (2) led in repentance and recommitment to the Lord (7:3,5); (3) was recognized as a judge (8:4); (4) had the influence to select Israel's first king (10:17–25); and (5) was mourned when he died (25:1).

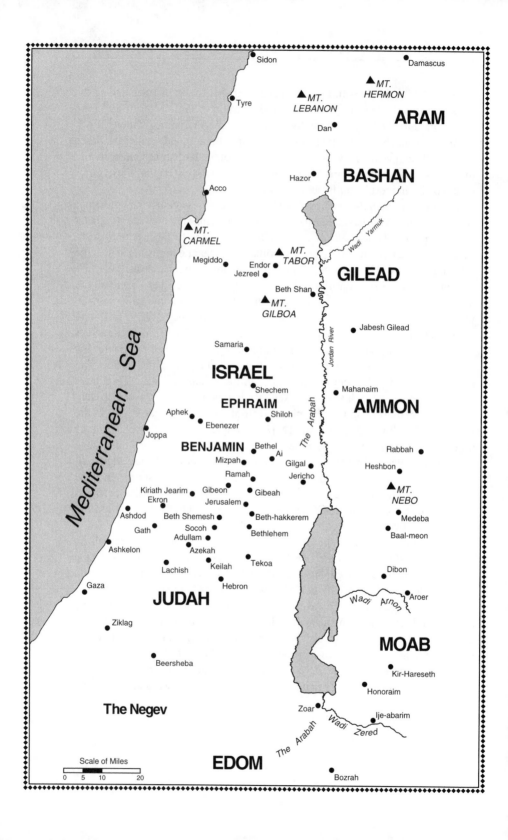

II. THE LORD GIVES ISRAEL A KING "SUCH AS ALL OTHER NATIONS HAVE" (8:1–14:51)

1. Samuel's Sons Are Rejected as Judges (8:1–3)
2. Israel's Elders Demand a King (8:4–6)
3. The Lord Grants the Elders' Sinful Request (8:7–22)
4. The Lord Selects Saul as King over Israel (9:1–12:25)
   (1) Saul Is Introduced (9:1–21)
   (2) Saul Is Honored (9:22–25)
   (3) Saul Is Privately Anointed (9:26–10:8)
   (4) Saul Is Overpowered by God's Spirit (10:9–13)
   (5) Saul Conceals His Anointing and Empowerment (10:14–16)
   (6) Saul Is Installed as King (10:17–27)
   (7) Saul Delivers Jabesh from the Ammonites (11:1–11)
   (8) Israel Confirms Saul's Kingship at Gilgal (11:12–15)
   (9) Samuel Admonishes Israel to Avoid Further Disobedience of God (12:1–25)
5. Saul Demonstrates His Unfitness to Be Israel's King (13:1–14:46)
   (1) Saul Disobeys the Lord's Command to Wait for Samuel (13:1–16a)
   (2) Saul Makes a Foolish Vow before the Lord (13:16b–14:46)
6. Saul's Achievements and Family Line Are Summarized (14:47–52)

II. THE LORD GIVES ISRAEL A KING "SUCH AS ALL OTHER NATIONS HAVE" (8:1–14:51)

This second major section of 1, 2 Samuel[1] details the outworking of one of the Torah's most important predictions, the transfer of supreme social influence

---

[1] Much has been written by critical scholars concerning the existence of supposed pro- and anti-monarchical elements in this section of 1 Samuel. Reflective of this body of literature are S. R. Driver, *An Introduction to the Literature of the Old Testament,* 9th ed. (Edinburgh: T & T Clark, 1913), 175–77; E. Sellin, *Introduction to the Old Testament,* rev. and rewritten by G. Fohrer, trans. D. E. Green (Nashville: Abingdon, 1968), 219–20; and A. D. H. Mayes, "The Rise of the Israelite Monarchy," *ZAW* 90 (1978): 1–19. See also B. C. Birch, *The Rise of the Israelite Monarchy: The Growth and Development of 1 Sam 7–15* (Missoula: Scholars Press, 1976). More recent scholarship has looked for other explanations. Cf. Klein, who sees both viewpoints being expressed by the final, Deuteronomistic historian (Dtr) (*1 Samuel,* 78). Without denying the presence of varying viewpoints regarding kingship within the text, conservative evangelical scholars nevertheless retain a high degree of confidence in the text's historical accuracy (cf. J. Baldwin, *1 and 2 Samuel,* TOTC [Leicester/Downers Grove: InterVarsity, 1988], 82–84). For a reassessment of the situation from a literary perspective, cf. L. Eslinger, "Viewpoints and Points of View in 1 Samuel 8–12," *JSOT* 26 (1983): 61–76.

in Israelite culture from judges and Levites to kings. These chapters function as a historical commentary on Deut 16:18–17:20 and provide insights into both the proximate and underlying causes for Israel's immutable decision to be ruled by an earthly king. As presented in 1 Samuel 8, the following political, military, and spiritual factors underlay Israel's demand for a change of leadership:

1. The failure to establish a system producing an adequate number of qualified judges to lead Israel (8:3–5; cf. Deut 16:18). In particular, the ability of the judgeship system to provide a system of succession failed. Four different judges were mentioned in the Bible as having sons who held positions of leadership following their fathers' deaths. In three of the cases—Gideon's, Eli's, and Samuel's—the sons were portrayed as unworthy successors. In the one instance where apparently successful succession did occur—Jair—it does not appear to have been carried on past one generation (Judg 10:4).

2. The desire of the people to have a national, rather than local or regional, government (cf. 8:4). Samuel is the first judge in the Bible who was accorded truly national status—eleven times in the Hebrew Bible, Samuel is noted as leading all Israel or at least being influential throughout all Israel.[2] Biblical narrative accounts give no suggestion that any of the judges prior to Samuel ministered to all Israel.

Samuel's influence as both prophet and judge exceeded his regional boundaries, suggesting that he was a transitional figure, preparing Israel for more formal national leadership.[3] His leadership over extensive regions indicates that Israel was moving away from the Torah ideal of numerous simultaneous judgeships (Deut 16:18). Likely this situation came about because of a lack of qualified candidates in many localities (cf. 8:2–3), reflective of the generally degraded state of Israelite society at that time. While exercising less control than a king, Samuel's career seems to have been a necessary event in preparing Israel for monarchy.

3. The perceived need for more human military leadership in armed conflicts against other nations (cf. 8:20). Israel's elders considered the tribes' external military threats to be sufficiently serious to warrant a fundamental change in leadership style. It is reasonable to assume that economic considerations, especially the desire of wealthy Israelites to preserve their wealth from foreign confiscation, played a key role in the call for a strengthened military structure.

4. The desire of the people to have a form of national government that was "like the other nations" (cf. 8:5,20). The Torah had foreseen a day when Israel would desire a king "like the nations" (Deut 17:14) surrounding them, and in

---

[2] 1 Sam 3:20; 4:1; 7:3,5; 8:4; 10:20,25; 11:14–15; 25:1; 28:3.

[3] To the extent that Samuel performed a ceremony by which a descendant of Jesse received the Holy Spirit, as well as the fact that Samuel was the last major figure of an era, the prophet foreshadows John the Baptist.

the latter part of Samuel's career that day came. The Torah implicitly suggests that this event would be an undesirable one, since Israel was to be fundamentally different from the other nations; the Lord was to be their king, with the nation set apart for service to their divine monarch.[4]

5. The more fundamental reason for Israel desiring a king, however, was spiritual: the Israelites had rejected God as their king (8:7). The Bible indicates that the concept of the Lord's kingship over Israel was as old as the foundations of Israelite society, being traced to Moses (Deut 33:5) and acclaimed by non-Israelites (Num 23:21). Any attempt to have an earthly king to take the Lord's rightful place (cf. 8:20) would end catastrophically.

Remarkably enough, the Lord honored the people's request, giving them precisely what they requested—Saul, a king "such as all the other nations have" (cf. 8:5). Saul, son of Kish, was as physically impressive—even his height is reminiscent of the other nations (cf. 9:2; Num 13:28)—and spiritually blind as the pagans. Saul's unfitness to lead the Lord's people is foreshadowed already in the writer's opening narrative portrait of Israel's first king (9:3–10:16). There Saul is depicted as a bad shepherd, a metaphorical image in Semitic societies of an incompetent or ruinous leader.[5]

This dark hint is reinforced in the writer's selection of narrative details that illustrate spiritual incompetence of almost legendary proportions. Because of his spiritual obtuseness, Saul was able to live within five miles of Samuel, the most significant spiritual figure since Moses, and yet be completely ignorant of the prophet-reformer's existence. So complete was Saul's darkness that he had to be told by his servant that a prophet could help him, and even then Saul assumed that prophets needed to be hired to perform their divine task. He displayed a fundamental ignorance of basic Torah regulations in such areas as diet and military conduct, and when he did institute Torah-based reforms, he exempted himself from them. His hypocrisy was most glaring when he attempted to justify his failure to destroy the Amalekites (15:9; cf. Exod 17:14; Num 24:20; Deut 25:19) and when he sought guidance from sources explicitly forbidden by the Torah (28:3–19; cf. Exod 22:18; Lev 19:31; 20:6; Deut 18:10–14).

Clearly deliberate parallels are established between Saul and Achish, the Philistine king of Gath, further reinforcing the notion that Saul was a king "such as all the other nations have." Both were impressed with David and had him serve as a personal bodyguard; both believed David was a serious threat to Saul; and both misjudged David, though in opposite ways.

---

[4] For Torah passages suggesting Israel's separation from other nations, cf. Exod 19:5; Lev 18:30; Deut 7:6; 14:2; 18:9; 26:18. Numbers 23:21 suggests that Yahweh was Israel's king. For Israel's obligation to serve Yahweh, cf. Deut 6:13; 10:12; 13:4; 28:47.

[5] The leader-as-shepherd motif is extremely popular in the Bible, particularly in prophetic literature. Cf. Ps 78:72; Isa 44:28; 56:11; Jer 3:15; 6:3; 10:21; 12:10; 22:22; 23:1–4; 25:34–36; 43:12; 49:19; 50:6,44; Ezek 34:2,7–10,23; Mic 5:4; Nah 3:18; Zech 10:3; 11:8–17; 13:7.

The biblical writer passes judgment on Saul for his failure to live up to fundamental Torah guidelines. But more importantly the writer faults Israel for desiring a king who was not "after God's own heart," that is, wholeheartedly devoted to God.[6]

1. Samuel's Sons Are Rejected as Judges (8:1–3)

¹When Samuel grew old, he appointed his sons as judges for Israel. ²The name of his firstborn was Joel and the name of his second was Abijah, and they served at Beersheba. ³But his sons did not walk in his ways. They turned aside after dishonest gain and accepted bribes and perverted justice.

8:1–3 Samuel was the third Levitical judge mentioned in the Bible, Moses (Exod 18:13–26) and Eli (1 Sam 4:18) being the first two. When he grew old, Samuel obeyed the Torah (cf. Deut 16:18) by appointing judges—in this case his sons Joel and Abijah—to function as judges in Beersheba (vv. 1–2). The succession of Eli, Samuel, and his sons suggests that an attempt was being made to bring Israel back to the original Torah pattern of hierocracy, or at least rule by Levites (cf. Deut 17:8–13). Perhaps the belief was that Levites, members of the tribe divinely entrusted with the task of preserving the divine revelation and providing spiritual leadership for Israel, were uniquely qualified to provide the sort of leadership Israel truly needed.

Israel's experiment with hierocracy came to an abrupt halt, however, when Samuel's sons Joel and Abijah "turned aside after dishonest gain and accepted bribes and perverted justice" (v. 3). Their actions were clearly in violation of the Torah (cf. Exod 23:8; Lev 19:15; Deut 16:19) and were certain to create conflict in society.

2. Israel's Elders Demand a King (8:4–6)

⁴So all the elders of Israel gathered together and came to Samuel at Ramah. ⁵They said to him, "You are old, and your sons do not walk in your ways; now appoint a king to lead us, such as all the other nations have."

⁶But when they said, "Give us a king to lead us," this displeased Samuel; so he prayed to the LORD.

8:4–6 An influential delegation of Israel's tribal leaders (lit., "all the elders of Israel"[7]) came to Samuel at his home in Ramah to confront him with

---

[6] For further discussion cf. J. B. Payne, "Saul and the Changing Will of God," *BibSac* 129 (1972): 321–25; D. V. Edelman, *King Saul in the Historiography of Judah* (Sheffield: University of Sheffield, 1991); and V. P. Long, *The Reign and Rejection of King Saul: A Case for Literary and Theological Coherence* (Atlanta: Scholars Press, 1989).

[7] The group known as "all the elders of Israel" was last mentioned in Deut 31:28. The impression made by the biblical narrative is that prior to the present incident, Israel's collective tribal leadership had not acted in a coordinated way since Moses' death. The closest they came to this was the punitive expedition against Benjamin in Judg 19–21.

the failures of the existing form of government and to propose an alternative (v. 4). The fact that leaders from all tribes "gathered together" suggests the existence of some sort of ruling council or political body above the tribal level.

The elders began their meeting with Samuel by delineating the facts of the present: Samuel had entered his years of physical decline, and his successors did "not walk in [his] ways" (v. 5). The apparently imminent return to the dismal pattern of failed judgeships, which Israel had known for so many years, would not be tolerated by the people. An alternative pattern, one foreseen in the Torah and practiced by Israel's neighbors, was now demanded by the elders: "Appoint a king to lead us, such as all the other nations have." In spite of its apparent attractiveness, the elders' demand contained at least one aspect that violated a fundamental tenet of the Torah. Israel was to be distinct from the nations (cf. Lev 20:26; Num 23:9), and moves motivated by a desire to conform to pagan ways were bound to create problems. No doubt this request also was heavily motivated by the elders' desire to defeat oppressive enemies (cf. 12:12). However, it amounted to an attempt to accomplish through a political act that which could only be achieved through ongoing spiritual responsibility (cf. Judg 3:4).

Samuel is consistently portrayed as the ideal prophet. As such, he was necessarily a supporter of the Torah.[8] Not surprisingly, therefore, the elders' request "displeased Samuel" (v. 6; lit., "was evil in the eyes of Samuel"). Before formulating a response to the elders, however, the prophet wisely took the issue before the Lord in prayer.

3. The Lord Grants the Elders' Sinful Request (8:7–22)

[7]And the LORD told him: "Listen to all that the people are saying to you; it is not you they have rejected, but they have rejected me as their king. [8]As they have done from the day I brought them up out of Egypt until this day, forsaking me and serving other gods, so they are doing to you. [9]Now listen to them; but warn them solemnly and let them know what the king who will reign over them will do."

[10]Samuel told all the words of the LORD to the people who were asking him for a king. [11]He said, "This is what the king who will reign over you will do: He will take your sons and make them serve with his chariots and horses, and they will run in front of his chariots. [12]Some he will assign to be commanders of thousands and commanders of fifties, and others to plow his ground and reap his harvest, and still others to make weapons of war and equipment for his chariots. [13]He will take your daughters to be perfumers and cooks and bakers. [14]He will take the best of your fields and vineyards and olive groves and give them to his attendants. [15]He will take a tenth of your grain and of your vintage and give it to his officials and attendants. [16]Your menservants and maidservants and the best of your cattle and donkeys he

---

[8]Cf. D. Stuart, *Hosea-Jonah*, WBC (Waco: Word, 1987), xxxi–xlii.

will take for his own use. [17]He will take a tenth of your flocks, and you yourselves will become his slaves. [18]When that day comes, you will cry out for relief from the king you have chosen, and the LORD will not answer you in that day."

[19]But the people refused to listen to Samuel. "No!" they said. "We want a king over us. [20]Then we will be like all the other nations, with a king to lead us and to go out before us and fight our battles."

[21]When Samuel heard all that the people said, he repeated it before the LORD. [22]The LORD answered, "Listen to them and give them a king."

Then Samuel said to the men of Israel, "Everyone go back to his town."

These verses represent one of the most significant connective links bonding the history and theology of the Torah to those of the Latter Prophets. Here the Lord establishes the thesis that Israel's history "from the day I brought them up out of Egypt until this day" was one continuous experience of "forsaking me and serving other gods" (v. 8). Against this backdrop, Israel's demand for an earthly king is presented as merely the latest instance of their long-standing pattern of rejection.

This tragic consistency in Israel's relationship with the Lord presaged an ominous future for Israel. As envisioned by Samuel, the earthly king that Israel demanded would assume rights otherwise reserved for the Lord, Israel's divine king; he would demand a "tithe" of Israel's grain, vintage, and flocks (vv. 15,17; cf. Lev 27:30,32); he would lay claim to their land and even their own beings (vv. 11–14,16; cf. Lev 25:23). Unlike the Lord, however, human kingship would not result in deliverance for Israel but rather oppression reminiscent of what the people had experienced under Egypt (cf. Exod 2:23), Aram Naharaim (cf. Judg 3:9), Moab (cf. Judg 3:15), and the Midianites (cf. Judg 6:6–7).

In a move that would determine the shape of Israel's history from that day forward, Israel's elders ignored Samuel's warning and restated their demand for a human king. Consistent with his pattern of fulfilling even Israel's sinful requests (cf. Num 11:18,31), the Lord acceded to their will. A troubling future for Israel was thus assured.

8:7–9 The narrator was careful to note that Samuel waited for the Lord to weigh in before taking any actions on the matter. The Lord's directives to the elderly prophet were threefold: (1) heed the people's request (v. 7; lit., "Hear in the voice of the people"), but (2) "warn them solemnly" (v. 9; lit., "warning you shall warn them"), and (3) inform them of the consequences associated with their demand. These instructions are surprising in view of the underlying condition that prompted the elders' request.

Samuel was stung by the people's rejection of his efforts, but the source of their demand was not to be found in their relationship with him or his sons. Instead, it lay in their troubled relationship with God; Israel had rejected the Lord as their king (cf. Num 14:11). The people's demand for an earthly king represented the political manifestation of a spiritual problem.

8:10–18   Having received the word of the Lord, the prophet carried it back "to the people who were asking for a king" (v. 10). Then in the third-longest recorded speech by Samuel in the Bible (eighty-five words in the Hebrew) he provided the people with a sober description of what they could expect from a king. Dominating Samuel's characterization of Israelite kings is the portrayal of the oppressive control they would take of Israelite lives, families, and possessions. In short, kings would be "takers" who would diminish others to further their own interests (cf. Deut 17).[9]

As Samuel pointed out, the decision to have a permanent king meant much more than the addition of one person to the circle of power in Israel. It entailed the establishment of a permanent, multitiered bureaucratic institution utilizing the services of thousands of individuals. To underwrite this form of government, vast quantities of personal and family resources would have to be given over to the king.

Human resources of every description would be required for the maintenance of a monarchy. As listed by Samuel, two primary categories of governmental employees would be needed, military and administrative support personnel. Military personnel included those who would serve in the royal honor guard (v. 11); those who would comprise the cavalry, a strategic military strike force (v. 11); those in a professional officer corps (v. 12); those involved in weapons production (v. 12); and those charged with the maintenance of a strategic food supply (v. 13).

Administrative support positions included those involved with the general maintenance of a high quality of life for the royal family and officials, most of whom would have been relatives of the king.[10] From the ranks of the general population would have to come those who would serve as cooks and bakers (v. 13), perfumers (v. 13), and general laborers (v. 16).

In addition to human resources, large quantities of material would be needed to sustain the bureaucracy. Though the king would own many fields (v. 14; cf. Eccl 2:5–6), the burden of providing a permanent food supply for this institution would fall on the population at large. The people would have to hand over a "tithe" of their grain, vintage, and flocks (vv. 15,17). In addition

---

[9] This is encoded grammatically in two lexical distinctives: (1) the extensive use of the third masculine singular pronominal suffix on nouns and prepositions (fourteen of eighty-five words, or one word in every six in the speech, had a suffix referring to the king); the suffixes all indicate possession by or the interests of the king; (2) in the extensive use of verbs denoting acquisition—לקח and עשׂה (six of the seventeen finite verbs in the speech were occurrences of these two verbs).

[10] Kings ordinarily chose family members for key positions in their administrations. Both Saul's son Jonathan and his uncle Abner were generals in his army (1 Sam 13:2; 14:5); David's nephews Joab and Abishai, as well as his own sons, played key roles in his government (cf. 2 Sam 8:16–17; 23:18).

to food, the royal institution would need a sustained supply of beasts of burden (v. 16), the engines of field labor and commerce.

Placing this heavy burden on the backs of the citizens of Israel's twelve tribes would have the practical effect of reducing them to slaves (v. 17). As a result, the people would "cry out for relief from the king" (v. 18) as though he were an enemy. However, the Lord would not grant them a respite at that time. Israel would one day be freed from the burden of a royal bureaucracy, but only after outside forces had reduced the royal bastions to rubble.

8:19–22 In spite of the prophet's sober warning, the people "refused to listen to Samuel" and reaffirmed their demand for "a king over us" (v. 19). Their previously stated sinful desire to be "like all the other nations" (see comments on 8:5) was now augmented by the additional sin of desiring to remove the Lord from his position at the head of Israel's armies (cf. Deut 1:30; also Exod 14:14,25; 15:3; Num 10:35; Deut 3:22; 4:20; 20:1–4). The narrator's portrayal of Israel's rejection of Samuel's warnings is reminiscent of the Torah language depicting Pharaoh's stubborn refusal to submit to Moses; both "did not hear" (v. 19) so as to heed (cf. Exod 7:4,13,16,22; 8:15,19[Hb. 11,15]; 9:12; 11:9).

In dutiful fulfillment of his mediatorial role as a prophet (cf. Num 27:5), Samuel repeated the peoples' words "before the LORD" (v. 21), that is, in the worship center at Ramah (cf. Isa 37:14). The Lord agreed to their request and commanded the prophet to "give them a king" (v. 22).

Their request having been granted, Samuel dismissed the "men of Israel" to their homes.[11] Thus was set in motion the events that gave Israel a king who was far more "like all the other nations" had than anyone could have imagined.

4. The Lord Selects Saul as King over Israel (9:1–12:25)

The Lord, the God who answers prayer, responded to Israel's demands for a king by giving them Saul. The narrator's portrait of Israel's first king is artfully equivocal in these four chapters. On the one hand, Saul is described as materially well-to-do and physically impressive; he was able to inspire a following among the Israelites, skillful in battle, and gracious in victory. On the other hand, he was genealogically linked with the most depraved tribe of the period of the judges and is depicted as pastorally incompetent, spiritually ignorant and disobedient, and, at times, oddly irrational. On balance, the portrait is a troubling one and foreshadows the sad outcome that awaits the man and the nation. In keeping with the Torah prophecy (cf. Gen 49:10), the tribe of Ben-

---

[11] R. Polzin has suggested that "Samuel is being portrayed here trying to delay or subvert the Lord's command even as he wants to appear fulfilling that command" (*Samuel and the Deuteronomist* [San Francisco: Harper & Row, 1989], 87). This interpretation misses the point: as Yahweh's true prophet, Samuel must first receive word from Yahweh before choosing a new king.

jamin's representative would not retain kingship for his tribe.

Structural similarities in the introduction and biographies of Saul and Samuel suggest that the writer was inviting a comparison/contrast between these two individuals. Both individuals were introduced with extensive genealogies. Both came from the same region of the country and rose from obscurity to national prominence. Both had names etymologically linked to the same verb, one meaning "requested."[12] Both led Israel in battle against the Philistines. Both built altars to the Lord. Yet as the Saul narratives progress, the contrasts between Saul and Samuel in matters of supreme importance for the writer will far outweigh the similarities. Whereas Samuel was for the writer the embodiment of leadership in submission to the Lord, Saul was a clear example of leadership at odds with the Lord.

(1) Saul Is Introduced (9:1-21)[13]

¹There was a Benjamite, a man of standing, whose name was Kish son of Abiel, the son of Zeror, the son of Becorath, the son of Aphiah of Benjamin. ²He had a son named Saul, an impressive young man without equal among the Israelites—a head taller than any of the others.

³Now the donkeys belonging to Saul's father Kish were lost, and Kish said to his son Saul, "Take one of the servants with you and go and look for the donkeys." ⁴So he passed through the hill country of Ephraim and through the area around Shalisha, but they did not find them. They went on into the district of Shaalim, but the donkeys were not there. Then he passed through the territory of Benjamin, but they did not find them.

⁵When they reached the district of Zuph, Saul said to the servant who was with him, "Come, let's go back, or my father will stop thinking about the donkeys and start worrying about us."

⁶But the servant replied, "Look, in this town there is a man of God; he is highly respected, and everything he says comes true. Let's go there now. Perhaps he will tell us what way to take."

⁷Saul said to his servant, "If we go, what can we give the man? The food in our sacks is gone. We have no gift to take to the man of God. What do we have?"

⁸The servant answered him again. "Look," he said, "I have a quarter of a shekel of silver. I will give it to the man of God so that he will tell us what way to take."

---

[12] However, "Samuel" is interpreted to mean "Requested from God"; whereas Saul's name means "[He who was] Requested." The presence of the theophoric element in Samuel's name—as well as its absence from Saul's—is reflective of the essential difference between the two leaders: Samuel's life and career were marked by the presence of God; Saul's were not.

[13] For highly skeptical evaluations of the historicity of this section, cf. B. C. Birch, "The Development of the Tradition on the Anointing of Saul in I Sam. 9:1–10:16," *JBL* 90 (1971): 55–67; and J. M. Miller, "Saul's Rise to Power: Some Observations Concerning 1 Sam. 9:1–10:16; 10:26–11:15; and 13:2–14:46," *CBQ* 36 (1974): 157–74. In their tendency to find multiple traditions and folktales blended together by a later editor, they are instructive as paradigms of modern skeptical approaches to the text.

⁹(Formerly in Israel, if a man went to inquire of God, he would say, "Come, let us go to the seer," because the prophet of today used to be called a seer.) ¹⁰"Good," Saul said to his servant. "Come, let's go." So they set out for the town where the man of God was.

¹¹As they were going up the hill to the town, they met some girls coming out to draw water, and they asked them, "Is the seer here?"

¹²"He is," they answered. "He's ahead of you. Hurry now; he has just come to our town today, for the people have a sacrifice at the high place. ¹³As soon as you enter the town, you will find him before he goes up to the high place to eat. The people will not begin eating until he comes, because he must bless the sacrifice; afterward, those who are invited will eat. Go up now; you should find him about this time."

¹⁴They went up to the town, and as they were entering it, there was Samuel, coming toward them on his way up to the high place.

¹⁵Now the day before Saul came, the LORD had revealed this to Samuel: ¹⁶"About this time tomorrow I will send you a man from the land of Benjamin. Anoint him leader over my people Israel; he will deliver my people from the hand of the Philistines. I have looked upon my people, for their cry has reached me."

¹⁷When Samuel caught sight of Saul, the LORD said to him, "This is the man I spoke to you about; he will govern my people."

¹⁸Saul approached Samuel in the gateway and asked, "Would you please tell me where the seer's house is?"

¹⁹"I am the seer," Samuel replied. "Go up ahead of me to the high place, for today you are to eat with me, and in the morning I will let you go and will tell you all that is in your heart. ²⁰As for the donkeys you lost three days ago, do not worry about them; they have been found. And to whom is all the desire of Israel turned, if not to you and all your father's family?"

²¹Saul answered, "But am I not a Benjamite, from the smallest tribe of Israel, and is not my clan the least of all the clans of the tribe of Benjamin? Why do you say such a thing to me?"

9:1–2 As in the case of Samuel, Saul's formal introduction is preceded by the introduction of his father. Kish, like Elkanah, was supplied with a four-generation genealogy (cf. 1:1). He was "a man of standing" (v. 1; Hb. lit., "powerful man of strength/might/wealth"[14]); the use of this phrase, in combination with the notation that the family owned slaves, donkeys, and oxen (cf. 11:5), suggests that Saul came from one of the most influential families in Benjamin.

Besides his favorable family situation, Saul himself was "an impressive young man [Hb. *bāḥûr wāṭôb;* lit., "chosen and good"] without equal among the Israelites" (v. 2). The feature that most obviously set Saul apart from other Israelites was his physical appearance; he was "a head taller than any of the

[14] The phrase גִּבּוֹר חַיִל is translated variously in the NIV: "mighty warrior" in Judg 11:1; "brave man" in 1 Sam 16:18; "man of standing" here, 1 Kgs 11:28, and Ruth 2:1; "valiant soldier" in 2 Kgs 5:1 and 2 Chr 17:17; "brave warrior" in 1 Chr 12:29 (Eng., 26) and 1 Chr 28:1; "able troops" in 2 Chr 13:1; and "fighting men" in 2 Chr 25:6 and 32:21.

others." Although this characteristic would normally be considered an asset, the narrator may have included this detail as a subtle indictment of Israel's first king. Saul is the only Israelite specifically noted in the Bible as being tall; elsewhere it was only Israel's enemies whose height was noted (cf. Num 13:33; Deut 1:28; 2:10; 9:2; 1 Sam 17:4). Israel had asked for a king "like all the other nations" (8:20), and the Lord was giving them the desires of their heart, even down to the physical details!

9:3–10 Saul's unfitness to serve as the shepherd of the Lord's flock is further suggested in the unusual narrative recounted here. Semitic leaders throughout ancient times were often referred to as shepherds;[15] the Torah's most significant patriarchs—Abraham, Isaac, Jacob, Moses—were also depicted as skillful shepherds. Yet here Saul is portrayed unflatteringly as an incompetent shepherd. So great was his ineptness that he could not even find a few large animals (v. 3; Hb. *hāʾătōnôt,* "she-asses") that had wandered away from his father's house—ones that ultimately returned home without Saul's assistance even as he was searching for them (9:20; 10:2)! With the aid of a slave (Hb. *ʿebed*) Saul searched exhaustively in the territory of Benjamin and southern Ephraim, including "the area of Shalisha" (= Baal Shalishah? cf. 2 Kgs 4:42) and "the district of Shaalim" (v. 4), probably both regions twenty miles or less from Gibeah, Saul's hometown.

After a frustrating and fruitless three-day search, Saul and his slave entered "the district of Zuph" (v. 5), the prophet Samuel's home region located some five miles from Gibeah. There Saul recommended that the search be called off, being concerned that his "father will stop thinking about the donkeys and start worrying about us." Saul's servant, however, suggested an alternative plan that ultimately prevailed. Recognizing that the nearby man of God was a "highly respected" (v. 6; Hb. *nikbād,* lit. "honored") individual whose prophetic word was uncannily accurate, he proposed that they seek Samuel's help in their search.

Saul was initially unwilling to visit a prophet, however, because he lacked payment to hire his services. Saul's objection was overcome when his slave offered to pay a quarter of a shekel of silver (approx. three grams) to the prophet "so that he will tell us what way to take." With that issue settled, the pair set out for Ramah, "the town where the man of God was" (v. 10).

At least three features are remarkable about the brief interchange between Saul and his servant in vv. 6–10. First is the future king's profound ignorance of Samuel. Though Samuel lived nearby and was known to "all Israel" (3:20; 4:1), even Saul's young slave (Hb. *naʿar*), he was unknown to Saul. Second is Saul's failure to consider seeking divine help in the trials of life. It was Saul's

---

[15] For references to pastoral imagery used to describe leaders in other ancient Semitic cultures, cf. *ANET,* 164–65, 177–78.

slave, not Saul himself, who recognized the need for spiritual help in coping with their problems. The future king's life at this point was devoid of a spiritual sensitivity that looked to the Lord for help. Third is Saul's assumption that spiritual favors had to be bought; though some unscrupulous prophets might have demanded this (cf. Mic 3:11; Acts 8:20), no true servant of the Lord would.[16]

Verse 9 is significant mainly because of the information it provides regarding the time of 1, 2 Samuel's *final* composition. Clearly the overall work was written late enough in time for the common term for a man of God to have changed from "seer" (Hb. *rōʾeh*) to "prophet" (Hb. *nābîʾ*).[17]

9:11–13 The fact that Saul and his servant "met some girls coming out to draw water" (v. 11) as they approached the city suggests that they arrived in Ramah/Ramathaim in the early evening, just prior to sundown (cf. Gen 24:11). Timeless social customs in the Middle East prevented men from having much contact with women in public, but women were permitted to speak even with total strangers under the circumstances presented here (cf. also Gen 24:13–27; 29:9–12; John 4:7–26).

Being an itinerant judge for the region (cf. 7:16–17), Samuel visited his hometown only occasionally. The altar that he had previously constructed there, likely "at the high place" (Hb. *bāmâ*), had apparently become a sacred site that served as a local substitute for the ruined worship center at Shiloh (cf. comments on 7:17).

As a respected elderly Levite, Samuel was given special recognition at the local religious observance (cf. Deut 14:27–29), including the honor of pro-

---

[16] The suggestion by S. M. Paul ("1 Samuel 9,7; An Interview Fee," *Bib* 59 [1978]: 542–44) that this payment was necessary in order to gain information from Samuel seems contrary to the recorded practice of other genuine prophets of Yahweh. More likely, Saul's anxiety concerning payment was portrayed in order to demonstrate his own spiritual ignorance.

[17] The verbal noun רֹאֶה, a *qal*-stem participle of the most common verb in Hb. meaning "see," characterizes prophets as individuals with both insight and foresight. The noun נָבִיא appears to be a *peʿal*-stem participle from a verb whose meaning is still uncertain. Suggested meanings include "one who is in a prophetic ecstasy," "one who is filled with spirit." Cf. *CHAL,* s.v. נָבִיא; R. D. Culver, "*nābîʾ,*" *TWOT,* 544. The suggestion by J. B. Curtis ("A Folk Etymology of *nābîʾ,*" *VT* 29 [1979]: 491–93) that the term נָבִיא is meant by the text to mean "to bring a gift" can be safely rejected; for rebuttal cf. S. Shaviv, "*nābîʾ* and *nāgîd* in 1 Samuel ix 1–x 16," *VT* 34 (1984): 108–13. See also *TDOT,* KB[3] (Eng.). Biblical evidence provides no definite indication about when the transition from רֹאֶה to נָבִיא in common parlance occurred. Clearly the biblical writer assumed that it occurred after the time of the events recorded here. The fact that Gad (1 Chr 29:29), Iddo (2 Chr 9:29), Hanani (2 Chr 16:10), Jehu (2 Chr 19:2), and Amos (7:12) were all identified as seers suggests the change occurred no earlier than the eighth century B.C. The use of נְבִיאִם in the Torah and reference to Abraham, Aaron, and Moses as such (cf. Gen 20:7; Exod 7:1; Num 11:29; 12:6; 13:2,4–5; Deut 18:15,20,22; 34:10) may suggest that (1) both terms were widely known early in Israelite linguistic history; (2) both terms had different semantic content at an early period; or (3) the Torah received its final editing after the time of Amos.

nouncing a blessing over the sacrifice (cf. Deut 10:8; 21:5; 2 Chr 30:27). The ritual would have been part of the evening sacrifice to be held at sundown (cf. Deut 16:6).

9:14–18 Having walked up the hill from the well, Saul and his servant entered the city gate just as Samuel was "on his way up to the high place." A providential encounter ensued between these three men. To delineate this point, the narrator notes that on the previous day the Lord "had revealed to Samuel" (v. 15; lit., "uncovered Samuel's ear") that he would send him "a man from the land of Benjamin" (v. 16). Deeper than any mortal motives driving the encounter were the currents of divine will: the Lord was fulfilling his promise to give Israel their new leader (Hb. *nāgîd*), who would deliver (Hb. *hôšîaʿ*) Israel from "the hand of the Philistines."[18]

God's words to Samuel regarding Saul in v. 17 are filled with irony: the Hebrew verb *ʿṣr*, translated here as "govern," can equally well mean "restrain/hold back/hinder" or even "imprison." The core meaning is "to restrain/constrict." In the majority of its forty-six occurrences in the Hebrew text the word possesses a negative connotation, suggesting imprisonment (2 Kgs 17:4; Jer 33:1), sterility (Gen 20:18), silencing (Job 4:2), or holding back (2 Kgs 4:24). In fact, 9:17 is the only location in Scripture where the word can be taken to mean "rule." By employing the verb here, the writer was suggesting that the Lord had determined to use Saul's career as a means of punishing the nation. Saul would literally fulfill the various meanings of this verb. Even as he governed Israel, his policies and behavior would hinder the welfare of the nation and act as a sort of barrier separating Israel from God's best for them.

Particularly striking in the instructions to Samuel in vv. 16–17 is the Lord's fourfold repetition of the phrase "my people." Though he had placed Saul in a position of authority over Israel, the Lord was in no way relinquishing his own claim to the nation: Israel would remain the Lord's own treasured possession (cf. Exod 19:5; Deut 7:6; 14:2; 26:18). At his finest Saul would be a mere caretaker of God's flock (cf. 1 Pet 5:2).

One function of the Saul narratives is to depict the spiritual unfitness of the man who would serve as Israel's first king. In so doing the writer demonstrates that Saul is spiritually, as in other ways, "a king such as all the other nations have." Emblematic of Saul's spiritual blindness is his initial encounter with Samuel. Though Samuel was the most famous and honored spiritual leader in Israel since the time of Moses, when Saul looked at him he saw only a stranger. The contrast between Saul and Samuel is striking: Samuel, the man of spiritual insight (the "seer"), knew all about an obscure young man even before he met

---

[18] Some scholars suggest the presence of a promonarchichal document in this section that clashes conceptually with a supposed antimonarchical document underlying the previous section. Cf. n. 1 in this chapter for further details.

up with him; Saul, the paragon of spiritual blindness, knew nothing of the most famous man in Israel even after he encountered him. The narrative motif of Saul's incapacity to see the true nature of people would later be expressed in the context of his relationships with Jonathan, David, and Ahimelech. He would misjudge Jonathan to be an unworthy son and traitor; David, a treacherous revolutionary; and Ahimelech, a co-conspirator against the throne. All of these misreadings of others resulted in tragedy, both for Saul and others.

9:19–20 Samuel's response to Saul's inquiry provides the young man with far more than he requested. Instead of being given directions to the seer's house, Saul was given the seer himself. In addition, he received a prestigious invitation to a sacrificial meal, free information regarding the lost donkeys (cf. vv. 7–8), and the intimation of a fabulous destiny. Instead of learning about his father's donkeys, he would learn about himself. The prophet's words contained a subtle condemnatory note,[19] but they were on the whole extremely positive. At the same time, they were perplexing to Saul.

9:21 Saul's response ignores his original motive for seeking out the prophet and suggests that his initial concerns had been replaced by a larger issue: why did Israel want him, a Benjamite, to be king? Benjamin was a notorious tribe that had been nearly eliminated through fratricidal wars in the not-too-distant past (cf. Judg 20:35,48). Furthermore, Saul's clan (Matri, cf. 10:21) was by his own admission "the least of all the clans of the tribe of Benjamin." This latter statement may merely reflect customary deference (cf. 24:14; 2 Sam 9:8), or it may be true in ways other than numeric or material. Saul apparently had numerous living relatives (10:14,21), and his father, Kish, was well-to-do, possessing land (11:5), servants (9:3), oxen (11:7), and donkeys (9:3).

Perhaps in the presence of Samuel the seer, Saul was reckoning spiritually: his clan was the least spiritual clan of the most sin-stained tribe. Reinforcing this possibility was the fact that Saul came from Gibeah, a Benjamite town whose citizens (Saul's forebears?) had committed one of the most heinous crimes in Israelite history (cf. Judg 19:22–26). D. F. Payne surmises that humanly speaking someone from Benjamin would have been a good choice. Its location between Ephraim and Judah would help "reduce rivalries" and "unify Israel in the struggle against the Philistines." Saul, therefore, could have

---

[19] Embedded in Samuel's words to Saul in v. 20 is a subtle wordplay that betrays the prophet's understanding of the events now unfolding: the word translated in the NIV as "desire" is a noun derived from the verb חָמַד, elsewhere translated as "covet" (cf. Exod 20:17). Though this noun form occurs in Genesis to 2 Kings only here and is normally used in a positive sense (e.g., Jer 3:19; Hag 2:7), it can also be used to refer to an object of sinful desire (cf. Dan 11:37). Especially in view of previous statements (8:6–18), the interrogative phrase "to whom is all the desire of Israel?" should be equally understood to mean "for whom is all the sinful craving of Israel?" Thus Saul, like quail in a previous generation (cf. Num 11:4–34), becomes God's judgmental response to Israel's sinful craving.

been "the ideal king for Israel, and at this point in time there was nothing to stop him achieving true greatness."[20] It was not to be, but the fault was in himself.

(2) Saul Is Honored (9:22-25)

[22]Then Samuel brought Saul and his servant into the hall and seated them at the head of those who were invited—about thirty in number. [23]Samuel said to the cook, "Bring the piece of meat I gave you, the one I told you to lay aside."
[24]So the cook took up the leg with what was on it and set it in front of Saul. Samuel said, "Here is what has been kept for you. Eat, because it was set aside for you for this occasion, from the time I said, 'I have invited guests.'" And Saul dined with Samuel that day.
[25]After they came down from the high place to the town, Samuel talked with Saul on the roof of his house.

9:22–23 Samuel is not recorded as responding to Saul's questions. Instead, Samuel assumed the role of gracious host to the travelers and set about tending to their needs. As host to the strangers in the city, Samuel was responsible for providing them with food (cf. Gen 19:2–3). Thus Samuel brought Saul to the worship center and, as a proper Middle Eastern host, gave him a seat of honor (v. 22). The exact nature of the sacrificial event attended by Samuel and his guests is unknown. The text suggests that the thirty or so men who attended were there by invitation; perhaps it was a new moon sacrifice limited to members of Samuel's clan (cf. 20:18,28–29). The site of the banquet was a rectangular room (Hb. *liškâ*) that opened into a courtyard, apparently part of a sanctuary associated with the high place in Ramah.

9:24–25 Since the Lord had told Samuel that he was sending him a guest (v. 16), the faithful prophet had duly prepared for the visitor's arrival, even setting aside the choicest portion of the sacrificial animal, "the leg with what was on it" (v. 24), for Saul's enjoyment.[21]

Following the meal a nocturnal conversation ensued between Saul and the prophet on the roof of Samuel's residence. The roof, always flat in ancient Israel, functioned in warm, dry weather as useful living space (cf. Deut 22:8). Following the conversation Samuel once again acted as the thoughtful host, permitting Saul to sleep in this preferred location, where breezes would have made the night more pleasant.

---

[20] D. F. Payne, *I and II Samuel*, DSB (Philadelphia: Westminster, 1982), 46.

[21] This portrayal of Samuel as Saul's generous host to Yahweh's guests nullifies claims by some that Samuel was deliberately disobeying God in an effort to prevent Saul from achieving kingship in Israel. Cf. Polzin, who suggests that Yahweh had to overcome "Samuel's subversive short-circuiting of the LORD's will in chapter 8" by making Saul "come to Samuel" through the unlikely circumstance of lost donkeys (*Samuel and the Deuteronomist*, 90).

(3) Saul Is Privately Anointed (9:26–10:8)

[26]They rose about daybreak and Samuel called to Saul on the roof, "Get ready, and I will send you on your way." When Saul got ready, he and Samuel went outside together. [27]As they were going down to the edge of the town, Samuel said to Saul, "Tell the servant to go on ahead of us"—and the servant did so—"but you stay here awhile, so that I may give you a message from God."

[1]Then Samuel took a flask of oil and poured it on Saul's head and kissed him, saying, "Has not the LORD anointed you leader over his inheritance? [2]When you leave me today, you will meet two men near Rachel's tomb, at Zelzah on the border of Benjamin. They will say to you, 'The donkeys you set out to look for have been found. And now your father has stopped thinking about them and is worried about you. He is asking, "What shall I do about my son?"'

[3]"Then you will go on from there until you reach the great tree of Tabor. Three men going up to God at Bethel will meet you there. One will be carrying three young goats, another three loaves of bread, and another a skin of wine. [4]They will greet you and offer you two loaves of bread, which you will accept from them.

[5]"After that you will go to Gibeah of God, where there is a Philistine outpost. As you approach the town, you will meet a procession of prophets coming down from the high place with lyres, tambourines, flutes and harps being played before them, and they will be prophesying. [6]The Spirit of the LORD will come upon you in power, and you will prophesy with them; and you will be changed into a different person. [7]Once these signs are fulfilled, do whatever your hand finds to do, for God is with you.

[8]"Go down ahead of me to Gilgal. I will surely come down to you to sacrifice burnt offerings and fellowship offerings, but you must wait seven days until I come to you and tell you what you are to do."

9:26–27 Rising about daybreak, Samuel summoned Saul from the roof back into the interior of the house so that final preparations could be made for the journey back home. As a proper host, Samuel then accompanied both Saul and the servant to the edge of the city (cf. Gen 18:16); but in a break with customary practice, Samuel asked Saul to stay behind while sending his servant on ahead. The reason Samuel gave was provocative: "so that I may give you a message from God" (v. 27), a message that was to take the dual forms of a symbolic gesture as well as a spoken word.

10:1–8 In his longest recorded speech to an individual (147 words in Hb.), Samuel accomplished three things: he (1) revealed that Saul was God's choice to be Israel's first king, (2) laid out for Saul a series of confirmatory signs, and then (3) intimated to Saul the proper relationship that was to exist between king and prophet in Israel.

Samuel's "message from God" first took the form of anointing, an action heretofore reserved for sacred objects (cf. Lev 8:10–11,30; Num 7:1) and Aaronic priests (Lev 8:30). The act of pouring a flask of specially prepared olive oil on Saul's head apparently symbolized the staking of a divine claim on

him, as well as the outpouring of the Lord's enabling Spirit into the newly designated king's life.[22] Payne notes: "In Egyptian culture it was the custom to
anoint vassal kings, i.e., minor kings who owed allegiance to the great king of
Egypt; in this light we may see the king of Israel not as a king in his own right
but as the vassal of Yahweh, who is envisaged as the true king of Israel."[23]
Though Samuel anointed Saul, it was in fact the Lord who was responsible for
designating Saul as the leader "over his inheritance" (v. 1). The Lord termed
him "leader" (Hb. *nāgîd*) and not "king" here, though the term evidently
implied kingship (cf. 1 Sam 12:13) and should not be taken here as a status
inferior to that of king. Payne suggests it may mean "king-designate" or "king-
to-be."[24] Samuel's kissing of Saul was an expression of respect for and acceptance of the Lord's anointed (cf. Gen 29:13; 33:4; 45:15; Exod 4:27; 18:7).

Samuel's artful casting of the affirmation "The LORD anointed you leader
over his inheritance" (v. 1) in the form of a question probably resonated with
Saul's own uncertainties.[25] To dispel doubts concerning the Lord's claim on
the young man's life, Samuel provided Saul with an unprecedented series of
validating signs that would be accomplished almost immediately—even
before Saul could return to his own home. This early confirmation would in
theory help Saul accept his new status immediately and thus prepare him to
accept his role as Israel's king when it was publicly bestowed on him.

The confirmatory signs would take the form of encounters with three suc-
cessively larger and religiously more significant groups of men. Having left the
one man Samuel, Saul would encounter two men with connections to his family; next, he would meet three pilgrims on their way to Bethel, a worship center
in Ephraim; finally, on the outskirts of Gibeah-of-God he would come upon a
band of prophets. While in the presence of this third group Saul would have a
climactic fourth encounter, this time with the Lord's Spirit. Saul's encounters
with the three groups of men parallel his encounters with Samuel at Ramah.
The following chart clarifies the semantic parallels between Saul's meetings
with Samuel and the others.

---

[22] For further discussion on the significance of anointing, cf. R. L. Harris, who suggests that the
term implied "separation for God's service" and "divine enablement," among other things ("מָשַׁח"
in *TWOT*, 530).

[23] D. F. Payne, *I and II Samuel*, DSB (Philadelphia: Westminster, 1982), 50.

[24] Ibid.

[25] The use of the Hb. adverbial particle הֲלוֹא is customarily employed in contexts where the
answer is understood to be in the affirmative. Cf. L. J. de Regt, "Rhetorical Questions in the Book
of Job," in *Biblical Hebrew and Discourse Linguistics*, ed. R. Bergen (Dallas: SIL, 1994), 365: "In
Biblical Hebrew in general, הֲלוֹא occurs in questions when an affirmative answer is implied (cf.
Latin *nonne*)." Cf. also B. K. Waltke and M. O'Connor, *An Introduction to Biblical Hebrew Syntax*
(Winona Lake: Eisenbrauns, 1990), 684.

Saul informed of donkeys' return (9:20)	Saul informed of donkeys' return (10:2,9)
Saul receives the food of sacrifices (9:24)	Saul receives the food of sacrifices (10:4,9)
Saul receives the holy anointing in the presence of a prophet (10:1)	Saul receives the Spirit of the Lord in the presence of prophets (10:6,10)

This replay of events in Saul's life would underline the significance of his encounter with Samuel and at the same time confirm the veracity of the divine word spoken through the prophet.

Saul's first confirmatory sign would authenticate Samuel's word concerning the issue that had motivated Saul to seek the prophet in the first place; two men near Rachel's tomb[26] would inform him of the return of the donkeys and the mounting anxiety for Saul's safety back in his father's household. The second sign would confirm the authenticity and legitimacy of Samuel's act of anointing Saul: three men on their way to a Yahwistic worship center in Bethel (cf. Judg 20:18,26; 21:2) would present Saul with food designated for use by one who was anointed. Though "the two loaves of bread" (v. 4) were originally intended by the pilgrims as a gift for an anointed Aaronic priest, Saul's acceptance of the food would require him to accept the legitimacy of his own anointing. The third encounter would confirm Samuel's assertion that the Lord had also anointed Saul (v. 1). In the presence of a group of prophets, "the Spirit of the LORD will come upon you in power and you will prophesy with them" (v. 6).

In addition to the three prophecies, Samuel also gave Saul his first lesson about the relationship that was to exist between Israel's king and Yahweh's prophet. Under the Lord's inspiration, Samuel and the later prophets had the right to prescribe royal behavior (cf. 1 Kgs 20:13,22). Furthermore, the plans of Saul (and all Israelite kings who would come after him) were to be subordinate to the prophetic word: "You must wait . . . until I come to you and tell you what you are to do" (v. 8). In Israel's monarchy royal authority was derived and secondary; the king was always to be under the Lord's authority. Since the Lord's true prophets were conduits through which the divine word came to kings, these prophets were in a functionally superior position to royalty. Royal power would

---

[26] According to the biblical text (v. 2), the location of the tomb of Rachel, wife of the patriarch Jacob, was on the border between the tribal territories of Benjamin and Ephraim. Based on Gen 35:19, a postbiblical tradition has located the tomb south of Jerusalem, near Bethlehem. This location conflicts with the present Scripture and is considered inaccurate.

have divinely set limits, and the Lord's prophets would define those limits. Samuel's words to Saul were thus the opening volley in an enduring struggle between human political will and divinely inspired religious conscience.

(4) Saul Is Overpowered by God's Spirit (10:9–13)

⁹As Saul turned to leave Samuel, God changed Saul's heart, and all these signs were fulfilled that day. ¹⁰When they arrived at Gibeah, a procession of prophets met him; the Spirit of God came upon him in power, and he joined in their prophesying. ¹¹When all those who had formerly known him saw him prophesying with the prophets, they asked each other, "What is this that has happened to the son of Kish? Is Saul also among the prophets?"

¹²A man who lived there answered, "And who is their father?" So it became a saying: "Is Saul also among the prophets?" ¹³After Saul stopped prophesying, he went to the high place.

10:9–10 As Saul turned to leave, "God changed [lit., "overturned"] Saul's heart" (v. 9).

The writer assumes the occurrence of the first two predicted events and depicts only the climactic final one. When Saul passed through "Gibeah of God" (NKJV, "the hill of God,"; NRSV, "Gibeath-elohim"), an otherwise unknown site in Benjamite territory[27] "where there is a Philistine outpost" (v. 5), Saul and his servant encountered an itinerant group of prophets playing musical instruments and prophesying. God's Spirit overpowered the formerly spiritually undistinguished Saul, so that he spontaneously "joined in their prophesying" (v. 10).

10:11–13 Saul's uncharacteristic behavior shocked "those who had formerly known him," and they reacted in disbelief: "What is this that has happened to the son of Kish? Is Saul also among the prophets?" (v. 11). It also gave rise to ridicule, expressed in a cryptic response to the previous rhetorical questions: "And who is their father?" (v. 12).

In these latter words an unnamed resident of Gibeah seems to have made a cynical wordplay on the meaning of the Hebrew word "father," a term used to indicate both genetic relationship—parenthood (v. 11)—and social relationship—authority over a group of prophets (cf. 2 Kgs 2:12; 6:21; 13:14). Though the meaning of the response is contested,[28] it seems intended to degrade Saul

---

[27] Some have suggested that the Gibeah mentioned here is the same city as Saul's hometown. Cf. Baldwin, *1 and 2 Samuel,* 91; R. Gordon, *I and II Samuel* (Grand Rapids: Zondervan, 1986), 117. Although this is possible, I do not consider it likely. The terminology "Gibeah of God" seems to be posited in deliberate contrast to the "Gibeah of Saul" (cf. 1 Sam 11:4; 15:34; 2 Sam 21:6). Others associate it with Geba. Cf. R. Klein, *1 Samuel,* WBC (Waco: Word, 1983), 91.

[28] H. W. Hertzberg (*I and II Samuel,* trans. J. S. Bowden, OTL [Philadelphia: Westminster, 1964], 86) interprets it to mean, "How does a reasonable man, well placed in civic life, come to be in this eccentric company?" For alternate interpretations cf. especially discussions by P. K. McCarter, Jr., *I Samuel,* AB (New York: Doubleday, 1980), 184; and Klein, *1 Samuel,* 92–93.

and the prophetic movement in general by raising derisive questions about the circumstances of Saul's birth. The logic underlying the saying probably was as follows: To be a prophet, one might be expected to have a father who is a prophet (cf. Amos 7:14). Yet Kish is not a prophet. Thus either Saul and, by extension, his prophetic brotherhood are not really prophets ("Is Saul among the prophets?") or Saul is only apparently the son of Kish but was actually conceived in an adulterous relationship between his mother and the head of the prophetic band.

Saul's experience at Gibeah parallels an important pneumatic event recorded in the Torah (cf. Num 11:16–18,25). In both cases individuals not previously associated with the prophetic movement had the Spirit come upon them in the presence of recognized prophets, and in both cases the nonprophets temporarily manifested the gift of prophecy. The repetition of this sequence of events here and elsewhere in 1 Samuel (cf. 19:18–24) suggests that the Lord's prophets were dynamic conduits through which the divine Spirit might overflow into the lives of others around them with powerful, if temporary, effects.[29] After his unique experience at Gibeah, "Saul stopped prophesying" (cf. Num 11:25) and continued on his way "to the high place" (v. 13). Perhaps he went there to offer up the bread presented to him earlier (cf. v. 3).

(5) Saul Conceals His Anointing and Empowerment (10:14–16)

[14]Now Saul's uncle asked him and his servant, "Where have you been?"

"Looking for the donkeys," he said. "But when we saw they were not to be found, we went to Samuel."

[15]Saul's uncle said, "Tell me what Samuel said to you."

[16]Saul replied, "He assured us that the donkeys had been found." But he did not tell his uncle what Samuel had said about the kingship.

10:14–16 Returning to his hometown, Saul was approached by his uncle, probably Ner (cf. 14:50), who "asked him and his servant, 'Where have you been?'" (v. 14). Saul indicated that they had been in various places in the region but had ultimately gone to Ramah to visit Samuel. Mention of the prophet's name sparked further inquiry from Saul's uncle: "Tell me what Samuel said to you" (v. 15). Saul's response was honest, though deceptively incomplete: the prophet had informed them that the donkeys had been found. What Saul did not say was more significant than what he said: "he did not tell his uncle what Samuel had said about the kingship" (v. 16). Thus at this time none of Saul's servants or family members were aware of Saul's divine selection; it remained a secret shared only by Saul and Samuel. David's kingship

---

[29] Consistent with this observation is 2 Kgs 13:21. The Kings passage suggests that in at least one case spiritual powers that influenced the lives of others were attributed to a prophet even after death.

likewise would have a two-stage beginning. Both were selected as kings by the Lord, yet the kingship of both was hidden from their family members for a period of time.

(6) Saul Is Publicly Installed as King (10:17–27)

[17]Samuel summoned the people of Israel to the LORD at Mizpah [18]and said to them, "This is what the LORD, the God of Israel, says: 'I brought Israel up out of Egypt, and I delivered you from the power of Egypt and all the kingdoms that oppressed you.' [19]But you have now rejected your God, who saves you out of all your calamities and distresses. And you have said, 'No, set a king over us.' So now present yourselves before the LORD by your tribes and clans."

[20]When Samuel brought all the tribes of Israel near, the tribe of Benjamin was chosen. [21]Then he brought forward the tribe of Benjamin, clan by clan, and Matri's clan was chosen. Finally Saul son of Kish was chosen. But when they looked for him, he was not to be found. [22]So they inquired further of the LORD, "Has the man come here yet?"

And the LORD said, "Yes, he has hidden himself among the baggage."

[23]They ran and brought him out, and as he stood among the people he was a head taller than any of the others. [24]Samuel said to all the people, "Do you see the man the LORD has chosen? There is no one like him among all the people."

Then the people shouted, "Long live the king!"

[25]Samuel explained to the people the regulations of the kingship. He wrote them down on a scroll and deposited it before the LORD. Then Samuel dismissed the people, each to his own home.

[26]Saul also went to his home in Gibeah, accompanied by valiant men whose hearts God had touched. [27]But some troublemakers said, "How can this fellow save us?" They despised him and brought him no gifts. But Saul kept silent.

10:17–19 In response to the peoples' desire to have Samuel "set a king over us" (v. 19), the prophet summoned the people to Mizpah (v. 17), one of Samuel's four centers of judicial activity. Ironically, the site chosen for the installation of Saul the Benjamite as king was also the site where Israel had previously covenanted to exterminate the tribe of Benjamin (cf. Judg 20:1–11). Ultimately this act would also mean the death of Benjamites, in this case the most honored of Benjamin's remaining tribesmen (cf. 31:2). Samuel knew it was God's will to select Saul as king, but he also understood that the day's events were motivated by Israel's rejection of God as king.

At the public convocation in Mizpah, Samuel acted not as judge but as prophet. His first act in the assembly was not to proclaim Israel's new leader but to reveal the Lord's prophetic judgments. In classic prophetic fashion Samuel began with an indication of his oracle's true origin: "This is what the LORD, the God of Israel, says" (v. 17). What followed were words of severe condemnation.

The oracle opened with a litany of the Lord's key saving acts on Israel's behalf, as described in the Torah. The choice of words in v. 18 creates subtle yet deliberate links to the Sinai covenant itself (cp. Exod 20:2) and suggests that the root of Israel's present problems was violation of the first commandment given at Sinai (v. 19a). This failure to keep the most basic requirement of Israel's covenant with King Yahweh could only result in devastating judgment, especially since the alternative to divine leadership was to have a human "king over us."

10:20–21a The process utilized here to identify the king was meant to emphasize that Israel's next leader was selected by divine prerogative, not human manipulation. As presented here, however, it serves a second function: it reinforces the notion that Saul's selection was a divine judgment against Israel. The only other occasion in which an individual was selected using a method like that described in vv. 20–21 was when Achan was identified following a previous disastrous act of rebellion against the Lord (cf. Josh 7:16–18).

10:21b–24 Curiously, when Saul son of Kish was chosen, "he was not to be found" (v. 21). Human efforts failed to locate Saul, and it was only after inquiring of the Lord that they learned that he had "hidden himself among the baggage" (v. 22), probably a location at the perimeter of the camp.

Saul's actions, however odd, were consistent with the portrayal of Saul to this point; previously the king-designate had shut out both his servant (9:27) and his uncle (10:16) from any knowledge of his destiny. Saul's vacancy at his own coronation suitably foreshadows a reign that would vacate responsibilities associated with the exercise of godly rule and perhaps suggests the lack of wisdom of those who preferred such a king to Yahweh. At the same time, divine assistance in the search for Saul reinforced the conclusion that Saul was indeed the Lord's answer to Israel's demand for a king "like the other nations."

The narrator's choice of details in describing the people's first view of their new king is thematically significant: "as he stood among them he was a head taller than any of the others" (v. 23). Elsewhere in Scripture only noncovenant peoples are noted as being tall.[30] Through the narrator's selection of this feature as the only attribute used to describe Saul, he successfully linked Saul with those who represent a threat to the safety and integrity of the Lord's covenantal people. A further wedge is driven between Saul and the rest of Israel in Samuel's words: "there is no one like him among all the people" (v. 24). All this being true, Saul still was "the man the LORD has chosen," and the people responded with enthusiastic shouts of "Long live the king!" (lit., "May the king live").

10:25–27 In what has been judged to be one of the turning points of Isra-

---

[30] Pre-Israelite residents of Canaan (Num 13:32–33), Anakites (Deut 2:10,21; 9:2), a Philistine (1 Sam 17:4), an Egyptian (1 Chr 11:23), Cushites (Isa 18:7), Sabeans (Isa 45:14), and Amorites (Amos 2:9) are all described in terms of their superior height. Only Saul among the Israelites was so described.

elite history,[31] the faithful judge Samuel declared to the people "the [divine] judgment of the kingship" (v. 25; *mišpaṭ hammĕlukâ*, NIV, "regulations of the kingship")[32] (cp. *mispăt hammelek* in 8:9,11). In keeping with the stipulations set forth in the Torah, Samuel the Levite made available to the new king "a copy of this law, taken from that of the priests, who are Levites" (Deut 17:18). The exact content of this document is unknown; it may have been a copy of at least a section of the Mosaic legal materials or perhaps an expansion of the materials in Deuteronomy. Like other sacred documents, it was "deposited . . . before the LORD."[33] That Samuel's document was the first one explicitly deposited before the Lord since the time of Joshua serves as a silent indictment of the entire period of the Judges. At the same time it elevates Samuel to the highest category of prestige and honor in orthodox Israelite religious history.

At the conclusion of the day's events Samuel, as God's spokesman, was still in charge, dismissing the people, including Saul, who returned to Gibeah (v. 26). Since no capital city had yet been established for an Israelite monarch, Saul's hometown became the de facto first capital of Israel. The beginnings of a standing military force—a necessary component for effective national leadership—are seen as Saul was "accompanied by valiant men [Hb. *haḥayil*, "the strength"] whose hearts God had touched." God's action in these men's lives demonstrates that the Lord was supplying his anointed with the vital resources needed to fulfill his responsibilities.

Saul was not without his detractors, however, as "some troublemakers" (lit., "sons of Belial," translated "wicked men" in Deut 13:14 (Eng., 13); Judg 19:22; 20:13; 1 Sam 2:12; 25:17; 30:22; and "scoundrels" in 1 Kgs 21:10,13; 2 Chr 13:7) "ridiculed him and brought him no gifts" (v. 27). In spite of compelling evidences that the Lord had indeed chosen Saul as Israel's king, these individuals rejected the outcome of the events and withheld all support from their new ruler, including tokens of goodwill customarily presented to newly installed authorities. Admirably, Saul's first act as an oriental monarch was one of grace; he "kept silent" in response to the critics'

---

[31] Z. Ben-Barak places this event on a par with the Sinai covenant act of Exodus 24 and Joshua's assembly of the Israelites at Shechem (Josh 24). He understands the event to serve as the basis of the new style of government in Israel ("The Mizpah Covenant [1 Sam 10:25]—The Source of the Israelite Monarchy Covenant," *ZAW* 91 [1979]: 30–43).

[32] In general agreement with the NIV, D. F. Payne translates the phrase as "the rights and duties of the kingship" (*I and II Samuel*, 52–53). McCarter opts for "the Law of the Kingdom" (*I Samuel*, 193).

[33] Other documents "deposited before the LORD" included documents penned by Moses (cf. Exod 24:7, "the Scroll of the Covenant"; Deut 31:26, "the Scroll of this Law") and Joshua (cf. Josh 24:26, "the Scroll of the Law of God"). The exact nature and content of each of these documents remains unknown. The fact that several individuals over a considerable period of time created such documents may suggest something about the growth of the OT canon. Almost certainly these documents were utilized in some way in the production of the final form of the Hebrew Bible.

effrontery instead of ordering their deaths (cf. Prov 16:14).

(7) Saul Delivers Jabesh from the Ammonites (11:1–11)

[1]Nahash the Ammonite went up and besieged Jabesh Gilead. And all the men of Jabesh said to him, "Make a treaty with us, and we will be subject to you."
[2]But Nahash the Ammonite replied, "I will make a treaty with you only on the condition that I gouge out the right eye of every one of you and so bring disgrace on all Israel."
[3]The elders of Jabesh said to him, "Give us seven days so we can send messengers throughout Israel; if no one comes to rescue us, we will surrender to you."
[4]When the messengers came to Gibeah of Saul and reported these terms to the people, they all wept aloud. [5]Just then Saul was returning from the fields, behind his oxen, and he asked, "What is wrong with the people? Why are they weeping?" Then they repeated to him what the men of Jabesh had said.
[6]When Saul heard their words, the Spirit of God came upon him in power, and he burned with anger. [7]He took a pair of oxen, cut them into pieces, and sent the pieces by messengers throughout Israel, proclaiming, "This is what will be done to the oxen of anyone who does not follow Saul and Samuel." Then the terror of the LORD fell on the people, and they turned out as one man. [8]When Saul mustered them at Bezek, the men of Israel numbered three hundred thousand and the men of Judah thirty thousand.
[9]They told the messengers who had come, "Say to the men of Jabesh Gilead, 'By the time the sun is hot tomorrow, you will be delivered.'" When the messengers went and reported this to the men of Jabesh, they were elated. [10]They said to the Ammonites, "Tomorrow we will surrender to you, and you can do to us whatever seems good to you."
[11]The next day Saul separated his men into three divisions; during the last watch of the night they broke into the camp of the Ammonites and slaughtered them until the heat of the day. Those who survived were scattered, so that no two of them were left together.

Saul's first major undertaking as Israel's king was a positive one. In this passage he is shown fulfilling the primary purpose for a king as envisioned by the Israelite elders, namely, to "go out before us and fight our battles" (8:20). Israel's victory over the Ammonites under Saul's inspired leadership (vv. 6–11) is reminiscent of some of the most glorious military moments in the period of the Judges (cf. Judg 3:10; 6:34–7:25; 11:29–33). Thus in connection with the previous description of Saul's frame (10:23), the present section demonstrates the Lord's faithfulness in fulfilling every aspect of Israel's vision of what a king should be: Saul was a king "such as all the other nations have" (8:5) who could lead Israel in battle.

The standard Hebrew text, and therefore all but the most recent of Bible versions, presents what is possibly an abridged version of the original account of Saul's encounter with the Ammonites. The Qumran manuscript 4QSam[a] as well as Josephus (*Ant.* 6.5.1) add a short paragraph of information now found in several modern versions (10:27b–11:1a).[34] The information contained in this paragraph is irrelevant to the central purpose of the story and may introduce a chronological problem into the narrative flow (cf. 10:8; 13:8–14). Especially in view of its omission from the standard Hebrew text, it may be safely ignored.[35]

11:1–3 Saul's first opportunity to exercise his royal responsibilities came as Ammonites besieged Jabesh Gilead (v. 1).[36] The inhabitants of Jabesh Gilead had initially attempted to handle the problem themselves, offering the aggressor the chance to "make a treaty with us, and we will be subject to you." The Israelites' pact likely would have called for taxes being paid to Nahash (= "Snake") in exchange for withdrawal and a moratorium on further attacks. Nahash agreed to their terms with one important addendum: that he gouge out everyone's right eye (v. 2). This mass facial disfigurement would have brought "disgrace on all Israel," to say nothing of deep humiliation and handicap for each mutilated individual.

From Nahash's standpoint, however, the removal of the most prized eye of each Jabesh Gileadite would have two advantages: it would preserve the Israelites' capacity to perform agricultural tasks (and thus generate taxable revenue), yet it would drastically reduce their ability to wage war by taking away their depth perception and reducing their field of vision.

Instead of immediately rejecting Nahash's counteroffer, the Jabesh Gileadites artfully negotiated for two additional concessions: first, additional time—seven days; and second, an opportunity to "send messengers throughout Israel" (v. 3). In exchange for this compromise, they would agree to "surrender" peacefully to subjugation and mutilation "if no one comes to rescue us."

Perhaps Nahash doubted Jabesh Gilead would receive help from the western tribes of Israel since those tribes had previously failed to lend support for a defense against the Ammonites (cf. Judg 11:4–11), and the Jabeshites had withheld support from the western tribes at an earlier point in Israelite history

---

[34] The text of the NRSV's additions is as follows: "Now Nahash, king of the Ammonites, had been grievously oppressing the Gadites and the Reubenites. He would gouge out the right eye of each of them and would not grant Israel a deliverer. No one was left of the Israelites across the Jordan whose right eye Nahash, king of the Ammonites, had not gouged out. But there were seven thousand men who had escaped from the Ammonites and had entered Jabesh-gilead. About a month later . . ." Other recent versions that include this information are the NEB and NAB.

[35] Cf. Gordon's useful discussion on the appropriateness of including this passage in modern versions. After surveying modern scholarly opinion, he concludes that "the wise course for the present . . . is to reserve judgement on the status of these additional lines in 4QSam[a]" (*I and II Samuel*, 64). Baldwin favors its inclusion in modern versions but notes that "it will not add substantially to the meaning of the text" (*I and II Samuel*, 96).

[36] Jabesh Gilead was a settlement east of the Jordan River and twenty miles south of the Sea of Galilee (modern Abu Kharaz? [so McCarter and Baldwin], or Miryamin? [so Driver]).

(cf. Judg 19–21). Perhaps he also believed Ammon could defeat any force Israel might muster and that a victory against a larger foe would simply mean greater spoil for himself and his nation. For whatever reason, Nahash agreed to the offer. However, it proved to be a deadly miscalculation.

11:4–6 The citizens of Jabesh Gilead wisely sent messengers to Saul at Gibeah.[37] Saul and the city of Gibeah possessed strong family and historical links with Jabesh Gilead (cf. Judg 21:1–23) and thus were predisposed to responding with urgency to the plea for help, but they also joined in the Jabeshites' grief (v. 4). Furthermore Saul, the newly ordained king, was also the only Israelite who had control of a standing army at the time (cf. 10:26).[38]

Graphic evidence for the humble beginnings of Israel's monarchy is seen in that the news came to the king as he "was returning from the fields, behind his oxen" (v. 5). In his first days as monarch Saul still actively participated in farming, his preregnal occupation.[39] No doubt this would have been necessary during the time of transition to an established monarchy, before the government could be financed by tribal levies.

Saul's outrage at their words was magnified by the energizing power of God's Spirit, who "came upon him in power" (v. 6). The writer's statement that God's Spirit was powerfully over Saul prepares the reader to expect a successful outcome for Saul's undertaking; nowhere in biblical Hebrew narrative does the divine Spirit come over a person without an act or word resulting that helps God's people. At the same time, however, the narrator artfully casts a shadow over Saul's moment of glory by referring to the divine presence as "the Spirit of God," not "the Spirit of Yahweh/the LORD." Though both phrases refer to the same being, this subtle change in language deprives Saul of direct association with Israel's covenant God. Five Israelites are mentioned as having "the Spirit of the LORD" come over them, but in Genesis to 2 Kings[40] the only other person said to have "the Spirit of God" come over him is Balaam, a non-Israelite (cf. Num 24:2) who ultimately brought harm to Israel (Num 31:16).

11:7–8 In an act reminiscent of one performed by a Levite in the Book of Judges (19:29), Saul summoned the Israelite tribes to war by butchering two valuable agricultural animals (v. 7). Calls to involvement in geographically limited conflicts had been mostly unsuccessful in Israelite history (cf. Judg

---

[37] Josephus (*Ant.* 6.5.2) asserted that the messengers went to other cities as well, "city by city," not merely Gibeah.

[38] Payne denies that Saul had a standing army at this time (*I and II Samuel*, 55).

[39] The mention of Saul's farming activity may be intended as a further hint of the biblical writer's negative evaluation of Saul. Previously Saul has been portrayed as an incompetent shepherd (cf. comments on 9:3); now he is portrayed as a farmer, a link that connects him with Cain (Gen 4:2).

[40] Othniel (Judg 3:10), Gideon (Judg 6:34), Jephthah (Judg 11:29), Samson (Judg 14:6,19; 15:14), and David (1 Sam 16:13).

5:16–17; 8:1; 12:2–3; 21:5); yet Saul's coercive threat proved effective, for "the terror of the LORD [*pahad yhwh;* cf. Isa 2:10,19,21; 2 Chr 14:13 (Eng. 14); 17:10] fell on the people." The Israelites' anxiety may have been increased when they remembered the punishment inflicted on a city—ironically, on Jabesh Gilead—that had once refused a similar call to assemble (Judg 21:5). Saul's slaughter of his oxen may have symbolized his entrance into full-time kingship.

The Israelites were to follow "Saul and Samuel" (v. 7). In spite of Saul's new title, Samuel remained the proven and respected leader who had led Israel for a generation. A time would come later when the ministry paths of Saul and Samuel would diverge (cf. 15:26–35), but for now they worked together effectively in confronting a common enemy.

The army gathered "at Bezek" (modern Khirbet Ibziq), twelve miles northeast of Shechem in the tribal territory of Manasseh. The site was a favorable one because it was only about ten miles west of Jabesh Gilead. The number of men mentioned as assembling for war was the second largest in Genesis to 2 Kings (v. 8).[41] Only the number of Israelites assembling for war against Benjamin was greater (Judg 20:2,17). The separate counts provided for Israel and Judah suggest that the tribal schism first hinted at in the Book of Joshua (11:21) was growing. It also sets the stage for difficulties that would plague David's rise to national kingship (cf. 2 Sam 2:10–11) and ultimately split the country (1 Kgs 12:19–20).

11:9–11 Under the leadership of Saul and Samuel, the assembled forces prepared for war against the Ammonites. Jabesh Gilead's messengers carried back an audacious pledge from the group to their besieged comrades (v. 9). The message contained two vital pieces of military intelligence: confirmation of armed Israelite intervention and an indication that the primary attack would occur before dawn.

Encouraged by these two strategic pieces of information, the men of Jabesh immediately began spreading disinformation designed to disarm the Ammonites psychologically (v. 10). By indicating that they would submit peacefully to the will of Nahash and his army after sunrise the next day, the Jabeshites encouraged the Ammonites to drop their guard and celebrate with abandon during the night—exactly when vigilance was most needed.

Following a time-tested strategy (cf. Judg 7:16; 9:43), "Saul separated his men into three divisions" (v. 11) so as to produce a multisided, simultaneous attack on the enemy camp. Then "during the last watch of the night"—somewhere between 2 A.M. and 6 A.M.—they attacked the Ammonite camp and

---

[41] The LXX offers much higher counts: 600,000 for Israel and 70,000 for Judah; Josephus (*Ant.,* 6.5.3) suggests 700,000 for Israel. The text of 4QSam[a], though fragmentary, supports 70,000 for Judah. Nevertheless, these numbers probably are not the ones in the autographic text: well-meaning transcribers in antiquity probably corrupted the numbers.

slaughtered their army. So successful was the attack that no unified group of survivors remained.

(8) Israel Confirms Saul's Kingship at Gilgal (11:12–15)

[12]The people then said to Samuel, "Who was it that asked, 'Shall Saul reign over us?' Bring these men to us and we will put them to death."

[13]But Saul said, "No one shall be put to death today, for this day the LORD has rescued Israel."

[14]Then Samuel said to the people, "Come, let us go to Gilgal and there reaffirm the kingship." [15]So all the people went to Gilgal and confirmed Saul as king in the presence of the LORD. There they sacrificed fellowship offerings before the LORD, and Saul and all the Israelites held a great celebration.

11:12–15 The Israelites were impressed with Saul's able management of the Ammonite crisis. He had fulfilled their expectations for one who could lead Israel successfully in battle (cf. 8:20), and so they desired to renew their commitments to the new leader and the new form of government. In the process they wanted to squelch all opposition to Saul and Israel's new direction. Approaching Samuel, who was at the time Israel's only universally recognized leader, they revealed their plan to "put . . . to death" (v. 12) those who had opposed Saul's kingship.

Saul, who apparently was in Samuel's company at the time of the request (cf. v. 7), interrupted the discourse. Majestically he intervened to avert a lynching, and thus spared the lives of his subjects. Instead of focusing on the evil of men, Saul encouraged the people to focus on the goodness of God, "for this day the LORD has rescued Israel" (v. 13).

Samuel affirmed Saul's suggestions, and instructed the group to assemble at Gilgal (v. 14). Since Gilgal had served as both an administrative and religious center (cf. Josh 5:2–10; 14:6; 1 Sam 7:16), and was a border settlement linking the tenuously aligned southern and northern tribes (cf. Josh 15:7), it was a fitting site to reestablish Saul's claim to kingship over all Israel. The event had both religious and political significance (v. 15).

In every other narrative instance in the Hebrew Bible, "fellowship offerings" (Hb. šĕlāmîm, trad. "peace offerings") were accompanied by burnt offerings (cf. Josh 8:31; Judg 20:26; 21:4; 1 Sam 10:8, etc.); however, in the present case they apparently were not. The reason for this break from the usually observed pattern seems to be related to the purpose of the occasion; Israel was holding "a great celebration" of their new king and new form of government. Eating was—and still is—a significant part of relationship establishment and religious celebrations, and fellowship offerings were voluntary sacrifices meant to be consumed in a festive meal. Thus it was appropriate to offer large quantities of them at this event.

(9) Samuel Admonishes Israel to Avoid Further Disobedience of God (12:1–25)

[1]Samuel said to all Israel, "I have listened to everything you said to me and have set a king over you. [2]Now you have a king as your leader. As for me, I am old and gray, and my sons are here with you. I have been your leader from my youth until this day. [3]Here I stand. Testify against me in the presence of the LORD and his anointed. Whose ox have I taken? Whose donkey have I taken? Whom have I cheated? Whom have I oppressed? From whose hand have I accepted a bribe to make me shut my eyes? If I have done any of these, I will make it right."

[4]"You have not cheated or oppressed us," they replied. "You have not taken anything from anyone's hand."

[5]Samuel said to them, "The LORD is witness against you, and also his anointed is witness this day, that you have not found anything in my hand."

"He is witness," they said.

[6]Then Samuel said to the people, "It is the LORD who appointed Moses and Aaron and brought your forefathers up out of Egypt. [7]Now then, stand here, because I am going to confront you with evidence before the LORD as to all the righteous acts performed by the LORD for you and your fathers.

[8]"After Jacob entered Egypt, they cried to the LORD for help, and the LORD sent Moses and Aaron, who brought your forefathers out of Egypt and settled them in this place.

[9]"But they forgot the LORD their God; so he sold them into the hand of Sisera, the commander of the army of Hazor, and into the hands of the Philistines and the king of Moab, who fought against them. [10]They cried out to the LORD and said, 'We have sinned; we have forsaken the LORD and served the Baals and the Ashtoreths. But now deliver us from the hands of our enemies, and we will serve you.' [11]Then the LORD sent Jerub-Baal, Barak, Jephthah and Samuel, and he delivered you from the hands of your enemies on every side, so that you lived securely.

[12]"But when you saw that Nahash king of the Ammonites was moving against you, you said to me, 'No, we want a king to rule over us'—even though the LORD your God was your king. [13]Now here is the king you have chosen, the one you asked for; see, the LORD has set a king over you. [14]If you fear the LORD and serve and obey him and do not rebel against his commands, and if both you and the king who reigns over you follow the LORD your God—good! [15]But if you do not obey the LORD, and if you rebel against his commands, his hand will be against you, as it was against your fathers.

[16]"Now then, stand still and see this great thing the LORD is about to do before your eyes! [17]Is it not wheat harvest now? I will call upon the LORD to send thunder and rain. And you will realize what an evil thing you did in the eyes of the LORD when you asked for a king."

[18]Then Samuel called upon the LORD, and that same day the LORD sent thunder and rain. So all the people stood in awe of the LORD and of Samuel.

[19]The people all said to Samuel, "Pray to the LORD your God for your servants so that we will not die, for we have added to all our other sins the evil of asking for a king."

²⁰"Do not be afraid," Samuel replied. "You have done all this evil; yet do not turn away from the LORD, but serve the LORD with all your heart. ²¹Do not turn away after useless idols. They can do you no good, nor can they rescue you, because they are useless. ²²For the sake of his great name the LORD will not reject his people, because the LORD was pleased to make you his own. ²³As for me, far be it from me that I should sin against the LORD by failing to pray for you. And I will teach you the way that is good and right. ²⁴But be sure to fear the LORD and serve him faithfully with all your heart; consider what great things he has done for you. ²⁵Yet if you persist in doing evil, both you and your king will be swept away."

Samuel's career of public service as Israel's Judge and prophet reached its zenith at this Gilgal assembly. Having been given full moral authority through a public exoneration of his character and conduct, Samuel used the occasion to unleash his full prophetic arsenal; he proclaimed stern warnings, called forth portents from nature, and issued one of the most sobering assessments of Israel's past, present, and future found in biblical Hebrew narrative. On the whole, the chapter represents one of the theological climaxes of the Former Prophets, and takes its rightful place alongside such similarly toned sections as Joshua 24, Judges 2, 1 Kings 8, and 2 Kings 17. The thematic significance of this section is underscored by the fact that three of Samuel's six longest recorded utterances are presented here, including his lengthiest speech (205 words in Hebrew).

12:1–5 Now that Israel's new national leader had been duly confirmed and celebrated, Samuel closed the books on his own lengthy tenure of service as a leader for all Israel. He began by reminding the people that he had cooperated with them in the transition to a new system of leadership. In fact, it was he who "set a king over" Israel (v. 1). This was accomplished when Samuel was "old and gray" (v. 2; cf. Josh 23:1–2), and was carried out even though it meant a great loss of prestige and significance for his own family.

Samuel's sons had failed to uphold the tradition of leadership established by their father (cf. 8:3–4) and so had driven the final nail in the coffin of the judgeship system prescribed in the Torah (cf. Deut 16:18). As a result, Samuel's sons were "with" the people (v. 2) rather than being "over" them (v. 1).

Holding court one last time with the people of Israel, Samuel's final act as judge was to put himself on trial. In this case Samuel was the defendant, the people were prosecutors, and "the LORD and his anointed" (v. 3) were the enforcing authorities. Noting that his public career had been a lengthy one, "from my youth until this day" (v. 2), Samuel invited anyone with just cause to "testify against me" (v. 3). If he had failed to live up to Moses' example (cf. Num 16:15) or had violated the Torah's standards of conduct (cf. Lev 6:2,4 [Hb. 5:21,23]; Deut 16:19), he would "make it right" (v. 3) at this time.

However, the people accounted Samuel's conduct as Israel's Judge to be faultless. With the Lord and Saul "his anointed" (v. 5) as witnesses, the people declared that Samuel had not "cheated or oppressed" them, nor had he "taken anything from anyone's hand" (v. 4; contrast Samuel's sons in 1 Sam 8:3). The example of Israel's last Judge would thus contrast sharply with that of Israel's kings, who would often cheat and oppress them and would take the people's sons, daughters, produce, and animals (cf. 8:11–16; 14:52).

12:6–9 Having been exonerated by the people as Israel's Judge, Samuel here asserted himself as Israel's prophet. In the longest single quotation of the Hebrew Bible attributed to Samuel, the prophet delivered a stern admonition and warning (vv. 14–15), flanked by a historical introduction (vv. 6–13) and the calling forth of a portent of divine disfavor (vv. 16–17). In a manner reminiscent of other Old Testament prophetic messages,[42] Samuel cast his message in a juridical mold and symbolically put Israel on trial. The assembled people were called to stand and hear the evidence (v. 7); divine testimony in the form of a sign from nature was also part of the event.

Samuel began by presenting a panorama of God's "righteous acts" from the time of Moses up until the present day. Five illustrations from Israel's past were employed to remind Israel of two simple yet profound theological truths: first, it is the Lord alone (not kings or armies or weapons or alliances) who rescues his people from foreign oppressors, though he does so through specially chosen human beings. Second, Yahweh rescues his people in response to their prayers and repentance. It is perhaps significant that three of the six deliverers mentioned by Samuel were Levites (Moses, Aaron, and Samuel) and that these individuals both initiate and conclude the list.[43]

12:10–17 Beginning with the Torah's most famous example of oppres-

---

[42] Cf. J. Blenkinsopp, "The Prophetic Reproach," *JBL* 90 (1971):267–78; and M. DeRoch, "Yahweh's *rîb* against Israel: A Reassessment of the So-called 'Prophetic Lawsuit' in the Preexilic Prophets, *JBL* 102 (1983):563–74.

[43] There is a subtle but consistent emphasis on the role of Levites in the events of both the Torah and the Former Prophets. Of course the Torah records the circumstances of Levi's birth (Gen 29:34) and his activities regarding Shechem (Gen 34:25–31); it also places special emphasis on the lives of Moses, Aaron, and Aaron's sons, as well as the duties and privileges of the Levites and Aaronic priests in almost the entirety of Exodus-Deuteronomy. This emphasis on the role of priests and Levites, though less conspicuous, is also present in the Former Prophets: cf. Josh 3:3–17; 4:3–18; 6:4–16; 8:33; 14:1–5; 17:4; 18:7; 19:51; 20:6; 21:1–42; 22:13–32; Judg 17:5–13; 18:3–31; 19:1–20:5; 1 Sam 1:1–4:22; 6:13–7:1; 7:3–10:25; 11:12–12:25; 13:8–14; 14:3,19,36–37; 15:1–3,10–35; 16:1–13; 21:1–9[2–10 Hb.]; 22:6–23; 23:6–12; 28:3,11–19; 30:7–8; 2 Sam 8:17; 15:24–30,35–36; 17:15–21; 19:11[12 Hb.]; 20:25–26; 23:20–22; 1 Kgs 1:7–8,19,25–26,32–39,42–45; 2:22–35; 4:2–5; 8:3–11; 12:31; 2 Kgs 11:4–17; 12:2–16[3–17 Hb.]; 16:10–16; 17:27–28; 19:2; 22:4–14; 23:2–9,24; 25:18. This suggests the possibility or even probability that Levitical authors and/or editors were involved in the production of these portions of the Hebrew Bible.

sion, supplication, and deliverance—the Exodus event, Samuel notes that though human agency was employed to accomplish the work, the liberators acted at the Lord's bidding: he "appointed" (v. 6), and he "sent" (v. 8) them. The Lord had provided this deliverance in response to their cry for help (cf. Exod 2:23). Though Moses and Aaron oversaw only the settlement of Israelite tribes east of the Jordan, they had in effect "settled them in this place."

The Lord's acts of deliverance did not cease once Israel entered the Promised Land; four of Samuel's five examples provide testimony to God's active presence among Israel within the land. Before mentioning these examples, however, the prophet was careful to clarify the reason for Israel's need of rescue. It was not because Israel served a weak god; rather, it was because Israel served a jealous and just God (cf. Exod 20:5; Deut 32:4). The nation had broken the first and most important requirement of the Sinai covenant— "they forgot the LORD their God" (v. 9; cf. Deut 8:11). Having done so, the Lord brought upon them one of the prescribed penalties of the covenant, foreign oppression (cf. Deut 28:25,29,33); "he sold them into the hand of" (v. 9) their enemies (v. 9).[44] Three geographically diverse enemies used by the Lord are listed by Samuel; one to the north (Hazor), one to the southwest (Philistia), and one to the east (Moab). The inclusion of these diverse regions probably is meant to be representative of all Israel's oppressors.

As a result of their suffering and loss, Israel "cried out" (v. 10; Hb. z^cq) to the Lord in anguish. Of great significance is the fact that their plea was not expressed as an explicit call for help; instead, it was an admission that they had violated the terms of the Sinai covenant. Their basic offense was twofold and complementary in nature: "we have forsaken" (Hb. ^czb, "abandoned, left") "the LORD, and served the Baals and the Ashtoreths" (v. 10). Israel's troubles were the direct result of one fundamental sin; they had violated the sacred relationship with their divine King. When they turned aside from devotion to the Lord, the people had not created a spiritual vacuum in their lives; instead, they had replaced the one God with many gods, filling their lives with a polytheistic fertility cult marked by devotion to Canaanite male ("Baals") and female deities ("Ashtoreths").

Yet when Israel repented, the Lord responded graciously to the peoples' pleas. In response to Israel's repentant words, the Lord "delivered" (Hb. nṣl, "rescued") them (v. 11). He did so by sending human agents—"Jerub-Baal,

---

[44] On three occasions the book of Judges indicates that Yahweh "sold" (מכר) Israel into the hands of specific enemies. Interestingly, these three references relate to Israel being oppressed by the three enemies Samuel mentioned here: Moab (Judg 3:12); the leaders of Hazor (Judg 4:2); and the Philistines (Judg 10:7). One possible inference from this precise correspondence is that 1, 2 Samuel was written with an awareness of the wording of the book of Judges. Rabbinic tradition, in fact, declares that Samuel wrote both Judges and Samuel (cf. *Baba Bathra* 14b).

Barak (Hb. "Bedan"),[45] Jephthah, and Samuel"[46]—who led Israel to impressive victories over their enemies. These human deliverers—and the freedom that they won for the nation—did not come as a result of the people's demands; instead, they were the by-product of Israel's return to the Lord.

Israel's oft-repeated pattern of repentance and return to the Lord in the face of a foreign threat was broken, however, in their demand for an earthly king (v. 12). Instead of first repenting of their sin, with the certain knowledge that the Lord would afterwards raise up a deliverer for them, they attempted to gain the benefits of a right relationship without actually returning to Yahweh. Far from being an act of repentance, their demand for a king (v. 13) was an act of insidious rebellion. Through their sin the people had "chosen" to have a king "such as all the other nations have" (8:5), and the Lord "set a king over" those who conformed to their choice. Samuel recognized their act for what it was and warned the people of the consequences of continued rebellion (v. 15).

However, Samuel also makes it clear that Israel could experience blessing under the new system of government, but that blessing was possible only as long as the Lord's position of superiority in society and religion was retained. Even the king must be a servant of the Lord.

Before the assembled group Samuel announced that the Lord would confirm the prophet's indictment with a "great thing" (Hb. *haddābār haggādôl;* lit., "the great word") that all present could see. Though this convocation was occurring during wheat harvest in the early part of the dry season (May-June), at Samuel's request the Lord would send a rainstorm (v. 17). This highly unusual meteorological event would be a sign, helping Israel to realize how displeased the Lord was that they had "asked for a king" (v. 17).

12:18–25 In a manner reminiscent of his Levitical predecessor, Moses (cf. Exod 9:23), Samuel called upon the Lord to bring thunder and rain. Exactly as predicted and requested, "the LORD sent thunder and rain" (v. 18), an event that would have damaged the heads of ripe grain, thereby causing

---

[45] The Hebrew text here does not use the name "Barak." This reading is supplied by the translators on the basis of context (cf. v. 9), the LXX, and the Syriac. "Bedan" is found nowhere else in Scripture; if it is not a textual corruption (the Hebrew letters 'daleth' (ד) and 'final nun' (ן)are similar to 'resh' (ר) and 'final kaph' (ך) or an alternate designation of Barak, it may refer to an otherwise unknown Israelite military leader. Other suggestions include Samson (an old rabbinical suggestion), Abdon and Jephthah. For a discussion of this issue, cf. H. Jacobson, "The Judge Bedan (1 Samuel xii 11)," *VT* 42 (1992):123–24; J. Day, "Bedan, Abdon, or Barak in 1 Samuel xii 11?" *VT* 43 (1993):261–64; and H. Johnson, "Bedan and Barak Reconsidered," *VT* 44 (1994):108–9.

[46] The Syriac, as well as the Lucianic recension of the LXX, substitutes the name Samson for Samuel: McCarter (*I Samuel,* 208) and NRSV accept this alternate reading. Clearly "Samuel" is the *lectio difficilior* but may for that reason also be the preferable reading. For an alternative view regarding the *lectio difficilior* principle, cf. B. Albrektson, "Difficilior Lectio Probabilior—A Rule of Textual Criticism and Its Use in OT Studies," *OTS* 21 (1981): 5–18.

grains of wheat to fall to the ground and the harvest to be reduced. The timing and nature of this occurrence were so striking that "all the people stood in awe of" (Hb. *yrʾ;* lit., "feared") not only the Lord but also Samuel (v. 18).

Why were the Israelites so moved by this event? Because they understood this disruption of the God-ordained pattern for the natural world to mirror Israel's disruption of the God-ordained pattern of relationship that was to exist between the nation and the Lord. As Israel moved out of her proper relational orbit with the Lord, the Lord had ordained that nature would move out of its proper orbit with the people (cf. Lev 26:19–22; Deut 28:18,22–24). The present demonstration terrified the Israelites, for they understood it to be a precursor of the more severe disturbances of nature prescribed in the Torah.[47]

The event produced the desired effect, a contrite confession of sin (v. 19). It is important to note here that the request for a king was not in itself sinful; the Torah envisioned a day in which Israel would decide to have a monarchy and made provisions for the establishment of this institution (cf. Gen 17:6; Deut 17:14–20). But for Israel to entrust its future to a human deliverer instead of anchoring it in their relationship with the Lord was both wicked and futile. Appropriately, Israel asked Samuel to pray that the Lord would not strike them all dead (v. 19).

Relying on the paradigm of history, Samuel allayed Israel's fears of imminent destruction. Israel had sinned many times in the past, yet the Lord had mercifully and patiently endured their misconduct. He had responded this way before and would do so again "for the sake of his great name" (v. 22; cf. Pss 25:11; 79:9; 106:8; 143:11; Isa 48:9; Jer 14:7,21; Ezek 20:9,22; Dan 9:19), not because of Israel's worthiness. Israel's previous efforts had never been the basis for God's selection of the nation, and their failures would not send him away. Israel was inextricably held in the iron grip of God's love (v. 22; cf. Rom 5:8; Titus 3:5–7).

The nation had not chosen this relationship with the Lord; nevertheless, because of it Israel possessed inescapable and eternal responsibilities. The nation's ongoing tasks were threefold: to "serve the LORD with all your heart" (vv. 21,24; cf. Deut 10:12; 11:13); "to fear the LORD" (v. 24; cf. Deut 6:2,13; 10:12); and to "consider" (lit., "see") "what great things he has done for you" (v. 24). This final task involved expectantly looking for evidences of the Lord's presence in the arena of national life, and giving due recognition to him for the attendant blessings. Taken as a whole, these three obligations required a total involvement of each person; they mandated external, observable activity as

---

[47] The Torah indicated that Yahweh would use famine, not floods, to bring judgment on Israel. However, within the Torah (Genesis 6–9) rains were used as a judgment on sin. Samuel may well have understood the mind-set that produced Israel's request to be as wicked as that of Noah's contemporaries (cf. Gen 6:5). Thus the use of rain instead of famine would have proven to be an especially harsh indictment of Israel's sin.

well as internal motivations, attitudes, and perceptions.[48]

Deities other than Yahweh might prove enticing, but they are all "useless idols" (Hb. *hattōhû;* lit., "the nothingness/emptiness").[49] Being nonentities, they offered no benefits and certainly no deliverance (v. 21).

As a Levite in the tradition of Moses, Samuel possessed two additional responsibilities, prayer and instruction. The Torah required Levites to instruct the people in the Lord's Law (cf. Deut 24:8; 33:10). Likewise, Samuel was duty-bound to pray for Israel. Throughout his lifetime Samuel had been a prophet like Moses (cf. introductory comments preceding 1:1); thus it was appropriate and even morally necessary that Samuel should follow Moses' example of prayer for the nation's welfare.[50] Thus, for Samuel to fail to pray— that is, to bring the people's needs before God—or to fail to teach—to bring God's words before the people—would be a sin (v. 23).

The final sentence Samuel spoke to an all-Israelite assembly is perhaps the most ominous of his career. In eight words (Hebrew) it summarizes the judgments of the Torah and foresees the ultimate futility of Israel's experiment with kingship. "If you persist in doing evil, both you and your king will be swept away" (v. 25). The verbal phrase translated in the NIV as "persist in doing evil" (lit., "if bringing about evil you should do evil") is an emphatic one, meant to heighten the emotional intensity of the prophet's warning. The message is a pointed one, and strikes at the heart of Israel's problem. The nation's real threat was not external, that is, one that could be faced and defeated by a king who would go out and lead Israel in battle (cf. 8:20). Rather it was internal and spiritual. The malignant faith condition that caused Israel to demand a king in preference to restoring a relationship with God was what would ultimately cause the nation to "be swept away" (v. 25; a form of *sāpâ*). No king, however mighty, could stop the tide of divine judgment that would roll against Israel in the day of the Lord's wrath.

---

[48] No doubt the biblical writer was speaking to his audience, us, through Samuel's words in this section. He intended all people possessing faith in the one true God to heed Samuel's admonition.

[49] The noun תֹהוּ does not denote "idol"; it is the same word used in Gen 1:2 to describe the vacant condition of the universe before God began performing the creative acts associated with the first week of creation. Samuel's avoidance of any term referring explicitly to idols is in keeping with a common prophetic practice (cf. Jer 18:15; Jonah 2:8[9 Hb.], Eng.). The use of substitute terms and phrases permitted them to avoid mentioning any deity other than Yahweh and thus to fulfill the letter of the Torah's command (cf. Exod 23:13).

[50] On four separate occasions the Torah uses the verb פלל to indicate that Moses prayed for Israel (Num 11:2; 21:7; Deut 9:20,26). On other occasions Moses is also portrayed as interceding in prayer for the nation (cf. Exod 32:11–14). No other leader in Israel's history is explicitly mentioned in Scripture as having prayed intercessory prayers for the nation so frequently.

5. Saul Demonstrates His Unfitness to Be Israel's King (13:1–14:46)

From a secular standpoint Saul was ideally equipped to be king; he was regal in appearance, had a demonstrated capacity to protect Israel's material interests by devising and executing successful military strategies, and enjoyed popular support. However, as this section makes clear, Saul and his kingship were fatally flawed and doomed to failure. From the standpoint of Samuel and the biblical narrator, the reason for Saul's failure is simple: the king was a spiritual rebel against the Lord's word. Saul is portrayed in this section as committing two of the most serious types of sin that are possible in a religious system grounded in revelation: rejection of the divine word, expressed here through active disobedience, and supplementation of the divine word with additional authoritative instruction. The former is manifested in his disobedience to the Lord's command issued in 10:8; the latter, in the imposition of foolish additional requirements on Israelite soldiers beyond those prescribed by the Torah. Through these early actions Saul established a pattern of disobedience and poor judgment from which he would not deviate. As a result, his dynasty would cease upon his death.

The author makes a powerful thematic statement through his selection and arrangement of material at this point in the book. By placing a story of royal disobedience immediately after a stern warning against "doing evil" (12:25), the audience easily connects Samuel's promise that "your king will be swept away" (12:25) with the prophet's pronouncement that "your kingship [NIV, "kingdom"] will not endure" (13:14).[51] The didactic purpose underlying the narrator's art is clear. Through the skillful use of historical narrative the author affirms the central tenet of the Torah: keep the Lord's command and he will establish you (13:13); rebel against his word and you will lose both your heritage and your destiny (13:14).

(1) Saul Disobeys the Lord's Command to Wait for Samuel (13:1–16a)[52]

¹Saul was [thirty] years old when he became king, and he reigned over Israel [forty-] two years.

²Saul chose three thousand men from Israel; two thousand were with him at Micmash and in the hill country of Bethel, and a thousand were with Jonathan at Gibeah in Benjamin. The rest of the men he sent back to their homes.

---

[51] This assertion is in keeping with the conclusions reached by J. Martin, "Studies in 1 and 2 Samuel, Part I—The Structure of 1 and 2 Samuel," *BibSac* 141 (1984): 28–42.

[52] For suggestions on the preaching value of this chapter, cf. R. A. Culpepper, "Narrative Criticism as a Tool for Proclamation: 1 Samuel 13," *RevExp* 84 (1987): 33–40; and T. G. Smothers, "Historical Criticism as a Tool for Proclamation," *RevExp* 84 (1987): 23–32.

³Jonathan attacked the Philistine outpost at Geba, and the Philistines heard about it. Then Saul had the trumpet blown throughout the land and said, "Let the Hebrews hear!" ⁴So all Israel heard the news: "Saul has attacked the Philistine outpost, and now Israel has become a stench to the Philistines." And the people were summoned to join Saul at Gilgal.

⁵The Philistines assembled to fight Israel, with three thousand chariots, six thousand charioteers, and soldiers as numerous as the sand on the seashore. They went up and camped at Micmash, east of Beth Aven. ⁶When the men of Israel saw that their situation was critical and that their army was hard pressed, they hid in caves and thickets, among the rocks, and in pits and cisterns. ⁷Some Hebrews even crossed the Jordan to the land of Gad and Gilead.

Saul remained at Gilgal, and all the troops with him were quaking with fear. ⁸He waited seven days, the time set by Samuel; but Samuel did not come to Gilgal, and Saul's men began to scatter. ⁹So he said, "Bring me the burnt offering and the fellowship offerings." And Saul offered up the burnt offering. ¹⁰Just as he finished making the offering, Samuel arrived, and Saul went out to greet him.

¹¹"What have you done?" asked Samuel.

Saul replied, "When I saw that the men were scattering, and that you did not come at the set time, and that the Philistines were assembling at Micmash, ¹²I thought, 'Now the Philistines will come down against me at Gilgal, and I have not sought the LORD's favor.' So I felt compelled to offer the burnt offering."

¹³"You acted foolishly," Samuel said. "You have not kept the command the LORD your God gave you; if you had, he would have established your kingdom over Israel for all time. ¹⁴But now your kingdom will not endure; the LORD has sought out a man after his own heart and appointed him leader of his people, because you have not kept the LORD's command."

¹⁵Then Samuel left Gilgal and went up to Gibeah in Benjamin, and Saul counted the men who were with him. They numbered about six hundred.

¹⁶Saul and his son Jonathan and the men with them were staying in Gibeah in Benjamin,

13:1 As in the narratives of seventeen other kings of Israel and Judah, the author marked his transition into a discussion of core events of a king's activities by inserting a chronological note containing the king's age at the time of ascension to the throne as well as the duration of his reign.[53] The Hebrew text regarding Saul (lit., "Saul was the son of a year [= one year old] when he became king, and he ruled over Israel two years") contains problems that have caused translators and commentators to deal creatively with this

---

[53] Cf. 2 Sam 2:10 (Ish-Bosheth); 5:4 (David); 1 Kgs 14:21 (Rehoboam); 2 Kgs 8:17 (Jehoram), 26 (Ahaziah); 11:1 (Joash); 15:2 (Azariah), 33 (Jotham); 16:2 (Ahaz); 18:2 (Hezekiah); 21:1 (Manasseh), 19 (Amon); 22:1 (Josiah); 23:21 (Jehoahaz), 36 (Jehoiakim); 24:8 (Jehoiachin), 18 (Zedekiah).

verse.[54] The NIV states that Saul's age was "thirty," E. H. Merrill suggests he was forty; yet these are merely guesses and are unsupported by any text.[55] Especially in light of Acts 13:21, it is best to regard the extant Hebrew text as corrupted at this point and avoid speculation regarding Saul's age at the time of his ascension to Israel's throne.

The NIV's declaration that Saul "reigned over Israel forty-two years" represents an attempt to align this verse with Paul's reckoning (Acts 13:21), yet it may contradict the writer's intentions at this point. Perhaps the writer purposely used the smaller number to indicate that Saul reigned only two years before the Lord disqualified him from kingship (cf. 15:26); Paul's larger number would then represent the number of years Saul functioned as king, in spite of his rejection by the Lord.

13:2–7 True to the elders' wishes (cf. 8:20), Saul set about the task of defending Israel against foreign enemies. The apparent objective of the troop deployments described here was the removal of a Philistine administrative center at Geba in the Israelite heartland; the presence of this enemy outpost less than three miles from Israel's original capital would have constituted a severe threat to the early Israelite monarchy. Furthermore, since Geba was a city set aside for the Aaronic priesthood (cf. Josh 21:7), the return of this city to Israelite hands would have been a way of strengthening the worship of the Lord in Israel. The necessary first steps in this mission were assembling and deploying an armed force. Accordingly, "Saul chose three thousand men from Israel" (v. 2) for the job, and divided them up into two groups.

Saul took command of the larger force, some "two thousand" men, and stationed them at Micmash (modern Mukhmas), about 4.5 miles northeast of the capital city of Gibeah. The location was strategic, since it was near a crucial pass on the Way to Ophrah, a road in Israel's central highlands that led to Geba. Saul's firstborn son Jonathan was given command of the remaining men, who were stationed "at Gibeah in Benjamin," Israel's capital at this time. Though others had volunteered for this military campaign, Saul chose not to use them and sent them "back to their homes."

Jonathan's forces attacked the Philistines at Geba (v. 3) and, based on both Israelite and Philistine reactions, apparently met with considerable success. As

---

[54] In an effort to remain congruent with the Hebrew text, a targum stated, "Like a one-year-old who has no sins was Saul when he became king" (McCarter, *1 Samuel*, 222). The LXX[B] omitted the verse entirely. Josephus variously declared the length of Saul's reign to be twenty (*Ant.* 10.8.4) and forty years (*Ant.* 6.14.9); Acts 13:21 states that Saul reigned forty years. M. Noth (*History of Israel*, trans. P. Ackroyd [New York: Harper & Row, 1960], 176–77) notes that the figure of two years fits the Deuteronomist's chronological framework; but Klein (*1 Samuel*, 125) suggests that the number two may apply only to Saul's control over Judah, as opposed to all Israel.

[55] E. H. Merrill, "1 Samuel," in *Bible Knowledge Commentary: Old Testament*, ed. J. F. Walvoord and R. B. Zuck (n.p.: Victor, 1985), 431–55.

a result of the assault, the Israelites had "become a stench to the Philistines," that is, had inflamed the passions of the Philistines to the point of retaliation (cf. Gen 34:30; Exod 5:21; 1 Sam 27:12; 2 Sam 10:6; 16:21). As a result, they immediately "assembled to fight Israel" (v. 5). The Israelites trumpeted news of Jonathan's attack "throughout the land" (v. 3) and mustered a large force "at Gilgal" (v. 4) in preparation for the expected Philistine response.

Though Israel anticipated a Philistine counterattack, they were totally unprepared for the magnitude of the Philistine reaction: "three thousand chariots,[56] six thousand charioteers, and soldiers as numerous as the sand on the seashore" (v. 5) were dispatched to Micmash, where they took possession of the site of Saul's original military camp. The Philistines' occupation of Saul's base appears to have been a tit-for-tat response to the Israelite occupation of their former center of operations at Geba. When the Israelites witnessed this overwhelming show of Philistine force, they understood "that their situation was critical" (v. 6); troop defections (cf. 14:21) and mass desertions quickly resulted. The deserters either hid (v. 6) or left the Promised Land entirely, going east of the Jordan (v. 7). Saul and the rest of the troops who did not leave "remained at Gilgal," where they were "quaking with fear" (v. 7).

13:8–16a In accordance with the Lord's word (cf. 10:8), Saul was in Gilgal, where he anxiously awaited the passage of the "seven days" (v. 8) and the prophet Samuel's arrival.[57] The king's timely obedience to Samuel's directive to go to Gilgal had likely saved his life since to have remained at Micmash would have meant certain defeat at the hand of the Philistines.

However, Saul's obedience was only partial; he had also been directed to

---

[56] The figure three thousand is based on readings found in the Lucianic recension of the LXX and the Syriac. The MT states that the Philistines deployed thirty thousand chariots. This figure may safely be regarded as an error introduced in the process of textual transmission since there would have been an insufficient number of charioteers to use them. Elsewhere in Scripture the largest chariot force mentioned is seventeen hundred (2 Sam 8:4); even wealthy King Solomon possessed only fourteen hundred chariots (1 Kgs 10:26). It is quite possible, therefore, that the figure of three thousand is also the result of a corrupt textual tradition.

[57] Youngblood ("1, 2 Samuel," 655) and Klein (*1 Samuel,* 126) are in apparent agreement with my interpretation of the chronology here. However, other evangelical biblical scholars indicate that there is no connection between the command issued by Samuel in 10:8 and the present narrative. Merrill ("1 Samuel," 445) indicates that there was a two-year gap between 10:8 and 13:8 (cf. his interpretation of 13:1). Gordon (*I and II Samuel,* 133) states that "an interval of many years separates" these two sections; apparently troubled by some implications of this conclusion, however, he goes on to affirm that "there is the closest literary link between the instruction given in 10:8 and this meeting" and that "plainly the earlier verse is meant to key the whole question of Saul's exercise of kingship and of his failed dynastic hopes (cf. vv. 13f.), to the issue of obedience." Baldwin (*1 and 2 Samuel,* 104) suggests that 13:8 refers to "a similar instruction [to 10:8] given for this occasion also," supporting this with the postulation of a practice of Samuel "to come within seven days in any time of crisis"—an admirable but unconvincing suggestion since many crises would have required faster response times, and Samuel is nowhere else recorded as having done this.

wait until Samuel arrived and administrated over the prescribed sacrifices. Since sacrifices were normally offered up twice a day, in the early morning and at twilight (cf. Num 28:1–6), Samuel could have arrived at any time on the seventh day and still fulfilled his role in the process.[58] Unfortunately Saul did not give Samuel an opportunity to do so but offered the "burnt offering" (v. 9; Hb. ʿōlâ) himself. Before the king could offer up the "fellowship offerings" (Hb. šĕlāmîm), however, he was interrupted by Samuel's arrival (v. 10). Saul "went out to greet" (v. 10; lit., "to bless"[59]) the prophet.

Samuel's curt response in the form of a question—"What have you done?" (v. 11; cf. Gen 3:13)—makes clear that the prophet was not interested in social niceties at this time. Saul responded to the question defensively, blaming three other parties for his act of disobedience: his soldiers, who "were scattering"; Samuel, who "did not come at the set time"; and the Philistines, who "were assembling at Micmash" (v. 11). He was "compelled" (lit., "forced himself") to perform the sacrifice because he feared that the Philistines would attack him before he had "sought the LORD's favor" (v. 12). It is ironic—and symptomatic of Saul's spiritual dullness—that the king believed he could obtain the Lord's favor through an act of disobedience.

Brushing aside Saul's excuses, Samuel condemned the king's actions as those of a fool. No line of reasoning, however compelling, could ever justify disobedience to the Lord. Saul had disobeyed the Lord's "command" (v. 13) and had to suffer the penalties. The employment of the term "command" (miṣwâ), used elsewhere to refer to Torah mandates (cf. Exod 24:12, etc.), places Samuel's words spoken in his role as a prophet of Yahweh on the same plane as the laws given through Moses at Sinai. This equating of the authority of Samuel's words with those of Moses, through the use of miṣwâ is in keeping with the theology of the Former and Latter Prophets, which recognizes every word spoken through divine inspiration as being equally authoritative (cf. Pss 19:8; 89:31; 112:1; 119:6,10,19,60,96,115,131,166,176).

The prophet mentioned two consequences resulting from Saul's disobedience, one with long-range implications and one with immediate implications. First, the Lord voided plans to prosper the Saulide dynasty's future: "He would have established your dynasty ["kingdom"] for all time. But now your dynasty ["kingdom"] will not endure" (vv. 13–14). As in the case of the dynastic promises made to David, there was a conditional dimension to the agreement that

---

[58] At least one scholar has concluded that Samuel deliberately broke his appointment at Gilgal in order to sabotage Saul's kingship; cf. Polzin, *Samuel and the Deuteronomist*, 129–31. This position is to be rejected because it is unsupported by the text—he did in fact arrive on the seventh day—and contrary to the spirit of the Samuel narratives, which consistently portray Samuel as a faithful servant of Yahweh.

[59] The writer's depiction of Saul "blessing" Samuel while placing a curse on himself through an act of disobedience is an apparent employment of irony.

required obedience to the Lord for covenant fulfillment (cf. 1 Kgs 11:11).[60]
Second and more immediately, "the LORD has sought out a man after his own
heart and appointed him leader of his people" (v. 14). The term translated as
"leader" (Hb. *nāgîd*) is the same one used earlier to describe Saul's present
position as king (cf. 9:16; 10:1). Unlike Saul, this new leader would be a man
"after [the Lord's] own heart," a phrase that may refer (1) to the person's profound commitment to the Lord or (2) to the fact that the Lord had selected that
person.[61]

The events included in the telling of this episode serve to create a tragic parallel between Saul and Adam (cf. Gen 3). Both men were the heads of their
respective social institutions; both violated commands given them by the Lord;
both expressed an unwillingness to take personal responsibility for their
actions. Because of sin Adam lost the opportunity for eternal life in the garden;
for the same cause Saul lost the opportunity for an enduring dynasty in the
Promised Land. These parallels are not accidental but result from a consistent
theological perspective that views loss of position and privilege as inevitable
consequences of violating the Lord's commandments.

"Samuel left Gilgal" (v. 15), apparently without offering up any of the sacrifices he had come to make (cf. 10:8). The Hebrew text indicates that the
prophet went to Gibeah, an assertion lacking in the LXX, while Saul and
"about six hundred" men apparently went to reinforce Jonathan's forces at
"Geba ["Gibeah"] of Benjamin" (v. 16).[62]

(2) Saul Makes a Foolish Vow before the Lord (13:16b–14:46)

**while the Philistines camped at Micmash. [17]Raiding parties went out from the
Philistine camp in three detachments. One turned toward Ophrah in the vicinity of
Shual, [18]another toward Beth Horon, and the third toward the borderland over-
looking the Valley of Zeboim facing the desert.**

**[19]Not a blacksmith could be found in the whole land of Israel, because the Phi-
listines had said, "Otherwise the Hebrews will make swords or spears!" [20]So all
Israel went down to the Philistines to have their plowshares, mattocks, axes and
sickles sharpened. [21]The price was two thirds of a shekel for sharpening plowshares and mattocks, and a third of a shekel for sharpening forks and axes and for
repointing goads.**

[60]Cf. the discussion regarding the conditional nature of dynastic covenants in A. E. Hill and
J. H. Walton, *A Survey of the Old Testament* (Grand Rapids: Zondervan, 1991), 198–99.

[61]For further discussion of translation options, cf. McCarter, *I Samuel*, 229.

[62]The NIV rejects the MT reading at this point, justifying their decision by suggesting that
"Geba" is a variant of "Gibeah" (cf. NIV n. at 13:16). However, Gibeah and Geba are clearly
treated as two separate locations in this episode (cf. 13:2–3) and are elsewhere translated as such
by the NIV. Jonathan had just stormed Geba (13:3), and it was militarily appropriate to consolidate
the Israelite hold on this city before withdrawing the troops. Perhaps the site was also more defensible than Gibeah, due to its location and possible Philistine construction at the site.

²²So on the day of the battle not a soldier with Saul and Jonathan had a sword or spear in his hand; only Saul and his son Jonathan had them.
²³Now a detachment of Philistines had gone out to the pass at Micmash.

¹One day Jonathan son of Saul said to the young man bearing his armor, "Come, let's go over to the Philistine outpost on the other side." But he did not tell his father.
²Saul was staying on the outskirts of Gibeah under a pomegranate tree in Migron. With him were about six hundred men, ³among whom was Ahijah, who was wearing an ephod. He was a son of Ichabod's brother Ahitub son of Phinehas, the son of Eli, the LORD's priest in Shiloh. No one was aware that Jonathan had left.
⁴On each side of the pass that Jonathan intended to cross to reach the Philistine outpost was a cliff; one was called Bozez, and the other Seneh. ⁵One cliff stood to the north toward Micmash, the other to the south toward Geba.
⁶Jonathan said to his young armor-bearer, "Come, let's go over to the outpost of those uncircumcised fellows. Perhaps the LORD will act in our behalf. Nothing can hinder the LORD from saving, whether by many or by few."
⁷"Do all that you have in mind," his armor-bearer said. "Go ahead; I am with you heart and soul."
⁸Jonathan said, "Come, then; we will cross over toward the men and let them see us. ⁹If they say to us, 'Wait there until we come to you,' we will stay where we are and not go up to them. ¹⁰But if they say, 'Come up to us,' we will climb up, because that will be our sign that the LORD has given them into our hands."
¹¹So both of them showed themselves to the Philistine outpost. "Look!" said the Philistines. "The Hebrews are crawling out of the holes they were hiding in." ¹²The men of the outpost shouted to Jonathan and his armor-bearer, "Come up to us and we'll teach you a lesson."
So Jonathan said to his armor-bearer, "Climb up after me; the LORD has given them into the hand of Israel."
¹³Jonathan climbed up, using his hands and feet, with his armor-bearer right behind him. The Philistines fell before Jonathan, and his armor-bearer followed and killed behind him. ¹⁴In that first attack Jonathan and his armor-bearer killed some twenty men in an area of about half an acre.
¹⁵Then panic struck the whole army—those in the camp and field, and those in the outposts and raiding parties—and the ground shook. It was a panic sent by God.
¹⁶Saul's lookouts at Gibeah in Benjamin saw the army melting away in all directions. ¹⁷Then Saul said to the men who were with him, "Muster the forces and see who has left us." When they did, it was Jonathan and his armor-bearer who were not there.
¹⁸Saul said to Ahijah, "Bring the ark of God." (At that time it was with the Israelites.) ¹⁹While Saul was talking to the priest, the tumult in the Philistine camp increased more and more. So Saul said to the priest, "Withdraw your hand."
²⁰Then Saul and all his men assembled and went to the battle. They found the Philistines in total confusion, striking each other with their swords. ²¹Those Hebrews who had previously been with the Philistines and had gone up with them to their camp went over to the Israelites who were with Saul and Jonathan.

²²When all the Israelites who had hidden in the hill country of Ephraim heard that the Philistines were on the run, they joined the battle in hot pursuit. ²³So the LORD rescued Israel that day, and the battle moved on beyond Beth Aven.

²⁴Now the men of Israel were in distress that day, because Saul had bound the people under an oath, saying, "Cursed be any man who eats food before evening comes, before I have avenged myself on my enemies!" So none of the troops tasted food.

²⁵The entire army entered the woods, and there was honey on the ground. ²⁶When they went into the woods, they saw the honey oozing out, yet no one put his hand to his mouth, because they feared the oath. ²⁷But Jonathan had not heard that his father had bound the people with the oath, so he reached out the end of the staff that was in his hand and dipped it into the honeycomb. He raised his hand to his mouth, and his eyes brightened. ²⁸Then one of the soldiers told him, "Your father bound the army under a strict oath, saying, 'Cursed be any man who eats food today!' That is why the men are faint."

²⁹Jonathan said, "My father has made trouble for the country. See how my eyes brightened when I tasted a little of this honey. ³⁰How much better it would have been if the men had eaten today some of the plunder they took from their enemies. Would not the slaughter of the Philistines have been even greater?"

³¹That day, after the Israelites had struck down the Philistines from Micmash to Aijalon, they were exhausted. ³²They pounced on the plunder and, taking sheep, cattle and calves, they butchered them on the ground and ate them, together with the blood. ³³Then someone said to Saul, "Look, the men are sinning against the LORD by eating meat that has blood in it."

"You have broken faith," he said. "Roll a large stone over here at once." ³⁴Then he said, "Go out among the men and tell them, 'Each of you bring me your cattle and sheep, and slaughter them here and eat them. Do not sin against the LORD by eating meat with blood still in it.'"

So everyone brought his ox that night and slaughtered it there. ³⁵Then Saul built an altar to the LORD; it was the first time he had done this.

³⁶Saul said, "Let us go down after the Philistines by night and plunder them till dawn, and let us not leave one of them alive."

"Do whatever seems best to you," they replied.

But the priest said, "Let us inquire of God here."

³⁷So Saul asked God, "Shall I go down after the Philistines? Will you give them into Israel's hand?" But God did not answer him that day.

³⁸Saul therefore said, "Come here, all you who are leaders of the army, and let us find out what sin has been committed today. ³⁹As surely as the LORD who rescues Israel lives, even if it lies with my son Jonathan, he must die." But not one of the men said a word.

⁴⁰Saul then said to all the Israelites, "You stand over there; I and Jonathan my son will stand over here."

"Do what seems best to you," the men replied.

⁴¹Then Saul prayed to the LORD, the God of Israel, "Give me the right answer." And Jonathan and Saul were taken by lot, and the men were cleared. ⁴²Saul said, "Cast the lot between me and Jonathan my son." And Jonathan was taken.

⁴³Then Saul said to Jonathan, "Tell me what you have done."

So Jonathan told him, "I merely tasted a little honey with the end of my staff. And now must I die?"

⁴⁴Saul said, "May God deal with me, be it ever so severely, if you do not die, Jonathan."

⁴⁵But the men said to Saul, "Should Jonathan die—he who has brought about this great deliverance in Israel? Never! As surely as the LORD lives, not a hair of his head will fall to the ground, for he did this today with God's help." So the men rescued Jonathan, and he was not put to death.

⁴⁶Then Saul stopped pursuing the Philistines, and they withdrew to their own land.

13:16b–23 Having established Micmash as their base camp, the Philistines sent out "raiding parties" (v. 17; Hb. *hamašḥît*; lit., "the destroyer/ spoiler") to control three of the roads that provided access to Micmash, one going northwest to Ophrah, one going southwest to Beth Horon, and one going east to the Valley of Zeboiim. A fourth detachment was sent later "to the pass at Micmash" (v. 23) to prevent Israelite troops moving north from Geba. These Philistine troop deployments had the double benefit of securing the Philistine camp at Micmash while at the same time sealing off Saul's camp at Geba from any reinforcements that might come from Israelite tribes to the north.

Clearly, Saul and his troops were very much at risk with the largest recorded Philistine army camped less than two miles away and all hope of assistance from the northern tribes being denied them. The situation was made even worse by the great disparity between Israelite and Philistine armaments. The Philistines possessed large numbers of metal weapons.[63] But by strictly controlling Israel's access to metallurgical technology and technicians, the Philistines effectively limited the entire Israelite arsenal to weapons made of wood and stone—arrows, slings, javelins, clubs, knives, and the like. Israel's weapons could certainly be deadly, but they were inferior to those made of bronze and iron, the strategic metal of that day. The Philistine embargo was so effective that when armed conflict broke out between Israel's royal army and the Philistines, "only Saul and his son Jonathan" had a metal "sword or spear" (v. 22).

The Philistines' control of Israel's access to metal also meant that Israel had no blacksmiths (v. 19). The men of Israel even had to rely on the Philistines to have their agricultural tools serviced—a step necessary to prevent metal in these implements from being reshaped into offensive weapons (cf. Joel 3:10). The Philistines used their monopoly on technology for economic gain as well, charging as much as a pim ("two-thirds of a shekel") of silver, about eight grams, for simple repairs. No doubt this fee was considered outrageous and had the effect of oppressing Israel economically as well.

---

[63] For examples of iron implements recovered from four Philistine sites in Palestine, cf. G. E. Wright, "Philistine Coffins and Mercenaries," *BA* 22 (1959): 54–66.

14:1–5 The author carefully included details regarding the magnitude of the Philistine threat and the minimal level of Israel's military readiness in 13:5–23 in order to provide an effective backdrop for the theologically rich narrative account of chap. 14. Clearly, from a human standpoint Israel's situation was hopeless: the Israelite band was dispirited; it was cut off from its northern comrades; and it was vastly outnumbered by a nearby enemy that possessed thousands of chariots, horses, and soldiers with superior armaments. Yet as the present narrative demonstrates, "The LORD rescued Israel that day" (14:23; cf. Exod 14:30) as the direct result of a single individual's bold faith. The point of the passage is also the point of Exodus 14, to which some interesting parallels exist;[64] no situation is hopeless for Israel because Yahweh is Israel's God, and "nothing can hinder the LORD from saving" (v. 6). Furthermore, as this passage demonstrates, faith-filled human initiative can serve as an entrance point for the Lord's saving action.

In the first instance of what will be a persistent pattern throughout the remainder of 1 Samuel, the narrator draws a sharp contrast between Jonathan and his father. Here the contrast is in how they express their relationship with Yahweh in a military context. Whereas Saul the commander publicly dishonored the Lord through fear-inspired disobedience, Jonathan the warrior would bring honor to the Lord through his fearless faith. Jonathan's faith in the face of a military threat (cf. Deut 20:1) activates the Torah promise of Deut 28:7.

The narrative of chap. 14 opens at a point chronologically and geographically detached from the events of chap. 13. Saul and his troops are now back in Gibeah, and the king has established a public royal court complete with armed guards and an Aaronic priest in attendance. Apparently lacking a fit administrative building in Gibeah, Saul practiced a court custom known in Israel since the time of the Judges (cf. Judg 4:5) and presided outdoors, "under a pomegranate tree in Migron" (v. 2)[65] on the outskirts of the royal city. Accompanying him

---

[64] The present passage and Exod 14 have at least the following commonalities: (1) Israel was being pursued by a large force featuring a sizable chariot force; (2) Israel was blocked from escape by a seemingly insuperable barrier; (3) Israel panicked when the large force approached them; (4) Yahweh intervened in the natural order to dispirit Israel's enemy; (5) a single individual acted in faith to help bring about a divine act of deliverance; (6) the narrator concluded by noting "That day Yahweh saved Israel." Despite the obvious differences between the passages, I believe the author shaped the present account through the selective use of historical details in order to create a deliberate parallel with Exod 14. If such is the case, then the theological purpose of this present section is to reinforce and make historically relevant the message of the Torah; 1Sam 13:5–14:23 could thus be marshalled as further evidence to suggest that the Torah existed in a fixed literary form prior to the writing of the Former Prophets.

[65] The term "Migron," from the Hb. root גרן ("threshing floor"), may simply refer to a smooth, polished rock surface usually reserved for threshing located just outside the main entrance to the city. Cf. McCarter's translation "on the threshing floor" (*I Samuel*, 232). Because cities were built on hills and threshing required abundant wind, such as was most likely to be present on hilltops, threshing floors for cities were often located near the entrance to a city. Cf. also 1 Kgs 22:10.

were "about six hundred men" (v. 2; cf. 13:15) and Eli's grandson Ahijah, who as a descendant of Aaron "was wearing an ephod" (v. 3), the official dress of an ordained Yahwistic priest (cf. Exod 28:4).

The focal events were set in motion when Jonathan acted independently of his father by initiating a small, covert military mission "to the Philistine outpost on the other side" (v. 1). Going north on the road to Micmash, Jonathan and his armor-bearer encountered a Philistine outpost overlooking a narrow pass in the Wadi Suweinit flanked by two steep rock outcroppings (lit., "tooth of bedrock"). The site was well-known to the locals, who had even given names to the rock formations: "Bozez" (meaning unknown) and "Seneh" (= "Shrub" [?]; v. 4).

14:6–10 As they approached the Philistine camp, Jonathan reaffirmed his intentions to "go over to the outpost of those uncircumcised fellows" (v. 6). The derisive term $h\bar{a}^{c}\bar{a}r\bar{e}l\hat{\imath}m$, translated as "uncircumcised fellows," has religious connotations, highlighting the fact that the Philistines were outside the covenant of Yahwistic faith (cf. Gen 17:10–14). Jonathan also used this time of pre-battle preparation to reaffirm his faith with a prayerful utterance ("Perhaps the LORD will act in our behalf"; v. 6) and a confession of confidence in Yahweh's power to bring victory against all odds ("Nothing can hinder the LORD from saving, whether by many or by few"; v. 6; cf. Rom 8:31).

Jonathan received encouragement from his armor-bearer, who was with him "heart and soul" (v. 7). The armor-bearer's response, more eloquent in the Hebrew (lit., "I [am] with you like your heart [is with you]"), is a pledge of total support for whatever actions Jonathan might take. This degree of loyalty would be needed, especially in view of Jonathan's blueprint for action.

Jonathan's plan for fighting the Philistines defied all military logic. First, he would give up the element of surprise: "We will cross over toward the men and let them see us" (v. 8). Second, he would avoid a skirmish with the Philistines if they abandoned their position of strategic superiority on the hilltop and exhausted themselves coming down to his position. On the other hand, he would attack if they challenged him to scale the sheer rock wall and then take them on. The plan is so absurd that if it did succeed it could only be because "the LORD has given them into our hands" (v. 10). Jonathan may have intended the phrase "the LORD has given them" as a wordplay on his own name, since it was expressed with a form of ntn and $yhwh$, the two lexical roots comprising his name.

14:11–14 The two men proceeded in accordance with Jonathan's plan (v. 11). The Philistines, who were mildly surprised by this foolhardy act, responded derisively, comparing "the Hebrews" to brute beasts "crawling out of the holes they were hiding in." They then taunted Jonathan and his armor-bearer with an artful double entendre, inviting them to "come up to us and we will teach [="inflict punishment on"] you" (v. 12; cf. Judg 8:16).

Jonathan interpreted the Philistines' words as the divine confirmation that the Lord would make him victorious (v. 12). Ordering his armor-bearer to follow (v. 12), the two began a difficult climb that required "hands and feet" (v. 13). Perhaps the task was made even more challenging by stones and arrows rained down on them from the Philistines.

Against all odds, Jonathan and his companion arrived safely at the top with enough strength and stamina to challenge and exterminate a squad of armed Philistines. When the battle was over, "some twenty men" (v. 14) lay dead in a tract of land no larger than what a yoke of oxen could plow in half a day (NIV "about half an acre"; NRSV "an area half a furrow long in an acre of land").

News of Jonathan's stunning victory over the hostile forces spread quickly to the main Philistine camp, situated little more than one-half mile away. The massacre of twenty well-armed comrades by two Israelites surely would have been taken by the Philistines as an omen that their gods were not with them in the present campaign. This conclusion was reinforced by a perfectly timed tremor that served as evidence that the Lord, the God of Israelite lands, was moving against those who had violated his space.

14:15–17 As a result the Philistines were struck with "a panic sent by God" (v. 15; cf. NRSV, "great panic"), which led to a headlong retreat (v. 16). Learning of this activity through his intelligence network, Saul mustered the forces to determine who was responsible for the incident that touched off the Philistine stampede. He quickly discovered "it was Jonathan and his armor-bearer" (v. 17).

14:18–23 With the Philistine forces terrified and on the run, the time was right for the Israelites to attack. But according to the Torah, no Israelite army was to enter battle prior to a priestly address (Deut 20:4–5). With an apparent awareness of this requirement, Saul ordered the Aaronic priest Ahijah to "bring the ark of God" (v. 18).[66] While the king and the priest were in front of the army, "the tumult in the Philistine camp increased" (v. 19).

Sensing that he was about to lose a golden opportunity to rout the enemy, Saul did the unthinkable—he ordered Ahijah to suspend his priestly activities before they were completed. This incredible interruption of the divine pattern—an action without precedent in the Bible—was intended to enable Israel to win an even greater victory over the Philistines. But for readers who were informed by the Torah, it meant that Saul was unfit to fulfill the task of leading Israel against their enemies (cf. 8:20). It also added one more image in the narrative montage that depicts Saul as spiritually benighted and insensitive to the Lord's ways. Furthermore, in light of Israel's diminished victory against the

---

[66] The LXX substitutes the phrase "ephod of God" (Hb. אֵפוֹד אֱלֹהִים) for the "ark of God" (אֲרוֹן אֱלֹהִים); Josephus (*Ant.* 6.7.3) follows this tradition as well. The fact that the phrase "ephod of God" is absent from the entire Hebrew Bible, whereas the phrase "ark of God" occurs thirteen times, suggests the MT reading is superior.

Philistines, it reinforced a fundamental teaching of the Torah; any breach of the Lord's instruction diminishes the good that could have resulted (cf. 14:30).

When Saul and his men reached the Philistines, he found them fighting themselves (v. 20). This self-destruction can be attributed to a blunder the Philistines had made earlier: they had permitted some "Hebrews" (v. 21)[67] with divided loyalties to join their ranks. When the tide of battle turned in Israel's favor, the non-Philistines "went over to the Israelites who were with Saul and Jonathan" (v. 21). Now soldiers wearing Philistine markings and wielding Philistine weapons were fighting Philistines—with disastrous consequences for Israel's enemies! It was a mistake the Philistines would never make again (cf. 29:3–9).

The Philistines made a mad dash westward "beyond Beth Aven" (v. 23) to return to their homeland. Saul's forces swelled as other Israelites, previously immobilized by fear and hopelessness, joined them (v. 23). Though many Israelites had participated in the battle that day, including former turncoats and deserters, the narrator does not give Israel credit for the victory. Instead, it was the Lord who "rescued Israel that day" (v. 23). Much as he had previously used another unlikely Israelite military force to demonstrate his power to deliver Israel from an overwhelming army (cf. Judg 7:6,16–25), so he reaffirmed here that "nothing can hinder the LORD from saving, whether by many or by few" (v. 6).

14:24–30 The Torah did not require soldiers to refrain from eating during battle; it was a command conceived of by Saul in an apparent effort to gain the Lord's favor. Saul's zeal is understandable; because victory over Israel's oppressors could only be accomplished with the Lord's help, it was appropriate for Israel's soldiers to prepare for battle by consecrating themselves. On the other hand, Saul's use of the phrase "my enemies" (v. 24) may suggest that his motivation for fighting the Philistines was personal vengeance, not zeal for the Lord.

Other military leaders in Israel placed certain religious requirements on their men prior to battle: David, for example, required those accompanying him on military missions to follow Torah holiness regulations while on task (cf. 21:5), particularly those regarding sexual abstinence (cf. Exod 19:15). However, Saul's demand that his soldiers deny themselves food at the very time when caloric needs were at their greatest was ill-conceived. As a result of Saul's misguided and foolish zeal "the men of Israel were in distress that day" (v. 24).

The focus of the battle left the roads and entered the woods as the Philistines

---

[67] The author's use of הָעִבְרִים instead of the expected בְּנֵי יִשְׂרָאֵל here is no doubt intended derogatorily. The willingness of these individuals to transfer their loyalties to the Philistines had proven that they were unworthy to be called by a covenant name. Cf. Baldwin, *1 and 2 Samuel,* 108–9.

attempted to evade the Israelites. In the forests of the "land flowing with milk and honey" (Exod 3:8, etc.) ground bees were prevalent, and honey, an efficient and convenient source of energy, was "on the ground" (v. 25). Though the Israelite soldiers "saw the honey oozing out" (v. 26) from disturbed nests, they were afraid to eat it (v. 26).

Jonathan, however, disobeyed his father and violated the oath in ignorance. The action reinvigorated him, a fact expressed by the Hebrew idiom "his eyes brightened" (v. 27; cf. Ps 13:3 [Eng. 13:4]).

Jonathan's actions did not go unnoticed, and a nearby soldier informed him of the oath his father forced the army to take, the accompanying curse, and the unfortunate results. Using theologically significant vocabulary, Jonathan responded that his "father has made trouble for the country" (v. 28). The Hebrew word translated "made trouble" (Hb. ʿākar) was used to describe actions by Achan, an individual who had impaired a previous Israelite army's military campaign (Josh 7:25). Achan died under God's judgment for "troubling" (ʿākar) Israel (Josh 7:26); Jonathan's reuse of this term here casts an ominous shadow on Saul's destiny. But Jonathan did not stop his criticism there; in assessing his father's actions, Jonathan noted that his father's foolishness had prevented an even greater triumph (v. 30).[68]

14:31–34 In spite of the impediment of Saul's misguided zeal, the Israelites achieved a great victory, pursuing the Philistines a distance of some fifteen miles. Naturally, after this exceptional undertaking, "they were exhausted" (v. 31). Evening had come and the battle was over, so the men were released from the terms of their vow and could now eat.

Immediately the famished forces "pounced on the plunder" (v. 32) and slaughtered ritually clean animals that were among the spoil. However, in their haste they butchered the animals "on the ground" rather than suspending them so as to permit the blood to drain properly. As a result, they ate meat "together with the blood." Saul, who either did not know that eating blood was a sin (cf. Gen 9:4; Lev 3:17; 7:26; etc.)[69] or was simply unaware of his men's actions, was told by an unnamed individual that "the men are sinning against the LORD."[70]

---

[68] The NASB's rendering of the phrase לֹא רָבְתָה מַכָּה as "has not been great" incorrectly invites the reader to conclude that Jonathan was casting aspersions on the quality—not magnitude—of Saul's victory. With the employment of רָבָה Jonathan is indicating a diminished size of victory.

[69] In view of other Scriptures that depict Saul as spiritually dark (cf. comments on 9:6; 13:11–12; 14:19,24; 15:8–9; 28:8–12), it seems safe to conclude that Saul was simply ignorant of the Torah requirements concerning the consumption of blood.

[70] The motif of Saul's blindness is extended there, as an unnamed individual had to point out to Saul that his men were violating the Torah. For other instances of Saul's spiritual blindness, cf. 9:6–8; 14:45; 22:13; 28:7–19. For more secular examples of his inability to perceive correctly, cf. 17:58; 24:4–16; 26:12–17.

The king condemned the soldiers for their sinful conduct and took steps to end it. First, he provided an elevated surface—"a large stone" (v. 33)—on which the animals could be butchered. Then he sent messengers among the ranks, ordering them to slaughter the animals there (v. 34). Finally, he provided a spiritual context for his commands, telling them that "eating meat with blood still in it" was a "sin against the LORD." Saul's efforts were effective; beginning that night the men brought their animals to the rock for slaughter.

14:35–37 Though no judgmental statements accompany the note that this was Saul's first altar, the tone of the note may be subtly condemnatory. Perhaps the writer is indicating that Saul was responsible for the construction of a high place at which sacrificial worship occurred, a practice that was forbidden for Israel once they entered the Promised Land (Deut 12:13–14).

Even as the men were finishing their fleshy feast, Saul was drawing up plans for a predawn raid on the Philistines to take more plunder and "not leave one of them alive" (v. 36). The soldiers, who had gotten a taste of Philistine spoils, supported the king's proposal. But Ahijah suggested that Saul's blueprint be approved by the Lord first. Saul agreed and inquired of God, perhaps through Ahijah's use of the Urim and Thummim. Much to Saul's frustration, however, "God did not answer him that day." The absence of a definite answer from the Lord in response to Saul's question suggests three outcomes were possible in a consultation involving revelatory devices: yes, no, and neither (cf. also 28:6).

14:38–42 Saul concluded that the Lord was silent because he was displeased with someone's actions (cf. Job 35:12; Isa 1:15; Ezek 1:18; Mic 3:4; Zech 7:13). But whose? Without hesitation Saul began an investigation to uncover the sin (v. 38).

Commentators normally assume that Ahijah used the Urim and Thummim in a formal process to determine the guilty party,[71] though none of these details are mentioned in the Hebrew. To the contrary, the Hebrew verb in v. 42 translated "cast" (lit., "cause to fall"; there is no word for "lot" in Hb. here) is plural, indicating that more than one individual was required. Perhaps here as elsewhere (cf. Neh 11:1) non-Levites such as "leaders of the army" (v. 38) and Saul and Jonathan dropped objects to the ground in such a way as to determine God's will (cf. Prov 16:33)—since God was the overseer of all nature, he was understood to control the falling lots in such a way as to reveal his will.

Following Saul's prayer for divine guidance, the process of determining guilt was carried out in two stages. Initially a trial by lot was conducted to see if the sin lay with the royal family or the army of Israel (v. 41). Then a selection was made between the king and Jonathan, using the same method (v. 42).

---

[71] Cf. NRSV, as well as McCarter's reconstruction of 14:38–42 and relevant comments (*I Samuel*, 244, 247–48) for a more confident affirmation of this proposal. Both of these follow a rendering based on the LXX. Cf. also Klein, *1 Samuel*, 140.

14:43–46 The guilty person having thus been identified, it was now time to discover the nature of his offense. Jonathan's sin was not that he had broken a vow, for he had never promised to fast that day. Instead he had placed himself under his father's curse because he had "merely tasted a little honey" (v. 43).

What follows is one of the most instructive passages in the Former Prophets regarding the limitations of human kingship. Prior to Saul the Lord was Israel's only king (cf. 12:12). The Lord is "a great king" (Mal 1:14), and whatever the Lord curses is cursed indeed (Gen 12:3). Saul was now Israel's king; and Saul, like the Lord, had the power to curse. But unlike the Lord, Saul did not have the power to enforce his curse. The curse of a king, like every other royal utterance, was ultimately the word of a human being and thus mired in the frailties of the human condition. In this case the power of the royal curse was shattered by nameless "men" (v. 45) who said "Never!" to the king's demand that Jonathan be slain. The men thus "rescued" (Hb. *pdh*; lit., "redeemed," a word filled with theological implications) the king's son. Even oaths spoken by earthly kings (v. 44) were the product of human breath and could be quashed. A royal oath could be overruled by another's oath sworn by "the life of Yahweh" ("As surely as the LORD lives"). Thus, Jonathan's faith-filled actions had inadvertently brought about the defeat of two enemies of Yahweh's purposes— one external, the Philistines, and one internal, a misguided Israelite king.

Taken as a whole, 14:24–45 is a stunningly effective critique of all monarchies. This passage showcases a spectrum of frailties and follies that beset monarchies. Using Saul, Israel's first monarch, as an example, the narrative demonstrates that kings could lead Israel into battle, but they could also diminish a nation's capacity to achieve victory. Kings could build altars for their subjects to sacrifice to God, but they could not guarantee an encounter with the divine. They could utter powerful words—curses and oaths—but lacked the power to bring about their fulfillment.

After Saul was rebuffed by his soldiers, he ended the battle and let the remaining Philistines get away (v. 46). Though Israel had won a victory on that day, Saul—and consequently kingship—had suffered a humbling defeat.

6. Saul's Achievements and Family Line Are Summarized (14:47–52)

[47]After Saul had assumed rule over Israel, he fought against their enemies on every side: Moab, the Ammonites, Edom, the kings of Zobah, and the Philistines. Wherever he turned, he inflicted punishment on them. [48]He fought valiantly and defeated the Amalekites, delivering Israel from the hands of those who had plundered them.

[49]Saul's sons were Jonathan, Ishvi and Malki-Shua. The name of his older daughter was Merab, and that of the younger was Michal. [50]His wife's name was Ahinoam daughter of Ahimaaz. The name of the commander of Saul's army was Abner son of Ner, and Ner was Saul's uncle. [51]Saul's father Kish and Abner's

father Ner were sons of Abiel.
⁵²All the days of Saul there was bitter war with the Philistines, and whenever Saul saw a mighty or brave man, he took him into his service.

14:47–48   This pair of verses presents a summary of Saul's entire military career. It resembles the more abbreviated formulaic notices found in the concluding descriptions of later kings' reigns,[72] though it is more detailed. The presence of a career summary at this point in the Saul narrative is a bit puzzling; it probably is best explained by the fact that in the very next episode Saul lost his status as the Lord's anointed leader for Israel. From the narrator's perspective Saul was no longer Israel's true king, though he would function as head of state for years to come.

Saul's military exploits included wars against enemies on the east (Moab, Ammon, Edom), the north ("the kings of Zobah"), the west ("the Philistines"), and the south (the Amalekites were a desert group who ranged to the south of Israel). Saul was made king by the Israelites because they wanted military leadership against their enemies (8:20); and, more than any other leader mentioned in the Former Prophets since the time of Joshua, he was successful (v. 47).

14:49–51   A short note provides information regarding Saul's family and military administration. Three of Saul's four sons—perhaps only those born to his wife Ahinoam (v. 50)—are mentioned: "Jonathan, Ishvi and Malki-Shua" (v. 49). Elsewhere Ishvi is the same as Ish-Bosheth (2 Sam 2:10) and Esh-Baal (1 Chr 8:33). The reason for Abinadab's (cf. 31:2) omission from this list is unclear; perhaps he was the son of a concubine (Rizpah?; cf. 2 Sam 21:8) and therefore ineligible for inheritance rights. Saul's two daughters Merab and Michal, mentioned here for the first time, will play important roles in the dynastic politics of later narratives.

As was—and still is—the custom in Near Eastern Semitic societies, family members were appointed to key governmental positions. In the Saulide dynasty Abner, who apparently was a cousin to Saul from his father's side of the family tree, was made commander of the army (v. 50).[73]

14:52   Though Saul fought limited battles against many foreign nations, the Philistines posed the most persistent threat to Israel during this period of the eleventh century B.C. Not surprisingly, therefore, "there was bitter war with the Philistines" throughout Saul's reign. To keep Israel's military in a state of readiness against this continuing threat, Saul instituted a system of conscription, thus fulfilling Samuel's ominous prophecy (8:11).

---

[72] Cf. 1 Kgs 14:30; 15:6–7; 22:45; 2 Kgs 14:28; etc.

[73] First Chronicles 9:35 supports the contention that Abner was Saul's cousin, since it lists Kish and Ner as brothers. However, 1 Chr 8:29–33 seems to suggest that Abner was Saul's uncle. It is possible, nevertheless, to read this passage in a manner not incompatible with either 1 Sam 14:51 or 1 Chr 9:35. Cf. J. A. Thompson, *1, 2 Chronicles,* NAC (Nashville: Broadman & Holman, 1994), 101.

III. THE LORD GIVES ISRAEL A KING "AFTER HIS OWN HEART"
(1 Sam 15:1–2 Sam 1:27)
1. The Lord Rejects Saul (15:1–35)
2. The Lord Elevates and Empowers David (16:1–13)
   (1) The Lord Has Samuel Anoint David (16:1–13a)
   (2) The Lord's Spirit Comes upon David Powerfully (16:13b)
3. The Lord Blesses David, the Courtier, but Frustrates Saul
   (16:14–20:42)
   (1) The Lord Oppresses Saul and Uses David to Bring
       Deliverance (16:14–23)
   (2) David Rescues Israel from a Philistine Giant (17:1–58)
   (3) The House of Saul Honors Saul and Elevates David (18:1–5)
   (4) Saul Begins to Perceive David as a Threat (18:6–9)
   (5) Saul Attempts Unsuccessfully to Murder David (18:10–12)
   (6) David Becomes Saul's Son-in-Law (18:13–30)
   (7) Saul Attempts to Have Jonathan Murder David (19:1–7)
   (8) David Continues to Defeat the Philistines (19:8)
   (9) Saul Again Attempts to Murder David (19:9–10)
   (10) Michal Rescues David from Saul (19:11–17)
   (11) God's Spirit Rescues David from Saul and His Troops
        (19:18–24)
   (12) Jonathan Protects and Covenants with David (20:1–42)
4. The Lord Blesses David the Fugitive but Judges Saul (21:1–29:11)
   (1) The Lord's Priest at Nob Assists David (21:1–9)
   (2) David Is Saved from the Philistines (21:10–15)
   (3) David Receives Assistance from the King of Moab (22:1–5)
   (4) Saul Slaughters the Lord's Priests at Nob (22:6–19)
   (5) David Rescues the Lord's Priest Abiathar (22:20–23)
   (6) David Rescues Keilah from the Philistines (23:1–6)
   (7) David Escapes from Saul in the Arabah (23:7–29)
   (8) David Spares Saul at En Gedi (24:1–22)
   (9) Aside: Samuel's Death Is Noted (25:1)
   (10) The Lord Spares David from Sin against Nabal (25:2–44)
   (11) David Spares Saul at the Hill of Hakilah (26:1–25)
   (12) David Hides from Saul and Resumes Israel's Conquest of
        Canaan (27:1–12)
   (13) David Becomes Achish's Bodyguard (28:1–2)
   (14) Saul Consults a Medium (28:3–25)

    (15) David Is Exempted from Fighting against Israel's Forces
           (29:1–11)
  5. David Conquers the Amalekites as the Philistines Defeat Saul
      (30:1–31:13)
    (1) David Defeats the Amalekites (30:1–31)
    (2) The Philistines Devastate Israel and the House of Saul
           (31:1–13)
  6. David Responds to Tragedy in the House of Saul (2 Sam 1:1–27)
    (1) David Executes Saul's Killer (1:1–16)
    (2) David Laments Devastation in the House of Saul (1:17–27)

───────   **III. THE LORD GIVES ISRAEL A KING**   ───────
"AFTER HIS OWN HEART" (1 Sam 15:1–2 Sam 1:27)

The previous chapter brought to a conclusion a major section of the narratives of 1, 2 Samuel. Chapter 14 highlighted different aspects of King Saul's military conduct and achievements so as to demonstrate that the Lord had given Israel exactly what they were looking for in a king. Saul's obtuseness and clumsiness in matters of faith, as well as his capacity to make blustery oaths he could not fulfill, showed him to be "a king such as all the other nations have" (8:5). On the other hand, his zeal in mobilizing and deploying Israel's armed forces showed him to be one who would "go out before us and fight our battles" (8:20). Now that the Lord had given Israel what they wanted, the time had come to give Israel what they needed.

The reader has already been informed that the Lord had "sought out a man after his own heart and appointed him leader of his people" (13:14). In this section the reader witnesses the unfolding of the Lord's plan to do just that.[1] After

---

[1] Some scholars understand 1 Sam 15 to 2 Sam 5 to be an originally independent section of text known as the "History of David's Rise"; cf. N. P. Lemche, "David's Rise," *JSOT* 10 (1978): 2–25. Other scholars understand this hypothetical "History of David's Rise" to begin at 16:14; cf. L. Rost, *The Succession to the Throne of David*, trans. M. D. Rutter and D. M. Gunn (Sheffield: Almond, 1982); P. K. McCarter, Jr., "The Apology of David," *JBL* 99 (1980): 489–504; R. Klein, *1 Samuel*, WBC (Waco: Word, 1983), xxxi. McCarter understands this section to have been originally composed during David's reign to defend him against six distinct charges leveled by his critics: (1) that he sought to advance his own career as a courtier at Saul's expense; (2) that he was a deserter; (3) that he was an outlaw; (4) that he was a Philistine mercenary; (5) that he was in part responsible for Saul's death; and (6) that he was in part responsible for Abner's death. J. C. VanderKam suggests further that the section also defends David against charges that he was responsible for the death of Ish-Bosheth ("Davidic Complicity in the Deaths of Abner and Eshbaal: A Historical and Redactional Study," *JBL* 99 [1980]: 521–39). Because of the complex literary linkages that bind the narratives of 1 Sam 15–2 Sam 5 to the rest of the chapters in 1, 2 Samuel, I remain unconvinced that the section ever existed as a separate literary entity.

Saul mishandled a matter of profound spiritual and cultural significance, he was publicly rejected as king by Samuel, the most respected leader of the Yahwistic faith in his day.

The Lord's plan to give the nation a man after his own heart, like so many of his other plans throughout history, emerged in a most unforeseen way. It began with a boy herding sheep near a small rural settlement at the southern fringes of Israelite-controlled territory. Initially overlooked by his father Jesse and even the prophet Samuel, David was nevertheless chosen by the Lord to become Israel's greatest king. While still too young to be permitted to fight in battle, he was set aside for divine service through sacred anointing. David soon proved his fitness in both the spiritual and material realms by defeating an evil spirit and a Philistine giant. Initially he was celebrated as a favorite of King Saul at the royal court but soon was scorned as the king's enemy when his constant successes caused him to become more popular than his master.

Saul's curses, however, could not stop the Lord's blessings. In spite of Saul's opposition, David married the king's daughter and became best friends with Saul's firstborn son. When forced to flee from his earthly sovereign, the man after God's own heart was rescued by his heavenly king: the Lord's Spirit, prophets, and priests all provided him with guidance, provision, and protection during David's days of fleeing from Saul.

Saul's vendetta against David led him to take away David's first wife (Saul's daughter) and deny David access to his best friend Jonathan. Saul employed Israel's military might against David and forced his son-in-law to seek refuge in two foreign countries—Moab and Philistia—as well as in the desertlike wilderness of Judah. In spite of it all, David twice passed up opportunities to kill Saul and even employed the services of his six-hundred-man militia to defeat Israel's enemies and give gifts to Israel's citizens. Until Saul's death David remained utterly loyal to his earthly king.

As the Lord's true servant, David redeemed his time as a fugitive by fulfilling the Torah mandates to war against the Amalekites and conquer the pre-Israelite inhabitants of the Promised Land. At the same time, he readied himself for the day when he would be made king of the Israelites by forging an effective fighting force and making alliances with key Israelite families.

As this section concludes, Saul's sin spawned a military defeat that brought his reign to an abrupt conclusion. Yet all was not lost, for following this midnight in Israelite history came the bright dawn of King David.

1. The Lord Rejects Saul (15:1–35)

[1]Samuel said to Saul, "I am the one the LORD sent to anoint you king over his people Israel; so listen now to the message from the LORD. [2]This is what the LORD Almighty says: 'I will punish the Amalekites for what they did to Israel when they waylaid them as they came up from Egypt. [3]Now go, attack the Amalekites and

totally destroy everything that belongs to them. Do not spare them; put to death men and women, children and infants, cattle and sheep, camels and donkeys.'"

⁴So Saul summoned the men and mustered them at Telaim—two hundred thousand foot soldiers and ten thousand men from Judah. ⁵Saul went to the city of Amalek and set an ambush in the ravine. ⁶Then he said to the Kenites, "Go away, leave the Amalekites so that I do not destroy you along with them; for you showed kindness to all the Israelites when they came up out of Egypt." So the Kenites moved away from the Amalekites.

⁷Then Saul attacked the Amalekites all the way from Havilah to Shur, to the east of Egypt. ⁸He took Agag king of the Amalekites alive, and all his people he totally destroyed with the sword. ⁹But Saul and the army spared Agag and the best of the sheep and cattle, the fat calves and lambs—everything that was good. These they were unwilling to destroy completely, but everything that was despised and weak they totally destroyed.

¹⁰Then the word of the LORD came to Samuel: ¹¹"I am grieved that I have made Saul king, because he has turned away from me and has not carried out my instructions." Samuel was troubled, and he cried out to the LORD all that night.

¹²Early in the morning Samuel got up and went to meet Saul, but he was told, "Saul has gone to Carmel. There he has set up a monument in his own honor and has turned and gone on down to Gilgal."

¹³When Samuel reached him, Saul said, "The LORD bless you! I have carried out the LORD's instructions."

¹⁴But Samuel said, "What then is this bleating of sheep in my ears? What is this lowing of cattle that I hear?"

¹⁵Saul answered, "The soldiers brought them from the Amalekites; they spared the best of the sheep and cattle to sacrifice to the LORD your God, but we totally destroyed the rest."

¹⁶"Stop!" Samuel said to Saul. "Let me tell you what the LORD said to me last night."

"Tell me," Saul replied.

¹⁷Samuel said, "Although you were once small in your own eyes, did you not become the head of the tribes of Israel? The LORD anointed you king over Israel. ¹⁸And he sent you on a mission, saying, 'Go and completely destroy those wicked people, the Amalekites; make war on them until you have wiped them out.' ¹⁹Why did you not obey the LORD? Why did you pounce on the plunder and do evil in the eyes of the LORD?"

²⁰"But I did obey the LORD," Saul said. "I went on the mission the LORD assigned me. I completely destroyed the Amalekites and brought back Agag their king. ²¹The soldiers took sheep and cattle from the plunder, the best of what was devoted to God, in order to sacrifice them to the LORD your God at Gilgal."

²²But Samuel replied:

"Does the LORD delight in burnt offerings and sacrifices
  as much as in obeying the voice of the LORD?
To obey is better than sacrifice,
  and to heed is better than the fat of rams.
²³For rebellion is like the sin of divination,

and arrogance like the evil of idolatry.
Because you have rejected the word of the LORD,
   he has rejected you as king."
   [24]Then Saul said to Samuel, "I have sinned. I violated the LORD's command and your instructions. I was afraid of the people and so I gave in to them. [25]Now I beg you, forgive my sin and come back with me, so that I may worship the LORD."
   [26]But Samuel said to him, "I will not go back with you. You have rejected the word of the LORD, and the LORD has rejected you as king over Israel!"
   [27]As Samuel turned to leave, Saul caught hold of the hem of his robe, and it tore. [28]Samuel said to him, "The LORD has torn the kingdom of Israel from you today and has given it to one of your neighbors—to one better than you. [29]He who is the Glory of Israel does not lie or change his mind; for he is not a man, that he should change his mind."
   [30]Saul replied, "I have sinned. But please honor me before the elders of my people and before Israel; come back with me, so that I may worship the LORD your God." [31]So Samuel went back with Saul, and Saul worshiped the LORD.
   [32]Then Samuel said, "Bring me Agag king of the Amalekites."
   Agag came to him confidently, thinking, "Surely the bitterness of death is past."
   [33]But Samuel said,
"As your sword has made women childless,
   so will your mother be childless among women."
And Samuel put Agag to death before the LORD at Gilgal.
   [34]Then Samuel left for Ramah, but Saul went up to his home in Gibeah of Saul. [35]Until the day Samuel died, he did not go to see Saul again, though Samuel mourned for him. And the LORD was grieved that he had made Saul king over Israel.

In this section Israel's first king was given the high privilege of fulfilling a prophecy made in the days of Moses, that of annihilating the Amalekites (cf. Exod 17:14–16; Num 24:20). With this special opportunity came special responsibility, and unhappily Saul proved unwilling to carry it out faithfully.

In one of the most distressing passages in the Former Prophets, the Lord here deposes Saul from his position as the royal shepherd of the Lord's people. God's immutable action was taken as punishment for Saul's failure to fulfill Torah commands. It serves as an object lesson of how seriously God reacts to willful disobedience.

15:1–3 The Saul narratives resume here following the succinct overview of Saul's military career, family, and administration that concluded the previous chapter. The absence of chronological details makes it impossible to determine when these events occurred, though it probably was early in Saul's royal career, not far removed in time from the incident of 13:9–14.

The account opens with the elderly prophet Samuel approaching the king unbidden to issue a startling command. The importance of the command is highlighted by the formal introduction given to it. Before revealing the Lord's command, Samuel first emphasized his credentials as an instrument by whom the Lord had previously touched Saul's life: "I am the one the LORD sent to anoint you king over his people Israel" (v. 1).[2] Second, the prophet emphasized the divine origin of the message he was now communicating to the king: "This is what the LORD Almighty [lit., "Yahweh of Armies"] says" (v. 2).[3] This phrase, first found here and present only in the Former and Latter Prophets (seventy-six times), is always used by a prophet to introduce an authoritative revelation.

The message itself began with a rehearsal of the events and prophetic judgments recorded in Exod 17:8–16 (cf. also Num 24:20; Deut 25:17–19). In the Torah Yahweh had stated that he would "completely blot out the memory of Amalek from under heaven" (Exod 17:15) and would "be at war against the Amalekites from generation to generation" (Exod 17:16). Now Yahweh was giving Saul the awesome responsibility of fulfilling these Torah prophecies. Saul, who was noted for his military leadership, was ideally suited for carrying out this challenging task.

The command required Saul to "attack the Amalekites and totally destroy everything that belongs to them" (v. 3). The destruction was to include "men and women, children and infants, cattle and sheep, camels and donkeys." This kind of warfare, called *ḥerem*, was practiced only against peoples who had come under the Lord's severest judgment (e.g., Jericho).[4] It required the destruction of all people and possessions captured in battle. The task was a solemn and holy one since those Israelites who carried it out functioned as the Lord's agents of judgment. The soldiers were not to profit from their assignment through the acquisition of slaves or booty; like Aaronic priests who offered up burnt offerings *(ʿōlāh)* to the Lord, they were to receive no compensation for their efforts other than the satisfaction of having fulfilled a divinely mandated mission.

15:4–6 Telaim (v. 4) was a site probably located in the Negev of Judah. The second-largest force under Saul's command mentioned in the Bible— 210,000 men—was brought together for this solemn duty.[5] The city of Amalek

---

[2] Klein suggests that the employment of the word מֶלֶךְ ("king") in the Samuel speech here instead of the word נָגִיד ("prince") "may indicate a separate literary history for the two accounts" (*1 Samuel*, 148). Such changes in vocabulary, however, may be more indicative of thematic intentions of a single writer than proof of multiple authorship.

[3] For meaning of צְבָאוֹת, "armies, hosts," see J. E. Hartley, "צָבָא *(ṣābāʾ)*," *TWOT* 2:749–51.

[4] For further information regarding *ḥerem* cf. D. Kidner, "Old Testament Perspectives on War," *EvQ* 57 (1985): 99–113, and R. Gordon's treatment in his commentary (*1 and II Samuel* [Grand Rapids: Zondervan, 1986], 147–48). Gordon suggests that this concept is applicable for Christians only in a spiritualized sense, in doing battle with nonphysical "principalities" and "powers" (cf. Eph 6:12). Also see L. Lohfink, "חָרַם *ḥāram;* חֵרֶם *ḥērem*," *TDOT* 5:180–99.

[5] Klein raises the possibility that the large number was mentioned in order to demonstrate Saul's "lack of excuse for failing to carry out the full command of Yahweh" (*1 Samuel*, 149).

(v. 5) is also an unknown site probably located south or southwest of Judah. The ravine where Saul "set an ambush" probably was the Brook of Egypt (modern Wadi 'el-`Arish), which served as a major road in the region. His troops were now poised for a frontal attack on the major Amalekite settlement as well as an attack on the Amalekites attempting to escape the main Israelite force. Before initiating an attack, however, Saul warned the Kenites, a nearby nomadic tribe with whom the Israelites had friendly dealings (cf. Judg 1:16; 4:11), to evacuate the area, which they did. Saul's consideration for the Kenites was motivated by their "kindness to all the Israelites when they came up out of Egypt" (v. 6). Although this incident is not recounted anywhere in Scripture, the issue was an important one for Israel since they remembered those peoples who had refused them passage through their land (e.g., Edom, Moab, etc.).

15:7–9 The preparations having been made, Saul's attack extended "all the way from Havilah to Shur" (v. 7),[6] an expression apparently referring to the entire geographic extent of Ishmaelite territory (cf. Gen 25:18), a distance stretching from Arabia to Egypt. Such a widespread attack would have been technically possible due to the large numbers of Israelite troops mustered. This massive, sweeping attack was successful, and since no prisoners were to be taken, "all" Amalekites who were caught were "totally destroyed with the sword" (v. 8)—all, that is, except Agag, the Amalekite king (v. 9).

Though Agag was only one man, Saul's decision to "spare" him represented a flagrant violation of the Lord's command (the same verb, *ḥāmal,* is used in v. 3 and can also mean "feel compassion"—e.g., Exod 2:6; Ezek 16:5). So significant was Saul's action to the writer that he recounted it twice, using two different verbs to describe the same event; Saul both "took Agag king of the Amalekites alive" (v. 7) and "spared Agag" (v. 8).[7]

Joining Saul in his disobedience was "the army" (v. 9), who also spared "the best of the sheep and cattle, the fat calves and lambs—everything that was good." But they did not totally disregard the Lord's command; whatever they did not want for themselves, they obediently gave over to God's annihilating judgment (cf. 2 Sam 12:4, where Nathan's "rich man" spared *[ḥāmal]* his own sheep and slaughtered the poor man's lamb). This self-serving selective obedience by both Saul and those under his command represented an early attempt—repeated countless times throughout history—to pursue gain under the guise of serving God. As it always does, it would ultimately prove futile.

---

[6] McCarter departs from both the MT and LXX traditions to substitute "wadi" for "Havilah" (*I Samuel,* 258, 261). While the proposal has some semantic merit, it is totally lacking in any textual support. Since the MT accords with Gen 25:18 and makes equally good, if not better, semantic sense, McCarter's suggestion is to be rejected.

[7] This narrative technique is used occasionally elsewhere in Hebrew to mark "peak" or climactic actional moments within a story. The Hebrew Bible's most outstanding example of the employment of this technique is found in the account of the universal flood, esp. Gen 7:10–23.

15:10–12 This incomplete compliance with the divine command prompted the Lord to give a further message to Samuel. This "word of the LORD" (v. 10) came to Samuel in the night as a revelation of judgment similar in some ways to one he had received in Eli's behalf (1 Samuel 3). The message apparently was lengthy (cf. vv. 16–19,22–23,26); however, the only portion that is presented as a direct quotation from the Lord is found in v. 11. This passage provides a remarkable window into God's emotions and concerns regarding Saul's kingship.

First of all, God was "grieved" that he "made Saul king."[8] The only other occasion in Scripture where the Lord stated that he was "grieved" (from *nḥm*) over peoples' actions was when he observed the wickedness of humanity that led to the universal flood (Gen 6:7). The employment of the term here suggests that the Lord was deeply concerned—or, as H. V. D. Parunak asserts, suffered emotional pain[9]—regarding choices Saul made of his own volition. In addition to the lexical linkage between v. 11 and Gen 6:7, there are also similarities in the clause and phrase structures.

The degree of similarity suggests that the writer was making a deliberate connection between the Genesis and Samuel narratives. Certainly similarities exist between the outcomes of the stories. The sins of humanity in Genesis 6 caused the Lord to destroy the sinners, yet they also gave rise to the Lord's selection of Noah, a man with a remarkable heart for God (cf. Gen 6:8,10). Saul's sins here destroyed his kingship, yet they also served as a springboard for the Lord's selection of David, a man after God's own heart. Clearly both passages teach that God is aware of and responsive to choices made by people, reacting favorably only when people choose the option of obedience to the divine will.

Second, the Lord revealed that the source of his grief was Saul's failure to follow his instructions completely. Saul's partial obedience might have been acceptable to his contemporaries, but when weighed in the divine balances, it was found wanting. Nothing short of strict obedience to the Lord's instructions was acceptable; anything less produced grief in heaven and pain and loss on earth.

Samuel, who was uniquely in tune with God's heart, "was troubled" (lit., "became angry") when the Lord informed him of Saul's actions. In a sleepless, agonizing night "he cried out to the LORD." The term translated "cried out" (Hb. *zāʿaq*) refers to an intense expression of grief or anxiety (cf. 1 Sam 4:13;

---

[8] The KJV here translates the *niphal* of ‮נחם‬ as "repenteth," which sounds to us as though Yahweh were somehow morally negligent in an action he had performed, a conclusion clearly incompatible with orthodox Christian theology. For a good discussion of the translational and theological issues involved in this passage, cf. R. F. Youngblood, "1, 2 Samuel," EBC 3:553–1104 (Grand Rapids: Zondervan, 1992), 675.

[9] H. V. D. Parunak, "A Semantic Survey of *NHM*," *VT* 56 (1975): 519.

7:8; 8:18; 12:8,10), doubtlessly mirroring the Lord's displeasure.

Rising at the first light of dawn (cf. Gen 22:3), Samuel set out to carry God's message to Saul (v. 12), but Saul was not where the prophet had expected to find him. Instead the king had set out on a journey that took him initially deep into the Negev to Carmel (Khirbet 'el-Kirmil, seven miles south of Hebron), where he "set up a monument in his own honor" (v. 12) commemorating the recent victory he had achieved in the area. Yet Saul had not remained there; instead, he had gone "down to Gilgal," an important military staging site that was also of great religious significance at this time (cf. 1:15; 7:16; 10:8; 13:4–15). The sequencing of Saul's actions—performing acts of self-interest prior to those of devotion to God—was reflective of his entire life.

15:13–15 When Samuel learned of Saul's location, he proceeded to Gilgal for a second, fateful confrontation with the errant king. As on the earlier occasion (13:10), Saul initiated the dialogue with a blessing. However, in a departure from the first Gilgal meeting, Saul did not wait for Samuel to respond but immediately proceeded to brag about his obedience (lit.), "I have established Yahweh's words." For Samuel, and for the readers who are aware of the Lord's words to Samuel in v. 10, Saul's words are bitterly ironic. The king has indeed "established Yahweh's words," but the words he "established" are regarding disobedience (v. 10), not obedience (v. 3).

Saul's boast of obedience was singularly unconvincing to Samuel since evidence to the contrary was "bleating" and "lowing" in their ears. Hearing these sounds that indicated a violation of *ḥerem* warfare, Samuel asked Saul for an explanation.

As in the previous confrontation between Saul and Samuel at Gilgal, the king blamed others for any sins that were committed: it was not Saul but "the soldiers" (v. 15) who "spared the best of the sheep and cattle." But even so, he said, their violation of the ban was only apparent. These animals were not killed in the heat of battle, it is true; but their slaughter was only delayed so that Yahweh might be glorified. They would be used as a "sacrifice to the LORD your God."

15:16–19 Samuel had had enough of Saul's contorted reasoning and excuse making. Before the king could make further excuses, Samuel cut him off to announce the Lord's word. In the three verses that follow, Samuel reminded the king that though he was now "head of the tribes of Israel" (v. 17), he could take no credit for it. It was the Lord who had taken him from being a nobody to being "king over Israel" (v. 17). The Lord gave Saul that position so that he might serve as the Lord's agent in carrying out the "mission" (v. 18) to wipe out the wicked Amalekites. Unfortunately, instead of destroying wickedness, Saul increased it by doing "evil in the eyes of the LORD" (v. 19).

15:20–21 Saul, however, did not see it that way. As far as he was concerned, he "did obey the LORD" (v. 20). Indeed, he went on the Lord's mission and carried out a campaign against the Amalekites marked by acts of *ḥerem* ("completely destroyed the Amalekites"). In the course of the battle Saul had succeeded in capturing "Agag their king" whom he "brought back"; in addition, the best of the livestock was set aside for sacrifice at a historic worship center. As Saul portrayed it, the army over which he exercised command had at least substantially fulfilled the requirements of *ḥerem* warfare.

Nevertheless, the fact remained that Saul and those under his leadership had disobeyed the Lord's command: they "took . . . the best of what was devoted to God" (v. 21). And Samuel, as God's unyielding spiritual advocate, could not permit God's primary political and military representative to get by with only partial obedience. Partial obedience was in fact disobedience. Saul's sin was the sin of Achan, who had also spared the choicest of *ḥerem* plunder from destruction (cf. Josh 7:21). Achan and his family died for his sin; Saul's sin would bring him misery and death and would cause his family's loss of kingship.

15:22–23 In the most eloquent and memorable recorded quotation coming from Samuel's lips, God's judgment was pronounced against the king. The prophet's words are expressed poetically in a series of four pairs of lines, with the climactic words of judgment being found in the final pair. Samuel began with a two-line rhetorical question that was asked in such a way as to expect a negative answer.[10] He followed with the brief (three words in Hebrew) yet profound maxim that summarizes a central tenet of the Torah: "obedience surpasses sacrifice" ("to obey is better than sacrifice"; v. 22). This truth is reinforced by the words "to heed is better than the fat of rams."[11] Clearly the Torah integrated sacrifice into the life of obedience to God; however, it never envisioned it as a substitute for obedience.

The third couplet (v. 23a) provides two of the three logical premises that underlie the serious punishment announced at the conclusion of the final couplet. The first line of the third couplet states that "rebellion" (Hb. *merî;* v. 23), or willful disobedience, is as serious a sin as the capital "sin of divination." The conclusion of the couplet declares that "arrogance," or insubordination (Hb. *ʾaven*), is equivalent to "idolatry" *(tĕrāpîm),* presumably since it

---

[10] For further information on rhetorical questions, cf. L. J. de Regt, "Functions and Implications of Rhetorical Questions in the Book of Job," in *Biblical Hebrew and Discourse Linguistics,* ed. R. D. Bergen (Dallas: SIL, 1994), 361–73.

[11] McCarter suggests that these lines express "the characteristic prophetic mistrust of sacrifice (or any ritual practice) as a substitute for obedience to divine command" (*I Samuel,* 270). Implicit in McCarter's words is the assumption of a tension between the prophetic and priestly communities in Israel, between a group that stressed righteousness through faith-motivated obedience to the prophetic revelation and one that stressed righteousness through faith-filled obedience to the ritual code. McCarter's position ignores the fact that Samuel himself—as a Levite (cf. 1 Chr 6:22–26)—was from the priestly community and frequently performed ritual sacrifice himself (cf. 1 Sam 10:8; 11:15; 16:3,5).

likewise involves the removal of Yahweh from his rightful place in every person's life, or as A. F. Kirkpatrick notes, "It elevates self-will into a god."[12] Interestingly, before Saul's life ended, he and a member of his family would be connected with both divination (cf. 28:7–19) and *tĕrāpîm* (cf. 19:13).

In the climactic final couplet (v. 23b) Samuel provided two crucial items: the most important premise leading up to the judgment against Saul and the judgment itself. The third and last premise preceding Samuel's announcement of punishment was the most personal one: "you have rejected the word of the LORD." Saul had "rejected" (Hb. *mā'as*) God's word by refusing to fulfill the stern requirements of God's command and permitting those under his charge to do the same (see the use of *mā'as* in Num 11:20; 14:31; and especially Lev 26:15,43).

The judgment against Saul was curt (two words in Hebrew) and extremely serious: the Lord "has rejected you as king." The form of the Hebrew verb used here (a perfect conjugation) suggests that Saul's rejection was already an accomplished fact. God's rejection of Saul's position of authority was caused by Saul's rejection of God's authoritative Word.

15:24–26 Belatedly, Saul acknowledged that he "sinned" (v. 24). In his response he used a verb that expresses the concept of "missing the mark" (Hb. *ḥāṭā'; *cf. Judg 20:16; Prov 19:2).[13] He missed the mark when he "violated" (lit., "passed over") both "the word of the LORD" (lit., "Yahweh's mouth") and Samuel's "instructions"; the prophet's words apparently were accepted by Saul as equal in authority to the Lord's words, just as Samuel intended them to be (cf. v. 2).

What had motivated Saul to move away from obedience to God's command? Fundamentally it was misdirected fear: instead of fearing the Lord as required by the Torah (cf. Lev 19:14; 25:17; Deut 6:13,24; 10:12,20), Saul "was afraid of the people" (cf. Mark 11:32; John 7:13). Because of that misguided fear, Saul "listened to the voice of" ("gave in to") the people instead of listening to the Lord's voice as required by the Torah (cf. Deut 27:10). Perhaps the desire to achieve economic gain by sparing Agag in exchange for ransom or trade concessions from the Amalekites had also led Saul into sin (cf. 1 Tim 6:10).

Saul understood the gravity of the prophet's words and dropped to his knees (cf. 1 Sam 15:27), begging Samuel to "forgive [his] sin." What he apparently did not know was that forgiveness was an act that could not be performed by the prophet but only by the Lord himself, usually in response to an act by an

---

[12] A. F. Kirkpatrick, ed., *The First Book of Samuel,* CB (Cambridge: University Press, 1891), 145.
[13] Cf. G. H. Livingston, "חָטָא," in *TWOT* 1:277–78 (Chicago: Moody, 1980), 277.

Aaronic priest.[14] Saul also requested that Samuel return with him so that the king could "worship the LORD."

Samuel rejected Saul's plea because not to do so would be to buttress Saul's claim to power over Israel, a position that had now been denied him by God. Emphasizing the primary point of the just-announced divine oracle, Samuel restated the crucial facts: Saul had disobeyed the Lord in a matter of utmost importance, as he had consistently disobeyed the Lord on previous occasions, and the Lord had now rejected him as king.

15:27–29 As the prophet "turned to leave" (v. 27) Gilgal, Saul grabbed the "hem" (Hb. *kānāp,* lit., "corner") of his robe. The Torah required tassels to be present on this portion of the robe as symbolic reminders of all of the Lord's commands (cf. Num 15:38–39), and it was likely the tassel that Saul actually grabbed. When Saul "tore" the corner tassel from Samuel's robe, he dramatically symbolized his breach of the Lord's command. Samuel immediately picked up on the significance of Saul's act and pronounced a further oracle of divine rejection. Using imagery appropriate to the situation, he added the time element in the Lord's judgment: "today" (v. 28). Though Saul might continue to act as Israel's king, "one better" than Saul, that is, one more careful than Saul to keep the Lord's commands, was being given to the kingdom of Israel.

Though some warnings sent from God were conditional in nature (cf. Jonah 3:4,10), this one was not. Through various experiences Saul had shown that he was spiritually incorrigible, in spite of previous warnings and penalties (cf. 13:13–14); as a result, his punishment would not be altered. Though the Lord "was grieved" (v. 11; *nhm*), he would not "change his mind" *(nhm).* The surety of the Lord's words was based in the stability of the divine nature.

To emphasize the finality of the judgment against Saul, Samuel created a new title for Yahweh, *nēṣaḥ,* "the Everlasting One" (NIV "the Glory")[15] and attached it to an indirect quotation from the Torah (cf. Num 23:19): "the Everlasting one does not lie or change his mind" (v. 29). Words of judgment spoken against Saul by an eternal God would stand unchanged forever.

15:30–33 Saul, desperate to retain his position of authority over the people, repeated and expanded his petition to Samuel. In an apparent effort to appease the prophet and regain his support, Saul confessed for the second time that he "sinned" and yet still wanted to worship the Lord. He requested once again that Samuel come with him and "honor" (Hb. *kbd*) him before Israel. Saul

---

[14] According to the Torah (cf. Lev 4:20,26,31,35; 5:10,16,18; 6:7; 19:22; Num 15:28), an ordained Aaronic priest could perform an act of atonement by which an individual may have his sins forgiven. However, nowhere in the Bible is it stated that Samuel was an Aaronic priest, though he was a Levite. Saul's request of Samuel probably was yet one more instance where the king revealed his ignorance of spiritual matters.

[15] The term נֶצַח has the translation options of "glory," "success," and "lastingness." Cf. *CHAL,* s.v. נֶצַח. In this context "lastingness" seems most appropriate.

recognized that he needed the endorsement of Israel's spiritual patriarch to rule the people effectively.

Saul's penitence and persistence paid off, at least to this extent: "Samuel went back with Saul" (v. 31).[16] In return Saul kept his word and "worshiped the LORD." Thus Saul was able to maintain the appearance of an undamaged relationship with the Lord.

However, in a gesture suggestive of his loss of divine favor, Saul was not permitted to complete the task given him by God. Instead, elderly Samuel performed one final action at Gilgal befitting his role as Israel's judge, that is, as one charged with the responsibility of carrying out the Lord's judgments. Calling "Agag king of the Amalekites" forward, Samuel pronounced an oracle of unrelenting judgment against a second king and then "put Agag to death before the LORD." The verb translated "put to death" *(šāsap)* is used only here in the Hebrew Bible and seems to suggest that Agag was cut to pieces (similar to *nātaḥ* in 11:7).[17]

The Hebrew text describing Agag's approach to his death is problematic: "Agag came to him *maʿădannōt* [NIV, "confidently"; others suggest "trembling," "in fetters," or even "cheerfully"],[18] and Agag said [to himself?], "Truly [*ʾākēn,* a word often introducing a statement contrary to expectations; e.g., Gen 28:16; Exod 2:14; Isa 45:15; 53:4; Jer 3:20; Zeph 3:7] the bitterness of death has turned aside." There is disagreement concerning the manner of Agag's approach and also the nature of his utterance. McCarter follows the LXX in translating Agag's last recorded words as a question—"Would death have been as bitter as this?"[19] The NIV follows the MT in translating it as an exclamatory clause. Agag seems to express surprise that he is not to be killed, a conclusion that may have based on his being brought before a prophet rather than a soldier.

15:34–35 Following the completion of this gruesome task, "Samuel left for Ramah" (v. 34), his hometown; Saul returned to "his home" and seat of power, "Gibeah of Saul."[20] The separation that occurred between the Lord's

---

[16] S. Greehnow understands Samuel to have sinned by capitulating to the request of the sinful king ("Did Samuel Sin?" *GTJ* 11 [1970]: 34–40). However, the absence of any hint of condemnation of Samuel in the biblical text regarding his actions in this matter makes Greehnow's assertion a dubious one.

[17] Cf. KB^3, 1486, s.v. שׁסף.

[18] For a discussion of translational issues involved, cf. Klein, *1 Samuel,* 260, and R. G. Bratcher, "How Did Agag Meet Samuel (1 Samuel 15:32)?" *BT* 22 (1971): 167–68. Bratcher's suggestions are diametrically opposed to those of the NIV translators. Kirkpatrick (*First Book of Samuel,* 147) suggests "cheerfully."

[19] Cf. McCarter, *I Samuel,* 260, 264–65.

[20] J. Baldwin (*1 and 2 Samuel,* TOTC [Leicester: InterVarsity, 1988], 117), summarizing previous twentieth-century archaeological excavations of Tell el-Ful (ancient Gibeah), suggests that Saul by this time lived in a large rectangular fortress that had a defensive tower at one corner. Cf. also W. F. Albright, *The Archaeology of Palestine* (Harmondsworth: Penguin, 1949), 121.

anointed and his prophet as they departed from Gilgal was to be permanent.

But though Saul was gone from Samuel's field of view, he was not gone from his heart: "Samuel mourned for him" (v. 35). The word translated "mourned" (Hb. *ʾābal*) suggests an intense emotional reaction in response to a distressing turn of events (cf. Exod 33:3) or death (cf. 2 Sam 19:1). Significantly, Saul's sin not only weighed heavily on Samuel but it also affected the Lord, who "was grieved that he had made Saul king over Israel."[21] In combination with v. 11 this note regarding the Lord's grief frames the judgment narrative of vv. 12–35 and sets the tone for its interpretation. In view of the double use of this verb with the Lord as its subject, chap. 15 must be viewed as one of the darkest passages of the Former Prophets. As clearly as any passage in the Bible, it shows how seriously God takes the failings of those he places in positions of authority (cf. Heb 13:7; Jas 3:1; also 2 Sam 11:27; 12:7–12).

2. The Lord Elevates and Empowers David (16:1–13)

Saul's work for God had ended, but God's work would go on. The Lord had already "sought out a man after his own heart and appointed him leader of his people" (13:14). This chapter portrays the unfolding of God's plan as it centered in the person of David.

At one level this chapter presents an interesting historical narrative about how one of Saul's adversaries outwitted the king to anoint a royal rival. But the writer's intention was clearly to present more than historical fact. This chapter is not so much about Samuel and David as it is about God. It portrays the Lord's infinite and effortless superiority to all things human. The ways of the Lord confound even the greatest spiritual intellects and frustrate all earthly forces that would stand in his way. This chapter provides one of the most fascinating examples of the Lord's inclination to choose "the lowly things of this world and the despised things—and the things that are not—to nullify the things that are" (1 Cor 1:28). When this story concludes, an unlettered rural shepherd boy has become the Lord's anointed—"a brave man and a warrior" (v. 18) who uses his supernaturally enhanced abilities to overpower even evil spirits.[22]

(1) The Lord Has Samuel Anoint David (16:1–13a)

¹The LORD said to Samuel, "How long will you mourn for Saul, since I have rejected him as king over Israel? Fill your horn with oil and be on your way; I am sending you to Jesse of Bethlehem. I have chosen one of his sons to be king."

²But Samuel said, "How can I go? Saul will hear about it and kill me."

The LORD said, "Take a heifer with you and say, 'I have come to sacrifice to the

---

[21] For a related discussion cf. K. Mathews, *Genesis 1–11:26,* NAC (Nashville: Broadman & Holman, 1996), 340–41.

[22] See L. Eslinger, "A Change of Heart: 1 Sam 16," in *Ascribe to the Lord,* ed. L. Eslinger & G. Taylor (Sheffield: Academic Press, 1988).

LORD.' ³Invite Jesse to the sacrifice, and I will show you what to do. You are to anoint for me the one I indicate."

⁴Samuel did what the LORD said. When he arrived at Bethlehem, the elders of the town trembled when they met him. They asked, "Do you come in peace?"

⁵Samuel replied, "Yes, in peace; I have come to sacrifice to the LORD. Consecrate yourselves and come to the sacrifice with me." Then he consecrated Jesse and his sons and invited them to the sacrifice.

⁶When they arrived, Samuel saw Eliab and thought, "Surely the LORD's anointed stands here before the LORD."

⁷But the LORD said to Samuel, "Do not consider his appearance or his height, for I have rejected him. The LORD does not look at the things man looks at. Man looks at the outward appearance, but the LORD looks at the heart."

⁸Then Jesse called Abinadab and had him pass in front of Samuel. But Samuel said, "The LORD has not chosen this one either." ⁹Jesse then had Shammah pass by, but Samuel said, "Nor has the LORD chosen this one." ¹⁰Jesse had seven of his sons pass before Samuel, but Samuel said to him, "The LORD has not chosen these." ¹¹So he asked Jesse, "Are these all the sons you have?"

"There is still the youngest," Jesse answered, "but he is tending the sheep."

Samuel said, "Send for him; we will not sit down until he arrives."

¹²So he sent and had him brought in. He was ruddy, with a fine appearance and handsome features.

Then the LORD said, "Rise and anoint him; he is the one."

¹³So Samuel took the horn of oil and anointed him in the presence of his brothers,

16:1–3[23] In the previous chapter the Lord had spoken through Samuel about another; here the Lord spoke to Samuel about Samuel. In the midst of Samuel's mournful depression God gave him a word of motivational reproof (cf. Exod 10:3,7; Num 14:27; 1 Sam 1:14; 2 Sam 2:26; 1 Kgs 18:21) and a job to do, one that Youngblood terms "the capstone to Samuel's career."[24] Perhaps to dispel doubts that may have arisen in the prophet's mind, the Lord first confirmed the stern prophetic word spoken by Samuel against Saul, the most powerful man in Israelite society: "I have rejected him as king over Israel" (v. 1). Having said this, God then gave the prophet a divine mission spelled out in specific terms. Samuel was first to "fill" an animal horn flask with specially prepared olive oil (cf. Exod 30:23–25). Then he was to take it along on a journey "to Jesse of Bethlehem" for a specific reason: Samuel was

[23] R. North suggests that 16:1–13a is the first of three accounts of David's rise to power ("David's Rise: Sacral, Military or Psychiatric?" *Bib* 63 [1982]: 524–44). Each account originates from one of the hypothetical Pentateuchal sources: E (16:1–13), D (16:14–23), and J (chap. 17). While commendably creative, the proposal is without textual merit and may be safely rejected. McCarter affirms the presence of multiple traditions regarding David's entrance into Saul's court. He suggests that the oldest tradition is that of David coming "to court as a musician and royal weapon-bearer" (*I Samuel*, 282).

[24] Youngblood, *1, 2 Samuel*, 686.

to anoint "one of his sons to be king."

Samuel's task was simple yet dangerous. As Israel's kingmaker and most esteemed servant of the Lord, Samuel's actions were of great interest to Saul. If Samuel were to make an unexpected journey, especially one to a location outside of his normal judicial circuit, it would likely be reported to the king. Saul would then certainly view Samuel's actions for what they were—a threat to Saul's own claim to the throne.

Consequently, the Lord gave Samuel an additional task that would help mask the central purpose of his trip to Bethlehem. Samuel was to make a sacrifice in that region and would "take a heifer" along for that purpose. As a levitical judge, Samuel was authorized to sacrifice such an animal as part of a ritual that atoned for an unsolved murder committed in a rural region (cf. Deut 21:1–9). Thus Samuel's journey to a rural region with a sacrificial animal accompanying him would not have raised undue suspicions.[25]

16:4–5 Perhaps the elders "trembled" at the sight of Samuel because they interpreted Samuel's arrival with a heifer as an indication that a murder had occurred in their territory and that a legal action was being initiated; Youngblood suggests the elders were "awed by his formidable reputation," established in part by his recent execution of Agag.[26]

In preparation for the sacrifice Samuel instructed the elders to "consecrate" themselves, that is, to place themselves in a condition of ritual cleanness. Entering into ritual cleanness normally involved bathing, putting on clean clothes, the temporary suspension of all sexual activity, as well as avoidance of contact with any dead body.[27] Samuel then went to the house of Jesse, where he personally invited him and his sons to the sacrifice and oversaw their consecration.

16:6–10 An unspecified amount of time later, Samuel began the anointing ceremony, the central purpose of his trek to Bethlehem. However, as this event began, the prophet was portrayed not knowing the Lord's will; this is the only time in biblical narrative when Samuel was shown in this uncomfortable position. Samuel was forced, therefore, to initiate the search for "the man after the Lord's heart" with only the use of his own insight. When he "saw Eliab,"[28] Jesse's firstborn son (cf. 17:13), he was impressed by "his appearance or his

---

[25] On the potential ethical problem associated with Samuel's deception, cf. W. C. Kaiser, Jr., *Toward Old Testament Ethics* (Grand Rapids: Academie, 1983), 225–27.

[26] Youngblood, *1, 2 Samuel*, 683.

[27] The Torah does not provide an explicit set of guidelines for consecration but does have several passages that either portray individuals who received instructions concerning consecration or discuss ritual cleanness. Cf. Exod 19:10,14; Lev 7:19–21; 15:2–33; Num 19:11–22; Deut 23:10–11. Cf. G. J. Wenham, who argues that any action that would cause a "life liquid" (i.e., blood or semen) to be lost from the body resulted in ritual uncleanness ("Why Does Sexual Intercourse Defile (Lev 15,18)?" *ZAW* 95 [1983]: 432–44).

[28] Eliab is also knowOn as Elihu (cf. 1 Chr 27:16).

height" (v. 7) and concluded that "the LORD's anointed stands here before the LORD" (v. 6). After all, Samuel had previously been led by God to anoint an individual who possessed exceptional height (cf. 10:23).

But before Samuel could uncork the horn and pour oil on Eliab's head, the Lord ended his silence. First, he informed Samuel that Eliab had been rejected as Israel's next king. Then, in a particularly memorable statement the Lord uttered one of the most important statements in all of Scripture regarding divine concerns and human capacities. God first affirmed his fundamental "otherness": "the LORD does not look at the things man looks at" (v. 7). Neither the Lord's considerations nor his abilities are the same as those of humans; whereas "man looks at the outward appearance" (lit., "the eyes"), "the LORD looks at the heart." The Lord alone has the capacity to observe and judge a person's "heart" (Hb. *lēb*), that is, one's thoughts, emotions, and intents.[29] On God's scales these matters outweigh all other aspects of a human life.

The firstborn having been rejected, "Jesse called Abinadab" (v. 8), his second born (17:13), "and had him pass in front of Samuel." But he, like his younger brother "Shammah" (v. 9),[30] was "not chosen." In fact, though four additional sons of Jesse passed in front of Samuel for possible anointing, the Lord had "not chosen these" (v. 10) either.

16:11–13a The prophet's experience seemed to contradict his revelation, and it resulted in a perplexing situation. On the one hand, the Lord revealed that he had chosen a son of Jesse to be king (v. 1); on the other hand, he had rejected every son paraded before Samuel. In an effort to resolve the confusion, Samuel asked Jesse if he had any other sons. As it turned out, Jesse's "smallest" (Hb. *haqqāṭān*; NIV, "youngest") son had been excluded from the event; he was out "tending the sheep" (v. 11).

Jesse's description of the omitted son—David—as "smallest" places him in strong contrast to the rejected king. Since the Lord had just told Samuel not to consider "his height" (v. 7), the prophet was predisposed to interpret this description positively and perhaps as an indicator that the small shepherd would indeed be the Lord's anointed. With urgency he requested that Jesse's remaining son be brought in.

When David was brought in from the field, his favorable physical traits were immediately obvious: he was first of all "ruddy" (v. 10; Hb. *ʾadmônî*), either possessing red-tinted hair or a bronze complexion; he possessed "a fine appearance" (lit., "beauty of eyes"); and he was "handsome." However—especially in light of v. 7—these physical assets were no proof that David was God's choice; at best they were irrelevant. What mattered was the young man's heart, and only God could judge that. The Lord removed all suspense from the situa-

---

[29] On the Hebrew word for "heart," cf. A. Bowling, "לֵבָב," in *TWOT* I:466–67.
[30] Shammah is elsewhere known as Shimea (cf. 1 Chr 2:13).

tion with his word to Samuel: "Anoint him; he is the one."

Obediently, Samuel opened the "horn of oil" (v. 12) and decanted its contents on David's head before his brothers and the elders of Bethlehem. The shapeless, invasive fluid used in the ceremony served fittingly as a symbol of the mystical presence of God. As the oil worked its way into the individual's hair and pores, it symbolized the divine presence entering into the one being anointed.

When David, the youngest of the sons in Jesse's family (cf. 1 Chr 2:13–15), was selected as the Lord's anointed, he joined a venerable crowd of Torah patriarchs selected by God in a way that confounded social norms. Other men who were not firstborn but who were selected by the Lord over their more socially powerful older brothers include Seth, Noah, Isaac, Jacob, Joseph, Ephraim, Moses, and perhaps Abraham. It seems that the biblical record deliberately creates the impression that Yahweh prefers to use disenfranchised members of society—earlier in 1 Samuel the barren woman Hannah and the child Samuel—to do his most significant work (cf. Mark 10:31; 1 Cor 1:27).

(2) The Lord's Spirit Comes upon David Powerfully (16:13b)

and from that day on the Spirit of the LORD came upon David in power. Samuel then went to Ramah.

16:13b In David's case more than mere symbolism was present in the anointing ceremony: "The Spirit of the LORD came upon David in power" (v. 12), even as had been the case previously with Saul (cf. 10:10).[31] What is more, it stayed with him "from that day on"; this made David's anointing superior to Saul's (cf. v. 14). The coming of the Spirit, an event that was primarily spiritual in nature, had major implications for the political future of Israel; after this event the political landscape of Israel would be forever different.

3. The Lord Blesses David, the Courtier, but Frustrates Saul (16:14–20:42)

This section provides an early indication of the magnitude of the Lord's blessings on David's life. David, newly empowered by the Lord's Spirit, is called into service at Saul's royal court in Gibeah. In this his situation is not unlike that of the youthful Samuel, who in a former day also served faithfully at the power center of the troubled anointed leader he would someday succeed.

The young man David soon proved to be both a blessing and a threat to his

---

[31] H. W. Hertzberg perceptively notes that OT and NT narratives centered around significant heroes of the faith, including David, "are largely narrated as a history of the Spirit of God with them" (*I and II Samuel*, OTL [Philadelphia: Fortress, 1964], 140).

royal master, Saul. On the one hand, David was the only Israelite capable of delivering Saul from spiritual oppression and Israel from an intimidating Philistine giant. On the other hand, David's success so intimidated Saul that the king found it necessary to try to kill Israel's brightest young hero. When his own weapon twice failed to find its mark, Saul sought the help of his firstborn son, his youngest daughter, and even the Philistines. However, because of the Lord's gracious hand of protection, every attempt failed: David was rescued at every turn, sometimes by the very ones Saul enlisted to kill him.

The theme of the section, repeated on four occasions (16:18; 18:12,14,28), is "the LORD was with David." Truly it was the Lord's presence in David's life (cf. 16:13) that preserved and prospered him during this time of personal crisis. When the section ends, David has married into the royal family, established a covenant with the heir-apparent to Saul's throne, and become Israel's favorite and most successful military leader.

(1) The Lord Oppresses Saul and Uses David to Bring Deliverance (16:14–23)[32]

[14]Now the Spirit of the LORD had departed from Saul, and an evil spirit from the LORD tormented him.

[15]Saul's attendants said to him, "See, an evil spirit from God is tormenting you. [16]Let our lord command his servants here to search for someone who can play the harp. He will play when the evil spirit from God comes upon you, and you will feel better."

[17]So Saul said to his attendants, "Find someone who plays well and bring him to me."

[18]One of the servants answered, "I have seen a son of Jesse of Bethlehem who knows how to play the harp. He is a brave man and a warrior. He speaks well and is a fine-looking man. And the LORD is with him."

[19]Then Saul sent messengers to Jesse and said, "Send me your son David, who is with the sheep." [20]So Jesse took a donkey loaded with bread, a skin of wine and a young goat and sent them with his son David to Saul.

[21]David came to Saul and entered his service. Saul liked him very much, and David became one of his armor-bearers. [22]Then Saul sent word to Jesse, saying, "Allow David to remain in my service, for I am pleased with him."

[23]Whenever the spirit from God came upon Saul, David would take his harp and play. Then relief would come to Saul; he would feel better, and the evil spirit would leave him.

---

[32] J. T. Willis suggests that this section and 18:5 consist of materials inserted by a final redactor and that they were incorporated into the present text to demonstrate theological points regarding David that were of central interest to that editor ("The Function of Comprehensive Anticipatory Redactional Joints in I Samuel 16–18," *ZAW* 85 [1973]: 294–314). This conclusion is possible, based on the evidence, but by no means certain.

16:14–20 David's new status before the Lord stood in sharp contrast to Saul's. When the Lord rejected Saul as king (15:23,26; 16:1), "the Spirit of the LORD had departed from" (v. 14) him as well.[33] Saul had lost the empowering reality behind the anointing that had marked his selection for divine service earlier (cf. 10:1,10). But Saul's condition now was far worse than being without the Lord's Spirit, for "an evil spirit from the LORD tormented him." The Hebrew word translated "evil" (Hb. $r\bar{a}^c\hat{a}$) has a wide range of meanings from "misery" to "moral perverseness."[34] Thus, it is possible—and perhaps preferable—to interpret the text not to mean that the Lord sent a morally corrupt demon[35] but rather another sort of supernatural being—an angel of judgment (cf. 2 Kgs 19:35)—against Saul that caused him to experience constant misery.[36]

Saul's tortured state was not an accident of nature, nor was it essentially a medical condition. It was a supernatural assault by a being sent at the Lord's command, and it was brought on by Saul's disobedience.[37]

The astounding declaration by the writer in vv. 14–15 reflects a worldview that bears further examination. God, the Creator of the universe, had issued a series of behavioral decrees applicable to all humanity, but especially to Israel, and these were revealed supremely in the Torah. The Torah was a path of life, and obedience to the Torah resulted in life and blessing. To disobey Torah requirements was to leave the path of life and enter into the realm of judgment and death. Through his repeated disobedience to the Torah requirements Saul had entered into a living, personal judgment that God brought against him. This punishment was carried out by a divinely created agent of judgment, "an evil [or "troubling"] spirit from the LORD."[38]

This is the only time in the Old Testament that an individual is noted as being tormented by a troubling/evil spirit. Evidence that the writer considered Saul's condition to be unusual is provided by the fact that the verb that

---

[33] D. Howard, Jr., understands the simultaneous transfer of the Spirit from Saul to David as not only a symbol of the transfer of political power but also a reflection of God's disapproval of Israel's manner of establishing the monarchy ("The Transfer of Power from Saul to David in 1 Sam 16:13–14," *JETS* 32 [1989]: 473–83).

[34] Cf. *TWOT* 2.856.

[35] Cf. Youngblood's option, "alien spirit" (*1, 2 Samuel*, 688).

[36] The verb בעת, translated "tormented," has recently been examined more closely in J. Hoftijzer, "Some Remarks on the Semantics of the Root b^ct in Classical Hebrew," in *Pomegranates and Golden Bells*, ed. D. P. Wright et al. (Winona Lake: Eisenbrauns, 1995), 777–83. He concludes that the word refers to an experience of extreme fear and incapacitation.

[37] W. Brueggemann suggests that Saul's "disturbance has to do with alienation rooted in a theological disorder" and is "both theological and psychological" (*First and Second Samuel*, IBC [Louisville: John Knox, 1990], 125).

[38] This line of reasoning could also be used to explain the enigmatic word spoken to King Ahab by the prophet Micaiah (cf. 1 Kgs 22:19–23).

describes Saul's condition (Hb. *bāᶜat*) is used nowhere else in a narrative framework clause in the Torah or Former Prophets; furthermore, the combination of grammatical and lexical features in this clause is rated as the most abnormal in the narrative framework of 1, 2 Samuel.[39]

Though Saul was the one being troubled by the spirit, the writer portrays him as being inert in dealing with it. It was "Saul's attendants" (v. 15), not Saul himself, who correctly diagnosed his condition; it also was they who suggested an effective treatment for helping him "feel better" (v. 16). Their remedy was one known in Israelite circles to have power in the spiritual world (cf. 2 Kgs 3:15), the playing of harp music. By listening to harp music "when the [troubling]/evil spirit comes" (v. 16), Saul "will feel better."

The suggestion seemed reasonable to Saul, and he immediately ordered a search for "someone who plays well" (v. 17). But even before a search party could be organized, an unnamed royal servant suggested that they seek "a son of Jesse of Bethlehem who knows how to play the harp" (v. 18). This individual—David—had numerous other qualifications that befit a person who would serve as a royal aide. Militarily, "he is a brave man and a warrior"; socially, "he speaks well"; physically, "he "is a fine-looking man"; and spiritually, "the LORD is with him." The mention of this last trait puts David in company with Isaac, Joseph, Joshua, and Samuel (cf. Gen 26:28; 39:2–3,21,23; Josh 6:27; 1 Sam 3:19).

On that recommendation Saul sent a message to Jesse ordering him to deliver his son over to the royal court. Dutifully, Jesse complied. The food that he sent—"a donkey loaded with bread,[40] a skin of wine and a young goat" (v. 20)—probably was meant to serve as David's provisions since there was as yet no formal taxation system to support people serving in the nation's political and military establishment.

16:21–23 David came to Saul at Gibeah and "entered his service" (lit., "stood before his face"), and it was not long before the king "loved *[ᵓāhab]* him greatly" ("liked him very much"). So impressed was Saul with this well-recommended shepherd that he decided to make David a permanent member of his court. Saul assigned him a coveted role as "one of his armorbearers." In this position David was kept close to the king and was thus able to respond imme-

---

[39] The fact that the clause is so different from other biblical Hebrew narrative clauses meant that this clause would have been more difficult to process mentally and therefore would have required more attention by a Hebrew speaker reading or listening to the text. As a result the material would have seemed to be "highlighted." This technique of encoding important and unusual information in grammatically exceptional structures is practiced in human communication of all languages. Cf. R. Bergen, "Evil Spirits and Eccentric Grammar: A Study of the Relationship between Text and Meaning in Hebrew Narrative," in *Biblical Hebrew and Discourse Linguistics* (Dallas: SIL, 1994), 320–35.

[40] For a discussion of the phrase לֶחֶם חֲמוֹר cf. D. Tsumura, "*ḥămôr leḥem* (1 Samuel xvi 20)," *VT* 42 (1992): 412–14.

diately "whenever the spirit from God came upon Saul" (v. 23). Gordon cites Qumranic evidence to suggest that David's songs were accompanied by singing as well.[41] Though David's musical efforts were effective in providing relief for Saul, the writer understood that David's success was due to the fact that the Spirit of the Lord was with him in power (vv. 13,18).

David's soothing remedy for Saul's malady was simple yet effective. The Hebrew verb forms in v. 23 suggest that Saul was attacked numerous times by the tormenting spirit; Scripture records two such additional instances (18:10; 19:9), and likely there were others.

The three concluding verses of chap. 16 depict David's first encounter with the one who would soon devote his life to trying to kill him. The verses play an important role in the larger scheme of 1, 2 Samuel, for they serve as the first evidence that David was a loyal, trustworthy servant of Saul who used his abilities to benefit the king. In spite of Saul's repeated efforts to kill David, Israel's next king made absolutely no efforts to bring down Saul's dynasty. In fact, David performed feats in Saul's behalf that no one else could, and the king initially appreciated David's efforts. Any deterioration in the relationship between Saul and David would not be David's fault.

(2) David Rescues Israel from a Philistine Giant (17:1–58)

[1]Now the Philistines gathered their forces for war and assembled at Socoh in Judah. They pitched camp at Ephes Dammim, between Socoh and Azekah. [2]Saul and the Israelites assembled and camped in the Valley of Elah and drew up their battle line to meet the Philistines. [3]The Philistines occupied one hill and the Israelites another, with the valley between them.

[4]A champion named Goliath, who was from Gath, came out of the Philistine camp. He was over nine feet tall. [5]He had a bronze helmet on his head and wore a coat of scale armor of bronze weighing five thousand shekels; [6]on his legs he wore bronze greaves, and a bronze javelin was slung on his back. [7]His spear shaft was like a weaver's rod, and its iron point weighed six hundred shekels. His shield bearer went ahead of him.

[8]Goliath stood and shouted to the ranks of Israel, "Why do you come out and line up for battle? Am I not a Philistine, and are you not the servants of Saul? Choose a man and have him come down to me. [9]If he is able to fight and kill me, we will become your subjects; but if I overcome him and kill him, you will become our subjects and serve us." [10]Then the Philistine said, "This day I defy the ranks of Israel! Give me a man and let us fight each other." [11]On hearing the Philistine's words, Saul and all the Israelites were dismayed and terrified.

[12]Now David was the son of an Ephrathite named Jesse, who was from Bethlehem in Judah. Jesse had eight sons, and in Saul's time he was old and well advanced in years. [13]Jesse's three oldest sons had followed Saul to the war: The firstborn was

---

[41] Gordon (*I and II Samuel*, 153), commenting on the apocryphal psalm 11QPsa27.

Eliab; the second, Abinadab; and the third, Shammah. ¹⁴David was the youngest.
The three oldest followed Saul, ¹⁵but David went back and forth from Saul to tend
his father's sheep at Bethlehem.

¹⁶For forty days the Philistine came forward every morning and evening and
took his stand.

¹⁷Now Jesse said to his son David, "Take this ephah of roasted grain and these
ten loaves of bread for your brothers and hurry to their camp. ¹⁸Take along these
ten cheeses to the commander of their unit. See how your brothers are and bring
back some assurance from them. ¹⁹They are with Saul and all the men of Israel in
the Valley of Elah, fighting against the Philistines."

²⁰Early in the morning David left the flock with a shepherd, loaded up and set
out, as Jesse had directed. He reached the camp as the army was going out to its
battle positions, shouting the war cry. ²¹Israel and the Philistines were drawing up
their lines facing each other. ²²David left his things with the keeper of supplies, ran
to the battle lines and greeted his brothers. ²³As he was talking with them, Goliath,
the Philistine champion from Gath, stepped out from his lines and shouted his
usual defiance, and David heard it. ²⁴When the Israelites saw the man, they all ran
from him in great fear.

²⁵Now the Israelites had been saying, "Do you see how this man keeps coming
out? He comes out to defy Israel. The king will give great wealth to the man who
kills him. He will also give him his daughter in marriage and will exempt his
father's family from taxes in Israel."

²⁶David asked the men standing near him, "What will be done for the man who
kills this Philistine and removes this disgrace from Israel? Who is this uncircumcised Philistine that he should defy the armies of the living God?"

²⁷They repeated to him what they had been saying and told him, "This is what
will be done for the man who kills him."

²⁸When Eliab, David's oldest brother, heard him speaking with the men, he
burned with anger at him and asked, "Why have you come down here? And with
whom did you leave those few sheep in the desert? I know how conceited you are
and how wicked your heart is; you came down only to watch the battle."

²⁹"Now what have I done?" said David. "Can't I even speak?" ³⁰He then turned
away to someone else and brought up the same matter, and the men answered him
as before. ³¹What David said was overheard and reported to Saul, and Saul sent
for him.

³²David said to Saul, "Let no one lose heart on account of this Philistine; your
servant will go and fight him."

³³Saul replied, "You are not able to go out against this Philistine and fight him;
you are only a boy, and he has been a fighting man from his youth."

³⁴But David said to Saul, "Your servant has been keeping his father's sheep.
When a lion or a bear came and carried off a sheep from the flock, ³⁵I went after
it, struck it and rescued the sheep from its mouth. When it turned on me, I seized
it by its hair, struck it and killed it. ³⁶Your servant has killed both the lion and the
bear; this uncircumcised Philistine will be like one of them, because he has defied
the armies of the living God. ³⁷The LORD who delivered me from the paw of the
lion and the paw of the bear will deliver me from the hand of this Philistine."

Saul said to David, "Go, and the LORD be with you."

[38]Then Saul dressed David in his own tunic. He put a coat of armor on him and a bronze helmet on his head. [39]David fastened on his sword over the tunic and tried walking around, because he was not used to them.

"I cannot go in these," he said to Saul, "because I am not used to them." So he took them off. [40]Then he took his staff in his hand, chose five smooth stones from the stream, put them in the pouch of his shepherd's bag and, with his sling in his hand, approached the Philistine.

[41]Meanwhile, the Philistine, with his shield bearer in front of him, kept coming closer to David. [42]He looked David over and saw that he was only a boy, ruddy and handsome, and he despised him. [43]He said to David, "Am I a dog, that you come at me with sticks?" And the Philistine cursed David by his gods. [44]"Come here," he said, "and I'll give your flesh to the birds of the air and the beasts of the field!"

[45]David said to the Philistine, "You come against me with sword and spear and javelin, but I come against you in the name of the LORD Almighty, the God of the armies of Israel, whom you have defied. [46]This day the LORD will hand you over to me, and I'll strike you down and cut off your head. Today I will give the carcasses of the Philistine army to the birds of the air and the beasts of the earth, and the whole world will know that there is a God in Israel. [47]All those gathered here will know that it is not by sword or spear that the LORD saves; for the battle is the LORD's, and he will give all of you into our hands."

[48]As the Philistine moved closer to attack him, David ran quickly toward the battle line to meet him. [49]Reaching into his bag and taking out a stone, he slung it and struck the Philistine on the forehead. The stone sank into his forehead, and he fell facedown on the ground.

[50]So David triumphed over the Philistine with a sling and a stone; without a sword in his hand he struck down the Philistine and killed him.

[51]David ran and stood over him. He took hold of the Philistine's sword and drew it from the scabbard. After he killed him, he cut off his head with the sword.

When the Philistines saw that their hero was dead, they turned and ran. [52]Then the men of Israel and Judah surged forward with a shout and pursued the Philistines to the entrance of Gath and to the gates of Ekron. Their dead were strewn along the Shaaraim road to Gath and Ekron. [53]When the Israelites returned from chasing the Philistines, they plundered their camp. [54]David took the Philistine's head and brought it to Jerusalem, and he put the Philistine's weapons in his own tent.

[55]As Saul watched David going out to meet the Philistine, he said to Abner, commander of the army, "Abner, whose son is that young man?"

Abner replied, "As surely as you live, O king, I don't know."

[56]The king said, "Find out whose son this young man is."

[57]As soon as David returned from killing the Philistine, Abner took him and brought him before Saul, with David still holding the Philistine's head.

[58]"Whose son are you, young man?" Saul asked him.

David said, "I am the son of your servant Jesse of Bethlehem."

Easily the most beloved story in 1, 2 Samuel—indeed, in all the Former

Prophets—is the account of David killing Goliath.[42] So compelling and well-known is the drama that it has become the primary historical metaphor in Western culture for describing any individual or group who overcomes seemingly insurmountable odds to defeat an oppressor.

But the biblical narrative is not primarily a story about human courage and effort; instead, it is about the awesome power of a life built around bold faith in the Lord. Like the story of Jonathan earlier (cf. 14:1–23), this account demonstrates the power of a single faith-filled life to inspire an entire army to victory and the vulnerability of all who "defy the armies of the living God" (vv. 26,36) when confronted by individuals who possess courageous faith in the Lord. As McCarter states, "It is Yahweh who gives victory, and he may give it to the weak (Israel) in order that his power might be known to all."[43]

The popularity and power of this historical account from David's life is not accidental. The writer deliberately employed certain narrative techniques that cause this story to achieve special prominence in the reader's/listener's mind. First of all, he made the account longer[44] than any other Davidic narrative relat-

---

[42] As is predictably the case, biblical scholars have given careful consideration—and often negative evaluations—to this popular story, especially in light of the sizable differences that exist between the LXX and the MT versions, as well as the claim of 2 Sam 21:19 that Elhanan killed Goliath. S. J. DeVries proposes a complicated development of the story that incorporates two different recensions along with midrashic expansion and other editorial additions, with the net result that the present narrative is not to be understood as historically accurate ("David's Victory over the Philistine as Saga and as Legend," *JBL* 92 [1973]: 23–36). H. Jason suggests that the narrative be regarded as a romantic epic ("The Story of David and Goliath: A Folk Epic?" *Bib* 60 [1979]: 36–70). McCarter, who assumes the story is essentially unhistorical in its present form, suggests a four-stage history in the development of the story: (1) an original "old story of an Israelite victory over the Philistines near Socoh, which Saul led but in which David played a prominent role, overshadowing the king; (2) the historical account's essential displacement by a "highly idealized and symbolic" "popular legend of young David's victory"; (3) the insertion of "certain details—the name of the Philistine, the distinctive metaphor about the shaft of the spear (v 7)—. . . from a similar legend about Elhanan"; and (4) the somewhat heavy-handed interpolation of a "complete, alternative account of David's arrival and victory over Goliath" (*I Samuel,* 298). McCarter's position, however, is highly speculative and equally presumptive in its assumed ability to detect such editorial revision and error in Scripture. The MT account may reasonably be accepted as historically accurate. For further treatment of the differences between the MT and LXX versions of the account, consult the Introduction to this commentary.

[43] McCarter, *I Samuel,* 297.

[44] The Codex Vaticanus of the LXX omits vv. 12–31,41,48b,50, part of 51, and 55–58—about eighty percent of the MT account. This fact has led some scholars to speculate that the MT represents a conflation of two originally independent accounts, only one of which is present in the LXX[B]. Cf. E. Tov, "The David and Goliath Saga," *BibRev* 2 (1986): 34–41. McCarter (*I Samuel,* 308) assumes the portions missing from the LXX were added to the MT during the fourth century B.C. On the other hand, Polzin presents a compelling argument on literary grounds favoring the integrity of the MT's rendition of David's encounter with Goliath (*Samuel and the Deuteronomist,* 161–76). The predominant view among OT scholars today is that the LXX[B] is the original version, a conclusion I reject. For further discussion see the introductory section of this commentary.

ing to a single battle with a foreign enemy (912 words in Hebrew).[45] Second, he placed more quotations in it than in other stories (twenty-two), including the longest quotation in 1, 2 Samuel placed on the lips of a named foreigner (Goliath, thirty-three words; 17:8–9). He also provided descriptions of normally omitted aspects of the narrative; for example, the pieces and weight of Goliath's armor, the number of cheeses and loaves of bread brought to the commander, the process of David's acquisition of slingstones, and David's removal of a sword from its scabbard. Furthermore, the account contains details that create apparent tensions with its narrative context: for example, David's absence from Saul's court after he was made a permanent courtier (v. 17; cf. 16:22) and Saul's nonrecognition of David (v. 55; cf. 16:21). These details force the reader to ponder the narrative after its reading and thus make the story more memorable and more likely to be studied further.[46]

17:1–3 We cannot know how soon the events of this chapter occurred after the previous events. However, enough time must have passed for Saul to have changed his policy toward David, permitting him to return to Bethlehem. It also may have been long enough for the youthful David to mature and change significantly in appearance, though not long enough for David to have become old enough for military service (=age twenty; cf. Num 1:3; also 1 Sam 17:33).

As this account opens, the Philistines had assembled their army in the west frontiers of Judah "at Socoh," about eight miles east of Gath and fifteen miles west of Bethlehem, and then "pitched camp" two miles west of Socoh at "Ephes Dammim." Though no free-flowing water exists here, the camp's proximity to a major Philistine city meant that provisions would not be a problem for Israel's enemy.

In response to the Philistine invasion, Saul's army assembled in the Valley of Elah (v. 2; lit., "Valley of the [cultically significant] Tree"), directly opposite the Philistine camp. Separating the two camps geographically was a wadi, a usually dry river bed. Separating the Israelites from the Philistines psychologically, as the following verses indicate, was a chasm of fear.

17:4–7 Among the Philistine ranks was a remarkable soldier named Goliath, a name of possibly Hittite or Lydian origin.[47] He was a "man between the two" (NIV, "champion"). This phrase, used only here in the Old Testament,

---

[45] As is typically the case in effective narrative art, the narrator lengthened the account with the inclusion of nonnarrative information. Among the inclusions are descriptions of Goliath and his armor (vv. 4–7) as well as information regarding David's genealogy (vv. 12–14).

[46] Certain scholars have interpreted these tensions as indications that the present story of David defeating Goliath is actually a combination of independent and perhaps contradictory accounts. Cf. Klein's discussion (*1 Samuel*, 173–74). Such a conclusion fails to do justice to the author's literary skill and in fact tacitly charges the author of 1 Samuel with literary incompetence.

[47] For further discussion of Goliath's name cf. McCarter, *1 Samuel*, 291; W. F. Albright, *CAH* II:30.

apparently refers to an individual who fought to the death in representative
combat with an opponent from a foreign army. One-on-one combat as a substitute for combat between two full armies apparently was not regularly practiced
in Semitic societies; it probably was more commonly employed by the Philistines.[48]

Goliath's most remarkable feature was his height; he was (lit.) "six cubits
and a span" (= nine feet, nine inches) tall.[49] Whether this measure refers to
Goliath in or out of uniform is immaterial; his physical stature was awesome
and psychologically overpowering, especially to the typically small Israelites.

Adding to Goliath's overwhelming appearance as a fighter was his combat
gear. At a time when most Israelite soldiers wore only basic clothing in battle
(cf. 13:22), Goliath was sheathed in metal. His head was covered with "a
bronze helmet" (v. 5). In ancient Egyptian artwork Philistine soldiers are
depicted wearing a feathered headdress, not a helmet;[50] Goliath's headgear
therefore was apparently atypical, designed for the special needs of representative combat. Protecting his trunk was "a coat of scale armor weighing five
thousand shekels" (= 126 pounds). Completing his body armor were "bronze
greaves" (v. 6) or knee and shin protectors. A covering of this weight and composition would have drastically reduced Goliath's ability to respond with
quickness and agility in close combat and suggests that he did not expect a skirmish involving hand-to-hand combat.

Goliath's weaponry was as overwhelming in appearance as his height and
armor. He had "a bronze scimitar" (Hb. *kîdôn*; NIV, "javelin"), a curved sword,
"slung on his back." In addition, he had a spear whose "shaft was like a
weaver's rod." This description may relate to the size and weight of the spear's
shaft or, more probably, to the fact that it had a loop of cord attached to it.[51] At
the head of Goliath's spear was a massive "iron point" that weighed "six hun-

---

[48] Cf. R. de Vaux, "Single Combat in the Old Testament," in *The Bible and the Ancient Near East,* trans. D. McHugh (Garden City: Doubleday, 1971), 122–35, who cites numerous examples from the ancient world in which such contests took place.

[49] The Lucianic recension of the LXX, the Codex Vaticanus, 4QSam[a], and Josephus (*Ant.* 6.171) state that Goliath was only four cubits and a span in height (= 6 ft. 6 in.). This lower figure appears to be a pious emendation designed to increase the text's credibility. Changing this figure, however, creates problems with Goliath's combat gear; e.g., a fifteen-pound spearhead. Clearly the original writer intended to portray Goliath as a person of almost superhuman proportions. D. Kellermann works from the assumption that Goliath suffered from gigantism and suffered from limitations associated with that condition. David exploited the visual problems associated with gigantism in bringing about Goliath's death, according to Kellerman ("Die Geschichte von David und Goliath im Lichte der Endokrinologie," *ZAW* 102 [1990]: 344–57).

[50] Cf. J. B. Pritchard, ed., *The Ancient Near East: Volume I: An Anthology of Texts and Pictures* (Princeton: Princeton University Press, 1958), plate 92.

[51] For further discussion cf. Y. Yadin, "Goliath's Javelin," *PEQ* 86 (1955): 58–69; and L. Krinzetki, "Ein Beitrag zur Stilanalyse der Goliathperikope (1 Sam 17,1–18,5)," *Bib* 54 (1973): 187–236.

dred shekels" (= 15.1 lbs.). Iron was the preferred metal for implements of warfare because it was strong, nonmalleable, and could retain a sharp edge much better than bronze. A weapon of this massive weight, while intimidating in appearance, would have been quite awkward to use; it was apparently designed mainly to intimidate.

As if all this were not enough, Goliath also had a "shield bearer" who "went ahead of him." Two primary styles of shields were used in ancient Near Eastern warfare; a smaller, round shield (Hb. *māgēn*) and a larger, rectangular body shield *(ṣinnâ)*. Goliath's assistant protected him with the second type.

This passage presents the longest description of military attire in the Old Testament. Goliath's physical stature, armor, weaponry, and shield bearer must have made him appear invincible. However, the reader has just been warned against paying undue attention to outward appearances. The detailed description of Goliath's external advantages here suggests that chap. 17 was intended in part to serve as an object lesson in the theology of the previous chapter (cf. 16:7).

17:8–11 As Goliath stepped forth between the two armies, he spoke insolently to the Israelites. First, he questioned their resolve in defending themselves against the army now camped on their lands: if they were unwilling to engage in combat with Goliath, why did they line up for battle? (v. 8).

Second, he educated them concerning the practice of representative combat. The concept was simple: a soldier chosen from the Israelite ranks was to fight to the death with Goliath. The results of the high-stakes contest were also clearcut: the nation represented by the dead soldier would become subject to the nation represented by the victor. The fact that Goliath is recorded as explaining the practice to the Israelites suggests that they had not previously participated in a contest like this; the fact that the Philistines later reneged on the agreement (cf. 18:30) suggests that representative combat was not taken seriously even by those who advocated it.

Third, Goliath insulted the Israelites: "I heap shame on [Hb. *ḥrp*; NIV, "defy"] the ranks of Israel!" The giant's dramatic presentation, complete with costume, actions, and words, achieved its desired effect: "Saul and all the Israelites were dismayed and terrified" (v. 11; cf. also Deut 1:21; 31:8; Josh 8:1; 10:25; 2 Chr 20:15,17; 32:7; Isa 51:7; Ezek 2:6).

17:12–15 The narrative focus shifts to David, who is reintroduced to the reader in this section. Here David's genealogical record is stated explicitly for the first time—it was only implicit prior to this point. Ephrathah, an important matriarch in the Judahite clan (cf. 1 Chr 2:19; 4:4), was the mother of Hur, who was an influential figure in the history of Bethlehem, and a relative of Jesse.

"Jesse had eight sons," and "David was the youngest" (v. 14); these assertions are in tension with 1 Chr 2:13, though not contradicted by it. Though 1 Chr 2:13 notes only seven sons of Jesse and states that David was the seventh, the differences between the passages may simply be a matter of reckoning. If Jesse had a son who died, especially one who died as a minor, the Chronicler's omission of that son could merely be the result of a difference in criteria for inclusion in the genealogical record.

Jesse "was old and well advanced in years" (v. 12) at the time of this Philistine incursion into Judahite territory. Consequently, he was exempted from military service. His sending only "the three oldest" (v. 14) of his sons to serve in Saul's army suggests one or both of two possibilities. The other sons, including David, may have been under the age of twenty, the minimum age for military service in Israel (cf. Num 1:3,19); or perhaps families were required to provide no more than three sons for military service, in which case the three eldest would have been given preference for this task.[52]

Though David had earlier been called a warrior (16:18) and was made a permanent courtier (16:22), he was denied a role in Saul's army assembled at the Valley of Elah. Instead he played a support role, "going back and forth from Saul" (v. 15) in short-term stints (note his use of a tent for a temporary residence, v. 54) that required David to be gone perhaps as little as one night (cf. v. 54). David's responsibilities within Saul's army may have been reduced when three of Jesse's other sons went on active duty. This certainly would have helped Jesse, who needed David to "tend his . . . sheep" now that the other sons had to be away for a lengthy period of time.

17:16–24 The standoff between the encamped armies of the Philistines and Israelites continued for at least "forty days" (v. 16), a situation that would have strained the resources of the impoverished Israelite monarchy. This lengthy standoff also would have made life difficult for individual Israelite families since this event would have occurred during the spring or summer, when adult males would have been needed for agricultural chores. At the beginning and end of each day during that time, Goliath stepped forward to taunt the Israelites.

The families of the soldiers supplied the rations for their relatives and others in the ranks. David bore the responsibility of transporting the foodstuffs to his three brothers as well as "the leader of the thousand" ("commander of their unit"). Meat, a rarity in the typical ancient Israelite diet, was not included among the provisions.

Jesse also asked David to check to see how the patriarch's sons were faring and to "take their token" (NIV, "bring back some assurance from them"). The "token" (Hb. "*arubbâ*) probably was a form of compensation given to families who helped underwrite the army's expenses, perhaps a sort of promissory note

---

[52] Supporting this contention is the fact that only three of Saul's sons were killed in a single battle with the Philistines (31:2); at least one of his sons was spared the battlefield experience (2 Sam 2:8) during the family's fateful encounter with the Philistines.

redeemable for a certain portion of plunder that might be taken from the Philistines in the event of an Israelite victory; alternatively, it was "to confirm the safe delivery of the gifts and that his brothers are still alive."[53]

At the first sign of morning light on the horizon David "left the flock with a shepherd." The inclusion of this subtle detail in the text highlights the fact that David was a "good shepherd"—a significant metaphorical image of a good leader (cf. John 10:1–21)—and increases the contrast between David and Saul (cf. previous notes on chap. 9).

Though the journey exceeded fifteen miles, David arrived at the Israelite camp early in the morning, "as the army was going out to its battle positions shouting the war cry" (v. 21; cf. Josh 6:16) but avoiding any open conflict. Matching the Israelites' movements were the Philistines, who "were drawing up their lines" to create a standoff. Dutifully, David first handed the provisions over to the supply officer and then "ran to the battle lines" and "checked on his brothers' condition" (v. 22; NIV, "greeted his brothers").

Being on the front lines at this hour of the morning, David was able to witness Goliath, "the champion from Gath" (v. 23), as he took his place between the two armies. David heard Goliath's words, and perhaps for the first time in his life he heard the Lord being ridiculed. David also saw his fellow Israelites' reactions to this desecration: "they all ran from him in great fear" (v. 24).

17:25–30 Word had been spread among the soldiers that Saul had determined that Israel should take up Goliath's challenge. Though the king would not personally fight the giant, he would handsomely reward anyone who successfully did so. The offer to "give him his daughter in marriage" (v. 25) was particularly appealing, for it would provide access to additional, unnamed privileges reserved for the royal household.

David was deeply disturbed that a Philistine, who was uncircumcised and therefore outside of a covenant relationship with the Lord, would so boldly heap shame on (NIV, "defy"; v. 26) "the armies of the living God." Goliath's words were not just an insult directed against the Israelite army; they were also an assault on "the living God,"[54] since the army was composed of members of the Lord's covenant community. Having missed out on the details of the king's response to Goliath because of his duties in Bethlehem, David asked for and received further information from "the men standing near him" (v. 26).

David's interest in this matter proved irritating to Eliab, perhaps because of his fear of Goliath, and he caustically accused David of having a haughty and wicked heart that motivated him to abandon his duty to the family's livestock for the sake of watching others die in battle. Of course, Eliab's accusation was

---

[53] For the latter opinion, cf. Hertzberg, *1 and 2 Samuel*, 150.

[54] The appellation אֱלֹהִים חַיִּים was first used in the Torah (Deut 5:26) in a context that emphasizes God's immanence and power. Perhaps David's use of it here was meant to highlight those ideas as well.

false. The author perhaps included it in the narrative to demonstrate the correctness of the Lord's decision to reject Eliab as Israel's next king (cf. 16:7). Like Eli and Saul, Eliab lacked the ability to make proper judgments about others—his "heart" was not right. Eliab's harsh words against his younger brother also strengthen the parallels that exist between David and Joseph, a young man in the Torah who also experienced family criticism prior to saving the Israelites (cf. Gen 37:8).

The concluding clause of David's response to Eliab is brief but problematic. The literal Hebrew—"[Is] it not [a] word/matter?"—is translated variously by major contemporary versions: NKJV: "Is there not a cause?" NRSV: "It was only a question"; NIV: "Can't I even speak?" I am inclined to translate David's response to Eliab loosely in the following way: "What have I done to offend you now? I happen to have been asking about a very important matter." Having ended his brief conversation with Eliab, David returned to his investigation of the matter and received confirmation of the details.

17:31–37 David's outrage sparked by Goliath's blasphemies, as well as his keen interest in the particulars of the royal offer, did not escape the attention of others. Details of David's reaction were even "reported to Saul, and Saul sent for him" (v. 31).

David's words to the king express youthful idealism in its full flower. First he exhorted those around him—all of whom were older than he—to stop being disheartened (lit., "Let not the human heart fall"). Then he proposed an astonishing solution to Israel's dilemma: he himself would "go and fight" Goliath.

Saul immediately rejected David's offer. Then, speaking with the battle-tested voice of reason, he reminded David of some obvious but apparently overlooked facts: "You are only a boy, and he has been a fighting man from his youth" (v. 33). Saul's reference to David's adolescence suggests that David was under twenty years of age, the earliest age at which an Israelite was permitted to serve in the military (cf. Num 1:3; 26:2).

Saul's royal rejection of David's offer should have concluded the meeting. However, David's idealism was exceeded only by his determination and his faith in the Lord. Consequently, he continued his efforts to change the king's heart. This time David dropped his sermonizing, choosing instead to emphasize his credentials and experience: literally, "[A] shepherd was your servant" (v. 34) who had already been victorious in two previous mortal combats, one with a lion and one with a bear. In each case David "went after" the marauding beast and "struck it." Then, when the enraged animal "turned on" David, he "seized it by its hair, struck it, and killed it."

To David's way of thinking, "the uncircumcised Philistine" had reduced himself to the level of a brutish animal "because he . . . defied the armies of the living God" (v. 36). Thus, fighting Goliath would be just another fight with a wild beast. The Lord had delivered David "from the hand ["paw"] of the lion and the hand ["paw"] of the bear," and he would deliver him "from the hand of this Philistine" (v. 37).

David's faith and courage were as extraordinary as his logic was simple. The king, disarmed by David's impressive presentation, decided to make what was perhaps the greatest military gamble of his career and accept David's offer. In a word of blessing that was certainly also a prayer, Saul asked that "the LORD be with" David in his fight.

17:38–40 In addition to the prayerful blessing, Saul also gave David the use of Israel's finest offensive and defensive military gear, the king's own. Saul's battle gear included a basic "tunic" worn next to the skin, "a coat of armor" worn over the cloth garment,[55] a helmet, and a sword.

David allowed Saul to put the armor on him. Ironically, Saul's actions confirmed and foreshadowed the royal status God promised David: the Lord had clothed David with the Spirit that enabled kingship; now Saul clothed David with the symbols that exemplified kingship. Yet David was unable to grow accustomed to Saul's military gear, and he removed it. The writer's inclusion of the clothing incident probably was meant to serve two functions: first, to preserve an unusual but interesting occurrence in the background of the Goliath event, indicating the greater value of divine enablement over human devices; second and more importantly, to symbolize David's rejection of Saul's approach to kingship. Saul chose to dress in royal clothing "such as all the other nations have"; David would wear none of it. Instead, he would identify with the great shepherd-leaders of the Torah—Abraham, Isaac, Jacob, and especially Moses—and live by faith in the promises of God (cf. Heb 11).

Accordingly, David armed himself as a shepherd would have, with a stick and a sling. He "took his staff in his hand" (v. 40). The stick, while a crude weapon, could have afforded some protection in close combat. David also took some stones from the bottom of the wadi. Because the stones were intended for use "with his sling" in battle, they probably were about the size of typical ancient Near Eastern slingstones—as big as tennis balls.[56]

The weapons David gathered for use against Goliath—the stick and the stones—were not products of human artifice; rather, they were shaped by God. As such, the author may have included these details as a counterpoint to 13:19–

---

[55] The Codex Vaticanus of the LXX omits any mention of armor. However, armor is included in the MT, the Syriac, and other major recensions of the LXX; and its description should be considered part of the autographic text.

[56] Examples of ancient Near Eastern slingstones are on display in the Lachish exhibit at the British Museum. Photographs of slingstones from Middle Eastern cultural sites can be seen in *The Ancient Near East: An Anthology of Texts and Pictures*, ed. J. B. Prichard (London: Princeton: 1958), plate 101; and *New Encyclopedia of Archaeological Excavations in the Holy Land*, ed. E. Stern (New York: Simon & Schuster, 1993), 2:463. A Middle Eastern slingstone from the private collection of D. Dorsey at the Evangelical School of Theology weighs approximately 450 grams, very much in line with those on display elsewhere.

22; the Philistines feared and relied on weapons pulled from human forges, but David would conquer them with divinely manufactured weapons. Armed with these provisions, David "approached the Philistine."

17:41–44 The events of the fatal confrontation now unfold rapidly as Goliath and his shield bearer advanced toward David. As Goliath drew near, he noticed for the first time the details of his opponent. Looking David in the face, he "saw that he was only a boy, ruddy and handsome" (v. 42). Winning a contest against a crudely armed, underage challenger would not be particularly prestigious for the Philistine giant, "and he despised" David.

In order to make the most of the contest, however, Goliath began a psychological assault. First, he insulted David's most prominent weapon—the stick in his hand, suggesting that it was an instrument fit only for spanking a dog. Next, he "cursed David by his gods" (v. 43). The author's use of the term "cursed" (Hb. *qālal*) here is theologically significant;[57] readers knowledgeable of the Torah would know that by cursing this son of Abraham, Goliath was bringing down the Lord's curse on himself (cf. Gen 12:3)—a favorable outcome to the battle (from an Israelite perspective!) was thus assured. Finally, Goliath threatened to kill David, dishonor his corpse, and then deny him an honorable burial.

17:45–47 Undaunted by the Philistine's words, David launched a verbal counterattack. He began by demonstrating that he was not going into the battle ignorantly: he was fully aware of Goliath's arsenal—"sword, spear, and scimitar" (v. 45; "javelin"). David also proved he was aware of the greatest of his own military resources, "the name of the LORD Almighty, the God of the armies of Israel" (cf. Ps 18:10–12).[58]

Furthermore, David expressed an awareness that Goliath had committed a capital crime by insulting, and thus blaspheming, the God of Israel. According to the Torah, any individual guilty of blasphemy—even a non-Israelite—must be stoned (Lev 24:16). Perhaps this was an underlying reason why David chose the weapon he did in confronting the Philistine;[59] even before serving as Israel's king, David would prove himself to be a diligent follower of the Torah and thus a man after the Lord's heart. At the same time, of course, David's use

---

[57] K. A. Mathews explains that קלל can mean to "despise" or "show contempt" but like ארר can have the force of verbal imprecation as here (*Genesis 1–11*, NAC [Nashville: Broadman & Holman, 1996], 394–95). V. P. Hamilton notes that at least six different Hb. words are translatable as "curse": ארר, קלל, אלה, קבב, נקב, זעם. Given this fact, the author's decision to render a non-Hebrew's insult with קלל seems all the more deliberate and theologically relevant.

[58] Brueggemann suggests that David's employment of the name יהוה צְבָאוֹת "means to allude to the entire memory of Yahweh's deliverances of Israel in the past" (*First and Second Samuel*, 132).

[59] Whether or not Goliath's blasphemy was the primary reason for David's use of the slingstone to kill Goliath, the writer of 1, 2 Samuel has certainly gone to considerable lengths elsewhere in the presentation of David's life to demonstrate that this king was scrupulous in his observance of Torah regulations—with one tragic exception (2 Sam 11:3–4).

of the sling and stone also must have been motivated by the fact that he was skillful in their use and the weapon was especially suited for exploiting Goliath's vulnerabilities.

As David viewed it, Goliath was outnumbered and would soon be overpowered, for the Lord would fight with David against the giant. In the battle that would occur "this day" (v. 46), the Lord would "hand [Goliath] over" to David; then for his part the young shepherd would "strike [Goliath] down and cut off [his] head." David's efforts would not be limited to slaying Goliath; he also would slaughter and humiliate the Philistine army. Yet the Philistines would not die in vain. In fact, their destruction would serve a high theological purpose; it would be a revelatory event by which "the whole world will know that there is a God in Israel" (cf. Josh 2:10–11). Achieving a depth of insight remarkable for a person of any age, young David perceived that the events of this day would give rise to narrative accounts that would reveal the Lord's power and reality to all who might hear them. Eyewitnesses to the ensuing battle would learn an additional truth from the Lord, "that it is not by sword or spear that the LORD saves, for the battle is the LORD's" (v. 47; cf. 2:9–10; 13:22; Jer 9:23–24; Zech 4:6).

David, the Lord's anointed one, discerned a theological purpose in warfare. This perspective is one that must be examined because it is of utmost importance for understanding the mind-set of orthodox Israelites in the Old Testament. For David—and, we judge, for all Old Testament Israelites of true faith in God—armed conflict was fundamentally a religious event.[60] Only when the Lord willed it were Israelites under David's command to engage in it (cf. 2 Sam 5:19). And when the Lord ordained battle for David's troops, it was to be performed in accordance with divine directives (cf. 2 Sam 5:23–25). Furthermore, because soldiers were performing God's work, only individuals who were in a state of ritual purity were to participate in military missions (cf. 1 Sam 21:5). The Lord was the one who gave victory to David and his troops in battle (cf. v. 47; 2 Sam 22:30,36,51), and thus the Lord alone was worthy of praise for David's and Israel's military successes (2 Sam 22:47–48).

17:48–51 The conflict reached a climax as words ceased and both parties moved toward one another for battle. David was clearly the more dynamic combatant; whereas as Goliath merely "walked" (Hb. *hālak*; v. 48), David "ran quickly" (lit., "hastened and ran") to meet him.

David's weapon of choice against Goliath (the sling) provided him with a tremendous advantage over the weapons at Goliath's disposal. All of Goliath's weapons were of value only in close combat; even the giant's spear, because it weighed over fifteen pounds, could not have been used effectively against an opponent standing more than a few feet away. On the other hand, David could

---

[60] See T. Longman III and D. G. Reid, *God Is a Warrior* (Grand Rapids: Zondervan, 1996).

use his sling with deadly force from comparatively great distances. With his
youthful vigor and unencumbered by heavy armor and weaponry, David could
quickly move to locations from which he could hurl the tennis-ball-sized stones
directly at Goliath.

Taking a single stone, David felled the Philistine with facility and deadly
accuracy.[61] The rock was hurled with such great force that it crushed the frontal
bone of Goliath's cranium and "sank into his forehead." In accordance with the
requirement of the Torah (cf. Lev 24:16), "without a sword in his hand he
struck down the Philistine and killed him" (1 Sam 17:50).

David had achieved a stunning victory over the Philistine. Immediately after
Goliath died, David followed the battlefield customs of the day (cf. 31:9) by
stripping the dead man of his weapon and decapitating the corpse. These final
acts against the giant served as undeniable proof to the Philistines "that their
hero was dead." In shock and confusion, "they turned and ran" in a westerly
direction, away from the Israelites.

17:52–54 Energized by David's undreamed-of success and the sight of
panic-stricken Philistines, the army of Israel chased the Philistines westward
until they came "to a valley" (NIV, "to the entrance of Gath")[62] and then along
the coastal plain "to the gates of Ekron," a distance exceeding ten miles. Strag-
glers from the fleeing army were caught and executed all the way to the protective confines of Gath and Ekron.

When the chase concluded, the Israelites returned to plunder the abandoned
Philistine camp in the Valley of Elah. David's battlefield trophies consisted of
the Philistine's head (v. 54), "which he brought to Jerusalem," and his weapons, which he put "into his own tent."[63] No doubt David had taken the tent for
his journey along with the provisions of food. Later he would dedicate the most
prized of the weapons to the Lord (cf. 21:9).

Why David brought Goliath's head to Jerusalem is unclear, since the city
was not under Israelite control at the time. Perhaps David brought the gruesome remains of Israel's most feared enemy to Jerusalem to intimidate the

---

[61] A. Deem argues that the word מִצְחוֹ should be translated "his greave," not "his forehead"
("'. . . and the stone sank into his forehead.' A Note on 1 Samuel xvii 49," *VT* 28 [1978]: 349–51).
This suggestion, however, is not supported by any ancient translations, nor has it been followed by
modern versions. Furthermore, it seems illogical to assume that David's primary offensive efforts
would have been directed against an armored portion of Goliath. The traditional translation is
clearly preferable.

[62] The NIV follows the Codex Vaticanus and Lucianic recension of the LXX to substitute Γεθ
("Gath") for the MT גַּיְא ("valley"). This departure from the MT reading seems unnecessary, since
the Hebrew reading makes good logical and geographic sense; the Philistines would have naturally
fled westward following the wadi/valley until it opened in the coastal plain closer to Ekron.

[63] Hertzberg emends בְּאָהֳלוֹ to בְּאָהֳלֵי and then interprets it to mean that David placed Goliath's sword in "the tent-sanctuary of Yahweh" (*I and II Samuel,* 154). This creative suggestion can
be safely rejected since it lacks textual support.

city's inhabitants; mounting the Israelite war trophy in a conspicuous location would certainly demonstrate to this long-time nemesis that Israel was a nation to be feared.[64] The fact that Jerusalem was the first city David attacked after he became king of all Israel (cf. 2 Sam 5:6) suggests that he had prioritized the conquest of the city for some time.

A second possible reason for selecting Jerusalem as the site for depositing Goliath's head was because it was the major city in the frontier separating the northern tribes from their somewhat alienated Israelite brothers to the south (cf. Josh 15:8),[65] and thus a neutral place where both Israelite groups could go to divide up the spoils of war. His tribal forebears had also used the site as a place to bring prizes of war prior to their (temporary) conquest of the city (Judg 1:7–8). Israelites were apparently permitted to enter the city (cf. Judg 19:11), and it is reasonable to assume that the Jebusites had worked out a coexistence with the Israelites who ringed their settlement. Klein suggests that the note regarding David bringing Goliath's head to Jerusalem may refer to an event that occurred years later, following David's conquest of the city.[66]

17:55–58 The writer makes use of flashback in vv. 55–56. Here Saul is depicted conversing with Abner, his commander (v. 55) prior to David's encounter with Goliath. At that time the king ordered his general to find out what family "that young man" belonged to (v. 56).

Verses 57–58 return to the narrative strand and thus the time and geographic location in v. 54. David was "still holding the Philistine's head" (v. 57), and it is reasonable to assume that Saul had relocated the Israelite base camp at Jerusalem, a site only about four miles from his capital city. At this site the conquering hero was brought before Saul, who asked him directly his father's name.

Contrary to the opinions of some, the portrayal of Saul's inquiry does not provide convincing evidence of contradictory accounts being blended together.[67] A writer/redactor as skillful as the one who put together 1 Samuel

---

[64] Baldwin affirms this first option as a possibility when she suggests that David could be "giving this important city reason to recognize Israel's dominance" (*1 and 2 Samuel*, 128).

[65] Evidence of incipient tensions between Judah and Israel are present throughout the earlier portions of the Former Prophets (cf. Josh 11:21; 1 Sam 11:8; also 18:16). They also are seen in the separate mention of these two Israelite entities in v. 52.

[66] Klein, *1 Samuel*, 181. I reject this position on grammatical grounds. The paired clauses of v. 54b—a *waw*-consecutive-plus-suffixal imperfect clause and an object-fronted perfect clause—suggest David's activities with Goliath's head and weapons occurred at essentially the same time. Cf. R. Bergen, "Varieties and Functions of *Waw*-plus-subject-plus-perfect-verb Sentence Constructions in the Narrative Framework of the Pentateuch" (Ann Arbor: University Microfilms, 1986).

[67] Cf. the structure and comments of McCarter's commentary in dealing with chap. 17 (*1 Samuel*, 284–309). McCarter treats 17:1–11,32–40,42–48a,49, and 51–54 as elements of one narrative strand (pp. 284–98) and 17:12–31,41,48b,50,55–58; 18:1–5,10–11,17–19, and 29b–30 as a second, post-fourth-century B.C. narrative strand.

to 2 Kings would likely not have been so literarily clumsy as to botch one of the most dramatic narrative accounts to be found in the Bible.

A more satisfying reading of the text here is one that sees one or more important plot functions for this flashback section. First, it was included to confirm the accuracy of reports David had heard about Saul's offer to provide a tax exemption for the family of the Israelite who killed Goliath (v. 25). Saul asked David for his father's name so that he could properly formulate an edict in behalf of Jesse's family and perhaps also so that he could learn more about the family background of the one who had earned the right to become the king's son-in-law.

In a different direction this passage may also function to demonstrate that the Lord's Spirit was no longer with Saul. Being devoid of the divine Spirit, Saul also was intellectually incompetent. The image presented in vv. 55–58 of a king who cannot remember details related to one of his most beloved and trusted courtiers (cf. 16:21–22) contrasts strikingly with King David later, who, empowered by the Lord, was like an angel of God "to know everything that is in the land" (2 Sam 14:20).

(3) The House of Saul Honors and Elevates David (18:1–5)

¹After David had finished talking with Saul, Jonathan became one in spirit with David, and he loved him as himself. ²From that day Saul kept David with him and did not let him return to his father's house. ³And Jonathan made a covenant with David because he loved him as himself. ⁴Jonathan took off the robe he was wearing and gave it to David, along with his tunic, and even his sword, his bow and his belt.
⁵Whatever Saul sent him to do, David did it so successfully that Saul gave him a high rank in the army. This pleased all the people, and Saul's officers as well.

18:1–5 Immediately after David's conversation with the king, his relationship with the royal family changed forever. For one thing, Saul's first-born son found in David a soul mate, and "Jonathan's soul was tied to David's soul" (NIV, "Jonathan became one in spirit with David"; v. 1). This was understandable because David and Jonathan had much in common; they were both courageous and capable young warriors who possessed profound faith in the Lord. Both had initiated faith-motivated attacks against militarily superior Philistines that had resulted in great victories for Israel.

Jonathan, like his father Saul (16:21), "loved" (Hb. *ʾāhab*; v. 3) David. That love inspired him to make a covenant with David, one that was expressed with extravagant gifts to the new celebrity. In a single day David had acquired the finest sword in the Philistine army as well as one of the finest swords in Israel's armory; he had been permitted to wear the king's clothing in the time of conflict and was given princely clothing in times of peace. The fact that Jonathan gave David the garb and armaments originally reserved for the heir to Saul's throne clearly possesses symbolic and thematic significance. In an apologetic vein, it also provides an explanation of how David came to possess these coveted tokens of power.

Not only did David's relationship with Jonathan evolve that day, but so did his relationship with the king. He became a member of the royal household and as such did not prove disappointing.

The term translated "caused to prosper/did successfully" (a form of *śākal*) is theologically significant; according to the Torah (Deut 29:8 [Eng., 29:9]), those who would keep the words of the Sinai covenant would "prosper in everything" they did. The author's employment of language that brings this Torah promise to mind is not accidental. The comment in v. 5 underscores the claim made elsewhere (16:13) that David was a man under the control and direction of the Lord's Spirit—the same Spirit who had brought into being the Sinai covenant and rewarded its adherents with prosperity.

In a manner reminiscent of Joseph, another man who prospered because the Spirit of God was in him (cf. Gen 41:38–40), David was rewarded with a position of great responsibility: "a high rank in the army." Saul's action was met by the approval of "all the people and Saul's officers as well."

(4) Saul Begins to Perceive David as a Threat (18:6–9)

⁶When the men were returning home after David had killed the Philistine, the women came out from all the towns of Israel to meet King Saul with singing and dancing, with joyful songs and with tambourines and lutes. ⁷As they danced, they sang:

**"Saul has slain his thousands,
and David his tens of thousands."**

⁸Saul was very angry; this refrain galled him. "They have credited David with tens of thousands," he thought, "but me with only thousands. What more can he get but the kingdom?" ⁹And from that time on Saul kept a jealous eye on David.

18:6–9 David's—and thus Saul's—phenomenal success was celebrated by all. After the Philistine campaign was concluded and the army was returning, grateful mothers, wives, and daughters met them with expressions of appreciation. The triumphant soldiers were treated to the sights and sounds of women "singing and dancing." The word "lutes" (Hb. *šališîm*), used only here in a context of revelry, is a derivative of the word for "three"; it may refer to a three-sided or three-stringed musical instrument, or it may be a musical term for a kind of poetry.

In accordance with an ancient Israelite custom (cf. Exod 15:21; Judg 5:1–31), the women composed songs with lyrics that memorialized the men's military successes. Five words (in Hebrew)—two lines—of the poem celebrating the present triumph are preserved. The poetry possesses characteristics typical of ancient Near Eastern poetry: parallelism and the use of a fixed word pair, "thousand" (ʾelep) and "ten thousand" (rĕbābâ).[68]

Saul's reaction to this couplet was predictable and intense. Even more than angry, it "was evil in his eyes" ("galled him") because he connected the mention of David with Samuel's prophecy of a previously anonymous "neighbor" of Saul to whom the Lord had given the kingdom of Israel (cf. 15:28). As a result, Saul watched David with jealousy.

The writer's use of the verb translated "kept a jealous eye" (Hb. ʿôyēn) probably is intended as a double entendre involving a similar-sounding word meaning "transgressed" (Hb. ʿwn).[69] The effect of this subtle wordplay is to inform the reader that from this point on Saul would carefully observe David for the purpose of committing sins against him.

(5) Saul Attempts Unsuccessfully to Murder David (18:10–12)

[10]The next day an evil spirit from God came forcefully upon Saul. He was prophesying in his house, while David was playing the harp, as he usually did. Saul had a spear in his hand [11]and he hurled it, saying to himself, "I'll pin David to the wall." But David eluded him twice.

[12]Saul was afraid of David, because the LORD was with David but had left Saul.

18:10–12 Saul wasted no time in attempting to eliminate David as Israel's next king. At the royal quarters in Gibeah, during an apparently tranquil scene, an "evil/tormenting spirit from God came forcefully upon Saul."[70] The narrator's portrayal of Saul prophesying under the influence of an evil/troubling spirit identifies Saul as a false prophet (cf. 1 Kgs 22:21–23) and therefore one who was not to be feared (Deut 18:22). Like Goliath (cf. 1 Sam 17:7), a previous adversary of David, "Saul had a spear in his hand."

Not once, but twice Saul hurled the spear at David with the intention of pinning him to the wall (v. 11). David's willingness to remain in the room long enough for Saul to retrieve the spear after the failed first attempt and then take a second shot at him portrays the incredible depth of David's loyalty to the king and his commitment to helping Saul overcome his torments.

Ironically, the spear episode incited fear—not in David, but in Saul. Saul

---

[68] For other uses of the fixed word pair אלף, רבבה cf. Deut 32:30; Ps 91:7; Mic 6:7.

[69] The ketiv reading here is actually עון ("transgression"), although the pointed qere' form is עוֹיֵן, a qal participle form of עין, "to eye, keep an eye(?)."

[70] Baldwin suggests that Saul's prophetic activity consisted of an "experience of ecstasy" (1 and 2 Samuel, 130).

reasoned correctly that the only way the young man was able to evade the point of his spear at such close range was that "the LORD was with David but had left Saul" (v. 12).

(6) David Becomes Saul's Son-in-Law (18:13–30)

[13]So he sent David away from him and gave him command over a thousand men, and David led the troops in their campaigns. [14]In everything he did he had great success, because the LORD was with him. [15]When Saul saw how successful he was, he was afraid of him. [16]But all Israel and Judah loved David, because he led them in their campaigns.

[17]Saul said to David, "Here is my older daughter Merab. I will give her to you in marriage; only serve me bravely and fight the battles of the LORD." For Saul said to himself, "I will not raise a hand against him. Let the Philistines do that!"

[18]But David said to Saul, "Who am I, and what is my family or my father's clan in Israel, that I should become the king's son-in-law?" [19]So when the time came for Merab, Saul's daughter, to be given to David, she was given in marriage to Adriel of Meholah.

[20]Now Saul's daughter Michal was in love with David, and when they told Saul about it, he was pleased. [21]"I will give her to him," he thought, "so that she may be a snare to him and so that the hand of the Philistines may be against him." So Saul said to David, "Now you have a second opportunity to become my son-in-law."

[22]Then Saul ordered his attendants: "Speak to David privately and say, 'Look, the king is pleased with you, and his attendants all like you; now become his son-in-law.'"

[23]They repeated these words to David. But David said, "Do you think it is a small matter to become the king's son-in-law? I'm only a poor man and little known."

[24]When Saul's servants told him what David had said, [25]Saul replied, "Say to David, 'The king wants no other price for the bride than a hundred Philistine fore-skins, to take revenge on his enemies.'" Saul's plan was to have David fall by the hands of the Philistines.

[26]When the attendants told David these things, he was pleased to become the king's son-in-law. So before the allotted time elapsed, [27]David and his men went out and killed two hundred Philistines. He brought their foreskins and presented the full number to the king so that he might become the king's son-in-law. Then Saul gave him his daughter Michal in marriage.

[28]When Saul realized that the LORD was with David and that his daughter Michal loved David, [29]Saul became still more afraid of him, and he remained his enemy the rest of his days.

[30]The Philistine commanders continued to go out to battle, and as often as they did, David met with more success than the rest of Saul's officers, and his name became well known.

18:13–16 His first attempt at killing David having failed, Saul tried a different tactic. David was removed from the protected confines of the royal res-

idence and was sent to lead Saul's troops in battle. These circumstances clearly
posed risks for both David's reputation and his well-being. Failure to perform
his duties successfully even once on the battlefield would reduce or erase
David's prestige and popularity and perhaps even end his life. However, David
was successful in carrying out every assignment "because the LORD was with
him." David's divinely assisted success in these military campaigns had two
effects on others: it added to Saul's fears, and it increased the people's love for
David.

18:17–19 Knowing that David's chances of being killed increased in proportion to the amount of time spent on the battlefield, Saul cunningly honored
his offer to give his daughter in marriage to the one who slew Goliath (cf.
17:25). However, Saul's offer was subtly nuanced; David was to be given
Saul's "older daughter Merab" (v. 17), but not as a reward for past accomplishments as had been implied in the original proposal. Instead she would be
acquired with the dual currencies of ongoing military service and zeal for the
Lord. Though David might not be motivated to risk his life in order to gain the
hand of the king's daughter in marriage, perhaps he could be persuaded to do
so as a demonstration of his commitment to the Lord. If David accepted the
offer, Saul could passively "let the Philistines" destroy his most feared adversary. Thus, David's love for God could be used to destroy God's youthful
anointed one.

A historical precedent existed for David to accept the conditions set by Saul
for gaining entrance into the royal family: Jacob had once used work as an
alternative to paying the customary bride price for a wife (cf. Gen 29:15–19);
so could David. David, who was indeed a gifted and enthusiastic warrior for
the Lord, was not troubled by the stipulations in the king's agreement; he would
fight in behalf of his God with or without the opportunity to win a royal bride.
Yet David refused the offer because of another consideration: David possessed
an undistinguished genealogy, so that he felt unqualified to "become the king's
son-in-law" (v. 18).[71] Saul was from a wealthy family; David was not. Saul
was king of Israel; David was a rural shepherd who possessed Moabite blood
(cf. Ruth 4:13–17).

David could not be dissuaded in the matter, so Merab "was given in marriage to Adriel of Meholah" (v. 19). This union produced five sons who were
later killed by the Gibeonites (2 Sam 21:8–9) as a lingering result of Saul's sin.

18:20–25 Not to be stymied, Saul saw in his "daughter Michal" (v. 20) a
third means of destroying David. Saul learned to his delight (lit., "it was
straight in his eyes") that this daughter "was in love with David." David had

---

[71] G. W. Coats understands David's statement "Who am I, and what is my family that I should
become the king's son-in-law?" (v. 18) as an example of a standard self-abasement/insult formula
that would be standardly employed in the presence of a social superior, especially royalty (cf.
"Self-Abasement and Insult Formulas," *JBL* 89 (1970): 14–26.

previously eluded the king's spear and the Philistines' weapons, but perhaps he could be ensnared and ruined by a woman. As Saul envisioned it, David would be facing a double threat: "the hand of the Philistines" (v. 21) and Michal herself, who would be a "snare to him." Michal could be a snare in two ways: first, she could motivate David to place his life at extreme risk in battle with the Philistines; second, she could corrupt David spiritually.

The term translated as "snare" (Hb. *môqēš*) is a theologically significant one, used three times in the Torah to describe the dangers of idols and idol worshipers (Exod 23:33; 34:12; Deut 7:16). Perhaps Saul was spiritually astute enough to recognize that in marriage his daughter's idolatrous inclinations (cf. 19:13) could easily lead David astray, in which case David would become the Lord's enemy and come to a disastrous end. Thus Saul was especially eager to provide David with "a second opportunity" to become a "son-in-law" to the king and spoke to David directly about it.

Saul reinforced his offer to David with a covert disinformation campaign. Previously David had heard from unnamed servants of Saul about the offer regarding Goliath; now from similar sources he would be informed of important particulars regarding the marriage offer. Of greatest priority, David was to be told that "the king is pleased with you" (v. 22); David would surely interpret this to mean that Saul was willing to overlook David's undistinguished background, thus clearing the way for David to "become [Saul's] son-in-law."

When David heard these words, however, he balked. Saul may be willing to disregard social proprieties, but David could not; he was "a poor man and little known" (v. 22). So for a second time he refused the offer to join the royal family.

Saul extended the offer to David a third time, this time providing David with an honorable means of overcoming all other shortcomings. David's "price for the bride" (v. 25)—and thus for the right to become the king's son-in-law—was "a hundred Philistine foreskins," implying one hundred Philistine deaths. As an added inducement, the offer was presented to David as a patriotic duty; David must fight the Philistines to help the king "take revenge on his enemies."

18:26–30 David's mind was changed; he was now "pleased to become the king's son-in-law" (v. 26; lit., "the matter was straight[ened out] in his eyes"). A deadline was set for David to meet the challenge, but before it came, David had succeeded abundantly (v. 27).[72] Then in a macabre ceremony David "pre-

---

[72] The Codex Vaticanus and Lucianic recensions of the LXX state that David killed a hundred Philistines. McCarter (*I Samuel*, 316) accepts the lower figure, citing 2 Sam 3:14 as his justification. However, 2 Sam 3:14 and the present passage suggest that David understood the מֹהַר to be one hundred Philistine foreskins (cf. v. 25). There is no substantive reason to doubt that the MT preserves the original reading. To the contrary, the larger number emphasizes David's commitment to Saul and his zeal for pleasing his master, thus underscoring the thesis that David was Saul's loyal servant throughout his lifetime.

sented the full number" of severed portions of Philistine genitals to the king "so
that he might become the king's son-in-law." The fact that David exceeded by
a hundred the required number of deaths underscores David's commitment to
the king and his eagerness to join the royal family. Saul had no choice but to
give David "his daughter Michal in marriage."

Because Saul was an eyewitness to David's prodigious success, he "realized
[knew] that the LORD was with David" (v. 28). That, added to the fact that two
of his own children were now bonded to David in friendship and love, rekindled Saul's anxieties concerning David. Michal's love for David had not eliminated him as a menace as had been hoped; instead, it had brought him into the
inner circle of legitimate contenders for the throne. As Saul viewed things,
David had now become the most serious threat to the Saulide dynasty, and so
"he remained his enemy the rest of his days" (v. 29).

Saul's efforts against the Philistines, including those involving David, were
not sufficient to stem the tide of Philistine aggression against Israel. But David
continued to go out to battle, even though he had already gained the coveted
marital status. And when he went, he exceeded all others in victories.[73] As a
result, David's name "was highly acclaimed" (NIV "became well known").

(7) Saul Attempts to Have Jonathan Murder David (19:1–7)

[1]Saul told his son Jonathan and all the attendants to kill David. But Jonathan
was very fond of David [2]and warned him, "My father Saul is looking for a chance
to kill you. Be on your guard tomorrow morning; go into hiding and stay there. [3]I
will go out and stand with my father in the field where you are. I'll speak to him
about you and will tell you what I find out."

[4]Jonathan spoke well of David to Saul his father and said to him, "Let not the
king do wrong to his servant David; he has not wronged you, and what he has done
has benefited you greatly. [5]He took his life in his hands when he killed the Philistine. The LORD won a great victory for all Israel, and you saw it and were glad.
Why then would you do wrong to an innocent man like David by killing him for no
reason?"

[6]Saul listened to Jonathan and took this oath: "As surely as the LORD lives,
David will not be put to death."

[7]So Jonathan called David and told him the whole conversation. He brought
him to Saul, and David was with Saul as before.

---

[73] The word translated by the NIV here as "met with . . . success" is שׂכל, a verb that elsewhere
may mean "possess understanding/wisdom." The occurrence of the verb here marks the fourth time
in this chapter the verb is used with David as a subject (cf. also vv. 5,14,15). This verb is used to
describe David more than any other person in the Hebrew Bible. Possession of this characteristic
is elsewhere associated with a knowledge of the Torah (Ps 119:99). The author's repeated employment of the verb to describe David is likely meant to reinforce the theme of David as a man of the
Torah—in other words, a man after God's own heart.

19:1–5 With great deliberateness and exactness the writer chronicles Saul's growing efforts to eliminate David. Although he initially loved David (16:21), Saul came to fear him (18:12) and then to seek his death. Saul's attempts began with a murderous thought (18:11), then progressed to awkward homicidal acts hidden from public view (18:11). Saul then crafted a wider and more artful plan that involved public lies (18:22) and a small circle of people, including servants and a daughter. The circle of involvement widened when this effort failed. Dropping all ruses, Saul now explicitly ordered Jonathan and all his servants to "kill David" (19:1).

When Jonathan heard his father's words, an internal collision occurred between the young man's love for David and his desire to please his father. Jonathan had known his father to issue poorly conceived commands in the past (cf. 14:29). He had also had his own life spared when others stood up against his father's rash words (14:39–45). Now, when he sensed that a heroic young life like his own was at risk, Jonathan acted to spare David's life.

First, he "warned" (v. 2) David by revealing Saul's intentions and timetable for murder. Next, he formulated a plan of escape for David. Finally, he proposed a plan to gather further information from the king and pass it along to David.

Jonathan fulfilled his part in the plan as he "spoke well of David to Saul" (v. 4). He urged the king to reconsider his plans for David and provided Saul with several reasons for doing so. The first reason was David's innocence; that is, he had committed no crime against the crown that would require his death. Second, on the positive side David had been of great help to Saul by killing a dreaded enemy. Third, Saul should spare David's life to avoid committing a serious sin, that of shedding innocent blood.

19:6–7 Jonathan's impeccable reasoning achieved—for the time being— the desired result: Saul "listened to Jonathan" (v. 6). The king took a solemn oath "by the life of Yahweh" (NIV, "as surely as the LORD lives") to underscore his decision that "David will not be put to death."

Having negotiated the reconciliation, Jonathan went at once to David to inform him of his success and accompany David back to the royal household. As a result, "David was with Saul as before" (v. 7). For the time being, at least, David was spared by the efforts of Jonathan, the man who had perhaps the most to gain from David's death.

(8) David Continues to Defeat the Philistines (19:8)

⁸Once more war broke out, and David went out and fought the Philistines. He struck them with such force that they fled before him.

19:8 Philistine attacks on Israel punctuated the eleventh century B.C. as these two peoples fought for undisputed control of Palestine's southern coastal plain and Shephelah region. When the Philistines once again went on the offensive, Israel's youthful commander David, as before (cf. 18:5,14,27,30), (lit.) "dealt them a great blow" so that "they fled before him."

(9) Saul Again Attempts to Murder David (19:9–10)

⁹But an evil spirit from the LORD came upon Saul as he was sitting in his house with his spear in his hand. While David was playing the harp, ¹⁰Saul tried to pin him to the wall with his spear, but David eluded him as Saul drove the spear into the wall. That night David made good his escape.

19:9–10 David's return to Gibeah and the royal residence following battle did not mean a lessening of dangers for David, for a tormenting/evil "spirit from the LORD"[74] (v. 9) had once again come upon Saul. The "spear in his hand" served as a clear indication that Saul was having problems; only a deeply troubled individual would sit armed for war inside the safest house in Israel! As was the custom during these difficult times in Saul's life (cf. 16:23), "David was playing the harp" in the king's presence.

David was keenly aware of Saul's threatening behavior in the past (cf. 18:10–11); accordingly, he surely had prepared himself for any irrational acts that might ensue. Thus, when "Saul tried to pin him to the wall with his spear" (v. 10), David escaped. Unlike the previous similar incident, however, David did not remain in Saul's presence to provide him with a second opportunity to take his life; he returned to his own residence and later that night would even depart the city (cf. v. 12).

(10) Michal Rescues David from Saul (19:11–17)

¹¹Saul sent men to David's house to watch it and to kill him in the morning. But Michal, David's wife, warned him, "If you don't run for your life tonight, tomorrow you'll be killed." ¹²So Michal let David down through a window, and he fled and escaped. ¹³Then Michal took an idol and laid it on the bed, covering it with a garment and putting some goats' hair at the head.

¹⁴When Saul sent the men to capture David, Michal said, "He is ill."

¹⁵Then Saul sent the men back to see David and told them, "Bring him up to me in his bed so that I may kill him." ¹⁶But when the men entered, there was the idol in the bed, and at the head was some goats' hair.

¹⁷Saul said to Michal, "Why did you deceive me like this and send my enemy away so that he escaped?"

Michal told him, "He said to me, 'Let me get away. Why should I kill you?'"

19:11–13 In his demonic passion Saul "sent men" (v. 11) to kill David when he left his house the next morning. But Michal was aware of her father's

---

[74] Cf. discussion at 18:10.

plan and, like her brother, "warned" David of the danger and urged him to flee before morning (cf. v. 2). She even facilitated his escape by letting David down through an unguarded window. Then in an act that revealed as much about her spiritual condition as it did about her commitment to her husband, Michal "took a teraphim" ("idol") and used it to deceive Saul's cohorts.

The reference here to a teraphim, apparently a large anthropomorphic idol,[75] is the second one in 1 Samuel. Ominously, the prophet Samuel previously had suggested that Saul's rebellious acts were equitable to the "evil of teraphim" (15:23). Through the present compelling scene and without the intrusion of didactic commentary, the writer suggests that Michal was as much a spiritual rebel as her father. This observation foreshadows an outcome for Michal's life that is the feminine counterpart to Saul's. Michal's father lost his opportunity to establish a dynasty; Michal lost her opportunity to establish a family (2 Sam 6:23). When read in connection with Psalm 59,[76] Michal's action creates a strong contrast with those of her husband; whereas Michal trusted in a teraphim to save David, David trusted in the Lord (cf. Ps 59:9–10,16–17).

In spite of the negative implications of the teraphim, the sequence of actions performed by Michal creates links between her and those of previous biblical heroines. In each case these allusions identify David in particularly favorable comparisons. Jacob too was saved by a woman who had possession of teraphim and deceived her father during a desperate search (cf. Gen 31:19–35). Moses also was saved through the efforts of the daughter of a wicked ruler (cf. Exod 2:6–10). Furthermore, David's escape echoed that of the spies saved by Rahab, who were let down through a window at night by a woman who lied to a king (Josh 2:2–15).

In both this instance and the one involving Jonathan earlier in the chapter, members of Saul's own family took the lead in scheming to protect David's life. In both instances David was portrayed as the passive conspirator in the attempts to undermine Saul's will. Saul's own children were the ones who initiated and executed plans in David's behalf to derail their father's purposes.

The author's careful description of the circumstances surrounding David's deliverances are not without purpose; they reinforce the claim that David did not usurp the throne from Saul. Leading members of Saul's own family loved and supported David throughout his rise to power and even played leading roles in David's ascent.

---

[75] J. Tropper suggests that a teraphim was utilized in ancestor worship and as an aid for use in magical healing rituals ("Trpym, rituels de guerison et culte des ancestres d'aprés 1 Samuel XIX 11–17 et les textes parvalleles d'Assur et de Nuzi," *VT* 37 [1981]: 340–61).

[76] The canonical tradition expressed in the preface to Psalm 59 explicitly connects this psalm to the present incident. The NIV's preface to Psalm 59, which is not assigned a verse number, is actually v. 1 of the MT.

19:14–17   The next morning Saul's messengers entered David's residence. However, the socially powerful daughter of the king refused to grant the men access to David's room, claiming he was ill. Being understandably hesitant to act against the objections of a royal family member, they returned to Saul empty-handed.

But Saul was still under the malignant influence of the tormenting spirit and would not be dissuaded by circumstances of health. If David was too sick to walk to his death, then he must be brought to Saul "in his bed" (v. 15)! It might also be that David was only pretending to be ill. Returning to David's house, therefore, the men who entered did not find in the bed one who was about to die; instead, they found one who had never lived.

Saul, of course, demanded an explanation. Michal was therefore called upon to answer for her role in the teraphim deception and David's escape. Her response was convenient, if not convincing; she acted as she did because David threatened her with death. Her defense could not be tested, for there were no witnesses. Besides, it was useful for Saul to accept her claim—if David had threatened a member of the royal household, he was doubly worthy of death.

(11) God's Spirit Rescues David from Saul and His Troops (19:18–24)

[18]When David had fled and made his escape, he went to Samuel at Ramah and told him all that Saul had done to him. Then he and Samuel went to Naioth and stayed there. [19]Word came to Saul: "David is in Naioth at Ramah"; [20]so he sent men to capture him. But when they saw a group of prophets prophesying, with Samuel standing there as their leader, the Spirit of God came upon Saul's men and they also prophesied. [21]Saul was told about it, and he sent more men, and they prophesied too. Saul sent men a third time, and they also prophesied. [22]Finally, he himself left for Ramah and went to the great cistern at Secu. And he asked, "Where are Samuel and David?"

"Over in Naioth at Ramah," they said.

[23]So Saul went to Naioth at Ramah. But the Spirit of God came even upon him, and he walked along prophesying until he came to Naioth. [24]He stripped off his robes and also prophesied in Samuel's presence. He lay that way all that day and night. This is why people say, "Is Saul also among the prophets?"

19:18–21   When David fled from the king, he did not return to his home; perhaps he feared betrayal there. Instead, he went three miles away to seek help from Samuel at Ramah. Samuel was able to provide David with empathy, since Samuel had also known the possibility of death at the hands of Saul (cf. 16:2). He also could supply spiritual encouragement, since he was the prophet who had received the revelation of David's selection as Israel's next king.

The two of them apparently left Samuel's house to take up temporary residency at "Naioth." The term translated by the NIV here as a geographic name literally means "dwellings/habitations" and may refer to a religious compound within Ramah, perhaps even the one mentioned in 9:22.

Accurate reports regarding David's whereabouts soon reached the king, and he immediately "sent men to capture" his fugitive son-in-law (19:19). Saul's servants entered Naioth, yet no indication is given that they located David. Instead, they saw Samuel and a group of prophets prophesying, perhaps the same group Saul had encountered earlier (cf. 10:5).

Before they could initiate a search for David within the group, however, they were captured by God's Spirit and compelled to join the prophets.[77] This activity so absorbed the men that they were unable to continue with their royal mission. God's Spirit, which had previously marked David for kingship over Israel, now acted to preserve David for that task.

But Saul was not to be deterred from his goal of eradicating David. As a second group entered that stronghold of the Spirit, they too were overcome and failed to apprehend David. Increasingly more desperate, Saul sent a third group of men into this mismatched clash between flesh and Spirit, with identical results. The Spirit of God was gently invincible;[78] those who had entered into Naioth under the influence of the ruler of Israel now found themselves under the infinitely greater influence of the ruler of the universe.

19:22–24 As a last resort Saul "himself left for Ramah" (v. 22), ordinarily about a ninety-minute journey. On the road he passed by a major regional water source, "the great cistern at Secu." He asked people who had come there to fill their water jars, some of whom probably were from Ramah (cf. 9:11), where he might find Samuel and David. Having received the answer, he proceeded to Naioth (v. 23).

But in a climactic tour de force, the Spirit of God made a mockery of the most ardent efforts of David's opponent. Saul's first servants had not begun prophesying until they arrived at Naioth; however, Saul began prophesying as "he walked along" some distance from Naioth. Then when he actually arrived at his destination, the Spirit of God so overwhelmed him that "he stripped off his robes" (v. 24) as he continued to prophesy "in Samuel's presence."[79] The triple employment of the Hebrew phrase *gam hûʾ* (lit., "even he"; not fully noted in the NIV) in vv. 23–24 emphasizes the fact that Israel's most powerful citizen was subjugated by the power of God.

---

[77] Brueggemann's speculation may be correct that the men's behavior was "some kind of ecstatic experience that causes the messengers to break out of normal, acceptable patterns of behavior and engage in frenzied or eccentric conduct not expected of the king's servants" (*First and Second Samuel*, 145).

[78] Contrast God's treatment of the soldiers King Ahaziah sent against Elijah (cf. 2 Kgs 1:9–12).

[79] The narrator's comment here creates a tension with 15:35, where the MT notes that "Samuel did not again see Saul until the day of his death." McCarter uses this as evidence of the late insertion of 19:18–24 into 1 Samuel (*1 Samuel*, 330). Perhaps, however, Samuel refused to look upon the naked and humiliated king who lay there in the compound.

Saul's loss of royal attire in the presence of God's Spirit presented a powerful image confirming the prophetic judgments Samuel made earlier (cf. 15:23,28). God had rejected Saul as king, so in God's presence Saul would not be permitted to wear the clothing of royalty. Saul had "rejected the word of the LORD" (15:23), so now in an ironic twist he would be condemned to be a mouthpiece for that word.

Saul remained "naked" (Hb. ʿārōm; NIV, "that way"; a grave shame in the ancient Near East) and in a prophetic trance "all that day and night." His actions, so out of keeping with his background and character, gave new life to the proverb coined when Saul was first anointed king over Israel (cf. 10:11), "Is Saul also among the prophets?" As Youngblood points out, the proverb now also distances Saul from the royal office.[80]

(12) Jonathan Protects and Covenants with David (20:1–42)

¹Then David fled from Naioth at Ramah and went to Jonathan and asked, "What have I done? What is my crime? How have I wronged your father, that he is trying to take my life?"

²"Never!" Jonathan replied. "You are not going to die! Look, my father doesn't do anything, great or small, without confiding in me. Why would he hide this from me? It's not so!"

³But David took an oath and said, "Your father knows very well that I have found favor in your eyes, and he has said to himself, 'Jonathan must not know this or he will be grieved.' Yet as surely as the LORD lives and as you live, there is only a step between me and death."

⁴Jonathan said to David, "Whatever you want me to do, I'll do for you."

⁵So David said, "Look, tomorrow is the New Moon festival, and I am supposed to dine with the king; but let me go and hide in the field until the evening of the day after tomorrow. ⁶If your father misses me at all, tell him, 'David earnestly asked my permission to hurry to Bethlehem, his hometown, because an annual sacrifice is being made there for his whole clan.' ⁷If he says, 'Very well,' then your servant is safe. But if he loses his temper, you can be sure that he is determined to harm me. ⁸As for you, show kindness to your servant, for you have brought him into a covenant with you before the LORD. If I am guilty, then kill me yourself! Why hand me over to your father?"

⁹"Never!" Jonathan said. "If I had the least inkling that my father was determined to harm you, wouldn't I tell you?"

¹⁰David asked, "Who will tell me if your father answers you harshly?"

¹¹"Come," Jonathan said, "let's go out into the field." So they went there together.

¹²Then Jonathan said to David: "By the LORD, the God of Israel, I will surely sound out my father by this time the day after tomorrow! If he is favorably disposed toward you, will I not send you word and let you know? ¹³But if my father is

---

[80] Youngblood, *1, 2 Samuel*, 717.

inclined to harm you, may the LORD deal with me, be it ever so severely, if I do not let you know and send you away safely. May the LORD be with you as he has been with my father. [14]But show me unfailing kindness like that of the LORD as long as I live, so that I may not be killed, [15]and do not ever cut off your kindness from my family—not even when the LORD has cut off every one of David's enemies from the face of the earth."

[16]So Jonathan made a covenant with the house of David, saying, "May the LORD call David's enemies to account." [17]And Jonathan had David reaffirm his oath out of love for him, because he loved him as he loved himself.

[18]Then Jonathan said to David: "Tomorrow is the New Moon festival. You will be missed, because your seat will be empty. [19]The day after tomorrow, toward evening, go to the place where you hid when this trouble began and wait by the stone Ezel. [20]I will shoot three arrows to the side of it, as though I were shooting at a target. [21]Then I will send a boy and say, 'Go, find the arrows.' If I say to him, 'Look, the arrows are on this side of you; bring them here,' then come, because, as surely as the LORD lives, you are safe; there is no danger. [22]But if I say to the boy, 'Look, the arrows are beyond you,' then you must go, because the LORD has sent you away. [23]And about the matter you and I discussed—remember, the LORD is witness between you and me forever."

[24]So David hid in the field, and when the New Moon festival came, the king sat down to eat. [25]He sat in his customary place by the wall, opposite Jonathan, and Abner sat next to Saul, but David's place was empty. [26]Saul said nothing that day, for he thought, "Something must have happened to David to make him ceremonially unclean—surely he is unclean." [27]But the next day, the second day of the month, David's place was empty again. Then Saul said to his son Jonathan, "Why hasn't the son of Jesse come to the meal, either yesterday or today?"

[28]Jonathan answered, "David earnestly asked me for permission to go to Bethlehem. [29]He said, 'Let me go, because our family is observing a sacrifice in the town and my brother has ordered me to be there. If I have found favor in your eyes, let me get away to see my brothers.' That is why he has not come to the king's table."

[30]Saul's anger flared up at Jonathan and he said to him, "You son of a perverse and rebellious woman! Don't I know that you have sided with the son of Jesse to your own shame and to the shame of the mother who bore you? [31]As long as the son of Jesse lives on this earth, neither you nor your kingdom will be established. Now send and bring him to me, for he must die!"

[32]"Why should he be put to death? What has he done?" Jonathan asked his father. [33]But Saul hurled his spear at him to kill him. Then Jonathan knew that his father intended to kill David.

[34]Jonathan got up from the table in fierce anger; on that second day of the month he did not eat, because he was grieved at his father's shameful treatment of David.

[35]In the morning Jonathan went out to the field for his meeting with David. He had a small boy with him, [36]and he said to the boy, "Run and find the arrows I shoot." As the boy ran, he shot an arrow beyond him. [37]When the boy came to the place where Jonathan's arrow had fallen, Jonathan called out after him, "Isn't the arrow beyond you?" [38]Then he shouted, "Hurry! Go quickly! Don't stop!" The

boy picked up the arrow and returned to his master. [39](The boy knew nothing of all this; only Jonathan and David knew.) [40]Then Jonathan gave his weapons to the boy and said, "Go, carry them back to town."
[41]After the boy had gone, David got up from the south side [of the stone] and bowed down before Jonathan three times, with his face to the ground. Then they kissed each other and wept together—but David wept the most.
[42]Jonathan said to David, "Go in peace, for we have sworn friendship with each other in the name of the LORD, saying, 'The LORD is witness between you and me, and between your descendants and my descendants forever.'" Then David left, and Jonathan went back to the town.

20:1–3 After witnessing four attempts on his life in one day, David certainly had no reason to doubt Saul's determination to kill him. Yet to escape the king's attacks, David would have to abandon the two most significant people in his life, his best friend Jonathan and the wife of his youth, Michal. Even if he were to escape and live, would life be worth living under those circumstances?

Hoping he was wrong but fearing he was right, David "fled from Naioth at Ramah and went to Jonathan" (v. 1) to discuss the matter further. Perhaps the fault was David's; perhaps he had committed some "transgression" (Hb. ʿavôn; NIV, "crime") or "sin" (Hb. ḥaṭṭāʾt; NIV, "have wronged") against Saul. If so, then he could repent, make reparations, and so end the nightmarish attacks; his life of love and friendship could return to him once more.

David's melancholic musings seemed like nonsense to Jonathan, and he rejected the conclusions. If anyone should know Saul's thought processes, it was Jonathan, for Saul did not "do anything, great or small, without confiding in" (v. 2) Jonathan.

But David, who had "wisdom like that of an angel of God" to "discern good and evil" (2 Sam 14:17,20), saw what Jonathan could not. The cold facts of the situation pointed to only one conclusion: Saul was passionately determined to kill David. In fact, at that moment David was "only a step" ahead of "death." Yet Saul had insulated Jonathan from the deadly scheme so his son would not "be grieved" (v. 3; cf. v. 34).

20:4–10 Jonathan, like David, had much to lose if the accusations against Saul proved true; he would forgo the companionship of his best friend and experience alienation from his father. In an effort to put the matter to rest, he agreed to cooperate with David in the investigation. Whatever plan David might put forth, Jonathan would follow it.

David, the man described more frequently than any other in the Old Testament as possessing success-inducing wisdom (śkl; cf. 18:5,14,15,30), had an ingenious ploy to force Saul to reveal his true intentions toward David. The plan was simple yet effective. It proactively safeguarded David by sequestering him, and it avoided any use of force. Granted, Jonathan would have to tell his father a lie, but not one that would violate either the letter or spirit of the Torah, since its purpose was to preserve innocent life. For his part David would merely absent himself from the royal court for two days. In so doing he would fail to be present at the sacrificial meals associated with an ordinary new moon festival (cf. Num 10:10).[81]

Jonathan's role would be more complicated. Most of the time during the next two days he was to be merely a passive observer of his father. However, when Saul commented on David's absence, Jonathan was to convey a respectable—though specious—excuse to account for David's empty chair at the meals. After that he was to note Saul's reaction: a positive response to Jonathan's words would mean that David "is safe" (v. 7); a hostile response would mean that Saul was "determined to harm" David.

Apart from that plan, however, David had another proposal—one that could eliminate the need for the previous one. David asked Jonathan himself to kill him before Saul could—if Jonathan was aware of any "transgression in" David's life (v. 8; NIV, "if I am guilty"). Reminding Jonathan that he had established a solemn "covenant of Yahweh" (NIV, "covenant . . . before the LORD") with David, he asked his friend to "deal faithfully" (NIV, "show kindness") with him in this matter.

Jonathan reacted strongly against David's second proposal: "Never" (v. 9) would he himself take David's life. So strongly did Jonathan value his friend's life that he would immediately let David know if he "had the least inkling"[82] that his "father was determined to harm" him.

Now that David had been exonerated by Jonathan, the pair could work out the remaining details associated with David's first proposal. The final issue was figuring out the particulars of how David would be covertly warned in the event Saul still intended to kill him.

20:11–17 A remarkable transformation occurs in the narrative beginning at v. 11 and extending through v. 23 as David, the most dynamic character in 1, 2 Samuel, becomes a silent and passive presence on the story line. A total of 162 Hebrew words occur in four different quotations in this section, but all of them are spoken by Jonathan. The two longest quotations attributed to Jonathan in the Old Testament (seventy-six and seventy-seven Hebrew words) also are present here. Furthermore, these quotes contain nine mentions of Yahweh's name, an unusually high number for a stretch of text extending only thirteen verses.

These facts suggest that the author intended this stretch of text to be more

---

[81] The festival being celebrated would not have been the Feast of Trumpets (cf. Num 29:1; Lev 23:24) since this event lasted a week and the meal served on the second day of the month was not one that required ritual cleanness (cf. v. 27).

[82] The construction uses an inf. abs. followed by the imperfect of יָדַע, lit., "knowing I will know." For similar constructions with יָדַע, cf. Gen 15:13; 43:7; Josh 23:13; 1 Sam 20:3; 28:1; Jer 40:14. See also *IBHS* §35.3.1g.

than just the simple completion of a plan to convey Saul's thoughts about David. In fact, this section may be viewed as the thematic centerpiece of the story of Jonathan. Several content-based reasons can be given to support this contention.

First, this section shows that Jonathan, the individual next in the dynastic succession to be king after Saul, was also the one who took responsibility for David's escape from Saul. Of his own accord Jonathan swore two oaths before the Lord (vv. 12–13) that he would obtain the information David needed, pass it along in a timely manner, and if necessary, "send" David "away safely" (v. 13). Since it was Jonathan who came up with the plan and swore the oaths, this scene negates any claim that David duped or coerced others into participating in this flight from the king.

Second, this section depicts the establishment of a covenant between the house of David and the house of Jonathan that would later lead David to defy conventional wisdom regarding the elimination of potential rivals to the throne.[83] Under the terms of the agreement, when David became king he was to show the son of Saul "unfailing kindness like that of the LORD" (v. 14), seeing to it that Jonathan would "not be killed" in a purge. Furthermore, David must "never terminate the commitment to be loyal" (v. 15; NIV, "not cut off your kindness") to Jonathan's descendants—their lives, too, must be spared. David later honored the terms of this agreement; instead of killing off all members of the Saulide dynasty, David gave Jonathan's son Mephibosheth great wealth and a place at the royal table (cf. 2 Sam 9:7,10). He even spared Mephibosheth's life when there was reasonable suspicion that he participated in a revolt against David (cf. 2 Sam 19:25–29).

Third, this section contains the first indication that the Lord would someday grant David success on an international scale. Jonathan's requests assume that the Lord would "cut off every one of David's enemies from the face of the earth" (v. 15)[84] This glimmer of prophetic insight in Jonathan's words would later be explicitly affirmed by the narrator (2 Sam 8:14). Jonathan's words unwittingly were at the same time condemnatory of his father, who had only recently called David his "enemy" (cf. 19:17).

In this way Jonathan "made a covenant" (Hb. *kārat*; lit., "cut") "with the house of David" (v. 16). The treaty sought the mutual welfare of both parties and was motivated by the noble kind of love enjoined in the Torah (Hb. *ʾāhāb*;

---

[83] Examples of Israelites killing off potential rivals to the throne include Abimelech (Judg 9:5), Solomon (1 Kgs 2:25,46), Baasha (1 Kgs 15:29), Elah (1 Kgs 16:11), Omri (1 Kgs 16:22), Jehu (2 Kgs 10:11), and Athaliah (2 Kgs 11:1).

[84] Gordon suggests that the phrase "David's enemies" is almost certainly euphemistic for David himself" (*I and II Samuel*, 167). This perspective seems to miss the thrust of Jonathan's statements here; he was expressing unmitigated love for David and therefore was deliberately avoiding any wish—even a hidden one—for David's demise.

Lev 19:18), for Jonathan loved David "as he loved himself" (v. 17).

20:18–23 Here Jonathan provided the specific details about how he would pass the vital information along to David. Because Saul and the royal household observed the Torah-prescribed new moon festival (cf. Num 10:10), David would be expected to participate in its ritual meals. His absence would certainly be noted because his seat would be empty (v. 18). Nevertheless, David was to bide his time until the third day—"the day after tomorrow" (v. 19), and then wait for Jonathan at the place where David "hid when this trouble began." More precisely, David was to "wait by the stone Ezel" (lit., "the stone, the departure"; v. 19), apparently a rock outcropping significant or unusual enough to have been named.[85]

On the third day Jonathan, accompanied by a young servant, would journey to that location for some target practice. The king's son would strategically "shoot three arrows" (v. 20) to the side of David's lair. The impact point of the arrows, and especially the words Jonathan would shout to his attendant, would convey the essential information to David.

If the signal was given indicating that it was safe to return to Gibeah, David needed to be absolutely certain that the information was accurate and trustworthy. Knowing this, Jonathan swore a solemn oath by the "life of Yahweh" (NIV, "as surely as the LORD lives") that he would not lead David to return unless he knew that "there is no danger" (v. 21).

In case it was necessary to inform David of a continued threat against him in Gibeah, then David "must go" (v. 22). This turn of events would be tragic for both Jonathan and David, but they could deal with it if they viewed it from the proper perspective. Demonstrating rare spiritual acumen, Jonathan provided a remarkable theological framework in which to cope with the possible tragedy of separation. If it happened, it would be because "the LORD has sent you away." The Lord had permitted painful separations in the lives of Torah patriarchs (cf. Gen 28:5; 37:28), yet each had ultimately resulted in the preservation of life and the increase of blessing. If the Lord were to permit such an experience in David and Jonathan's life, it must also be for these unchanging divine purposes.

In addition, Jonathan reminded David that the Lord was overseeing the relationship that existed between them. God might permit their physical separation, but he would preserve their relationship. David and Jonathan's commitment to

---

[85] The name could have been given to the stone as a result of the events described in this chapter. The LXX as well as the Syriac substitute the word "that" for the name "Azel" (הָאָ֫זֶל). To do so they seem to have edited the Hebrew consonants to read הַלָּ֫ז. S. R. Driver (*Notes on the Hebrew Text of Samuel*, 2d ed. [1912; reprint, Winona Lake: Alpha, 1984], 167–68) and McCarter (*I Samuel*, 333, 337) emend the Hb. to read הָאַרְגֹּב הַלָּזֶה and thus translate it as "that mound." All of this seems unnecessary. In view of the Benjamite tendency to name significant geographic features in the region (cf. 14:4), the MT reading can be safely retained.

loyalty and mutual protection would remain "forever" (Hb. *ᶜad ᶜôlām*; v. 23).

20:24–29 Those moving words having been uttered, the crucial events were now about to take place. David dutifully "hid in the field" (v. 24), and at the time of the ritually significant first meal of the new month, "Saul sat down to eat." The king sat "by the wall" (v. 25), a location of prominence but perhaps more importantly a spot that afforded him greater protection from assassination attempts. Around the table were seats for Jonathan,[86] Abner, and David. Of course, "David's place was empty."

Though Saul noted David's absence, he reasoned that David had somehow become "ceremonially unclean" (v. 26) and so "said nothing that day." Saul's actions reflect positively on David, for the king assumed that David would follow Torah regulations as a matter of course. David, a devout man, was absent at a ritual meal; the Torah prohibited the consumption of a ritual meal during times of ritual uncleanness (Lev 7:20–21), so "surely he is unclean." This ceremonial uncleanness could be caused by accidental contact with anything ritually unclean or detestable, including such diverse things as forbidden insects (Lev 11:24), moist seeds that had come in contact with a dead animal (Lev 11:38), another unclean person (Lev 15:11), and a human corpse (Num 19:14–16), to name but a few. Seminal emissions, including those resulting from routine marital contact (Lev 15:16,18) as well as certain skin diseases (Lev 13:11,36), would also have caused David to be in a state of ritual uncleanness.

But Saul was forced to reject his previous hypothesis when "on the second day of the month" (v. 27)—a nonholy day—David skipped a meal that could be eaten by ceremonially unclean individuals. As David had suspected, Saul expressed concern about David's absence. The king began his investigation by interrogating David's best friend—"his son Jonathan"—with words that mark a dramatic shift in attitude, one of alienation and hostility. No longer did Saul mention David by name; instead, his son-in-law had become the "son of Jesse." This marks the first recorded instance where Saul refers to David in this manner, but it will be by no means the last (cf. also vv. 30–31; 22:7,8,9,13).

In response to Saul's subtly hostile inquiry, Jonathan presented the cover-up story as convincingly as possible: the son of Jesse was "observing a sacrifice" in Bethlehem with the family of Jesse. David was not acting subversively or secretly in this matter; he went because a family member "ordered" him to, and he had sought permission from a member of the royal family before making the trek.

20:30–34 When Jonathan lied to his father regarding David's absence, "Saul's anger flared up" (v. 30). Furthermore, Saul distanced himself from

---

[86] The MT does not mention seating for Jonathan but assumes it in v. 34. The NIV's "opposite Jonathan" is based on the LXX; the MT states that "Jonathan arose" when his father sat at the royal table. It is reasonable to assume, with McCarter (*I Samuel*, 338), that the original Hebrew reading was וַיִּקְדַּם, not the current וַיָּקָם.

Jonathan: no longer was the royal heir referred to as "my son" (cf. 14:39–42); he had now become the "son of a perverse and rebellious woman" (20:30). Saul now accused his dynastic heir of being in league with the very one whom Saul believed would destroy the family dynasty.

In an apparent effort to bring Jonathan back to his side, Saul appealed to three powerful motivators: shame, guilt, and greed. First, he noted that Jonathan's scandalous betrayal was bringing about personal "shame." Second, in an attempt to elicit feelings of guilt, Saul noted that Jonathan's actions were also bringing shame on "the mother who bore you" (lit., "the shame of the nakedness of your mother"), that is, Ahinoam (cf. 14:50), whom he himself had just shamed by calling her "perverse and rebellious." Third, Saul appealed to his son's greed, noting that "as long as the son of Jesse lives on this earth, neither you nor your kingdom will be established" (v. 31).

Having thrust these three barbs into Jonathan's soul, Saul then issued a royal command, ordering his son to "send and bring" David, "for he must die!" Surely Jonathan must have felt as though he had betrayed his father and dishonored his mother; surely he must have felt some urge to claim the amenities of royalty for himself. Any one of these emotions could have motivated him to break his commitment to David and obey his father's edict.

Remarkably, however, Jonathan resisted all urges to the contrary (cf. Ps 15:4) and defended David. The defense took the form of asking his father two parallel questions that hit at the heart of Saul's responsibilities as God's representative: "Why should he be put to death? What has he done?" (1 Sam 20:32). As king over God's people and thus chief enforcer of the Torah (cf. 1 Kgs 1:3), Saul must not execute the innocent (Exod 23:7), and David had not committed any capital offense.

However, Saul was no longer acting as God's representative; matters of justice were being subordinated to the king's mad drive to eliminate David. Since Saul's son had chosen to identify himself with David, he must be treated like David. Thus, "Saul hurled his spear at him to kill him" (1 Sam 20:33). Though Saul's spear missed him, Jonathan got the point—"his father intended to kill David."

Immediately Jonathan left the room "in fierce anger" (v. 34) and spent the remainder of the day fasting and grieving. The reason for Jonathan's understandable reactions is not one that could have been anticipated; Jonathan did not grieve because of the humiliating or murderous treatment accorded him by his father but because of "his father's shameful treatment of David." Jonathan's reaction thus serves as one of the purest displays of human loyalty found in the annals of human history.

20:35–42 The next morning Jonathan fulfilled his commitment to David by conveying the unhoped-for news. Taking his bow, some arrows, and a "small boy with him" (v. 35), he went out to the rendezvous point and initiated the agreed-upon ritual. Jonathan sent the lad running into the field and then "shot an arrow beyond him" (v. 36) to establish an appropriate context for uttering the coded words. When the boy, now some distance away, stopped to pick up the arrow, Jonathan pretended to misinterpret the boy's actions and thus shouted out the prearranged signal to flee. So as to remove all doubt, he also added a series of three commands with unmistakable significance for David: "Hurry! Go quickly! Don't stop!" (v. 38). Unaware of the significance of any of this, the boy simply "picked up the arrow and returned to his master." Jonathan then brought the target practice to an abrupt end, sending the boy and his weapons "back to town" (v. 40). Thus Jonathan was disarmed when David came out of hiding to meet him (cf. v. 8), a condition underscoring his benevolent intentions toward David.

In the solitude of the empty field, David and Jonathan met together face-to-face. Expressions of respect and mutual commitment marked their encounter. In the gravity of the moment David initially spoke no words. Instead, he silently displayed subservience and utmost respect for his friend by bowing before Jonathan three times—the greatest number of times anyone in the Bible is depicted as performing this act in a single encounter.[87]

Jonathan countered David's symbolic expression of subordination with one that implied acceptance as a respected peer—he kissed him (cf. 2 Sam 14:33). In this case kisses were exchanged because they also functioned as expressions of farewell (cf. Gen 31:55; Acts 20:37). The pathos of the moment is evident in the fact that they also "wept together." The observation "David wept the most" emphasizes David's loyalty and commitment to the heir-apparent of the Saulide dynasty and thus blunts implied accusations that King David tried to exterminate his predecessors.

Jonathan seemed to understand that this encounter would be a watershed; never again would these two best friends enjoy an easy, informal camaraderie. In his final moments with David he urged him to "go in peace"—an expression of goodwill used elsewhere in the Old Testament in situations involving extended or permanent separations (cf. Exod 4:18; 2 Kgs 5:19). Though David and Jonathan would be physically separated from one another, they would remain inseparably joined by the oath they swore in the Lord's name (v. 42). Furthermore, their commitment would be intergenerational, continuing between their "descendants forever." Having affirmed that commitment, the two friends left each others' presence for the next-to-last time.

---

[87] Amarna Letters indicate that multiple prostrations were a common means of expressing subservience and loyalty to an authority. A formulaic phrase often found in them was "At the feet of the king, my lord, seven times, seven times I fall" (cf. EA 234, 244, 250, 254, 270, 271, 286 in *ANET,* 483–90).

4. The Lord Blesses David the Fugitive but Judges Saul (21:1–29:11)

These nine chapters depict David's "wilderness experience." As Israel's wilderness experience followed an exodus from a foreign king, so David's followed an exodus from a king "such as all the other nations have." And as the wilderness for Israel preceded possession of the Promised Land, so for David it preceded possession of a promised kingdom. Furthermore, during this wilderness period David experienced events that in crucial ways paralleled those of the Israelites following their expulsion from Egypt—pursuit by the armed forces of the king they were fleeing, a hostile encounter with the Midianites, an attempted foray into Moab, and yet the Lord's protection against all human foes.

These connections between David's life and the Israelites' experiences recorded in the Torah not only magnify the story of David to one of epic proportions, but they also create the expectation that the Lord would ultimately give David the fulfillment of all the good promises made to him.

(1) The Lord's Priest at Nob Assists David (21:1–9)

[1]David went to Nob, to Ahimelech the priest. Ahimelech trembled when he met him, and asked, "Why are you alone? Why is no one with you?"

[2]David answered Ahimelech the priest, "The king charged me with a certain matter and said to me, 'No one is to know anything about your mission and your instructions.' As for my men, I have told them to meet me at a certain place. [3]Now then, what do you have on hand? Give me five loaves of bread, or whatever you can find."

[4]But the priest answered David, "I don't have any ordinary bread on hand; however, there is some consecrated bread here—provided the men have kept themselves from women."

[5]David replied, "Indeed women have been kept from us, as usual whenever I set out. The men's things are holy even on missions that are not holy. How much more so today!" [6]So the priest gave him the consecrated bread, since there was no bread there except the bread of the Presence that had been removed from before the LORD and replaced by hot bread on the day it was taken away.

[7]Now one of Saul's servants was there that day, detained before the LORD; he was Doeg the Edomite, Saul's head shepherd.

[8]David asked Ahimelech, "Don't you have a spear or a sword here? I haven't brought my sword or any other weapon, because the king's business was urgent."

[9]The priest replied, "The sword of Goliath the Philistine, whom you killed in the Valley of Elah, is here; it is wrapped in a cloth behind the ephod. If you want it, take it; there is no sword here but that one."

David said, "There is none like it; give it to me."

21:1–6   Nob was a city probably located atop Mount Scopus, just northeast of Jerusalem and about two miles south of David's Naioth hideout.[88] Though not a Levitical city, the small settlement was populated by descendants of Aaron the priest (cf. 22:19), who operated a Yahwistic worship center there. Members of Saul's retinue did come to the sanctuary from time to time (cf. v. 7); McCarter suggests it was "the most sacred shrine of Saul's kingdom" and perhaps "a kind of official state sanctuary."[89] But the royal son-in-law's arrival at this time elicited a troubled response. Ahimelech,[90] who oversaw the sanctuary, "trembled" when David unexpectedly arrived alone. Perhaps Ahimelech was aware of the recent events at Naioth (cf. 19:19–24), in which the lives of Yahwistic prophets were endangered by David's presence, and he feared a repetition of these events at Nob. Knowing that David was commander of the royal bodyguard (22:14), he thought it unusual for David to be "alone," that is, without the king. Accordingly, he plied David with two questions that probed into the circumstances of his visit.

David's answer may be taken as self-serving deception or as a shrewd but honest use of language. David noted first that "the king charged me with a certain matter" (v. 2; Hb. v. 3). What he failed to clarify in his opening words to Ahimelech, however, was the name of the king to which he was referring. If it was King Yahweh (cf. 8:7; 12:12), and I am inclined to believe it was since David is elsewhere recorded referring to God as king (cf. Pss 5:2; 20:9; 24:7–10; 29:10; 68:24; 145:1), then David was telling the truth.

Secrecy and solitude were essential aspects of the special mission given him by King Yahweh. Other men would join him in this undertaking, but they were to meet David later. Due to the matter's urgency and haste, David was now several miles from Gibeah and had made no provision for food. Boldly he asked Ahimelech for "five loaves of bread, or whatever you can find" (v. 3; Hb. v. 4). Receiving food from others while on a journey is a time-honored tradition in the Middle East (cf. Gen 18:3–8; 19:3; Judg 19:20–21), so David's request was not exceptional.

There was one problem associated with honoring David's request; Ahimelech did not "have any profane bread on hand" (v. 4; Hb. v. 5; NIV, "ordinary bread"), that is, bread that might be offered to non-Levites without

---

[88] Cf. Y. Aharoni and M. Avi-Yonah, *The Macmillan Bible Atlas,* rev. ed. (New York: Macmillan, 1977), 62.

[89] McCarter, *I Samuel,* 366.

[90] Mark 2:26 suggests that this event occurred "in the days of Abiathar the high priest"—an assertion seemingly at odds with the present statement. Several scholars have provided alternatives to the conclusion that a genuine misstatement of fact is present in the NT at this point. E.g., Youngblood, who suggests that Mark's statement should be translated "'in the account of Abiathar the high priest' . . . especially since Abiathar was the only survivor of the slaughter of the priests of Nob (22:20) and in fact became much more noteworthy than his father" ("1, 2 Samuel," 728).

any special consideration. However, he did possess "some holy bread" (NIV, "consecrated bread")—that is "bread of the Presence that had been removed from before the LORD and replaced by hot bread" (v. 6; Hb. v. 7; cf. Exod 25:30). This replacement of the bread may have occurred in connection with the new moon festival celebrated a day or two earlier (cf. 20:24,27). Under normal circumstances the Torah required that such food be consumed only by "Aaron and his sons . . . in a holy place" (Lev 24:9).

Yet specific Torah laws might be set aside if higher-level considerations warranted, especially the preservation of life.[91] As a vested Aaronic priest, Ahimelech possessed authority to interpret and apply Torah guidelines to specific cases and could do so with some latitude. Since food was necessary for life and David and his men had no food, it was consistent with Torah principles to provide David and his men the means to sustain their lives.

Ahimelech ruled that David and his men could eat bread reserved for Levites if they did so in a Levite-like way—that is, with due consideration for ritual purity laws. Levites could eat the Bread of the Presence only in the holy place and thus were required to be ritually clean. Since David and his men were supposedly on a military mission, they could not be expected to keep all the ritual cleanliness laws, especially those regarding contact with corpses (Num 19:14–16). However, it was reasonable to ask men on military missions to keep ritual cleanliness laws that related to sexual contact (Lev 15:18). That having been agreed to, David was given the consecrated bread.

David's statement that "the men's things are holy even on missions that are not holy" (v. 5; Hb. v. 6) suggests that he considered Israelite warfare to be a task that should be performed only by consecrated servants of the Lord. Earlier David had been motivated to fight Goliath because the Philistine had "defied the armies of the living God" (17:36), a reason that was at least partly theological. When he entered into battle against Goliath, he did so "in the name of the LORD Almighty" (17:45)—that is, with due regard to his relationship with the Lord. Apparently David transferred his personal practices to those under his command, requiring them to be in proper relationship

---

[91] This principle of setting aside Torah laws in certain, limited circumstances for the sake of higher-level considerations was practiced from the time of Moses onward. An example within the Torah is seen in Lev 10:12–20, where a violation of Lev 6:16 was permitted, with the judgment having been rendered by Moses himself. Another example is the work performed by priests on the Sabbath as part of the required sacrificial ritual (cf. Num 28:9). First-century Judaism practiced this principle as well as they practiced Sabbath circumcision (cf. John 7:22) and Sabbath-day rescues of animals and persons whose life and well-being was threatened (cf. Luke 14:5). Jesus, the supreme interpreter of the Torah for Christians, also accepted this time-honored principle. For Jesus, irregularities in the implementation of specific Torah regulations were justifiable as long as they were performed to accomplish a greater good or to save life (cf. Mark 3:4). In keeping with this principle Jesus permitted and even perpetrated certain violations of the Sabbath and dietary laws (cf. Matt 12:9–13; Mark 7:19).

with God during all missions.

21:7–9   Earlier Saul had fought against the Edomites (cf. 14:47); perhaps
Doeg was a prisoner of war who had proven unusually useful to Saul. Alternatively, he may have been a mercenary. The purpose of Doeg's presence at Nob
is not clearly understood by modern interpreters, but it may be related to some
form of punishment or penance.[92]

Besides food, David needed a weapon; thus, he inquired about obtaining
"a spear or a sword" (v. 8; Hb. v. 9). It is reasonable to assume that David
asked about these items because he had deposited Goliath's weapons there
earlier as a gift of dedication (cf. Lev 27:14ff.). Such gifts could be returned
to the one who had given them, though a redemption payment would normally have been required. Ahimelech, who had carefully preserved David's
dedicated item "wrapped in a cloth behind the ephod" (v. 9; Hb. v. 10),
granted David permission to reclaim it, which he did without hesitation.

(2) David Is Saved from the Philistines (21:10–15)

[10]That day David fled from Saul and went to Achish king of Gath. [11]But the servants of Achish said to him, "Isn't this David, the king of the land? Isn't he the one
they sing about in their dances:

"'Saul has slain his thousands,
   and David his tens of thousands'?"

[12]David took these words to heart and was very much afraid of Achish king of
Gath. [13]So he pretended to be insane in their presence; and while he was in their
hands he acted like a madman, making marks on the doors of the gate and letting
saliva run down his beard.

[14]Achish said to his servants, "Look at the man! He is insane! Why bring him
to me? [15]Am I so short of madmen that you have to bring this fellow here to carry
on like this in front of me? Must this man come into my house?"

21:10–15   In an effort to find sanctuary "from Saul" (v. 10; Hb. v. 11) and
yet avoid endangering the lives of family and friends, David "went to Achish
king of Gath," some twenty-three miles west southwest of Nob.

However, David's arrival in the city aroused suspicions among the royal servants there. Achish's attendants were poorly informed yet ironically insightful
concerning David—they mistakenly called him "the king of the land" (v. 11;
Hb. v. 12). At the same time, they were aware of his status as a Hebrew folk
hero who was celebrated with song and dance.

---

[92] Cf. Baldwin, *1 and 2 Samuel*, 138; and Hertzberg, *I and II Samuel*, 180. Others suggest it
was for religious purposes, perhaps to celebrate a holy day; cf. Kutsch, "Die Wurzel ʿṣr im Hebräis-
chen," *VT* 2 (1952): 65–67.

Knowing what was being said about him,[93] David realized that his life was as much at risk in the royal court of Gath as it was in the royal court of Gibeah. Consequently, he found it necessary to act with the same wisdom here that enabled him to survive in Saul's court. For the present situation he used a different tactic: "he changed his perception in their eyes" (v. 13, Hb. v. 14; NIV, "he pretended to be insane in their presence").

This was accomplished by vandalous acts against public property and demeaning acts against his own person. He abused public property in Gath by "making marks on the doors of the gate,"[94] perhaps writing nonsensical graffiti or symbols associated with cultic curses. He also treated himself disgracefully by "letting saliva run down his beard." The beard was an obvious and important symbol of manhood in that culture,[95] and desecration of one's own beard—especially with spit (cf. Num 12:14; Deut 25:9; Job 17:6; 30:10)—would be an obvious indication of derangement within the context of their culture.

David's act was certainly convincing to Achish, who pronounced the foreigner "insane" (v. 14; Hb. v. 15). Thus he convinced the Philistines that he was no longer a threat to them. Payne even suggests that insanity was viewed as a divine affliction and rendered someone taboo—not to be harmed.[96] Launching into a tirade against his courtiers, Achish questioned why they had even allowed David into the royal palace. Achish's suggestion that there was an ample supply "of madmen" (v. 15; Hb. v. 16) in Gath need not be taken literally, though people with unusual characteristics (e.g., excessive height, twenty-four digits; cf. 17:4; 2 Sam 21:20) were certainly associated with that city.

David's success places him in a category with Abraham and Isaac, who also outwitted a Philistine king when they sensed their lives were threatened (cf. Gen 20:2; 26:7). His actions also sharpened the contrast between himself and Saul. David took upon himself the trappings of insanity to hide his sanity; Saul surrounded himself with the trappings of sanity to cloak his insanity.[97]

---

[93] It is conceivable that David had a working knowledge of the Philistine language. In fact, the Philistines may have just adapted Canaanite language. Furthermore, an extensive Philistine population was situated only a few miles west of David's hometown. Also the Philistines were politically and economically dominant in many of the regions of Judah and Benjamin.

[94] The LXX suggests that David "drummed" against the doors; McCarter suggests David "spat" against them (*I Samuel*, 354–55).

[95] Any mistreatment of one's beard by others through cutting or pulling was considered a humiliating insult (cf. Isa 7:20; 15:2; 50:6). Desecrating another's beard could even be justification for going to war (cf. 2 Sam 10:4–8).

[96] Payne, *I and II Samuel*, 113.

[97] McCarter (*I Samuel*, 358) suggests 21:11b–16 "might even be said to *contradict* the story of David's sojourn in Philistia, insofar as it shows how he and Achish failed to strike an acquaintance." He also notes that Budde viewed this as a midrashic reinterpretation of chap. 27. But if Achish viewed David's pretense as evidence of a divine spirit's influence on him, he would not have gained a jaundiced view of David that would have prevented David's later acceptance in the city.

(3) David Receives Assistance from the King of Moab (22:1–5)

¹David left Gath and escaped to the cave of Adullam. When his brothers and his father's household heard about it, they went down to him there. ²All those who were in distress or in debt or discontented gathered around him, and he became their leader. About four hundred men were with him.
³From there David went to Mizpah in Moab and said to the king of Moab, "Would you let my father and mother come and stay with you until I learn what God will do for me?" ⁴So he left them with the king of Moab, and they stayed with him as long as David was in the stronghold.
⁵But the prophet Gad said to David, "Do not stay in the stronghold. Go into the land of Judah." So David left and went to the forest of Hereth.

22:1 Leaving Gath, David went ten miles east to the cave of Adullam in Judahite territory. David's "brothers and his father's household" (v. 1) learned of his return to their region and left their home in Bethlehem to join him there. No doubt they were motivated to do this not because of their great love of David but because of their fear of reprisals by Saul.

22:2 In addition to his family, "about four hundred" (v. 2) individuals who lived on the ragged edge of society came to David's outpost in the Israelite frontier lands. Included among this group were "all who were in distress or in debt or discontented." Those who for various reasons had failed to integrate into the fabric of society may have thought to find in David a leader who could understand them and who would help them create a society insulated from those from whom they were alienated. Alternatively, they may have thought David would help them get revenge on the society they had left. At this point David and his band have some of the characteristics of the group centered around Jephthah, another Israelite who was forced to leave Israelite society, only to return later as its leader (cf. Judg 11:3).

22:3–5 David and his group did not long remain in Judah but instead "went to Mizpah in Moab" (v. 3), an otherwise unknown site somewhere east of the Dead Sea. Mizpah, whose name literally means "watchtower," was apparently the fortified city of residence at the time for "the king of Moab." In a personal audience with the Moabite king, David requested that his father and mother be granted sanctuary in Moab until David learned "what God will do" for him.

The king granted David's request, perhaps for two reasons: first, because he was honoring the ancient practice of providing sanctuary for adversaries of enemies (cf. 1 Sam 27:4–5; 1 Kgs 11:17–18; 12:2; 2 Kgs 25:26) and second, because David had a Moabite great-grandmother (cf. Ruth 4:13–17). The provision of protection for David's family lasted "as long as David was in the stronghold" (Hb. *meṣûdâ*). No consensus exists among scholars about the location of the stronghold; options include a site in Moab (perhaps Mizpah itself), modern Masada just west of the Dead Sea, and the cave of Adullam.[98] The comment by Gad in v. 5 suggests that David and his men resided in a Moabite fortress.

However, the stay was only temporary because the prophet Gad admonished David to depart for Judah. The command is stated as a categorical prohibition, using a clause structure parallel to that employed in the Ten Commandments (cf. Exod 20:4–5,12–17).[99] The reason for the strong wording is simple: the Torah prohibited the establishment of friendly treaties with Moabites (cf. Deut 23:2–6). As a true prophet of the Lord, Gad's duty was to help others understand and heed the Torah. If David established such a treaty with the king of Moab, he would violate the Torah and so risk bringing judgment on himself and all who were with him.

Understanding Gad's admonition to possess divine authority, David obediently "left and went to the forest of Hereth," an unidentified area west of the Dead Sea. Apparently, David's family and followers also accompanied him to that location. The forest location would have provided excellent protection against large, organized forces that Saul might bring against them. In obeying the Torah—even though it meant leaving a stronghold built by human hands, David would find himself in a far safer stronghold, Yahweh himself (cf. 2 Sam 23:14; Pss 18:2 [Hb. v. 3]; 31:3 [Hb. v. 4]; 144:2).

The prophet Gad, first mentioned here, appears to have been a member of David's band of followers. Gad later informed David of punishment for a violation of the Lord's will (cf. 2 Sam 24:11–14) and also produced archived records of David's life (1 Chr 29:29), which suggests the prophet had a long tenure of service to David.

(4) Saul Slaughters the Lord's Priests at Nob (22:6–19)

⁶Now Saul heard that David and his men had been discovered. And Saul, spear in hand, was seated under the tamarisk tree on the hill at Gibeah, with all his officials standing around him. ⁷Saul said to them, "Listen, men of Benjamin! Will the son of Jesse give all of you fields and vineyards? Will he make all of you commanders of thousands and commanders of hundreds? ⁸Is that why you have all conspired against me? No one tells me when my son makes a covenant with the son of Jesse. None of you is concerned about me or tells me that my son has incited my servant to lie in wait for me, as he does today."

⁹But Doeg the Edomite, who was standing with Saul's officials, said, "I saw the son of Jesse come to Ahimelech son of Ahitub at Nob. ¹⁰Ahimelech inquired of the

---

[98] Cf. Gordon (*I and II Samuel*, 173), Baldwin (*1 and 2 Samuel*, 140), McCarter (*I Samuel*, 355), and Klein (*1 Samuel*, 219), who favor a Moabite location; Y. Aharoni and M. Avi-Yonah prefer Masada (*The Macmillan Bible Atlas*, rev. ed. [New York: Macmillan, 1977], 62).

[99] "The imperfect with לֹא represents a more emphatic form of prohibition than the jussive with אַל (GKC §107:o).

LORD for him; he also gave him provisions and the sword of Goliath the Philistine."

[11]Then the king sent for the priest Ahimelech son of Ahitub and his father's whole family, who were the priests at Nob, and they all came to the king. [12]Saul said, "Listen now, son of Ahitub."

"Yes, my lord," he answered.

[13]Saul said to him, "Why have you conspired against me, you and the son of Jesse, giving him bread and a sword and inquiring of God for him, so that he has rebelled against me and lies in wait for me, as he does today?"

[14]Ahimelech answered the king, "Who of all your servants is as loyal as David, the king's son-in-law, captain of your bodyguard and highly respected in your household? [15]Was that day the first time I inquired of God for him? Of course not! Let not the king accuse your servant or any of his father's family, for your servant knows nothing at all about this whole affair."

[16]But the king said, "You will surely die, Ahimelech, you and your father's whole family."

[17]Then the king ordered the guards at his side: "Turn and kill the priests of the LORD, because they too have sided with David. They knew he was fleeing, yet they did not tell me."

But the king's officials were not willing to raise a hand to strike the priests of the LORD.

[18]The king then ordered Doeg, "You turn and strike down the priests." So Doeg the Edomite turned and struck them down. That day he killed eighty-five men who wore the linen ephod. [19]He also put to the sword Nob, the town of the priests, with its men and women, its children and infants, and its cattle, donkeys and sheep.

22:6–10 Saul, who had previously issued an order to all those in his service to kill David (cf. 19:1), received a report "that David and his men had been discovered" (v. 6). At the time he was conducting royal business outdoors in a time-honored manner (cf. Judg 4:5). The geographically prominent location (a hilltop), the presence of Saul's throne under a type of tree associated with the worship of Yahweh (cf. Gen 21:33), and the spear in the king's hand all lent authority and dignity to the conduct of royal affairs at that site.

Mention of David's name caused Saul to launch into a half-crazed tirade against "all his officials standing around him." Saul addressed his officials as "men of Benjamin" (v. 7), indicating that he had given positions of highest authority in his government only to kinsmen.[100] Appealing to their tribal loyalty as well as to their greed, he suggested that they had much to lose if "the son of Jesse"—a Judahite—became king in Saul's place. Through the use of

---

[100]This was—and remains—the common practice in Middle Eastern governments. Many, if not all, of David's top officials were family members (cf. 2 Sam 8:16–18): his military leaders Joab and Benaiah were certainly from Judah; Jehoshaphat was a prominent name in Judahite genealogies, though it cannot be established beyond doubt that the Jehoshaphat serving in David's court was from Judah; and, of course, David's sons were also in the court.

two rhetorical questions he indicated that a nonfamily member would not grant them such favors as he had done.

This being the case, Saul expressed consternation with the fact that his family members had not been more supportive of his efforts to dispose of this supposed threat to his kingship. Their inaction amounted to a massive conspiracy against the crown, and proof of this lay in the fact that no one had informed Saul that his own son Jonathan had made "a covenant with the son of Jesse" (v. 8; cf. 18:3). Their silence proved to him that none of them was concerned about him.

In his rage Saul's distorted thinking took a peculiar turn as he accused his own son of being the ringleader of the anti-Saul conspiracy. As Saul now envisioned it, David was not actually Saul's primary enemy—he was merely a pawn in a regicidal scheme hatched by Jonathan! Apparently Saul considered it plausible that Jonathan had hired David as a hit man in a plan to become king in his father's stead (cf. 2 Kgs 19:37). Such distorted thinking may help to explain why Saul attempted to murder Jonathan only days before (cf. 20:33).

Saul not only was distorted in his perception of Jonathan's actions, but he misunderstood David's as well; he thought David was at that moment lying "in wait," seeking to kill him at the first opportunity.

Saul's Israelite officials remained silent during and after the king's diatribe. The awkward silence was finally broken when a foreigner, "Doeg the Edomite, who was standing with Saul's officials" (v. 9), came forward with some information regarding David's visit to Nob. In addition to previously known aspects of David's interaction with Ahimelech—the fact that he "gave him provisions and the sword of Goliath" (v. 10)—Doeg also revealed that "Ahimelech inquired of the LORD for him."

This new information gives rise to two very different conclusions. First, it suggests that David was deeply committed to submitting to and receiving help from the Lord during his time of trouble. Second, from Saul's perspective it indicated that Ahimelech was using the unique powers of his office to give aid to an enemy of the king—anyone might supply David with food and a weapon, but only an Aaronic priest could inquire of the Lord.

22:11–15 Saul's perverted mind concluded from Doeg's report that the conspiracy against him was far larger than previously imagined. Now it was not just a son and a son-in-law out to kill him; hundreds of people, including the entire priestly establishment at Nob, were marshaled against him! In an effort to quash the revolt and deprive it of divine assistance, Saul "sent for the priest Ahimelech son of Ahitub and his father's whole family" (v. 11).

Obediently, the adult males of the priestly family made the hour-long trip west northwest to Gibeah, "to the king." Not knowing the nature of the king's request, perhaps these Ithamarites (cf. 1 Chr 24:6), relatives of the Elide family, imagined that they would once again be permitted to care for the ark of the covenant. But the king's first words spoken to Ahimelech dashed whatever hopes they might have held.

In the formal setting of the royal court, Saul held a trial in which he was the prosecutor and the family of Ahitub, represented by Ahimelech, were the defendants. Refusing to mention the name of his new adversary in conversation, Saul addressed Ahimelech as "son of Ahitub" (v. 12). He then named additional coconspirators, suggesting that the priests[101] had "conspired against" him. As Saul interpreted the events at Nob, Ahimelech's actions, supported by the other priests, had strengthened David's hand so that he "has rebelled" and now "lies in wait for" (v. 13) the king.

Stunned by the king's insane accusations, Ahimelech gave a four-pronged response. First, he provided a fivefold defense of David: far from being Saul's enemy, David was (1) "your servant," (2) "loyal," (3) "the king's son-in-law," (4) "captain of your bodyguard," and (5) "highly respected in your household" (v. 14). Second, Ahimelech characterized his priestly actions toward David as routine. Although it was true that he "inquired of God for" David, this "was not the first time" (v. 15). Third, the priest affirmed his loyalty to Saul, calling himself "your servant." Finally, Ahimelech declared his noninvolvement in any plot against Saul: he "knows nothing at all about this whole affair."

22:16–19 Unfazed by Ahimelech's rebuttal, Saul found the entire family of Ahitub guilty and pronounced sentence against them. Using the stern language of the Torah in pronouncing the punishment (cf. Gen 2:17; 20:7), Saul declared "dying you shall die" (v. 16; NIV, "you shall surely die"). This judgment applied to the "whole family."

Immediately the king ordered them executed. The men who received this command were presumably Saul's bodyguards, who only days before had been under David's command (v. 14). David had previously stated that these men were careful to observe cleanliness regulations (21:5), implying that they were devout followers of the Lord. Not surprisingly, therefore, Saul's attendants "were not willing to raise a hand to strike the priests of the LORD."

Perhaps one other reason for their disobedience to a direct order from the king was their rejection of the premise on which the death sentence was based. According to Saul, the priestly family of Ahitub had to die "because they too have sided with David" in a plot against the king. Saul's attendants loved and respected David (16:18; 18:5,22,30), and they knew him to be devoted to the king's welfare. There was no conspiracy against the king, so the priests had no reason to die.

This is now the second recorded instance where those under Saul's leadership refused to carry out a foolish royal order (cf. 14:44–45). It reinforces the

---

[101] The Hebrew verbs in Saul's accusation contain second-person plural subject suffixes, suggesting that Saul was indicting the entire priestly community.

Israelite understanding that earthly kings possessed finite powers and that Israelites must "obey God rather than men" (Acts 5:29).

Understanding the Israelites' reluctance to kill Yahwistic priests and the limits of power the Israelites had imposed on the royal office, Saul turned to a non-Israelite to "turn and strike down the priests" (v. 18). As an Edomite, Doeg had no compunctions about fulfilling the order;[102] accordingly "he killed eighty-five men who wore the linen ephod," that is, duly authorized leaders in the worship of Yahweh.[103] Perhaps, as Hertzberg suggests,[104] Doeg used this event to get revenge on the priests of Nob for the detention he faced at the sanctuary earlier (cf. 21:7).

The slaughter did not end there, however. Apparently with Saul's approval (cf. v. 21), Doeg also slaughtered the inhabitants of Nob, including men, women, children, and livestock (v. 19). This kind of mass execution, elsewhere termed *herem*, was authorized in the Torah only for use against non-Yahwistic peoples living in Canaan who would otherwise teach the Israelites to sin against the Lord (cf. Deut 20:17–18). The perpetration of this act against a city of Aaronic priests—those who taught Israelites to avoid sinning against Yahweh—was an unspeakable crime. Saul's stunning inversion of the revealed will of the Lord in this instance is consistent with the text's portrayal of Saul as a king "such as all the other nations have" (8:5).

Doeg's actions constitute the second time in 1 Samuel that Aaronic/Ithamarite priests were killed by foreigners as the result of Israelite sin (cf. 4:10–11). There is an essential difference between the two situations, however. On the earlier occasion it was the wickedness of the priests that caused their death, whereas in the latter it was the wickedness of the priest's king.

(5) David Rescues Yahweh's Priest Abiathar (22:20–23)

[20]But Abiathar, a son of Ahimelech son of Ahitub, escaped and fled to join David. [21]He told David that Saul had killed the priests of the LORD. [22]Then David said to Abiathar: "That day, when Doeg the Edomite was there, I knew he would be sure to tell Saul. I am responsible for the death of your father's whole family. [23]Stay with me; don't be afraid; the man who is seeking your life is seeking mine also. You will be safe with me."

Providentially, one of the Aaronic priests, "Abiathar, a son of Ahimelech son of Ahitub escaped" (v. 20). Now a fugitive from Saul, Abiathar found it expe-

---

[102] Edomites are frequently portrayed in the OT as a group of people at cross-purposes with Yahweh and his people. Cf. Gen 27:41–45; 32:1–21; Exod 15:15; Num 20:14–21; 2 Sam 8:13–14; 2 Kgs 8:20–22; 14:7; Pss 52; 83; Jer 49:9–16; Joel 3:18–19; Amos 1:11–12; 9:12; Ezek 35; Mal 1:3.

[103] The LXX asserts 305 men died; Josephus (*Ant.*, 6:260) gives the number as 385.

[104] Hertzberg, *I and II Samuel*, 180.

dient to abandon Israelite society and "join David" at Keilah (cf. 23:6)[105] in the territory of Judah. When he arrived at David's camp, he told him "that Saul had killed the priests of the LORD" (v. 21). The report was accurate, for even though Saul did not actually wield the sword, it was his mandate that brought about the slaughter.

Without mentioning Saul's role in the tragedy, David acknowledged that he himself was significantly "responsible for the death of" (v. 22) Abiathar's clan. He was accountable, not because of anything he had done, but because of something he had not done; David failed to kill Doeg although he had reasonable suspicions that he would inform Saul about David's activities in Nob. David's admission of homicidal negligence could not bring the dead back to life, but it could motivate him to give special consideration to the lone survivor of the massacre. Accordingly, David asked Abiathar to "stay with" him, assuring the priest that he would "be safe with" David. Abiathar accepted the offer (cf. 23:6).[106]

(6) David Rescues Keilah from the Philistines (23:1–6)

[1]When David was told, "Look, the Philistines are fighting against Keilah and are looting the threshing floors," [2]he inquired of the LORD, saying, "Shall I go and attack these Philistines?"

The LORD answered him, "Go, attack the Philistines and save Keilah."
[3]But David's men said to him, "Here in Judah we are afraid. How much more, then, if we go to Keilah against the Philistine forces!"
[4]Once again David inquired of the LORD, and the LORD answered him, "Go down to Keilah, for I am going to give the Philistines into your hand." [5]So David and his men went to Keilah, fought the Philistines and carried off their livestock. He inflicted heavy losses on the Philistines and saved the people of Keilah. [6](Now Abiathar son of Ahimelech had brought the ephod down with him when he fled to David at Keilah.)

23:1–4 Less than three miles south of the cave of Adullam was the fortified city of Keilah (Khirbet Qila). A walled city located in the agriculturally productive Shephelah region of Judah, Keilah represented a desirable prize for the Philistines. It was only about twelve miles east southeast of Gath and was relatively isolated from other Israelite cities. These details, in combination with the time of year—early summer, either during barley or wheat harvest—meant

---

[105] When read in light of 23:6, it becomes clear that the events of 22:6–23 occurred simultaneously with 23:1–5. David was in the forest of Hereth in 22:5; Abiathar did not come to David there, however; instead it was at Keilah that Abiathar joined him (23:6). Furthermore, no mention is made of David using Abiathar's revelatory ephod prior to David's arrival at Keilah.

[106] According to the canonical introduction of Psalm 52, David also used this occasion to compose a psalm. Psalm 52 contrasts Doeg's lack of faith and woeful destiny with David's faith and bright destiny.

that Keilah was an attractive and vulnerable target for Philistine plunderers.

David, who was presumably with his troops in the forest of Hereth (cf. 22:5) at the time of the Philistine attack, was informed of the events at Keilah. In the tradition of previous Spirit-anointed deliverers,[107] David responded to the news with a desire to lead his fellow Israelites in battle against the enemy.

Before going into battle, Israelites would normally await a confirmation that the Lord would give the enemy into their hands (cf. Judg 1:2; 3:28; 4:14; 7:15; 1 Sam 14:12). In keeping with this tradition, David formally "inquired of the LORD" (v. 2), and received word that he should "attack the Philistines and save Keilah." The method David used to discern God's will is unknown; perhaps he was acting as a prophet (cf. 2 Sam 23:2; Acts 4:25). According to v. 6 David did not have the ephod until Abiathar met him at Keilah.[108] Whatever method David used, it did not seem to be satisfactory to David's men; they were unconvinced by the words of David's supposed revelation. The command to go "against the Philistine forces" (v. 3), an army with superior armaments and greater numbers, did not seem divinely inspired. In fact, David's troops were even "afraid" of doing battle with the comparatively weaker Israelite army under Saul's command—how much more so the Philistines. The men's concerns caused David to go before the Lord "once again" (v. 4). As before, the Lord responded favorably to David's request, promising him success.

23:5–6 Armed with that confirmatory word, "David and his men went into battle. Exactly as promised, the Israelites defeated the Philistines and captured the Philistines' "livestock" as booty. The captured Philistine livestock may have been flocks brought to the region of Keilah to consume the Israelites' pasture lands and grain fields; alternatively, they may have been beasts of burden the Philistines intended to use to carry off Israelite possessions.

While David was at Keilah, a large number of individuals joined his ranks (cf. v. 13). Of those who came to him there, none was more important to him than "Abiathar son of Ahimelech" (v. 6). Abiathar's presence in David's camp was especially important because he had "brought the ephod." Abiathar's ephod was presumably like the cultic garment mentioned in the Torah (cf. Exod 28:6–35) that had attached to it a pouch containing the revelatory Urim and Thummim. Thus with Abiathar's arrival David now had acquired access to the only revelatory device sanctioned by the Torah (cf. Num 27:21). The deficiencies and questions that plagued David's previous efforts to know God's will (cf. vv. 2–4) were dealt with in a convincing way.

---

[107] Cf. Othniel (Judg 3:10), Gideon (Judg 6:34), Jephthah (Judg 11:29), Samson (14:6,19; 15:14), and Saul (1 Sam 11:6).

[108] The NIV's translation of the perfect form הֵבִיא as a pluperfect ("had brought") creates difficulties, since v. 6 indicates Abiathar brought David the ephod "at Keilah," which he could not have done until after David took the city. Therefore, the point of v. 6 is that David did not have the ephod until after the battle.

(7) David Escapes from Saul in the Arabah (23:7–29)

⁷Saul was told that David had gone to Keilah, and he said, "God has handed him over to me, for David has imprisoned himself by entering a town with gates and bars." ⁸And Saul called up all his forces for battle, to go down to Keilah to besiege David and his men.

⁹When David learned that Saul was plotting against him, he said to Abiathar the priest, "Bring the ephod." ¹⁰David said, "O LORD, God of Israel, your servant has heard definitely that Saul plans to come to Keilah and destroy the town on account of me. ¹¹Will the citizens of Keilah surrender me to him? Will Saul come down, as your servant has heard? O LORD, God of Israel, tell your servant."

And the LORD said, "He will."

¹²Again David asked, "Will the citizens of Keilah surrender me and my men to Saul?"

And the LORD said, "They will."

¹³So David and his men, about six hundred in number, left Keilah and kept moving from place to place. When Saul was told that David had escaped from Keilah, he did not go there.

¹⁴David stayed in the desert strongholds and in the hills of the Desert of Ziph. Day after day Saul searched for him, but God did not give David into his hands.

¹⁵While David was at Horesh in the Desert of Ziph, he learned that Saul had come out to take his life. ¹⁶And Saul's son Jonathan went to David at Horesh and helped him find strength in God. ¹⁷"Don't be afraid," he said. "My father Saul will not lay a hand on you. You will be king over Israel, and I will be second to you. Even my father Saul knows this." ¹⁸The two of them made a covenant before the LORD. Then Jonathan went home, but David remained at Horesh.

¹⁹The Ziphites went up to Saul at Gibeah and said, "Is not David hiding among us in the strongholds at Horesh, on the hill of Hakilah, south of Jeshimon? ²⁰Now, O king, come down whenever it pleases you to do so, and we will be responsible for handing him over to the king."

²¹Saul replied, "The LORD bless you for your concern for me. ²²Go and make further preparation. Find out where David usually goes and who has seen him there. They tell me he is very crafty. ²³Find out about all the hiding places he uses and come back to me with definite information. Then I will go with you; if he is in the area, I will track him down among all the clans of Judah."

²⁴So they set out and went to Ziph ahead of Saul. Now David and his men were in the Desert of Maon, in the Arabah south of Jeshimon. ²⁵Saul and his men began the search, and when David was told about it, he went down to the rock and stayed in the Desert of Maon. When Saul heard this, he went into the Desert of Maon in pursuit of David.

²⁶Saul was going along one side of the mountain, and David and his men were on the other side, hurrying to get away from Saul. As Saul and his forces were closing in on David and his men to capture them, ²⁷a messenger came to Saul, saying, "Come quickly! The Philistines are raiding the land." ²⁸Then Saul broke off his pursuit of David and went to meet the Philistines. That is why they call this place Sela Hammahlekoth. ²⁹And David went up from there and lived in the strongholds of En Gedi.

23:7–13 From his information-gathering network Saul learned that David was at Keilah (v. 7). Saul took this as a divinely engineered circumstance that would enable him to capture David. Accordingly, "Saul called up all the people" (v. 8; NIV, "his forces") to attack Keilah and seize David. Reports of this massive conscription order came to David, who immediately sought the Lord's will by means of the ephod.

As portrayed by the biblical writer, the central event in the Keilah episode of vv. 7–13a is David's pursuit of divine counsel by means of the ephod; 48 of the 103 Hebrew words in this section (47 percent) are used to depict this one seemingly minor incident. The author used the ephod-based interchange between David and the Lord to achieve several results relevant to the themes and theological intents of the book. First, the incident demonstrated David's reliance on the Lord; though David was Israel's greatest military hero, he would make no military move without divine approval. Second, the success David experienced in communicating with the Lord demonstrated the vitality of his relationship with the God of Israel. Third, the short narrative heightened the contrast between David and Saul; Saul would repeatedly fail to establish a link with the Lord, while David would have easy and extended dialogue with him. Finally, it demonstrated the effectiveness of the Torah-prescribed means of receiving divine counsel.

Presumably Keilah's residents had heard what Saul had done to Nob's citizens (cf. 22:18–19) and feared he would do the same to them if they were perceived to be supporting David. Certainly David wished to avoid inflicting harm on his group or on the people of the city. Consequently, he and his men left quickly before Saul could set out against him there. David's course of action produced the intended effect: Saul "did not go" to Keilah and destroy it. At the time of his retreat from the city, David's band numbered "about six hundred"— a 50-percent increase from the time when he was at Adullam (cf. 22:2).

23:14–18 Having saved Keilah through his timely departure, David now needed to act in such a way as to protect his followers. The strategy he chose involved three key elements; first, frequent relocation—he "kept moving from place to place"; second, preference for remote frontier areas such as "the Desert of Ziph" (v. 14), some sixteen miles south of Bethlehem; and third, residing in easily defensible locations—"the desert strongholds" of the central mountain regions. Although "Saul searched" for David and his men "day after day," God worked through David's plan to keep the group safe.

One of the locations in which David and his men stayed was "Horesh in the Desert of Ziph" (v. 15), an otherwise unknown location. While there, David "learned that Saul had come out to take his life."[109] Jonathan was as well

---

[109] Youngblood (*1, 2 Samuel*, 744) has followed many others in emending the MT's וַיַּרְא ("and then he saw," from רָאָה) to וַיִּרָא ("and then he feared," from יָרֵא). The verb רָאָה, however, can mean more generally "to perceive," and so the MT makes perfect sense.

informed about David's location as his father (cf. 20:2). Unencumbered by the limitations of traveling with a large armed force, Jonathan was able to get "to David at Horesh" (v. 16) before his father could. His purpose was as noble as his commitment to David; he "strengthened his hand in God" (NIV, "helped him find strength in God").

Jonathan encouraged his friend by reminding him of the trustworthy promise the Lord had made to him earlier—"you will be king over Israel" (v. 17), and then by suggesting some implications of this divine promise. Because the Lord was overseeing David's rise to kingship, David had no need to "be afraid." Because the Lord was with David, Saul would not "lay a hand on" him. Because it was the Lord's decision to install David in the nation's highest political office, David was not revolting against the Saulide dynasty as Saul had charged; thus it would be possible for David to fulfill the divine plan and maintain harmonious relations with the Saulides. Jonathan could "be second" to David in the new order. The Lord's plans for David were not hidden (cf. 2 Sam 5:2), nor were they the product of David's imagination: even Saul knew them.

During this final recorded meeting, David and Jonathan confirmed and extended commitments they had made to each other on previous occasions (cf. 18:3–4; 20:14–16). Afterward "Jonathan went home," apparently choosing not to join—or being barred from joining (cf. 20:30)—his father's militia in the task of tracking down David. For his part, "David remained at Horesh."

23:19–20 Both David and Saul had intelligence-gathering networks that included people from opposing tribes. David had received crucial information regarding Saul's activities and intentions from Jonathan, a Benjamite (cf. 20:35–39); here Saul received valuable information about David from "the Ziphites" (v. 19), who were Judahites associated with the family of Caleb (cf. 1 Chr 2:42).[110] Not waiting for Saul to threaten them with destruction, the Ziphites took the initiative and "went up to Saul at Gibeah" to inform the king of David's whereabouts. The information they provided was quite detailed, specifying even the exact hill.

That the Ziphites would provide this information to remove the threat of destruction by Saul's forces is understandable. But the enthusiastic support they offered Saul is less so; they virtually begged Saul to come down (lit., "for every desire of your soul, O king, you must come down!"). Furthermore, they voluntarily committed themselves to hand David "over to the king." David's noble reaction to this betrayal by fellow tribesmen is recorded in Psalm 54. The tone of this psalm reflects the words of encouragement given him by Jonathan.

---

[110] The writer of 1 Samuel elsewhere notes that a Calebite, Nabal, was a troublemaker for David (cf. 25:3). Calebites also inhabited Bethlehem (cf. 1 Chr 2:51), and so David probably had relationships with this clan throughout his life. Perhaps there had been a falling out between the Calebites and the rest of the tribe of Judah at some early point in the history of the tribe, which would help explain the ready assistance the Calebite city of Ziph provided to Saul at this time.

It also suggests that David would not use this situation as a justification for personally avenging the traitors; he would leave vengeance to God (cf. Ps 54:2; also Deut 32:35).

23:21–25 Saul responded to the Ziphites' offer in a manner that is, from a spiritual standpoint, predictably inappropriate. The Ziphites had just betrayed the Lord's anointed, yet Saul stated they were "blessed to Yahweh" (v. 21; NIV, "the LORD bless you") because of this act in Saul's behalf.

Then Saul asked the Ziphites to "go and probe again" (v. 22; NIV, "go and make further preparation") into David's situation and then return to him (v. 23). Saul especially had need of three vital pieces of information: first, he needed to know "where David usually goes"; this would be useful in determining possible locations for attacking David during his routine activities. Second, he needed to know "who has seen him," that is, what individuals and/or groups had been cooperating with him and supplying him with necessities for survival. No doubt Saul would be displeased to learn that his own son was among those who had assisted David in the desert. Finally, he needed to know "about all the hiding places he uses" (v. 23). This information would be vital in case Saul wished to make a predawn raid on David's camp, as he had done previously against the Philistines (cf. 11:11).

Once Saul had received this valuable data from the Ziphites, he would use it to track David "down among all the clans of Judah." The king needed help in acquiring this information because David "is very crafty" (ʿārôm yaʿrîm). The verb phrase expressing Saul's perception of David creates an ironic wordplay with the narrator's description of Saul, who was said to be ʿārôm, "naked," in 19:24. David's "craftiness" permitted him to remain hidden from view; Saul's caused him to be shamefully exposed to all.

Obediently the Ziphites left Gibeah ahead of Saul (v. 24). Shortly thereafter Saul and his men began their pernicious game of cat-and-mouse. Meanwhile, David and his men had moved about five miles south of Ziph to an area near the wealthy Nabal's city of residence (cf. 25:2). Then when David learned of Saul's southward movements, "he went down to the rock" in the Maon wilderness, apparently a natural formation particularly desirable for defensive purposes. Guided by intelligence reports from the Ziphites, Saul responded to David's movements by leading the royal troops "into the Desert of Maon."

23:26–29 The confrontation almost came to a head when Saul and his men arrived at David's desert mountain sanctuary and began scaling "one side of the mountain" (v. 26). A deadly battle pitting Israelite against Israelite seemed inevitable, and yet it probably was David's to win.[111] After all, he was Israel's

---

[111] An alternate interpretation of this event understands David and his men to be confronted by a superior force that was on the verge of overwhelming them. In that view the remarkable feature of the event is that the Lord's anointed was saved by the report of Philistine aggression. Either interpretation is possible, but (obviously) I prefer the one presented in the main text.

greatest military leader, and he and his troops held the high ground in the battlefield of their own choosing. Nevertheless, David had no desire to risk killing
Yahweh's anointed king (cf. 1 Sam 24:10; 26:9,11,23; 2 Sam 1:14–16). Consequently, David had his troops abandon their advantageous site and begin a militarily foolish but theologically wise retreat, "hurrying to get away from Saul."

"Saul and his forces were closing in on David and his men to capture them"
when a providential and urgent report arrived, indicating that "the Philistines
are raiding the land." Obedient to the royal mandate given him by the Israelite
elders (cf. 8:20), Saul reluctantly and temporarily abandoned his personal vendetta. National interests were given precedence over personal ones, and the
fight with David was set aside for another day.

In recognition of this remarkable prevention of a bloody civil war, the rock
outcropping on which these events occurred came to be known as "the Promontory of the Parting" (NIV, "Sela Hammahlekoth"). Following this narrow
escape, David and his men traveled east to the rugged hills west of the Dead
Sea "and lived in the strongholds of En Gedi" (= "The Spring of the Young
Goat"; v. 29; Hb. 24:1). In this area David and his men had isolation, protection, and, because of the En Gedi spring, an adequate supply of fresh water.

(8) David Spares Saul at En Gedi (24:1–22)[112]

[1]**After Saul returned from pursuing the Philistines, he was told, "David is in the
Desert of En Gedi."** [2]**So Saul took three thousand chosen men from all Israel and
set out to look for David and his men near the Crags of the Wild Goats.**
[3]**He came to the sheep pens along the way; a cave was there, and Saul went in to
relieve himself. David and his men were far back in the cave.** [4]**The men said, "This
is the day the LORD spoke of when he said to you, 'I will give your enemy into your
hands for you to deal with as you wish.'" Then David crept up unnoticed and cut
off a corner of Saul's robe.**
[5]**Afterward, David was conscience-stricken for having cut off a corner of his
robe.** [6]**He said to his men, "The LORD forbid that I should do such a thing to my
master, the LORD's anointed, or lift my hand against him; for he is the anointed of
the LORD."** [7]**With these words David rebuked his men and did not allow them to**

---

[112] The predominant opinion of modern OT scholarship is that this account represents the first
of two retellings of an event modified in its details in chap. 26. Among writing scholars who hold
to this opinion are Smith (*Samuel*, 216), Hertzberg (*I and II Samuel*, 207), McCarter (*I Samuel*,
379), Klein (*I Samuel*, 236), and Brueggemann (*First and Second Samuel*, 166). McCarter
assumes that the present chapter is a modification of the supposedly older account found in chap.
26, though much disagreement exists concerning the priority of accounts (*I Samuel*, 379, 386–87;
cf. Klein's discussion, *I Samuel*, 237). Scholars who assume that two different events are recorded
in chaps. 24 and 26 include Kirkpatrick (*First Book of Samuel*, 243–44) and Baldwin (*I and 2 Samuel*, 154). Gordon, while appearing to favor the existence of two separate events, notes that "the
apologetic function of the narratives is, in any case, unimpaired, whichever view we adopt" (*I and
II Samuel*, 178).

attack Saul. And Saul left the cave and went his way.

[8]Then David went out of the cave and called out to Saul, "My lord the king!" When Saul looked behind him, David bowed down and prostrated himself with his face to the ground. [9]He said to Saul, "Why do you listen when men say, 'David is bent on harming you'? [10]This day you have seen with your own eyes how the LORD delivered you into my hands in the cave. Some urged me to kill you, but I spared you; I said, 'I will not lift my hand against my master, because he is the LORD's anointed.' [11]See, my father, look at this piece of your robe in my hand! I cut off the corner of your robe but did not kill you. Now understand and recognize that I am not guilty of wrongdoing or rebellion. I have not wronged you, but you are hunting me down to take my life. [12]May the LORD judge between you and me. And may the LORD avenge the wrongs you have done to me, but my hand will not touch you. [13]As the old saying goes, 'From evildoers come evil deeds,' so my hand will not touch you.

[14]"Against whom has the king of Israel come out? Whom are you pursuing? A dead dog? A flea? [15]May the LORD be our judge and decide between us. May he consider my cause and uphold it; may he vindicate me by delivering me from your hand."

[16]When David finished saying this, Saul asked, "Is that your voice, David my son?" And he wept aloud. [17]"You are more righteous than I," he said. "You have treated me well, but I have treated you badly. [18]You have just now told me of the good you did to me; the LORD delivered me into your hands, but you did not kill me. [19]When a man finds his enemy, does he let him get away unharmed? May the LORD reward you well for the way you treated me today. [20]I know that you will surely be king and that the kingdom of Israel will be established in your hands. [21]Now swear to me by the LORD that you will not cut off my descendants or wipe out my name from my father's family."

[22]So David gave his oath to Saul. Then Saul returned home, but David and his men went up to the stronghold.

24:1–7 After Saul had responded militarily to the latest outbreak of Philistine aggression, he returned to Gibeah to focus on David. When his intelligence network informed him of David's whereabouts, he immediately assembled an elite fighting force "from all Israel and set out to look for David and his men" (v. 2; Hb. v. 3). Having made a journey of more than thirty miles, the royal troops centered their efforts in the vicinity of the "Crags of the Wild Goats," an otherwise unidentified rock outcropping near the Dead Sea.

As the troops made their way down a path cut by shepherds driving their flocks, they came to a series of "sheep pens along the way" (v. 3; Hb. v. 4)—suggesting a favorable campsite for Saul's men—and a nearby cave. There Saul "went in to relieve himself" (lit., "to cover his feet").[113] Providentially, the cave that Saul chose to use was the same one in which David and his men

---

[113] This Hebrew idiom refers to the Israelite practice of disposing of human excrement in a sanitary manner through covering it over with dirt (cf. Deut 23:13).

were hiding.[114] Saul's vulnerability during this private moment was extreme, and David's soldiers knew it. In fact, the situation was so extraordinary that David's men concluded God made it happen to fulfill the prophetic words, "I will give your enemy into your hands for you to deal with as you wish" (v. 4; Hb. v. 5). This prophecy is not mentioned elsewhere in Scripture and probably represents an example of false prophecy (cf. 1 Kgs 22:11–16); alternatively, it may have been a genuine prophecy relating to non-Israelite enemies misapplied to Saul.

David moved stealthily to Saul's location and used his weapon aggressively against the king. However, the aggression was symbolic in nature; he "cut off a corner of Saul's robe." This act was far from meaningless because David's confiscation of a portion of the royal robe signified the transfer of power from the house of Saul to the house of David. Furthermore, by removing the corner of the robe, David made Saul's robe to be in a state of noncompliance with Torah requirements (cf. Num 15:38–39; Deut 22:12); thus, Saul's most obvious symbol of kingship was made unwearable. In essence, David had symbolically invalidated Saul's claim to kingship.[115]

David immediately recognized the powerful implications of his act and was conscience stricken (v. 5; Hb. v. 6). By voiding Saul's claim to kingship, he was at some level lifting his hand against "the anointed of the LORD" (v. 6; Hb. v. 7). This was more than an act against the king; it was rebellion against the Lord, who had commanded Israelites not to curse their rulers (Exod 22:28), and had previously punished Israelites who had expressed a rebellious attitude against constituted authority (cf. Num 12:2–15; 16:1–35).

Having repented of his own actions, David then worked to prevent his men from sinning in a similar manner (v. 7; Hb. v. 8). Meanwhile, Saul, who somehow remained oblivious to all of this, returned to his men.

24:8–15 A most remarkable confrontation occurred in this moment of vulnerability for Saul and David. The section of text stretching over vv. 8–21 contains the longest recorded quotes by both David (114 Hebrew words) and Saul (sixty-seven Hebrew words) found in 1 Samuel. The amount of space the author devoted to these two quotations suggests that he considered them to be

---

[114] The reference to David and his men in the cave connects this series of events with Pss 57; 142. Both of those psalms express David's profound reliance upon and exultant faith in God. In those compositions David confesses that Yahweh, not the natural fortification, is his refuge (Pss 57:1; 142:5)—one which in fact proved most secure.

[115] Gordon notes that "in Mesopotamia the hem of a person's garment could be used in the person's absence as a means of authentication" and speculates accordingly that David interpreted his actions toward Saul as "tantamount to a violation of Saul's—sacrosanct (6)—person" (*I and II Samuel,* 179). Along this line, note the comment by V. H. Matthews: "The rather elaborate hems with suspended tassels found on most garments in the ancient Near East symbolized the ranks of kings and their advisers as well as the military" (*Manners and Customs in the Bible* [Peabody, Mass.: Hendrickson, 1988], 119).

thematically central. Close inspection of these quotations does not disappoint us, for they are seen to contain at least two major items: David's most passionate affirmation of loyalty to the king and Saul's confession that David would be Israel's next king.

While Saul was still within earshot of the cave, David emerged from its dark recesses and "called out to Saul" (v. 8; Hb. v. 9). This action was perilous, since it betrayed the location of David and his men. However, the risks were not extreme, since Saul was away from his camp (cf. Deut 23:12) and therefore his army: if need be, David and his men could capture Saul before the king could rejoin his troops and muster them for battle.

David prefaced his major quotation with a short but significant call, as well as an action directed to Saul. Rather than cursing his ruler, David honored him by calling him both "my lord" and "the king." Rather than falling upon Saul in a murderous attack, David fell upon the ground "and prostrated himself with his face to the ground." Following these verbal and actional signals of loyalty to the king, David uttered what is perhaps the most passionate and eloquent plea for reconciliation between persons recorded in all ancient literature.

In his appeal David tactfully avoided accusing Saul of being the one who initiated hurtful actions against him. It was not Saul but unnamed "men" (v. 9; Hb. v. 10) who concocted the idea that "David is bent on harming" the king. Having affirmed his support for Saul and disavowed a belief that Saul was ultimately responsible for the present problem, David then brought forward evidence to suggest that the premise upon which the attacks against David were based was entirely false.

With the skill of an expert lawyer, David carefully laid out both eyewitness and material evidence to make his case, and then used it to lead Saul to an unavoidable conclusion. First, he discussed the eyewitness evidence. He pointed out that the evidence was fresh: it was based on events of "this day" (v. 10; Hb. v. 11). Furthermore, it was evidence that was directly available to Saul: "you have seen with your own eyes." David then carefully walked Saul through the immediately past events, supplying details to emphasize the extreme danger from which the king was delivered: "the LORD delivered you into my hands," and some of David's men even "urged" David to kill the king. As part of this presentation David emphasized his saving actions on the king's behalf: "I spared you."

More importantly, David also declared his motive for sparing the king: it was because he respectfully recognized that Saul "is the LORD's anointed." David treated the king properly, not because of anything the king had done or might do, but because of what the Lord had done. David's respect for human authority was based on his respect for divine authority.

Second, David presented material evidence to support the interpretation of events just given: a "piece of your robe in my hand" (v. 11; Hb. v. 12). If there was any doubt in Saul's mind about how close his brush with death really was, this evidence would remove it. Saul's own royal garment would remind him that David "cut off the corner of" the robe, "but did not kill" him.

Finally, David led Saul to the desired verdict: he was "not guilty of wrongdoing or rebellion." David skillfully concluded his case for exoneration by quoting an ancient proverb (v. 13; Hb. v. 14: cf. Matt 7:16,20). Since David did not carry out an evil deed against the king, it followed that David was not an evildoer. Thus he was no threat to Saul, and the king should stop treating David as if he were.

To this point, however, Saul had been hunting David down, and this was wrong. Even so, David would not seek to avenge the king for "the wrongs" done against him; his "hand will not touch" Saul. But in attempting to kill an innocent man, Saul was violating the Torah and was in danger of bringing divine wrath upon himself (cf. Exod 23:7). The Lord, who is a judge with greater authority than any earthly king, would "judge between" David and Saul and "avenge the wrongs" (v. 12; Hb. v. 13). Thus David was actually pleading for Saul to save himself, not just to spare David.

As he began to conclude his presentation to Saul, David's language rose to the level of poetry. Using a series of two synonymously parallel couplets externally linked through the key word "after," he attempted to put the king's recent efforts in perspective (literally):

> After whom goes forth Israel's king?
> After whom are you seeking?
> After a lifeless dog?
> After a single flea?

With these words David tacitly accused the king of acting like a fool and squandering precious national resources. Yet the employment of rhetorical questions and unflattering comparisons of himself to a dead dog and a flea—all expressed in a poetic framework—helped to make David's criticisms more palatable and poignant.[116]

David brought his address to a thundering conclusion by employing five consecutive hortatory clauses that have the Lord as the subject. This sustained appeal to the Lord is unparalleled in the Former Prophets and is rivaled only by the language of the Psalms. In these words David moved his focus away from Saul to look to an authority high above the king. He appealed to the Lord to (1) "be our judge, (2) "decide" the dispute, (3) "consider" his cause, (4) "uphold" it, and finally (5) "vindicate" him (v. 15; Hb. v. 16).

24:16–21 Saul, who was apparently far enough away from the cave that he could not see the face of the one addressing him, attempted to confirm David

---

[116] Baldwin suggests that these lines were intended to warn Saul that he had actually "taken on the LORD, who will show David to be in the right" (*1 and 2 Samuel,* 145).

as the source of the words just spoken. That David's words had a great impact on the king is apparent. Formerly he had refused even to mention the name of his enemy (cf. 20:27,30–31; 22:7–9,13); now he called him "David" (v. 16; Hb. v. 17). Formerly David was Saul's son-in-law (cf. 18:21); now he is "my son."[117] Saul was now emotionally broken and "wept aloud."

Then the king launched into the longest unbroken quote credited to him in Scripture (sixty-seven Hebrew words). He began by exonerating David, noting that the young man was "more righteous than" himself (v. 17; Hb. v. 18; cf. Gen 38:26; Hab 1:13); whereas David treated Saul "well" (Hb. *haṭṭôbâ*), that is, in an ethically commendable manner; Saul had treated David "badly" (Hb. *hārā'â*), that is, wickedly (cf. Gen 44:4; 1 Sam 25:21; Pss 35:12; 38:20; 109:5; Prov 17:13; Jer 18:20).

David's actions toward Saul defied military logic: "the LORD delivered" the king into David's hands, yet he "did not kill" him (v. 18; Hb. v. 19). Furthermore, his actions defied common sense: conventional wisdom advises killing one's enemy when found, but David let Saul "get away unharmed" (v. 19; Hb. v. 20). In gratitude for this, Saul pronounced a blessing on his son-in-law, asking the Lord to "reward" him richly.

Then, as if he just recalled that the Lord had already promised David a reward, he affirmed God's royal intentions for the younger man: "you will surely be king" (v. 20; Hb. v. 21; cf. 15:28; 16:12). In making this confession, Saul confirmed the words of his son Jonathan (cf. 23:17). Rekindling for a moment his prophetic powers (cf. 10:10; 18:10; 19:24), Saul also predicted that Israel would flourish under David: it "will arise in your hands" (NIV, "be established").

Saul was emotionally crushed by the circumstances and in this state set aside all pretense of superiority to David. Begging him to grant two requests, he first asked that his successor "not cut off my seed" (v. 21; Hb. v. 22; NIV, "descendants")—that is, that David not follow the ancient Near Eastern custom of exterminating all descendants of his dynastic predecessor (cf. discussion at 20:14). Second, he requested that David not "wipe out my name from my father's family," a request closely related to the first but emphasizing the preservation of a link between Saul and his forebears.

Without hesitation "David gave his oath to Saul" (v. 22). In so doing he was confirming the oath he had made previously with Jonathan (cf. 20:14–17,42). David would later fulfill this commitment by giving sanctuary—indeed a position of honor and a generous inheritance—to Mephibosheth (cf. 2 Sam 9:1–13; 19:29; 21:7).

---

[117] R. Lawton argues that the author's inclusion of language that portrays a filial relationship between Saul and David was intended to reinforce the theme that David was Saul's legitimate successor ("Saul, Jonathan and the 'Son of Jesse,'" *JSOT* 58 [1993]: 35–46).

As this encounter between the present and future kings of Israel ended, "Saul returned home" to Gibeah. However, David chose not to return to his wife and home, probably fearing that the fire of Saul's insane enmity toward him would be rekindled. Instead, he "and his men went up to the stronghold."

(9) Aside: Samuel's Death Is Noted (25:1)

¹Now Samuel died, and all Israel assembled and mourned for him; and they buried him at his home in Ramah.
Then David moved down into the Desert of Maon.

While David was in the southern regions of Judah, his elderly friend and spiritual counselor, Samuel, died. The prophet's death meant the loss of a national resource and marked the end of an era in Israelite history. Appropriately, "all Israel"—perhaps including David and his men—"assembled and mourned for him." Samuel was accorded an honorable burial in his house "in Ramah,"[118] a site connected by popular—though probably inaccurate—tradition with modern Nebi Samwil. Shortly thereafter "David moved down into the Desert." Exactly which desert he moved to is disputed; the Hebrew text states it was Paran, normally understood to be in the central portion of the Sinai peninsula, extending up to Kadesh Barnea. The NIV, following the LXX and the logic of geographic proximity, states it was the "Desert of Maon," one of David's favored lairs (cf. 23:24–25).

Favoring the Paran location is the fact that David's life is deliberately presented as a parallel to the history of Israel; this portion of David's life is more closely parallel with Israel if he, like Israel, spent time in the Desert of Paran (cf. Num 10:12ff.). Furthermore, the Desert of Paran, which included Kadesh Barnea, was situated on the southern border of tribal territories allotted to Judah (cf. Josh 15:3) and thus provided the most isolated location within David's homeland for hiding from Saul.

(10) The Lord Spares David from Sin against Nabal (25:2–44)

²A certain man in Maon, who had property there at Carmel, was very wealthy. He had a thousand goats and three thousand sheep, which he was shearing in Carmel. ³His name was Nabal and his wife's name was Abigail. She was an intelligent and beautiful woman, but her husband, a Calebite, was surly and mean in his dealings.
⁴While David was in the desert, he heard that Nabal was shearing sheep. ⁵So he sent ten young men and said to them, "Go up to Nabal at Carmel and greet him in my name. ⁶Say to him: 'Long life to you! Good health to you and your household!

And good health to all that is yours!

⁷"'Now I hear that it is sheep-shearing time. When your shepherds were with us, we did not mistreat them, and the whole time they were at Carmel nothing of theirs was missing. ⁸Ask your own servants and they will tell you. Therefore be favorable toward my young men, since we come at a festive time. Please give your servants and your son David whatever you can find for them.'"

⁹When David's men arrived, they gave Nabal this message in David's name. Then they waited.

¹⁰Nabal answered David's servants, "Who is this David? Who is this son of Jesse? Many servants are breaking away from their masters these days. ¹¹Why should I take my bread and water, and the meat I have slaughtered for my shearers, and give it to men coming from who knows where?"

¹²David's men turned around and went back. When they arrived, they reported every word. ¹³David said to his men, "Put on your swords!" So they put on their swords, and David put on his. About four hundred men went up with David, while two hundred stayed with the supplies.

¹⁴One of the servants told Nabal's wife Abigail: "David sent messengers from the desert to give our master his greetings, but he hurled insults at them. ¹⁵Yet these men were very good to us. They did not mistreat us, and the whole time we were out in the fields near them nothing was missing. ¹⁶Night and day they were a wall around us all the time we were herding our sheep near them. ¹⁷Now think it over and see what you can do, because disaster is hanging over our master and his whole household. He is such a wicked man that no one can talk to him."

¹⁸Abigail lost no time. She took two hundred loaves of bread, two skins of wine, five dressed sheep, five seahs of roasted grain, a hundred cakes of raisins and two hundred cakes of pressed figs, and loaded them on donkeys. ¹⁹Then she told her servants, "Go on ahead; I'll follow you." But she did not tell her husband Nabal.

²⁰As she came riding her donkey into a mountain ravine, there were David and his men descending toward her, and she met them. ²¹David had just said, "It's been useless—all my watching over this fellow's property in the desert so that nothing of his was missing. He has paid me back evil for good. ²²May God deal with David, be it ever so severely, if by morning I leave alive one male of all who belong to him!"

²³When Abigail saw David, she quickly got off her donkey and bowed down before David with her face to the ground. ²⁴She fell at his feet and said: "My lord, let the blame be on me alone. Please let your servant speak to you; hear what your servant has to say. ²⁵May my lord pay no attention to that wicked man Nabal. He is just like his name—his name is Fool, and folly goes with him. But as for me, your servant, I did not see the men my master sent.

²⁶"Now since the LORD has kept you, my master, from bloodshed and from avenging yourself with your own hands, as surely as the LORD lives and as you live, may your enemies and all who intend to harm my master be like Nabal. ²⁷And let this gift, which your servant has brought to my master, be given to the men who follow you. ²⁸Please forgive your servant's offense, for the LORD will certainly make a lasting dynasty for my master, because he fights the LORD's battles. Let no wrongdoing be found in you as long as you live. ²⁹Even though someone is pursuing you to take your life, the life of my master will be bound securely in the bundle of

the living by the LORD your God. But the lives of your enemies he will hurl away as from the pocket of a sling. [30]When the LORD has done for my master every good thing he promised concerning him and has appointed him leader over Israel, [31]my master will not have on his conscience the staggering burden of needless bloodshed or of having avenged himself. And when the LORD has brought my master success, remember your servant."

[32]David said to Abigail, "Praise be to the LORD, the God of Israel, who has sent you today to meet me. [33]May you be blessed for your good judgment and for keeping me from bloodshed this day and from avenging myself with my own hands. [34]Otherwise, as surely as the LORD, the God of Israel, lives, who has kept me from harming you, if you had not come quickly to meet me, not one male belonging to Nabal would have been left alive by daybreak."

[35]Then David accepted from her hand what she had brought him and said, "Go home in peace. I have heard your words and granted your request."

[36]When Abigail went to Nabal, he was in the house holding a banquet like that of a king. He was in high spirits and very drunk. So she told him nothing until daybreak. [37]Then in the morning, when Nabal was sober, his wife told him all these things, and his heart failed him and he became like a stone. [38]About ten days later, the LORD struck Nabal and he died.

[39]When David heard that Nabal was dead, he said, "Praise be to the LORD, who has upheld my cause against Nabal for treating me with contempt. He has kept his servant from doing wrong and has brought Nabal's wrongdoing down on his own head."

Then David sent word to Abigail, asking her to become his wife. [40]His servants went to Carmel and said to Abigail, "David has sent us to you to take you to become his wife."

[41]She bowed down with her face to the ground and said, "Here is your maidservant, ready to serve you and wash the feet of my master's servants." [42]Abigail quickly got on a donkey and, attended by her five maids, went with David's messengers and became his wife. [43]David had also married Ahinoam of Jezreel, and they both were his wives. [44]But Saul had given his daughter Michal, David's wife, to Paltiel son of Laish, who was from Gallim.

25:2–8 Dwelling in the region of Maon was Nabal, a "very wealthy" (v. 2) Calebite. As the incident opened, he had his animals moved about a mile north of Maon to Carmel, a site previously mentioned in connection with a monument Saul built to himself (cf. 15:12). There he was shearing his sheep, a process that may be carried out twice annually, in the spring and early fall.

Nabal, whose name means "[intellectually and/or ethically] foolish," was a member of the Calebite clan,[119] an esteemed family in Judah that was apparently responsible for the founding of David's hometown of Bethlehem (cf.

---

[119] The Calebites are prominently mentioned in the Former Prophets (cf. Josh 14:6–14; 15:13–19; 21:12; Judg 1:12–20; 3:9–11) and have both Caleb and Othniel as heroic family members. The prestige of the family is reflected in the amount of genealogical information provided for it in 1 Chronicles (2:9,18–54).

1 Chr 2:51); he was certainly one of David's kinsmen. However, he was not an honorable man, being "hard and evil (v. 3; Hb. *qāšeh* and *raʿ*; NIV, "surly and mean") in his dealings." Nabal's wife was Abigail (= "My father [is] joy"), one who was both "good of understanding and beauteous of form" (NIV, "intelligent and beautiful"). The root word used to express "intelligent" here (Hb. *śkl*) is the same one used previously to describe David (18:5,30); this subtle lexical connection begins to lay a foundation for future connections that will arise between these two individuals. While a bond is being established between David and Abigail, the author uses another pair of descriptors to drive a wedge between Nabal and his wife; whereas she is "good [of understanding]" (Hb. *ṭôb*), he is "evil" (Hb. *raʿ*). This sharp contrast likewise serves as a subtle foreshadowing of future events.

From his desert lair David "heard that Nabal was shearing sheep" (v. 4) in Carmel. During a recently completed stay in the Desert of Maon (23:24–25), David had used his men to act as a security force for this relative's servants and animals (v. 16). Now during the present festive time of taking profit from the animals that David and his men had protected, David "sent ten young men" bearing a treaty-like personal statement to his wealthy kinsman. This statement included the pronouncement of a blessing on Nabal and his servants, a review of the history of the relationship between David's group and Nabal's group, and a request for due compensation.

First, David instructed his men to extend a blessing to Nabal and his household, wishing the man "long life" and "good health." Ironically, Nabal would be denied both (cf. vv. 37–38) because of his mistreatment of the one who sent the blessing.

Second, David's men were to remind/inform Nabal that during the time they protected the wealthy man's servants and flocks, David's forces "did not mistreat them," and "nothing of theirs was missing" (v. 7). The value of David's protection is suggested by a previous narrative account, which noted that after the Philistines attacked nearby Keilah, they were in possession of livestock (23:5).

Third, David's men were to make a request for an unspecified but appropriate gift to be given in return for the protection provided and also as a gesture of support and goodwill during this "good day" (NIV, "festive time"). Nabal was to give David's men—lit., "your servants"—and "your son David" whatever he could find. David's reference to himself as Nabal's son emphasizes the kindred and amicable relationship that David believed to exist between the two Judahites. At the same time, it provides another link between Nabal and Saul (cf. 24:16) and thus strengthens the thematic value of this chapter.

25:9–13 Nabal responded to this message delivered "in David's name" (v. 9) in a manner consistent with his "surly and mean" (v. 3) character. Rather than supporting David, arguably the most famous (and infamous!) member of his tribe at this time, Nabal rebuffed him. He rejected the significance of "this son of Jesse" (v. 10) and implied that David and his troops were nothing more than a band of rogue slaves who had broken "away from their masters." Nabal implied that David and his men were individuals who had abandoned those charged with their care; as such he felt no obligation to take the "bread and water, and the meat" he had set aside for his own slaves and "give it to men coming from who knows where" (v. 11). R. Youngblood incisively notes that Nabal's speech in v. 11 contains eight first-person references ("I," "my"),[120] a clear indication that the writer is emphasizing the wealthy man's sinful self-centeredness in this affair.

When "David's men turned around and went back" to Paran, all that the delegation of ten brought to David were the contemptuous words Nabal had spoken. David's response was instant and heated: "Put on your swords!" Mustering two-thirds of his troops, David led them up to get revenge on Nabal. The remainder stayed behind to protect the supplies and perhaps also wives and children who were a part of the group at that time (cf. 27:3).

25:14–19 While the events of vv. 12–14 were still in progress,[121] an unnamed servant went to his master's wife to report Nabal's shameful treatment of David's men. Though the servant's immediate concern was to convey the implications of Nabal's actions, fully half of the words in the quotation (twenty-eight of fifty-six Hebrew words) were used to extol David and his men. This high proportion suggests that the underlying theme-related reason for the author's inclusion of this quotation was to supply the reader with additional details concerning David's virtue.

David's men were "very good" (Hb. *ṭôbîm mĕᵓōd*; v. 15) to Nabal's servants. Previously Jonathan had noted that David's actions were "very good" toward Saul (19:4; NIV, "benefited you greatly"). The servant's use of semantically parallel phrasing here suggests that men under David's command took on the favorable characteristics of their leader (cf. also 21:5). These men "did not mistreat" Nabal's servants, and thanks to them "nothing was missing" from Nabal's flocks. In fact, under his leadership David's men "were a wall around" (v. 16) Nabal's possessions and workers by night and by day.

From these details David the good shepherd of sheep is shown to be a vigilant shepherd of shepherds also. Even as he had formerly protected his flocks from marauders (cf. 17:34–35), so now he protected keepers of flocks from marauders. The image presented here is that of a leader who is demonstrably fit to "shepherd" the Lord's people (cf. 2 Sam 7:7).

Nabal's servant urged Abigail to consider carefully the substance of his

---

[120] Youngblood, "1, 2 Samuel," 755–56.

[121] Simultaneity is implicit in the employment of a so-called "nominal" clause to convey the narrative framework information of v 14. From semantic clues in the text as well, one can safely assume that the events of vv. 14–19 were simultaneous with those of vv. 12–13.

report and then respond appropriately. The matter was urgent, for "disaster is hanging over" (v. 17) the entire household because of Nabal's foolish actions. Losing no time, Abigail immediately set about preparing a generous gift of foodstuffs for David and his men (v. 18). This amount of food would not have been enough to feed six hundred men plus their families for any length of time, but it did represent a sizable token of appreciation and support for a fellow Judahite.

Once the provisions were prepared and assembled, Abigail had them taken to David, and she followed soon after. Abigail's initiative and independence were certainly rare for a married woman in the ancient Near East. In this case it was downright scandalous, since it entailed a clandestine meeting with one of her husband's enemies.

25:20–22 Abigail's encounter with David occurred in a remote "mountain ravine" (v. 20), when she, riding on a donkey, met "David and his men descending toward her." David was venting his frustrations regarding Nabal as Abigail approached. David's high level of aggravation with Nabal is evident in the fact that he referred to him merely as "this fellow" (v. 21). By refusing to mention his adversary's name, he was acting somewhat like Saul in his tirades against David (cf. 20:27,30,31; 22:7–9,13).

Verses 21–22 present what may be the bitterest recorded declaration coming from David's lips in 1, 2 Samuel. In his venomous speech David did three things: first, he evaluated the efforts he put forth to protect Nabal's property to have been "useless" (v. 21; Hb. *laššeqer*—lit., "to the lie"); second, he analyzed his interaction with Nabal as being a matter of "good" being paid back with "evil"; finally, he vowed to kill every "male of all who belong to" Nabal.

David even took an oath to emphasize the degree to which he was committed to bringing about a vengeful death to Nabal and his male clan members. Interestingly, however, David's oath was not taken in the Lord's name, and—contrary to the LXX's and NIV's rendering—it was not stated in such a way as to bring any judgment on himself in case the vow was broken. According to the MT, the opening text of David's oath is: "Thus may God do to David's enemies, and thus may he add" (v. 22). David's oath form is admittedly irregular, but it reflects a degree of wisdom; it avoids the risk of taking the Lord's name in vain (cf. Exod 20:7), and it insulates David from disastrous consequences in the event the vow is not fulfilled. In fact, it essentially obligated God to kill any enemies that David himself might fail to kill. Interestingly, after failing to carry out his vow, David would later praise the Lord for the divinely wrought act of fatal justice against Nabal (v. 39). David's skill in wording his oath[122] helped

---

[122] My position regarding David's oath is not supported by other scholars at this time. The more popular position is to understand the MT's wording to be an example of a supposed scribal habit of modifying the autographic text to protect David's reputation (see comments at 2 Sam 12:14).

him avoid the folly and ultimate tragedy of Saul's oath (cf. 14:44).[123]

25:23–31   Abigail's encounter with David is one of the most remarkable female-initiated encounters between a man and a woman in the Bible.[124] Bearing many similarities with David's encounter with the wise woman of Tekoa,[125] it began without words when Abigail "quickly got off her donkey and bowed down before David with her face to the ground" (v. 23). This self-abasing expression of deep respect was immediately followed by a nonverbal plea for mercy as "she fell at his feet" (v. 24; cf. Mark 5:22,33; 7:25). Only after these acts did she begin to speak.

Abigail's words reinforced the acts that preceded them. In the longest speech by a woman in the Old Testament (153 Hebrew words),[126] Abigail did three remarkable things: (1) she successfully interceded in behalf of her husband, (2) she prophetically revealed David's destiny as the founder of a dynasty and vanquisher of enemies, and (3) she prevented David from bringing judgment down on himself through an egregious violation of the Torah.

Abigail's intercessory words began with a confession of "sin" (v. 24; Hb. *ʿāwōn*; NIV, "blame"). Without excusing her husband's acts, she nevertheless accepted the blame for David's mistreatment by a member of her clan. Nabal was known to be "wicked" (v. 25; Hb. *bĕliyyaʿal*), and he lived up to "his name—"his name is Fool, and folly goes with him" (fool/folly = *nābāl/nĕbālâ*). Abigail implied to David that since she knew these facts about her husband, she should have been more watchful to protect her husband from himself. Unfortunately, in the present instance she "did not see the men" David sent and thus became blameworthy.

However, the Lord interceded in the present situation to avoid a catastrophe for everyone: "the LORD has kept" David "from bloodshed and from avenging" himself (v. 26)—a statement that applies most immediately to Abigail's intervention but also applies to David's treatment of Saul in 24:3–22. By withholding due payment for services, Nabal had violated the Torah (cf. Lev 19:13; Deut 24:15) and wronged David. Nevertheless, the Torah reserved for the Lord alone the right to avenge wrong in this case (cf. Lev 19:18; Deut 24:15; 32:35).

In an effort to remove any reason for David to continue his pursuit of Nabal, Abigail brought David and his men a "blessing" (v. 27; Hb. *bĕrākâ*; NIV,

---

[123] It can be argued that one of the reasons Saul had to die was because he had called down a curse on himself in the name of Yahweh when he broke a foolish oath he had made at 14:39.

[124] Other significant female-initiated contacts between genders include Adam and Eve (Gen 3), Judah and Tamar (Gen 38), Deborah and Barak (Judg 4), Ruth and Boaz (Ruth 3), and the woman who anointed Jesus with perfume (Matt 26:6–13).

[125] Cf. D. M. Gunn, "Traditional Composition in the 'Succession Narrative,'" *VT* 26 (1976): 221–22; also Youngblood, "1, 2 Samuel," 758.

[126] The so-called Song of Deborah (Judg 5:2–31) is actually longer (352 Hb. words), but the words of the song were sung by Deborah and Barak—not Deborah alone.

"gift") designed to supplant the insults that had come from her husband. Having softened David with her gracious words and the generous supply of provisions, she then boldly ordered David to "forgive your maidservant for the rebellion" [!] (v. 28; NIV, "please forgive your servant's offense") she had instigated against him.

Abigail's strong words of implicit self-condemnation strike a dissonant chord in the narrative, for she never high-handedly sinned against David—only her husband Nabal did. By taking responsibility for his actions, she effectively became a martyr in behalf of her churlish husband. However, by doing so she hoped to deflect David's anger before anyone was hurt.

To encourage David to choose the path of peace and forgiveness in this matter, Abigail brought before David a prophetic vision of his destiny. David should act magnanimously in the present situation because God has designed a majestic future for him—the Lord would "certainly make a lasting dynasty for" him.[127] However, the Lord reserved this destiny only for one who "fights the LORD's battles"; if David were to squander his resources by redressing petty wrongs, then "wrongdoing" (lit., "evil"; Hb. rā'â) would be accounted to him "as long as you live."

Abigail encouraged David to put the recent events in perspective; David could tarnish or destroy God's future plans for him if he acted foolishly in the present. Besides, David had no need to defend himself in such matters because the Lord would watch over him: "David's life will be bound securely in the bundle[128] of the living by the LORD your God" (v. 29). Not only would the Lord protect David but he also could be trusted to dispose of David's enemies, hurling them "away as from the pocket of a sling." Abigail's brilliant use of the sling metaphor no doubt brought to David's mind a sling the Lord once used to dispense with an enemy much more imposing than Nabal (cf. 17:47–50).

The Lord would not only make an end to David's enemies, but he would do for him "every good thing he promised concerning him" (v. 30), including fulfilling the prophetic word spoken by Samuel that David would be "leader over Israel" (cf. 13:14). Since David would surely someday be king, he should not sow future trouble for himself by placing "on his conscience the staggering burden of needless bloodshed" (v. 31) or of having "saved" (NIV, "avenged") himself.

One of the most unusual aspects of Abigail's remarkable speech was her request that David "remember your handmaid" (NIV, "servant"). As used here

---

[127] Polzin notes the similarity that exists between Abigail's words here regarding David's destiny and Rahab's words regarding Israel's destiny (*Samuel and the Deuteronomist*, 208; cf. Josh 2:9). The parallel is real and reinforces the connection between Israel and David as the metaphorical representative of Israel.

[128] The term "bundle" (Hb. צְרוֹר) is believed by some to mean "document" and thus is the equivalent to the Book of Life (cf. Phil 4:3; Rev 3:5; 13:8; 17:8; 20:12,15; 21:27; 22:19).

the term "remember" (Hb. *zākar*) means to "act favorably in behalf of." It is uncertain, however, what sort of favor David could have bestowed on another man's wife in that society, except perhaps the granting of special privileges for her children (cf. 2 Kgs 4:13–37; Matt 20:20–21).

One of the most noteworthy aspects of Abigail's speech was her repeated use of the term translated "my lord" (Hb. *ʾădonî*). Her fourteen uses of the term are both ironic and prophetic since the word also means "my husband."

25:32–35   David, simultaneously chided and encouraged by Abigail's words, responded with a threefold beatitude (not discernible in the NIV), each element of which began with the word "blessed" (Hb. *bārûk/bĕrûkâ*). First, he declared "the LORD, the God of Israel" (v. 32) blessed (NIV, "praise") for putting it in Abigail's heart to come to David. Then he declared Abigail's "perceptiveness" (v. 33; NIV, "good judgment"), which was so evident within her words, to be blessed. Finally he declared Abigail herself to be blessed (v. 33), since she deterred David "from bloodshed" and "avenging" himself with his "own hands."

Abigail's outrageous actions—including negating her husband's intentions in a matter, assuming moral culpability for actions in which she took no part, giving away part of the family fortune as a gift to one of her husband's enemies, and acting as a prophet and theologian—saved the day for everyone. Had she not been willing to violate the social expectations placed on her, "not one male [lit., "no one left urinating against the wall"] belonging to Nabal would have been left alive at daybreak" (v. 34). As Polzin notes,[129] this providential intervention sharpened the contrast between David and Saul: David spared the clan of those who offended him, but Saul wiped the clan out that offended him (cf. chap. 21).

Having provided Abigail with a blessing, "David accepted from her hand what she had brought him" (v. 35). Then he confirmed orally the commitment to turn his armed force back and encouraged her to "go home in peace."

25:36–39a   When Abigail returned to her home in Carmel that evening, "Nabal was in the house holding a banquet" (v. 36) of the lavish sort traditionally associated with the annual sheep shearing event (cf. 2 Sam 13:23–28). Thus, even though she had triumphant news for the clan, she was unable to share it because Nabal's "heart was good upon him" (NIV, "was in high spirits"), and he was "very drunk."

The narrator notes that Nabal's banquet was "like that of a king." The comparison of Nabal's feast to a royal feast deliberately invites the reader to make a comparison of Nabal to Saul.[130] Such a comparison reveals significant simi-

---

[129] Polzin, *Samuel and the Deuteronomist*, 211.

[130] For a different treatment of the relationship between Nabal and Saul, cf. R. Gordon, "David's Rise and Saul's Demise: Narrative Analogy in 1 Sam 24–26," *TynBul* 31 (1980): 37–64.

larities. Both were socially powerful individuals who were members of wealthy families; both had benefited from David's actions, yet both acted hostilely against David; both had female clan members who married David and acted to help him avoid a personal catastrophe; both had their lives spared by David. And, as the narrative will later show, both died under God's judgment.

Nabal's descent into judgment began the next morning when he "was sober"[131] (v. 37) and Abigail told him about the recent events relating to David and his men. When he heard these words, "his heart/mind/intellect/emotions [Hb. *lēb*] died inside of him" (NIV, "his heart failed him"), "and he became like a stone." In more contemporary medical terms, Nabal may have experienced a stroke that resulted in a coma. Whatever the case, "ten days later" Nabal died (v. 38). But the writer was careful to note that the ultimate cause of Nabal's death was not an unfortunate medical problem: "The LORD struck Nabal." His death came as the direct result of personally administered divine judgment (cf. Acts 12:23); David's oath was fulfilled (1 Sam 25:22, Hb. text).

News of Nabal's sudden death reached David in his isolated desert lair. But he did not exult over his enemy's death. Instead, the surprising reaction was a benediction laden with theological instruction. For the second time in this chapter (cf. v. 32) David declared the Lord to be blessed. Here the Lord is declared blessed because of his actions as judge and pastor. In his role as arbiter of human disputes the Lord had vindicated David and punished Nabal. The Lord also was blessed because of his pastoral watchcare for David's soul; "he has kept his servant from doing wrong."

25:39b–44 So impressed was David with Abigail during his confrontation with her only a few days earlier that he decided to ask Nabal's widow "to become his wife."[132] It is not discernible from the text whether David was intentionally acting as a kinsman-redeemer here (cf. Deut 25:5, though the term *gōʾēl* is not used here). Under normal circumstances the adult male most closely related to the deceased man would have fulfilled this role, though this did not always happen (cf. Ruth 4:1–11). Supporting the possibility that David was acting as a kinsman-redeemer is the fact that the only child known to have come from Abigail was fathered by David (Kileab/Daniel; cf. 2 Sam 3:3; 1 Chr 3:1), and that this child was never mentioned in the Biblical text as a contender for the throne of David. The absence of any payment of bridal money (cf. 1 Sam 18:25) by David may also reinforce the conclusion that David—a fellow

---

[131] A wordplay with Nabal's name may be present in the biblical statement (lit.) "in the going out of the wine from Nabal." The consonants of Nabal's name, נבל, can be repointed to mean "wineskin" (נֵבֶל). Cf. Gordon, "David's Rise and Saul's Demise," 51.

[132] Baldwin (*1 and 2 Samuel*, 152), in agreement with J. D. Levenson ("1 Samuel 25 as Literature and as History," *CBQ* 40 [1978]: 27), suggests that David's actions here foreshadow his later immoral actions with Bathsheba. However, the differences so outweigh the similarities in the narrative portrayal that no useful comparison can be made.

Judahite—was fulfilling the role of kinsman-redeemer by pursuing childless Abigail's hand in marriage.

When David's servants presented his proposal to Abigail, she responded with humble acquiescence; "she bowed down with her face to the ground" (v. 41) before David's men. Abigail's manner of giving a favorable spoken response typified proper oriental humility. Though David asked her to become his wife *(ʾiššâ)*, she did not offer herself for that honorable role, for that would be claiming too much privilege (cf. Prov 25:6–7; Matt 23:10–11; Luke 14:8–10); instead, she made herself available as his slave *(šipḥâ)* who would assume the lowly responsibility of washing "the feet of my master's servants." Of course, she fully expected David to abide by the terms of his—not her own—offer!

Without delay Abigail made preparations for a second encounter with David. Indicative of her personal wealth, she rode her own donkey and was "attended by five maids" (v. 42)—more than any other Israelite woman in the Bible is said to have had. Traveling under the guard of "David's messengers," she arrived at David's camp and there "became his wife."[133] The New Testament practice of friends of the bride going out to meet the groom (cf. Matt 25:1–10) may be reflected in this Old Testament passage.

Indicative of David's growing prestige and power, Abigail was technically his third wife. Marrying Nabal's widow gave David legitimate claim to Nabal's position and wealth (cf. 2 Sam 12:8; 16:21–22) and thus probably was of strategic importance in David's later rise to power in Hebron (2 Sam 2:4), a town in the vicinity of Carmel.

Previously David "had also married Ahinoam of Jezreel" (v. 43), a Judahite woman from a town located in the region of the Wilderness of Ziph. Ahinoam became the mother of David's firstborn son, Amnon (cf. 2 Sam 3:2).

Meanwhile, Saul had taken David's first wife Michal and given her in marriage "to Paltiel son of Laish, who was from Gallim" (v. 44), an otherwise unidentified city believed to be located in Judah.[134] Saul probably forced Michal into an involuntary divorce and remarriage following her (apparently) fabricated report of David's life-threatening treatment of her (cf. 19:17); however, she may have requested the divorce herself.

(11) David Spares Saul at the Hill of Hakilah (26:1–25)

[1]The Ziphites went to Saul at Gibeah and said, "Is not David hiding on the hill of Hakilah, which faces Jeshimon?"

---

[133] Levenson argues that the central historical significance of chap. 25 is David's marriage to Abigail since it provided him with an increased power base in Judah ("1 Samuel 25 as Literature and as History," 11–28).

[134] Cf. Aharoni and Avi-Yonah, *Macmillan Bible Atlas,* map 130.

²So Saul went down to the Desert of Ziph, with his three thousand chosen men of Israel, to search there for David. ³Saul made his camp beside the road on the hill of Hakilah facing Jeshimon, but David stayed in the desert. When he saw that Saul had followed him there, ⁴he sent out scouts and learned that Saul had definitely arrived.

⁵Then David set out and went to the place where Saul had camped. He saw where Saul and Abner son of Ner, the commander of the army, had lain down. Saul was lying inside the camp, with the army encamped around him.

⁶David then asked Ahimelech the Hittite and Abishai son of Zeruiah, Joab's brother, "Who will go down into the camp with me to Saul?"

"I'll go with you," said Abishai.

⁷So David and Abishai went to the army by night, and there was Saul, lying asleep inside the camp with his spear stuck in the ground near his head. Abner and the soldiers were lying around him.

⁸Abishai said to David, "Today God has delivered your enemy into your hands. Now let me pin him to the ground with one thrust of my spear; I won't strike him twice."

⁹But David said to Abishai, "Don't destroy him! Who can lay a hand on the LORD's anointed and be guiltless? ¹⁰As surely as the LORD lives," he said, "the LORD himself will strike him; either his time will come and he will die, or he will go into battle and perish. ¹¹But the LORD forbid that I should lay a hand on the LORD's anointed. Now get the spear and water jug that are near his head, and let's go."

¹²So David took the spear and water jug near Saul's head, and they left. No one saw or knew about it, nor did anyone wake up. They were all sleeping, because the LORD had put them into a deep sleep.

¹³Then David crossed over to the other side and stood on top of the hill some distance away; there was a wide space between them. ¹⁴He called out to the army and to Abner son of Ner, "Aren't you going to answer me, Abner?"

Abner replied, "Who are you who calls to the king?"

¹⁵David said, "You're a man, aren't you? And who is like you in Israel? Why didn't you guard your lord the king? Someone came to destroy your lord the king. ¹⁶What you have done is not good. As surely as the LORD lives, you and your men deserve to die, because you did not guard your master, the LORD's anointed. Look around you. Where are the king's spear and water jug that were near his head?"

¹⁷Saul recognized David's voice and said, "Is that your voice, David my son?"

David replied, "Yes it is, my lord the king." ¹⁸And he added, "Why is my lord pursuing his servant? What have I done, and what wrong am I guilty of? ¹⁹Now let my lord the king listen to his servant's words. If the LORD has incited you against me, then may he accept an offering. If, however, men have done it, may they be cursed before the LORD! They have now driven me from my share in the LORD's inheritance and have said, 'Go, serve other gods.' ²⁰Now do not let my blood fall to the ground far from the presence of the LORD. The king of Israel has come out to look for a flea—as one hunts a partridge in the mountains."

270 * 271 21Then Saul said, "I have sinned. Come back, David my son. Because you considered my life precious today, I will not try to harm you again. Surely I have acted like a fool and have erred greatly."
22"Here is the king's spear," David answered. "Let one of your young men come over and get it. 23The LORD rewards every man for his righteousness and faithfulness. The LORD delivered you into my hands today, but I would not lay a hand on the LORD's anointed. 24As surely as I valued your life today, so may the LORD value my life and deliver me from all trouble."
25Then Saul said to David, "May you be blessed, my son David; you will do great things and surely triumph."
So David went on his way, and Saul returned home.

26:1–4 Saul's Judahite allies the Ziphites, a Calebite subclan, continued to supply the king with valuable intelligence reports of David's whereabouts. Perhaps they were motivated in the present instance by jealousy; David's marriage to the richest member of the Calebite clan may have been perceived as a usurpation of rights reserved for one of their own. In the present situation the Ziphites "went to Saul at Gibeah" and informed him that David was "hiding on the hill of Hakilah, which faces Jeshimon" (v. 1), an unidentified site in the general area east of Ziph where they had previously spotted David (cf. 23:19).

Acting on the basis of their information, "Saul went down to the Desert of Ziph" (v. 2). As before (cf. 24:2), Saul was accompanied by "his three thousand chosen men of Israel." Saul had his soldiers camp at a site that provided security, a strategic view of the region, and mobility for his troops (v. 3). However, David remained hidden from view "in the desert."

Though David remained isolated and inaccessible to those seeking his life, he did send out scouts (v. 4) who came close enough to the royal troops to learn "that Saul had definitely arrived."[135]

26:5–7 Armed with the knowledge of Saul's location, David and a select group of men stole into Saul's camp that night. Under the cloak of darkness, David may have been going there to gather additional information about the one who threatened him (cf. Judg 7:10–15). His covert efforts were rewarded, for he was able to identify the key personnel leading the forces as well as the exact location and arrangement of the camp: on this expedition Saul was accompanied by his cousin Abner. The arrangement of Saul's camp, combined with the location of the camp at the top of a hill, would have provided Saul with maximum protection.

Possessing this information, David was now in a position to use a favored military tactic that Saul also had employed, that of making a predawn raid on

---

135 McCarter (*1 Samuel,* 405) and R. Thornhill ("A Note on *ʾl-nkwn* in 1 Sam XXVI.4, *VT* 14 [1964]: 462–66) interpret the admittedly difficult phrase אֶל־נָכוֹן (NIV, "definitely"; marg. n. "to Nacon") as a corruption of אֶל־הֲכִילָה, "to Hakilah." This follows the LXX and Josephus (*Ant.* 6.13.9).

a hostile camp (cf. Judg 7:9–25; 1 Sam 11:11). David chose not to pass up this opportunity and asked two men, including Ahimelech the Hittite, if they cared to accompany him. Though Ahimelech had a Hittite background, his name was Semitic; this, added to the fact that he was in David's circle of trusted associates, suggests that his family had adopted Israelite cultural and religious practices, including the worship of Yahweh. Failing this, it would be hard to understand why David would have permitted this man to be part of his group (cf. Deut 7:1–4; 20:17).[136]

David's objective in this nocturnal expedition was to make an incursion into the very center of the camp. Abishai, David's nephew (cf. 1 Chr 2:16), agreed to accompany him on this dangerous journey. Making their way past the perimeter to Saul, they found his spear, symbol of his authority and power, "stuck in the ground near his head," where he could quickly grab it in an emergency. Situated nearby him were "Abner and the soldiers."

26:8–11 Abishai interpreted their remarkable success in penetrating the defenses as proof that "God has delivered your enemy into your hands" (v. 8). Wishing to be a good steward of the opportunity, he requested the honor of killing David's enemy for him, offering to pin Saul "to the ground with one thrust of my spear."

David responded to Abishai's theologically based proposal with a convincing theological counterargument. Saul must be left untouched, for no one "can lay a hand on the LORD's anointed and be guiltless" (v. 9). As David perceived it, the situation presented a divine trial—an opportunity to demonstrate restraint and goodwill toward one of the Lord's anointed leaders, not vengeance on a human foe. It was not David's role to punish the servant of another. "Yahweh lives" (v. 10; NIV, "As the LORD lives"), and so "Yahweh will strike" his servant Saul in his own time and way, either through nonviolent or violent means. The incident with Nabal had just affirmed David's convictions regarding the Lord's sovereignty in judgment.

Because of his fear of the Lord, David was prevented from laying "a hand on the LORD's anointed" (v. 11). But that did not mean he could not lay hands on the property of Lord's anointed, especially if it saved lives and prevented needless bloodshed. Accordingly, he commanded Abishai to take Saul's "spear"—symbol of his power in society—and "water jug"—symbol of his life-sustaining resources. Having thus symbolically stripped Saul of both his social standing and life, they left.

26:12–16 David and Abishai accomplished this entire act of bravado in secrecy: "No one saw or knew about it, nor did anyone wake up" (v. 12). Yet

---

[136] Throughout the Former Prophets, individuals who came from problematic national groups were permitted to live among the Israelites as long as they converted to Yahwism; e.g., Rahab (Josh 2:10–13) and Ruth (Ruth 2:12).

the writer does not credit this achievement to human skill or stealth; as in previous crises (cf. 17:46–47; 23:12–14), it was the Lord who was at work on David's behalf. The means the Lord used were diverse—a perfectly aimed stone, a word of revelation, "a deep sleep"—but in each case the result was the same. The Lord once again demonstrated his incredible capacity to provide exactly what was needed to rescue his saints.

Going down the hill of Hakilah and then ascending another "hill some distance away" (v. 13), David began the climactic stage of his "assault" on Saul and his men, the verbal assault. In the predawn darkness David's voice echoed across the canyon as "he called out to the army and to Abner son of Ner" (v. 14), Saul's cousin and most powerful aide, and awakened them from their supernatural slumber. Then as they groped their way to consciousness, David began to taunt them with a series of four questions and a pronouncement of judgment.

Abner responded to David's first question by inquiring about the identity of this one who would dare to disturb the king's sleep. David refused to reveal his name; instead, he plied Abner with a pair of contemptuous questions. First, he questioned Abner's manhood: "You're a man, *aren't you?*" (v. 15; italics added). Next, he raised questions about Abner's competency as Israel's most powerful soldier: "Why didn't you guard your lord the king" when "someone came to destroy" him? Having reminded the soldier Abner that such negligent conduct "is not good" (v. 16), David spoke as a judge at a court martial and declared Saul's entire elite force to be "sons of death" (NIV, "deserve to die") for their failure to "guard . . . the LORD's anointed."[137] To verify this grave charge, David urged Abner to confirm the absence of "the king's spear and the water jug that were near his head."

26:17–20 Saul, by now awake, tentatively proposed an answer to Abner's question (cf. v. 14): "Is that your voice, David my son?" (v. 17). Saul's question echoes a previous one (cf. 24:16) and strengthens the parallels that exist between the events of chaps. 24 and 26. David confirmed the accuracy of the king's conjecture and then raised a series of questions and conjectures designed to probe and resolve the conflict separating the two men. First, David asked "why" Saul was "pursuing his servant" (v. 18). David's next two questions assumed that Saul's answer to the first question was that David was worthy of death. But if David had committed some awful crime, what was it? "What evil" was in his "hand" (NIV, "What wrong am I guilty of")?

Before permitting Saul to respond, David asked the king to listen as he

---

[137] F. Cryer suggests that the essential difference between chaps. 24 and 26 is that in the former chapter David requires Saul's death, whereas here he requires Abner's death ("David's Rise to Power and the Death of Abner: An Analysis of 1 Samuel xxvi 14–16 and Its Redaction-Critical Implications," *VT* 35 [1985]: 385–94). In spite of the explicit biblical claim to the contrary (2 Sam 3:37), Cryer suggests that David actually ordered Abner's death.

uttered a solemn two-part prayer designed to put an end to the conflict that had created so much grief for David. In the first part of his prayer David assumed the possibility that the trouble in his life was of his own making; perhaps because of some sin he committed "the LORD has incited" Saul to pursue David (v. 19). If that was the case, David prayerfully requested that the Lord accept a freewill offering to restore the broken relationship and end the strife.

In the second part of his prayer David expressed the possibility that "men"—not God—were the source of his problem. In such a case, David prayed that God would judge them for their sin—that they "be cursed before the LORD." The sin of such men was to seek to drive David from the Lord and the blessings that accompanied a relationship with the true God. As a member of the covenant community David had a "share in the LORD's inheritance," that is, either the right to a plot of land entrusted to his family by the Lord, the Promised Land as a whole, or membership in the covenant community.[138] Inseparably linked to this gift of land, David had an obligation to fulfill the terms of the covenant relationship with the Lord, especially the requirement to serve the Lord (cf. Exod 20:2–4; 23:25; Deut 6:13; 10:12,20; 11:13; 13:4). But wicked men had "driven" David away from that which the Lord had given him, and now they were trying to make him "serve other gods." Those who encouraged David to serve other gods were acting like false prophets, who were under God's curse and were to be put to death (cf. Deut 13:1–5).

David implied that Saul, not God, was the source of his problem. Accordingly, he pleaded with the king not to let his "blood fall to the ground far from the presence of the LORD" (v. 20), that is, not to force David to continue to live in exile. Reiterating a theme expressed in his first encounter with Saul in the Desert of Ziph (cf. 24:14), David asked Saul to put his present actions in proper perspective. The king was squandering precious national resources "to look for a flea," to hunt "a partridge,"[139] and he should stop it.

26:21–25 As before, David's actions and words brought Saul to a temporary state of repentance and reconciliation. He confessed he had "sinned" and urged his "son" to "come back" (v. 21). This time, however, the words rang hollow, even though they were accompanied by words of vigorous self-condemnation and the promise not "to harm" David "again."

David, who knew Saul better than Saul knew himself, accepted the king's words for what they were—sincere, deadly lies. Accordingly, David tacitly turned down the invitation to return. Instead, he asked the king to have one of

[138] H. Forshey suggests the phrase "the LORD's inheritance" actually refers to the people of Yahweh, not to a geographic location ("The Construct Chain Nahalat *YHWH/Elohim*," *BASOR* 220 [1975]: 51–53). Gordon understands the phrase to refer to the land of Israel (*I and II Samuel*, 189).

[139] McCarter correctly notes (*I Samuel*, 408) that David was making a wordplay using הַקֹּרֵא (here = "partridge"). In v. 14 Abner used the same term to mean "who calls." Thus David became "the partridge"/"the one who calls" in the mountains.

his "young men come over" to David and retrieve "the king's spear" (v. 22).

This gracious offer by the triumphant David was accompanied by a brief discourse on the "law of spiritual sowing and reaping," the last recorded words spoken by David to his royal father-in-law. The major premise in David's closing words is that "Yahweh returns to a man his righteousness and faithfulness" (v. 23; NIV, "the LORD rewards every man for his righteousness and faithfulness"), a statement that foreshadows Paul's assertion in Gal 6:7. Because David acted righteously and faithfully by sparing "the LORD's anointed" when "the LORD delivered" him into David's hands, David could humbly expect and pray that the Lord would "value [his] life and deliver [him] from all trouble" (v. 24; cf. Ps 54:7).

As if to confirm his premise, David's gracious acts toward Saul were returned to him in the form of gracious words of blessing and promise. In Saul's last recorded words to his son-in-law, he declared David "blessed" and confidently predicted a glorious future for David. Having uttered those words, both men parted ways, never to see each other again in life.

(12) David Hides from Saul and Resumes Israel's Conquest of Canaan (27:1–12)

¹But David thought to himself, "One of these days I will be destroyed by the hand of Saul. The best thing I can do is to escape to the land of the Philistines. Then Saul will give up searching for me anywhere in Israel, and I will slip out of his hand."

²So David and the six hundred men with him left and went over to Achish son of Maoch king of Gath. ³David and his men settled in Gath with Achish. Each man had his family with him, and David had his two wives: Ahinoam of Jezreel and Abigail of Carmel, the widow of Nabal. ⁴When Saul was told that David had fled to Gath, he no longer searched for him.

⁵Then David said to Achish, "If I have found favor in your eyes, let a place be assigned to me in one of the country towns, that I may live there. Why should your servant live in the royal city with you?"

⁶So on that day Achish gave him Ziklag, and it has belonged to the kings of Judah ever since. ⁷David lived in Philistine territory a year and four months.

⁸Now David and his men went up and raided the Geshurites, the Girzites and the Amalekites. (From ancient times these peoples had lived in the land extending to Shur and Egypt.) ⁹Whenever David attacked an area, he did not leave a man or woman alive, but took sheep and cattle, donkeys and camels, and clothes. Then he returned to Achish.

¹⁰When Achish asked, "Where did you go raiding today?" David would say, "Against the Negev of Judah" or "Against the Negev of Jerahmeel" or "Against the Negev of the Kenites." ¹¹He did not leave a man or woman alive to be brought to Gath, for he thought, "They might inform on us and say, 'This is what David did.'" And such was his practice as long as he lived in Philistine territory. ¹²Achish trusted David and said to himself, "He has become so odious to his people, the

Israelites, that he will be my servant forever."

27:1–4   After the confrontation with Saul had ended, David begrudgingly came to the conclusion that as long as he remained in the land, the king would continue to pursue him until he was "destroyed by the hand of Saul" (v. 1). The only way to put an end to Saul's pathological game of hide-and-seek was to move to the land of the Philistines. So he and his troops, along with their families (cf. v. 3; 30:2–3), went to Gath, some twenty-five miles northwest of the Desert of Ziph.[140]

David's latest action marked the second time he had fled to Gath in order to escape Saul (cf. 21:10). Yet this time both David's circumstances and his reception were different. The first time he had entered Gath armed and alone from the royal household in Gibeah—a circumstance that appeared threatening to Achish, who knew nothing of the conflict between Saul and David.

However, this time David was entering as an infamous outlaw—a would-be usurper of Saul's throne who was so feared by the Israelite monarch that he had repeatedly sent thousands of men into the desert to track David down. The Philistines' awareness of this conflict is evidenced by their timing a raid on Israel to coincide with one of Saul's forays against David (cf. 23:27–28). Acting in accordance with the timeless dictum "My enemy's enemy is my friend," the Philistine ruler welcomed David, his men, and their families into his territory and probably considered them to be mercenaries (cf. 28:1).

Family members accompanying David into Philistine territory included "his two wives: Ahinoam of Jezreel and Abigail of Carmel" (v. 3). No doubt David took them along for two reasons: first, to protect them from persecution and abuse at the hands of Saul and his sympathizers and, second, to enjoy their companionship. David had learned the hard way what Saul would do to wives he left behind in Israelite territory (cf. 25:44). After learning of the flight of David and his group to Gath, Saul "no longer searched for him" (v. 4). David's present plan, like all the ones before, succeeded admirably.

Achish's commitment to grant asylum was a considerable one, since David's entire group must have consisted of more than a thousand individuals—a large enough group to have disrupted life in Gath and created resentment among some of the city's residents. No doubt David was aware of this and recognized the threat it posed to his ability to remain beyond Saul's grasp in Philistia. Furthermore, David probably was uncomfortable being too near an uncircumcised king who was as much his enemy as his ally. David had not for-

---

[140] Because of the near-disastrous situation David faced when asked by Achish to go to war against Saul (cf. 28:1; 29:2), Payne suggests that the writer may have meant "the reader to draw the lesson that David should have consulted a priest or prophet before marching into Philistine territory to offer Achish his services" (*I and II Samuel,* 140). If this line of reasoning is accepted, then David's actions are somewhat analogous to those of Abraham in Egypt (Gen 12:10–20).

gotten his own remarkable past or his prophetic destiny; and as the prophet-anointed, Spirit-empowered successor to Saul, he must be about his Father's business, even in exile. That business could be conducted much more easily away from Achish's view.

27:5–7 Hiding his true reasons under a cloak of humility, David approached Achish and told him he was unworthy to "live in the royal city with" the mighty king. Instead of living in prestigious Gath, David requested that "a place be assigned" to his group of exiles "in one of the country towns" (v. 5). Achish, who probably was both flattered by David's words and relieved to have an excuse to move the group of foreigners away from his city's food and water resources, "gave him Ziklag" (v. 6). Ziklag (modern Tel Seraᶜ?)[141] was located about twenty-five miles southwest of Gath in what was technically territory assigned to both the tribes of Simeon (cf. Josh 19:5) and Judah (cf. Josh 15:31). Though the city was allotted to the Israelites, they had never conquered it. Yet David's cleverness did what previous military campaigns failed to do; it brought Ziklag into Israelite hands, "and it has belonged to the kings of Judah ever since." Thus David redeemed his time in exile, using it to resume Israel's conquest of Canaan.

David and his group apparently entered Gath ca. 1012 B.C.[142] They "lived in Philistine territory a year and four months" (v. 7),[143] after which time David returned to Israel to become king.

27:8–12 At his isolated base of operations in Philistine-controlled Judah, David was out from under the watchful eye of Achish. Ever the faithful servant of the Lord, David used this opportunity to pursue the Torah mandate to conquer the Promised Land. "David and his men went up and raided" (v. 8) three different groups. God had given the land of "the Geshurites," located in Judah's tribal allotment, to Israel; however, Israel had failed to take control of that region (cf. Josh 13:1–2). The Lord had also commanded Israel to eliminate "the Amalekites" (cf. Exod 17:15–16; Deut 25:17–19). Saul had failed to accomplish the task (cf. chap. 15), but David heeded the Torah mandate. "The Girzites"[144] are otherwise unknown, but like the Geshurites and Amalekites, "had lived in the land extending to Shur and Egypt" and thus were partially in territory that legitimately belonged to Judah.

---

[141] The location of Ziklag is much disputed. Proposed sites include Tel Ḥalif (so F. M. Abel), Tel Seraᶜ (so B. Mazar, Y. Aharoni, Z. Kallai, and E. D. Oren), Tel Massos, and Tell es-Sebaᶜ (so V. Fritz). Cf. J. D. Seger, "Halif, Tel," in *New Encyclopedia of Archaeological Excavations in the Holy Land* (New York: Simon & Schuster, 1993), 553–59; E. D. Oren, "Sera, Tel," idem, 1329–35; and V. Fritz, "Where Is David's Ziklag?" *BAR* 19 (1993): 58–61.

[142] Cf. discussion regarding chronology in the introductory section.

[143] The LXX states that the period of time was only four months.

[144] The *qere* (וְהַגִּזְרִי) of the MT metathesizes two consonants in the *ketiv* (וְהַגִּרְזִי) and reads "the Gezerites."

As such, the Geshurites, Girzites, and Amalekites were under the ban commanded by the Torah (Deut 20:16–17); none of them was to be spared by the Israelites in warfare. David, the man after the Lord's heart (cf. 12:24; Acts 13:22), was careful to follow the prescribed rules of warfare. Thus, whenever "he attacked an area" (v. 9) inhabited by these peoples, "he did not leave a man or woman alive." However, he did take the booty—"sheep and cattle, donkeys and camels, and clothes," part of which he presented "to Achish" on his periodic visits to Gath.

In his visits to the Philistine royal city David would have a personal audience with Achish. As the king was receiving his share of David's spoils, he would ply the Israelite warlord with questions regarding the location of his plundering activities. David's cunning and deceitful answers suggested that he was raiding territories in the Promised Land that were under Israel's control—"the Negev of Judah," "the Negev of Jerahmeel," and "the Negev of the Kenites" (v. 10). The answer seemed credible to Achish, for none of David's victims survived who "might inform" the king to the contrary.

David's scheme was ingenious and effective. His conscious use of deceit was arguably the lesser of two evils: granted that lying is wrong and to be avoided (cf. Lev 19:11; Col 3:9), in this case David's deception saved lives and thus fulfilled the Spirit of the Torah. Not only did it enable hundreds of Israelites to avoid a deadly confrontation with Saul, but it also helped Israel fulfill military assignments left undone since the days of Moses.[145]

Achish was thoroughly taken in by David's skillful lies and therefore "trusted David" (v. 12). The words—along with the generous gifts of plunder—made the Philistine king conclude that David had become "odious to his people" and would therefore be forced to be Achish's gift-bearing "servant forever."

Thus, David's obedience to the Torah warfare regulations caused him to prosper. In this section the writer subtly contrasts David's actions toward the Amalekites with Saul's. David's killing of all the Amalekites he encountered brought about blessing and life. On the other hand, when Saul disobeyed the Torah and consciously spared an Amalekite, he experienced a curse and loss of position.

(13) David Becomes Achish's Bodyguard (28:1–2)

[1]In those days the Philistines gathered their forces to fight against Israel. Achish said to David, "You must understand that you and your men will accompany me in the army."

[2]David said, "Then you will see for yourself what your servant can do."

---

[145] Cf. discussion at 20:4 regarding the tension between the biblical mandate to speak the truth and the need to preserve life.

Achish replied, "Very well, I will make you my bodyguard for life."

While David was in Ziklag, "the Philistines gathered their forces to fight against Israel" (v. 1). Perhaps one of the reasons they decided to attack Israel at this time was the mistaken belief that David had weakened his own nation through the ongoing raids he conducted. Achish certainly considered David to be a valuable asset in any conflict with Israel and so ordered David and his men to "accompany" the Philistine army into battle.

David's superlative skill in deceptive speech is demonstrated in his response to Achish's potentially disastrous order: "You will see for yourself what your servant can do" (v. 2). What exactly did David mean by these words? Would Achish see what David could do *for* Israel's enemies or what he could do *to* Israel's enemies? What Achish heard in these words probably is something different from what David actually meant, though this miscommunication was certainly what David intended. Achish obviously took the words to mean something favorable for the Philistines, for he offered to make David his "bodyguard [lit., "keeper for my head"] for life." Achish's words are ironic—David had already kept one Gathite's head (cf. 17:54), but he did so only after he removed it from Goliath's body!

The narrative skills of the writer are on display in this section as the reader is left in suspense regarding David's fate. Will the Lord's anointed actually fight against the Lord's people? Will David join forces with Achish and the Philistines? Stay tuned (cf. 29:1–11)!

(14) Saul Consults a Medium (28:3–25)

³Now Samuel was dead, and all Israel had mourned for him and buried him in his own town of Ramah. Saul had expelled the mediums and spiritists from the land.

⁴The Philistines assembled and came and set up camp at Shunem, while Saul gathered all the Israelites and set up camp at Gilboa. ⁵When Saul saw the Philistine army, he was afraid; terror filled his heart. ⁶He inquired of the LORD, but the LORD did not answer him by dreams or Urim or prophets. ⁷Saul then said to his attendants, "Find me a woman who is a medium, so I may go and inquire of her."

"There is one in Endor," they said.

⁸So Saul disguised himself, putting on other clothes, and at night he and two men went to the woman. "Consult a spirit for me," he said, "and bring up for me the one I name."

⁹But the woman said to him, "Surely you know what Saul has done. He has cut off the mediums and spiritists from the land. Why have you set a trap for my life to bring about my death?"

¹⁰Saul swore to her by the LORD, "As surely as the LORD lives, you will not be punished for this."

¹¹Then the woman asked, "Whom shall I bring up for you?"

"Bring up Samuel," he said.

[12]When the woman saw Samuel, she cried out at the top of her voice and said to Saul, "Why have you deceived me? You are Saul!"

[13]The king said to her, "Don't be afraid. What do you see?"

The woman said, "I see a spirit coming up out of the ground."

[14]"What does he look like?" he asked.

"An old man wearing a robe is coming up," she said.

Then Saul knew it was Samuel, and he bowed down and prostrated himself with his face to the ground.

[15]Samuel said to Saul, "Why have you disturbed me by bringing me up?"

"I am in great distress," Saul said. "The Philistines are fighting against me, and God has turned away from me. He no longer answers me, either by prophets or by dreams. So I have called on you to tell me what to do."

[16]Samuel said, "Why do you consult me, now that the LORD has turned away from you and become your enemy? [17]The LORD has done what he predicted through me. The LORD has torn the kingdom out of your hands and given it to one of your neighbors—to David. [18]Because you did not obey the LORD or carry out his fierce wrath against the Amalekites, the LORD has done this to you today. [19]The LORD will hand over both Israel and you to the Philistines, and tomorrow you and your sons will be with me. The LORD will also hand over the army of Israel to the Philistines."

[20]Immediately Saul fell full length on the ground, filled with fear because of Samuel's words. His strength was gone, for he had eaten nothing all that day and night.

[21]When the woman came to Saul and saw that he was greatly shaken, she said, "Look, your maidservant has obeyed you. I took my life in my hands and did what you told me to do. [22]Now please listen to your servant and let me give you some food so you may eat and have the strength to go on your way."

[23]He refused and said, "I will not eat."

But his men joined the woman in urging him, and he listened to them. He got up from the ground and sat on the couch.

[24]The woman had a fattened calf at the house, which she butchered at once. She took some flour, kneaded it and baked bread without yeast. [25]Then she set it before Saul and his men, and they ate. That same night they got up and left.

This section presents what another writer considered perhaps the darkest moment in Saul's life, his deliberate violation of one of the most serious prohibitions in the Torah (cf. 1 Chr 10:13–14). By turning to a medium to receive guidance for his life, Saul committed a capital offense (cf. Lev 20:6). Less than twenty-four hours after he did so, he was dead—a sobering reminder of the swiftness and surety of the Lord's punishment for any who violate the divine word.

28:3–5 These verses review known facts and present additional background materials necessary for understanding one of the strangest and most sordid events in Saul's life. First, the author reminds the reader that at this time "Samuel was dead" (v. 3; cf. 25:43). Furthermore, he had been dead long enough to have been buried and have an appropriately long mourning period.

Second, the writer indicates that Saul had previously made a commendable effort to abide by the Torah in the matter of expelling "mediums and spiritists from the land." Mediums (Hb., *ʾōbôt*)[146] and spiritists (Hb., *yiddĕʿōnîm*) were individuals who claimed the ability to contact the dead, either serving as intermediaries through whom the dead would speak (cf. Isa 8:19) or rousing the dead to speak for themselves.[147] This note establishes Saul's clear understanding that it was forbidden for Israelites to consult these individuals, a fact necessary for understanding the severity and speed of the punishment meted out to him.

In this section we also learn more details about the Philistine forces poised to attack Israel. At the time when Saul consulted the medium, they had "set up camp at Shunem" (v. 4), a town in the tribal territory of Issachar some seventy-five miles north northeast of Gath. Shunem was located on a hill next to the Via Maris, the major trade route passing through the Promised Land. The Philistines desired to control this region, which included the Valley of Jezreel, since it would provide them with considerable revenue from caravans using the highway.

To oppose the Philistines, "Saul gathered all the Israelites and set up camp at Gilboa," likely a mountain just south of Shunem that overlooked the Via Maris and the Valley of Jezreel through which it passed.[148] From that vantage point Saul could view Philistine troop movements in relative safety. However, Saul was not prepared to cope with what he observed: when he saw the size of "the Philistine army, he was afraid; terror filled his heart" (v. 5).

28:6–7 Quite properly, Saul first "inquired of the LORD" (v. 6), seeking guidance in dealing with the Philistines.[149] However, the Lord "did not answer him by dreams," that is, through a personal revelation given directly to him. Nor did the Lord respond by means of the "Urim," that is, with the revelatory device that could only be used with the assistance of an Aaronic priest (cf. Exod 28:30; Num 27:21). This is not surprising since Saul had slain many of the Aaronic priests, and the only named surviving priest from Nob—one who possessed an ephod—had fled to David (cf. 22:18–20). Furthermore, the Lord did

---

[146] For more information regarding mediums, cf. H. A. Hoffner, "אוֹב, *ʾobh*," *TDOT* 1:130–34.

[147] Cf. Isa 29:4. For scholarly literature on the cult of the dead see T. J. Lewis, *Cults of the Dead in Ancient Israel and Ugarit*, HSM (Atlanta: Scholars Press, 1989). On the cult in Judah see E. M. Bloch-Smith, "The Cult of the Dead in Judah: Interpreting the Material Remains," *JBL* 111 (1992): 213–24.

[148] For an alternate viewpoint regarding the location of Gilboa, cf. H. Bar-Deroma, "Ye Mountains of Gilboa," *PEQ* 102 (1970): 116–36, who suggests that Gilboa was located much farther to the south, near modern Tel Aviv.

[149] The comment in 1 Chr 10:14 that Saul died because he "did not inquire of the LORD" does not contradict this passage. Instead, it affirms the contention of 1 Sam 28 that Saul's final source of guidance was not Yahweh.

not answer by means of "prophets." Saul did not receive a prophetic word for two reasons: first, because Samuel was dead, and second, he had lost the support of the prophets when Samuel, the leading prophet of Israel in his generation and the leader of a group of prophets (cf. 19:20), had declared Saul's kingship had ended (cf. 15:24,28–29).

Having cut himself off from the Lord through personal disobedience, as well as his abuse of both the priestly and prophetic institutions in Israel, Saul turned to a non-Yahwistic alternative for guidance. He ordered "his attendants" to find "a woman who is a medium so he could "go and inquire of her" (v. 7). From them he learned of just such a woman "in Endor" (modern Khirbet Safsafeh) six miles away and two miles northeast of the Philistine camp.

28:8–11 A measure of Saul's desperation—and his willingness to sin against the Lord—in the present situation is seen in the fact that he went to the medium, even though he had to steal his way past the Philistine camp to get there. In order to make the journey as safe as possible, however, "Saul disguised himself, putting on other clothes" (v. 8). The absence of royal clothing and jewelry insulated him from scrutiny by Philistine soldiers patrolling the roads in the area and shielded his true identity from the medium. In order to reduce the journey's risks even further, Saul waited until after the sun had set to begin the trip, and he was accompanied by two bodyguards.

Arriving at the medium's house safely, Saul asked the woman to "consult a spirit" and to "cause the one whom I say to you to come up to me" (NIV, "bring up for me the one I name"). At first the woman refused, suspecting that these men were agents from the king who had "set a trap" (v. 9) to kill her. Saul's efforts to purge the land of those who led in banned revelatory practices (cf. Exod 22:18; 19:31; 20:6,27; Deut 18:10–11) were based in the Torah and perhaps had been inspired by Samuel (cf. 1 Sam 10:25).

To calm the woman's fears, "Saul swore to her by the LORD" that she would not be punished for her activities. Yet for the informed reader, Saul's words to the medium are just one more manifestation of his lifelong spiritual incongruities (literally)—"By the life of Yahweh, there will not occur for you a transgression in this matter." In fact, Saul's oath invoked the Lord to grant immunity to one who broke the Lord's command—it turned God against himself. Such an oath was not only foolish but actually blasphemous.

After the medium received this solemn word of assurance from Saul, she proceeded about her task. Asking the disguised king whom she should "bring up" (v. 11), Saul requested the prophet "Samuel." If it was indeed because of Samuel's efforts that Saul had attempted to rid the land of mediums, his request here is particularly ironic. Presently she "saw Samuel" (v. 12).

Questions naturally arise at this point: Did the medium actually make contact with a living spirit-being, and if so, was it really the prophet Samuel?[150] While this matter is not likely to be settled to everyone's satisfaction, the following observations can be made. First, the plain statement of the Hebrew text is that she did in fact see Samuel. Second, the medium reacted to Samuel's appearance as though it was a genuine—and terrifying—experience: she "cried out at the top of her voice." Her strong reaction also suggests that Samuel's appearance was unexpected; perhaps this was the first time she had ever actually succeeded in contacting the dead. Third, the speeches attributed to Samuel contained allusions to a prior interchange between the two, allusions that would have been appropriate only for the real Samuel to have made. Fourth, Samuel's role and message as a prophet, so much a part of his ministry in life, was unchanged in his encounter with Saul here.

Indeed, a straightforward reading of the biblical account suggests the possibility that mediums may possess the capacity to contact dead persons and establish lines of communication between the living and the dead. This view is not explicitly rejected elsewhere in Scripture; the Torah prohibits necromancy not because it is a hoax but because it promotes reliance on supernatural guidance from some source other than the Lord.

An alternative reading of this passage suggests that it was not the skill of the medium but rather a unique act of God that brought Saul into contact with Samuel. The medium did not possess the capacity to disturb a dead saint; but God, as "a sign of his grace,"[150] permitted Saul to have one last encounter with the prophet who had played such a determinative role in the king's career.

28:12–14 With the appearance of Samuel the medium came to understand that her customer was actually King Saul. Undaunted by the fact that his deception had been discovered, Saul asked the woman not to fear, but to continue with her task. The fact that he asked the medium what she could see suggests that Saul himself was prevented from viewing the spirit, though he was able to speak with the prophet directly. The woman claimed that she saw "gods arising from the earth" (v. 13; NIV, "a spirit coming up out of the ground"), perhaps from a pit in the room dug for the purpose of necromancy.[152] The NIV's rendering of the woman's response masks the fact that the subject is *ʾĕlōhîm*, a word normally used to refer to a divine being and that the subject's verb is plural, a situation that regularly occurs in the MT

---

[150] Along this line, cf. T. Figart, "Saul, the Spiritist, and Samuel," *GTJ* 11 (1970): 13–29; and K. A. D. Smelik, "The Witch of Endor," *Vigiliae Christianae* 33 (1979): 160–79, who catalog different interpretations of this event. Rabbinic interpretations include: (1) an actual raising of Samuel by the wicked means of necromancy; (2) a deception perpetrated by the necromancer; (3) God causing either Samuel or a demon to appear; and (4) a demon acting apart from God to deceive Saul. Additional suggestions include (5) a vision produced by hallucinatory drugs; (6) a psychologically induced illusion; and (7) a Satanic impersonation.

[151] Payne, *I and II Samuel*, 145.

[152] Cf. H. A. Hoffner, *TDOT* 1:131–32.

when a pagan god is the referent.[153] In the present instance it seems reasonable to conclude that the medium's words reflected a pagan belief that Samuel had become a "god"—a spirit-being possessing capabilities beyond those
of mortals—following his death. The writer, wishing to demonstrate linguistically that she was speaking heretically, employed a plural verb form with
the subject *ʾĕlōhîm.*

Saul apparently was confused by the woman's answer, so he asked her to
provide additional descriptive details of what she saw: "What does he look
like?" (v. 14). Her imprecise answer—"an old man wearing a robe"—was nevertheless convincing to Saul. The word used to describe Samuel's garment here
(Hb., *mĕʿîl,* = "sleeveless robe") is the same one used previously to describe
the garment the prophet was wearing when Saul grabbed and tore its hem
(15:27). Out of respect for the prophet who had provided guidance during previous times of confusion and crisis in Saul's life (cf. 9:19–20; 15:1–3), "Saul
bowed down and prostrated himself with his face to the ground."

28:15–19 Unmoved by Saul's show of submission and humility, Samuel
asked for an explanation of why Saul "disturbed" (v. 15) the prophet by causing
him to come up. Saul apparently assumed that the prophet was unaware of
events occurring in the land of the living, so he proceeded to explain about the
Philistine threat and the fact that God had "turned away" from him. Having
failed to contact the Lord "either by prophets or by dreams," he then sought to
learn "what to do" from the most insightful man he had ever known, Samuel.

Samuel did not provide Saul with the information he desired. Instead, he
reassumed his role as the Lord's prophet and picked up where he had left off in
his judgment of the king (cf. 15:22–25). He reintroduced the topic of obedience
to the Lord by probing Saul's motives: If Saul knew that the Lord had turned
away from him and become his adversary, "why" (v. 16) did he choose to make
the Lord even angrier by violating the Torah's ban on consulting the dead (cf.
Lev 19:31; 20:6; Deut 18:14)?

Without waiting for an answer, Samuel proceeded to interpret the course of
events in Saul's reign from a prophetic perspective. He reminded Saul that prophetic judgments had been pronounced against him because of disobedience in
the past. Now at this stage in Saul's life it was clear that "the LORD has done
what he predicted" (v. 17; cf. 15:26–29). As prophesied, "the LORD has torn the
kingdom out of" Saul's hands and given it "to David"—in spite of Saul's
relentless and bloody efforts to prevent it.

Saul had lost the right to rule Israel because of disobedience to the Lord's
words in the Torah; the king did not "carry out his fierce wrath against the Ama-

---

[153] The NIV is inconsistent in doing this; previously, in Exod 32:4, the translators encountered
a similar construction involving the use of אֱלֹהִים as subject of a plural verb when it did not refer
to Yahweh. In that verse they took the verse to refer to "gods," though the context suggests it was
a reference to a single idol.

lekites" (v. 18; cf. Deut 25:17–19). Now Saul had repeated the same basic sin
of disobedience to the Torah by consulting the dead. As a result, punishment
must follow. Saul's present sin was private and concealed in darkness; however, its consequences would be public and massive. In this case "the LORD
will hand over both Israel and you to the Philistines." In keeping with the seriousness of the present breach, Saul would also lose his family and his own life:
"tomorrow you and your sons will be with me" (v. 19; cf. Lev 20:6).

28:20–25 The words were more than the king could bear: "immediately
Saul fell full length on the ground, filled with fear" (v. 20). Saul's collapse was
caused not only by the dead prophet's words of mortal judgment but also by the
fact that "he had eaten nothing all that day and night." Apparently Saul was
maintaining his foolhardy practice of fasting during times of battle (cf.
14:28);[154] Klein suggests it was because the fast was "in preparation for this
conjuring session."[155] The stress associated with confronting the Philistine
threat, in addition to the efforts expended in making the risky six-mile trip to
the medium's house, had sapped his body's energy and left him no reserve.

When the medium witnessed her king's collapse, she immediately tried to
assist him. Referring to herself as "your maidservant" and identifying herself
as one who had already risked her life to help the king, she offered to prepare
him a meal so that he might "eat and have the strength to go on" (v. 22).

Saul initially "refused" (v. 23) the woman's offer, apparently because it
would mean breaking a vow associated with his fast. However, "his men joined
the woman in urging him" to take some nourishment, and eventually "he listened to them." He got up and "sat on the couch," a low piece of furniture on
which one might recline while eating (cf. Esth 7:8) but which also was used
regularly as a bed (cf. 19:13).

When Saul agreed to the woman's offer of food, she immediately set about
preparing a meal consisting of meat from a hastily butchered "fattened calf"
and freshly "baked bread without yeast" (v. 24). Any meal that included meat
was special in ancient Israel, but one that included meat from a stall-fed animal
was truly exceptional—a feast "fit for a king" (cf. Amos 6:4).

The woman's generous gift of food in behalf of the king and his men is reminiscent of Abigail's even more bounteous gift to David and his men (cf. 25:18–
27). The comparison of the women's gifts invites a comparison of the women:
whereas Saul was nurtured by a woman under the Lord's curse (cf. Lev 20:27),
David was nurtured by a woman under the Lord's blessing (25:33).

---

[154] The biblical text never accuses Saul of being irreligious, just reckless in his application of
religion to life. Saul repeatedly "turned to the right and the left" in his religious expression, sometimes adding supplemental regulations to those already imposed by the Torah (e.g., requiring soldiers to fast before battle), sometimes ignoring Torah regulations (e.g., sparing Amalekites,
practicing necromancy).

[155] Klein, *1 Samuel*, 272.

After the meal was prepared—which perhaps took a considerable amount of time—Saul and his men "ate" (v. 25). Sometime before dawn, then, they left Endor to slip past Philistine lines and return to their camp on Mount Gilboa.

(15) David Is Exempted from Fighting against Israel's Forces (29:1–11)

[1]The Philistines gathered all their forces at Aphek, and Israel camped by the spring in Jezreel. [2]As the Philistine rulers marched with their units of hundreds and thousands, David and his men were marching at the rear with Achish. [3]The commanders of the Philistines asked, "What about these Hebrews?"

Achish replied, "Is this not David, who was an officer of Saul king of Israel? He has already been with me for over a year, and from the day he left Saul until now, I have found no fault in him."

[4]But the Philistine commanders were angry with him and said, "Send the man back, that he may return to the place you assigned him. He must not go with us into battle, or he will turn against us during the fighting. How better could he regain his master's favor than by taking the heads of our own men? [5]Isn't this the David they sang about in their dances:

"'Saul has slain his thousands,
   and David his tens of thousands'?"

[6]So Achish called David and said to him, "As surely as the LORD lives, you have been reliable, and I would be pleased to have you serve with me in the army. From the day you came to me until now, I have found no fault in you, but the rulers don't approve of you. [7]Turn back and go in peace; do nothing to displease the Philistine rulers."

[8]"But what have I done?" asked David. "What have you found against your servant from the day I came to you until now? Why can't I go and fight against the enemies of my lord the king?"

[9]Achish answered, "I know that you have been as pleasing in my eyes as an angel of God; nevertheless, the Philistine commanders have said, 'He must not go up with us into battle.' [10]Now get up early, along with your master's servants who have come with you, and leave in the morning as soon as it is light."

[11]So David and his men got up early in the morning to go back to the land of the Philistines, and the Philistines went up to Jezreel.

29:1–5 Beginning with this section the author steps back in time a few days and returns to the story thread last encountered in 28:2. This is discernible from the fact that at the beginning of this episode the Philistine forces are still assembled by the waters of the Yarkon River "at Aphek" (v. 1), whereas in 28:4 they have moved to Shunem. David is with the Philistine forces at the more southerly site, while Saul and his forces "camped by the spring in Jezreel" (v. 1). Apparently Saul chose this favorable site—one that provided the Israelite forces with a ready supply of water as well as food—because they anticipated northerly Philistine troop movements designed to take control of the Valley of Jezreel, a vital segment of the major trade route connecting Egypt with Mesopotamia.

As the Philistine forces pulled out of the supply center at Aphek "with their units of hundreds and thousands, David and his men" (v. 2) accompanied them. Since they had been residing in Philistine-controlled territory by permission of Achish king of Gath (cf. 27:2–6), they were "marching at the rear with Achish."

However, when the other Philistine commanders learned that "Hebrews" (v. 3) were in their ranks, they immediately raised some serious questions— and with good reason. In a previous battle against Saul and the Israelites, the Philistines had allowed some Hebrews who had been under their protection to join their army, and the results had been catastrophic. Hebrew soldiers wearing Philistine markings and armed with Philistine weapons had turned against their hosts in the heat of battle and had begun killing them (cf. 14:21). The chaos and confusion that resulted from that mistake caused the Philistines to kill many of their own men (cf. 14:20).

Though Achish was no doubt keenly aware of that military disaster, he was convinced that David and his men would not recreate it. After all, the Philistine king had observed David "for over a year" (v. 3) and had received gifts of plunder from him purported to have come from Israelite settlements. Through it all, Achish had "found no fault in" David. In fact, Achish was so confident of David's loyalty that he had made him his bodyguard for life (cf. 28:2).

However, the other Philistine military commanders were skeptical and "furious" (Hb., *qāṣap*; NIV, "angry"; v. 4) with Achish for endangering the lives of their soldiers by putting "an officer of Saul king of Israel" (v. 3) in the Philistine army. Abandoning the protocol of deference usually accorded a king, the commanders ordered Achish to "send the man back."[156] Otherwise, David "might become an adversary" (Hb., *śāṭān*; NIV, "he will turn against") to the Philistines "during the fighting."

The commanders understood that David had a motive for betraying his Philistine hosts—the desire to "regain his master's favor." In a possible allusion to David's treatment of Goliath's corpse (cf. 17:51,57), they suggested that David would purchase Saul's favor with the currency of "the heads of our own men." David certainly had demonstrated the capacity to kill Philistines. In fact, so effective was David in battle against the Philistines that his exploits were celebrated in both song and dance among the Israelites (cf. 18:6–7).

29:6–11 Achish acquiesced to the demands of his fellow Philistines. Calling his trusted bodyguard before him, the king tactfully informed David of his expulsion from the Philistine army. Achish began with an effusive affirmation of David's service record. "As surely as the LORD lives," David had proven

---

[156] A more respectful way to ask a king to act is through the employment of jussive verb forms (i.e., "Let the king ..."; cf. 26:19). Here, however, a bald-faced imperative verb form is employed.

himself "reliable" (v. 6)—and certainly financially profitable (cf. 27:9); the Philistine king had "found no evil" (Hb., *rāʿâ*; NIV, "fault") in him. Then revealing the rift that existed between the commanders, Achish noted that "in the eyes of the rulers you are not[157] good" (Hb., *ṭôb*; NIV, "the rulers don't approve of you")—even though he personally "would be pleased to have" David serve beside him in battle. Having provided this affirming introduction, Achish issued three brief orders to David: "return" to Ziklag, "go peacefully," and "do nothing the Philistine rulers would consider evil" (v. 7).

Ironies abound in Achish's relationship with David. A study of the author's portrayal of the Philistine king suggests that Achish was intended to serve simultaneously as a type and a foil for Saul. Both kings made David their personal bodyguard (cf. 22:14; 28:2); both were impressed with David, particularly his fighting abilities, yet both ended up removing him from the ranks of their armies; both were responsible for David's making his abode in southern Judah; and both badly misjudged David. Saul considered David his mortal enemy, yet he was in fact his most loyal subject; Achish considered David his most trusted subject, yet he was in fact his most dangerous enemy. Both kings also made inappropriate use of oaths taken in the Lord's name (cf. 14:39; 29:6). The parallels between Saul and Achish suggest that Saul was indeed a king "such as all the nations have" (cf. 8:5).

Using David as the link that bound these two kings together also invites comparisons between David and these men. In such comparisons David is seen to be superior—the only figure of truly royal stature in the triangle of men. In the presence of Achish and Saul, David is seen for what he is, the man after God's heart (cf. 13:14; Acts 13:22).

David responded to his dismissal with an appropriate—although undoubtedly feigned—expression of displeasure. Inquiring into the nature of his offense against the Philistines, he asked to know what complaints had been filed "against your servant" that prevented him from being able to "go and fight against the enemies" (v. 8).

The enemies David wanted to fight against were those of "my lord the king," words that were perhaps intentionally ambiguous. The situation would lead us (and especially Achish) to assume he was referring to Achish his king. But David may have been thinking secretly of Saul as his lord and king (cf. 24:8; 26:17). Or was David's reference to king Yahweh? The reader is left to weigh David's past activities in the courts of both earthly kings, in addition to his spiritual heart, to determine against whom he would have fought in the upcoming battle.

---

[157] McCarter (*I Samuel*, 426), following the LXX, omits the לֹא from his text. D. Deboys—more plausibly—argues that such an omission is unnecessary ("1 Samuel xxix 6," *VT* 39 [1989]: 214–19).

Having issued the difficult orders to David, Achish returned to his compliments. Though other leaders believed differently, to Achish David was "as good as an angel of God" (v. 9). Even so, this "angel" must fly away from the Philistines and "leave in the morning as soon as it is light" (v. 10), taking the entire Israelite contingent with him. Maintaining his image as an ideal servant, David obeyed. He got his troops up before sunrise, went south "back to the land of the Philistines" (v. 11), while the Philistines proceeded north "up to Jezreel."

The events of this chapter must be viewed as the providential supply of an alibi, excusing David from any involvement in the death of king Saul. This chapter answers any who might have accused David of conspiring with the Philistines to bring about the downfall of the Saulide dynasty. The events indicate that David could not and did not assist the Philistines in armed hostilities against the Israelites or their king. In fact, on the day of Saul's death David and his men were a hundred miles away killing Amalekites,[158] fulfilling a Torah command that Saul had neglected (cf. 15:18–19; Exod 17:15–16; Deut 25:17–19).

5. David Conquers the Amalekites as the Philistines Defeat Saul (30:1–31:13)

This relatively brief section presents the simultaneous actions and yet contrasting destinies of Israel's first two kings, Saul and David. On the one hand, David was here fulfilling the mandate of the Torah regarding the Amalekites and receiving the resulting blessing of a restored family and the increase of possessions. On the other hand, at the very moment David was enjoying success and blessing, Saul was experiencing the full force of a Torah curse, including the loss of his family and possessions.

Both David and Saul were fighting traditional enemies of Israel in the events recorded in this section, and both men sought divine guidance in their respective undertakings. To the south, David consulted the only form of revelation sanctioned by the Torah before going forth to slaughter the Amalekites, who had temporarily dispossessed David and his men of their families and worldly goods during a lightning raid on Ziklag. To the north Saul sought insight from a medium, a revelatory means expressly forbidden by the Torah, before waging war against the Philistines. As a result of Saul's sinful actions, the Lord used the Philistines as agents of divine judgment to bring down on Saul's head the just punishment for his rejection of the Torah (cf. 1 Chr 10:13–14).

When this pivotal series of events concludes, Saul and all his credible heirs to the throne are dead;[159] David, on the other hand, is poised to become Israel's

---

[158] Cf. chart at 2 Samuel 1.

[159] The writer's portrayal of Saul's son Ish-Bosheth is that of a sleepy (2 Sam 4:5), intimidated (2 Sam 3:11,14–15) individual who is dominated by a more competent and assertive relative (2 Sam 2:8–9). Ish-Bosheth was as regally incompetent as his father was spiritually incompetent.

king and to establish a dynasty as all of his heirs are restored to him.

(1) David Defeats the Amalekites (30:1–31)

[1]David and his men reached Ziklag on the third day. Now the Amalekites had raided the Negev and Ziklag. They had attacked Ziklag and burned it, [2]and had taken captive the women and all who were in it, both young and old. They killed none of them, but carried them off as they went on their way.

[3]When David and his men came to Ziklag, they found it destroyed by fire and their wives and sons and daughters taken captive. [4]So David and his men wept aloud until they had no strength left to weep. [5]David's two wives had been captured—Ahinoam of Jezreel and Abigail, the widow of Nabal of Carmel. [6]David was greatly distressed because the men were talking of stoning him; each one was bitter in spirit because of his sons and daughters. But David found strength in the LORD his God.

[7]Then David said to Abiathar the priest, the son of Ahimelech, "Bring me the ephod." Abiathar brought it to him, [8]and David inquired of the LORD, "Shall I pursue this raiding party? Will I overtake them?"

"Pursue them," he answered. "You will certainly overtake them and succeed in the rescue."

[9]David and the six hundred men with him came to the Besor Ravine, where some stayed behind, [10]for two hundred men were too exhausted to cross the ravine. But David and four hundred men continued the pursuit.

[11]They found an Egyptian in a field and brought him to David. They gave him water to drink and food to eat— [12]part of a cake of pressed figs and two cakes of raisins. He ate and was revived, for he had not eaten any food or drunk any water for three days and three nights.

[13]David asked him, "To whom do you belong, and where do you come from?"

He said, "I am an Egyptian, the slave of an Amalekite. My master abandoned me when I became ill three days ago. [14]We raided the Negev of the Kerethites and the territory belonging to Judah and the Negev of Caleb. And we burned Ziklag."

[15]David asked him, "Can you lead me down to this raiding party?"

He answered, "Swear to me before God that you will not kill me or hand me over to my master, and I will take you down to them."

[16]He led David down, and there they were, scattered over the countryside, eating, drinking and reveling because of the great amount of plunder they had taken from the land of the Philistines and from Judah. [17]David fought them from dusk until the evening of the next day, and none of them got away, except four hundred young men who rode off on camels and fled. [18]David recovered everything the Amalekites had taken, including his two wives. [19]Nothing was missing: young or old, boy or girl, plunder or anything else they had taken. David brought everything back. [20]He took all the flocks and herds, and his men drove them ahead of the other livestock, saying, "This is David's plunder."

[21]Then David came to the two hundred men who had been too exhausted to follow him and who were left behind at the Besor Ravine. They came out to meet David and the people with him. As David and his men approached, he greeted

them. ^{22}But all the evil men and troublemakers among David's followers said, "Because they did not go out with us, we will not share with them the plunder we recovered. However, each man may take his wife and children and go." ^{23}David replied, "No, my brothers, you must not do that with what the LORD has given us. He has protected us and handed over to us the forces that came against us. ^{24}Who will listen to what you say? The share of the man who stayed with the supplies is to be the same as that of him who went down to the battle. All will share alike." ^{25}David made this a statute and ordinance for Israel from that day to this.

^{26}When David arrived in Ziklag, he sent some of the plunder to the elders of Judah, who were his friends, saying, "Here is a present for you from the plunder of the LORD's enemies."

^{27}He sent it to those who were in Bethel, Ramoth Negev and Jattir; ^{28}to those in Aroer, Siphmoth, Eshtemoa ^{29}and Racal; to those in the towns of the Jerahmeelites and the Kenites; ^{30}to those in Hormah, Bor Ashan, Athach ^{31}and Hebron; and to those in all the other places where David and his men had roamed.

30:1–5 "David and his men" traveled southward along the coastal plain some fifty-five miles, arriving at "Ziklag on the third day" (v. 1). In their absence, however, the Amalekites had burned David's recently acquired city to the ground. This attack on David's base of operations was no doubt in retaliation for assaults David and his men had carried out against the Amalekites during the past sixteen months (cf. 27:8) and was timed to coincide with David's expected northern tour of duty.

Before the Amalekites burned the city, however, they had taken captive all its inhabitants (v. 2). In doing this the Amalekites' actions were reminiscent of ancient Mesopotamian invaders, who also had attacked a city in the territorial region of Judah (cf. Gen 14:11–12), and invite a comparison of David's actions with those of Abraham in a previous day. None of the Amalekites' captives had been killed, perhaps because they were intended as bargaining chips with David or for sale in slave markets (cf. Amos 1:6,9). Their act of kidnapping, however, was a capital offense according to the Torah (cf. Exod 21:16), and David would not countenance this especially personal violation of the Lord's revealed will.

As David and his men made their way back to Ziklag, they were no doubt elated and relieved at being exempted from a treasonous encounter with their fellow Israelites. However, the upbeat mood vanished when they arrived at Ziklag (v. 3). Tragedy rivaling that of Job (cf. Job 1:12–19) was multiplied six hundred times over as each man discovered the loss of all his possessions and the disappearance of spouses and children. So overwhelming was the discovery that "David and his men"—some of the toughest men on the planet—wept until they were exhausted (v. 4). David now found himself bereft of all three of his wives: Michal, who had been taken away by Saul (cf. 25:44), and now Ahinoam of Jezreel, and Abigail (v. 5).

30:6–8 The Israelite soldiers grieved especially over the loss of their "sons and daughters" (v. 6). As they speculated about the abuse and pain their children may have faced at the hands of the Amalekites, the men became "bitter in spirit." The bitterness soon turned to raging anger and found a focus in David, whom "the men were talking of stoning." David "was greatly distressed" by all of this, as any leader would have been when faced with a tragedy that was in part of his own making. Nevertheless, he did not let the situation master him; instead, he "found strength in the LORD his God" (cf. 23:16).

One reason for that strength lay in the fact that David had the freedom to communicate with the living God. David could not reach out to the Philistine army for help in pursuing the Amalekites, nor could he rely on the armies of Israel; yet he could—and did—reach up to Yahweh of Armies to request help. With the aid of Abiathar the priest, David "inquired of the LORD" (v. 8) by means of "the ephod" (v. 7). Likely David did so by means of the Urim, or Urim and Thummim,[160] which were kept in a breastpiece attached to the ephod (cf. Exod 28:28–30). In answer to David's question about the advisability and probable success of a mission to pursue the Amalekites, the Lord indicated that David and his men would "certainly overtake them and succeed in the rescue." No doubt David's faith in this divine word did help him "find strength"!

The author skillfully used vv. 6–8 to draw yet one more sharp distinction between David and Saul. During a time of great distress both men sought supernatural guidance for battle. Chronologically, they probably were seeking guidance on the very same day. However, one defied the Torah; the other utilized its gracious provision. Saul sought help from a medium and received the promise of death; David sought help through an Aaronic priest using the ephod and received the promise—later fulfilled—of life and blessing.

30:9–10 Acting on the divine assurance provided them, "David and the six hundred men with him" (v. 9) traveled perhaps sixteen miles south until they "came to the Besor Ravine" (modern Wadi Ghazzeh [?]), the largest and deepest wadi in the heartlands of southern Judah. At this point one-third of David's troops, "two hundred men" (v. 10), halted their pursuit of the Amalekites, for they "were too exhausted to cross the ravine." This is not surprising, for prior to their sixteen-mile race after the adversary they had marched several miles to Ziklag and then exhausted themselves emotionally dealing with the discovery of lost possessions and family. However, after regrouping the forces

---

[160] The Bible does not indicate how these revelatory devices were utilized. It is possible that certain types of inquiries could be answered with the use of only one stone, the Urim, while others required the use of both stones. Lending credence to this speculation is the fact that on two occasions only the Urim is mentioned as being needed for revelation (Num 27:21; 1 Sam 28:6). For further discussion of the Urim and Thummim, cf. C. F. Armerding, "The Breast-plate of Judgment," *BibSac* 118 (1961): 54–58; E. Robertson, "The 'Urim and Tummim': What Were They?" *VT* 14 (1964): 67–74; and E. Lipinski, "'Urim and Thummim," *VT* 20 (1970): 195–96.

"David and four hundred" other men who still possessed the capacity to carry on the task "continued the pursuit."

30:11–15 As David's forces continued their southwesterly trek, "they found an Egyptian in a field" (v. 11). The man was half-dead when he was discovered, but David realized that this individual might be able to provide him with crucial information regarding the Amalekites. The man was given food and drink, a more sumptuous meal than the usual rations of a soldier on patrol and one that may have been the envy of David's own men. It was doubtless made all the tastier for the Egyptian because he had been starving.

The writer's detailed description of an Egyptian captive's meal in the midst of one of the most tension-filled narratives in 1 Samuel certainly seems odd and perhaps inappropriate. In fact, if this narrative was intended only to be a record of David's military exploits it would be. However, the writer possessed multiple agendas in putting this narrative together. By showing David's kind and gracious treatment of this Egyptian sojourner, the author demonstrated that even in the midst of personal tragedy David was sensitive to Torah injunctions regarding the treatment of aliens, particularly Egyptians (cf. Exod 22:21; 23:9; Lev 19:34; Deut 23:7).

This incident with the unnamed Egyptian sojourner thus measures the circumference of David's soul. David was wracked with emotional pain, but he was not so wrapped up in his own problems that he could not help another person in need. The greatness of David's character is seen in the greatness of his provision for an alien in need.

David's obedient act of kindness toward the Egyptian produced benefits for all. For his part the Egyptian "was revived." To David's benefit the Egyptian provided information and assistance that enabled the Israelites to see the fulfillment of the Lord's promise (v. 8). In the course of his interrogation David learned that the man was an abandoned slave (v. 13) who had materially participated in the Amalekites' military operations at Ziklag.

From the Egyptian David also learned that the Amalekite raiding party's itinerary was extensive and included raids on three different regions: (1) "the Negev of the Kerethites" (v. 14), a coastal area inhabited by allies of the Philistines who possessed Cretan roots (cf. Ezek 25:16); (2) "the territory belonging to Judah," part of the holdings of David's ancestral tribe east of Ziklag; and (3) "the Negev of Caleb," a special allotment of Judah's territory centered around Hebron (cf. Josh 14:13–14; 15:13–15).

In spite of the fact that the Egyptian to whom he had been so gracious was also one who had helped destroy his village, David asked a remarkable favor of him: "Can you lead me down to this raiding party?" (v. 15). David was now placing the success or failure of his entire military mission—to say nothing of the hopes of six hundred families for reunion and restoration—in the hands of a man he had known for only an hour, one who had admitted to torching

David's possessions. It was a dangerous gamble, but it also was David's best hope, one that apparently had been sent to him by the providential hand of God.

The Egyptian, knowing that he also had much at risk in this venture, asked for some assurances of protection before agreeing to David's terms. He required David to take an oath "before God" that he would not be executed for what he had done, nor would he be returned to the Amalekites.

30:16–20 Apparently David agreed to these terms, for the foreigner "led David down" (v. 16) to the Amalekite camp.

In their drunken, celebratory state the Amalekites were out of battle formation, "scattered over the countryside," and in no condition for combat. David's men, though nearing exhaustion, were highly motivated and newly energized by the discovery of their enemy in such a vulnerable state. Seizing the opportunity, David led his men in a lightning raid on the camp and "fought them from dusk until the evening of the next day" (v. 17).[161]

David's incredible risks and efforts paid off handsomely for the Israelites, as two major objectives were met. First, the Amalekite army was all but wiped off the face of the earth. So completely were the Amalekites nullified by David's efforts that they were not mentioned again as an opponent of Israel until the time of Hezekiah (716–687 B.C.; cf. 1 Chr 4:43).[162]

Second, David and his men recovered the persons and possessions the Amalekites had previously seized. In fact, so complete was the restoration that "nothing was missing" (v. 19); everything was brought back into Israelite control. Especially significant was the fact that the Israelite prisoners of war were set free, including David's wives and everyone else, "young or old, boy or girl."

Because of the magnitude of their victory, David's troops took control of large quantities of goods and livestock left behind by the Amalekites. Much of this booty had previously been owned by the Kerethites, Calebites, and other Judahites. However, David and his men came into possession of it by right of

---

[161] N. Collins suggests that a better translation of this phrase is "fought them from twilight just before dawn, until soon after sunset in the evening, following the start of their [i.e., the Amalekites'] new calendar day" ("The Start of the Pre-exilic Calendar Day of David and the Amalekites: A Note on 1 Samuel xxx 17," *VT* 41 [1991]: 203–10).

[162] W. Brueggemann (*First and Second Samuel*, 203) seems to misinterpret the thrust of the passage here when he notes that "an outsider might observe that David is more ruthless than the Amalekites, for they 'killed no one' (v. 2)" and that "the Amalekites are resented for taking spoil; Saul is rejected for taking spoil; David is saluted and championed for doing the same! David is subject to none of the restrictions, held accountable to none of the old norms." The Torah required that kidnappers be killed (Exod 21:16) and also that theft be punished not only with the return of the stolen object but also with the exacting of an additional penalty payment (cf. Exod 22:7). Thus David was fulfilling the terms of the Torah in these two matters—to say nothing of fulfilling the Torah prophecies regarding the elimination of Amalekites (cf. Exod 17:16; Num 24:20) in doing what he did.

conquest—after all, they were the ones who put their lives on the line to attack the Amalekites, and it was already lost to the previous owners.

As leader of the strike force, David received the largest portion of the booty; "he took all the flocks and herds" (v. 20). Most, if not all, of these animals would have come from the Amalekite raids on sites other than Ziklag. The remaining "property" (Hb., *miqneh;* NIV, "other livestock") was to be divided up among David's troops.

30:21–25   As the victorious band made its way northward, the troops eventually returned to the two hundred men left behind (v. 21). When David met them, "he inquired about their welfare" (NIV, "greeted them"); as a good general he was concerned that these temporarily disabled soldiers would be recovering. Significantly, he did not rebuke them or deride them for failing to participate in the raid on the Amalekites.

David's conciliatory attitude, however, was not shared by all of the other four hundred men who accompanied him into battle. Some wicked men resented the fact that these two hundred had not joined in the heat of battle. In their opinion those who fought should "not share" the plunder with those who sat on the sidelines. Each nonparticipant might be allowed to "take his wife and children" back, but there should be no reward beyond that.

David intervened in the developing confrontation and in the process created a "statute and ordinance" (v. 25) regarding the distribution of plunder that was to be followed by Israelite armies for centuries thereafter—literally, "from that day to this" (v. 25). Simply stated, the policy was that "the share of the man who stayed with the supplies is to be the same as that of him who went down to battle" (v. 24). This policy was based on three foundational premises.

The first presupposition was theological in nature: all plunder gained in battle was ultimately a gracious gift from the Lord (v. 23). Thus, David rejected the view that booty was payment to a worker for services performed in battle. By viewing plunder as sacred gift, not secular gain, David highlighted the truth that "the battle [and its perhaps lucrative outcome] is the LORD's" (17:47). In theory, all of the Lord's people might be eligible to partake of the Lord's gifts.

The second presupposition was also theological in nature, designed to provide a better perspective on plunder: booty was actually one of the lesser gifts provided by the Lord to those who actively fought in war. Two things were more important than material gain in war: personal protection and the defeat of the enemy. Resentment among the front-line fighters stemming from a less-than-expected share of plunder was blunted when one realized that the Lord had already provided them two other gifts of greater value.

The third presupposition is that of corporate equality. This presupposition recognizes that (1) successful military operations require the performance of many different tasks, some of which must be done away from the heat of battle; (2) each job is vital to the success of the whole effort; and (3) therefore "all" team members should "share alike" (v. 24) in the fruits of success.

30:26–31   When David returned to the war-scarred village of Ziklag, he wisely chose to invest some of his newly acquired resources in building relationships with "the elders" (v. 26) who controlled settlements located throughout southern Judah. Perhaps he did so with the intention of creating a network of treaties that would allow him to move his sizable band of soldiers and their families back into Judahite territory, away from the bad memories and destruction of Ziklag.

But there may have been another reason. The fact that David presented his gift to them as a "present [Hb., bĕrākâ; "blessing"] for you from the plunder of the LORD's enemies" suggests that he was also using this gift as an announcement of his messianic status. David was the Lord's anointed (cf. 16:12–13); but rather than proclaim his status with mere words, he would announce it with deeds. As would be expected of the Lord's anointed, David had fought the Lord's enemies (cf. Exod 17:15–16; Deut 25:17–19). As would be expected of the Lord's anointed, he was now bringing blessing to the Lord's people. David's use of the phrase "the LORD's enemies" in preference to "the Amalekites" provides the key to this interpretation. It casts David's military exploits as a "crusade"—that is, essentially theological in nature—not a "conquest"—that is, fundamentally profane and secular. His actions against the Amalekites were not vengeance for burned houses and displaced families; rather, they were acts of spiritual obedience—the fulfillment of ancient Torah mandates and the fulfillment of timeless prophecies.

David sent gifts to a significant number of settlements scattered throughout southern Judah: fourteen cities or clan territories are specified, though gifts were also sent to "other places" (v. 30). David, however, did not send any gifts to Philistine or Kerethite cities. No doubt they were excluded because they were not members of God's covenant community. Thus, David seems to have considered two factors when determining who received these blessings from the Lord: whether or not the Lord was the official God of the settlement and whether or not they were "places where David and his men had roamed" (v. 31) during David's period of internal exile.

The majority of the villages mentioned in vv. 27–29 remain unidentified by modern researchers. The "Bethel" (v. 27; lit., "House of God"; LXX, "Beth Sur") mentioned here is not the site named by Jacob (cf. Gen 28:19), which is located in the tribal territory of Ephraim; instead, it would have been in southern Judah. "Ramoth Negev" (lit., "Heights of Negev") is mentioned nowhere else in Scripture. "Jattir" is a location in Judah's hill country set aside for the Aaronic priests (cf. Josh 15:48; 21:14) but is otherwise unknown. "Aroer" (v. 28) is an unidentified Judahite settlement—not the former city of Sihon in Reubenite territory east of the Jordan (cf. Josh 12:2). "Siphmoth" is an unknown site. "Eshtemoa" is a city set aside for the Aaronic priesthood (cf.

Josh 21:14) in southern Judah, not otherwise known. "Racal" (v. 29; LXX, "Carmel") is also unknown. "The towns of the Jerahmeelites and the Kenites" were apparently settlements in the Simeonite district of central southern Judah. "Hormah" (v. 30; lit., "Destruction") was a site in the Simeonite region of Judah (cf. Josh 15:30; 19:4) the Israelites had conquered on at least three occasions (cf. Num 21:3; Josh 12:14; Judg 1:17). "Bor Ashan" (LXX, "Beersheba") and "Athach" (LXX, "No") are not mentioned elsewhere in the Bible and remain unidentified. "Hebron" (v. 31), the largest and most historically significant city in southern Judah, was both a center for the Aaronic priesthood and a designated city of refuge (cf. Josh 20:7; 21:11). The fact that David sent gifts to three different sites associated with the Levites suggests that the future king was both giving a tithe, and more, of the battlefield acquisitions and also making special efforts to curry favor with this significant element in Israelite society.

(2) The Philistines Devastate Israel and the House of Saul (31:1–13)

¹Now the Philistines fought against Israel; the Israelites fled before them, and many fell slain on Mount Gilboa. ²The Philistines pressed hard after Saul and his sons, and they killed his sons Jonathan, Abinadab and Malki-Shua. ³The fighting grew fierce around Saul, and when the archers overtook him, they wounded him critically.

⁴Saul said to his armor-bearer, "Draw your sword and run me through, or these uncircumcised fellows will come and run me through and abuse me."

But his armor-bearer was terrified and would not do it; so Saul took his own sword and fell on it. ⁵When the armor-bearer saw that Saul was dead, he too fell on his sword and died with him. ⁶So Saul and his three sons and his armor-bearer and all his men died together that same day.

⁷When the Israelites along the valley and those across the Jordan saw that the Israelite army had fled and that Saul and his sons had died, they abandoned their towns and fled. And the Philistines came and occupied them.

⁸The next day, when the Philistines came to strip the dead, they found Saul and his three sons fallen on Mount Gilboa. ⁹They cut off his head and stripped off his armor, and they sent messengers throughout the land of the Philistines to proclaim the news in the temple of their idols and among their people. ¹⁰They put his armor in the temple of the Ashtoreths and fastened his body to the wall of Beth Shan.

¹¹When the people of Jabesh Gilead heard of what the Philistines had done to Saul, ¹²all their valiant men journeyed through the night to Beth Shan. They took down the bodies of Saul and his sons from the wall of Beth Shan and went to Jabesh, where they burned them. ¹³Then they took their bones and buried them under a tamarisk tree at Jabesh, and they fasted seven days.

31:1–6 This section resumes the narrative story line of 28:25. As in chap. 28, the events are set in the area of Jezreel, Saul and the Philistine army are central in the action, and the time is only hours after Saul's meal with the medium. In accordance with Samuel's prediction (cf. 28:19), the Philistines defeated

Israel. They pursued Saul's army as they made a hasty retreat up to their base camp, "and many" Israelites "fell slain on Mount Gilboa" (31:1).

Not content merely to push the Israelites back, the Philistines wanted to bring an end to the dynastic family that had caused them so much trouble over the past forty years (cf. Acts 13:21). Now at last they scored a dramatic success: Saul's three oldest sons all died at the hands of the Philistines, and Saul himself was overtaken by "the archers" (v. 3), who "wounded him critically."

Saul knew that his time to die had come. The Philistines were quickly advancing from the position where the fatal arrow had been launched, and they would overrun the king's position in only minutes. Saul was keenly aware of the ancient Near Eastern customs regarding the treatment of mortally wounded enemy soldiers on the battlefield—including the mutilation or removal of genitalia (cf. 18:27) and decapitation (cf. 17:51). Wishing to deny "these uncircumcised fellows" (v. 4) the opportunity to "abuse" him and subject him to a torture-execution, Saul ordered his armor-bearer to deliver a swift and merciful death blow with his sword. In this way Saul was acting like the tragic character Abimelech (cf. Judg 9:54), the original wicked Israelite "king" (cf. Judg 9:6). However, the assistant "was terrified and would not do it," perhaps because he feared the consequences of harming the Lord's anointed (cf. 26:9–11). Consequently, "Saul took his own sword and fell on it," thus becoming like the tragic figure Eli, who also "fell" at his death.[163] In a tragic show of solidarity with his king, Saul's armor-bearer followed his example and took his own life (31:5).

Samuel's haunting words (28:19), less than twenty-four hours old, were resoundingly echoed in v. 6; "Saul and his three sons and his armor-bearer and all his men died together that same day" (v. 6).

31:7–10 Israelites living in the Jezreel valley area, as well as those in the nearby Transjordan territory of Manasseh soon learned of the crushing Israelite defeat. Realizing that their blanket of military protection disappeared when "the Israelite army had fled" and that the king and all his designated successors had been slaughtered, "they abandoned their towns and fled." Rather than defending their lives and possessions against the rampaging Philistine army, they wisely opted to become war refugees.

The next day "the Philistines came and occupied" the abandoned towns of Issachar and Manasseh in order to profit as fully as possible from their military success. No doubt the victorious army looted the hastily abandoned Israelite

---

[163] Saul's action represents the second of six recorded suicide or assisted-suicide attempts in the Bible (cf. also Judg 9:54 [Abimelech]; 1 Sam 31:6 [Saul's armor-bearer]; 2 Sam 17:23 [Ahithophel]; 1 Kgs 16:18 [Zimri]; Matt 27:5; Acts 1:18 [Judas]). Though the Bible does not explicitly prohibit such actions, each portrayal of this practice is replete with tragic overtones. The Bible seems to suggest that suicide or assisted-suicide is a desperate act by a deeply troubled individual. None of the individuals who resorted to this action is portrayed as a role model for the pious. Even Ahithophel, perhaps the most praised of the lot, is shown to have done this as the direct result of a treacherous act against Yahweh's anointed.

homes and villages as long as they remained in the area.

Part of the looting process involved returning to the battlefield the day after the battle "to strip the dead" (v. 8). In the process they came across the corpses of "Saul and his three sons" on Mount Gilboa. The bodies of the royal family members being left overnight on the battlefield suggests the magnitude of the Israelite defeat; efforts usually were made to remove such prominent individuals before the enemy could get them (cf. 1 Kgs 22:34–38; 2 Kgs 23:30).

When the Philistines discovered Saul's remains, "they cut off his head and stripped off his armor" as war prizes. The armor was later placed "in the temple of the Ashtoreths" (v. 10),[164] probably as a thank offering to a protectress deity or perhaps in fulfillment of a vow.[165] The naked, decapitated bodies of Saul and his three sons were then sent a few miles east to Beth Shan, a former Israelite village in the Jezreel valley area, where they were fastened "to the wall."

At the same time, the Philistines sent messengers to proclaim the news in the temple of their idols and among their people" (v. 9) that they had won a major victory over the Israelites, decimated Israel's dynastic family, and gained control of the most strategic portion of the Via Maris in Palestine.

31:11–13 Though most of the Israelites in the region reacted to the Philistine victory with fear and flight, "the people of Jabesh Gilead" (v. 11) did not, perhaps because theirs was a walled city (cf. 11:1). When news of the disgraceful treatment of the royal family's bodies reached Jabesh, "all their valiant men journeyed through the night to Beth Shan" (v. 12). The trek was difficult and dangerous, especially at night, since Beth Shan was about fifteen miles away and one had to ford the Jordan River and enter Philistine-held territory to get there.

However, the squadron succeeded in their efforts. Once at Beth Shan, the men managed to retrieve the bodies of the royal family and to transport them "to Jabesh." There they "burned"—but did not actually incinerate—the bodies on a funeral pyre until the fleshy portions had been consumed.[166] Afterward

---

[164] The temple location is unknown. Aharoni assumes that the temple of Ashtoreths was at Beth Shan (*The Archaeology of the Land of Israel*, 121). Also note the mention of גֻּלְגָּלְתֹּ, "skull," in 1 Chr 10:10. Cf. K. N. Schoville, *Biblical Archaeology in Focus* (Grand Rapids: Baker, 1978), 332.

[165] According to 1 Chr 10:10 Saul's head was "hung up . . . in the temple of Dagon."

[166] Unlike the Egyptians (cf. Gen 50:2,26), the Israelites were not concerned to try to preserve the flesh of a dead member of their society. But the preservation and proper interment of the bones was vital to demonstrate proper respect for the deceased. To prevent wild animals from consuming the rotting flesh and thus risk losing or destroying the bones (cf. 2 Sam 21:10–11), it was acceptable to cook/burn the fleshy portions enough to facilitate removal of the bones. Completely incinerating a body, however, was considered an abominable desecration (cf. Amos 2:1). For archaeological evidence of ancient Semitic cremation techniques, cf. W. Zwickel ("1 Sam 31,12f. und der Quadratbau auf dem Flughafengelände bei Amman," *ZAW* 105 [1993]: 165–74), who finds evidence that individuals were ritually cremated at moderate temperatures in such a way as to preserve their bones. R. Gordon (*I and II Samuel*, 204) notes that a Jewish Targumic tradition indicates that the Jabesh Gileadites merely burned spices in behalf of the deceased, thus not applying heat to the bodies. Though this is an ancient suggestion, it seems misguided and is certainly lacking in textual support.

they removed the bones of the four men from the fire for burial (v. 13). The final association of Saul with a tamarisk was possibly a symbolic gesture, made out of consideration for the fact that he had previously conducted royal proceedings under this type of tree (cf. 22:6). Out of respect for their fallen leaders the people of Jabesh then "fasted seven days."

Though the efforts of the citizens of Jabesh Gilead were considerable and apparently exceeded those of any other Israelite city, they were thoroughly appropriate. After all, the city had once been rescued from humiliation at the hands of foreigners by Saul's efforts on their behalf (cf. 11:1–11). In addition, Saul may have had genealogical ties with individuals within Jabesh Gilead (cf. Judg 21:10–12; 2 Sam 21:12–14). David would later commend the Gileadites for their heroic act of loyalty to Saul (cf. 2 Sam 2:5–7).

6. David Responds to Tragedy in the House of Saul (2 Sam 1:1–27)

In this section David spontaneously displays his loyalty, respect, and admiration for his fallen king. David learns of Saul's death from an Amalekite—perhaps a shiftless deserter from the armies of his own countrymen—who brags that he delivered the deathblow to Israel's king and produces convincing evidence to support his claim.

Consistent with his policy of respecting the royal messianic office, David kills the Amalekite. Grief stricken, David then utters the most stirring tribute to fallen companions recorded in the Bible. The words stand as a monument to David's solidarity with Israel's first dynastic family and demonstrate why he was such a fitting choice to be Israel's next king.

(1) David Executes Saul's Killer (1:1–16)

[1]After the death of Saul, David returned from defeating the Amalekites and stayed in Ziklag two days. [2]On the third day a man arrived from Saul's camp, with his clothes torn and with dust on his head. When he came to David, he fell to the ground to pay him honor.

[3]"Where have you come from?" David asked him.

He answered, "I have escaped from the Israelite camp."

[4]"What happened?" David asked. "Tell me."

He said, "The men fled from the battle. Many of them fell and died. And Saul and his son Jonathan are dead."

[5]Then David said to the young man who brought him the report, "How do you know that Saul and his son Jonathan are dead?"

[6]"I happened to be on Mount Gilboa," the young man said, "and there was Saul, leaning on his spear, with the chariots and riders almost upon him. [7]When he turned around and saw me, he called out to me, and I said, 'What can I do?'

[8]"He asked me, 'Who are you?'

" 'An Amalekite,' I answered.

Table 4: Order of Events (1 Sam 30 to 2 Sam 1:2)

Day	Reference	Event
(Before)	28:4a	Philistines assemble for war
	29:1a	Philistines gather forces at Aphek
	28:4d	Saul gathers Israelites for war
	28:4e	Israelites set up camp at Gilboa
	29:1b	Israelites camp at Jezreel
1	29:2	Philistine rulers march from Aphek, with David in formation
	29:3	Philistine rulers exclude David from Philistine force
2	29:10–11	David and men leave in early morning after first day's march with the Philistines
4	28:4b	Philistines come [to Shunem]
	28:4c	Philistines set up camp at Shunem
	28:5	Saul sees Philistines, becomes terrified
	28:7	Saul seeks but fails to receive guidance from Yahweh
	28:8	Saul goes to medium in Endor at night; speaks with Samuel, learns of his impending death
	28:25	Saul returns from Endor to Gilboa at night
	30:1	David and his men reach Ziklag at end of a three-day march; discover Ziklag destroyed
	30:7–8	David seeks guidance from Yahweh using Abiathar and the ephod
	30:17	David and his men conduct dusk raid on Amalekites
5	30:17	David fights Amalekites till evening, recovers plunder and family
	31:1–6	Philistines rout Israel
	31:2–6	Philistines kill Saul and sons
6	31:8	Philistines cut off Saul's head, strip him of his armor
	31:10	Philistines fasten Saulides' bodies to Beth Shan wall
	31:11–12	Jabesh Gileadite men remove Saulides' bodies
	30:26	David and his men return to Ziklag
	2 Sam 1:1	David returns from defeating the Amalekites
7–8	2 Sam 1:1	David and his men stay in Ziklag two days
	30:26–31	David sends gifts to elders of Judah
9	2 Sam 1:2	Amalekite informs David of Saul's death

[9]"Then he said to me, 'Stand over me and kill me! I am in the throes of death, but I'm still alive.'

[10]"So I stood over him and killed him, because I knew that after he had fallen he could not survive. And I took the crown that was on his head and the band on his arm and have brought them here to my lord."

[11]Then David and all the men with him took hold of their clothes and tore them. [12]They mourned and wept and fasted till evening for Saul and his son Jonathan, and for the army of the LORD and the house of Israel, because they had fallen by the sword.

[13]David said to the young man who brought him the report, "Where are you from?"

"I am the son of an alien, an Amalekite," he answered.

[14]David asked him, "Why were you not afraid to lift your hand to destroy the LORD's anointed?"

[15]Then David called one of his men and said, "Go, strike him down!" So he struck him down, and he died. [16]For David had said to him, "Your blood be on your own head. Your own mouth testified against you when you said, 'I killed the LORD's anointed.'"

1:1–4 Saul, the first all-Israelite king,[167] was dead. He died battling the Philistines on Mount Gilboa at the very time David was doing battle against the Amalekites. Telling the stories of Saul and David more-or-less simultaneously in one book required an artful interlacing of the narratives. The events of 2 Samuel 1 should be linked to 1 Sam 30:31; 1:1 actually resumes the time line of 30:26, with the events of 30:27–31 apparently occurring simultaneously with the events of 2 Sam 1:1b–27.[168] The table on p. 285 suggests the order of events in this section of 1, 2 Samuel.

On David's third day back in Ziklag, no doubt as David and his men were busy putting their households in order following the Amalekite destruction of their settlement, "a man arrived from Saul's camp" (v. 2). David must have

---

[167] Abimelech is the first Israelite mentioned in the Bible who is said to have ruled as king over Israel (cf. Judg 9:6). However, his domain was quite limited—Shechem and Beth Millo.

[168] The chronological disconformities present in 1 Samuel 28 to 2 Samuel 1—interruptions of the time line as well as restatements of events—are typical of biblical Hebrew narratives at actional peaks. McCarter notes simply that the present form of this section is a "prophetically revised arrangement" (*1 Samuel*, 437). The greatest example of chronological restatement is found in the story of the flood, particularly Genesis 7. Other prime examples include Genesis 1–2 and Joshua 3. Though the narrative irregularities present in these sections have been interpreted as evidences pointing to the conflation of multiple recensions of texts, a more linguistically literate perspective understands them to be standard literary features designed to highlight moments of key actional significance in a story. For further information cf. R. E. Longacre, *An Anatomy of Speech Notions* (Lisse: Peter de Ridder, 1976); "Discourse Peak as Zone of Turbulence," in *Beyond the Sentence: Discourse and Sentential Form,* ed. J. R. Wirth (Ann Arbor: Karoma, 1985), 51–98; and N. Winther-Nielsen, "The Miraculous Grammar of Joshua 3–4," in *Biblical Hebrew and Discourse Linguistics,* ed. R. Bergen (Dallas: SIL, 1994), 300–319.

realized immediately that the man was bearing bad news, for he was displaying the customary outward signs of grief, "clothes torn and with dust on his head" (cf. 1 Sam 4:12; 2 Sam 13:31; Job 2:12). David could tell from the foreign messenger's appearance that one of the armies had suffered a tragic defeat. But because he did not know the messenger, it was impossible to discern from mere appearances which side had lost—perhaps it was Achish and the Philistines who had been slaughtered.

Before providing verbal details of his news, the messenger "came to David," falling "to the ground to pay him honor" (v. 2). David then began his meeting with the unnamed stranger by inquiring from where he had come. The man indicated that he had "escaped from the Israelite camp" (v. 3). News from the northern battlefield was particularly important to David since it would contain information regarding people, whether Israelites or Philistines, who were playing key roles in shaping his life. Quite naturally, therefore, David asked to know "what happened" (v. 4).

What the messenger described was indeed a military rout—the entire Israelite army fleeing from battle, with many injured and dead. Worst of all, King Saul and the primary heir to the throne, "his son Jonathan," were dead.

1:5–10 The messenger's claims—if true—were so serious and tragic that David refused to accept them at face value; instead he probed into the credibility of the messenger's information source.

The messenger stated that the report had come from his own eyewitness experience; he confirmed it with three different forms of evidence: the report of a personal sighting, the report of a conversation with the king, and a token from the king's own person. Two visual details were mentioned, the first of which was a sighting of the king. Mention of Saul in connection with his spear certainly lent an air of credibility to the young man's claim, since Saul and his spear were inseparable (cf. 1 Sam 13:22; 18:10–11; 19:9–10; 20:3; 22:6; 26:7–22). Second, the graphic details of "chariots and riders almost upon him" must have increased the believability of the claim as well, since David would have been well aware of the Philistine armaments sent to the northern battlefield.

The report of a private conversation with Saul by the messenger also provided evidence of credible information from the messenger. Saul had inquired about the identity of the young man and ordered the Amalekite to "stand over" him and "kill" him (v. 9), for although the king was "in the throes of death," his "soul was still in" him (NIV, "I'm still alive"). Obediently, the young foreigner followed the king's orders and thus became the first foreigner to kill an anointed Israelite (cf. 1 Sam 22:18). The Amalekite implied he acted out of compassion, knowing that "after [Saul] had fallen he could not survive."

The ironies of this event are not lost on the reader. Saul had lost his kingship because he had failed to kill an Amalekite king (cf. 1 Sam 15:9,26); now an Amalekite that Saul had failed to eliminate would kill this Israelite king.

Saul had been ordered to kill the Amalekites—now he ordered an Amalekite to kill him.

The Amalekite's third and most convincing form of evidence pointing to the death of Saul was material: the young man presented David "the crown" (Hb., *nēzer*; v. 10) that had been on Saul's head and the "band" (Hb., *ʾeṣʿādâ*) "on his arm." The presence of these personal tokens of royalty in the hands of a foreigner removed all doubt concerning Saul's death and provided compelling evidence of a personal encounter between the messenger and Saul.

In spite of the evidence presented by the Amalekite, contradictions—or at least tensions—do seem to exist between the account of Saul's death in 1 Sam 31:4–5 and the one presented in vv. 8–10. Was the Amalekite lying? Was he merely an opportunistic thief who robbed battlefield corpses before the Philistines could strip them? Had he accidentally stumbled across Saul's corpse and imagined he could trade the jewelry and information for a great reward? Or are there multiple and incompatible sources that have been awkwardly bound together by a redactor?[169] Many scholars assume the Amalekite concocted the story; others, especially commentators writing around the beginning of the twentieth century, accept it as truthful.[170]

On the other hand, the writer gives no indication that David questioned the veracity of the Amalekite's account; on the contrary, he acted on the assumption that the words were true. Furthermore, the foreigner's description of Saul with his spear seems to be that of an eyewitness. Finally, the Amalekite's story best accounts for the fact that the Philistines did not gain possession of Saul's crown or armlet. Thus, vv. 6–10 are most reasonably understood as a truthful retelling of 1 Sam 31:4–5, with the inclusion of additional details regarding the final moments of Saul's life. The reader can conclude that Saul inflicted on himself a blow that, given sufficient passage of time, would have killed him; however, his death was hastened by the Amalekites' efforts.

---

[169] For a useful overview of multiple-source theories, as well as a conservative evaluation of them, cf. B. Arnold, "The Amalekite's Report of Saul's Death: Political Intrigue or Incompatible Sources?" *JETS* 32 (1989): 289–98.

[170] Cf. Baldwin: "The reader knows that his story does not tally with the events already recorded" (*1 and 2 Samuel*, TOTC [Leicester: InterVarsity, 1988], 176); McCarter: "The contradiction is deliberate, a result of the writer's self-conscious portrayal of the Amalekite messenger as a liar" (*II Samuel*, 64); Anderson: "It must have been fairly clear to the readers that the Amalekite was exaggerating his own role in this particular episode" (*2 Samuel*, 5); Hertzberg: "His account does not tally with that of ch. 31" (*I and II Samuel*, 236); Gordon: "He will be executed as a regicide . . ., but he was more probably a common looter with some facility in story-telling" (*I and II Samuel*, 209); and Youngblood: "Josephus . . . errs in his basic assumption that the Amalekite was telling the truth" (*1, 2 Samuel*, 806). But see Smith: "The easiest hypothesis is that the Amalekite fabricated his story. But the whole narrative seems against this" (*Samuel*, 254); and Kirkpatrick: "It is not necessary to regard this as a lie of the Amalekite" (*The First Book of Samuel*, 51). Brueggemann is noncommittal on the point, suggesting that "there is no way to adjudicate the question of the historicity of either narrative" (*First and Second Samuel*, 213).

This narrative account not only provides interesting historical data but also clears David of any suspicions that may have been aroused by his possession of Saul's royal jewelry. David acquired them not by participating in the battle against Saul but by executing Saul's killer.

1:11–16   When David learned that his most determined enemy was dead, he did not rejoice. Instead, he and his men expressed profound grief in response to the news. The anguish was not only for Saul's death but also for the royal family and because the defeat at Gilboa was indeed a national tragedy.

In the midst of his grief, however, David did not fail to perform his duty to obey the Torah, which prescribed the death of all Amalekites (cf. 15:18–19; Exod 17:15–16; Deut 25:17–19). Before acting against the messenger, David confirmed the man's nationality: he was indeed "the son of an alien, an Amalekite" (v. 13). David had just conducted a holy war campaign against the Amalekites in fulfillment of Torah commands. Now when he learned that a member of the Amalekite nation had also played a direct role in the death of Israel's king—"the LORD's anointed" (v. 14)—David did not hesitate to execute judgment on him. Destroying the Lord's anointed was tantamount to rejecting the Lord, since it represented the ultimate rejection of his designated leader.

No doubt the Amalekite expected David to reward him. However, instead of crowning him with honor, David decreed that "your blood be on your head" (v. 16), that is, that the Amalekite bear full responsibility for participating in Saul's untimely death. Since he "killed the LORD's anointed," David ordered one of his men to "strike him down" (v. 15). The logic was that of the lex talionis; as the man had done, so it would be done to him (cf. Exod 21:23–25; Lev 24:19–21; Deut 19:21). The unnamed soldier obeyed David's command, with the result that the Amalekite "died."

(2) David Laments Devastation in the House of Saul (1:17–27)[171]

[17]David took up this lament concerning Saul and his son Jonathan, [18]and ordered that the men of Judah be taught this lament of the bow (it is written in the Book of Jashar):
   [19]"Your glory, O Israel, lies slain on your heights.
      How the mighty have fallen!

   [20]"Tell it not in Gath,
      proclaim it not in the streets of Ashkelon,

---

[171] For further discussion regarding David's lament, cf. W. Shea, "David's Lament," *BASOR* 221 (1976): 41–44; idem, "Chiasmus and the Structure of David's Lament," *JBL* 105 (1986): 13-25; D. Stuart, *Studies in Early Hebrew Meter,* HSM 13 (Missoula: Scholars Press, 1976), 187–95; and D. Zapf, "How Are the Mighty Fallen! A Study of 2 Samuel 1:17-27," *GTJ* 5 (1984): 95-126.

lest the daughters of the Philistines be glad,
lest the daughters of the uncircumcised rejoice.

[21]"O mountains of Gilboa,
may you have neither dew nor rain,
nor fields that yield offerings [of grain].
For there the shield of the mighty was defiled,
the shield of Saul—no longer rubbed with oil.
[22]From the blood of the slain,
from the flesh of the mighty,
the bow of Jonathan did not turn back,
the sword of Saul did not return unsatisfied.

[23]"Saul and Jonathan—
in life they were loved and gracious,
and in death they were not parted.
They were swifter than eagles,
they were stronger than lions.

[24]"O daughters of Israel,
weep for Saul,
who clothed you in scarlet and finery,
who adorned your garments with ornaments of gold.

[25]"How the mighty have fallen in battle!
Jonathan lies slain on your heights.
[26]I grieve for you, Jonathan my brother;
you were very dear to me.
Your love for me was wonderful,
more wonderful than that of women.

[27]"How the mighty have fallen!
The weapons of war have perished!"

Having the unambiguous tokens of Saul's death—the royal crown and arm-let (cf. v. 10)—in his possession, David was overwhelmed by the reality of the royal family's destruction. Yet as in the case of the author of Lamentations, David's agony works catalytically. His pain creates one of the most sensitive and moving expressions of mourning ever penned or uttered. Gordon praises the passage as "one of the finest specimens of Hebrew poetry in the Old Testament."[172] David's words not only express his personal grief, but that of all Israel as well.

1:17–18   David's "lament" (Hb., *qînâ*), entitled "Bow" (v. 2; cf. also v. 22),[173] was for both "Saul and his son Jonathan" (v. 17). Though its meter deviates from the unbalanced three-plus-two meter traditionally associated

---

[172] Gordon, *I and II Samuel*, 201.
[173] The literal reading of 1:18a is, "And he [David] said to teach the sons of Judah Bow."

with Hebrew dirge poetry,[174] its content places it directly in this category.

David "ordered that the men of Judah be taught this lament" (v. 2), perhaps because of its subject matter, since it paid tribute to Israel's first royal family and dealt with the larger and ever-relevant issue of loved ones dying in war. David's decision had the effect of bringing this composition into the canon of literature that defined ancient Israelite society. This piece of oral and written literature played the valuable roles of preserving the memory of a crucial event in Israelite history while reinforcing the office of kingship through its portrayal of the king as the agent through whom prosperity was brought to Israel.

The poem was preserved not only here but also in "the Book of Jashar" (cf. Josh 10:13). This piece of literature, literally entitled "the Scroll of the Righteous," is no longer extant; it is believed to have been a work that "dealt with the heroic exploits of the Israelites."[175]

1:19–20 The mournful tribute to Saul and Jonathan began with a powerful image taken from nature: "The gazelle, O Israel, on your high places has been struck dead" (NIV, "Your glory, O Israel, lies slain on your heights"; v. 19). The image of a majestic buck, master of the rugged hills of Israel, lying dead in a place of prominence and seeming protection, vividly reflects the tragic reality of Saul's death. With the deaths of Saul and Jonathan, it was the case that "the mighty have fallen."

Adding to the power of David's poetry is the use of double entendre: the same word translated here as "the gazelle" (Hb. ṣĕbî) also can mean "the glory." With a single word David praised the Saulide dynasty twice.

Though the fact of Saul's death must have been delightful to the Philistines, David issued a poetic warning to the returning Philistine soldiers whom David must have observed passing by Ziklag on their way to nearby Philistine settlements: "Tell it not in Gath" and do not "proclaim it in the streets of Ashkelon" (v. 20). Doing so would only pour salt in wounded Israelite souls, since it would inevitably cause "the daughters of the uncircumcised" to "rejoice" (cf. Exod 15:20–21; Judg 11:34; 1 Sam 18:6–7).

1:21 Having addressed the Philistines, David now speaks to the "mountains of Gilboa." The grammar of v. 21a is artfully contorted and mirrors the wrenching of David's soul in this hour of grief;[176] the Hebrew literally reads,

---

[174] Cf. D. Stuart, *Studies in Early Hebrew Meter,* 15. Besides the content of this poem, the employment of אֵיךְ ("How") in the opening distich is also characteristic of קִינָה poetry (cf. Jer 9:19 [Hb. v. 18]; Lam 1:1; 2:1; 4:1).

[175] Cf. D. L. Christensen, "Jashar, Book of," *ABD* 3:646–47; A. A. Anderson, *2 Samuel,* WBC (Waco: Word, 1989), 14; Baldwin, *1 and 2 Samuel,* 178.

[176] The opening plural construct form הָרֵי, which requires a nonprefixed noun to follow, is instead followed by a noun possessing a prepositional prefix (בַגִּלְבֹּעַ). McCarter, who notes it as an "unusual construction," suggests that the early Greek copyists who produced the Lucianic recension of the LXX were working from a text that had been grammatically "corrected" by the omission of the בַ preposition in the phrase. Such "corrections," whether ancient or modern, reduce the emotional content and impact of the original (*II Samuel,* 69).

"Mountains of—in the Gilboa, No dew and no rain upon you, and fields of offerings."[177] The terse constructions and absence of any verb in v. 21a suggest that David was reduced to gasping utterances during this tragic moment.

David called for the mountains of Gilboa to be denied life-giving liquid because it was on them that Saul's life fluids were poured out. Yet David did not yet mention Saul's death directly; instead he referred to a desecration of the anointed "Shield of the mighty ones." His use of "shield" *(māgēn)* is cleverly ambiguous, since the term may refer either to a benevolent being (cf. Gen 15:1) or a piece of defensive weaponry. Both an anointed man (cf. 1:14) and an anointed (Hb., *māšîaḥ*; NIV, "rubbed with oil") weapon fell on Gilboa, and the mountain would never be the same again. Indeed, the only references to Gilboa in Scripture are in connection with the death of Saul (cf. 1 Sam 28:4; 31:1–8; 2 Sam 1:6; 21:12; 1 Chr 10:1,8).

1:22–24 Before directly mentioning the battlefield deaths of Saul and Jonathan, David first recounted their honorable distinctions. Both Jonathan and Saul were renowned for their battlefield prowess. "The bow of Jonathan" (v. 22)—metonymous for Jonathan himself—had once saved David's life (cf. 1 Sam 20:36–39) but was also responsible for pouring out "the blood of the slain" and felling "the flesh of the mighty" (cf. 1 Sam 14:13–14). "The sword of Saul" likewise "did not return unsatisfied." Jonathan and Saul were further praised by David as individuals who possessed not only skill but also speed and strength in battle: "they were swifter than eagles" and "stronger than lions" (v. 23).

The success of "Saul and Jonathan" off the battlefield was also impressive; in society they "were loved and endeared" (v. 23; NIV, "gracious"). They were both men of character, who possessed a sense of loyalty and faithfulness to the nation and each other to the extent that even "in death" *pro patria* "they were not parted."

Though the Philistine daughters were to remain silent (v. 20), the "daughters of Israel" by contrast were to "weep for Saul" (v. 24). They were to mourn the loss of the one who "clothed you in scarlet and finery, who adorned your garments with ornaments of gold." Saul should not be thought of as having personally distributed such manifestations of wealth as clothing colored with

---

[177] The phrase translated in the NIV as "fields that yield offerings of gain" has been the subject of much scholarly debate, although popular Eng. versions are in general agreement on its rendering: NRSV, "bounteous fields"; NKJV, "fields of offerings." McCarter, concluding that "no satisfactory interpretation of the received text has been achieved," emends the text to create a parallel with a Ugaritic poem about Aqhat and thus creates the reading "flowing of the deeps" (*II Samuel,* 70). I reject his considerable efforts to make David's emotion-charged poetry more smooth and simple. For an argument in favor of retaining difficult lines of poetry in an unemended state, cf. F. I Andersen, "The Poetic Properties of Prophetic Discourse in the Book of Micah," in *Biblical Hebrew and Discourse Linguistics,* ed. R. Bergen (Dallas: SIL, 1994), 520–28.

imported dyes and brooches of worked gold; but his military successes provided a stable society that permitted the Israelites to acquire wealth through agriculture, trade, and conquest.

1:25–26 David returns to the mournful thesis of the lament, first expressed in v. 19, as he grieves that "the mighty have fallen in battle" (v. 25). The reuse of the phrase here, with its expansion through the addition of the phrase "in battle," suggests that vv. 25–26 are the thematic center of the poem. Among the dead was David's soul mate "Jonathan," who "lies slain on your heights." The mention of his best friend's death elicits the most personal expression of grief found in the poem. In v. 26 it is David, not the daughters of Jerusalem, who weeps. David has lost his "brother," a kindred spirit who was "very dear to" him.

With the death of Jonathan, David lost his most trusted confidant and companion. Jonathan's affirmations of support (cf. 1 Sam 18:3–4; 19:1–7; 20:1–42; 23:16–18) had come at key moments in David's life and were deeply appreciated. To David, Jonathan's "love . . . was wonderful, more wonderful than that of women." David's very personal expression of emotion here should not be taken as evidence of a homosexual liaison with Jonathan;[178] rather, it is a manifestation of the parameters of social relations that existed in ancient Israelite society. Marriages in ancient Israel took place primarily for the benefit of the tribe—to increase the size and strength of the social group through procreation (cf. Gen 1:28) and to increase its prosperity through the establishment of advantageous formal ties with other families (cf. Gen 34:21–23). A man's wife was his partner in procreation and parenting, but not necessarily his best friend, confidant, or social peer. For David, Jonathan was the peer, friend, and confidant that no wife could ever have been in that society; and his untimely death left a gaping hole in David's soul.

1:27 The elegy ends chiastically, repeating the phrase that had marked its beginning (v. 19) and thematic peak (v. 25). It hauntingly reminds us of the painful outcome of war, any war—through it "the mighty have fallen." The reference to "the weapons of war" that "have perished" metonymically refers to the deaths of Saul and Jonathan (cf. v. 22).

---

[178] Cf. D. M. Gunn, who suggests that "Jonathan's intensive and exclusive devotion to David is strongly suggestive of a homosexuality which in turn would represent a denial of Saul's dynastic hopes. Thus in this sense also David as the object of Jonathan's love may be seen to have 'cut off' Saul's descendants" (*The Story of King Saul* [Sheffield: University of Sheffield, 1980], 93). Gunn's observations are misguided and misleading; while Jonathan clearly had a deep friendship with David, there is no evidence to suggest a sexual aspect. Rather the Bible explicitly maintains that Jonathan (as well as David) had a heterosexual relationship that produced at least one son, Mephibosheth/Meribaal (cf. 2 Sam 9:3). Thus, Jonathan's relationship with David was in no way limiting Saul's dynastic hopes.

IV. DAVID REIGNS AS KING (2:1–20:26)
  1. The Judahites Anoint David King at Hebron (2:1–4a)
  2. David Woos Supporters of the House of Saul (2:4b–7)
  3. The House of Saul Relinquishes Its Claim on Israel's Throne
     (2:8–4:12)
     (1) Abner Establishes Ish-Bosheth as King over Israel (2:8–11)
     (2) Conflict Erupts between the Houses of Saul and David
         (2:12–3:1)
     (3) David Builds His Family in Hebron (3:2–5)
     (4) Abner Switches His Loyalty to David (3:6–21)
     (5) Joab Murders Abner (3:22–27)
     (6) David Proves His Innocence in Abner's Death (3:28–39)
     (7) Recab and Baanah Murder Ish-Bosheth (4:1–7)
     (8) David Executes Ish-Bosheth's Murderers (4:8–12)
  4. All the Tribes of Israel Anoint David King at Hebron (5:1–5)
  5. The Lord Blesses David (5:6–10:19)
     (1) David Conquers Jerusalem (5:6–8)
     (2) The Lord Blesses David as King in Jerusalem (5:9–16)
     (3) David Defeats the Philistines Twice (5:17–25)
     (4) David Brings the Ark of God to Jerusalem (6:1–23)
     (5) David Desires to Build a Temple for the Lord (7:1–3)
     (6) The Lord Makes Eternal Promises to the House of David
         (7:4–17)
     (7) David Praises the Lord (7:18–29)
     (8) The Lord Gives David Victory Over All His Enemies (8:1–14)
     (9) David Establishes a Righteous and Just Administration
         (8:15–18)
     (10) David Fulfills His Commitment to Jonathan (9:1–13)
     (11) David Conquers an Ammonite-led Coalition (10:1–19)
  6. The Lord Judges David (11:1–20:26)
     (1) David Does Evil in the Lord's Sight (11:1–27)
     (2) Nathan Announces the Lord's Judgment and Forgiveness
         (12:1–14)
     (3) The Lord Expresses Judgment and Forgiveness (12:15–25)
     (4) David Defeats and Subjects the Ammonites (12:26–31)
     (5) Amnon Rapes Tamar (13:1–22)
     (6) Absalom Murders Amnon, Then Flees to Geshur (13:23–39)
     (7) David Is Reconciled with Absalom (14:1–33)

295

(8) Absalom Leads a Treasonous Revolt against David (15:1–12)
(9) David Goes into Exile beyond the Jordan River (15:13–17:29)
(10) David's Forces Quell Absalom's Revolt (18:1–19:8)
(11) David Returns to Jerusalem (19:9–43)
(12) Sheba Revolts Unsuccessfully against David (20:1–22)
(13) Aside: David's Key Administrative Officials (20:23–26)

─────── IV. DAVID REIGNS AS KING (2:1–20:26) ───────

This section stands as the narrative peak of 1, 2 Samuel and one of the thematic centers of the Former Prophets. Here David, the most significant character in the Former Prophets—the human character who serves as the subject of more clauses than any other in the Old Testament[1]—climbs to the pinnacle of his career and then tumbles from that lofty height through a complicated series of events initiated by his own sin. In the process David, the man after the Lord's heart, fulfills major Torah prophecies regarding the rise of the tribe of Judah to rulership over Israel (cf. Gen 49:10), the determination of the place where the Lord would put his Name for his dwelling (Deut 12:5), the acquisition of territories promised to Israel since the days of Abraham (Gen 12:7; 15:18–21; 17:8), and the destruction of Moab, Edom, and Amalek (Num 24:17–21).

At the same time, the life of David is transformed by the writer into a metaphor for the nation of Israel. His conquest of the land; a period of rich blessing, desolation, and exile caused by sin; and return to the land following a time spent east of the Promised Land all make the portrayal of this period of his life a tableau depicting the Lord's blessings, judgments, and restorative mercy. This portion of 2 Samuel is not only a historically accurate and detailed account of David's rise and fall, but also a profound object lesson in Torah theology and a metaphor of hope for later Israel.

1. The Judahites Anoint David King at Hebron (2:1–4a)

[1]In the course of time, David inquired of the LORD. "Shall I go up to one of the towns of Judah?" he asked.
The LORD said, "Go up."

---

[1] 638 times in the corpus of narrative framework (nonquotational materials) consisting of Genesis to Deuteronomy as well as 1, 2 Samuel. By contrast, the second most commonly occurring human subject in the same material is Moses, who is the subject 554 times. In that same stretch of material God is the subject 943 times.

David asked, "Where shall I go?"

"To Hebron," the LORD answered.

²So David went up there with his two wives, Ahinoam of Jezreel and Abigail, the widow of Nabal of Carmel. ³David also took the men who were with him, each with his family, and they settled in Hebron and its towns. ⁴Then the men of Judah came to Hebron and there they anointed David king over the house of Judah.

2:1–3 After an appropriate expression of grief for his former father-in-law and his best friend, David consulted the Lord for guidance in his own life. Saul's death had removed the only obvious roadblock to David's return to Israelite territory, but David needed divine guidance to affirm or overrule his intentions. Furthermore, if it was the Lord's will for David to return, he needed a confirmation of the timing and location of a repatriation. Thus, it was appropriate that David's first act following the mourning period for the house of Saul was "not recruitment, strategy, or public relations" but rather "to inquire of Yahweh."[2] Based on David's previous practice (cf. 1 Sam 23:9–12; 30:7–8), it is likely that he "inquired of the LORD" with the assistance of Abiathar and the ephod.

David first asked if it was appropriate to "go up to one of the towns of Judah" (v. 1), the tribal territory of his ancestors and the location of the Israelites most likely to support him in his efforts to claim Saul's throne. The Lord confirmed that it was appropriate to "go up" at that time.

The site chosen by the Lord for David to reestablish his Israelite residency was Hebron, the city termed by J. G. Baldwin as "the most distinguished of Judah's cities."[3] Three factors favored David's settlement in this city; it was the largest city of refuge in the region (cf. Josh 21:13); it was a Calebite city (Josh 14:14; 15:13), and it was a city set aside for the Aaronic priesthood (Josh 21:13). As a city of refuge, Hebron was specifically set aside as a haven for one who had been falsely accused of murder—and there were no doubt those in Israel who believed David played a role in Saul's death. The size of the city seems to have been crucial as well because many people accompanied David in his return to Israel. Among these were David's two wives as well as the six hundred soldiers and their families. Perhaps the fact that David had married the widow of a Calebite (1 Sam 25:3) made his acceptance easier in Hebron as well. In addition the presence and status of Abiathar, an Aaronic priest, within David's group must have increased the readiness of the inhabitants of Hebron to accept him.

David's sizable group, which may have numbered more than a thousand, appears to have overwhelmed the city of Hebron itself. As a result, many in the returning group had to settle in "the cities of Hebron" (NIV, "its towns"), that

---

[2] W. Brueggemann, *First and Second Samuel*, IBC (Louisville: John Knox, 1990), 219.
[3] J. G. Baldwin, *1 and 2 Samuel*, TOTC (Leicester: InterVarsity, 1988), 183.

is, the unwalled villages in the immediate vicinity.

2:4a   After David was planted back in Israel, the Lord's previously revealed plan for David to shepherd his people began to blossom. Included among the group who came to anoint David may have been some who had witnessed David's original anointing by Samuel (cf. 1 Sam 16:5–13). Though some Judahites had previously opposed David (cf. 1 Sam 23:19–24; 26:1), no hint of tribal opposition was present at this time.

David's support, however, was limited; only those Israelites who had the closest blood ties to him were present at his anointing in Hebron. Although he no doubt enjoyed the support of at least some of the Levites (David had gained a reputation as a protector of priestly interests; cf. 1 Sam 22:20–23), David was not recognized as king of all Israel at this time.[4]

2. David Woos Supporters of the House of Saul (2:4b–7)

When David was told that it was the men of Jabesh Gilead who had buried Saul, [5]he sent messengers to the men of Jabesh Gilead to say to them, "The LORD bless you for showing this kindness to Saul your master by burying him. [6]May the LORD now show you kindness and faithfulness, and I too will show you the same favor because you have done this. [7]Now then, be strong and brave, for Saul your master is dead, and the house of Judah has anointed me king over them."

David understood that the Lord had selected him to be the leader of all Israel and took prudent steps to make that happen. He began as his predecessor did, by making a contact with Jabesh Gilead.

2:4b–6   David, the newly anointed king of Judah, heard about the brave actions of the Jabesh Gileadites, "who had buried Saul" (v. 4) and his three slain sons (cf. 1 Sam 31:11–13). The men of Gilead had been motivated by their respect and appreciation for the slain king (cf. 1 Sam 11:1–11). David was impressed by this courageous act, for it mirrored his own respect for the royal family. Accordingly, "he sent messengers to the men of Jabesh Gilead" affirming them with the message (lit.), "Blessed are you to Yahweh." Their burial of Saul was an act of loving loyalty (*ḥesed*, NIV "kindness"). In return he assured them of the Lord's *ḥesed* and *ʾemet* ("faithfulness") as well as his own.[5] David's kind words sent to them by his personal emissary must have relieved the concerns of some, for David was reputed to be an enemy of Saul and therefore a

---

[4] H. P. Smith asserts that David was able to rise to power in Hebron because "the Philistines allowed him to extend his kingdom so far" (*The Books of Samuel*, ICC [Edinburgh: T & T Clark, n.d.], 266). However, the extent of the Philistines' toleration of David at this time is questionable, since he accepted the role of "king over the house of Judah" (2:4), and the Philistines had previously considered David a threat when he was associated with Israelite kingship (cf. 1 Sam 21:11).

[5] David selected terms taken from Yahweh's own self-description found in the Torah (cf. Exod 34:6).

potential adversary of the Gileadites.

2:7 Having reached out to these loyal supporters of Saul's regime, David encouraged them to "be strong and brave" (lit., "strengthen your hands and become men of power/virtue"). He urged them to accept the fact that Saul their "master [was] dead" and move beyond their grief. Though the one who had brought them deliverance and protection was gone, the Lord had raised up another to take Saul's place. The "house of Judah" had already anointed David "king over them," and David would gladly be Jabesh Gilead's king as well.

3. The House of Saul Relinquishes Its Claim on Israel's Throne (2:8–4:12)

According to this crucial section, active opposition to David's bid for kingship over all Israel temporarily coalesced around Saul's surviving son, Ish-Bosheth. Empowered by Saul's cousin Abner, Ish-Bosheth made a bid to rule the territories formerly under the control of his father. Unfortunately for the house of Saul, King Ish-Bosheth proved to be essentially inert and decidedly incompetent: though he reigned two years, the writer depicts him performing only three acts—wrongly accusing Abner of misconduct, giving his sister back to David, and lying on his bed.

David extended his rule over all Israel with the assistance of a Benjamite, Ish-Bosheth's rebuffed general Abner. Abner negotiated privately with David, reunited David with his Saulide wife Michal, and then acted as an intermediary between the Judahite king and key groups in the north; thus David was poised to take control of tribal territories that had previously proved resistant. The untimely and violent deaths of Abner and Ish-Bosheth complicated the process, but David's skillful handling of these crises kept the process of his rise to power on track. As a result David experienced the fulfillment of the Lord's promise to make him king of all Israel; the shepherd of Jesse's flock to become the shepherd of the Lord's flock Israel.

(1) Abner Establishes Ish-Bosheth as King over Israel (2:8–11)

⁸Meanwhile, Abner son of Ner, the commander of Saul's army, had taken Ish-Bosheth son of Saul and brought him over to Mahanaim. ⁹He made him king over Gilead, Ashuri and Jezreel, and also over Ephraim, Benjamin and all Israel.

¹⁰Ish-Bosheth son of Saul was forty years old when he became king over Israel, and he reigned two years. The house of Judah, however, followed David. ¹¹The length of time David was king in Hebron over the house of Judah was seven years and six months.

2:8–9 In an effort to revitalize the Saulide dynasty and thus to retain his position as Israel's most powerful military leader, Abner had taken Ish-Bosheth,[6] Saul's only surviving son, to Mahanaim to anoint him as king.[7] Abner was Saul's cousin (1 Sam 14:50) and apparently his closest confidant (1 Sam 20:25; 26:7), so it was appropriate that he act loyally in behalf of his cousin/commander/friend. Mahanaim, a site whose remains have not yet been identified with certainty, was a Levitical city assigned to the Merarites (cf. Josh 21:38) east of the Jordan in the territory of Gad and had been associated with the patriarch Jacob (cf. Gen 32:2). Since it was east of the Jordan, it had likely escaped the ravages of the Philistines and thus provided relative safety and stability for reestablishing the monarchy in Israel.

Because of recent defeats at the hands of the Philistines as well as David's influence in Judah, the Israelite territories over which Ish-Bosheth's grip was most secure were relatively limited: "Gilead" (v. 9), the territory east of the Sea of Galilee; "the Ashuri," probably a reference to the tribal territory of Asher; "Jezreel," the region recently oppressed by the Philistines (1 Sam 29:1,11); and of course "Benjamin," Ish-Bosheth's and Abner's tribal homeland. However, Ish-Bosheth's claim of authority extended over "all Israel."

2:10–11   At the age of forty Ish-Bosheth would have been qualified to have fought in the fateful battle against the Philistines on Mount Gilboa with his father and three brothers (cf. 1 Sam 31; Num 1:36). Perhaps he had been purposely exempted, however, in order to assure a direct heir to the throne in case of a battlefield catastrophe like the one that actually occurred.

Ish-Bosheth laid claim to Israel's throne "two years" before he was murdered. These two years may correspond to the sixth and seventh years of David's reign at Hebron.[8] Two textual reasons support this contention: first, David was said to have ruled over only the house of Judah while he lived in Hebron (v. 11; 5:4); and second, 5:1–9 suggests that David moved his capital city to Jerusalem almost immediately after being anointed as king over all Israel.

---

[6] Ish-Bosheth's name means "Man of shame," a name that seems to have been a sort of nickname given him by the writer and perhaps others. Elsewhere in Scripture (cf. 1 Chr 8:33; 9:39) he is called "Esh-Baal," an appellation that means "[The] Fire of Baal" or perhaps "Man of Baal" (so Noth, *Die israelitischen Personennamen im Rahmen der gemeinsemitischen Namengeburg* [1928; reprint, Hildesheim: Olms, 1966], 138–39), or even "Baal Exists" (so W. F. Albright, *Archaeology and the Religion of Israel*, 5th ed. [Garden City: Doubleday, 1969], 206).

[7] D. F. Payne makes the useful observation that Ish-Bosheth's rise to kingship evidently was undertaken "without any consideration for God's will in the matter; no prophet was consulted" (*I and II Samuel*, DSB [Philadelphia: Westminster, 1982], 163). The absence of any note on the part of the writer that divine leadership was involved in this event is a clear foreshadowing that a tragic end awaits Ish Bosheth's reign.

[8] Cf. R. F. Youngblood, "1, 2 Samuel," EBC 3:553–1104 (Grand Rapids: Zondervan, 1992), 824; and J. A. Soggin, "The Reign of ʾEshbaʿal, Son of Saul," in *Old Testament and Oriental Studies* (Rome: Pontifical Biblical Institute, 1975), 31–49. R. Gordon disagrees, suggesting that "we are probably to understand . . . that during [the first five-and-a-half] years David ruled both Judah and Israel from Hebron" (*I and II Samuel* [Grand Rapids: Zondervan, 1986], 214).

If the tribes of Israel apart from Judah were in fact without a king for more than five years, this would suggest that the Philistines controlled the region completely enough during that time to prevent the rise of any Israelite to the throne. In this scenario Abner, as the leading military figure in the northern tribes, would have functioned as the de facto head of state. Yet instead of installing himself as king, he—nobly—put a direct descendant of Saul on the throne when he sensed Israel's situation had sufficiently improved.

Ish-Bosheth's kingship was not recognized in the territory of Judah because they "followed David." After all, David was one of their own and had made the southern Judahite town of Hebron his capital city. In fact, Hebron remained David's royal city for "seven years and six months" (v. 11), apparently the amount of time it took for David to gain undisputed control of all Israel as well as to conquer Jerusalem.

(2) Conflict Erupts between the Houses of Saul and David (2:12–3:1)

[12]Abner son of Ner, together with the men of Ish-Bosheth son of Saul, left Mahanaim and went to Gibeon. [13]Joab son of Zeruiah and David's men went out and met them at the pool of Gibeon. One group sat down on one side of the pool and one group on the other side.

[14]Then Abner said to Joab, "Let's have some of the young men get up and fight hand to hand in front of us."

"All right, let them do it," Joab said.

[15]So they stood up and were counted off—twelve men for Benjamin and Ish-Bosheth son of Saul, and twelve for David. [16]Then each man grabbed his opponent by the head and thrust his dagger into his opponent's side, and they fell down together. So that place in Gibeon was called Helkath Hazzurim.

[17]The battle that day was very fierce, and Abner and the men of Israel were defeated by David's men.

[18]The three sons of Zeruiah were there: Joab, Abishai and Asahel. Now Asahel was as fleet-footed as a wild gazelle. [19]He chased Abner, turning neither to the right nor to the left as he pursued him. [20]Abner looked behind him and asked, "Is that you, Asahel?"

"It is," he answered.

[21]Then Abner said to him, "Turn aside to the right or to the left; take on one of the young men and strip him of his weapons." But Asahel would not stop chasing him.

[22]Again Abner warned Asahel, "Stop chasing me! Why should I strike you down? How could I look your brother Joab in the face?"

[23]But Asahel refused to give up the pursuit; so Abner thrust the butt of his spear into Asahel's stomach, and the spear came out through his back. He fell there and died on the spot. And every man stopped when he came to the place where Asahel had fallen and died.

[24]But Joab and Abishai pursued Abner, and as the sun was setting, they came to the hill of Ammah, near Giah on the way to the wasteland of Gibeon. [25]Then the

men of Benjamin rallied behind Abner. They formed themselves into a group and took their stand on top of a hill.

[26]Abner called out to Joab, "Must the sword devour forever? Don't you realize that this will end in bitterness? How long before you order your men to stop pursuing their brothers?"

[27]Joab answered, "As surely as God lives, if you had not spoken, the men would have continued the pursuit of their brothers until morning."

[28]So Joab blew the trumpet, and all the men came to a halt; they no longer pursued Israel, nor did they fight anymore.

[29]All that night Abner and his men marched through the Arabah. They crossed the Jordan, continued through the whole Bithron and came to Mahanaim.

[30]Then Joab returned from pursuing Abner and assembled all his men. Besides Asahel, nineteen of David's men were found missing. [31]But David's men had killed three hundred and sixty Benjamites who were with Abner. [32]They took Asahel and buried him in his father's tomb at Bethlehem. Then Joab and his men marched all night and arrived at Hebron by daybreak.

[1]The war between the house of Saul and the house of David lasted a long time. David grew stronger and stronger, while the house of Saul grew weaker and weaker.

2:12–13 At some unknown point during the last two years of David's reign in Hebron, "Abner son of Ner, together with the men of Ish-Bosheth son of Saul, left Mahanaim and went to Gibeon" (v. 12). The reason for Abner's expedition to Benjamite territory is not stated, but it seems probable that he was returning for one or more of four purposes: to have a war counsel with David's representatives, to enlist further pro-Saulide military support from the men of Benjamin (cf. v. 25), to establish a site back in Benjamite territory from which Ish-Bosheth could rule, and/or to mount an attack against David's forces who were establishing a presence in that area. Regardless of which option represents reality, it is clear that Abner expected hostilities to break out, for he had hundreds of armed troops in readiness nearby.

David's nephew "Joab son of Zeruiah" (v. 13) learned of Abner's troop movements and led "David's men" some twenty-three miles north to "the pool of Gibeon," a hand-carved reservoir thirty-seven feet in diameter and eighty-two feet deep,[9] to confront Abner and his soldiers. Gibeon, like David's capital city of Hebron, was a city set aside for Aaronic priests (cf. Josh 21:17; 1 Chr 6:60); following the destruction of Shiloh and Samuel's death, it also was recognized as the central Yahwistic shrine (cf. 1 Chr 16:39; 1 Kgs 3:4). Perhaps David's forces advanced into Gibeon to defend the Aaronic priests from another possible attack from Saulide forces desiring to punish the priests for

---

[9]Cf. J. B. Pritchard, "The Water System at Gibeon," *BA* 19 (1956): 66–75; and idem, *Gibeon, Where the Sun Stood Still* (Princeton, N. J.: Princeton University, 1962). Pritchard excavated el-Jib, site of the Gibeon pool and the city of Gibeon, between 1956 and 1960.

their apparent support of David.

Initially, a standoff resulted at the pool as Joab refused to allow Saul's forces to advance farther; "one group sat down on one side of the pool and one group on the other side."

2:14–16 The impasse was finally broken as Abner challenged Joab to have their forces engage in a deadly contest involving "hand to hand" (v. 14) fighting. When Joab agreed, a representative force from both sides was chosen— "twelve men for Benjamin," and "twelve men for David" (v. 15).

The contest ended almost as quickly as it had begun. Without the aid of bows, spears, lances, or slings, each soldier could rely only on his hands and "sword" (Hb. *ḥereb*; NIV, "dagger"). Advancing directly to confront his opponent, each man grabbed "his opponent by the head" (v. 16), then thrust his weapon "into his opponent's side," apparently producing a fatal wound. Sadly, all twenty–four men "fell together" in the indecisive contest.

The event was highly unusual in Israelite society; with the possible exception of the confrontation between David and Goliath (1 Samuel 17), no parallel to this contest exists in recorded Israelite history.[10] Nor was this extraordinary event forgotten; the site in Gibeon where it occurred was given the memorial name "Helkath Hazzurim"—literally, "the field of the hostilities."

2:17–23 Far from preventing a greater shedding of blood, the contest in Gibeon only heightened the tensions between the opposing forces. Immediately afterward a "very fierce" (v. 17) battle broke out that resulted in a resounding defeat for Ish-Bosheth's forces.

Three of David's nephews, "Joab, Abishai, and Asahel" (v. 18; cf. 1 Chr 2:16), played key roles in the events of this day. Asahel, who was a valiant soldier (cf. 23:24) and reputed to be "as fleet-footed [lit., "as light in his feet"] as a wild gazelle," pursued Abner in an effort to destroy the individual most responsible for sustaining Ish-Bosheth's claim to Israel's throne. So focused was he in his efforts to kill Ish-Bosheth's general that he turned "neither to the right nor to the left as he pursued him" (v. 19).

Both men entered the battle without benefit of chariot or riding animal; however, Abner was carrying weapons, whereas Asahel apparently was only lightly armed. Although Abner was much better armed than Asahel, he attempted to avoid a direct confrontation with him. Perhaps he did this so that he would be free to focus his attention on directing the troops; but when he learned that it was Asahel who was tracking him down, Abner had a second reason to evade a showdown—killing Asahel would irreparably damage his relationship with his respected peer (and adversary), Asahel's "brother Joab" (v. 22).

---

[10] F. C. Fensham suggests that this unique encounter may have been an ordeal, where the guilty party would be judged by God through death in the contest ("The Battle between the Men of Joab and Abner as a Possible Ordeal by Battle?" *VT* 20 [1970]: 356–57). Payne prefers to understand this as representative combat (*I and II Samuel*, 165).

In an effort to level the playing field for the inevitable showdown, Abner encouraged Asahel first to "take on one of the young men and strip him of his weapons" (v. 21). However, Asahel "refused to give up his pursuit" (v. 23). Instead, he chased Abner with even more determination and presently came within a few feet of overtaking him.

Compelled at last to use force to defend himself, Abner "thrust the butt"—that is, the blunt, nonaggressive side—"of his spear into Asahel's stomach."[11] Though the action probably was intended only to knock the wind out of his opponent, Asahel's charge was so energetic and Abner's thrust so powerful that "the spear came out through his back." Consequently, Asahel "died on the spot." The gruesome sight of one of David's most honored soldiers slain in such a freakish manner caused "every man" to stop "when he came to the place where Asahel had fallen."

2:24–28 Asahel's heroic brothers "Joab and Abishai" then took up the task left unfinished by their brother and "pursued Abner" (v. 24) until sunset. Their chase led them eastward "to the hill of Ammah." On that promontory they encountered forces from Benjamin, who had "rallied behind Abner" (v. 25) and taken a stand with him there on that easily defended site.

From his militarily advantageous position on the hilltop, "Abner called out to Joab" (v. 26). His message of reason encouraged Joab to consider the long-term consequences of pursuing the conflict against Abner and the supporters of Ish-Bosheth—it would "end in bitterness." After all, by hunting down the Benjamites they were in fact "pursuing their brothers." In a previous generation other Israelites had attacked and almost wiped out the Benjamites, but they had come to regret it (cf. Judg 21:2–3). Barring a change, the present situation would turn out the same way.

However, Joab took Abner's words to heart. Though he had intended to have his troops continue "the pursuit of their brothers until morning" (v. 27), he ordered "a halt" (v. 28) to the attack, and fighting was suspended.

2:29–32 Abner took advantage of the temporary cessation in hostilities as well as the cover of darkness to regroup his forces far away from Joab. Bringing his troops eastward down to "the Jordan," Abner and his men made an exceptional nocturnal crossing of the river and then proceeded along "the whole Bithron"—perhaps an alternate designation for the Jabbok ravine[12]—until they arrived back in Mahanaim.

Joab likewise withdrew from the battlefield, traveling approximately thirty miles to Hebron (cf. v. 32) during the night. Back in the safety of the city, Joab

[11] Images of ancient Near Eastern spears, each of which has a long blunt pole with a sharp metal (?) blade attached to one end, can be seen in *The Ancient Near East,* vol. 1, ed. J. B. Pritchard (Princeton, N.J.: Princeton University, 1958), plates 91, 95, 101, 102.

[12] The term בִּתְרוֹן is a hapax legomenon. Traditionally it has been translated something like "ravine"; however, some speculate that it means "morning"; cf. McCarter, *II Samuel,* 92.

mustered "all his men" (v. 30) and took a casualty count. Excluding Asahel, "nineteen of David's men were found missing" (v. 30); most of those had died in the initial standoff at the pool of Gibeon (cf. v. 16). If David's standing army at this time was still approximately six hundred men (cf. 1 Sam 23:13; 27:2; 30:9), this would have represented a loss of about three percent of his forces.

The writer indicates that David's troops had inflicted heavy casualties on the Benjamite forces in the course of the conflict—"three hundred and sixty" (v. 31) of Abner's men died that day. This suggests that when the fighting began in earnest, 348 Benjamites were killed compared with only seven of Joab's men—a rout by anyone's standards.

Before retreating from Benjamite territory, Joab's men retrieved his brother Asahel's corpse from the battlefield and returned it to Bethlehem, the ancestral home of the clan of his grandfather Jesse. There Asahel was buried "in his [grand?]father's tomb" (v. 32).

3:1 Though the previous incident was the only one detailed in the ongoing conflict, many more took place, for "the war between the house of Saul and the house of David lasted a long time." Nevertheless, the incident characterized the general course of the hostilities because throughout the two-year conflict "David grew stronger and stronger, while the house of Saul grew weaker and weaker." As characterized by the writer, the conflict was fundamentally between two families vying for undisputed control over one nation, not two nations at war with each other.

(3) David Builds His Family in Hebron (3:2–5)

²**Sons were born to David in Hebron:**
His firstborn was Amnon the son of Ahinoam of Jezreel;
³**his second, Kileab the son of Abigail the widow of Nabal of Carmel;**
the third, Absalom the son of Maacah daughter of Talmai king of Geshur;
⁴**the fourth, Adonijah the son of Haggith;**
the fifth, Shephatiah the son of Abital;
⁵**and the sixth, Ithream the son of David's wife Eglah.**
These were born to David in Hebron.

3:2–5 Through the use of a genealogical table, the writer demonstrated David's obedience to the Torah mandate to "be fruitful and multiply" (cf. Gen 1:28).

The writer indicates that David fathered children through six different wives. The Torah implicitly permitted kings to possess more than one wife, though they were not to have "many wives" (cf. Deut 17:17). Since David was not explicitly condemned for this number of wives, the writer may have considered David to be in compliance with the letter of the Torah in this matter, though he may certainly be viewed as having strayed from the biblical ideal (cf. 1 Tim 3:2; Titus 1:6). The diversity of David's harem suggests that he was deliberately using marriages for political, as well as familial, reasons; he was in fact skillfully consolidating his power base with them. Two of the wives, Ahinoam of Jezreel and Abigail of Carmel, were from families situated in southern Judah and thus could have played an important role in assuring his regional support.[13]

David's marriage to "Maacah daughter of Talmai king of Geshur" (v. 3) suggests that David established an alliance with a society east of the Jordan and immediately north of Ish-Bosheth's capital city of Mahanaim. The practical effect of such an alliance would be to double the number of potential threats to Ish-Bosheth's territorial claims—now Ish-Bosheth would have to be concerned with a northern ally of David, besides David himself. This added pressure would have helped to destabilize the Saulide regime.

The other wives—Haggith, Abital, and Eglah—are never depicted in biblical narrative as speaking or performing any actions. They are known elsewhere only for the fact that they bore David's children (cf. 1 Chr 3:2–3).

The genealogical list here also serves the practical function of delineating the line of dynastic succession. Thus, Amnon would have been the heir-apparent to the throne, followed by Kileab,[14] Absalom, Adonijah, Shephatiah, and Ithream. In the parallel list found in 1 Chr 3:1–3, the son of Abigail is called "Daniel," not Kileab. The variation may be due to an alternate appellation for Kileab. It is also possible that Kileab died and so was replaced in the list by a second son born to Abigail while David was still in Hebron. In such a case the surviving offspring might have retained his brother's position in the dynastic succession.

(4) Abner Switches His Loyalty to David (3:6–21)

6During the war between the house of Saul and the house of David, Abner had been strengthening his own position in the house of Saul. 7Now Saul had had a concubine named Rizpah daughter of Aiah. And Ish-Bosheth said to Abner, "Why did you sleep with my father's concubine?"

8Abner was very angry because of what Ish-Bosheth said and he answered, "Am I a dog's head—on Judah's side? This very day I am loyal to the house of your father Saul and to his family and friends. I haven't handed you over to David. Yet now you accuse me of an offense involving this woman! 9May God deal with Abner,

---

[13] See J. D. and B. Halpern, "The Political Import of David's Marriages," *JBL* 99 (1980): 507–18.

[14] This supposes that Kileab was not an heir raised up under the circumstances of levirate marriage in order to preserve the name of Nabal (cf. discussion at 1 Sam 25:39). However, my opinion is that Kileab was actually counted as the descendant of Nabal and therefore not eligible to be considered as a potential inheritor of David's throne. Reinforcing this conclusion is the fact that the name Kileab (כִּלְאָב) appears to be an artful combination of the first two letters of the names Caleb (כָּלֵב), Nabal's tribe of origin, and Abigail (אֲבִיגַיִל).

be it ever so severely, if I do not do for David what the LORD promised him on oath [10]and transfer the kingdom from the house of Saul and establish David's throne over Israel and Judah from Dan to Beersheba." [11]Ish-Bosheth did not dare to say another word to Abner, because he was afraid of him.

[12]Then Abner sent messengers on his behalf to say to David, "Whose land is it? Make an agreement with me, and I will help you bring all Israel over to you."

[13]"Good," said David. "I will make an agreement with you. But I demand one thing of you: Do not come into my presence unless you bring Michal daughter of Saul when you come to see me." [14]Then David sent messengers to Ish-Bosheth son of Saul, demanding, "Give me my wife Michal, whom I betrothed to myself for the price of a hundred Philistine foreskins."

[15]So Ish-Bosheth gave orders and had her taken away from her husband Paltiel son of Laish. [16]Her husband, however, went with her, weeping behind her all the way to Bahurim. Then Abner said to him, "Go back home!" So he went back.

[17]Abner conferred with the elders of Israel and said, "For some time you have wanted to make David your king. [18]Now do it! For the LORD promised David, 'By my servant David I will rescue my people Israel from the hand of the Philistines and from the hand of all their enemies.'"

[19]Abner also spoke to the Benjamites in person. Then he went to Hebron to tell David everything that Israel and the whole house of Benjamin wanted to do. [20]When Abner, who had twenty men with him, came to David at Hebron, David prepared a feast for him and his men. [21]Then Abner said to David, "Let me go at once and assemble all Israel for my lord the king, so that they may make a compact with you, and that you may rule over all that your heart desires." So David sent Abner away, and he went in peace.

3:6–11 During the two-year conflict "between the house of Saul and the house of David" (v. 6), the real power behind Ish-Bosheth's claims was his father's cousin Abner. It was Abner who had initiated his relative's rise to the throne (cf. 2:8–9), and it was he who sustained it through his military exploits.

However, Abner's motives for supporting the dynastic claims of this younger member of his clan may have been less than selfless. Perhaps Abner saw in Ish-Bosheth a person who could be manipulated and otherwise controlled, with the result that he himself would be the de facto ruler over Israel. The text's observation that Abner "had been strengthening his own position in the house of Saul" suggests that he was preparing to usurp his nephew's throne.

Whether or not Abner was actively plotting to claim the throne of Israel, Ish-Bosheth believed he was and set about identifying "evidence" to prove it. The son of Saul concluded that his older relative had had sexual contact with "Rizpah daughter of Aiah," (v. 7), a concubine in Saul's harem. This act, if it had actually occurred, would mean that Abner was exercising a privilege reserved for the king and thus was using that action to proclaim himself king (cf. 2 Sam 16:21–22).

However, the Bible never affirms that Abner had a sexual relationship with

Rizpah, only that Ish-Bosheth accused him of it.[15] Abner became "very angry because of what Ish-Bosheth said" (v. 8). His reaction to the king's allegation suggests that he considered it to be without merit. To have used a royal concubine would have been an "offense"—an act of betrayal; it would be the equivalent of being "on Judah's side" and—from an ancient Semitic perspective—as despicable as being "a dog's head."[16] But Abner considered himself to be "loyal to the house" of Saul as well as "to his family and friends."

If in fact Abner was telling the truth, then Ish-Bosheth's apparently unfounded accusation suggests that he possessed the same tendency to misperceive reality that his father had. Like Saul, Ish-Bosheth falsely accused his most loyal and capable soldier of treason.[17]

Ish-Bosheth's incendiary words against his most crucial supporter spelled the end of Abner's efforts to maintain the Saulide regime's grip on power.[18] Ish-Bosheth was exhibiting his father's insane tendencies, and Abner did not wish to inflict a second Saul on the nation. From now on he would redirect his efforts to "do for David what the LORD promised him" (v. 9). Rather than contest David's claim for the divine right to rule Israel, he would vigorously support it. Abner would use the resources he possessed to "transfer the kingdom from the house of Saul and establish David's throne over Israel" (v. 10); he would see to it that David ruled "from Dan" in the far north of the Promised Land "to Beersheba" in the south.

Abner's exasperated outburst intimidated Ish-Bosheth, who was now deeply "afraid of" (v. 11) his relative. Rather than execute his highest-ranking general for treason, "he was unable [NIV, "did not dare"] to say another word" about the incident. Perhaps the king's display of weakness and lack of courage in this

---

[15] Brueggemann assumes Abner actually did have sexual relations with Saul's concubine, doing so as "a defiant public, political challenge" to Ish-Bosheth (*First and Second Samuel,* 226). In drawing this conclusion he creates the more difficult task of explaining how such a supposedly ambitious man could negotiate so quickly and submissively with David, an even more determined would-be king over all Israel.

[16] The Torah considered a dog to be unclean (cf. Lev 11:26–28), and the animal was generally despised in ancient Palestine. The aggressive nature of wild dogs as well as their tendency to rove in packs around the villages (cf. 2 Kgs 9:35–36) made them a dangerous nuisance. In addition, the habit of dogs eating their vomit (cf. Prov 26:11), as well as the homosexual tendencies of male dogs (cf. Deut 23:18) probably added to their disrepute. A supreme insult was to call someone a dog (cf. 1 Sam 17:43; 24:14; 2 Sam 9:8; 16:9; 2 Kgs 8:13).

[17] This interpretation disagrees with Brueggemann (*First and Second Samuel,* 225), who understands Abner to have indeed raped Rizpah.

[18] Youngblood states that "the devastating defeat of Ish-Bosheth's men by David's men (2:30–31) has made its impact on Saul's cousin Abner. Ruthless and ambitious, Abner is a canny politician who sees the handwriting on the wall. He therefore sets about to transfer Ish-Bosheth's kingdom over to David" ("1, 2 Samuel," 832). In light of 3:6–10, which is almost certainly intended to present the decisive motive behind Abner's move to support David, Youngblood's position must be rejected.

matter only reinforced Abner's determination to put a truly fit king on Israel's throne.

3:12–14 Following the dispute with Ish-Bosheth, Abner began carrying out the terms of his oath. However, the undertaking was a sensitive one and had to be carried out with considerable diplomacy. After all, he had led military campaigns against David's regime for two years and had killed one of David's close relatives (cf. 2:23). Rather than approach David directly, therefore, Abner initiated contact by means of "messengers" sent "on his behalf to David" (v. 12). Through these representatives he proposed that David "make an agreement" [lit., "cut a covenant"] with him: David had made and kept agreements with Benjamites before, and apparently Abner had confidence that David would do it again. If David did so, Abner would use his influence to "bring all Israel over to" his former rival.

The proposed accord seemed quite desirable to David, who saw in it the opportunity to accomplish through diplomacy what could not be done through warfare, the voluntary unification of the nation under David's rule. However, David attached one requirement to the agreement. His motivation behind this shrewd request for Michal's return is apparent: by reestablishing the marital link between David and the house of Saul, David was legally repositioning himself back into the house of Saul. Thus, he was legitimizing his claim of being qualified to rule over territories once ruled by Saul.

With Abner's backing, David coordinated his response to Abner with an ultimatum to Ish-Bosheth. In it he demanded that the king of Israel hand over his sister to David, who was in fact his brother-in-law. David reminded Ish-Bosheth that Michal was, after all, David's rightful wife since he had "betrothed" (v. 14) her by paying "the price of a hundred Philistine foreskins" (cf. 1 Sam 18:25–27).

Now the Torah prohibited men from taking back wives they had previously divorced (cf. Deut 24:1–4). At the same time, the biblical narrator consistently portrayed David as a man obedient to the Torah. Consequently, it seems reasonable to assume that David considered himself legally married to Michal since his days in Saul's royal court. Since he had never divorced Michal, her relationship with Paltiel was technically an adulterous one. Thus David's demand to have Michal returned amounted to an act designed to restore a state of righteousness in the land.[19]

3:15–16 Ish-Bosheth, who is portrayed throughout the narratives of chaps. 2–3 as a weak and passive figure, did not resist David's demand, perhaps in part because he recognized the sinfulness of his father's actions in separating Michal from David (cf. 1 Sam 25:44).

Ish-Bosheth's order was not without heart-rending consequences. Paltiel,

---

[19] Cf. Gordon for an affirmation of this position (*I and II Samuel,* 219).

who had cooperated with Saul in depriving David of his rightful wife years before, refused to give her up. Instead, he "went with her, weeping behind her all the way to Bahurim" (v. 16), a village northeast of Jerusalem near the border between Judah and Benjamin. At that point Abner, perhaps accompanied by an armed military contingent, forced Paltiel to "go back home." Reluctantly, Paltiel complied.

3:17–18 Abner's activities on David's behalf took a significant turn when he "conferred with the elders of Israel" (v. 17). Though the "elders" possessed less authority than the king in a monarchical governmental structure, they probably were more esteemed and influential within their respective tribes than the king. It was the tribal elders who had demanded the creation of an Israelite monarchy in the first place (cf. 1 Sam 8:4–5), and support of David would guarantee his recognition as king throughout Israel.

Playing on their anxieties regarding the Philistines and other foreign threats, Abner tactfully nudged the power brokers to [re!]consider anointing David as their king. Surely during the intervening years following Saul's death the other tribal leaders thoughtfully considered the advantages of following the tribe of Judah's lead in making David, the most successful military commander in Israel's history, their king. Abner encouraged them to stop thinking about it and "do it" (v. 18).

Abner bolstered his recommendation with a revelatory word not previously mentioned in 1, 2 Samuel and associated with David. According to Abner, the Lord had "promised David" that he would work through David's life and ministry to rescue Israel from the Philistines and their other enemies. The closest parallel to this is found in 1 Sam 9:16, where this prophetic language had applied to Saul. The reference to the Lord's decision to use David as the only human vehicle for achieving the elders' stated objective (cf. 1 Sam 8:20) reinforces the conclusion that the Lord had rejected Saul and selected David as the central human agent responsible for bringing deliverance to Israel.

While the biblical text does not indicate the elders' response to Abner's plea here, it is clear that his words had a positive effect. This same group affirmed David's divine right to rule over them and took part in his anointing (cf. 5:2–3).

3:19–21 In a more general sense "Abner also spoke to the Benjamites in person" (v. 19). A special meeting with this group was crucial, since their acceptance of David as king could be accomplished only when they rejected one of their own. Because Abner was one of the most respected and powerful Benjamites, his support of David would have been critical to the cause of making David king over Benjamin.

The text suggests that Abner scored diplomatic successes in both of his meetings because afterwards he "went to Hebron to tell David everything that Israel and the whole house of Benjamin wanted to do." Wisely, Abner chose not to enter the territory of Judah without a detachment of "twenty" (v. 20) soldiers;

after all, he was the supreme commander of troops officially at war with Judah.

David treated Abner and his men not as enemies but as honored guests at the royal residence and "prepared a feast" for them. Having concluded an upbeat *tête-à-tête* with David, Abner requested permission to complete the transfer of national power into David's hands. This would be accomplished by calling an all-Israelite assembly so that the nation could "make a compact [lit., "cut a covenant"] with" (v. 21) David. At the proposed convocation David would be given the right to "rule over all that" his "heart desires."

David wholeheartedly approved of Abner's plan and sent him away from the southern royal city "in peace."

(5) Joab Murders Abner (3:22–27)

[22]Just then David's men and Joab returned from a raid and brought with them a great deal of plunder. But Abner was no longer with David in Hebron, because David had sent him away, and he had gone in peace. [23]When Joab and all the soldiers with him arrived, he was told that Abner son of Ner had come to the king and that the king had sent him away and that he had gone in peace.

[24]So Joab went to the king and said, "What have you done? Look, Abner came to you. Why did you let him go? Now he is gone! [25]You know Abner son of Ner; he came to deceive you and observe your movements and find out everything you are doing."

[26]Joab then left David and sent messengers after Abner, and they brought him back from the well of Sirah. But David did not know it. [27]Now when Abner returned to Hebron, Joab took him aside into the gateway, as though to speak with him privately. And there, to avenge the blood of his brother Asahel, Joab stabbed him in the stomach, and he died.

3:22–25 Soon after David successfully concluded the delicate negotiations with Abner (v. 22) at Hebron, the king was greeted with more good news of Joab's return from a successful raid. The plunder was most appreciated since it funded David's governmental activities, including the payment of his troops and extending his influence throughout the territory. Since David had no administrative system for gathering income, he continued his earlier practice of conducting raids against Israel's enemies to create the necessary revenues (cf. 1 Sam 27:8–11; 30:26), just as the rival king Ish-Bosheth did (cf. 2 Sam 4:2).

However, when Joab learned of the negotiations with Abner (v. 23), he was livid. Abner was Joab's most hated enemy, especially because of his role in Asahel's death (cf. 2:23). Joab did not believe this rival general could be trusted to provide sincere support for David, since Abner was a member of Saul's family. Furthermore, Abner also was the single greatest threat to Joab's own position of supreme military leadership; it is almost certain that David would give Abner key military responsibilities in exchange for his help in becoming king over all Israel. As a result, he angrily berated David for letting Abner return unharmed to Benjamite territory. He accused Abner of dishonesty and suggested that the true purpose of his visit was to gain military intelligence (v. 25).

3:26–27 Without waiting for orders from David, Joab left the king's presence and initiated a secret plan designed to permanently eliminate Abner as a threat. First, he dispatched "messengers after Abner" (v. 26), apparently to tell Abner that David wanted to speak with him further. The messengers met up with the Saulide general less than two miles northwest of Hebron at "the well of Sirah" (modern Ain Sirah[?]). Succeeding in convincing him to return to Hebron, they "brought him back" without David's knowledge.

Meanwhile, Joab was lurking in the recesses of the fortified gate structure at the entrance to Hebron. As Abner entered the royal city, Joab stepped out and "took him aside into the gateway, as though to speak with him privately" (v. 27). Abner's guard was down at the time, in part because of the peace agreement he had just negotiated with David and in part because he was in a city of refuge (cf. Josh 21:13), where the Torah strictly prohibited vengeful violence (cf. Num 35:24–25) without due process of law.

There Joab murdered Abner to avenge his brother Asahel. Now the Torah did permit surviving adult males in a murder victim's family to kill the murderer of their kinsman if circumstantial evidence warranted and it could be demonstrated that the killer was motivated by malice aforethought (cf. Num 35:20–21). But the fact that Abner was fleeing from Asahel when death occurred as well as the fact that the deathblow was administered with the blunt end of a spear suggest that no malice aforethought motivated Abner's actions. Following the Torah-mandated trial (cf. Num 35:24), Abner probably would have been exonerated and permitted to live out his days in a city of refuge like Hebron (Num 35:25). Joab's actions against Abner were not only unwarranted but a flagrant violation of God's law.

(6) David Proves His Innocence in Abner's Death (3:28–39)

28Later, when David heard about this, he said, "I and my kingdom are forever innocent before the LORD concerning the blood of Abner son of Ner. 29May his blood fall upon the head of Joab and upon all his father's house! May Joab's house never be without someone who has a running sore or leprosy or who leans on a crutch or who falls by the sword or who lacks food."

30(Joab and his brother Abishai murdered Abner because he had killed their brother Asahel in the battle at Gibeon.)

31Then David said to Joab and all the people with him, "Tear your clothes and put on sackcloth and walk in mourning in front of Abner." King David himself walked behind the bier. 32They buried Abner in Hebron, and the king wept aloud at Abner's tomb. All the people wept also.

33The king sang this lament for Abner:

"Should Abner have died as the lawless die?
34Your hands were not bound,

your feet were not fettered.
You fell as one falls before wicked men."
And all the people wept over him again.

[35] Then they all came and urged David to eat something while it was still day; but David took an oath, saying, "May God deal with me, be it ever so severely, if I taste bread or anything else before the sun sets!"

[36] All the people took note and were pleased; indeed, everything the king did pleased them. [37] So on that day all the people and all Israel knew that the king had no part in the murder of Abner son of Ner.

[38] Then the king said to his men, "Do you not realize that a prince and a great man has fallen in Israel this day? [39] And today, though I am the anointed king, I am weak, and these sons of Zeruiah are too strong for me. May the LORD repay the evildoer according to his evil deeds!"

3:28–39 When David heard of this wanton act of violence against Abner (v. 28), as a proper king he was obligated to uphold the Torah guidelines (cf. Deut 17:18–19), which in this case had clearly been violated. Rather than overlook the actions of his close relative and commanding general, therefore, David distanced himself and the Lord's people from Joab and instead placed a curse on him. Announcing that "I and my kingdom are forever innocent before the LORD concerning the blood of Abner son of Ner," David prayed that Abner's blood might "fall upon the head of Joab and upon all his father's house" (v. 29). David then invoked a curse calling for a variety of disasters to inflict Joab's household. The calamities David mentioned—"a running sore or leprosy," having a family member "who leans on a crutch[20] or who falls by the sword or who lacks food"—are essentially a summary of the litany of Torah curses directed against Israelites who violated Yahweh's covenant (cf. Lev 26:14–39; Deut 28:15–68). On his deathbed David would later cite Joab's murder of Abner as one of two reasons for ordering his general's execution (cf. 1 Kgs 2:5–6).

3:30–31a Joab properly bore the brunt of responsibility for Abner's death. However, he had not acted alone; "his brother Abishai" assisted in the deed; perhaps Abishai had led the delegation that called Abner back to Hebron. David implicated others—"all the people with" (v. 31) Joab—as accessories in the murder as well.

David then forced all who participated in any manner in Abner's murder to deny their inclination to exult over his death. Instead, they must take the lead in a mournful observance of Abner's death that commemorated him as a national hero. Each co-conspirator had to rip his "clothes and put on sackcloth

---

[20] The popular translation of פֶּלֶךְ as "spindle" or "distaff" (cf. Baldwin, Gordon, NASB, GNB, etc.) should be rejected in favor of the NIV's option. While male effeminacy—implicit in the word "spindle" (an implement used in that society by women)—would certainly be viewed as a curse, it is not mentioned as one in the Torah; however, loss of physical health is explicitly mentioned (cf. Deut 28:22,59–60).

and walk in mourning in front of" the bier carrying Abner's body.

David had been traumatized by the shocking turn of events that day. It had begun with bright promises for national unity and peace, yet it ended with the threat of deepening national division and conflict; it began with the cementing of a friendship but ended with the burying of a friend. As has been the case throughout history, a despicable deed of personal vengeance put a crimson stain on the fabric of society and threatened to tear it apart.

In the midst of this dark series of events, however, the author subtly encourages the reader not to conclude that the Lord's will for David had been thwarted. For the first time in the biblical narrative—and in the very midst of Abner's funeral procession, at that—the writer calls David "the king" (Hb. *hammelek*) in a nonquotational clause. For the writer—and thus for the astute reader—this tragedy transformed David; it provided a forum in which he could display his truly regal nature, and neither he nor the nation would ever be the same again. To reinforce David's new identity, the writer would refer to David as "the king" five more times in the next seven verses—only twice in those verses does he use David's personal name. Ironically, Abner did bring the kingdom to David.

3:31b–35 David played the most memorable role in Abner's funeral. Besides walking immediately "behind the bier" (v. 31) of his friend during the procession to the burial site, he "wept aloud at Abner's tomb" (v. 32)—an undignified but deeply touching form of conduct for a king. In addition, David composed and sang a "lament for Abner" (v. 33). The song highlights the heinous circumstances of Abner's death and vilifies his killers, calling them "wicked men" (v. 34). The power of the king's impassioned art overwhelmed "all the people," who "wept over" Abner again.

As if these previous actions on David's part were not enough, the king also took an oath to fast during the remainder of the daylight hours. Even as Abner's death had deprived David of the kingdom-sustaining help of his new ally, so it would also deprive him of food, the sustaining strength of his body. This form of self-denial out of respect for a dead opponent was certainly contrary to custom. In spite of the urging of "all the people" (NIV, "all"; v. 35), David refused to "taste bread or anything else" prior to sunset.

3:36–39 David's sincere yet astute actions did not go unnoticed by "all the people" (v. 36)—particularly the northern soldiers who had accompanied Abner on his peace mission to Hebron. David's respectful treatment of their slain leader, as well as "everything the king did" generally, "pleased them." As a result they concluded that "the king had no part in the murder of Abner son of Ner" (v. 37).

This conclusion was reinforced by David's prosaic tribute to Abner in which the king proclaimed him "a prince and a great man" (v. 38). The term translated in the NIV as "prince" (Hb. *śar*) is generally employed in the Hebrew to indicate an appointed leader, especially a military commander (cf. 4:2; 1 Sam 17:18)—not a direct descendant of the king.

David also contrasted his style of leadership as Israel's "anointed king" with that of Joab and Abishai, the "sons of Zeruiah" (v. 39). Whereas they were rash and rough (NIV, "strong"), David was sensitive and restrained (NIV, "weak"). He explicitly rejected their approach as being excessive. No doubt David's comments were meant to reassure the Israelites who had not yet accepted him as their king that he would avoid a bloody purge of those who had resisted his claim of sovereignty over all Israel.

(7) Recab and Baanah Murder Ish-Bosheth (4:1–7)

[1]When Ish-Bosheth son of Saul heard that Abner had died in Hebron, he lost courage, and all Israel became alarmed. [2]Now Saul's son had two men who were leaders of raiding bands. One was named Baanah and the other Recab; they were sons of Rimmon the Beerothite from the tribe of Benjamin—Beeroth is considered part of Benjamin, [3]because the people of Beeroth fled to Gittaim and have lived there as aliens to this day.

[4](Jonathan son of Saul had a son who was lame in both feet. He was five years old when the news about Saul and Jonathan came from Jezreel. His nurse picked him up and fled, but as she hurried to leave, he fell and became crippled. His name was Mephibosheth.)

[5]Now Recab and Baanah, the sons of Rimmon the Beerothite, set out for the house of Ish-Bosheth, and they arrived there in the heat of the day while he was taking his noonday rest. [6]They went into the inner part of the house as if to get some wheat, and they stabbed him in the stomach. Then Recab and his brother Baanah slipped away.

[7]They had gone into the house while he was lying on the bed in his bedroom. After they stabbed and killed him, they cut off his head. Taking it with them, they traveled all night by way of the Arabah.

4:1–3 The death of Abner meant the end of Ish-Bosheth's ability to retain the throne of Israel. Now no effective military opposition could be mounted against David's forces in the battle for control of the northern tribal areas. Furthermore, without Abner, Ish-Bosheth would be unable to fulfill the primary mandate Israel's elders had placed on their king; he could no longer go out before Israel and fight their battles (cf. 1 Sam 8:20). As a result, "all Israel became alarmed" (v. 1).

In this moment of vulnerability, Recab and Baanah, two of Ish-Bosheth's lesser military commanders, decided to use the king's reversal of fortunes to their advantage. Their responsibilities as "leaders of raiding bands" (v. 2) in Ish-Bosheth's army probably were identical to that of Joab's in David's army (cf. 3:22)—to fund the Israelite government by plundering nearby foreign settlements.

These two Benjamites had originated from Beeroth (modern Khirbet el-

Burj?), a former Gibeonite settlement located approximately four miles northwest of Jerusalem. They were descended from a family of Benjamites that had helped resettle Beeroth (cf. Josh 9:16–18) after the original inhabitants were forced to move to Gittaim, a less desirable location.[21]

4:4 The most important event of chap. 4 is the death of Ish-Bosheth. But in order to dispel the notion that might arise in the reader's mind that Ish-Bosheth's death meant the final destruction of the Saulide family, the writer inserts here a note concerning Mephibosheth, son of "Jonathan son of Saul." When Mephibosheth, known outside of 2 Samuel as Merib-Baal (cf. 1 Chr 8:34; 9:40), was "five years old," his father died (cf. 1 Sam 31:2) on the battlefield. In the ensuing chaos of a hasty flight from Philistines at the royal palace in Gibeah, Mephibosheth was inadvertently dropped by "his nurse," so that he "became crippled." The resulting permanent disability would play a role later in shaping the events of 2 Samuel (cf. 9:1–13; 16:1–4; 19:24–30).

4:5–7 Recab and Baanah returned to Ish-Bosheth's royal residence in Mahanaim. Entering the residence unhindered[22] under the premise they were getting "some wheat" (v. 6) from an interior storeroom, they entered Ish-Bosheth's bedroom instead. Once there they "stabbed him in the stomach" and then "cut off his head" (v. 7), a pair of actions designed not only to produce a quick and certain death but also to provide proof of the monarch's death. The circumstances of Ish-Bosheth's death are highlighted by repeating them with expansions in v. 7.[23]

With their gruesome trophy in hand, Recab and Baanah "traveled all night by way of the Arabah" (v. 7), a desolate pathway extending south from Mahanaim in the Jordan rift valley north of the Dead Sea. The men's timing and route permitted them to avoid detection by forces loyal to the house of Saul and at the same time arrive in Hebron as quickly as possible.

(8) David Executes Ish-Bosheth's Murderers (4:8–12)

[8]They brought the head of Ish-Bosheth to David at Hebron and said to the king, "Here is the head of Ish-Bosheth son of Saul, your enemy, who tried to take your life. This day the LORD has avenged my lord the king against Saul and his offspring."

---

[21] Noth's hypothesis that Recab and Baanah were vengeance-seeking Gibeonites serving in Ish-Bosheth's army is without merit, since the explicit claim of the text is that they were "sons of Rimmon . . . from the tribe of Benjamin" (v. 2). Cf. M. Noth, *The History of Israel,* trans. P. R. Ackroyd (New York: Harper & Row, 1960), 186.

[22] The LXX notes that a female doorkeeper had fallen asleep, thereby permitting Recab and Baanah to enter the palace undetected. Cf. RSV, Gordon's discussion favoring this (*I and II Samuel,* 222–23), and McCarter's translation and ensuing discussion (*II Samuel,* 123, 127–28).

[23] This narrative technique is frequently employed at significant actional moments in biblical Hebrew (cf. Gen 1:27; 7:11; Josh 4:10–11; 1 Sam 17:50).

[9]David answered Recab and his brother Baanah, the sons of Rimmon the Beerothite, "As surely as the LORD lives, who has delivered me out of all trouble, [10]when a man told me, 'Saul is dead,' and thought he was bringing good news, I seized him and put him to death in Ziklag. That was the reward I gave him for his news! [11]How much more—when wicked men have killed an innocent man in his own house and on his own bed—should I not now demand his blood from your hand and rid the earth of you!"

[12]So David gave an order to his men, and they killed them. They cut off their hands and feet and hung the bodies by the pool in Hebron. But they took the head of Ish-Bosheth and buried it in Abner's tomb at Hebron.

4:8 When Recab and Baanah reached Hebron, they went with pride straight "to David" with "the head of Ish-Bosheth." The men showed no signs of remorse for their murderous deed and apparently believed that they were serving as the Lord's agents of divine vengeance "against Saul and his offspring." Whatever their thinking may have been, they were crediting God with what was in fact a vile, sinful deed. No doubt they believed that a handsome reward awaited them for their success in eliminating this rival claimant to Israel's throne.

4:9–11 But the men's confident expectations were not based on an accurate understanding of David's respect for Saul and his family (cf. 1 Sam 24:12; 26:9–11; 2 Sam 1:14–16) or his commitment to the royal responsibility of upholding the teachings of the Torah (cf. Deut 17:19). Rather than commending and rewarding the men, David obligated himself by an oath in the Lord's name to "demand" their lives in punishment for their murder of Ish-Bosheth (v. 11).

David's decision to put the murderers to death was consistent with his previous treatment of the Amalekite who had sought an audience with David "in Ziklag" (v. 10) to announce his role in killing Saul (cf. 1:14–16). It was also consistent with Torah demands regarding "wicked men" who "have killed an innocent man in his own house and on his own bed" (cf. Gen 9:6; Exod 21:12; Lev 24:17; Num 35:31).

David did not want the help of murderous conspirators in furthering his career. Instead, he desired a career that was conceived and perfected by "the LORD" who "lives" (v. 9). In the past it was the Lord who had "delivered" David "out of all trouble," and David would now rely on the Lord—not Recab and Baanah—to bring him to an even higher level of success.

4:12 David had rendered his judgment on Recab and Baanah; now it was time to act. To express the fact that Recab and Baanah died under a divine curse (cf. Deut 21:22–23), David had his men "cut off their hands and feet" and then hang "the bodies by the pool in Hebron." By contrast, David showed respect for his murdered brother-in-law by burying Ish-Bosheth's head "in Abner's tomb at Hebron."

4. All the Tribes of Israel Anoint David King at Hebron (5:1–5)

[1] All the tribes of Israel came to David at Hebron and said, "We are your own flesh and blood. [2] In the past, while Saul was king over us, you were the one who led Israel on their military campaigns. And the LORD said to you, 'You will shepherd my people Israel, and you will become their ruler.'"

[3] When all the elders of Israel had come to King David at Hebron, the king made a compact with them at Hebron before the LORD, and they anointed David king over Israel.

[4] David was thirty years old when he became king, and he reigned forty years. [5] In Hebron he reigned over Judah seven years and six months, and in Jerusalem he reigned over all Israel and Judah thirty-three years.

5:1–2 Credible opposition to David's claim to kingship over all Israel died with Abner and Ish-Bosheth. Making David Israel's next monarch thus became Israel's only rational alternative. This conclusion was strengthened by four factors: David's impressive record of military successes while in service to Saul (cf. 1 Sam 18:13–14,30–31), prophetic revelations regarding David's destiny as Israel's leader (cf. 1 Sam 16:1; 2 Sam 3:9,18), Abner's endorsement of him (cf. 3:9–10,17–18), and his respectful treatment of the slain leaders of the Saulide dynasty (3:28–35; 4:12).

Israel's elders were aware of a word from the Lord revealing that David would "shepherd my people Israel" (v. 2). The text of the prophecy avoided calling David Israel's king; instead, it termed him a "ruler" (Hb. $n\bar{a}g\hat{\imath}d$), a term previously used to refer to Saul in his role as Israel's divinely appointed leader (cf. 1 Sam 9:16). Though the prophetic revelation regarding David in v. 2 was not presented in the preceding narratives, it is consistent with other biblical claims relating to him (cf. 1 Sam 13:14; 25:30; Ps 78:71).

The Lord's words must have been reassuring to the elders of Israel. First of all, the oracle affirmed that Israel was the Lord's possession—literally, "my people"; no earthly king could own them. Second, it stated that David's assigned role was that of "shepherd," that is, one appointed to defend, lead, and tend to the needs of those for whom he was responsible. The king-as-shepherd image has paternalistic overtones; shepherds are responsible for sheep, not sheep for the shepherd.

5:3 For these reasons and perhaps more, "all the elders of Israel" journeyed to David's capital city of Hebron to install him as their new king. There in the city of his royal residence David "made a compact" (lit., "cut a covenant") with these official representatives of all the tribes. The ceremony was carried out "before the LORD," suggesting that the ceremony was as religious in nature as it was political; in such a case, members of the Aaronic priesthood residing in Hebron would have played a significant role in the event. Following the ratification of the formal agreement, David was "anointed . . . king over Israel," an act probably performed by an authorized religious leader.

5:4–5   A formulaic insertion reflective of those of other kings (cf. 1 Sam 13:1; 2 Sam 2:10) notes that David came to occupy the Israelites' most powerful political position when he "was thirty years old" (v. 4). The total number of years he functioned as king over any part of Israel was "forty years." Seven and a half of those years David was king "over Judah" while he was "in Hebron" (v. 5). The balance of the time, "thirty-three years," was spent "in Jerusalem," from which David "reigned over all Israel and Judah." The proleptic mention of David reigning as king in Jerusalem anticipates the narrative of vv. 6–9. It also reinforces the impression that David's first act as king over all Israel was the establishment of a capital city in northern territory.

5. The Lord Blesses David (5:6–10:19)

This section of 1, 2 Samuel presents the apex of David's career. Here David conquers Jerusalem, the crown jewel of the Promised Land. Here also David establishes an effective administrative system and leads Israel to victory over all their enemies. David's virtue is also showcased as he fulfills his commitment to Jonathan by caring for his fallen comrade's only son, Mephibosheth. Most significantly, in a passage that has major implications for the Christian community, the Lord establishes an eternal covenant with David's family line.

In these chapters David is furthermore portrayed as the founder of the long-ago-prophesied worship center where the Lord would cause his name to dwell (cf. Deut 12:5). It is in this section also that David brings the ark of the covenant to Jerusalem and initiates the practice of offering blood sacrifices to the Lord there.

(1) David Conquers Jerusalem (5:6–8)

⁶The king and his men marched to Jerusalem to attack the Jebusites, who lived there. The Jebusites said to David, "You will not get in here; even the blind and the lame can ward you off." They thought, "David cannot get in here." ⁷Nevertheless, David captured the fortress of Zion, the City of David.

⁸On that day, David said, "Anyone who conquers the Jebusites will have to use the water shaft to reach those 'lame and blind' who are David's enemies." That is why they say, "The 'blind and lame' will not enter the palace."

5:6–8   As presented by the writer, David's first recorded act as king over united Israel was to establish a capital city that reflected the emerging national identity. Though Hebron, a city located deep within Judahite territory, had served David well for seven and a half years, maintaining it as the capital of all Israel would have implied a governmental bias for Judah that would have alienated the other tribes from their king and made a truly united nation much more difficult to achieve. Wisely, David chose to make Jerusalem, a city that bordered Judah but was technically in the territorial inheritance of the northern tribe of Benjamin (cf. Josh 18:28), his capital city. David's selection of a northern city for the national capital would have appeared to the non-Judahite tribes as a significant concession on his part and would have ingratiated the peoples to him.[24]

Of course, David's decision concerning Jerusalem was not without its challenges: this city in the south-central highlands of Israel was inhabited by Jebusites, a banned Canaanite group (cf. Exod 23:23; 33:2; 34:11; Deut 7:1–2; 20:17) whom Israelites of previous generations had unsuccessfully attempted to eradicate (cf. Josh 15:63; Judg 1:21). Thus, for David to make Jerusalem Israel's capital he first had to conquer it. Mustering his troops, "the king and his men marched to Jerusalem to attack the Jebusites who lived there" (v. 6).[25]

But there was a second, even more important reason for David to choose Jerusalem as his capital. For the Former Prophets, the standard for evaluating a king's reign was his obedience to the Lord (cf. 1 Kgs 15:3,11,26; 16:2, etc.). By David making his first recorded act as Israel's king that of fulfilling the long-neglected Torah command to dispossess the Jebusites and of reinitiating the crusade to eradicate them from the land (cf. Exod 23:23–24; Deut 7:1–2; 20:17), he was demonstrating his continuity with Moses and establishing himself as a king devoted to the Lord's demands (cf. Deut 17:19). David's courageous and immediate attention to this detail of the Torah reinforces the writer's thesis that David was indeed a man after God's own heart (cf. 1 Sam 13:14; 1 Kgs 11:4; also Acts 13:22). Jerusalem would become a trophy of obedience to the Lord for David and his descendants.

David's conquest of the Jebusites required him to deal with some daunting geographic obstacles. The relatively small walled city[26] was located atop the southeastern promontory of a steep, finger-shaped hill and was surrounded on three sides by valleys. It was located adjacent to a perennial spring (the Gihon) and was so well-protected by both natural and man-made

---

[24] Youngblood wrongly asserts that Jerusalem was a border city not included in the territories of any tribe and was thus "tied to no tribe" ("1, 2 Samuel," 855). In fact, Josh 18:28 explicitly places it in Benjamin.

[25] W. G. E. Watson suggests that the phrase הַיְבֻסִי יוֹשֵׁב הָאָרֶץ be emended, with the resulting translation "the Jebusite ruler of the city" ("David Ousts the City Ruler of Jebus," *VT* 20 [1970]: 501–2). The proposal unnecessarily complicates matters, for the parallel passage in 1 Chr 11:4–5 unambiguously means "the Jebusite[s] living [in] the land."

[26] Jebus covered approximately twelve acres. For further information on the archaeology of Jebusite Jerusalem, cf. K. Kenyon, *Digging up Jerusalem* (London: Benn, 1974), 83–97; B. Mazar, "Jerusalem in the Biblical Period," in *Jerusalem Revealed: Archaeology in the Holy City 1968–1974*, ed. Y. Yadin (New Haven: Yale University Press, 1976); and Y. Shiloh, *Excavations at the City of David 1978–1982*, Qedem Monograph (Jerusalem: Hebrew University, 1984); and Baldwin, *1 and 2 Samuel*, 199–202.

defenses that the Jebusites taunted David by saying that "even the blind and the lame can ward you off."[27] However, their derisive words proved premature because "David captured the fortress of Zion" (v. 7). "Zion" (meaning unknown) was apparently the Jebusite name for the hill and thus the walled portion of the hilltop Jebusite settlement. The narrative's lack of detail regarding Jerusalem's defeat—surprising for an event of such monumental significance—focuses the reader's attention on one fact: "David captured the fortress of Zion."

David's conquest of the city was considered a military marvel; his strategy is apparently delineated in v. 8. The NIV suggests that after examining the city's defenses, David concluded that "anyone who conquers the Jebusites will have to use the water shaft" (v. 8). The Hebrew text of this verse is fraught with difficulties, the major one being the meaning of *ṣinnôr;* suggested translations include "water shaft" (NIV), "grappling-iron" (NEB), "dagger" (LXX), "trident," "joint," "neck," and "windpipe."[28] Of all possibilities the NIV's rendering is the most popular today (cf. NASB, NRSV, NKJV, NLT) and apparently is corroborated by archaeological evidence.

If "water shaft" is the correct translation, then the reference may be to "Warren's tunnel," a narrow vertical shaft forty-nine feet long dug through rock, providing residents of the Zion fortress access to waters from the Gihon spring during times of siege.[29] Though difficult to climb, it proved to be the Achilles heel of the Jebusite fortress. Once key members of David's strike force had successfully entered the city by means of the shaft and secured this passageway, others would have poured into the heart of the city and brought about its subjugation.

In insulting David, the Jebusites had implicitly compared themselves to "the blind and the lame" (v. 6). David appears to have taken this as a Jebusite self-designation and used it to mock them in his statements found in v. 8; it is the "lame and blind who are David's enemies" (lit., "the hated ones of David's soul"). Furthermore, though not all Jebusites were killed in battle (cf. 24:16–24), the survivors were denied entry to "the house" (NIV, "palace"). The "house" may refer either to David's royal residence, that is, the entirety of the former Jebusite fortress, or perhaps a Yahwistic sanctuary. Especially in view of the context of this statement and because of his treat-

---

[27] H. P. Smith asserts that "in derision, the walls were manned by cripples" (*Samuel,* 287). That contention assumes that the Jebusites' taunt was intended to be taken literally—a possibility that can neither be affirmed nor denied.

[28] Y. Yadin, *The Art of Biblical Warfare* (New York: McGraw Hill, 1963), 268; W. F. Albright, "The *Ṣinnôr* in the Story of David's Capture of Jerusalem," *JPOS* 2 (1922): 286–90; McCarter (*II Samuel,* 140).

[29] For further information, cf. Kenyon, *The Bible and Recent Archaeology,* rev. ed. (Atlanta: John Knox, 1987), 92.

ment of the lame Mephibosheth (cf. 9:3–13), this verse cannot mean that David had contempt for physically challenged individuals.[30]

(2) The Lord Blesses David as King in Jerusalem (5:9–16)

⁹David then took up residence in the fortress and called it the City of David. He built up the area around it, from the supporting terraces inward. ¹⁰And he became more and more powerful, because the LORD God Almighty was with him.

¹¹Now Hiram king of Tyre sent messengers to David, along with cedar logs and carpenters and stonemasons, and they built a palace for David. ¹²And David knew that the LORD had established him as king over Israel and had exalted his kingdom for the sake of his people Israel.

¹³After he left Hebron, David took more concubines and wives in Jerusalem, and more sons and daughters were born to him. ¹⁴These are the names of the children born to him there: Shammua, Shobab, Nathan, Solomon, ¹⁵Ibhar, Elishua, Nepheg, Japhia, ¹⁶Elishama, Eliada and Eliphelet.

5:9–10 In renaming the conquered city after himself, David was following an Israelite practice first evidenced in the Torah (cf. Num 32:41–42; also 2 Sam 12:28).

David's decision to make Jerusalem the central administrative city for all Israel would mean that the twelve-acre site enclosed by the original Jebusite walls would not suffice for the buildings and population that would be needed. As a consequence, "he built up the area around" the fortress area, "from the *millô'* inward." The Hebrew term translates literally as "the filling" (NIV, "supporting terraces")[31] and suggests that part of David's project included bringing dirt and rock to the hilltop and depositing these inside massive cliffside retaining walls in order to create a larger, more level surface on which Jerusalem could be constructed.

David's unbroken string of successes both politically and militarily meant that he was becoming "more and more powerful" (v. 10). Yet the source of the king's success was not his personal competence or ingenuity. As both he (cf. Ps 23:4) and the narrator were careful to note, it was "because the LORD God

---

[30] Contra Gordon's interpretation of this passage (*I and II Samuel*, 51) and Brueggemann (*First and Second Samuel*, 241), who contrasts the "old Jerusalem of this text," in which "the blind and lame are excluded and despised," with "the new Jerusalem envisioned by the gospel," in which "all are welcomed and the blind and lame are transformed into full, welcomed, participants." Brueggemann's portrayal ignores some relevant facts: not only did David provide Mephibosheth, the nation's most famous invalid, with the practical status of a prince in Jerusalem (cf. 9:10,13), but Jesus unapologetically made conditional exclusion from the new Jerusalem a permanent feature in the landscape of Christian theology (cf. Matt 13:41–42,49–50; 25:41–46).

[31] L. E. Stager takes a minority position in rejecting the view that the *millo'* was a supporting terrace ("The Archaeology of the East Slope of Jerusalem and the Terraces of the Kidron," *JNES* 41 [1982]: 111–21). However, he has no firm opinion about what it might be.

Almighty was with him" (cf. also 1 Sam 18:12,14,28).

5:11–12 One measure of David's growing reputation is the fact that a regional monarch, "Hiram king of Tyre, sent" an ambassadorial delegation (Hb. *malʾākîm*) to David at Jerusalem (v. 11). Accompanying this official party was a group of skilled "carpenters and stonemasons," as well as a supply of "cedar logs." These human and material resources were used to build "a house [NIV, "palace"] for David" in the expanding city.

Hiram's generous gifts to David, coming as they were from one of the historically most powerful city-states of the eastern Mediterranean seaboard, helped David to know that the Lord "had exalted his kingdom." But David also understood that he had not received this unparalleled success so that he might experience personal aggrandizement; rather it was "for the sake of his [= the Lord's] people Israel." Some scholars believe that Hiram's gift may have come to David as many as twenty-five years after he had become Israel's king.[32]

5:13–16 A further evidence of David's increasing power, success, and divine blessing was the growth of the royal family. Probably in an effort to cement relationships with leading families of the various Israelite tribes, "David took more concubines and wives in Jerusalem" (v. 13). By marrying into the various families and then bringing the newly acquired wives to Jerusalem, he was giving the most influential families throughout the nation a stake in his success: the king's success was their success.

In order for David's strategy to succeed, it was necessary that each new wife and concubine be treated properly. This meant that each member of his harem be given a proper residence in the city of David—hence the need for a new palace and additional buildings—but also that each one have the privilege of giving birth to a royal son or daughter.

Elsewhere in Scripture (1 Chr 3:5) Shammua (or Shimea), Shobab, Nathan, and Solomon were noted to be sons of Bathsheba. No indication is given here or elsewhere in Scripture about the names of the women who bore the remaining children.

The list provided here is the shortest of three canonical lists of children born to David while he was in Jerusalem (cf. also 1 Chr 3:5–9; 14:4–6). Added to one or both of the other lists are Nogah and a second Eliphelet/Elpelet. In 1 Chr

---

[32] This is the position of Youngblood ("1, 2 Samuel," 853). Gordon notes that "Hiram I of Tyre did not become king until about 969 BC," which if true would necessitate the events of this section being placed very late in—if not past the end of!—David's reign (*I and II Samuel*, 228). I personally see no compelling reason to date this event in the latter portion of David's kingship. It certainly must have been built prior to 7:1–2. The assumption of a royal residence at the time of the ark's entrance into Jerusalem (6:20), as well as the existence of an inside location for a table large enough to accommodate David, his sons, and Mephibosheth (9:11), suggests the palace was built early rather than late in David's reign.

3:6 Elishua is called Elishama; in 14:6 Eliada is called Beeliada.[33]

The large number of children, particularly sons, born to David while he was in Jerusalem—five more than were mentioned in connection with Hebron—suggests that the Lord blessed David richly in this location and that the divine blessings bestowed at Jerusalem exceeded those given at Hebron. This is in keeping with the Torah teaching that productive wombs are a blessing resulting from obedience to the Lord's commands (cf. Lev 26:9; Deut 28:11); David's obedience in dispossessing the Jebusites resulted in increased numbers of offspring. The fact that David's successor (Solomon) was among those born in Jerusalem adds to the impression that the writer is using David's descendant list here to emphasize the divine blessing associated with the conquest of Jerusalem. At the same time, one cannot fail to hear in this passage—especially in the phrase "David took more concubines and wives" (v. 13)—another, more troubling message. True to Samuel's prophetic words, David had become a king who took the nation's daughters (1 Sam 8:13). In his acquisitions he came perilously close to violating the Torah's prohibition against taking many wives (Deut 17:17). In fact, it was his unauthorized acquisition of a wife that shattered his regency and took away still greater blessings that could have been his.

(3) David Defeats the Philistines Twice (5:17–25)

[17]When the Philistines heard that David had been anointed king over Israel, they went up in full force to search for him, but David heard about it and went down to the stronghold. [18]Now the Philistines had come and spread out in the Valley of Rephaim; [19]so David inquired of the LORD, "Shall I go and attack the Philistines? Will you hand them over to me?"

The LORD answered him, "Go, for I will surely hand the Philistines over to you."

[20]So David went to Baal Perazim, and there he defeated them. He said, "As waters break out, the LORD has broken out against my enemies before me." So that place was called Baal Perazim. [21]The Philistines abandoned their idols there, and David and his men carried them off.

[22]Once more the Philistines came up and spread out in the Valley of Rephaim; [23]so David inquired of the LORD, and he answered, "Do not go straight up, but circle around behind them and attack them in front of the balsam trees. [24]As soon as you hear the sound of marching in the tops of the balsam trees, move quickly, because that will mean the LORD has gone out in front of you to strike the Philistine

---

[33] Youngblood asserts that Beeliada (= "Baal/Owner/Master knows") was "doubtless the original name" ("1, 2 Samuel," 860). Should this speculation be true, it demonstrates that the writer of 1, 2 Samuel had at his disposal two substitutionary options for dealing with the theophoric element Baal: בֹּשֶׁת ("shame") and אֵל ("God"). Interestingly, the former option was reserved for the house of Saul, while the latter (more favorable) option was used with the house of David. As such it represents yet one more means of reinforcing the writer's contention that David was indeed the man after Yahweh's heart.

army." [25]So David did as the LORD commanded him, and he struck down the Philistines all the way from Gibeon to Gezer.

5:17 At an early but unspecified time after David was anointed king over all Israel—[34]prior to the building of David's palace in Jerusalem, "the Philistines" learned of David's change in status. During his seven years at Hebron they had considered him something of an ally, since he technically was at war with Israel's dynastic family. But when Ish-Bosheth died and David became Israel's king, the Philistine perception of him changed dramatically.

Now the focus of the Philistine military resources became eliminating David. As a result, "they went up in full force to search for him." Therefore "David heard about it and went down to the stronghold," probably the recently captured Jebusite fortress located within Jerusalem.[35]

5:18–21 The Philistines "spread out in the Valley of Rephaim," a steep-walled canyon less than a mile southwest of David's new home. The writer carefully notes that David "inquired of the Lord" (v. 19) before making the decision to attack the Philistines. Unlike Saul, he was careful to determine the Lord's will concerning any offensive action. David's inquiry into the divine will implicitly occurred with the assistance of an Aaronic priest (cf. 1 Sam 22:15; 23:2–6; 30:8), at least this is how David did it in every other recorded instance after Abiathar's entrance into David's ranks.

Thus the writer effectively credits David with the first employment of an Aaronic priest for sacerdotal activities in Jerusalem. This latter fact would doubtless have been of significance to the writer, who was careful to portray

---

[34] H. P. Smith (*Samuel*, 290) and C. Hauer ("Jerusalem, the Stronghold and Rephaim," *CBQ* 32 [1970]: 571–78) assume that David's encounters with the Philistines recorded in 5:17–25 occurred prior to his conquest of Jerusalem. In view of the author's placement of these narrative accounts after the account of Jerusalem's conquest and without indications otherwise, we may assume that these events occurred after David conquered Jerusalem.

[35] Disagreement exists concerning the location of "the fortress." H. W. Hertzberg (*I and II Samuel*, OTL [Philadelphia: Westminster, 1964], 275) believes it was Jerusalem. A commonly held scholarly view understands the site to be the same one David occupied during his flight from Saul (cf. 1 Sam 22:4–5; 24:22). The primary reason for accepting this view seems to be the author's employment of the verbal root יָרַד (= "went down"), assuming David could not descend to Zion. This conclusion ignores the fact that elsewhere in the OT יָרַד may refer to movement other than to a lower elevation (cf. Num 34:11; 1 Kgs 22:2; 2 Kgs 2:1–3). In a number of cases יָרַד means that only the initial part of a journey involved some loss of elevation. Therefore it is quite possible that David moved his camp from a nearby hill to a location within Zion itself. Alternatively, it may suggest that David moved from a camp north of and just outside of the Jebusite walled city into the fortress itself. Those who accept the view that the fortress refers to a site south of Bethlehem also assume that chronological displacement has occurred in the narrative, with the events of 5:17–25 occurring prior to David's conquest of Jerusalem. Cf. J. R. Vannoy, "Notes on 2 Samuel," NIVSB, ed. K. Barker (Grand Rapids: Zondervan, 1985), 431; H. P. Smith, *Samuel*, 290; McCarter, *II Samuel*, 157–58. It is more likely that the fortress is Zion, primarily because of references to the Valley of Rephaim and Gibeon (vv. 18,22,25), both of which are locations near Jerusalem.

David as the human agent responsible for establishing Jerusalem as the dwelling place for the Lord's name.

The Lord responded favorably to David's questions, commanding David to "go" and assuring him of victory over the Philistines. Accordingly, David went to a site of unknown provenance in the vicinity of the Valley of Rephaim, where he defeated the Philistines handily. David's attack was so successful and the enemy's retreat so hurried that "the Philistines abandoned their idols" [ʿăṣabbêhem, lit., "their grievous things"] there" (v. 21), a counterpoint to what the Israelites had done in a battle against the Philistines in a former generation (cf. 1 Sam 4:11). Following the battle, David named the location of the hostilities "Baal Perazim" (lit., "Lord of the breakings forth")[36] because "the LORD has broken out against my enemies before me." The king and his men also removed the idols from the territory, in keeping with the Torah command to rid the Promised Land of such offensive objects (cf. Num 33:52; Deut 7:5,25; 12:3). Though no mention is made of what David and his men did with the idols, it seems safe to assume they destroyed them.

5:22–25 Not to be deterred from their efforts to remove David as a threat to Philistine domination in the region, the Philistines gathered once again in the same place. David's first response to the renewed Philistine aggression was to inquire again of the Lord, no doubt with the aid of an Aaronic priest. The Lord affirmed David's inclination to fight the Philistines; in fact, he provided David with a strategy for victory as well as the promise of a miraculous intervention that would result in a resounding victory for Israel.

The Lord ordered David to use a tactic that maximized the element of surprise while at the same time cutting off the Philistines' only avenue of retreat. Israel's army was to "circle around behind" (v. 23) the Philistines and then "attack them in front of the balsam trees" (bĕkāʾîm).[37] There they were to delay the attack, however, until they heard "the sound of marching in the tops" of the vegetation (v. 24). This phenomenon, somewhat reminiscent of God's timely provision of thunder prior to another Israelite attack against the Philistines (1 Sam 7:10), may have been accomplished through an unusually strong gust of wind or through some more spectacular divine intervention in the natural order. Regardless, it was to be understood as a definite sign that the Lord had

---

[36] A. Mazar tentatively identifies Baal Perazim with Giloh, some four miles southwest of Jerusalem ("Giloh: An Early Settlement Near Jerusalem," *IEJ* 31 [1981]: 1–36).

[37] The NIV's translation of בְּכָאִים as "balsam trees" must be rejected. As has been helpfully pointed out by my late friend John Hunt, Josephus (*Ant.* VII.4.1) states that David's men were in the "grove of weeping" and furthermore that balsam was not introduced to Israel until the time of Sheba's visit to Solomon (*Ant.* VIII.6.6). Whether or not Josephus was correct, modern lexicographers (cf. *CHAL*, s.v. בָּכָא) also reject the translation "balsam tree." Versions and commentators have proposed various translations (e.g., KJV, NKJV, "mulberry"; REB, "aspen"; LXX, "[place of] weeping"; McCarter, "[asherahs of] Bachaim" [*2 Samuel*, 150]). For the present, it seems, the meaning of this term is lost.

"gone out in front of" (v. 24) his earthly forces "to strike the Philistine army." In language reflecting descriptions of the obedient heroes of the Torah (e.g., Noah, Gen 7:9,16; Abraham, Gen 21:4; and Moses, Exod 7:6), "David did as the LORD commanded him" (v. 25). The results of David's obedience were spectacular: he and his forces "struck down the Philistines all the way from Geba [NIV, "Gibeon"] to Gezer," a westward trek of more than twenty miles.

Especially significant in this event is that David deferred his attack until the Lord had gone out in front of Israel. In so doing, he was charting a course for the nation that differed fundamentally from the one the people had proposed during the days of Samuel. Previously the Israelites had asked to "be like all the other nations," with an earthly "king to lead us and to go out before us to fight our battles" (1 Sam 8:20). Under David's leadership (as under Moses' and Joshua's before him), the Lord—not a mortal king—would go out before the nation to fight their battles.

(4) David Brings the Ark of God to Jerusalem (6:1–23)[38]

¹David again brought together out of Israel chosen men, thirty thousand in all. ²He and all his men set out from Baalah of Judah to bring up from there the ark of God, which is called by the Name, the name of the LORD Almighty, who is enthroned between the cherubim that are on the ark. ³They set the ark of God on a new cart and brought it from the house of Abinadab, which was on the hill. Uzzah and Ahio, sons of Abinadab, were guiding the new cart ⁴with the ark of God on it, and Ahio was walking in front of it. ⁵David and the whole house of Israel were celebrating with all their might before the LORD, with songs and with harps, lyres, tambourines, sistrums and cymbals.

⁶When they came to the threshing floor of Nacon, Uzzah reached out and took hold of the ark of God, because the oxen stumbled. ⁷The LORD's anger burned against Uzzah because of his irreverent act; therefore God struck him down and he died there beside the ark of God.

⁸Then David was angry because the LORD's wrath had broken out against Uzzah, and to this day that place is called Perez Uzzah.

⁹David was afraid of the LORD that day and said, "How can the ark of the LORD ever come to me?" ¹⁰He was not willing to take the ark of the LORD to be with him in the City of David. Instead, he took it aside to the house of Obed-Edom the Gittite. ¹¹The ark of the LORD remained in the house of Obed-Edom the Gittite for

---

[38] Many OT scholars assume that this chapter was originally part of a literary unit sometimes termed "the Ark Narrative," consisting of 1 Samuel 4–6 and the present chapter. For further information cf. A. F. Campbell, *The Ark Narrative (1 Sam 4–6; 2 Sam 6): A Form-critical and Traditio-historical Study* (Missoula, Mont.: Scholars Press, 1975), and ibid., "Yahweh and the Ark: A Case Study in Narrative," *JBL* 98 (1979): 31–43. Some scholars assume the supposed composition was an unhistorical fabrication: cf. G. W. Ahlström, "The Travels of the Ark: A Religio-Political Composition," *JNES* 43 (1984): 141–49. For a skeptical evaluation of this theory and the implicit acceptance of the ark narrative as historically accurate, cf. Gordon, *I and II Samuel*, 24–26; and T. Kleven, "Hebrew Style in 2 Samuel 6," *JETS* 35 (1992): 299–314.

three months, and the LORD blessed him and his entire household.

¹²Now King David was told, "The LORD has blessed the household of Obed-Edom and everything he has, because of the ark of God." So David went down and brought up the ark of God from the house of Obed-Edom to the City of David with rejoicing. ¹³When those who were carrying the ark of the LORD had taken six steps, he sacrificed a bull and a fattened calf. ¹⁴David, wearing a linen ephod, danced before the LORD with all his might, ¹⁵while he and the entire house of Israel brought up the ark of the LORD with shouts and the sound of trumpets.

¹⁶As the ark of the LORD was entering the City of David, Michal daughter of Saul watched from a window. And when she saw King David leaping and dancing before the LORD, she despised him in her heart.

¹⁷They brought the ark of the LORD and set it in its place inside the tent that David had pitched for it, and David sacrificed burnt offerings and fellowship offerings before the LORD. ¹⁸After he had finished sacrificing the burnt offerings and fellowship offerings, he blessed the people in the name of the LORD Almighty. ¹⁹Then he gave a loaf of bread, a cake of dates and a cake of raisins to each person in the whole crowd of Israelites, both men and women. And all the people went to their homes.

²⁰When David returned home to bless his household, Michal daughter of Saul came out to meet him and said, "How the king of Israel has distinguished himself today, disrobing in the sight of the slave girls of his servants as any vulgar fellow would!"

²¹David said to Michal, "It was before the LORD, who chose me rather than your father or anyone from his house when he appointed me ruler over the LORD's people Israel—I will celebrate before the LORD. ²²I will become even more undignified than this, and I will be humiliated in my own eyes. But by these slave girls you spoke of, I will be held in honor."

²³And Michal daughter of Saul had no children to the day of her death.

6:1–2 David's twin victories against the Philistines guaranteed that Israel's enemy would be motivated to return and fight another day. David was especially aware that his decision to dispose of the Philistine gods (cf. 5:21) would invite reprisals, perhaps even a second Philistine attempt to take possession of the ark of the covenant (cf. 1 Sam 4:11; 5:1). An attack against Israel to acquire and destroy the ark would have been particularly attractive due to the fact that the ark was located only a few miles from their own territory. In an apparent effort to forestall any such undertaking by the Philistines, "David brought together out of Israel" (v. 1) a comparatively large force of "thirty thousand chosen men"—an elite force that was truly national (cf. 1 Chr 13:5), not merely tribal, in nature—"to bring up . . . the ark of God" (v. 2) and remove it to a safer location.³⁹ Since the days of Samuel's childhood, the ark was kept

---

³⁹ Here, as elsewhere, many scholars seriously question or reject the numerical data from the MT. Typical of this perspective is H. P. Smith, *Samuel,* 292. The LXX's number is even higher, stating that David had seventy thousand men. Typical of those who are skeptical of even the MT's number in H. P. Smith, *Samuel,* 292.

in a private residence in a small village in the northwestern regions of Judahite territory (cf. 1 Sam 7:1–2). Accordingly, David assembled the troops at "Baalah of Judah," otherwise known as Kiriath Jearim, the Israelite settlement in which the ark was situated (1 Sam 6:21–7:2).

David was especially concerned to prevent the ark from falling into enemy hands because of its significance for Israel's religion. The ark was the object most closely associated with Israel's God, a truth expressed by the writer's notation that the "Name—the name of Yahweh of Armies, He who is seated on the cherubim—is called upon it."[40] The ark contained the written agreement between Israel and the Lord (cf. Exod 25:16; 40:20; Deut 10:5; 1 Kgs 8:9), was a place of divine revelation (Exod 25:22; Num 7:89), and was in fact the Lord's throne (cf. 1 Sam 4:4; 2 Kgs 19:15; Pss 80:1; 99:1; Isa 37:16). An object of such overwhelming significance would certainly make a valuable prize for the Philistines and was worthy of the massive protective force called up by David.

6:3–5 David had the men "set the ark of God on a new cart" (v. 3), the employment of a new cart being a sign of respect for the holy object. As respectful and well-intended as David's effort was, however, it violated Torah guidelines regarding the transport of the ark (cf. Num 4:15; 7:9). In fact, David's actions in this matter were more like those of the spiritually ignorant Philistines (cf. 1 Sam 6:7,10).

Celebrating was accompanied by "songs"[41] and by harps, lyres, tambourines, sistrums and cymbals" (v. 5). The musical instruments included both stringed (harp and lyre) and percussion instruments (tambourine, sistrum [a type of rattle], and cymbal). Leading the procession was Ahio, one of the "sons of Abinadab" (v. 4), with his brother Uzzah "guiding the cart" from behind. The passage implicitly assumes that Ahio and Uzzah were Levites from the clan of Kohath (cf. Num 4:4–20).

6:6–7 As the oxcart was being pulled down the hill, an unforeseen tragedy occurred, as "the oxen stumbled" (NASB, "the oxen nearly upset *it*"). Instinctively, the levitical priest Uzzah reached out and "took hold of the ark of God" to stabilize and protect it. However, in so doing he committed a capital offense established in the Torah (cf. Num 4:15). Since he was not an Aaronic priest, he was prohibited from touching this holiest object in the Yahwistic faith. Uzzah's

---

[40] The difficult clause עָלָיו הַכְּרֻבִים יֹשֵׁב צְבָאוֹת יהוה שֵׁם שֵׁם אֲשֶׁר־נִקְרָא is to be understood as a construction parallel to Deut 28:10. As such, the preposition עָלָיו is not attached to יֹשֵׁב הַכְּרֻבִים but rather to שֵׁם נִקְרָא.

[41] The MT reads בְּכֹל עֲצֵי בְרוֹשִׁים, lit., "with all woods of cypress/fir/pine"—an apparent reference to the primary material out of which the musical instruments were constructed. The NIV, as well as almost all versions (but not NKJV or NASB), regularly substitutes the variant reading of 1 Chr 13:8, בְּכֹל עֹז וּשִׁירִים. Clearly a close consonantal connection exists between the two readings; neither enjoys the complete support of the LXX. Thus, translators are left to judge for themselves which—if either—of the MT readings best preserves the original. I prefer retaining the Samuel reading in Samuel and the Chronicles reading in Chronicles.

conscientious effort to protect the ark actually defiled it; accordingly, "the LORD's anger burned against Uzzah" (v. 7). Uzzah's act violated a divinely established taboo and was therefore "irreverent"; appropriately, "God"—not some impersonal force—"struck him down and he died there beside the ark of God." For the third time in the books of Samuel (cf. 1 Sam 5:3–12; 6:19–20), the Lord had demonstrated that he was capable of defending the ark. As on the second occasion, the threat was not from a Philistine but from Israelites who disobeyed Torah guidelines regarding proper treatment of the Lord's throne.

6:8–12 David, who had acted with noble intentions in the matter of moving the ark, was angry. The stated reason for David's emotional storm was "because the LORD had broken out against Uzzah" (v. 8)—a clause that could either mean that David was mad at God for killing Uzzah (unlikely, since God was merely enforcing the Torah) or that he was upset that Uzzah had acted in such a way as to cause God to bring fatal judgment to bear (more likely). An Israelite tragedy was exactly what he attempted to avoid, and when Uzzah died, the king memorialized the event by renaming the accident site "Perez Uzzah" (= "Uzzah's Breach"/"The Outburst against Uzzah").

Having witnessed a dramatic demonstration of the Lord's zeal to protect his holiness, David became "afraid of the LORD that day" (v. 9). His deepened respect for the Lord's power and for his willingness to use it against anyone who would violate the Torah caused David to ask, "How can the ark of the LORD ever come to me?" Brueggemann notes the fear generated by this event was positive, for "when people are no longer awed, respectful, or fearful of God's holiness, the community is put at risk."[42]

David's intention had been to move the ark "to be with him in the City of David" (v. 10). There in the former Jebusite fortress the ark would have been protected from any Philistine reprisals. Once in Jerusalem, it would have played a useful role in increasing the prestige of the newly established national capital by locating the divine throne in the same city as David's.[43] However, the recent turn of events had changed David's plans, perhaps because he feared that some further transgression would cause the Lord's judgment to destroy the new capital.

Accordingly, David ordered that the ark be taken to the house of a Levite[44]

---

[42] Brueggemann, *First and Second Samuel*, 249.

[43] J.-M. de Tarragon suggests that David was especially motivated to bring the ark to Jerusalem to provide a historic connection between Shiloh and Jerusalem and thus acting as a unifying force within the nation ("David et l'arche: II Samuel, VI," *RB* 86 [1979]: 514–23).

[44] Gordon (*1 and II Samuel*, 233) asserts that Obed-Edom was a Philistine from Gath who may eventually have been enrolled in the ranks of the Levitical priests. This position is questionable since the practice of adopting Philistine men into the holiest tribe of Israel—or into any Israelite tribe, for that matter—is not explicitly affirmed anywhere in the OT. Cf. Baldwin, who recognizes a probable Levitical origin of Obed-Edom (*1 and 2 Samuel*, 208).

(cf. 1 Chr 15:16–18), Obed-Edom the Gittite" (v. 11). He was associated with a location of uncertain identity that had an olive or wine press (Hb. *gat*). Perhaps Obed-Edom's residence was the closest levitical residence to the disaster; at that site, they hoped, further catastrophes could be avoided. The plan worked well; during the "three months" it was there, blessings—not curses—attended Obed-Edom and everything around him (v. 12; cf. 1 Chr 26:5). The blessing on Obed-Edom's household seemingly took the form of fertility (cf. 1 Chr 26:8).

When David learned that a proper levitical household might experience blessings "because of the ark of God," he concluded that Jerusalem, too, could benefit from the presence of the ark. So David completed his plans to bring the ark to the City of David. As in the first attempt three months prior, the ark's pilgrimage to Jerusalem was carried out "with rejoicing."

6:13–15 But there was one significant difference between the two attempts to transport the sacred throne; this time Levites carried it by hand (v. 13; cf. Num 4:15), not transporting it on a cart (cf. v. 3). Costly fellowship offerings[45] consisting of "a bull and a fattened calf" were offered to the Lord after the Levites "had taken six steps." This ritual pause after six steps suggests a symbolic significance, perhaps a sort of Sabbath rest, suggesting a consecration of the entire journey.[46]

For the occasion of this almost ten-mile journey, David had prepared both his capital city and himself. First, he had erected a special tent in Jerusalem that would house the ark (cf. v. 17). According to 1 Chr 16:39–40, this was done without removing the tent in Gibeon, which was still used to house the remainder of the sacred tabernacle furnishings.[47] Second, he prepared and wore special ritual garments: "a linen ephod" (v. 14), a piece of clothing otherwise reserved in Israelite society for priests and Levites (cf. Exod 28:6; 1 Sam 2:18; 22:18), and, according to 1 Chr 15:27, a "robe of fine linen."

David's use of the ephod suggests that he possessed the credentials of a

---

[45] The biblical text does not state what category of sacrifice was offered, but the Torah explicitly permitted the slaughter of a bull (שׁוֹר) for fellowship offerings (שְׁלָמִים); cf. Lev 4:10; 9:4,18. Certainly such a voluntary offering would have been appropriate on this occasion.

[46] Youngblood ("1, 2 Samuel," 873), following McCarter (*1 Samuel*) and R. A. Carlson (*David the Chosen King* [Stockholm: Almquist & Wiksell, 1964]), suggests that David had the priests offer sacrifices every six steps until the group arrived at the worship site in Jerusalem.

[47] David's desire to build a temple for Yahweh in Jerusalem after he had previously made provisions for the Yahwistic worship center in Gibeon—including the installation of Zadok as priest there (cf. 1 Chr 16:39)—suggests a change in plans regarding the structure of Israelite religion during his administration. For one or more reasons—a desire to fulfill the Torah's expectation that Yahwistic worship was to be centralized or his desire to increase the significance of Jerusalem— he took steps to move all, or at least the most important, Yahwistic activities to Jerusalem. Though he would later be denied the privilege of building the temple in Jerusalem, he took considerable efforts to facilitate the accomplishment of this task. Accordingly, at some point he transferred Zadok to serve at the Jerusalem tent (2 Sam 15:25–29), and provisions were stockpiled for the Jerusalem temple's construction (cf. 1 Chr 22:2–16).

priest.[48] How David attained sacerdotal status is not described in the Bible, but
the acquisition of priestly status "in the order of Melchizedek" by the Davidic
family line is hinted at in Ps 110:4.[49] If indeed this title applied to David as well
as one of his descendants (cf. Heb 7:14–21), he most likely acquired it by right
of conquest: having conquered Jerusalem, he became possessor of all the titles
and honors traditionally accorded to the king of the city. Melchizedek having
been Salem's/Jerusalem's priest-king of God Most High (cf. Gen 14:18; Heb
7:1)—that is, of Yahweh (cf. Gen 14:22), David as king of Jerusalem would
have become a priest of Yahweh. However, as a Yahwistic priest in the order of
Melchizedek, David would have been prohibited from performing his duties
explicitly reserved for the Aaronic priesthood (cf. comments on vv. 17–18). His
status as a Melchizedekian priest would not have restricted him from leading
in certain aspects of worship, and this he did with vigor: David "danced [lit.,
"was dancing"] before the LORD with all his might." His actions were accompanied by "shouts and the sound of trumpets" (v. 15). Trumpets—ones blown
by Levitical priests—had also been sounded during a movement of the ark in
the days of Joshua (cf. Josh 6:4–20).

6:16–19 Missing from the procession bringing the ark to Jerusalem was
"Michal daughter of Saul" (v. 16), who viewed the festivities from a palace
window. It is unclear why Michal was absent from the event, since other
women were permitted to be present (cf. v. 19), but the tone of the passage suggests that it was due to her jaded attitude toward the Lord and his anointed; previously she had been connected with the use of a teraphim, an object
considered an abomination to the Lord (cf. 1 Sam 15:23; 19:13). Michal could
have resented David for forcing her to leave Paltiel as well (cf. 3:14–16). During the triumphal moments when the ark passed through the streets of the royal
fortress, David's unbounded enthusiasm for his God expressed itself in "leaping and dancing before the LORD" (v. 16). His enthusiasm was not appreciated
by Michal. In her attitudes and actions she was truly a "daughter of Saul" (vv.
20,23) and not a wife of David.

Meanwhile, the celebrative group set the ark in its place of honor (v. 17; cf.
Ps 76:2 [Hb. v. 3]). Then David, once again acting sacerdotally, "sacrificed
burnt offerings and fellowships before the LORD." It is unclear from the text
whether David actually officiated at these sacrifices or merely directed Levites
to perform these tasks. If he did perform the sacrifices himself, he may have
been acting in accordance with a precedent set by Melchizedek.

Priestly parallels certainly exist between David and Melchizedek in two

---

[48] For a differing opinion cf. A. Phillips, "David's Linen Ephod," *VT* 19 (1969): 485–87, who
takes the position that David's linen ephod was in fact a brief loincloth, not a priestly garment. Cf.
E. H. Merrill, "Royal Priesthood: An Old Testament Messianic Motif," *BibSac* 150 (1993): 50–61.

[49] The notation of a possible linkage between David and Melchizedek is found also in Gordon,
I and II Samuel, 235.

other matters: pronouncing a blessing upon the Lord's people and providing a
food gift for those who had received the blessing (cf. Gen 14:18–19). As David
"blessed the people in [Hb. "by"] the name of the LORD Almighty" (v. 18),
Melchizedek blessed "Abram by God Most High, Creator of heaven and earth"
(Gen 14:19). Also Melchizedek brought Abram and his men "bread and wine"
(Gen 14:18); David "gave a loaf of bread, a cake of dates and a cake of raisins
to each person in the whole crowd of Israelites" (v. 19).

Both men and women participated in the climactic events of sacrifice and
gift-giving as the ark came to rest in its new home. After the participants each
had received a blessing and a token food gift from the Lord's royal priest, they
"went to their homes."

6:20–23 Following the conclusion of his public duties, David would not
neglect his own household on this day of blessing (v. 20). But even before he
could pronounce a word of blessing, Michal, daughter of Saul, began to berate
him. She first accused him of "disrobing in the sight of the slave girls of his servants"—thus exposing his nakedness. Second, she equated him with a "vulgar
fellow" [Hb. *rēqîm;* "empty/worthless one"; cf. Judg 9:4; 11:3; 2 Chr 13:7].
Implicitly she suggested that immoral sexual urges, not zeal for the Lord, had
motivated his enthusiastic activities in the festivities of the day.[50]

David rejected Michal's slanderous accusations; "it was before the LORD"
(v. 21)—not the young women—that David was celebrating. Furthermore, his
actions were appropriate for one who had been "appointed" by the Lord as
"ruler over the LORD's people Israel." David's celebratory acts earlier in the
day expressed the king's unbridled joy in having been selected by the Lord for
such significant service. Besides, assuming he was dressed as a properly outfit-
ted Yahwistic priest, David's energetic dancing could not have exposed his
nakedness and so violated the Torah's requirements (cf. Exod 20:26) since he
was wearing a linen undergarment. In rejecting David, Michal was also rejecting the Lord because it was he who "chose" David in preference to Michal's
"father or anyone from his house" to lead Israel. More probably, Michal's
rejection of David actually was symptomatic of an underlying problem in her
relationship with God.

Though David's pious actions might have resulted in some embarrassing
moments, David was willing to "become even more undignified" (v. 22), if
necessary, to honor the Lord. He would even allow himself to be "humiliated" (Hb. *šāpal*) in his own eyes for the Lord's sake. Elsewhere in the Old
Testament (cf. Prov 29:23) *šāpal* is understood as a virtue signifying proper

[50] J. R. Porter's hypothesis that David was participating in a syncretistic religious ritual that
blended together cultic copulation with orthodox Yahwism is without merit, since it runs counter
to the biblical presentation of David as a faithful man of the Torah, i.e., a man after Yahweh's heart
("The Interpretation of 2 Samuel vi and Psalm cxxxii," *JTS* 5 [1954]: 161–73). Furthermore, it is
a fanciful interpretation based on the viewpoint of Michal that the biblical text rejects (v. 23).

humility before the Lord. People of true faith, such as "these slave girls" who attended the Yahwistic celebration, would interpret David's actions for what they were—expressions of unrestrained, authentic faith; thus the king would "be held in honor" by people of faith. Like the people of profound faith throughout the ages, David was willing to risk being misunderstood and humiliated as he pursued a deeper relationship with God (cf. 1 Cor 3:18; 4:10).

As a result of this incident "Michal daughter of Saul had no children to the day of her death" (v. 23). In the Torah a blessing associated with obedience to the Lord is a fruitful womb (cf. Exod 23:26; Deut 7:14; 28:11). To an audience knowledgeable of the Torah, Michal's unproductive womb would have been interpreted as a curse sent against a disobedient wife—not as evidence of a husband's neglect of a marital duty.[51] Michal's lack of faith would mean that the house of Saul would be forever separate from Israel's eternal royal dynasty.

(5) David Desires to Build a Temple for the Lord (7:1–3)[52]

[1]After the king was settled in his palace and the LORD had given him rest from all his enemies around him, [2]he said to Nathan the prophet, "Here I am, living in a palace of cedar, while the ark of God remains in a tent."

[3]Nathan replied to the king, "Whatever you have in mind, go ahead and do it, for the LORD is with you."

The covenant between the Lord and David has been compared both to Amorite[53] and Hittite[54] treaties, as well as to the one established between the

---

[51] For an interpretation that views this verse as pointing to David's disassociation with Michal, cf. Baldwin, *1 and 2 Samuel,* 211, and McCarter, *II Samuel,* 187. But the verse implies an act of Yahweh, not an act of David.

[52] D. J. McCarthy, assuming this chapter to be the product of the Deuteronomist, considers it one of the most important passages in the so-called "Deuteronomic history" ("II Samuel 7 and the Structure of the Deuteronomic History," *JBL* 84 [1965]: 131–38). Taking a very different approach, W. J. Dumbrell interprets chaps. 6–7 in view of the Sinai covenant, understanding these chapters to play a crucial role in integrating the Israelite monarchical system into the Sinai covenant ("The Davidic Covenant," *RTR* 39 [1980]: 40–47). David and his royal descendants were to be reflectors and defenders of the Sinai covenant. Both of these insights clearly have merit; this is a chapter of supreme importance, and it provides information that integrates the Davidic dynasty into the religious and social dimensions of the Sinai covenant.

[53] Cf. G. E. Mendenhall and G. A. Herion, *ABD,* s.v. "Covenant," I:1188: "There is little reason to doubt that the prophet Nathan, in proclaiming the divine promise to David, was simply applying the age-old Amorite political theory of Jebus (now Jerusalem) to its new king (and now in the name of its new king's God, Yahweh)."

[54] Cf. F. C. Fensham, *IBD,* s.v. "Covenant," I:329: "The eternal throne of David's descendants can be paralleled to the promise in the form of a blessing in the Hittite vassal treaties, i.e., that the faithful vassal's sons would reign eternally on his throne."

Lord and Abraham (cf. Gen 15).[55] As noted by G. E. Mendenhall and G. A. Herion, the two primary similarities between God's commitments to Abraham and David are (1) that God is bound by an oath and (2) that God made a promise to the individuals. The agreement that God made with David sometimes has been termed a grant/promissory/oath-type covenant—a concept that suggests unconditionality—and sometimes a charter—a concept that emphasizes the role of the initiator while downplaying the responsibilities/role of the recipient.

7:1–3 The events of this section occurred sometime after Hiram's stonemasons and carpenters had built David's palace (cf. 5:11). They also took place after the Lord had given David "rest from all his enemies around him" and after the ark had been deposited in Jerusalem (cf. v. 2); thus, it was likely a period of at least a few years after David's conquest of the Jebusite city and probably after the events described in 8:1–14 and 10:1–19.[56] Having entered into a period of rest because of God's help (cf. Heb 4:3), David desired to provide a rest for God.

At that time David had a conversation with "Nathan the prophet" (v. 2), a previously unknown spokesman for the Lord who would come to play a major role in the course of David's life (cf. 12:1–25; 1 Kgs 1:11–45) and the preservation of Israelite history (cf. 1 Chr 29:29; 2 Chr 9:29). David was troubled that he, the Lord's servant, was honored and blessed by a palace, while the ark of God"—the Lord's locus on earth—was still in a tent (v. 2). It seemed inappropriate to David for an underling to be living in greater luxury than his divine master.

Near Eastern kings throughout history—certainly long before David's time—had devoted national resources to the enhancement of temples in order to honor their gods and secure divine blessing for themselves and their kingdoms.[57] Nathan saw no problem in David introducing this practice into the Israelite royal tradition. Accordingly, he encouraged the king to "go ahead and do it, for the LORD is with you" (v. 3). Since Nathan later received a word from God contrary to what he told David, however, it seems safe to assume that Nathan spoke without first consulting God in this matter.

---

[55] Cf. Gordon, *I and II Samuel,*236; also R. E. Clements, *Abraham and David: Genesis 15 and Its Meaning for Israelite Tradition* (London: SCM, 1967).

[56] For agreement with this position, cf. C. F. Keil and F. Delitzsch, *II Samuel,* trans. J. A. Martin (Grand Rapids: Eerdmans, n.d.), 341.

[57] Pre-Davidic efforts on the part of UR III period (ca. 2100–2000 B.C.) kings to construct/improve temples for national deities are found in the date formulae of cuneiform inscriptions. Cf. N. Scheider, *Die Zeitbestimmungen der Wirtschaftsurkunden von Ur III* (Rome: Pontifical Biblical Institute, 1936); and A. B. Mercer, *Sumero-Babylonian Year-formulae* (London: Luzac, 1946). An example of an Ur-Nammu period date formula is: "The year the foundation of the temple of Ningubla was laid." A Shulgi period date formula reads: "The year the foundation of the temple of Ninurta was laid." Typical of a Semitic king's recorded efforts to undertake construction projects in behalf of deities is the claim of Zakir of Hamat and Luʿath (early eighth-century B.C.): "I built houses for the gods everywhere in my country." Cf. *ANET,* 501–2.

(6) The Lord Makes Eternal Promises to the House of David (7:4–17)

[4]That night the word of the LORD came to Nathan, saying:

[5]"Go and tell my servant David, 'This is what the LORD says: Are you the one to build me a house to dwell in? [6]I have not dwelt in a house from the day I brought the Israelites up out of Egypt to this day. I have been moving from place to place with a tent as my dwelling. [7]Wherever I have moved with all the Israelites, did I ever say to any of their rulers whom I commanded to shepherd my people Israel, "Why have you not built me a house of cedar?"'

[8]"Now then, tell my servant David, 'This is what the LORD Almighty says: I took you from the pasture and from following the flock to be ruler over my people Israel. [9]I have been with you wherever you have gone, and I have cut off all your enemies from before you. Now I will make your name great, like the names of the greatest men of the earth. [10]And I will provide a place for my people Israel and will plant them so that they can have a home of their own and no longer be disturbed. Wicked people will not oppress them anymore, as they did at the beginning [11]and have done ever since the time I appointed leaders over my people Israel. I will also give you rest from all your enemies.

"'The LORD declares to you that the LORD himself will establish a house for you: [12]When your days are over and you rest with your fathers, I will raise up your offspring to succeed you, who will come from your own body, and I will establish his kingdom. [13]He is the one who will build a house for my Name, and I will establish the throne of his kingdom forever. [14]I will be his father, and he will be my son. When he does wrong, I will punish him with the rod of men, with floggings inflicted by men. [15]But my love will never be taken away from him, as I took it away from Saul, whom I removed from before you. [16]Your house and your kingdom will endure forever before me; your throne will be established forever.'"

[17]Nathan reported to David all the words of this entire revelation.

The events portrayed in this section may rightly be understood as the flowering of a Torah prophecy, the climax of David's life, and the foundation for a major theme in the writings of the Latter Prophets. Youngblood understands this section to be "the center and focus of . . . the Deuteronomic history itself"; Brueggemann sees it as "the dramatic and theological center of the entire Samuel corpus" and in fact "the most crucial theological statement in the Old Testament."[58] The Lord's words recorded here constitute the longest recorded monologue attributed to him since the days of Moses (197 words). The prodigious size of this divine pronouncement suggests that the writer intended it to be interpreted as centrally important—perhaps on a plane with the Torah itself.

The Lord's words spoken here demonstrate him to be the promise-keeping God; having prophetically placed the scepter in Judah hundreds of years earlier (Gen 49:10), he here secured its place within that tribe "until he comes to whom it belongs." Through the prophetic pronouncements of this chapter David is

---

[58] Youngblood, 1, 2 Samuel, 880; Brueggemann, First and Second Samuel, 253, 259.

made the founder of the only royal family the Lord would ever sanction in perpetuity; not only would he become the source of all Israel's uniquely favored dynastic line, but he would become the standard by which his descendants would be judged.

The covenant that the Lord established with the house of David became the nucleus around which messages of hope proclaimed by Hebrew prophets of later generations were built (cf. Isa 9:1–7; 11:1–16; 16:5; 55:3; Jer 23:5–6; 30:8; 33:15–26; Ezek 34:23–24; 37:24–25; Hos 3:5; Amos 9:11; Zech 12:7–8). To a people broken and humbled by invaders sent as agents of divine punishment, the Lord's promise to David of a kingdom that "will endure forever" (v. 16) was the seed of hope that resurrected a nation. The Lord's promise of an enduring house for David became Israel's assurance that God would once again lift the nation up and cause it to flourish anew.

The significance of the eternal covenant between the Lord and David for the New Testament writers cannot be overemphasized.[59] These words played an essential preparatory role in developing the messianic expectations that were fulfilled in Jesus. The hopes that were raised by the Lord's words—that God would place a seed of David on an eternal throne and establish a kingdom that would never perish—were ones that no Israelite or Judahite monarch satisfied, or even could have satisfied. But they were ones that the first-century Christians understood Jesus to fulfill.[60]

The Lord's words recorded here arguably play the single most significant role of any Scripture found in the Old Testament in shaping the Christian understanding of Jesus. The divine declarations proclaimed here through the prophet Nathan are foundational for seven major New Testament teachings about Jesus: that he is (1) the son of David (cf. Matt 1:1; Acts 13:22–23; Rom 1:3; 2 Tim 2:8; Rev 22:16, etc.); (2) one who would rise from the dead (cf. Acts 2:30; 13:23); (3) the builder of the house for God (cf. John 2:19–22; Heb 3:3–4, etc.); (4) the possessor of a throne (cf. Heb 1:8; Rev 3:21, etc.); (5) the possessor of an eternal kingdom (cf. 1 Cor 15:24–25; Eph 5:5; Heb 1:8; 2 Pet 1:11, etc.); (6) the son of God[61] (cf. Mark 1:1; John 20:31; Acts 9:20; Heb 4:14; Rev

[59] See, e.g., R. F. O'Toole, "Acts 2:30 and the Davidic Covenant of Pentecost," *JBL* 102 (1983): 245–58.
[60] Cf. D. Juel, *Messianic Exegesis: Christological Interpretation of the Old Testament in Early Christianity* (Philadelphia: Fortress, 1988).
[61] The theory put forth by liberal NT scholars that the first-century Christian community's doctrine of Jesus' theanthropic nature represents the syncretization of pagan mystery religions with Judaism cannot be sustained (cf. R. Bultmann, *Theology of the New Testament,* trans. K. Grobel [New York: Scribners, 1955], 128–33). The NT writers consistently employed Hebrew scriptures as the intellectual basis for their belief that Jesus was indeed the Son of God (cf. Heb 1:5; Acts 13:33). Cf. Youngblood, *1, 2 Samuel,* 891–92, for further treatment on the application of this text to Jesus Christ. Also cf. W. C. Kaiser, Jr. *Toward an Old Testament Theology* (Grand Rapids: Zondervan, 1978), 143–64; G. Van Groningen, *Messianic Revelation in the Old Testament* (Grand Rapids: Baker, 1990), 287–304.

2:18, etc.); and (7) the product of an immaculate conception, since he had God as his father (cf. Luke 1:32–35).

7:4–7 The Lord did not delay in correcting the word Nathan had given David. "That night" he instructed the prophet to convey a message to David that would dramatically change his life and the future of his dynasty forever.[62]

The divine revelation began with words of commendation for David; the Lord called the king "my servant" (Hb. ʿabdî; v. 5), a term used elsewhere in speeches by the Lord to refer to honored faithful patriarchs, prophets, Israel, and the Messiah.[63] However, immediately following this positive word, the Lord indicated by means of a rhetorical question that David was not to be the one to build God's house.

In fact, the Lord questioned the desirability of anyone building a permanent structure in which he might dwell—at least doing so unbidden and at that point in time.[64] When God "brought the Israelites up out of Egypt" (v. 6), he did so without any sort of a material residence—not even a tent. Even so, his presence among the Israelites was real and certainly impressive (cf. Exod 13:21–22). Before the Israelites left Mount Sinai, they obeyed the Lord's command and constructed a special skin "tent" that served as a divine "dwelling" place (cf. Exod 26:1–37; 40:34–38). Throughout the events following Israel's departure from Sinai, the Lord had never expressed displeasure with having a tent for his earthly domicile, nor did he ever order any of the Israelite "staffs" (v. 7; NIV, "rulers")[65]—the ancient symbol of authority used metonymically to signify a person with authority—to build him "a house of cedar." Even in the absence of

---

[62] A. A. Anderson concludes that "the best setting for the origin of vv. 5–7 is the early exilic period when the temple was reduced to rubble" and that "the purpose of this *vaticinium post eventum* was to serve as a literary device in order to provide a theological interpretation of a tragic event, i.e., the destruction of Yahweh's house" (*2 Samuel*, WBC [Waco: Word, 1989], 119). Such a perspective assumes that the canonical form of the text misrepresents the facts of history and that statements were formulated and then attributed to Yahweh—albeit for pious and noble reasons—that were not in fact spoken by Yahweh. This scholarly tendency to second-guess the claims of Scripture, a tendency sometimes present even among evangelical scholars, represents an unacceptable departure from the historically orthodox view of Scripture that accepts all canonical statements of Scripture as completely accurate as written. Certainly the Chronicler (cf. 1 Chr 17:4–6) accepted the words of Nathan presented in vv. 5–7 as historically accurate. It seems reasonable for those of us even further removed in time than he to be hesitant to reject his conclusion.

[63] Abraham (Gen 26:24); Jacob (Ezek 37:25); Moses (Num 12:7–8; Josh 1:2,7; 2 Kgs 21:8); Caleb (Num 14:24); Isaiah (Isa 20:3); Zerubbabel (Hag 2:23); Job (Job 1:8; 2:3; 42:8); Nebuchadnezzar (Jer 25:9; 27:6); Israel (Isa 41:9; 44:1–2,21; 49:3; Jer 30:10); and the Messiah (Isa 52:13; Zech 3:8).

[64] Cf. M. Ita, "A Note on 2 Sam 7," in *A Light unto My Path: Old Testament Studies in Honor of Jacob M. Myers*, ed. H. N Bream, R. D. Heim, and C. A. Moore (Philadelphia: Temple University, 1974), 406.

[65] The term שִׁבְטֵי is normally translated "tribes of" (cf. LXX, NKJV, NASB). However, none of the tribes of Israel was ever appointed to shepherd Israel. Consequently the NIV—and most recently NLT—opted for a translation that implies individual leaders.

an impressive building that people could see, the Lord's presence among them was discernible, especially as he acted through the leaders "whom I commanded to shepherd my people Israel."

7:8–11a Through David God had presented additional testimony to his presence among his people. David's meteoric rise to prominence and power in Israel—being taken "from the pasture and from following the flock to be ruler over my people Israel" (v. 8)—was compelling evidence of the Lord's presence. The Lord himself had brought David from the pasture; the Lord had made David ruler; the Lord had "been with" (v. 9) David wherever he had gone; and it was the Lord who had "cut off all" David's "enemies from before" him.

David did not need to construct an impressive but lifeless building in which the Lord could dwell; the Lord had already constructed an impressive living building in which to dwell, and that edifice was the life of David. Though the ark resided in a lifeless tent of skin, in a very real sense the Lord resided in the living tent of David.[66] And the Lord was not finished adorning his earthly dwelling place; he would make David's "name great, like the names of the greatest men of the earth"—a covenantal promise not made by the Lord to an individual since the days of Abraham (cf. Gen 12:2).

The Lord's words become eschatological in character as they describe the benefits that will accrue for Israel with the magnification of the house of David. David's rise to the ranks of the "greatest men of the earth" would mean that the Lord would provide Israel a secure and peaceful homeland (v. 10). In addition,[67] justice would prevail for the Lord's people: "wicked men will not oppress them anymore." The Lord planned a further benefit for David beyond those already mentioned: an era of tranquility awaited Israel's king, for the Lord would "also give" David "rest from all" his "enemies" (v. 11), an apparent reference to a continued and increased freedom from the threat of non-Israelite aggressors (cf. v. 1). These promises, however, were not fulfilled in David's lifetime; later prophets understood them to refer to a future period (cf. Isa 9:7; 16:5; Jer 23:5–6; 33:15–16).

7:11b–17 Even more significantly, "the LORD himself will establish a house" (v. 11)—that is, a dynasty—for David. David had sought to build a house (= temple) for the Lord, but the Lord would instead build a house (= dynasty) for David. The incredible blessings that the Lord both gave and pledged would not be set aside for some usurper to the throne. Instead, the Lord "will raise up your offspring [Hb. *zeraʿ*; lit., "seed"; cf. Gen 13:15] to succeed

---

[66] Later Yahwistic prophets referred to the Davidic dynasty as the "tent of David" (cf. Isa 16:5; Amos 9:11; Acts 15:16); the metaphor is appropriate to this passage.

[67] Disagreement exists among scholars about what מָקוֹם, "place," refers to. It probably refers to a peaceful homeland, i.e., the Promised Land; cf. D. F. Murray, "מָקוֹם and the future of Israel in 2 Samuel vii 10," *VT* 40 (1990): 298–320.

you" (v. 12). For the New Testament Christian community, this verse apparently was viewed as proof that Jesus was indeed the Messiah; God did indeed "raise up" Jesus (cf. Acts 2:30; 13:23), thus legitimizing him as the messianic son of David.[68] According to the prophecy, the royal successor would be one "who will come from your body."[69] The emphasis on an offspring/seed who would come from David's body links this covenant with the Abrahamic covenant (cf. Gen 15:4). As with David, so with the royal successor—the Lord would "establish his kingdom."

It would not be David but his successor who would "build a house for" (v. 13) the Lord. Viewed in its immediate historical context, the prophetic reference was to Solomon, who constructed the temple for the Lord in Jerusalem between 966 and 959 B.C. (cf. 1 Kgs 6:1–38).

The New Testament does not deny that some aspects of the prophetic revelation of v. 13 referred to Solomon (cf. Acts 7:47). But for the New Testament writers, the primary application of this verse was to Jesus, the ultimate "son of David" (e.g., Matt 1:1). One reason for this is that the Lord's promise to "establish the throne of his kingdom forever" seems to vault this portion of the prophecy beyond the bounds of Solomon's reign and give it eschatological and/or messianic overtones. The throne of Solomon's kingdom was not permanently established; in fact, his kingdom—in the strict sense of the word—ceased to exist immediately after his death (cf. 1 Kgs 11:31–38). This incongruity between divine prophecy and human history invited the New Testament writers to look to a different son of David for the fulfillment of the word.

In applying v. 13 to Jesus, the New Testament writers took their cue from Jesus himself. Three of Jesus' claims concerning himself allude to this verse. First, Jesus claimed he would build a temple (cf. Matt 26:61; 27:40; Mark 14:58; 15:29; John 2:19–22). Second, he claimed to possess an eternal throne (cf. Matt 19:28–29). Finally, he claimed to possess an imperishable kingdom (cf. Luke 22:29–30; John 18:36).

Of this promised descendant of David the Lord said "I will be his father, and he will be my son" (v. 14). Although some Old Testament interpreters suggest this may refer to an otherwise unreported practice whereby an Israelite king

[68] The Hebrew verb used here is קוּם, which in certain contexts is synonymous with חיה, "to live" (cf. Isa 26:14,19). The LXX verb in this phrase is ἀναστήσω, also translatable as "I will resurrect." For further discussion of this translation point, along with its messianic implications, cf. O. Betz, "Das messianischen Bewusstsein Jesu," *NovT* 6 (1963): 20–48.

[69] The prophetic verb forms (prophetic perfects) suggest that the individual who would become David's royal successor had not yet been born. This, of course, accords well with the facts surrounding Solomon. He was certainly much younger than any of the sons born in Hebron and probably was not the first son born to David in Jerusalem. Carlson, however, understands this as a reference to Absalom (*David the Chosen King*, 122).

was ritually "adopted" by the deity upon assumption to the throne,[70] the New Testament writers accepted the claim literally. Jesus is unambiguously understood in the New Testament to be the Son of God (Mark 1:1; John 20:31; Acts 9:20; Heb 1:5), an understanding fostered by Jesus' own self-claims (cf. Matt 27:43; Luke 22:70). In taking this verse literally and applying it to Jesus, the New Testament connected it with Jesus' virgin birth (cf. Luke 1:32).

The Lord indicated that he would punish David's seed "when he does wrong." Punishment would be "with the rod of men, with floggings inflicted by men." This warning restates the Torah's teaching that the Lord would punish disobedient covenant people with the instrumentality of human oppressors (cf. Lev 26:25; Deut 28:25,49–52): it was literally fulfilled in the case of Solomon (cf. 1 Kgs 11:14,23–26). Without affirming Jesus' need for punishment due to personal sin, the writer of the Book of Hebrews seems to suggest that this passage is likewise messianic (cf. Heb 5:8–9).

Though sin by David's descendants would bring punishment and alienation, it would not result in the Lord's withdrawal of love. In fact, the Lord's faithful, loving commitment (Hb. *ḥesed*) to David's descendants would "never be taken away" (v. 15). What God had done in removing the dynasty of Saul from Israel he would never do to the house of David, though because of sin David might later think it possible (cf. Ps 51:11 [Hb. v. 13]).

God would establish David's "house," "kingdom," and "throne . . . forever" (v. 16). Once again the facts of history demonstrated that the Davidic dynasty's grip on royal power in Israel was tenuous. Interloping Israelites (e.g., Athaliah; 2 Kgs 11:1–3) and foreign conquerors perforated Davidic claims to the throne. As a result, these verses also were understood eschatologically/messianically. In the New Testament they were explicitly applied to Jesus (Heb 1:8).

Nathan "reported to David all the words of this entire revelation" (v. 17). This may have come to the king in both oral and written forms (cf. 1 Chr 29:29; 2 Chr 9:29).

(7) David Praises the Lord (7:18–29)

¹⁸Then King David went in and sat before the LORD, and he said:

"Who am I, O Sovereign LORD, and what is my family, that you have brought me this far? ¹⁹And as if this were not enough in your sight, O Sovereign LORD, you have also spoken about the future of the house of your servant. Is this your usual way of dealing with man, O Sovereign LORD?

---

[70] Cf. McCarter, who cites Pss 2:7–8; 89:27–28 [Hb. 26–27] as evidence that Yahweh ritually adopted David, thus "qualify[ing] the king for the patrimony Yahweh wishes to bestow on him" (*II Samuel*, 207). In the present case, according to McCarter, "Israel becomes, in effect, the patrimonial estate of David's family," one that is both permanent and inalienable. Cf. also R. de Vaux, *Ancient Israel, vol. 1: Social Institutions*, trans. J. McHugh (New York: McGraw-Hill, 1961), 112–13.

²⁰"What more can David say to you? For you know your servant, O Sovereign LORD. ²¹For the sake of your word and according to your will, you have done this great thing and made it known to your servant.

²²"How great you are, O Sovereign LORD! There is no one like you, and there is no God but you, as we have heard with our own ears. ²³And who is like your people Israel—the one nation on earth that God went out to redeem as a people for himself, and to make a name for himself, and to perform great and awesome wonders by driving out nations and their gods from before your people, whom you redeemed from Egypt? ²⁴You have established your people Israel as your very own forever, and you, O LORD, have become their God.

²⁵"And now, LORD God, keep forever the promise you have made concerning your servant and his house. Do as you promised, ²⁶so that your name will be great forever. Then men will say, 'The LORD Almighty is God over Israel!' And the house of your servant David will be established before you.

²⁷"O LORD Almighty, God of Israel, you have revealed this to your servant, saying, 'I will build a house for you.' So your servant has found courage to offer you this prayer. ²⁸O Sovereign LORD, you are God! Your words are trustworthy, and you have promised these good things to your servant. ²⁹Now be pleased to bless the house of your servant, that it may continue forever in your sight; for you, O Sovereign LORD, have spoken, and with your blessing the house of your servant will be blessed forever."

7:18–20 David's response to the Lord's magnificent declarations was awestruck humility, solemnity, and bold faith. After hearing the Lord's words, David entered the sacred tent that housed the ark—perhaps by virtue of his priestly status (cf. discussion at 6:16–19)—and "sat before the LORD." There he spoke the second-longest monologue recorded from his lips in 1, 2 Samuel (198 words), exceeded only by the psalmodic recitation found in the appendix (22:2–51). Its similarity in size to the Lord's immediately preceding pronouncement—only one word longer in the Hebrew text—suggests it was literarily shaped so as to make David's response as thematically important as the divine words themselves. Indeed, the faith-filled response of the king serves as a model for all who receive unmerited blessing from the living God. Like David, all believers are implicitly encouraged to be humbled, pensive, and emboldened by the perception of God's incredible goodness expressed within their lives.

David's prayerful monologue, spoken while the king was in a sitting position,[71] begins with a note of wonder, as the king meditatively asked "Lord Yahweh" [NIV, "Sovereign LORD"], "Who am I, . . . and what is my house [NIV, "family"], that you have brought me this far?" David's question implicitly recognized that the Lord, not David, was the source of the transformation of the

---

[71] This is the only time in the Bible when a person is noted as praying in a seated position. McCarter cites a "rabbinic notion that only the Davidic kings were permitted to sit down in the temple court (Yoma 25)" (*2 Samuel*, 236).

lowly shepherd of Bethlehem into Israel's king. David's employment of the phrase "Lord Yahweh" here is the first of seven occasions in this monologue. This phrase appears for the first time in the Old Testament in a tête-à-tête between the Lord and Abram in which the Lord revealed the blessed future of Abram's family (cf. Gen 15). David's reuse of the relatively unusual appellation for God in a similar context seems deliberate. The lexical links between the Lord's compact with Abraham in the Torah and the one with David invite the reader to compare the two events and perhaps to accord them equal significance. Coming out of Abram's experience with God was the promise of land for Israel; out of David's experience came the promise of a leader for Israel within that land.

In spite of the magnitude of God's blessings already bestowed on the house of David, they were (lit.) "little" [NIV, "not enough"; NASB, "insignificant"] in comparison to those that would ultimately accrue. The Lord's blessings for David would not cease at that point in time; God had "also spoken about the future [NASB, "distant future"] of the house of your servant" (v. 19), and those pronouncements were favorable. In David's acknowledgment of God's concern for the king's descendants, he referred to himself as the Lord's servant/ slave, the first of ten times he would do so during this prayer to God. In so doing David was following a pious tradition of using the socially demeaning term as a badge of honor.[72] However, David is recorded in Old Testament narratives as having used the phrase more than any other person (13x), followed by his son Solomon (7x). The Lord's provision of insight into a family's fate was certainly not the deity's "usual way of dealing with man," but it was not unknown, especially among the patriarchs (cf. Gen 12:2–3; 15:4–21), priests (1 Sam 2:28–36; 3:11–18), and even kings (1 Sam 15:28).

7:21–22 Although David did not profess to understand why he had received the Lord's wonderful promises, he recognized that these promises had been given for a reason: not as a reward for David's righteousness but "for the sake of your word and according to your will" (v. 21). David did not indicate what "word" he was referring to, for the sake of which these promises had been given. In keeping with the larger purposes of the books of Samuel, we can speculate that he was alluding to a Torah promise, particularly one that links royal leadership with the tribe of Judah (cf. Gen 49:10).

David's failure to understand the Lord's gracious activity in no way minimized his recognition that it was a "great thing." It was made even greater by the fact that God had "made it known to your servant"; God's gift of this prophetic revelation added an additional reason to marvel at God's gracious

---

[72] Other individuals who were recorded in the OT as referring to themselves in this way during statements to Yahweh were Abram (Gen 18:3); Jacob (Gen 32:10); Moses (Exod 4:10; Num 11:11; Deut 3:24); Samson (Judg 15:18); Hannah (1 Sam 1:11); and Samuel (1 Sam 3:10).

activities in Israel's behalf.

In light of all this, David could only marvel at "how great" (v. 22) the Lord is; no being is or could be his equal. Only a divine being could possibly do or be all that David attributed to the Lord, but "there is no God but" the Lord. Thus Israel's God—One who makes promises in the Torah and then acts for their sake so as to fulfill them and who can speak of their fulfillment even before the events themselves—is without peer.

7:23–24 The Lord's unique status and his gracious covenant with Israel meant that his "people Israel" (v. 23) were also unique. They were "the one nation on earth that God went out to redeem as a people for himself" (cf. Amos 3:2). As the Lord had implied in his prophetic promise to Abram (cf. Gen 15:13–21), he had driven "out nations and their gods from before" Israel in the Promised Land[73] and had "redeemed" Israel "from Egypt." In making this confession David echoed a theme prominent in Moses' Deuteronomic monologues (cf. Deut 7:8; 9:26; 13:5; 15:15; 24:18). The Lord's actions on Israel's behalf, like those on behalf of David, were used "to make a name"—that is, to bring glory to God.

Through these actions the Lord had established his "people Israel as [his] very own forever" (v. 24). His covenant with Israel was an eternal one (Hb. ʿad ʿôlām), just as David's throne, dynasty, and kingdom were eternal (Hb. ôlām; cf. vv. 13,16). As promised to Abraham and thus to Israel, the Lord had indeed "become their God" (cf. Gen 17:8).

7:25–29 Having marveled at the Lord's work in his own life and on behalf of Israel, David now boldly commanded (*hiphil* imperative of *qûm*) the Lord to "keep forever the promise you have made concerning your servant and his house" (v. 25). Borrowing a literary device from the poetic genre, David used synonymous parallelism to underscore his mandate to the Lord: "do [qal imperative of *ʿāśāh*] as you have promised." This act of giving an order to God should not be viewed as an irreverent act on David's part; on the contrary, it was an act of great faith. David heard Nathan's prophecy and accepted it for what it was—a solemn promise from God. Through these commands David acknowledged that he believed and accepted what the Lord had said and was confidently asking God to do what he said he would do.

By fulfilling his promise to establish "the house of your servant David"

---

[73] Somewhat surprisingly, the NIV—unlike the NASB and NKJV—chose to depart considerably from the BHS text, opting instead to create a text here on the basis of the LXX and 1 Chr 17:21. The Hebrew text that was modified reads literally "wonders for your land and before your people, whom you redeemed from Egypt, from the nations and their gods." To arrive at this wording, the most significant change was the substitution of לְגֵרֵשׁ (cf. 1 Chr 17:21) for לְאַרְצְךָ. In its present form the NIV text deemphasizes certain aspects of Yahweh's accomplishments on Israel's behalf: not only did he redeem Israel from Egypt, but he redeemed them from other foreign threats, both nations and gods.

(v. 26), the Lord's name would be "great forever" because God's trustworthiness and goodness would be manifestly evident to all. As people—especially the covenant people of Israel—witnessed God's incredible display of mercy and favor to the family of David, they would "say, 'The LORD Almighty is God over Israel!' "

David did not wait for the historical outworking of the promises before making his confession of faith. He heard Nathan's prophecy and accepted it immediately as God's "revealed" word; therefore he found courage to offer his prayer and confession of faith. David's confession—"O Sovereign LORD, you are God" (v. 28)—mirrors that which he entreated other Israelites to proclaim.

The logic of David's faith was not complicated. It was a syllogism consisting of a major premise, a minor premise, and an implicit conclusion stated as a prayer request:

> *Major Premise:* The Lord's words "are truth" (Hb. *ʾemet*; NIV, "trustworthy")
>
> *Minor Premise:* The Lord "promised these good things to" David
>
> *Conclusion:* [Implicit: the Lord would "bless the house of" (v. 29) David]
>
> *Resulting Prayer:* "Be pleased to bless the house of your servant" David

The Lord had spoken a blessing upon David's family line, and "with your blessing the house of your servant will be blessed forever." David's simple acceptance of the Lord's word mirrors Abraham's (cf. Gen 15:6) and confirms that David was indeed a man after the Lord's own heart.

(8) The Lord Gives David Victory over All His Enemies (8:1–14)

¹In the course of time, David defeated the Philistines and subdued them, and he took Metheg Ammah from the control of the Philistines.

²David also defeated the Moabites. He made them lie down on the ground and measured them off with a length of cord. Every two lengths of them were put to death, and the third length was allowed to live. So the Moabites became subject to David and brought tribute.

³Moreover, David fought Hadadezer son of Rehob, king of Zobah, when he went to restore his control along the Euphrates River. ⁴David captured a thousand of his chariots, seven thousand charioteers and twenty thousand foot soldiers. He hamstrung all but a hundred of the chariot horses.

⁵When the Arameans of Damascus came to help Hadadezer king of Zobah, David struck down twenty-two thousand of them. ⁶He put garrisons in the Aramean kingdom of Damascus, and the Arameans became subject to him and brought tribute. The LORD gave David victory wherever he went.

⁷David took the gold shields that belonged to the officers of Hadadezer and brought them to Jerusalem. ⁸From Tebah and Berothai, towns that belonged to Hadadezer, King David took a great quantity of bronze.

⁹When Tou king of Hamath heard that David had defeated the entire army of Hadadezer, ¹⁰he sent his son Joram to King David to greet him and congratulate

him on his victory in battle over Hadadezer, who had been at war with Tou. Joram brought with him articles of silver and gold and bronze.

[11]King David dedicated these articles to the LORD, as he had done with the silver and gold from all the nations he had subdued: [12]Edom and Moab, the Ammonites and the Philistines, and Amalek. He also dedicated the plunder taken from Hadadezer son of Rehob, king of Zobah.

[13]And David became famous after he returned from striking down eighteen thousand Edomites in the Valley of Salt.

[14]He put garrisons throughout Edom, and all the Edomites became subject to David. The LORD gave David victory wherever he went.

Immediately after the writer recorded the phenomenal promises the Lord revealed to David, he began presenting materials that demonstrate their fulfillment.[74] The Lord had stated that he would provide a safe haven for Israel, one in which wicked men would be unable to oppress them (cf. 7:10). Now God is shown working through David to make these words a reality. In fact, the thematically central refrain of this section is, "The LORD gave David victory wherever he went" (vv. 6,14). The events mentioned in this section come from various periods in David's administration, most of which cannot be located at specific points in time.

8:1–2   The events described in this chapter were said to have occurred "in the course of time" (lit., "after thus"), an expression understood by Keil and Delitzsch to serve "as a general formula of transition to attach what follows to the account just completed, as a thing that happened afterwards."[75] Since the days of Samson, Israel's most oppressive enemy had been the Philistines. In order to demonstrate that the Lord was keeping his promise, it was appropriate to indicate that David triumphantly waged holy war against them. David's efforts were mightily successful (v. 1). Furthermore, he also enlarged Israel's presence in the Promised Land when he secured "Metheg Ammah from the control of the Philistines." The name "Metheg Ammah" is an unusual one, possessing the literal meaning "The Bridle of the Forearm/Cubit." No ancient city bearing this name has been discovered, and this has led some to speculate that the phrase is (1) the name of a topographical feature such as "common lands," not a city; (2) an idiomatic expression meaning "tribute"; (3) an idiomatic expression—or perhaps a textual corruption—meaning "a city of importance" (= Gath; cf. 1 Chr 18:1); or (4) an idiomatic expression meaning "the govern-

---

[74]Brueggemann's assertion that "in chapter 8 David outruns the mandate of the oracle" and in so doing is "indeed 'like all the nations'" misses the biblical writer's point (*First and Second Samuel,* 261). In his valiant military undertakings David was fulfilling Torah promises dating to the time of Abraham.

[75]C. F. Keil and F. Delitzsch, *II Samuel,* in *Commentary on the Old Testament,* trans. J. Martin (Grand Rapids: Eerdmans, n.d.), II:355.

ment."[76] David's efforts did not eradicate the Philistines, but after David's time they are never portrayed in the Old Testament as presenting a serious threat to Israel (cf. 1 Kgs 4:21; 15:27; 16:15; 2 Kgs 8:2–3; 18:8).

Besides dealing with Israel's greatest foreign threat to national security, David also waged war successfully against a traditional enemy that had opposed Israel since the days of Moses. In keeping with a Torah prophecy (cf. Num 24:17), King David "defeated the Moabites" (v. 2). In so doing David demonstrated that his commitment to obeying the Torah was greater than his family ties (cf. Ruth 4:13–21).

Through a policy that would be highly controversial and universally condemned today, David also eliminated any serious near-term military threat that might have been posed by the Moabites. In his successful campaign against them, David captured a number of prisoners of war. These he made to "lie down on the ground." Then he "measured them off with a length of cord" and put to death all the prisoners falling under two of every three lengths of cord. No parallels to David's action against the Moabites exists in Scripture.

In spite of all appearances, such an action probably was considered compassionate in contrast to the options of killing all the prisoners or selling them all as slaves to foreign nations. After all, many of David's enemies were permitted to live and return to their families. David's decisive action certainly benefited Israel economically because the survivors could return to work the fields of Moab and produce grain and livestock, a portion of which would be sent annually to David's court as "tribute."

8:3–8 Besides attacking enemies to the west and east, David channeled military efforts to the northeast as he "fought Hadadezer son of Rehob, king of Zobah" (v. 3), an area more than sixty miles north of the Sea of Galilee. The circumstances of David's encounter with this Aramean king are debated by scholars, due to geographical considerations and ambiguities in the Hebrew text.

One issue of uncertainty relates to the identity of the river. One Hebrew tradition (the *qere,* followed by the NIV) adds "Euphrates" (i.e., *pĕrāt*), whereas another (the *kethiv*) simply has "the river," allowing perhaps the Jordan or the Yarmuk. Another basic issue of uncertainty is the question of who "went to" the Euphrates River—was it David or Hadadezer? If it was David, what was he doing so far north at this time? And if it was Hadadezer, why was David contesting Hadadezer's activities so far away from Jerusalem? A third issue is what the person by the river was doing—was he going "to restore his control" of the

---

[76] The LXX suggests "tribute"; McCarter suggests "common lands" (*II Samuel,* 242–43). Baldwin suggests "a city of importance," referring to Gath (*1 and 2 Samuel,* 220); Keil and Delitzsch suggest "the government" (*II Samuel,* 355).

region (so NIV), or was he going to plant a stele there?[77]

This episode likely relates to a time when David led a military expedition to the Euphrates to fulfill another Torah promise, namely, that of extending Israel's territorial claims to the Euphrates (cf. Gen 15:18; Exod 23:31; Deut 1:7; 11:24). God had declared in the Torah that the land belonged to Israel, and Saul had made an attempt to conquer it (cf. 1 Sam 14:47); now David the man of the Torah went to stake a more credible claim on this region. Though David encountered opposition from Hadadezer, who likewise claimed control of the region, David and his forces handily defeated them. In the process the Israelite king "captured a thousand of [Hadadezer's] chariots, seven thousand charioteers,[78] and twenty thousand foot soldiers" (v. 4), thus drastically reducing the military threat of perhaps the most formidable opponent in the region of Aram.

In disposing of the captured military resources, David "hamstrung all but a hundred of the chariot horses." He probably did this for at least three reasons. First and foremost, the Torah prohibited Israelite kings from "acquiring great numbers of horses" (Deut 17:16). Second and most practically, the Israelite kingdom was not equipped to maintain thousands of horses: they had neither the government facilities nor the numbers of permanent government employees necessary to care for them. Furthermore, chariots—and therefore chariot horses—were useless for military purposes in much of the Israelite heartland because of the terrain: in cost-versus-benefit terms, they were a bad investment for a nation of rugged hills and brushy forests.

Israelite incursions into the territories traditionally controlled by Aramean city-states were met with opposition from more than one kingdom. "Arameans of Damascus" (modern Damascus) "came to help Hadadezer king of Zobah" (v. 5). However, like the army of Zobah they experienced a crushing defeat as "David struck down twenty-two thousand of them" (v. 5). Then, in an effort to consolidate his gains, David "put garrisons in the Aramean kingdom of Damascus." This permanent Israelite military presence in the region helped assure that the subjugated Arameans "brought tribute" annually to Jerusalem. David's success here represents the first recorded Israelite success in gaining control of Damascus. So significant was the event that the writer noted what every Israelite soldier involved in the campaign must have felt—"The LORD gave David victory" (v. 6).

Bringing Damascus under Israelite control was of immense financial significance to David's kingdom for two reasons. First, this city was the junction

---

[77] Recent versions, including the NRSV and NEB, as well as McCarter (*II Samuel,* 242, 247–48) translate יָד as "monument" (cf. in this regard 1 Sam 15:12). Regarding scholars who accept the Yarmuk as the river to which reference is being made, consult McCarter, *II Samuel,* 248.

[78] The MT here omits any mention of chariots, stating instead that David captured "1,700 horsemen" (cf. NASB). The NIV accepts the LXX reading here, since it is supported by 1 Chr 18:4 and Dead Sea Scroll evidence.

point for the Way of the Sea and the King's Highway, the two major caravan routes connecting Asia with Africa. By controlling this location and stationing garrisons along the caravan routes, Israel was able to collect revenues from itinerant merchants in exchange for safe passage on the roads. Second, David was able to tap the reserves of wealth already in place within the region. David did this in part by taking "the gold shields that belonged to the officers of Hadadezer" (v. 7) and bringing them to Jerusalem. These shields were likely ceremonial in function, stored in Damascus for use during courtly and religious festivities (cf. 1 Kgs 10:16–17; 14:26–28). David may have dedicated these objects to the Lord as *herem*, items irrevocably given over for service to the deity (cf. 2 Kgs 11:10; Lev 27:28). David also "took a great quantity of bronze" (v. 8) from the Aram-Zobahite towns of "Tebah and Berothai." The identity and location of Tebah is in doubt; in the MT the city is called Betah, but the NIV uses Tebah here to harmonize the passage with 1 Chr 18:8.[79] Berothai probably occupied the same site as modern Bereitan; in 1 Chr 18:8 it is called Cun.[80]

8:9–14   David's successful military exploits against both Zobah and Damascus intimidated leaders of the other Aramean city-states, causing them to take steps to appease David and establish nonaggression pacts with him. When, for example, "Toi [NIV, "Tou"; cf. 1 Chr 18:9] king of Hamath heard that David had defeated the entire army of Hadadezer" (v. 9), he sent a high-level delegation "to King David to greet him and congratulate him" on his recent successes. Heading the delegation was Toi's son and heir-apparent Joram (= "Yah is exalted"),[81] known elsewhere as Hadoram (= "Hadad is exalted"; cf. 1 Chr 18:10), "who brought with him articles of silver and gold and bronze." The importance of the persons and gifts sent to David suggest that Hamath was establishing a treaty with Israel in which Israel was the superior party.[82]

David, who recognized the Lord as the true source of his success, "dedicated these articles to the LORD" (v. 11), along with the plunder he had taken from

---

[79] The MT's reading בֶּטַח is questionable in light of the agreement of the Lucianic recension of the LXX and Syriac with 1 Chr 18:8, טִבְחַת. Of course, the possibility does exist that the city was known by both names.

[80] Since Chronicles was written later than 2 Samuel, it is possible that a subsequent military conquest had resulted in a name change for the city, from Berothai to Cun. Significant events (cf. Gen 28:19; 50:11), linguistic differences (cf. Gen 31:47), or changes in political control (cf. Num 32:42; Deut 3:14) often have resulted in new names for geographic entities.

[81] The Yahwistic theophoric element in Joram's name may be due to a name change associated with the establishment of a treaty with David and Israel. Since Israel was the superior party in this arrangement, it is conceivable that Toi's son had to demonstrate proper respect for Israel's deity. One way to do this would be through the assumption of an additional name; while he might have retained the name Hadoram, within the context of Israelite dealings he would have been known as Joram. For a somewhat similar situation cf. 2 Kgs 23:34, where the Egyptian pharaoh Necho renamed Eliakim Jehoiakim.

[82] Cf. A. Malamat, "The Kingdom of David and Solomon in Its Contact with Egypt and Aram Naharaim," *BA* 21 (1958): 101.

the other nations. According to 1 Chr 22:14, the cumulative amount of these acquisitions was staggering: one hundred thousand talents of gold (approx. 7.5 million pounds)[83] and one million talents of silver (approx. seventy-five million pounds). In keeping with Torah precedent (cf. Num 4:4), David assigned the Levites the task of protecting this immense wealth.

David's decision to give the silver and gold to the Lord rather than keep it for himself marked him as a true man of the Torah. The law required kings not to "accumulate large amounts of silver and gold" (Deut 17:17), and David's obedience to this basic requirement displayed his unalloyed heart for the Lord. At the same time, it provided a foil for his son Solomon, who amassed huge amounts of the precious metals for himself (cf. 1 Kgs 10:14–23) and ultimately developed a heart that strayed from the Lord (cf. 1 Kgs 11:4). David's sacrificial obedience here also provides a partial explanation of why David's reign was evaluated more positively than Solomon's by the writer of 1 Kings.[84]

David's military exploits also brought him east of the Dead Sea, where he killed eighteen thousand (v. 13) enemy troops. The identity of the enemy is disputed: Samuel states they were Arameans, but 1 Chr 18:12 indicates they were Edomites.[85] The NIV and most modern versions accept the Chronicles account as the superior one, mainly because of the reference to the "Valley of Salt," an area south of the Dead Sea. If the reference in the title of Psalm 60 is to this battle, then the Edomite reading is confirmed.[86]

Perhaps this dispute can be resolved by recognizing that the King's High-

---

[83] J. A. Thompson suggests that those numbers were intended "not to be taken literally," since "this sort of hyperbole is often used in ancient literature and speeches" and also because of "the round numbers" (*1, 2 Chronicles,* NAC [Nashville: Broadman & Holman, 1994], 166). In spite of this reasoning, I am still inclined to accept the figure as essentially accurate (permitting some rounding).

[84] In 1 Kgs 10:14–11:8 Solomon's reign is implicitly measured against the Torah's standards for kings (Deut 17:16–17). In each of the points of comparison Solomon is weighed in the balances and found wanting. David, on the other hand, is subjected to similar tests in 2 Sam 8:4–12 and passes them: he neither acquired large numbers of horses nor accumulates large amounts of silver and gold. Like Solomon, David practiced polygamy; yet the magnitude of Solomon's involvement in this practice (cf. 1 Kgs 11:3) dwarfs that of David.

[85] The MT of 1 Sam 8:13 speaks of אֲרָם, while 1 Chr 18:12 refers to אֱדוֹם. Ignoring vocalic differences, the essential difference between the two words is the upper right-hand corner of one letter (ד vs. ר).

[86] The primary problem in connecting Psalm 60 with this section is in the agents and numbers of battlefield casualties. In the psalm Joab "struck down twelve thousand Edomites," whereas in the present section David struck down eighteen thousand. A traditional way of dealing with this apparent discrepancy is to suggest that Abishai (six thousand casualties; cf. 1 Chr 18:12) and Joab (twelve thousand casualties) assisted David in the task but that David—as commander of the operation—was credited with all casualties inflicted on the enemy. If the MT's reading of 1 Sam 8:13 is accepted as accurate—and I am inclined to do so—then the Ps 60 reference need not be correlated with 8:13, though it is possible to attempt to do so.

way, a major trade route that was controlled by Arameans farther to the north, also ran through this area. It is conceivable that Aramean troops had extended their control into traditionally Edomite territory in order to gain revenues from the caravans passing through the region. Thus after David took control of the caravan routes in the region of Damascus, he would have had to wrest control of the Aramean-dominated sections to the south as well. Having taken control of the Edomite sections of the King's Highway, David "put garrisons throughout Edom" (v. 14). As a result, "all the Edomites became subject to David."

The section summarizing David's military exploits east of the Jordan ends as it began (cf. v. 6), by noting that the Lord "gave David victory wherever he went." From beginning to end, David's battlefield successes were the Lord's successes.

(9) David Establishes a Righteous and Just Administration (8:15–18)

¹⁵**David reigned over all Israel, doing what was just and right for all his people. ¹⁶Joab son of Zeruiah was over the army; Jehoshaphat son of Ahilud was recorder; ¹⁷Zadok son of Ahitub and Ahimelech son of Abiathar were priests; Seraiah was secretary; ¹⁸Benaiah son of Jehoiada was over the Kerethites and Pelethites; and David's sons were royal advisers.**

8:15–18 Justice and righteousness (Hb. *mišpāṭ* and *ṣĕdāqâ*) were primary attributes of the Lord's character (Job 37:23; Pss 33:5; 36:6; 99:4; 103:4; Isa 5:16; Jer 9:24; Mic 7:9) and were considered the two basic virtues that characterized every person and society that pleased the Lord (Ps 106:3; Prov 21:3 Isa 1:27; 9:7; 56:1; Ezek 18:5,27; 33:14–19); by possessing them an individual would avoid the Lord's judgments and receive covenant promises and blessings (Gen 18:19; Ps 106:3; Jer 22:15; Ezek 18:5,27; 33:14–19). Israelite leaders especially were expected to possess these traits (1 Kgs 10:9; 2 Chr 9:8; Isa 9:7). David's exemplary administration of justice over all Israel opened the way for the Lord's blessing to fall on the land.

David demonstrated his competency in administering justice and righteousness over all Israel by appointing competent leaders who would enforce the Lord's judgments. His nephew Joab (v. 16; cf. 20:23) was charged with the task of bringing divine justice militarily on those who opposed the Lord. Jehoshaphat was "recorder" (Hb. *mazkîr*; lit., "one causing to remember"), that is, one who chronicled David's administration and the discharge of the Lord's will, thus permitting future generations to "remember the wonders [Yahweh] has done" (Ps 105:5). He probably also bore the responsibilities of overseeing the archiving of official records and of disseminating royal commands. Seraiah, who served as "secretary" (Hb. *sôpēr,* v. 17), probably assisted him in these tasks.

Zadok and Ahimelech (v. 17) were both direct descendants of Aaron though through different families.[87] Their responsibility in David's cabinet was the proper implementation of Israelite worship, especially as it was administered in Jerusalem (cf. 2 Sam 15:24–35). Zadok also functioned as one of several court prophets (cf. 2 Sam 15:27).

Benaiah, a military hero of legendary proportions (cf. 23:20–21), was the son of a priest (cf. 1 Chr 27:5) from the southern Judahite city of Kabzeel (cf. 2 Sam 23:20; Josh 15:21). The Kerethites and Pelethites are usually understood to be non-Israelite soldiers of Cretan and Philistine extraction that served as a private militia for the king, the assumption being that mercenaries would have no vested interest in participating in treachery against the throne.[88] The Kerethites and Pelethites are always mentioned in connection with each other—as though they were a single group—and only in passages dealing with David's kingship; perhaps the group ceased to exist after David's death. David's appointment of a priest as the head of the Kerethites and Pelethites seems to reflect his characteristic concern to have Israelite military affairs conducted in accordance with the Lord's guidelines (cf. 1 Sam 21:5). Benaiah's priestly status probably also explains his mention after the Aaronic priests and prior to David's priestly sons.

David's sons served as priests (Hb. *kōhănîm*; NIV, "royal advisers"). Scholars have proposed various explanations of the actual role David's sons played as priests. Some, such as the NIV, take their interpretive cue from 1 Chr 18:17 and translate the term *kōhănîm* as though it conveyed a consultative role. G. J. Wenham proposes a textual emendation and suggests they were "administrators of the royal estates."[89] It is preferable, however, to interpret the term in light of David's presumed status as a priest in the order of Melchizedek (cf. comments on 6:14); accordingly, David's sons would have possessed the inherited title and performed whatever duties were associated with the office. Still others understand the term to refer to David's sons' participation in sacerdotal duties that could be performed by laypersons.[90] Although I know of no scholar who holds this position, a fourth—and unlikely—possibility is that David

---

[87] Cf. 1 Chr 24:6. Zadok was a descendant of Eleazar (cf. 1 Chr 6:3–9) and thus an inheritor of the Torah prophecies given to Phinehas (cf. Num 25:12–13). Abiathar was a descendant of Ithamar, son of Aaron, as well as Eli (cf. 1 Kgs 2:27).

[88] Cf. Baldwin, *1 and 2 Samuel*, 224. For a detailed treatment of the Kerethites, cf. M. Delcor, "Les Kéréthim et les Crétois," *VT* 28 (1978): 409–22. Delcor concludes that the Kerethites migrated from Crete to Palestine during the Davidic period.

[89] Cf. G. J. Wenham, "Were David's Sons Priests?" *ZAW* 87 (1975): 79–82. His emendation is based on the assumption that the word כֹּהֲנִים should be emended to שֹׁכְנִים.

[90] Cf. J. Mauchline, *1 and 2 Samuel*, NCB (London: Oliphants, 1971), 238; and C. E. Armerding, "Were David's Sons Really Priests?" in *Current Issues in Biblical and Patristic Interpretation: Studies in Honor of Merrill C. Tenney*, ed. G. F. Hawthorne (Grand Rapids: Eerdmans, 1975), 75–86.

bestowed the title on his sons in recognition of the Torah's assertion that Israel was to be a "kingdom of priests" (Exod 19:6): as a faithful son of the covenant, David was a priest, and by bestowing the title on his sons, he was dedicating them to faithful service to the covenant as well.

(10) David Fulfills His Commitment to Jonathan (9:1–13)[91]

[1]David asked, "Is there anyone still left of the house of Saul to whom I can show kindness for Jonathan's sake?"

[2]Now there was a servant of Saul's household named Ziba. They called him to appear before David, and the king said to him, "Are you Ziba?"

"Your servant," he replied.

[3]The king asked, "Is there no one still left of the house of Saul to whom I can show God's kindness?"

Ziba answered the king, "There is still a son of Jonathan; he is crippled in both feet."

[4]"Where is he?" the king asked.

Ziba answered, "He is at the house of Makir son of Ammiel in Lo Debar."

[5]So King David had him brought from Lo Debar, from the house of Makir son of Ammiel.

[6]When Mephibosheth son of Jonathan, the son of Saul, came to David, he bowed down to pay him honor.

David said, "Mephibosheth!"

"Your servant," he replied.

---

[91] Many scholars consider 2 Samuel 9–20, along with 1 Kgs 1–2, to be an originally separate narrative unit, popularly known as the Succession Narrative. Cf. L. Rost, *Die Überlieferung von der Thronnachfolge Davids*, BWANT III, 6 (Stuttgart: W. Kohlhammer, 1926; English trans.—*The Succession to the Throne of David* (Sheffield: Almond, 1982); J. W. Flanagan, "Court History or Succession Document? A Study of 2 Sam 9–20 and 1 Kings 1–2," *JBL* 91 (1972): 172–81. McCarter considers this section to be "court apologetic"—a series of narratives assembled during the period of Solomon to vindicate Solomon in his role as king of Israel ("Plots, True or False? The Succession Narrative as Court Apologetic," *Int* 35 [1981]: 355–67). K. W. Whitelam concludes that this supposed composition was designed to portray David as the ideal man for Israel's throne and thus terms it a "defence of David" ("The Defence of David," *JSOT* 29 [1984]: 61–87). A suspicious view of this hypothesis is expressed by P. R. Ackroyd, "The Succession Narrative (so-called)," *Int* 35 (1981): 383–96; Carlson, *David the Chosen King*, 131–39. For a literary treatment of the so-called Succession Narrative, cf. J. S. Ackerman, "Knowing Good and Evil: A Literary Analysis of the Court History I 2 Samuel 9–20 and 1 Kgs 1–2," *JBL* 109 (1990): 41–60; for a reader-response approach to this section of text, cf. W. S. Vorster, "Readings, Readers and the Succession Narrative: An Essay on Reception," *ZAW* 98 (1986): 351–62. For an example of theological exegesis that views the so-called Succession Narrative as a demonstration of the shift from a theocentric to an anthropocentric worldview in ancient Israel, cf. Brueggemann, "Life and Death in Tenth-Century Israel," *JAAR* 40 (1972): 96–109. I am unconvinced that an originally independent narrative entity as conceived by Rost, Flanagan, McCarter, and others ever existed. Certainly there were various written accounts that were utilized in the writing of 2 Sam 9–20; but their wording, arrangement, and predominant themes are the unique product of the author of 1, 2 Samuel.

[7]"Don't be afraid," David said to him, "for I will surely show you kindness for the sake of your father Jonathan. I will restore to you all the land that belonged to your grandfather Saul, and you will always eat at my table."

[8]Mephibosheth bowed down and said, "What is your servant, that you should notice a dead dog like me?"

[9]Then the king summoned Ziba, Saul's servant, and said to him, "I have given your master's grandson everything that belonged to Saul and his family. [10]You and your sons and your servants are to farm the land for him and bring in the crops, so that your master's grandson may be provided for. And Mephibosheth, grandson of your master, will always eat at my table." (Now Ziba had fifteen sons and twenty servants.)

[11]Then Ziba said to the king, "Your servant will do whatever my lord the king commands his servant to do." So Mephibosheth ate at David's table like one of the king's sons.

[12]Mephibosheth had a young son named Mica, and all the members of Ziba's household were servants of Mephibosheth. [13]And Mephibosheth lived in Jerusalem, because he always ate at the king's table, and he was crippled in both feet.

In this chapter David fulfills the pledge of familial support he made to Saul as well as to Jonathan son of Saul (cf. 1 Sam 18:3; 20:42; 23:18; 24:21–22), the one initially positioned in the Saulide dynasty as David's chief challenger for Israel's throne. Through this narrative the biblical writer portrays David as the supreme Israelite example of covenant faithfulness (Hb. *ḥesed*), the highest virtue in Hebrew society. Judged by David's own demanding criteria (cf. Ps 15:1,4), the king proved himself worthy to live on the Lord's holy hill by keeping his oath to Jonathan even though it ran the risk of hurting his own dynasty.

9:1–3 Established on the throne in Jerusalem after having effectively put down both internal and external opposition, David was now in a position to fulfill his commitment to "the house of Saul" (v. 1). Accordingly, at an unknown point in time but perhaps before the events of 2 Sam 21:1–10 (cf. esp. 21:7), he began a search for someone to whom he could "show kindness for Jonathan's sake." Ziba, a well-to-do (cf. v. 10) "servant of Saul's household" (v. 2) who apparently managed the former king's royal estate, was called in and questioned by the king.

The narrator's seemingly unnecessary repetition of David's question in v. 3 (cf. v. 1) is in fact significant in establishing the theme of this chapter. It underscores that David was not an enemy of "the house of Saul" (v. 3); in fact, he was an agent of "God's kindness" (Hb. *ḥesed;* "loving faithfulness") working to benefit Israel's former dynastic family.

9:4–10 Through his inquiry David learned that there was "still a son of Jonathan" (v. 4) apparently living with a wife and son (cf. v. 12) in a self-imposed internal exile "at the house of Makir son of Ammiel in Lo Debar." Makir, mentioned here for the first time, was a wealthy and powerful individual living east of the Jordan at Lo Debar (modern Umm ed-Debar?) in the Jordan river valley of Gilead. Later he proved to be one of David's most loyal supporters (cf. 17:27–29).

Mephibosheth, known outside of 2 Samuel as Merib-Baal[92] (cf. 1 Chr 8:34; 9:40), was "crippled in both feet" (v. 3) as a result of an accident in early childhood (cf. 4:4). David summoned him for appearance at the royal court. Appropriately—and perhaps somewhat awkwardly—the lame young man "bowed down" before the king "to pay him honor" (v. 6).

Using a dialogic script reflective of an interchange between a social superior and an inferior (cf. 1 Sam 3:9), David called out Mephibosheth's name; in turn, Mephibosheth referred to himself as "your servant." After establishing the sociological parameters of this relationship by giving the proper initial exchange, David issued a magnanimous decree that changed Mephibosheth's fortunes forever. First, David restored to the disfigured, exiled Saulide "all the land that belonged to . . . Saul" (v. 7). This would have meant that the family estate located about three miles north of Jerusalem in Gibeah would be returned to Mephibosheth. Second, David gave Mephibosheth a privilege that seemed to have perished the day his father Jonathan had died, the right to board at the king's table "always."[93] Saul had accorded David this dispensation during his youth (cf. 1 Sam 20:5); now David returned the favor. Third, David provided Mephibosheth with a large contingent of servants and material wealth. He ordered "Ziba, Saul's servant" (v. 9) along with his "fifteen sons and twenty servants" (v. 10), "to farm the land" that had originally belonged to Saul "and bring in the crops" for Mephibosheth so that Jonathan's son "may be provided for."

Mephibosheth's response to the king's magnanimous pronouncements was one of abject humility (cf. 2 Sam 7:18). After bowing down once again before David, he called himself "your slave" (v. 8; NIV, "servant"; Hb. ʿebed) and "a dead dog" (cf. 1 Sam 24:14).

9:11–13 Ziba, whose destiny had also been changed by the king's imperial edict, had no choice but to accept the new assignment—and this he did. However, when the opportunity presented itself, Ziba apparently tried to manipulate David to issue a different, more favorable edict (cf. 16:2–4).

---

[92] Cf. comments at 4:4. In keeping with the literary/theological tendency of extant copies of 1, 2 Samuel, Mephibosheth's name appears to have been modified from its original form. The name "Mephibosheth" appears to mean "From the mouth of shame," or possibly "One who scatters shame" (cf. McCarter, *II Samuel,* 124–25; S. R. Driver, *Notes on the Hebrew Text of Samuel,* 254). The name "Merib-Baal" means "He who contends with Baal." The theophoric element "Baal" has been expunged from all personal names in 1, 2 Samuel. It seems that this effort was carried out in accordance with the Torah requirement to avoid letting other gods' names be heard on the lips of a person of the Covenant (cf. Exod 23:13).

[93] Youngblood understands this provision for Mephibosheth "as a metaphor referring to house arrest" (*1, 2 Samuel,* 918). I understand it much more positively, as does Baldwin (*1 and 2 Samuel,* 227). Payne detects "mixed motives" (*I and II Samuel,* 197).

Mephibosheth—and presumably his entire family, including "a young son named Mica" (v. 12)—was permanently relocated back in Benjamite territory "in Jerusalem" (v. 13).[94] There Mephibosheth "always ate at the king's table" even though "he was crippled in both feet." David's acceptance of a lame man in his house confirms that the royal pronouncement banning "the lame" in the royal residence was intended as a figurative reference to an ethnic group, not mobility-impaired individuals (cf. comments at 5:8).

(11) David Conquers an Ammonite-led Coalition (10:1–19)

[1]In the course of time, the king of the Ammonites died, and his son Hanun succeeded him as king. [2]David thought, "I will show kindness to Hanun son of Nahash, just as his father showed kindness to me." So David sent a delegation to express his sympathy to Hanun concerning his father.

When David's men came to the land of the Ammonites, [3]the Ammonite nobles said to Hanun their lord, "Do you think David is honoring your father by sending men to you to express sympathy? Hasn't David sent them to you to explore the city and spy it out and overthrow it?" [4]So Hanun seized David's men, shaved off half of each man's beard, cut off their garments in the middle at the buttocks, and sent them away.

[5]When David was told about this, he sent messengers to meet the men, for they were greatly humiliated. The king said, "Stay at Jericho till your beards have grown, and then come back."

[6]When the Ammonites realized that they had become a stench in David's nostrils, they hired twenty thousand Aramean foot soldiers from Beth Rehob and Zobah, as well as the king of Maacah with a thousand men, and also twelve thousand men from Tob.

[7]On hearing this, David sent Joab out with the entire army of fighting men. [8]The Ammonites came out and drew up in battle formation at the entrance to their city gate, while the Arameans of Zobah and Rehob and the men of Tob and Maacah were by themselves in the open country.

[9]Joab saw that there were battle lines in front of him and behind him; so he selected some of the best troops in Israel and deployed them against the Arameans. [10]He put the rest of the men under the command of Abishai his brother and deployed them against the Ammonites. [11]Joab said, "If the Arameans are too strong for me, then you are to come to my rescue; but if the Ammonites are too strong for you, then I will come to rescue you. [12]Be strong and let us fight bravely for our people and the cities of our God. The LORD will do what is good in his sight."

[13]Then Joab and the troops with him advanced to fight the Arameans, and they fled before him. [14]When the Ammonites saw that the Arameans were fleeing, they fled before Abishai and went inside the city. So Joab returned from fighting the Ammonites and came to Jerusalem.

[94]Concerning the tribal assignment for Jerusalem, cf. Josh 18:28.

^{15}After the Arameans saw that they had been routed by Israel, they regrouped. ^{16}Hadadezer had Arameans brought from beyond the River; they went to Helam, with Shobach the commander of Hadadezer's army leading them.

^{17}When David was told of this, he gathered all Israel, crossed the Jordan and went to Helam. The Arameans formed their battle lines to meet David and fought against him. ^{18}But they fled before Israel, and David killed seven hundred of their charioteers and forty thousand of their foot soldiers. He also struck down Shobach the commander of their army, and he died there. ^{19}When all the kings who were vassals of Hadadezer saw that they had been defeated by Israel, they made peace with the Israelites and became subject to them.

So the Arameans were afraid to help the Ammonites anymore.

The present story serves as a significant foil to the previous episode. In both narratives David is shown expressing compassion and generosity toward individuals from the region of Gilead whose royal forebears had recently died. David's desire to bless both sons of the covenant, exemplified by Mephibosheth, as well as those outside the covenant circle, exemplified by Hanun, is evident here. Hanun's reactions to David's acts—which differ significantly from those of Mephibosheth—go far to throw favorable light on Mephibosheth.

King David's deep concern for the interests and concerns of his soldiers, as well as his military brilliance both tactically and in the heat of battle, are displayed in this chapter. The biblical writer portrays David here as a man who was willing to put significant national resources at risk in order to uphold justice (cf. 8:15).

David's continuing interaction with Aramean city-states also is portrayed in this chapter. Perhaps his interest in these national groups (cf. 8:3–14) was due in part to the fact that much revenue could be earned from controlling the international trade routes that ran through the region.

At the same time, this chapter provides a historical context for the events of chaps. 11–12. In concert with 12:26–31, this section frames, and thus highlights, the significance of David's sin and resulting judgment.[95]

10:1–2a "After this" (v. 1; NIV, "In the course of time")—that is, after David had fulfilled his commitment to Jonathan—Nahash "the king of the Ammonites died." Israel had previously defeated Nahash in battle (cf. 1 Sam 11:1–11), and David had apparently maintained a peace treaty with the Ammonites that recognized Israel as the superior party.

Out of proper respect for the passing of a head of state with whom he had established a treaty, "David sent a delegation to express his sympathy to Hanun" (v. 2), Nahash's son and successor. At the same time, David took steps to "show kindness to Hanun son of Nahash" and thereby confirm the continu-

---

[95] For a similar conclusion, cf. J. I. Lawlor, "Theology and Art in the Narrative of the Ammonite War (2 Samuel 10–12)," *GTJ* 3 (1982): 193–205.

ance of favorable relations between the nations.

10:2b–5 David's honorable intentions in sending the delegation to Rabbah Ammon were either misunderstood or cunningly rebuffed by the "military leaders [lit., "princes"] of the sons of Ammon" (v. 3; NIV, "Ammonite nobles"). This group of influential men convinced the new Ammonite king that David had sent the diplomatic entourage with ulterior, hostile motives.

Hanun believed the paranoid (or sinister?) report that came to him and acted accordingly. Rather than treating David's men with great respect as representatives of a superior party in a covenant treaty, he humiliated them egregiously and sent them back. Hanun's treatment of the men would have desecrated the men's bodies, their clothes, and their national mission.

Except for the performance of certain religious rituals (cf. Lev 14:9; Num 6:18: Ezek 5:1) or to express profound emotional distress (cf. Ezra 9:3), Israelite men always wore beards. To remove an Israelite male's beard forcibly was to force him to violate the Torah (cf. Lev 19:27) and to show contempt for him personally (cf. Isa 50:6).

Likewise, the removal of the extremities of a garment made that garment unacceptable by Torah standards (cf. Num 15:38; Deut 22:12) and had the effect of symbolically desecrating the law itself (cf. Num 15:39). Of course, the Ammonites' actions also dishonored the Israelite men by forcibly exposing their genitals to public view, a humiliating experience to men of that culture.

When David learned of the Ammonites' outrageous actions, he acted as a good shepherd of the Lord's flock, ministering first to the needs of his victimized men before tending to the Ammonites. He ordered the delegation to "stay at Jericho," the first Israelite settlement west of the Jordan on the main road back to Jerusalem, until their beards had grown back. This decree permitted the men to avoid multiplying their humiliation by having to appear in disgrace before their families and at the royal court in Jerusalem.[96]

10:6–8 The Ammonites no doubt calculated that their provocative actions would cause them to "become a stench in David's nostrils" (v. 6)—and their reasonings proved correct. Perhaps Hanun and his men had deliberately created an incident in order to break free of treaty obligations established between David and his father Nahash. In anticipation of an armed response from David, they hired an army of mercenaries from Beth Rehob, Zobah, Maacah, and Tob. These Aramean city-states, all regions north and east of the Sea of Galilee, were as much as 110 miles north of Rabbah Ammon. The hired forces would have traveled down the King's Highway to journey to Rabbah Amman and encounter the Israelite army. According to 1 Chr 19:6, Hanun paid one thousand talents (approx. 75,000 pounds) of silver to gain the services of these Arameans. The

---

[96] The Israelite custom regarding the appropriateness of facial hair at the royal court differed considerably from Egyptian protocol. Whereas the Israelite's full beard (cf. Lev 19:27) was his glory, it was apparently considered uncultured and unsuitable for Egyptians (cf. Gen 41:14).

practice of employing a mercenary force against enemies who were perceived to be superior was common in the ancient Near East; Israelites did this on numerous occasions throughout the royal period (cf. 1 Kgs 15:18–20; 2 Kgs 16:8–9; 2 Chr 25:5–6).

David learned of the menacing military activity in the vicinity of Aram, perhaps from the Israelite garrisons situated in the district of Damascus (cf. 8:14), who may have observed Ammonite caravans transporting silver. Taking the threat extremely seriously, he responded by sending Joab out with the Israelite army (v. 7).

David's forces under Joab crossed the Jordan river near Jericho, then pushed eastward and northward up toward Rabbah Ammon. An unexpected and dangerous military situation awaited the Israelites as they approached the vicinity of Ammon. Instead of a massive group of Arameans still north of them, about to join forces with the Ammonites at Rabbah, they found that the Arameans had arrived early and actually moved their forces some twenty miles south of Rabbah to Medeba (modern Madeba; cf. 1 Chr 19:7).[97]

Now the entire Israelite army was trapped between two formidable armies. "The Ammonites came out and drew up in battle formation at the entrance to their city gate" (v. 8), while the chariot-led (cf. 1 Chr 19:6) Aramean armies were poised to attack the Israelites from the rear.

10:9–12 When Joab became aware of the enemy's brilliant tactic of putting "battle lines in front of him and behind him" (v. 9), he was compelled to improvise a strategy that would permit him to deal with both threats simultaneously. His plan was to divide the Israelite troops, putting the most capable general and most "of the best troops in Israel" up against the greatest threat, while directing the remainder of the force against the weaker enemy. Joab himself took command of the elite Israelite force "and deployed them against the Arameans." He gave command of the second force to his brother Abishai with the understanding that if the Arameans proved to be "too strong for" (v. 11) Joab's forces, or if the Ammonites were "too strong for" Abishai's forces, then the two contingents would reunite and face the most immediate threat together.

Joab's plan was risky at best, and all involved knew it. Nevertheless, it seemed to be the best way to cope with the nasty surprise that had greeted Israel east of the Jordan. Accordingly Joab encouraged the troops to do three things: first, to "be strong" (v. 12)—that is, to utilize every personal resource at their disposal. Second, he urged them to "fight bravely for our people"—that is, to remember that their efforts on the battlefield would directly impact their families and the rest of Israel. Third, he encouraged them to fight bravely for "the

---

[97] Some biblical interpreters reject the textual assertions in 1 Chr 19:7 regarding Medeba, assuming "that this relates to David's conquest of Moab" (Aharoni and Avi-Yonah, *Macmillan Bible Atlas*, 67). Such a conclusion is not based on textual evidence and seems both arbitrary and unwarranted.

cities of our God"—that is, to fight in defense of the Lord's possessions, in this case the Promised Land and its cities.

Joab's third statement to the troops suggests that for him this battle was ultimately a religious conflict; it was a tangible expression of Israel's commitment to the Lord. So far the Ammonites had desecrated the Lord's people by their shameful treatment of the official delegation; however, if the Israelite troops failed to achieve a victory here, the Ammonites would be free to invade and desecrate the Lord's land, thus doing immeasurably more harm.

Joab concluded his prebattle statements by encouraging the Israelites to remember that the battle belonged to the Lord (cf. 1 Sam 17:47; 2 Chr 20:15). Over and above the Ammonites, the Arameans, and the Israelites stood the Lord, and he could be counted on to "do what is good in his sight."

10:13–14 After the strategy was devised and the troops properly encouraged, Joab's forces attacked the Arameans, who "fled before him." The Israelites' success against the Aramean forces portended disaster for the Ammonites, who had been closely monitoring the Arameans' battlefield fortunes. Realizing that their hopes of a decisive victory against the Israelites were dashed that day, "they went inside" (v. 14) the fortress city of Rabbah to avoid a similar defeat.

The Israelites, who had not wanted to fight the Ammonites in the first place, made no effort to lay siege to Rabbah at this time; that challenge would await another day (cf. 11:1). Instead, Joab ordered the troops to withdraw and returned to Jerusalem.

10:15–19 The Arameans probably feared military reprisals from David for their role in the failed Ammonite attempt. In an effort to deal with this predictable Israelite response, the Aramean coalition "regrouped" to mount a preemptive military strike. For this second operation Hadadezer, the previously conquered king of Zobah (cf. 8:5), bolstered the regional troops with "Arameans brought from beyond the River" (v. 16) Euphrates.

David's intelligence network in Aram again warned the king of this new threat. David responded appropriately by taking his army across the Jordan to Helam (v. 17; modern `Alma[?]), a site slightly more than thirty miles east of the Sea of Galilee.

At that location he was met by a vast force of chariots and foot soldiers. However, once again the Arameans' best efforts against the Israelites proved futile. In the end "they fled before Israel" (v. 17) and suffered massive casualties: "David killed seven hundred of their charioteers and forty thousand of their foot soldiers" (v. 18).[98] In addition, "he also struck down Shobach [or Shophach; cf. 1 Chr 19:16] the commander" of the multinational force so that "he died there."

---

[98] 1 Chr 19:18 puts this figure at seven thousand, which surely is a transmissional error entering the text sometime after the autographic texts had been completed. A further difference between the Samuel and Chronicles passage is the type of the forty thousand soldiers killed by David's forces: whereas in Chronicles they are foot soldiers (רַגְלִי), in Samuel they are horsemen (פָּרָשִׁים).

David's apparently unsought victories against the Aramean coalition had the desirable effect of greatly expanding Israel's influence over the territories north of Damascus, thus helping them fulfill the Torah promise first given to Abraham (cf. Gen 15:18). The vassal states previously controlled by Hadadezer of Zobah "made peace with the Israelites and became subject to them." This gave David an additional source of revenue, as well as strengthened control over both the Via Maris and the King's Highway, the two most important international roads of that region.

David's influence over the Arameans forced these kingdoms to cancel the mutual-assistance treaties they had previously established with the Ammonites; they now became "afraid to help the Ammonites anymore."

6. The Lord Judges David (11:1–20:26)

Chapter 11 is a watershed in the biblical writer's presentation of David's life. Up to this point, David has been portrayed as the ideal servant of the Lord, scrupulously obedient to every point of the law and zealous in his execution of each command. David's obedience resulted in the fulfillment of Torah promises and an outpouring of blessing on Israel beyond any previously known. Perhaps the most significant of the Torah promises fulfilled through David was the establishment of a dynastic covenant with messianic and eschatological implications (cf. Gen 49:10; Num 24:17).

In this section David becomes for a moment a rebel against the Lord's covenant, with devastating consequences. His twin sins of adultery and murder rent the tapestry of blessing woven so carefully in the previous narratives. Although David repented of the sins he had committed, irreparable damage had been done; the dynastic covenant promises graciously given to David remained, but the Torah blessings resulting from obedience vanished. In their place David began to experience the stern curses of the Torah, including loss of family (cf. Deut 28:18) and even exile (cf. Deut 28:64–67). In all of this David extended the metaphorical comparison between his life and the life of Israel: even as David lost his prestige and homeland through sin, so also would the nation.

If David's sin with its dread consequences is a metaphor of judgment for the nation of Israel through the exilic period, it is also a metaphor of hope. As chap. 20 concludes, David has returned to the environs of Jerusalem and is successfully engaged in the arduous task of rebuilding a nation. The Lord graciously brought David back from exile east of the Jordan, and the Lord would graciously bring Israel back to Jerusalem from its Babylonian exile.[99]

---

[99] For a useful treatment of this chapter from a literary perspective, cf. M. Sternberg, *The Poetics of Biblical Narrative* (Bloomington: Indiana University, 1985), 190–222.

(1) David Does Evil in the Lord's Sight (11:1–27)

[1]In the spring, at the time when kings go off to war, David sent Joab out with the king's men and the whole Israelite army. They destroyed the Ammonites and besieged Rabbah. But David remained in Jerusalem.

[2]One evening David got up from his bed and walked around on the roof of the palace. From the roof he saw a woman bathing. The woman was very beautiful, [3]and David sent someone to find out about her. The man said, "Isn't this Bathsheba, the daughter of Eliam and the wife of Uriah the Hittite?" [4]Then David sent messengers to get her. She came to him, and he slept with her. (She had purified herself from her uncleanness.) Then she went back home. [5]The woman conceived and sent word to David, saying, "I am pregnant."

[6]So David sent this word to Joab: "Send me Uriah the Hittite." And Joab sent him to David. [7]When Uriah came to him, David asked him how Joab was, how the soldiers were and how the war was going. [8]Then David said to Uriah, "Go down to your house and wash your feet." So Uriah left the palace, and a gift from the king was sent after him. [9]Uriah slept at the entrance to the palace with all his master's servants and did not go down to his house.

[10]When David was told, "Uriah did not go home," he asked him, "Haven't you just come from a distance? Why didn't you go home?"

[11]Uriah said to David, "The ark and Israel and Judah are staying in tents, and my master Joab and my lord's men are camped in the open fields. How could I go to my house to eat and drink and lie with my wife? As surely as you live, I will not do such a thing!"

[12]Then David said to him, "Stay here one more day, and tomorrow I will send you back." So Uriah remained in Jerusalem that day and the next. [13]At David's invitation, he ate and drank with him, and David made him drunk. But in the evening Uriah went out to sleep on his mat among his master's servants; he did not go home.

[14]In the morning David wrote a letter to Joab and sent it with Uriah. [15]In it he wrote, "Put Uriah in the front line where the fighting is fiercest. Then withdraw from him so he will be struck down and die."

[16]So while Joab had the city under siege, he put Uriah at a place where he knew the strongest defenders were. [17]When the men of the city came out and fought against Joab, some of the men in David's army fell; moreover, Uriah the Hittite died.

[18]Joab sent David a full account of the battle. [19]He instructed the messenger: "When you have finished giving the king this account of the battle, [20]the king's anger may flare up, and he may ask you, 'Why did you get so close to the city to fight? Didn't you know they would shoot arrows from the wall? [21]Who killed Abimelech son of Jerub-Besheth? Didn't a woman throw an upper millstone on him from the wall, so that he died in Thebez? Why did you get so close to the wall?' If he asks you this, then say to him, 'Also, your servant Uriah the Hittite is dead.'"

[22]The messenger set out, and when he arrived he told David everything Joab had sent him to say. [23]The messenger said to David, "The men overpowered us

and came out against us in the open, but we drove them back to the entrance to
the city gate. ²⁴Then the archers shot arrows at your servants from the wall, and
some of the king's men died. Moreover, your servant Uriah the Hittite is dead."
²⁵David told the messenger, "Say this to Joab: 'Don't let this upset you; the
sword devours one as well as another. Press the attack against the city and destroy
it.' Say this to encourage Joab."
²⁶When Uriah's wife heard that her husband was dead, she mourned for him.
²⁷After the time of mourning was over, David had her brought to his house, and
she became his wife and bore him a son. But the thing David had done displeased
the LORD.

11:1 David had met the challenge of the Ammonite rebellion following
Nahash's death (cf. 10:6–14), but he had not eliminated the Ammonite threat
of continued challenges to his authority. In their previous fight with Israel's
army the Ammonites had merely retreated behind the protective walls of Rabbah and remained essentially unscathed. The proximity of Ammon to the tribal
territories of Gad and Manasseh meant that David could not ignore this menacing neighbor; another, more focused military effort against them would be
necessary.

Consequently, the following "spring, at the time when the delegation had
gone forth [NIV, "when kings go off to war"],[100] David sent Joab out" to Rabbah Ammon a second time. David's timing for the military campaign was
important for two reasons. First, by picking the anniversary date of the humiliation of the Israelite envoy sent to convey condolences for Nahash's death (cf.
10:2), David left no doubt about the reason for this attack on Rabbah. Second,
late spring was the ideal time to conduct foreign military campaigns because of
improved weather conditions and the fact that the armies could be fed from the
wheat and barley ripening in Ammonite fields. For the campaign David made
Joab his agent to command both "the king's men"—perhaps the Kerethites and
Pelethites—"and the whole Israelite army."

The Israelites were eminently successful in the first phase of their campaign;
"they destroyed the Ammonites" who chose to stand their ground and defend
their city. In the second phase of Israel's efforts, the army "besieged Rabbah";
this process could easily take months or even years (cf. 2 Kgs 25:1–3)—a fact
of some relevance for the present narrative.

David "remained in Jerusalem" during all but the final phase of this cam-

---

[100] The NIV's rendering rejects the MT at this point, choosing to follow the variant textual traditions of the LXX, Vg, Josephus, and 1 Chr 20:1. However, the MT reading is both comprehensible and thematically useful here: it should not be rejected. M. Garsiel analyzes this story, working
from the standpoint that the unemended, surface reading of the MT is the preferred reading; his
approach is refreshing and fraught with implications useful to biblical studies in general ("The
Story of David and Bathsheba: A Different Approach," *CBQ* 55 [1993]: 244–62). Cf. also J. P.
Fokkelman, *Narrative Art and Poetry in the Books of Samuel,* vol. 1: *King David (II Sam. 9–20
and 1 Kings 1–2)* (Assen: Van Gorcum, 1981), 50–51, who also agrees with the MT's reading.

paign (cf. 13:29–30). The king's absence from the battlefield at this time should not be understood as dereliction of duty. David had previously remained in Jerusalem when the Ammonites were attacked (cf. 10:7). Furthermore, at some point in David's military career—quite possibly prior to the events of this passage—David's men had pleaded with him to avoid an active role in military campaigns (cf. 21:17) out of concern for the king's safety and the best interests of the nation.

11:2–5 "One evening"[101] (v. 2) during this period, David got up from his bed and walked around on the roof of the palace." The preferred portion of an Israelite house on warm evenings was the sturdy flat roof (cf. 1 Sam 9:25), where one might relax in the comparative comfort of cool breezes.

David's house probably was located on the highest ground within the old Jebusite fortress, and from his rooftop he would have had a commanding view of the city. From that vantage point, David "saw a woman bathing." Since no Israelite house had running water at that time, bathing often may have been performed privately, in the enclosed courtyard that was a part of many Israelite houses; alternatively, it may have been done openly near the city's public water source. There is no indication in the text that the woman deliberately positioned herself so as to entice David.[102]

David noticed that "the woman was very beautiful," and his desires were aroused. Accordingly, he "sent someone to find out about her" (v. 3; cp. 1 Sam 17:55–58). The messenger reported that the woman was "Bathsheba, the daughter of Eliam and the wife of Uriah the Hittite"; thus, she was the daughter of one of David's best fighters (cf. 23:34), the granddaughter of his most trusted counselor (cf. 16:23; 23:34), and the wife of one of his inner circle of honored soldiers (cf. 23:39). Since David was properly informed of this latter fact, for him to pursue Bathsheba further was already to commit adultery with her in his heart (cf. Matt 5:28).

Notwithstanding the Torah's prohibition (cf. Exod 20:14; Lev 18:20; Deut 5:18) and the fact that the penalty for adultery was death (cf. Lev 20:10; Deut 22:22), "David sent messengers to get her" (v. 4). Bathsheba "came to him," perhaps because she was naive or simply lacked the will to resist the powerful king's request, or perhaps because she desired to be unfaithful to her husband. The writer's omission of an explicit motive behind Bathsheba's action reinforces the conviction that this story is not so much about Bathsheba's actions

---

[101] Keil and Delitzsch suggest that the time was after David had taken "his mid-day rest" (*II Samuel*, 382).

[102] In spite of this, G. G. Nicol concludes that Bathsheba was shrewdly manipulating David for personal ends in this and other incidents throughout her life ("Bathsheba, A Clever Woman?" *ExpTim* 99 [1988]: 360–63). Keil and Delitzsch also fault Bathsheba because "she came without any hesitation and offered no resistance to his desires" (*II Samuel*, 383). However, the text merely omits any mention of hesitation and resistance; it does not affirm the position of Keil and Delitzsch.

but David's. David "slept with her," an idiomatic Hebrew expression indicating that he engaged in sexual intercourse with her. David's sinful encounter with Bathsheba occurred "after she had purified herself from her uncleanness" (cf. Lev 15:19), that is, during the part of her monthly cycle when she was not menstruating and thus was more likely to conceive,[103] which she did. When she had become aware of the bodily changes that accompanied the pregnancy, Bathsheba sent someone to David informing him of her situation.

11:6–9 Ever resourceful in adversity, David had a scheme for handling the present crisis. The plan was simple and essentially foolproof: bring Uriah back to Jerusalem temporarily, have him spend one intimate night with his wife, and then send him back to Rabbah. Approximately nine months later Bathsheba would have her child, Uriah would be ecstatic, and David would possess total deniability—no one, not even the servant who had brought Bathsheba to David, could prove that David fathered the child. With this plan in mind, David ordered Joab to "send me Uriah the Hittite," which he did.

With the first part of the plan successfully implemented, David initiated the second phase. Uriah, perhaps breathless from the hasty return to Jerusalem in response to the royal summons, entered the king's presence. Not knowing what urgent matter had necessitated this forty-plus-mile trip to Jerusalem, Uriah might have been somewhat surprised to find that the king merely wanted to know "how Joab was, how the soldiers were, and how the war was going" (v. 7). Such comparatively trivial information could have been acquired from any of the runners who kept David informed of the battle's progress—it certainly did not need to come from one of the Thirty (cf. 23:39).

In an effort to appear generous and appreciative of Uriah's efforts and information, David directed Uriah to "go down to your house and wash your feet" (v. 8). David's reference to footwashing was a suggestion that he receive gracious domestic hospitality (cf. Gen 18:4; 19:2; 24:32; 43:24) from his wife; implicitly it was an order to spend a night of marital intimacy with Bathsheba. To encourage the celebrative moment in the household, David sent "a gift"— probably of food and wine—to Uriah's residence. However, neither David's directive nor his gift achieved their intended purpose, for Uriah "did not go down to his house" (v. 9).[104]

Uriah's refusal to have sexual contact with his wife at this time was clearly an expression of his devotion to the Lord: all sanctioned military activity was a form of service to the Lord, and it required the Lord's blessing for success. In order to maximize the probability of receiving that blessing in military endeav-

---

[103] M. Krause suggests it was the fourteenth day within her (lunar-based) cycle ("II Sam 11,4 und das Konzeptionsoptimum," *ZAW* 95 [1983]: 434–37).

[104] Hertzberg suspects "that Uriah had wind of the affair" because of court gossip he had heard and that David's generosity confirmed his suspicions (*I and II Samuel*, 310). This opinion is not supported by any explicit statements in the text.

ors, David seems to have required soldiers carrying out military assignments to keep themselves in a state of ritual purity, which necessarily meant refraining from all sexual contact (cf. 1 Sam 21:5; Exod 19:15). If Uriah had had sexual relations with Bathsheba, he would have rendered himself temporarily unfit for military service (cf. Lev 15:18) and thus unfit for service to the Lord.

11:10–13 When David learned that "Uriah did not go home" (v. 10), he had the soldier brought before him and plied him with leading questions: Had he not "just come from a distance" that would have required him to be absent from his wife for a period of time? Why then did he not "go home?" David's questions were a thinly veiled attack on Uriah's virility designed to pressure him into temporarily setting aside larger commitments.

Undaunted by the king's wounding words, Uriah explained his action as the expression of solidarity with both the Lord and his comrades in arms.[105] His comrades—men with equally strong affections for their wives—were forced to be separated from their families by being encamped "in the fields." On oath Uriah declared he would not break faith with the others and afford himself the luxury of spending the evening with his wife.

In growing desperation David ordered Uriah to spend one more day in Jerusalem so that the king could try a different strategy. This time David would employ a scandalous but uncomplicated tactic: the king would make Uriah drunk, hoping that his servant would then sacrifice principle for baser instincts. David could have learned this technique, ironically enough, from a study of the Torah's account of the origins of the Ammonites (cf. Gen 19:30–38), the very people Uriah was now fighting.

"At David's invitation" (v. 13) on two consecutive evenings (cf. v. 12), therefore, Uriah "ate and drank" at the royal table and the king succeeded in making him drunk. Despite his chemically impaired reasoning, however, Uriah again refused to compromise his values. Instead of going home to sleep with Bathsheba, he spent the night among his master's servants."

11:14–15 All lesser measures having failed, David was now confronted with the horrible choice of either admitting that he committed a capital crime, thereby condemning himself to death, or ordering the death of one of his most valuable soldiers. Either way, someone would have to die, and since David was unwilling to order his own death, that someone was Uriah.

"The morning" (v. 14) after what must have been one of the most difficult nights in David's life, the king "wrote a letter to Joab and sent it with Uriah." Though ostraca were sometimes used for official military correspondence,[106]

---

[105] Youngblood translates the word בַּסֻּכּוֹת, "in tents," as "'in Succoth' (modern Deir Alla, a Transjordanian site almost forty miles northeast of Jerusalem)," since the ark never would have been put in a סֻכָּה, that is, an agricultural hut (*1, 2 Samuel,* 934).

[106] Cf. the Lachish ostraca, a collection of twenty-one letters written on broken pottery discovered at Lachish, which are examples of military correspondence. Cf. *ANET,* 321–22.

undoubtedly the letter that Uriah carried was either parchment or papyrus, sealed with the royal signet ring so that its contents would have been unknown to anyone but Joab. Uriah was unwittingly carrying his own death warrant.[107]

11:16–21 Joab complied with his uncle's orders, though he must surely have questioned them. Once the Israelite troops had sealed off Ammon by preventing all traffic in or out of the city, direct attacks against Rabbah's walls would have been unnecessary, since it was safer to wait until the people inside starved or voluntarily surrendered. Except for occasional desperate attacks from Ammonite forces venturing out of the city gate to try to break the siege or perhaps mercenary forces other than Arameans (cf. 10:19) hired by the besieged, the Israelite forces had little to fear.

Joab obediently ordered Uriah to attack the city at its strongest point—probably near the city gate. Exactly as David had hoped, Uriah was killed, but along with him several other of David's soldiers died needlessly.

As part of the ongoing task of keeping the king informed of the military operation's progress, "Joab sent David a full account of the battle" (v. 18). The news was not particularly good on this occasion, so Joab provided the messenger with a set of additional—albeit oblique—instructions. Whether the comparatively lengthy set of guidelines (fifty-three words, Joab's second-longest speech) was intended to be part of the cover-up or whether Joab genuinely feared some reprisal from the king cannot be discerned from the text. At any rate, Joab let the messenger know it was important to inform David that his "servant Uriah the Hittite is dead" (v. 21).

11:22–25 The messenger returned to Jerusalem with his report. The reader learns the tragic details of Uriah's death only as they are relayed to King David here. David's response was pastoral in tone as he instructed the messenger "to encourage Joab" (v. 25). David waxed philosophical as he quoted from an ancient proverb to remind Joab that war's unpredictable appetite sometimes consumes a nation's best men. Uriah's death was lamentable, but it must not cause the general to lose sight of the larger objective: Joab should "press the attack against the city and destroy it."

11:26–27 Commonly practiced Old Testament mourning customs included weeping (Hb. *bākâ;* cf. Jer 22:10; Ezek 24:17; Joel 1:8; Zech 12:10); wailing—that is, expressing a mournful, high-pitched cry (*ʾābal;* Jer 6:26); rolling in dust (cf. Ezek 27:30); modifying one's diet for a period of time (Jer 16:5; Ezek 24:17); and modifying one's garb, either putting on sackcloth or, in the case of a woman who lost her spouse, wearing garments that identified her as a widow (Gen 38:14; Jer 6:26; 49:3).

---

[107] For a study of the use of deception in the 2 Samuel narratives, cf. H. Hagan, "Deception as Motif and Theme in 2 Sm 9–20; 1 Kgs 1–2," *Bib* 60 (1979): 301–26. Hagan discusses eighteen different instances of deception.

The official mourning period for an individual might have varied in duration, depending on the social status of the deceased: Aaron and Moses were officially mourned for one cycle of the moon (cf. Num 20:29; Deut 34:8); Uriah's mourning period would not have exceeded that.

Though David's actions here toward Bathsheba have parallels with his treatment of Abigail (cf. 1 Sam 25:39–42), similar policies and motivations may distinguish the two. As perhaps in the case of Abigail, David may have been acting as a royal, surrogate kinsman-redeemer (Hb. *gōʾēl*). David might have claimed he was taking the *gōʾēl* responsibility on himself since Uriah was a foreigner who had no near kinsman living in Israel. As such, David would have assumed the lifelong responsibility of caring for the needs of Uriah's widow and was obligated to father a child in order to raise up an offspring to preserve the family line of the deceased (cf. Gen 38:8; Deut 25:5–6; Ruth 4:5). Such a pretext would have made David's actions toward Bathsheba following Uriah's death seem truly noble and would have accounted nicely for the birth of the son.

No matter how honorable and magnanimous David's actions may have appeared to some, however, what David had done "was evil in the eyes of Yahweh" [NIV, "displeased the LORD"]. The Lord had looked at David's heart (cf. 1 Sam 16:7) and seen the king's act for the despicable deed it was. The closest parallel to the writer's description of the Lord's reaction to David's behavior is found in the Torah's expression of the Lord's response to Onan's sexual misconduct (cf. Gen 38:10).[108] Onan died for his misbehavior; and David's penalty—though not yet revealed by the writer—could be expected to be equally severe.

(2) Nathan Announces the Lord's Judgment and Forgiveness (12:1–14)

[1]The LORD sent Nathan to David. When he came to him, he said, "There were two men in a certain town, one rich and the other poor. [2]The rich man had a very large number of sheep and cattle, [3]but the poor man had nothing except one little ewe lamb he had bought. He raised it, and it grew up with him and his children. It shared his food, drank from his cup and even slept in his arms. It was like a daughter to him.

[4]"Now a traveler came to the rich man, but the rich man refrained from taking one of his own sheep or cattle to prepare a meal for the traveler who had come to him. Instead, he took the ewe lamb that belonged to the poor man and prepared it for the one who had come to him."

[5]David burned with anger against the man and said to Nathan, "As surely as the LORD lives, the man who did this deserves to die! [6]He must pay for that lamb

---

[108] The apparently deliberate parallel between Yahweh's reactions to David and Onan reinforce the notion that David, like Onan, was improperly acting within the context of a *gōʾēl* relationship with a woman.

four times over, because he did such a thing and had no pity."

⁷Then Nathan said to David, "You are the man! This is what the LORD, the God of Israel, says: 'I anointed you king over Israel, and I delivered you from the hand of Saul. ⁸I gave your master's house to you, and your master's wives into your arms. I gave you the house of Israel and Judah. And if all this had been too little, I would have given you even more. ⁹Why did you despise the word of the LORD by doing what is evil in his eyes? You struck down Uriah the Hittite with the sword and took his wife to be your own. You killed him with the sword of the Ammonites. ¹⁰Now, therefore, the sword will never depart from your house, because you despised me and took the wife of Uriah the Hittite to be your own.'

¹¹"This is what the LORD says: 'Out of your own household I am going to bring calamity upon you. Before your very eyes I will take your wives and give them to one who is close to you, and he will lie with your wives in broad daylight. ¹²You did it in secret, but I will do this thing in broad daylight before all Israel.'"

¹³Then David said to Nathan, "I have sinned against the LORD."

Nathan replied, "The LORD has taken away your sin. You are not going to die. ¹⁴But because by doing this you have made the enemies of the LORD show utter contempt, the son born to you will die."

Nathan's divinely inspired pronouncement here tempers, though does not nullify, the incredible blessings promised to David and his dynastic house in chap. 7. David had sinned egregiously, and the Lord must judge it. The Lord's judgment is duly harsh yet merciful: David had committed a sin whose only stated penalty was death (cf. Lev 20:10; Deut 22:22), yet the Lord sovereignly promised that the king would not die.

The metaphorical comparison between the lives of David and Israel, so firmly established prior to this point, is extended in this incident. Israel had played the harlot with foreign gods, thereby committing a sin for which the Torah decreed death (cf. Deut 7:25–26). Yet after judging them and causing them to sacrifice much of the blessing that had been theirs, Yahweh the Merciful permitted them to live.

12:1–4 As on previous occasions (cf. 1 Sam 16:12–13; 2 Sam 7:4–17), when the Lord made a destiny-shaping pronouncement concerning David's life, he conveyed it through a prophet. In this instance "the LORD sent Nathan to David" (v. 1), apparently on the day that Bathsheba gave birth to the baby (cf. vv. 14,18).

Nathan conveyed the divine judgment against the king with superlative communicative skill. He began with a parable *(māšāl)*, in this case a simple, immediately comprehensible narrative designed to convey a truth that far exceeded its surface meaning. Such stories, not unlike political cartoons today, permitted persons of lesser social power to render judgment against the most powerful members of society.[109] Jotham had previously used one to condemn Abimelech's actions (cf. Judg 9:6–15) and judge a city; Ezekiel later used one to convey words of harsh judgment against Israel (cf. Ezek 17:2–10).

Nathan's story was about a rich man and a poor man. The rich man's wealth included "a very large number of sheep and cattle" (v. 2), suggesting that he—like David—was a shepherd. The poor man's penury was reflected in his lack of livestock; he "had nothing except one little ewe lamb he had bought" (v. 3). What the poor man lacked in material wealth he made up for in compassion. Truly the lamb was loved "like a daughter." The prophet's comparison of the poor man's ewe to a "daughter" (Hb. *bat*) who slept (Hb. *šākab*) in a man's arms creates a not-so-subtle lexical linkage between the beloved lamb and Bathsheba (Hb. *bat-šebaᶜ*), who previously was portrayed as sleeping (Hb. *šākab*; v. 4) in David's arms.

When the rich man in Nathan's story had a guest journey to his residence, he followed the Mediterranean rules of hospitality by preparing a sumptuous meal for the visitor (cf. Gen 18:5–8; 19:3). Yet when the rich man did so, he violated protocol and propriety (as well as the Torah) by using a stolen lamb for the purpose rather than his own.

12:5–6 David, acting in his role as presiding judge in Israel's royal court of justice, interrupted the narrative at this point to pronounce judgment against the sinful party. Enraged, David first expressed his instinctive feelings—"the man who did this deserves to die"—and then rendered a verdict duly prescribed by the Torah (cf. Exod 22:1)—"he must pay for that lamb four times over, because he did such a thing and had no pity" (v. 6). Because of the high-handed and cruel nature of the rich man's actions, the full Torah penalty would be imposed.[110] David's own Torah-violating behavior had not robbed him of his commitment to impose the requirements of the Torah on others!

12:7–10 Of course, when David condemned the rich man's sin, he also condemned himself, as Nathan emphatically declared. Then without waiting for a response from the stunned king, he launched into a stern judgment oracle consisting of three sections: first, a background section (vv. 7–8), where the

---

[109] A. Graffy suggests that the genre of Nathan's parable be entitled "self-condemnation parable" ("The Literary Genre of Isaiah 5,1–7," *Bib* 60 [1979]: 400–409). D. Daube asserts that this parable was actually one created by Davidic sympathizers to condemn Saul's action of taking Michal from David, but was utilized for a different purpose by Nathan ("Nathan's Parable," *NovT* 24 [1982]: 275–88). Daube's creative suggestion lacks any obvious textual support and can be confidently rejected.

[110] The LXX indicates that David set the penalty at sevenfold compensation, a reading accepted by McCarter (*2 Samuel*, 292, 299) and by P. W. Coxon ("A Note on 'Bathsheba' in 2 Samuel 12,1–6," *Bib* 62 [1981]: 247–50). However, the MT provides a reading quite in character with the portrayal of David as a covenant man, and this reading is accepted by Youngblood ("1, 2 Samuel," 943) and Baldwin (*1 and 2 Samuel*, 236–37).

Lord described the favorable treatment David had been accorded over the years; second, an enumeration of David's offenses, both Godward and manward (v. 9); and finally, a declaration of the penalties associated with David's offense (vv. 10–12).

The section begins with a lengthy oracle-initiation formula employed only rarely in Scripture.[111] By crediting the words to "the LORD the God of Israel," Nathan was establishing the judgment in a covenantal context. From Nathan's perspective, David had violated the sacred covenant established at Sinai between the Lord and the sons of Israel, of which David was one.

Before pronouncing sentence against the king, the Lord through his spokesman enumerated a list of benevolent actions he had performed on David's behalf. These undeserved blessings had provided David with (1) position—"I anointed you king over Israel"; (2) protection—"I delivered you from the hand of Saul"; (3) possessions—"I gave your master's house to you" (v. 8); (4) symbols of royal prestige and privilege—"your master's wives"; and (5) control over "the house of Israel and Judah."

From this list the reader learns for the first time that when David assumed kingship over all Israel, he took control of at least that portion of Saul's possessions that were acquired as a result of his kingship. David also gained exclusive rights to Saul's harem. This was a dramatic symbol of David's uncontested kingship, since to have rights over these women signified the acquisition of privileges previously reserved for Saul (cf. 16:21–22).

Then, in a verse that may be viewed as a key—a turning point—in the structure of 2 Samuel, the Lord furthermore suggested that David had not yet plumbed the depths of God's generosity in his behalf. After providing a relational context describing how David had been so richly blessed, the Lord made explicit the exact nature of the offenses committed. Fundamentally, David had rejected the terms of the relational framework that had bound the king to his God: David "had shown contempt for [NIV, "despise"] the word of the LORD by doing what is evil" (v. 9) in the Lord's eyes. David had made a mockery of the Ten Commandments, the central tenets of the Lord's covenantal relationship with Israel,[112] by committing the dual sins of murder and adultery.

---

[111] כֹּה אָמַר יהוה אֱלֹהֵי יִשְׂרָאֵל occurs only thirty-two times: Exod 5:1; 32:27; Josh 7:13; 24:2; Judg 6:8; 1 Sam 10:18; 2 Sam 12:7; 1 Kgs 11:31; 14:7; 17:14; 2 Kgs 9:6; 19:20; 21:12; 22:15; 22:18; 2 Chr 34:26; Isa 37:21; Jer 11:3; 13:12; 21:4; 23:2; 24:5; 25:15; 30:2; 32:36; 33:4; 34:2,13; 37:7; 42:9; 45:2. Among the Latter Prophets it occurs only in Isaiah (1x) and Jeremiah (13x).

[112] At least three clues in the Torah suggest that the Ten Words (Ten Commandments) were the centerpiece of the Sinai covenant established between Yahweh and Israel: (1) the placement of the Ten Words (Ten Commandments) at the very beginning of Yahweh's legal pronouncements coming forth from the top of Mount Sinai (cf. Exod 20); (2) the fact that only the Ten Words were written on the two stone tables Moses received from Sinai (cf. Exod 34:28); and (3) the fact that they are repeated nearly verbatim in Deuteronomy (chap. 5) Cf. E. H. Merrill, *Deuteronomy*, NAC (Nashville: Broadman & Holman, 1994), 139–40.

As is regularly the case with sin, David's transgression had not only violated his relationship with God (cf. Ps 51:4 [Hb. 51:6]), but it also had ravaged human relationships as well. When David sinned against the Lord by violating the covenant, he also had sinned against both a man and a woman: he "struck down Uriah the Hittite and took his wife" as his own, besides causing the deaths of the soldiers who had accompanied Uriah on his fateful mission.

David might have been tempted to claim that it was the Ammonites, not he, who killed Uriah; but the Lord shredded that defense by ruling that David killed "Uriah with the sword of the Ammonites." The hand of David that had penned the murderous order would bear responsibility for thrusting Uriah in the path of a deadly Ammonite weapon.

Uriah had died because of David's sin, but God decreed that death would enter David's life as well: "the sword will never depart from your house" (v. 10). This dark judgment presages fatal violence within David's family and can be seen as the literary motivation for chaps. 13–19 as well as 1 Kings 1–2. All told, four of David's sons would experience premature death—an unnamed son (cf. 12:18), Amnon (cf. 13:29), Absalom (cf. 18:14–15), and Adonijah (cf. 1 Kgs 2:25). Traditional Jewish and Christian interpretation of this passage has correlated the death of the four sons to be the "fourfold" of v. 6. To remove all doubt about why this would occur, Yahweh restated the fundamental cause: "You despised me and took the wife of Uriah the Hittite to be your own."

In the restatement of David's offenses, the Lord personalized the king's transgression against the deity. David had not merely despised the Lord's word; he had despised the Lord himself. The Lord and his Word were inseparable: to neglect or offend the word of the Torah—that is, the word of the Lord—was to neglect or offend the Lord. The writer's effortless equation of God with the written covenant in vv. 9–10 reflects an acceptance of Scripture as truly divine (cf. 2 Tim 3:16; 2 Pet 1:21).

12:11–12 A second wave of judgments were pronounced against David in v. 11 as Nathan declared what else "the LORD says." In this section judgment was proclaimed against David, not his house: "Out of your own household I am going to bring evil [NIV, "calamity"] upon you." In a striking display of the Torah concept of *lex talionis* (cf. Exod 21:24; Lev 24:20; Deut 19:21), David's sexual sins against another would give rise to sexual sins committed by another against David: "I will take your wives and give them to one who is close to you, and he will lie with your wives."[113]

When David pronounced judgment against the wicked rich man in Nathan's story, he had dictated that the Torah penalty be meted out against the man. In

---

[113] Anderson understands v. 11 to be "a prophecy after the event in order to provide a theological interpretation of Absalom's rebellion and, especially, of his appropriation of David's concubines" (*2 Samuel,* 163). This position, while intellectually attractive to the contemporary Western mind, is clearly at odds with the plain sense of the text and must be rejected.

keeping with the principle of a penalty that compensatorily exceeded the original act, the Lord performs a similar magnification: David "did it in secret, but I will do this thing in broad daylight before all Israel" (v. 12).

12:13–14 In a remarkable display of humility and contrition, David confessed his guilt in the single most significant dimension of his sinful act: "I have sinned against the LORD" (v. 13; cf. Ps 51:4 [Hb. v. 6]). David had certainly also sinned against Uriah, Bathsheba, and unnamed soldiers; but those offenses were derivative and secondary in nature. Had David not rebelled against the Lord's Word, these persons would not have been murdered or abused.

David's confession came with immediacy, without denial, and without excuse; the Lord's forgiveness was equally direct and unrestrained. It also was without cost: forgiveness was granted the king without requiring him first to make animal sacrifices or give great gifts to the Lord. In an unadorned fashion Nathan responded to David by declaring that "the LORD has taken away your sin."

The Lord's forgiveness was also accompanied by great mercy. The Torah declared that all murderers and adulterers must die (cf. Gen 9:6; Exod 21:12; Lev 20:10; 24:17; Deut 22:22); nevertheless, in what Baldwin terms "the turning-point in the life of David,"[114] the Lord declared that David was "not going to die." Why did the Lord choose not to enforce the unambiguous requirements of the Sinai covenant? There can be but one answer: because he is "the compassionate and gracious God, slow to anger, abounding in love and faithfulness, maintaining love to thousands, and forgiving wickedness, rebellion, and sin" (Exod 34:7). David lived for the same reason that the nation of Israel would live beyond its sin (cf. Deut 32:26–27; Hos 11:8).

The Lord forgave David and granted him the unmerited gift of life, but he did not remove all consequences resulting from David's sin. David's sin had "showed utter contempt for the LORD" (v. 14; NIV, "made the enemies of the LORD show utter contempt"[115]) and is lexically linked to the sin of Hophni and Phinehas (cf. 1 Sam 2:17). God slew Eli's sons for showing contempt (Hb. *nāʾaṣ*) for the Lord's offering, and in the case of David's contempt, his son would die.

---

[114] Baldwin, *1 and 2 Samuel*, 239.

[115] The NIV's translation is decidedly inaccurate here because it assumes a meaning of יְנֵאץ that cannot be confirmed anywhere else in Scripture. The literal rendering of the disputed phrase in the MT is "you have displayed utter contempt for the enemies of Yahweh." Because this reading is semantically dissonant with its context, it seems reasonable to conclude that the MT does not preserve the wording of the autographic text. Rather, the MT's text is the result of a pious insertion of the word אֹיְבֵי ("the enemies of") in order to soften the prophet's declaration concerning David's actions. In this regard, cf. also 1 Sam 25:22, which may also demonstrate this emendatory trait. For further discussion regarding pious scribal habits, cf. McCarter, *II Samuel*, 296.

(3) The Lord Expresses Judgment and Forgiveness (12:15–25)

[15]After Nathan had gone home, the LORD struck the child that Uriah's wife had borne to David, and he became ill. [16]David pleaded with God for the child. He fasted and went into his house and spent the nights lying on the ground. [17]The elders of his household stood beside him to get him up from the ground, but he refused, and he would not eat any food with them.

[18]On the seventh day the child died. David's servants were afraid to tell him that the child was dead, for they thought, "While the child was still living, we spoke to David but he would not listen to us. How can we tell him the child is dead? He may do something desperate."

[19]David noticed that his servants were whispering among themselves and he realized the child was dead. "Is the child dead?" he asked.

"Yes," they replied, "he is dead."

[20]Then David got up from the ground. After he had washed, put on lotions and changed his clothes, he went into the house of the LORD and worshiped. Then he went to his own house, and at his request they served him food, and he ate.

[21]His servants asked him, "Why are you acting this way? While the child was alive, you fasted and wept, but now that the child is dead, you get up and eat!"

[22]He answered, "While the child was still alive, I fasted and wept. I thought, 'Who knows? The LORD may be gracious to me and let the child live.' [23]But now that he is dead, why should I fast? Can I bring him back again? I will go to him, but he will not return to me."

[24]Then David comforted his wife Bathsheba, and he went to her and lay with her. She gave birth to a son, and they named him Solomon. The LORD loved him; [25]and because the LORD loved him, he sent word through Nathan the prophet to name him Jedidiah.

12:15–17 After making the grim pronouncement in the king's presence, Nathan went home. To emphasize the immediacy of God's judgment, the writer reports no intervening events between Nathan's departure from the royal court and the time when "the LORD struck the child that Uriah's wife had borne to David" (v. 15). The sober reality that this child was the product of a sinful union is highlighted by the fact that his mother was referred to as "Uriah's wife." Immediately the newborn son "became ill."

David the man of prayer (cf. Ps 109:4) "pleaded with God for the child" (v. 16). David's efforts on behalf of his beloved infant were intense, fueled both by a father's natural compassion for a sick child and by a profound confidence in God's mercy. Without hesitation the king "fasted and went into his house and spent the nights lying on the ground." David's self-denial and self-abasement probably should be interpreted as a demonstration of his remorse for the sins he had committed, carried out in an effort to gain a reprieve for his son. Alternatively, they may have been an effort to demonstrate to God that the child's recovery was more important to him than either food, comfort, or pride. David persisted in his actions in spite of the efforts of "the elders of his household"

(v. 17)—probably his royal counselors, who "stood beside him to get him up from the ground."

12:18–19 "On the seventh day" (v. 18)—that is, when the child was seven days old—he "died." The fact that the child died on the seventh day of his life is of great significance when considered in light of the Torah. Sons were not to receive circumcision, the physical sign of identification with the Lord's covenant, until the eighth day of their life (cf. Lev 12:3; also Luke 1:59; 2:21; Phil 3:5). David's son was conceived as a result of David's contempt for the Lord's covenant (cf. v. 9), so it was painfully fitting that the child should be permanently excluded from Israel's covenant community (cf. Gen 17:14). This seventh-day death may also explain why the child is never referred to by name; perhaps the child never received a name, since under normal circumstances naming might not occur until after the child received the covenant sign (cf. Luke 1:59–62).[116]

David had inflicted so much pain on himself during the time of the child's illness that his "servants were afraid to tell him that the child was dead." They feared that when he learned that his efforts to win a reprieve for his son had failed, "he may do something desperate" (Hb. *rāʿah*; lit., "evil, harm").

The servants' fears, however, proved unjustified. David, ever the astute interpreter of others' actions (cf. 1 Sam 20:1–3), "realized the child was dead" (v. 18) when he "noticed that his servants were whispering among themselves." His conclusion was confirmed when he asked the servants a direct question.

12:20–23 David surprised everyone, however, by his reaction to the news. Instead of doing something reckless and injurious, David ended his humiliation before the Lord and prepared to worship.[117] Even as David's unnamed son was being prepared for burial, David was grooming himself for a new life. And this new life would begin exactly where the king's earlier life had found its success and strength, in the presence of the Lord.

In a manner appropriate for a priest (cf. Exod 30:20; cf. Ps 110:4) David first washed himself and then "went into the house of the LORD and worshiped." In losing his son, David sought more than ever to gain a deeper relationship with his Heavenly Father. It is significant that David did not break his fast until after he had worshiped God; David's hunger for a right relationship with God exceeded his desire for culinary delights.

David's servants were mystified by the king's actions and boldly asked him why he was "acting this way" (v. 21). Whereas others rolled in the dust when a family member died, David had chosen to "get up"; though others might fast

---

[116] Of course, this passage states nothing about the spiritual destiny of the unnamed child. Physical circumcision or the lack thereof would not have affected the infant's eternal destiny (Gal 6:15).

[117] Hertzberg suggests that David accepted the child's death as a sacrifice (*I and II Samuel*, 316). This position cannot be justified on the basis of explicit scriptural statements.

(cf. Ezra 10:6), David ate.

David, whose life found its focus and fundamental motivations in God, explained his actions theologically. He knew that Yahweh was a God of great compassion and mercy (cf. Exod 34:6) who sometimes relented from executing harsh—but just—judgments; therefore, it was possible that the Lord would "let the child live" (v. 22). In order to encourage God to spare the child's life, therefore, the king had "fasted and wept" (v. 22). However, the child's life expired.

God had acted, and the child was "dead" (v. 23), never to be brought "back again." The child's death did not mean that God was unjust or unloving; on the contrary, it meant that the divine word spoken through the prophet was trustworthy (cf. v. 14)—a fact that must have provided a measure of comfort to the king. The Lord's word had not changed, and the Lord himself had not changed; divine grace was just as real after the death as it had been before. Neither David's sin nor the child's death had changed God's nature. Therefore, now that the child was gone David could and must get on with his life. Though David was now bereft of his son, the separation would be only temporary. There is to be heard a note of consolation in David's words "I will go to him."

12:24–25 David accepted these twin realities of God's grace and judgment and found himself comforted. Having been comforted by God, he was able to bring comfort (cf. 2 Cor 1:3–4) to "his wife Bathsheba" (v. 24). In a consoling act of intimacy, "David went to her and lay with her." Arms bereft of a child now embraced a king; and as a result Bathsheba "gave birth to a son."

The royal parents named their child "Solomon" (*šĕlōmô*, lit., "His [Yahweh's] Restoration/Peace"). Following the agony of death, the Lord had given him peace. The contrasts between the first child of David and Bathsheba's union and the second were sharp. Whereas the Lord fatally judged the first, "the LORD loved" the second.[118] Though the first died before it was old enough to be given a covenant name, the second received a name from the God of the covenant: the Lord "sent word through Nathan the prophet to name him Jedidiah" (v. 25; lit., "Beloved of Yahweh"). The etymological commonality between David's name and the name bestowed by God (both are based on the verb *dwd*) is a subtle hint to the reader that God had already set aside this child to be the next "David."[119] Later narratives prove the accuracy of this intimation.

(4) David Defeats and Subjects the Ammonites (12:26–31)

26Meanwhile Joab fought against Rabbah of the Ammonites and captured the royal citadel. 27Joab then sent messengers to David, saying, "I have fought against

---

[118] G. W. Coats suggests that the birth of Solomon following the tragedy of David's sin demonstrates God's propensity for creating a good future out of a bad past and bringing newness to the present without eliminating the tragedy of the past ("II Samuel 12:1–7a," *Int* 40 [1986]: 170–75).

[119] In agreement with this, cf. Fokkelman, *King David*, 92.

Rabbah and taken its water supply. [28]Now muster the rest of the troops and besiege the city and capture it. Otherwise I will take the city, and it will be named after me."

[29]So David mustered the entire army and went to Rabbah, and attacked and captured it. [30]He took the crown from the head of their king—its weight was a talent of gold, and it was set with precious stones—and it was placed on David's head. He took a great quantity of plunder from the city [31]and brought out the people who were there, consigning them to labor with saws and with iron picks and axes, and he made them work at brickmaking. He did this to all the Ammonite towns. Then David and his entire army returned to Jerusalem.

12:26–28 Meanwhile, the siege of Rabbah continued. Though the chronological relationship between the narrative of 11:27–12:25 and the present verse is unclear, apparently the process of starving Rabbah into submission had taken at least nine months and perhaps two years. Nevertheless, Joab's dogged persistence in the military undertaking paid off. At last he "captured the royal citadel" (v. 26; lit., "the city of the kingship"), apparently the heavily fortified subdivision of the city that contained the royal palace. In the process he also succeeded in capturing "its water supply" (v. 27; lit., "the city of the waters")—perhaps a fortification guarding the city's primary water supply—a feat virtually guaranteeing that the entire city would soon fall under Israelite control.

Now that the most difficult and dangerous portion of Rabbah's conquest had been accomplished, Joab "sent messengers to David" informing him of the key events and encouraging the king to "muster the rest of the people [NIV, "troops"] and besiege the city and capture it" (v. 28). David probably had remained in Jerusalem out of consideration for his safety (cf. 21:17) and also because of the need to attend to administrative and personal matters. As an additional incentive for the king to come, Joab indicated he would "take the city and it will be named after me" (cf. 5:9; Num 32:42) if David chose to remain in Jerusalem.

12:29–31 Accordingly, "David mustered all the people [NIV, "the entire army"] and went to Rabbah" (v. 29), a distance of more than forty miles, "and attacked and captured it." Having conquered the city, David received the possessions and privileges reserved for the king of the city. Among them was "the crown from the head of their king" (v. 30). The weight of the jewel-studded crown—"a talent of gold," that is, about seventy-five pounds—as well as the witness of some traditions of the LXX,[120] suggest that the crown was one normally set on a statue of either a former Ammonite king or their god Milcom (cf. 1 Kgs 11:5; 2 Kgs 23:13). In addition to taking possession of the most ostentatious symbol of Ammonite kingship, David also "took a great quantity of plunder from the city," which he dedicated to the Lord for later use in constructing

---

[120] The Codex Vaticanus, Codex Coislinianus, and Codex Basiliano-Vaticanus all transliterate מלכם as a personal name, either as "milcom" or "milcol."

the Jerusalem temple (cf. 8:11–12; 1 Chr 29:2–5).

After taking control of the most important and well-defended Ammonite city, David pressed the attack against "all the Ammonite towns" (v. 31). In the process he took many prisoners of war, "consigning them to labor with saws and with iron picks and axes," as well as "brickmaking."[121] These tasks are all related to the preparation of building materials and suggest that David was engaged in building or strengthening fortified structures throughout Israelite-held territory.

(5) Amnon Rapes Tamar (13:1–22)

¹In the course of time, Amnon son of David fell in love with Tamar, the beautiful sister of Absalom son of David.

²Amnon became frustrated to the point of illness on account of his sister Tamar, for she was a virgin, and it seemed impossible for him to do anything to her.

³Now Amnon had a friend named Jonadab son of Shimeah, David's brother. Jonadab was a very shrewd man. ⁴He asked Amnon, "Why do you, the king's son, look so haggard morning after morning? Won't you tell me?"

Amnon said to him, "I'm in love with Tamar, my brother Absalom's sister."

⁵"Go to bed and pretend to be ill," Jonadab said. "When your father comes to see you, say to him, 'I would like my sister Tamar to come and give me something to eat. Let her prepare the food in my sight so I may watch her and then eat it from her hand.'"

⁶So Amnon lay down and pretended to be ill. When the king came to see him, Amnon said to him, "I would like my sister Tamar to come and make some special bread in my sight, so I may eat from her hand."

⁷David sent word to Tamar at the palace: "Go to the house of your brother Amnon and prepare some food for him." ⁸So Tamar went to the house of her brother Amnon, who was lying down. She took some dough, kneaded it, made the bread in his sight and baked it. ⁹Then she took the pan and served him the bread, but he refused to eat.

"Send everyone out of here," Amnon said. So everyone left him. ¹⁰Then Amnon said to Tamar, "Bring the food here into my bedroom so I may eat from your hand." And Tamar took the bread she had prepared and brought it to her brother Amnon in his bedroom. ¹¹But when she took it to him to eat, he grabbed her and said, "Come to bed with me, my sister."

¹²"Don't, my brother!" she said to him. "Don't force me. Such a thing should not be done in Israel! Don't do this wicked thing. ¹³What about me? Where could I get rid of my disgrace? And what about you? You would be like one of the

---

[121] The *qere* reading of the MT translated by the NIV as "and he made them work at brickmaking" is וְהֶעֱבִיר אוֹתָם בַּמַּלְבֵּן, lit., "and he made them pass through the brick kiln." While this reading is a gruesome one, it is possible that this was indeed the punishment David inflicted on certain of the Ammonites. Cf. 2 Sam 8:2 for a similarly deadly punishment for David's enemies.

wicked fools in Israel. Please speak to the king; he will not keep me from being married to you." [14]But he refused to listen to her, and since he was stronger than she, he raped her.

[15]Then Amnon hated her with intense hatred. In fact, he hated her more than he had loved her. Amnon said to her, "Get up and get out!"

[16]"No!" she said to him. "Sending me away would be a greater wrong than what you have already done to me."

But he refused to listen to her. [17]He called his personal servant and said, "Get this woman out of here and bolt the door after her." [18]So his servant put her out and bolted the door after her. She was wearing a richly ornamented robe, for this was the kind of garment the virgin daughters of the king wore. [19]Tamar put ashes on her head and tore the ornamented robe she was wearing. She put her hand on her head and went away, weeping aloud as she went.

[20]Her brother Absalom said to her, "Has that Amnon, your brother, been with you? Be quiet now, my sister; he is your brother. Don't take this thing to heart." And Tamar lived in her brother Absalom's house, a desolate woman.

[21]When King David heard all this, he was furious. [22]Absalom never said a word to Amnon, either good or bad; he hated Amnon because he had disgraced his sister Tamar.

This narrative forges another link in the tragic chain of sin begun in chap. 11 as David's firstborn son (cf. 3:2) and heir-apparent committed an incestuous rape. The parallels between the king's sin and that of his son Amnon are numerous: both committed immoral acts outside of marriage with beautiful women (v. 1; 11:2) in the privacy of their own residences (v. 7; 11:4). Both women experienced great grief (v. 19; 11:26) because of the men's actions. Ultimately, both transgressions brought about death for sons of David (v. 29; 12:18). This carefully constructed narrative seems intended to demonstrate at least two truths: first, that God's prophetic word is true; second, that the sins of one generation imprint the next generation. Each sin not only fosters more sin, it also fashions it by providing precedents for others to follow.

13:1–2 Following David's successful completion of the Ammonite campaign, "Amnon" (v. 1), the firstborn son "of David, fell in love with Tamar," his "beautiful" half-sister born to David's wife Maacah (cf. 3:3). Unfortunately for Amnon, she was also the "sister of Absalom," David's third son.

Though Amnon was fascinated by Tamar's feminine charms, he was also "frustrated to the point of illness" (v. 2) with her. The stated reason for Amnon's frustration placards his own lack of character and parades Tamar's virtue: he was upset because "she was a virgin, and it seemed impossible for him to do anything to her." Tamar was implicitly portrayed as a woman of the Torah, for the Law required that unmarried women retain their virginity (cf. Deut 22:13–21).

In his readiness to compromise Tamar's virtue, however, Amnon was implicitly pagan. To emphasize the point, the biblical narrator deliberately patterns the portrayal of Amnon's actions and emotions after Shechem, an immoral Canaanite in the Torah. Shechem, like Amnon, was the firstborn son of a ruler who also raped the daughter of an Israelite leader and ended up dead (cf. Gen 34:2–3,26). Amnon is portrayed as one who chose the way of the Canaanite; thus, readers are prepared to accept the fact that he will suffer the fate of the Canaanite.

13:3–5 Encouraging Amnon in his sinful desires was "Jonadab son of Shimeah" (v. 3), his "companion" (NIV, "friend") and cousin. Jonadab was described as "a very wise [NIV, "shrewd"] man"; he was the only person in Scripture accorded this ostensibly complimentary description. The word translated in the NIV as "shrewd" is ḥākām, the term normally rendered in the positive sense as "wise." Yet, as events would soon demonstrate, Jonadab's wisdom was "earthly, unspiritual, of the devil" (Jas 3:15; cf. also Jer 4:22; 1 Cor 2:6).

Jonadab was concerned that his cousin was looking "haggard morning after morning" (v. 4), and spoke with him about it. He soon discovered that Amnon's problem was that he was "in love with Tamar," his "brother Absalom's sister." The narrator's restatement that Tamar was closely related to Amnon (cf. v. 1)— too close to permit a sanctioned sexual relationship (cf. Lev 18:11; 20:17; Deut 27:22)—emphasizes the fact that Amnon was contemplating an act strictly prohibited by the Torah. Amnon's so-called "love" was as perverse as Jonadab's so-called "wisdom"; it was a sensual craving for sexual gratification that was just as earthly, unspiritual, and devilish as Jonadab's wisdom.

Jonadab suggested a churlish plan for Amnon that was both simple and surefire: the king's son would "go to bed and pretend to be ill" (v. 5). Then when David visited his son, Amnon would petition the king to order Tamar to spend an extended amount of time in the privacy of Amnon's residence, satisfying the physical appetite of her half-brother. At an appropriate moment during Tamar's nurturing encounter with Amnon, he would compel her to satisfy his sexual appetite as well.[122]

13:6–7 The plan's initial phase worked perfectly. David, being the good father that he was, heard the report of his son's illness and postponed administrative matters long enough to visit the heir-apparent in his own residence. Apparently, each of the older royal sons was granted the privilege of having his own residence in the City of David (cf. vv. 7–8).

Amnon requested, and David agreed, that Tamar should "come and make some special bread"—perhaps in the courtyard oven of Amnon's residence—and that she feed it to Amnon herself. The "special bread" (Hb. lĕbibâ) was

---

[122] Fokkelman suggests that Jonadab was not actually encouraging Amnon to rape Tamar, only to have a private, amorous encounter (*King David*, 109).

apparently a heart-shaped cake or dumpling,[123] perhaps made of a dough laced with healing herbs.

13:8–11 As a proper daughter, Tamar obeyed her father's orders. When she arrived at Amnon's residence, dutifully she made the bread. However, "he refused to eat." Instead, he evicted everyone from the premises—everyone, that is, except Tamar.

When the two of them were alone in the privacy of his residence, Amnon ordered his half-sister to bring him the food and feed it to him in his bedroom. Instead of taking Tamar's food, however, Amnon "grabbed her" and begged his half-sister to lie with him.

13:12–13 Tamar resisted, both verbally and physically. Her first word in response to her half-brother's sinful request was "No" (v. 12; NIV, "Don't"). In fact, Tamar included a form of the word *no* in the first four consecutive clauses of her response to Amnon. She directly ordered him not to "rape" (a form of *ʿānâ;* NIV, "force") her. Then she appealed to his conscience, reminding him that what he was pursuing was "a wicked thing" that "should not be done in Israel."

Tamar's use of the phrase "should not be done" and of the term "wicked thing" (Hb. *nĕbālâ;* cf. 1 Sam 25:25, "folly") are an unmistakable allusion to the Torah's account of Shechem's rape of Dinah (cf. Gen 34:7). This skillful reference to a sordid chapter in patriarchal history not only forced Amnon to put his mind—at least momentarily—back into the sacred Scriptures, but also to consider the end result of Shechem's—and therefore, his own—actions.

Tamar also compelled Amnon to think about the lasting impact of his actions on both of their lives. Amnon's theft of her virginity would place on her a personal "disgrace" (v. 13) that she would never be able to "get rid of." It would ruin Amnon's reputation as well, causing him to be thought of as "one of the 'Nabals' [NIV, 'wicked fools'] in Israel"—perhaps a not-so-subtle allusion to another wicked man who died under the Lord's curse for having mistreated others (1 Sam 25).

Finally, Tamar urged Amnon to delay—not permanently forgo—his sexual gratification. If sexual intimacy with Tamar was his objective, she asserted that he might still have it. In fact, it could be his without the taint of disgrace or ruined reputation if he would first "speak to the king" and obtain permission to marry her.[124]

---

[123] Cf. W. L. Holladay, *CHAL,* s.v. לְבִבָה. McCarter presents evidence to suggest that the food being prepared was "hearty dumplings" (*II Samuel,* 322).

[124] Tamar's assertion that King David would "not keep me from being married to you" (v. 13) might not have actually proven accurate, should it have been put to the test. With the notable exception of the Bathsheba affair, David attempted to obey the teachings of the Torah scrupulously. Since the Torah forbade sexual relations between a half-brother and a half-sister (cf. Lev 18:11; 20:17; Deut 27:22), it is doubtful David would have sanctioned a marriage between Amnon and Tamar.

13:14–16   Unfortunately, Amnon was beyond being influenced by moral, religious, or rational considerations. Instead, he attacked Tamar. His sensual objective having been achieved with Tamar and his physical passions now spent, Amnon now "hated her with intense hatred" (v. 14). The winds of "love" (v. 1) which had propelled him so forcefully proved to be nothing more than gusts of lust. Feelings of guilt and shame heightened Amnon's emotions, so that he now "hated her more than he had loved her" (v. 15).

The Torah dictated that a man who had sexual intercourse with a virgin not pledged to be married to another was obligated to marry her and pay a financial penalty (cf. Exod 22:16–17; Deut 22:28–29). However, when Amnon ordered Tamar to "get up and get out" of his house, his actions following the rape indicated he did not intend to follow the Torah in this matter. Tamar, knowing that this kind of disregard for the Law only made the situation worse, pointed out that "sending" her "away would be a greater wrong than what you have already done to me" (v. 16). However, the morally reckless Amnon once again "refused to listen to her."

13:17–19   To hasten Tamar's eviction, Amnon "called his personal servant" (v. 17) and ordered him to "expel this one [NIV, "woman"], then bolt the door after her."

In keeping with the Torah's implicit expectation that fathers assume some responsibility in preserving their daughters' virginity until marriage (cf. Deut 22:13–21), David encouraged and rewarded his virgin daughters' sexual purity by providing each of them with a status-laden "richly ornamented robe" (Hb. *kĕtonet pāssîm*; cf. Gen 37:3). By maintaining their virginal status till marriage, the daughters preserved their chances of achieving the most favorable marital circumstances. Depending on the circumstances leading to their deflowering, daughters who prematurely lost their virginity might even lose their lives (cf. Deut 22:21).

Tamar had been wearing the distinctive dress of a royal virgin daughter when she was raped, but afterwards "she tore the ornamented robe" (v. 19), and overwhelmed by shock and grief, she "put her hand on her head . . . weeping" as she returned to her residence (cf. Jer 2:37).

13:20–22   Not long afterward, Tamar's "brother Absalom" spoke with her regarding the sordid experience in Amnon's residence. She confirmed that "Amnon" had been "with" her, humiliated her, and then abandoned her. Amnon's criminal activity condemned Tamar to live the life of "a desolate woman" because she was now disqualified from active consideration for any royal marriage contracts. Nevertheless, Absalom attempted to provide her with some comfort and consolation. He could neither give Tamar a husband nor be one to her, but he did provide her with two of the amenities associated with marriage—a place to live and the attendant promise of protection. He also counseled her not to "take this thing to heart," that is, to let the memory/

implications of the tragic event continue to dominate her thinking.

For his part, King David "was furious" (v. 21). The outrageous misconduct by his heir-apparent was both a shame and an embarrassment to the royal family. Nevertheless, there was little that the king could do in response to the situation. The only penalty prescribed in the Torah for Amnon was the payment of fifty shekels of silver (Deut 22:29), an insignificant sum for the king's son. While David could have also forced Amnon to marry Tamar (cf. Exod 22:16; Deut 22:29), doing so would have created an emotionally explosive situation that only multiplied the family's heartache: besides, the Torah prohibited marriage between near kinsmen (cf. Lev 18:11; 20:17; Deut 27:22). Thus David found himself in a posture of weakness in the matter. His situation had become uncomfortably similar to that of Eli, who also had to deal with errant offspring (cf. 1 Sam 2:22–25).[125]

Meanwhile, Absalom, who had cast himself as something of a kinsman-redeemer (a *gōʾēl*) in this matter, "hated Amnon because he had disgraced his sister Tamar (v. 22). Shrewdly, however, he "never said a word to Amnon, either good or bad." Absalom's rage would be expressed more cogently in due time.

(6) Absalom Murders Amnon, Then Flees to Geshur (13:23–39)

[23]**Two years later, when Absalom's sheepshearers were at Baal Hazor near the border of Ephraim, he invited all the king's sons to come there.** [24]**Absalom went to the king and said, "Your servant has had shearers come. Will the king and his officials please join me?"**

[25]**"No, my son," the king replied. "All of us should not go; we would only be a burden to you." Although Absalom urged him, he still refused to go, but gave him his blessing.**

[26]**Then Absalom said, "If not, please let my brother Amnon come with us."**

The king asked him, "Why should he go with you?" [27]**But Absalom urged him, so he sent with him Amnon and the rest of the king's sons.**

[28]**Absalom ordered his men, "Listen! When Amnon is in high spirits from drinking wine and I say to you, 'Strike Amnon down,' then kill him. Don't be afraid. Have not I given you this order? Be strong and brave."** [29]**So Absalom's men did to Amnon what Absalom had ordered. Then all the king's sons got up, mounted their mules and fled.**

[30]**While they were on their way, the report came to David: "Absalom has struck down all the king's sons; not one of them is left."** [31]**The king stood up, tore his clothes and lay down on the ground; and all his servants stood by with their**

[125] The LXX and 4QSam[a] add the following phrase, which further strengthens the negative portrayal of David in this incident: "But he [David] did not grieve the spirit of Amnon his son, because he loved him, because he was his firstborn." It is impossible to determine with certainty whether this statement is autographic, but it might well have been.

clothes torn.

[32]But Jonadab son of Shimeah, David's brother, said, "My lord should not think that they killed all the princes; only Amnon is dead. This has been Absalom's expressed intention ever since the day Amnon raped his sister Tamar. [33]My lord the king should not be concerned about the report that all the king's sons are dead. Only Amnon is dead."

[34]Meanwhile, Absalom had fled.

Now the man standing watch looked up and saw many people on the road west of him, coming down the side of the hill. The watchman went and told the king, "I see men in the direction of Horonaim, on the side of the hill."

[35]Jonadab said to the king, "See, the king's sons are here; it has happened just as your servant said."

[36]As he finished speaking, the king's sons came in, wailing loudly. The king, too, and all his servants wept very bitterly.

[37]Absalom fled and went to Talmai son of Ammihud, the king of Geshur. But King David mourned for his son every day.

[38]After Absalom fled and went to Geshur, he stayed there three years. [39]And the spirit of the king longed to go to Absalom, for he was consoled concerning Amnon's death.

13:23 The day of reckoning came "two years later." In connection with the sheepshearing and celebration (cf. 1 Sam 25:7–8) at the location some fourteen miles north of Jerusalem, Absalom "invited all the king's sons to come there."

13:24–27 Absalom himself had remained in Jerusalem, while his servants performed the laborious task of shearing the sheep. During those days, Absalom advanced his plot to avenge Amnon. The scheme began innocently enough, as Absalom requested that "the king and his officials please join" him at Baal Hazor for a time of celebration. Absalom's request was a calculated one, since David's acceptance of the offer would have ended his chances of killing Amnon during the event.

However, the gamble paid off as David graciously declined Absalom's petition. Even though Absalom "urged him, he still refused to go, but gave him his blessing" (v. 25). By this Absalom succeeded in manipulating his father into a defensive position of social obligation that almost forced David to say yes to Absalom's next request. The request came without delay and with the appearance of innocence: if the king himself would not come, then let him send "my brother Amnon" (v. 26), the king's heir-apparent in his place.

David, the ever-astute interpreter of human motivation (cf. 1 Sam 20:1–3), immediately was suspicious of Absalom's request and asked him "why" Amnon "should go" as the guest of honor. Absalom artfully rebuffed the king's attempts to probe the true motive by merely repeating the request. Thus for the second time—and both of them following his sin with Bathsheba—David is portrayed as having been deceived (cf. 12:1–7). Thus, David "sent with him

Amnon and the rest of the king's sons" (v. 27).

13:28–29 In these verses the narrative setting has changed from Jerusalem to the site of a banquet at Baal Hazor,[126] but the biblical writer omits any mention of the change so as to quicken the pace of the story at this key point. During this time of lively celebration, Absalom quietly set his treacherous plan in motion. The narrator's mention of the circumstances of sheepshearing, a banquet and its attendant revelry link this passage with 1 Samuel 25 and prepare the reader for the untimely death of a "Nabal" (= "wicked fool").

Absalom's servants apparently balked at the order to commit murder. After all, they knew what David had done to other men who had killed royalty (cf. 1:15–16; 4:9–12), and they probably feared he would do the same to them. Absalom encouraged them not to "be afraid," however; he himself would take responsibility for the murder, since it was he who had "given . . . this order."

With that assurance, "Absalom's men did to Amnon what Absalom had ordered" (v. 29). The revenge must have seemed doubly sweet to Absalom, for he had succeeded in using the very same tactics to destroy Amnon that Amnon had previously used to destroy Tamar. Like Amnon, he had deceptively manipulated the king into ordering one of his children into a trap; then in the midst of a meal he had overpowered the sibling and carried out a violent and wicked fantasy at their expense.

As soon as the attack on Amnon was carried out, David's other sons fled on their mules, the preferred mount for royalty at that time (cf. 18:9; 1 Kgs 1:33, 38, 44).[127] Their flight from Absalom was quite disorganized and must have taken them in different directions, as is evidenced by the fact that David could not dismiss or correct the erroneous initial account of the attack for some time.

13:30–31 The initial report King David received of the tragic incident was woefully inaccurate. David was told that "all of the king's sons" (v. 30) had died at the hands of Absalom, and that "not one of them is left." The king's first reaction to this horrifying report was to leave his royal throne; then he "tore his clothes and lay down on the ground" in a classic expression of grief and distress (cf. Josh 7:6; 2 Sam 12:16). Nathan's words regarding a sword of judgment that would not depart from his house (cf. 12:10) must have come flooding back to him at this time. "All" (v. 31) of David's servants also "stood by with their clothes torn"—no doubt they, too, felt shock and anguish at the reported murder of the royal heirs.

13:32–33 The first indication that the first report was faulty came from David's nephew "Jonadab son of Shimeah" (v. 32), who had apparently been

---

[126] 4QSam[a] adds the statement "and Absalom made a feast like the feast of a king." While the statement is lacking from the MT, it is interesting for its proleptic value.

[127] Mules (פְּרָדִים), were the product of breeding a donkey with a horse. Since the Torah (Lev 19:19) forbade the production of such animals in Israel, it is probable that these animals were imported from foreign nations. Solomon certainly imported mules (cf. 1 Kgs 10:25).

in the royal palace at the time of the dispatch. As Amnon's good friend and as a cousin to both Amnon and Absalom, Jonadab was aware of the extreme tension that existed between David's two sons. He knew that "Absalom's expressed intention ever since the day Amnon raped his sister Tamar" was to kill his half-brother. Confidently, therefore, he asserted that "only Amnon is dead" (v. 33), and that the king should dismiss "the report that all the king's sons are dead."

13:34–36 The first evidence that Jonadab's words were reliable came as one of David's watchmen saw a group coming down the hill into Jerusalem. The fact that the group was approaching Jerusalem from the west even though Baal Hazor was northeast of the royal city suggests that they had taken a circuitous return route and helps to explain why the report came to David much sooner than his sons did. The LXX, whose reading is followed by the NIV, inserts a clause that mentions "Horonaim," a twin site northwest of Jerusalem known elsewhere as Upper- and Lower Beth Horon. As the group continued its trek, it became possible to discern the individual's identities. As soon as Jonadab visually confirmed his previous assertion, he announced that "the king's sons are here" (v. 35).

With the exception of Absalom, who "had fled" (v. 34), the king's surviving sons entered grief stricken (v. 36). This unrestrained emotional outburst from those who had witnessed the killing served to intensify the emotions of the royal court. The "king, too, and all his servants" erupted in tears and "wept very bitterly."

13:37–39 Absalom, like his brothers, had also fled to a king. However, it was not to his father, but rather his grandfather (cf. 3:3; 1 Chr 3:2), "Talmai son of Ammihud, the king of Geshur" (v. 37) that Absalom went. Thus, the one who was apparently next in line to become Israel's king,[128] was living in exile in a region immediately east of the Sea of Galilee, some eighty miles northeast of Jerusalem.

David understandably remained in a state of grief over the death of his oldest son for quite some time. During David's three-year period of grief, Absalom lived in exile at Geshur. In fleeing Israel as a young man to avoid the wrath of a sitting king, Absalom's life paralleled that of his father: a younger David had once been forced to live as a refugee in non-Israelite territory to elude King Saul. David knew the pain and anxiety that resulted from separation from one's family and homeland, and perhaps it was the remembrance of those emotions that made "the spirit of the king" (v. 39) yearn "to go to Absalom." In addition, David had finally forgiven Absalom

---

[128] The absence of any mention of David's second-born son Kileab/Daniel outside of the genealogical lists of 2 Sam 3:3 and 1 Chr 3:1 suggests one of two possibilities: (1) that this individual died prior to the time of 2 Sam 13's events; or (2) that this individual was counted as the heir of Nabal. Cf. further discussion at 1 Sam 25:39b–43.

for killing his brother and was ready to be reconciled to the son who apparently stood next in line to become Israel's king.

(7) David Is Reconciled with Absalom (14:1–33)

[1]Joab son of Zeruiah knew that the king's heart longed for Absalom. [2]So Joab sent someone to Tekoa and had a wise woman brought from there. He said to her, "Pretend you are in mourning. Dress in mourning clothes, and don't use any cosmetic lotions. Act like a woman who has spent many days grieving for the dead. [3]Then go to the king and speak these words to him." And Joab put the words in her mouth.

[4]When the woman from Tekoa went to the king, she fell with her face to the ground to pay him honor, and she said, "Help me, O king!"

[5]The king asked her, "What is troubling you?"

She said, "I am indeed a widow; my husband is dead. [6]I your servant had two sons. They got into a fight with each other in the field, and no one was there to separate them. One struck the other and killed him. [7]Now the whole clan has risen up against your servant; they say, 'Hand over the one who struck his brother down, so that we may put him to death for the life of his brother whom he killed; then we will get rid of the heir as well.' They would put out the only burning coal I have left, leaving my husband neither name nor descendant on the face of the earth."

[8]The king said to the woman, "Go home, and I will issue an order in your behalf."

[9]But the woman from Tekoa said to him, "My lord the king, let the blame rest on me and on my father's family, and let the king and his throne be without guilt."

[10]The king replied, "If anyone says anything to you, bring him to me, and he will not bother you again."

[11]She said, "Then let the king invoke the LORD his God to prevent the avenger of blood from adding to the destruction, so that my son will not be destroyed."

"As surely as the LORD lives," he said, "not one hair of your son's head will fall to the ground."

[12]Then the woman said, "Let your servant speak a word to my lord the king."

"Speak," he replied.

[13]The woman said, "Why then have you devised a thing like this against the people of God? When the king says this, does he not convict himself, for the king has not brought back his banished son? [14]Like water spilled on the ground, which cannot be recovered, so we must die. But God does not take away life; instead, he devises ways so that a banished person may not remain estranged from him.

[15]"And now I have come to say this to my lord the king because the people have made me afraid. Your servant thought, 'I will speak to the king; perhaps he will do what his servant asks. [16]Perhaps the king will agree to deliver his servant from the hand of the man who is trying to cut off both me and my son from the inheritance God gave us.'

[17]"And now your servant says, 'May the word of my lord the king bring me rest, for my lord the king is like an angel of God in discerning good and evil. May the LORD your God be with you.'"

¹⁸Then the king said to the woman, "Do not keep from me the answer to what I am going to ask you."

"Let my lord the king speak," the woman said.

¹⁹The king asked, "Isn't the hand of Joab with you in all this?"

The woman answered, "As surely as you live, my lord the king, no one can turn to the right or to the left from anything my lord the king says. Yes, it was your servant Joab who instructed me to do this and who put all these words into the mouth of your servant. ²⁰Your servant Joab did this to change the present situation. My lord has wisdom like that of an angel of God—he knows everything that happens in the land."

²¹The king said to Joab, "Very well, I will do it. Go, bring back the young man Absalom."

²²Joab fell with his face to the ground to pay him honor, and he blessed the king. Joab said, "Today your servant knows that he has found favor in your eyes, my lord the king, because the king has granted his servant's request."

²³Then Joab went to Geshur and brought Absalom back to Jerusalem. ²⁴But the king said, "He must go to his own house; he must not see my face." So Absalom went to his own house and did not see the face of the king.

²⁵In all Israel there was not a man so highly praised for his handsome appearance as Absalom. From the top of his head to the sole of his foot there was no blemish in him. ²⁶Whenever he cut the hair of his head—he used to cut his hair from time to time when it became too heavy for him—he would weigh it, and its weight was two hundred shekels by the royal standard.

²⁷Three sons and a daughter were born to Absalom. The daughter's name was Tamar, and she became a beautiful woman.

²⁸Absalom lived two years in Jerusalem without seeing the king's face. ²⁹Then Absalom sent for Joab in order to send him to the king, but Joab refused to come to him. So he sent a second time, but he refused to come. ³⁰Then he said to his servants, "Look, Joab's field is next to mine, and he has barley there. Go and set it on fire." So Absalom's servants set the field on fire.

³¹Then Joab did go to Absalom's house and he said to him, "Why have your servants set my field on fire?"

³²Absalom said to Joab, "Look, I sent word to you and said, 'Come here so I can send you to the king to ask, "Why have I come from Geshur? It would be better for me if I were still there!" 'Now then, I want to see the king's face, and if I am guilty of anything, let him put me to death.'"

³³So Joab went to the king and told him this. Then the king summoned Absalom, and he came in and bowed down with his face to the ground before the king. And the king kissed Absalom.

14:1–3 "Joab son of Zeruiah" (v. 1), David's nephew and the commanding general of Israelite forces, had walked with his uncle through the deepest valleys of life and climbed with him to the heights of power in Israel. Because of his lifelong association with David, he knew how David thought; and in the present situation Joab knew that "the king's heart was upon [NIV, "longed for"] Absalom."

In an effort to help David and bring healing to the wounded family, Joab devised a plan. Though devious, the scheme was noble in purpose and not unprincipled in its implementation. Joab's strategy was essentially the same as that used successfully by Nathan (cf. 12:1–14): someone would obtain an audience with the king, seek judgment in a fictitious situation, let the king pronounce judgment, then compel the king to apply the judgment to himself.[129] Joab's hope was that David would have the good sense to implement in his own life the wise advice he had given others.

Accordingly, Joab enlisted the services of a woman from Tekoa (v. 2) to play a role requiring consummate dramatic skill.[130] Costumed as one in mourning, the Tekoite was to act as "a woman who has spent many days grieving for the dead." She was to come before King David to seek an authoritative judgment and in the process deliver in a convincing way a speech Joab had given to her.

In choosing this method of seeking to influence David, Joab implicitly acknowledged the power of human art—in this case the dramatic arts—for shaping the lives of people and so transforming human society. Artistic expression can move the heart of even a seemingly invincible oriental monarch.

14:4–7 The unnamed heroine accepted the assignment. As the king sat in the palace in Jerusalem performing the task of administering justice among the Lord's people, the woman appeared before him with appropriate humility and then pleaded for "help."

David responded favorably to her appeal and provided her with an opportunity to present her situation. She then began to present a *māšāl* teaching story daringly told in the first person.[131] In her dramatic performance of Joab's script, the woman presented herself as an Israelite "widow" (v. 5).

The plot of her story bears a remarkable similarity to the Torah's account of the first murder in human history (cf. Gen 4:8–16). As in the story of Cain and Abel, the present murder occurred as two brothers were alone "in the field" (v. 6). One brother killed the other, and after the murder occurred concerns were expressed that the killer might die at the hands of others.[132] In both cases

---

[129] For a detailed treatment of the present section, along with a treatment of its parallels with other OT narratives, cf. J. Hoftijzer, "David and the Tekoite Woman," *VT* 20 (1970): 419–44.

[130] The root חכם appears to be used here to mean "skillful," as in Exod 35:25, and is not necessarily a term meant to convey what we think of today as "wisdom." This is in keeping with the conclusions reached by G. G. Nicol, "The Wisdom of Joab and the Wise Woman of Tekoa," *Studia Theologica* 36 (1982): 97–104, who understands the woman's role in this episode to have been incidental. Taking a different tack, C. Camp ("The Wise Woman of 2 Samuel: A Role Model for Women in Early Israel?" *CBQ* 43 [1981]: 14–29) suggests that in pre- and early monarchic Israel the role of the wise woman was the most politically influential role a woman could legitimately be expected to play.

[131] For a discussion of מְשָׁלִים, cf. comments on 12:1–4.

[132] The Genesis account does not explicitly state that Cain feared his relatives would kill him. However, the implicit claim of the text is that everyone he might encounter would be related to him through Adam and Eve.

an appeal was made to an authority figure to save the killer's life. The parallels suggest that Joab deliberately crafted the tale in order to compel David to render the same verdict that the Lord issued in Cain's behalf.

PARALLELS BETWEEN JOAB'S TALE AND GEN 4:1–15

	Cain and Abel	Joab's Tale
Two brothers	Gen 4:1	v. 6
alone together in a field	Gen 4:8	v. 6
one killed the other	Gen 4:8	v. 6
concerns expressed about murderer being killed by others	Gen 4:14	v. 7
authority figure intervened to save murderer's life	Gen 4:15	v. 8
threat of retaliation for anyone contravening authority's decision	Gen 4:15	v. 10

Implicit in Joab's use of this parallel is the assumption that David had a masterful knowledge of the Torah, and that Joab—like Nathan before him (cf. 12:6)—counted on the king using it as an authoritative guide in formulating his legal decisions.

14:8–11 Just as Joab had hoped, David ruled that the son's life was to be spared. The king's decision to spare the murderer's life was not based on legal mandates in the Torah, for its explicit commands required the son's death (cf. Gen 9:6; Exod 21:12; Lev 24:17). Rather, the king's decision was based on a narrative account within the Torah.[133] The narrative account of the Lord's merciful intervention in Cain's behalf—in spite of legal guidelines to the contrary set forth by the Lord himself—provided an enlightening insight into the Lord's own application of covenantal law. Yahweh the Merciful (cf. Exod 34:5–7)—he who had spared both Cain and David (cf. 12:13) from Torah-mandated death sentences—had established the definitive precedent for David's commutation of the murderer's sentence. David was doubly justified in choosing to spare the son, because killing him would snuff out "the only burning coal" (v. 7) the

---

[133] The present account provides a useful insight into how narrative portions of the Torah were utilized in administering justice in ancient Israel. Because the narratives presented specific historical examples modeling the correct application of divine law, they possessed tremendous forensic value. In the present instance David clearly used the narrative as an interpretive guide to the specific commands regarding the treatment of a murderer.

woman had left, and leave her "husband neither name nor descendant on the face of the earth."

Accordingly, David assured the woman that he would "issue an order" (v. 8) in her behalf granting a reprieve for her son. The woman apparently expressed concerns that the king's disregard for the letter of the Law might not "let the king and his throne" (v. 9) be perceived as being "without guilt." After all, the Torah permitted an "avenger of blood" (v. 11) to track down and kill a murderer (cf. Num 35:12,19–21).

However, David assured her the matter would stand as he had decided it. Using an oath that ominously foreshadows the fate of Absalom (cf. 18:9), he swore that "not one hair of your son's head will fall to the ground." The king added forebodingly that any who challenged his decision "will not bother you again" (v. 10).

14:12–17 David had settled the legal dispute to his own satisfaction and expected the woman to depart (cf. v. 8). However, the woman violated courtly protocol by requesting to "speak a word to my lord the king" (v. 12). In spite of her disregard for the norms, however, David graciously permitted her to "speak."

In the lengthy (ninety-three words in the MT) speech that followed, the woman of Tekoa revealed the central thesis of her presentation before David. By failing to restore Absalom to the court of Jerusalem, David was acting "against" the interests of "the people of God"—for if, as it appears from the text, Absalom was the heir-apparent to the throne, then keeping Absalom in exile threatened the fledgling dynasty of David, and thus a continuation of quality leadership for Israel.

Speaking as a sage of Israel, the wise woman of Tekoa then juxtaposed two profound truths about life. First, she noted that death is a hallmark of the human condition. Her emphatic verbal statement that "we must surely die" (v. 15) is an apparent allusion to Gen 2:17; if that is the case, then she is restating the Torah teaching that God consigned all people to die. Second, she noted that although God requires every person's death, he does not try to "take away life; instead, he devises ways so that a banished person may not remain estranged from him" (v. 14). This irony—that God established a world system that requires death, but then works to contravene his own system by creating ways to spare life—provided David with a theological justification for becoming reconciled to Absalom. Since the Lord makes harsh judgments against sinners but then establishes mechanisms for reconciliation, the king—as the Lord's representative in matters of justice on earth—should do the same.

The woman confessed that her presentation to the king came from a heart filled with both fear and hope: "the people" (v. 15) had made her "afraid"—perhaps because of their pessimism regarding her chances for success in gaining a commuted sentence for her (fictitious) son. But David had given her hope that he might "do what his servant asks," and would "agree to deliver his servant from the hand of the man who is trying to cut off both" her and her (fictitious) son from "the inheritance God gave"[134] them (v. 16).

The wise woman concluded her central monologue with a plea, a statement of profound faith in David's wisdom, and a blessing for the king. Her plea was that David's judgment in her imaginary dilemma would "bring" her "rest" (v. 17). Her favorable comparison of David with "an angel of God in discerning good and evil" expressed confidence that the king would act as wisely as the Lord would—and did in the past—in the matter. The wise woman's blessing of David stands as the only example of a female pronouncing a blessing on a king in the Hebrew Bible.

14:18–20 The woman's not-so-subtle linkage of her tragic story with David's own personal tragedy convinced the king that she was acting in collaboration with a member of the royal family. Accordingly, he demanded that she reveal whether or not it was Joab. Knowing that to "turn to the right or to the left" in her answer could prove fatal, she confessed that it was David's "servant Joab who instructed" her "to do this and who put all these words into" her mouth. Though it was true that Joab had arranged the woman's performance and plea, his guiding purpose in it was simply "to change"—and improve— "the present situation" (v. 20).

14:21–22 Joab carried out his scheme in part to help David find an adequate justification for doing what his heart had been urging him to do (cf. 13:39). With Joab's help David had come to realize that reconciliation with his son was both consistent with the Torah and in the nation's best interests; thus, he agreed to "do it" (v. 21). Without delay, he ordered Joab to "bring back the young man Absalom."

Joab had risked both his position of honor in David's court, and perhaps even his own life in attempting to influence the king as he did. No doubt relieved that his gamble had paid off, Joab fell on his face before David. David had "granted his servant's request," to be sure; but in the process David had also satisfied his own yearnings. The healing process between father and son could now move to a new, albeit difficult, phase.

14:23–24 In accordance with the royal decree, Joab went to Geshur and brought Absalom back to Jerusalem" (v. 24). Absalom was permitted to return "to his own house" (v. 25) and possessions within the confines of the royal city. However, he was not permitted to "see the face of the king," in accordance with an edict issued by this father.

---

[134] For a discussion of translational issues involved in the phrase מִנַּחֲלַת אֱלֹהִים, cf. T. J. Lewis, "The Ancestral Estate (נחלת אלחים) in 2 Samuel 14:16," *JBL* 110 (1991): 597–612. Lewis concludes, in partial agreement with the NIV, that the phrase should be translated as "ancestral estate." Lewis's suggestion requires the translation of אלהים as "one who is deceased," assuming that the term was sometimes used that way in biblical Hebrew (cf. 1 Sam 28:13).

Why did David refuse to see his son Absalom after permitting him to return to Jerusalem? Perhaps a major reason was David's desire to imitate the Lord's example in dealing with Cain. Though the Lord spared Cain's life, Cain "went out from the face of the Lord" (Gen 4:16; NIV, "presence of the LORD"), and apparently was never again in the presence of the Lord. Since David had previously relied on the Cain narrative to guide his judgment in this matter (cf. comments on vv. 5–11), it was consistent for him to bar Absalom from his face as well.

The practical effect of David's action was highly negative for Absalom. His expulsion from the royal court undoubtedly meant that he—notwithstanding his position as the heir-apparent—had lost any claim to Israel's throne. By murdering his brother, Absalom had effectively removed himself from the chain of royal succession, even as Cain had removed himself from the line of blessing through a similar act.

14:25–27 Though Absalom had fallen out of favor with David, he was a popular figure among the other Israelites. One reason for his popularity was his physical appearance.

The biblical narrator's effort to describe Absalom's physical attractiveness is extraordinary and serves a thematic purpose. Previously the theologically oriented narrator has taught that people are not to look at outward appearance; instead they are to imitate the Lord by looking at "the heart" (cf. 1 Sam 16:7). Absalom's physical appeal assured that those untrained in godliness would be beguiled by him. In so doing, however, they would blind themselves to the Lord's ways and will. The narrator's emphasis on Absalom's appearance subtly warned of impending tragedy, both for Absalom and his followers.

In addition to being handsome, Absalom was a hairy man. In fact, when Absalom would "cut his hair from time to time" (v. 26) "its weight was two hundred shekels by the royal standard" (lit., "the stone of the king")—slightly more than five pounds, assuming the weight of a shekel to be 11.5 grams. To many of the Israelites of Absalom's day this must have served as evidence of virility. However, the narrator's mention of this aspect of Absalom's appearance implicitly draws an unflattering parallel with Esau (cf. Gen 25:25). Like Esau (cf. Gen 25:28), Absalom was a masculine, hairy son who was favored by his father; like Esau (cf. Gen 25:29–34), Absalom sacrificed his birthright through foolish actions at a meal, and ultimately caused much grief for his father (cf. Gen 28:8). Certainly the writer's emphasis on Absalom's hair would also have called to mind the tragic story of Samson.

The narrator criticizes Absalom subtly by clarifying the reason for his haircut; he would cut his hair "when it became too heavy for him." The Torah provided two primary reasons for a man to cut his hair: one was to give the hair to God following the successful completion of a Nazirite vow (cf. Num 6:18), and the other was to enter into a state of ceremonial cleanness before the Lord (cf.

Lev 14:8–9; Num 8:7). Absalom's stated motive for getting a haircut was totally devoid of any connection with service to Yahweh; it was secular and self-serving. This detachment of Absalom's act from any religious motivation underscores the profane nature of the man's life and reinforces the intimation that his life would end disastrously. Interestingly, his hair would play a significant role in that disastrous end (cf. 18:9).

A genealogical note in the text states that Absalom fathered "three sons and a daughter" (v. 27). This note, likewise, plays an important role in helping the reader evaluate Absalom's life. Although three sons would have been reckoned as a great blessing, by the time of Absalom's death all of them would be dead, so that Absalom had no male heir to continue his family line (18:18). The Torah declared that disobedience to the Lord would cause one's children to be cursed (Deut 28:18), and the narrator's indication that Absalom lost all three male heirs so early in life would reinforce the notion that he was indeed under the Lord's curse.

Absalom chose the name "Tamar" (lit., "Palm tree") for his "beautiful" daughter, apparently as a gesture of sympathy for his desolate and humiliated sister who resided with him in his residence (13:20). While this act might have been viewed as thoughtful and affirming by many, it had the effect of perpetuating painful memories in David's household for another generation. Every time Absalom thought or spoke his daughter's name he created another opportunity to relive the tragic chain of events that resulted in the five-year alienation from David, and so to increase the bitterness he held toward his father.

14:28–30 In effect Absalom was living in internal exile; he was restored to his former abode in the most important city in Israel, but he was restricted in his ability to move about. Not only did this situation affect Absalom in the present in that it prevented him from dining at the royal table, but it also affected his future in that he could not be considered as David's successor to the throne.

After tolerating two years of quiet frustration in internal exile, Absalom decided to bring it to an end by implementing a plan to restore fellowship with his father David. Since he could not approach David directly, he "sent for Joab in order to send him to the king" (v. 29). However, Joab repeatedly "refused to come."

Absalom was undaunted in his efforts to achieve the goal of being restored to his father. Ever the man of bold action, he established a plan designed to compel Joab to come to him: the king's son ordered "his servants" (v. 30), to go to "Joab's field" of barley and "set the field on fire." According to the Torah, Absalom would have to reimburse Joab for the lost harvest (cf. Exod 22:6), but Joab would have to come to him before he could get it. In doing a cost-versus-benefits analysis of the situation, Absalom concluded the price he would pay was worth the reconciliation it might bring about.

14:31-33 Absalom's plan to force a meeting with Joab worked. In the confrontation that followed, Absalom expressed his frustrations regarding the present limiting circumstances. He noted that life would be less oppressive for him in his grandfather's household in "Geshur" (v. 32) than it was in his father's royal city as things now stood.

But Absalom was in something of a dilemma: he did not want to depart from Israel, nor did he wish to live any longer in internal exile. Either he would experience a complete restoration of his former status in the royal household or he would die. And if Absalom had his way, it would be his father David who would decide his fate.

Having been confronted with Absalom's audacious demand, Joab dutifully "went to the king and told him" (v. 33) of Absalom's ultimatum. Absalom's power play worked—after five years of separation, "the king summoned Absalom" to come before him. With all the humility of a lowly slave, David's son "came in" to the king's presence "and bowed down with his face to the ground." However, David did not treat Absalom as a slave but as an equal: "the king kissed Absalom." This act demonstrated both David's respect and acceptance of his son.[135] Reconciliation had occurred. David had regained his son, and Absalom had regained his father.

(8) Absalom Leads a Treasonous Revolt against David (15:1-12)

[1]In the course of time, Absalom provided himself with a chariot and horses and with fifty men to run ahead of him. [2]He would get up early and stand by the side of the road leading to the city gate. Whenever anyone came with a complaint to be placed before the king for a decision, Absalom would call out to him, "What town are you from?" He would answer, "Your servant is from one of the tribes of Israel." [3]Then Absalom would say to him, "Look, your claims are valid and proper, but there is no representative of the king to hear you." [4]And Absalom would add, "If only I were appointed judge in the land! Then everyone who has a complaint or case could come to me and I would see that he gets justice."

[5]Also, whenever anyone approached him to bow down before him, Absalom would reach out his hand, take hold of him and kiss him. [6]Absalom behaved in this way toward all the Israelites who came to the king asking for justice, and so he stole the hearts of the men of Israel.

[7]At the end of four years, Absalom said to the king, "Let me go to Hebron and fulfill a vow I made to the LORD. [8]While your servant was living at Geshur in Aram, I made this vow: 'If the LORD takes me back to Jerusalem, I will worship

---

[135] Anderson notes in connection with the Absalom event that David's failure to implement the death penalty as punishment for the murder of Amnon indicates that "in David's time murder or, at least, fratricide was not strictly a sacral crime" (*2 Samuel*, 187). This suggests that the Torah—or at least the corpus of Sinai legal materials—did not exist in the tenth century B.C. Such a position is not supportable with the evidence presented elsewhere in 1, 2, Samuel.

the LORD in Hebron.'"
⁹The king said to him, "Go in peace." So he went to Hebron.

¹⁰Then Absalom sent secret messengers throughout the tribes of Israel to say, "As soon as you hear the sound of the trumpets, then say, 'Absalom is king in Hebron.'" ¹¹Two hundred men from Jerusalem had accompanied Absalom. They had been invited as guests and went quite innocently, knowing nothing about the matter. ¹²While Absalom was offering sacrifices, he also sent for Ahithophel the Gilonite, David's counselor, to come from Giloh, his hometown. And so the conspiracy gained strength, and Absalom's following kept on increasing.

15:1 Having been restored to a position of prominence in the royal city and household, Absalom began to assert his lofty ambitions. First of all, he acquired his own personal chariot and horses, thereby becoming the first Israelite specifically mentioned in the biblical text to do so. The prophet Samuel had stated that Israel's kings would someday use chariots and horses (1 Sam 8:11), though neither king Saul nor king David were portrayed in the biblical narratives as using them. However, each of the three sons of David who claimed kingship for himself acquired a chariot and horses (cf. 1 Kgs 1:5; 4:26). Absalom's acquisition of these highly visible symbols of royalty in the present narrative already foreshadows a treasonous rebellion against David.

The biblical narratives stretching from Exodus through this point in 2 Samuel are surprisingly negative in their portrayal of horses and chariots. The texts consistently depict only enemies of the Lord and his covenant people as having them. The Egyptians (cf. Exod 14:9–15:21; Deut 11:4; Josh 24:6), northern Canaanites (Josh 11:4–9; Judg 4:15; 5:19–22), and Arameans (8:4; 10:18) all used them unsuccessfully in battle against Israel. Thus, when Absalom linked them with himself, he was joining his ambitions with symbols of hostility against the Lord and Israel, and with ultimate failure.

In addition to the chariot and horses, Absalom employed "fifty men to run ahead of him." This contingent of young men—likely soldiers—added to his impressive presence wherever he went. Samuel had pessimistically indicated that Israel's kings would someday press young men into service in the way that Absalom did here (cf. 1 Sam 8:11; also 1 Kgs 1:5).

15:2–4 Since the time of Moses, a major function of Israel's highest-ranking leaders was to administer divine justice for the Lord's people (cf. Exod 18:13–16; Judg 4:4–5; 1 Sam 8:5; 1 Kgs 3:16–28; 7:7). Without yet declaring himself king, Absalom began carrying out this executive responsibility as though he were king. Shrewdly, "he would get up early" (v. 2)—that is, before sunrise—"and stand by the side of the road leading to the city gate" of Jerusalem, perhaps at a threshing floor (cf. 1 Kgs 22:10). By being stationed there even before the time of the morning sacrifice, Absalom was able to intercept all citizens seeking justice from David's court.

Absalom displayed consummate social and political acumen in his interactions with Israel's citizens. Before providing them any judicial services, he first of all expressed a personal interest in each person who had journeyed to the City of David. By first asking them "what town" they had come from, he made the people feel like he cared for them as individuals.

After listening to their concerns Absalom would support them in their case by telling them that their "claims are valid and proper" (v. 3). The same duplicity which had served Absalom so well in the past (cf. 1 Sam 13:24–27), was surely at work here, for at least some of the complaints that came before him must have been without merit.

Absalom also furthered his personal ambitions by fostering a sense of alienation between David's regime and the citizens who sought the king's help. By telling each distraught person he encountered that "there is no representative of the king to hear" their case, he created the false impression that David was neglecting a fundamental royal responsibility. By nurturing the impression that David was derelict in his duty, Absalom succeeded in creating an atmosphere of political discontent among the citizenry of the various tribes.

After creating a positive impression of himself and then alienating the Israelites from David, Absalom hinted that he would like to be given more authority in Israel. However, he wisely avoided openly expressing his desire to depose David and become Israel's next king—that would be treason: instead, he communicated the innocuous wish to be "appointed judge in the land" (v. 4).

15:5–6 Absalom's persuasive skills were not limited to his speech. "Whenever anyone approached him to bow down before him" (v. 5), Absalom would "take hold of him," thus preventing them from completing their act. In a sense, it was appropriate that Absalom stop them, since he was not truly a king and therefore should not be treated like one. However, once again it was Absalom's cunning duplicity, not his virtuous humility, that motivated him to act in this way.

After refusing to accept the respect normally accorded royalty, Absalom then displayed toward each person a sign of great respect and acceptance by kissing them. For many, this action by one who played the role of an empathetic, humble, and justice-minded monarch so convincingly, must have cemented their conviction that he, not David, deserved to be Israel's king. Thus he must have directly influenced hundreds—if not thousands—of individuals from all over Israel to support enthusiastically his bid for kingship. Indeed, before long "he stole the hearts of the men of Israel."

15:7–9 Absalom's practice of administering justice at the city gate was apparently carried out consistently for a period "of four years" (v. 7).[136] After

---

[136] The NIV emended the text to produce the reading "four," basing their reading on the Lucianic recension of the LXX, the Syriac, and Josephus (*Ant.* 7.9.1); the MT and other recensions of the LXX state that Absalom performed this activity for a period of forty years. R. Althann ("The meaning of ארבעים שנה in 2 Samuel 15,7," *Bib* 73 [1992]: 248–52) prefers to understand the time period as "forty days," a position supported by two MT manuscripts.

that time Absalom entered a new phase in his scheme to supplant David as Israel's king. Cunningly, he asked David for permission to "go to Hebron"— the same city in which David had been anointed as king over Judah (cf. 2:3–4)—in order to "fulfill a vow" he "made to the LORD." The vow reverberated with piety: "If the LORD takes me back to Jerusalem, I will worship the LORD in Hebron" (v. 8).

However, the fact that Absalom waited four years to fulfill the vow takes some of the luster off his halo. Since the Torah required vows to be fulfilled quickly (cf. Deut 23:21), Absalom's slackness in this matter should have raised questions about his true devotion to the Lord. To the wary, this unusual delay might also have raised doubts regarding Absalom's true motives.

But if David had any misgivings regarding Absalom's request, he did not express them. Since Hebron was also the city of Absalom's birth (3:2–3) and a significant religious center in Judah (cf. Josh 21:11–13), the request must not have seemed unreasonable to David. Besides, if he prohibited Absalom from fulfilling a sacred vow, he himself might have to bear the responsibility for forcing his son to disobey the Torah (cf. Num 30:2). Thus, Absalom "went to Hebron."

15:10–12 At Hebron Absalom found himself twenty miles away from his father and protected by strong walls. From this relatively safe base of operations Absalom moved quickly to usurp David's throne. He prepared for the public phase of his plot by sending "secret messengers throughout the tribes of Israel" (v. 10) to make a coordinated proclamation throughout the land. Once in place, they were to await "the sound of trumpets" and then announce simultaneously that "Absalom is king in Hebron." Implicit in this proclamation was a call to arms for those who supported Absalom in his efforts.

One of the most brilliant aspects of Absalom's plot to overthrow his father may have been his success in emptying Jerusalem of some of its most valuable administrators at the very time when David needed them most. "Two hundred men from Jerusalem had accompanied Absalom to Hebron" (v. 11). Each one had been hand-picked by Absalom and had come "quite innocently," being only "invited guests." Once inside the walls of Hebron, however, they became his hostages. Because these two hundred men were unable to assist David in his efforts to respond to the national emergency, the king was put at a severe disadvantage from the very beginning. Furthermore, if any of the two hundred men openly expressed support for David while in Hebron, they risked being killed.

Absalom's rebellion gained a powerful ally when "Ahithophel the Gilonite, David's counselor" (v. 12), switched allegiances and joined the traitor in Hebron. The narrator does not state why one of David's most valued administrators abandoned him; however, the fact that David had had unlawful sexual relations with Ahithophel's granddaughter and murdered her husband, Uriah, (cf. 11:3; 23:34) may have played a role in the decision. Other unnamed individuals also joined Absalom at Hebron, so that his "following kept on increasing" and "the conspiracy gained strength."

(9) David Goes into Exile beyond the Jordan River (15:13–17:29)

[13]A messenger came and told David, "The hearts of the men of Israel are with Absalom."
[14]Then David said to all his officials who were with him in Jerusalem, "Come! We must flee, or none of us will escape from Absalom. We must leave immediately, or he will move quickly to overtake us and bring ruin upon us and put the city to the sword."
[15]The king's officials answered him, "Your servants are ready to do whatever our lord the king chooses."
[16]The king set out, with his entire household following him; but he left ten concubines to take care of the palace. [17]So the king set out, with all the people following him, and they halted at a place some distance away. [18]All his men marched past him, along with all the Kerethites and Pelethites; and all the six hundred Gittites who had accompanied him from Gath marched before the king.
[19]The king said to Ittai the Gittite, "Why should you come along with us? Go back and stay with King Absalom. You are a foreigner, an exile from your homeland. [20]You came only yesterday. And today shall I make you wander about with us, when I do not know where I am going? Go back, and take your countrymen. May kindness and faithfulness be with you."
[21]But Ittai replied to the king, "As surely as the LORD lives, and as my lord the king lives, wherever my lord the king may be, whether it means life or death, there will your servant be."
[22]David said to Ittai, "Go ahead, march on." So Ittai the Gittite marched on with all his men and the families that were with him.
[23]The whole countryside wept aloud as all the people passed by. The king also crossed the Kidron Valley, and all the people moved on toward the desert.
[24]Zadok was there, too, and all the Levites who were with him were carrying the ark of the covenant of God. They set down the ark of God, and Abiathar offered sacrifices until all the people had finished leaving the city.
[25]Then the king said to Zadok, "Take the ark of God back into the city. If I find favor in the LORD's eyes, he will bring me back and let me see it and his dwelling place again. [26]But if he says, 'I am not pleased with you,' then I am ready; let him do to me whatever seems good to him."
[27]The king also said to Zadok the priest, "Aren't you a seer? Go back to the city in peace, with your son Ahimaaz and Jonathan son of Abiathar. You and Abiathar take your two sons with you. [28]I will wait at the fords in the desert until word comes from you to inform me." [29]So Zadok and Abiathar took the ark of God back to Jerusalem and stayed there.
[30]But David continued up the Mount of Olives, weeping as he went; his head was covered and he was barefoot. All the people with him covered their heads too and were weeping as they went up.
[31]Now David had been told, "Ahithophel is among the conspirators with

Absalom." So David prayed, "O LORD, turn Ahithophel's counsel into foolishness."

[32] When David arrived at the summit, where people used to worship God, Hushai the Arkite was there to meet him, his robe torn and dust on his head.

[33] David said to him, "If you go with me, you will be a burden to me. [34] But if you return to the city and say to Absalom, 'I will be your servant, O king; I was your father's servant in the past, but now I will be your servant,' then you can help me by frustrating Ahithophel's advice. [35] Won't the priests Zadok and Abiathar be there with you? Tell them anything you hear in the king's palace. [36] Their two sons, Ahimaaz son of Zadok and Jonathan son of Abiathar, are there with them. Send them to me with anything you hear."

[37] So David's friend Hushai arrived at Jerusalem as Absalom was entering the city.

[1] When David had gone a short distance beyond the summit, there was Ziba, the steward of Mephibosheth, waiting to meet him. He had a string of donkeys saddled and loaded with two hundred loaves of bread, a hundred cakes of raisins, a hundred cakes of figs and a skin of wine.

[2] The king asked Ziba, "Why have you brought these?"

Ziba answered, "The donkeys are for the king's household to ride on, the bread and fruit are for the men to eat, and the wine is to refresh those who become exhausted in the desert."

[3] The king then asked, "Where is your master's grandson?"

Ziba said to him, "He is staying in Jerusalem, because he thinks, 'Today the house of Israel will give me back my grandfather's kingdom.'"

[4] Then the king said to Ziba, "All that belonged to Mephibosheth is now yours."

"I humbly bow," Ziba said. "May I find favor in your eyes, my lord the king."

[5] As King David approached Bahurim, a man from the same clan as Saul's family came out from there. His name was Shimei son of Gera, and he cursed as he came out. [6] He pelted David and all the king's officials with stones, though all the troops and the special guard were on David's right and left. [7] As he cursed, Shimei said, "Get out, get out, you man of blood, you scoundrel! [8] The LORD has repaid you for all the blood you shed in the household of Saul, in whose place you have reigned. The LORD has handed the kingdom over to your son Absalom. You have come to ruin because you are a man of blood!"

[9] Then Abishai son of Zeruiah said to the king, "Why should this dead dog curse my lord the king? Let me go over and cut off his head."

[10] But the king said, "What do you and I have in common, you sons of Zeruiah? If he is cursing because the LORD said to him, 'Curse David,' who can ask, 'Why do you do this?'"

[11] David then said to Abishai and all his officials, "My son, who is of my own flesh, is trying to take my life. How much more, then, this Benjamite! Leave him alone; let him curse, for the LORD has told him to. [12] It may be that the LORD will see my distress and repay me with good for the cursing I am receiving today."

[13] So David and his men continued along the road while Shimei was going along the hillside opposite him, cursing as he went and throwing stones at him and showering him with dirt. [14] The king and all the people with him arrived at their destination exhausted. And there he refreshed himself.

¹⁵Meanwhile, Absalom and all the men of Israel came to Jerusalem, and Ahithophel was with him. ¹⁶Then Hushai the Arkite, David's friend, went to Absalom and said to him, "Long live the king! Long live the king!"

¹⁷Absalom asked Hushai, "Is this the love you show your friend? Why didn't you go with your friend?"

¹⁸Hushai said to Absalom, "No, the one chosen by the LORD, by these people, and by all the men of Israel—his I will be, and I will remain with him. ¹⁹Furthermore, whom should I serve? Should I not serve the son? Just as I served your father, so I will serve you."

²⁰Absalom said to Ahithophel, "Give us your advice. What should we do?"

²¹Ahithophel answered, "Lie with your father's concubines whom he left to take care of the palace. Then all Israel will hear that you have made yourself a stench in your father's nostrils, and the hands of everyone with you will be strengthened." ²²So they pitched a tent for Absalom on the roof, and he lay with his father's concubines in the sight of all Israel.

²³Now in those days the advice Ahithophel gave was like that of one who inquires of God. That was how both David and Absalom regarded all of Ahithophel's advice.

¹Ahithophel said to Absalom, "I would choose twelve thousand men and set out tonight in pursuit of David. ²I would attack him while he is weary and weak. I would strike him with terror, and then all the people with him will flee. I would strike down only the king ³and bring all the people back to you. The death of the man you seek will mean the return of all; all the people will be unharmed." ⁴This plan seemed good to Absalom and to all the elders of Israel.

⁵But Absalom said, "Summon also Hushai the Arkite, so we can hear what he has to say." ⁶When Hushai came to him, Absalom said, "Ahithophel has given this advice. Should we do what he says? If not, give us your opinion."

⁷Hushai replied to Absalom, "The advice Ahithophel has given is not good this time. ⁸You know your father and his men; they are fighters, and as fierce as a wild bear robbed of her cubs. Besides, your father is an experienced fighter; he will not spend the night with the troops. ⁹Even now, he is hidden in a cave or some other place. If he should attack your troops first, whoever hears about it will say, 'There has been a slaughter among the troops who follow Absalom.' ¹⁰Then even the bravest soldier, whose heart is like the heart of a lion, will melt with fear, for all Israel knows that your father is a fighter and that those with him are brave.

¹¹"So I advise you: Let all Israel, from Dan to Beersheba—as numerous as the sand on the seashore—be gathered to you, with you yourself leading them into battle. ¹²Then we will attack him wherever he may be found, and we will fall on him as dew settles on the ground. Neither he nor any of his men will be left alive. ¹³If he withdraws into a city, then all Israel will bring ropes to that city, and we will drag it down to the valley until not even a piece of it can be found."

¹⁴Absalom and all the men of Israel said, "The advice of Hushai the Arkite is better than that of Ahithophel." For the LORD had determined to frustrate the good advice of Ahithophel in order to bring disaster on Absalom.

¹⁵Hushai told Zadok and Abiathar, the priests, "Ahithophel has advised Absalom and the elders of Israel to do such and such, but I have advised them to

do so and so. [16]Now send a message immediately and tell David, 'Do not spend the night at the fords in the desert; cross over without fail, or the king and all the people with him will be swallowed up.'"

[17]Jonathan and Ahimaaz were staying at En Rogel. A servant girl was to go and inform them, and they were to go and tell King David, for they could not risk being seen entering the city. [18]But a young man saw them and told Absalom. So the two of them left quickly and went to the house of a man in Bahurim. He had a well in his courtyard, and they climbed down into it. [19]His wife took a covering and spread it out over the opening of the well and scattered grain over it. No one knew anything about it.

[20]When Absalom's men came to the woman at the house, they asked, "Where are Ahimaaz and Jonathan?"

The woman answered them, "They crossed over the brook." The men searched but found no one, so they returned to Jerusalem.

[21]After the men had gone, the two climbed out of the well and went to inform King David. They said to him, "Set out and cross the river at once; Ahithophel has advised such and such against you." [22]So David and all the people with him set out and crossed the Jordan. By daybreak, no one was left who had not crossed the Jordan.

[23]When Ahithophel saw that his advice had not been followed, he saddled his donkey and set out for his house in his hometown. He put his house in order and then hanged himself. So he died and was buried in his father's tomb.

[24]David went to Mahanaim, and Absalom crossed the Jordan with all the men of Israel. [25]Absalom had appointed Amasa over the army in place of Joab. Amasa was the son of a man named Jether, an Israelite who had married Abigail, the daughter of Nahash and sister of Zeruiah the mother of Joab. [26]The Israelites and Absalom camped in the land of Gilead.

[27]When David came to Mahanaim, Shobi son of Nahash from Rabbah of the Ammonites, and Makir son of Ammiel from Lo Debar, and Barzillai the Gileadite from Rogelim [28]brought bedding and bowls and articles of pottery. They also brought wheat and barley, flour and roasted grain, beans and lentils, [29]honey and curds, sheep, and cheese from cows' milk for David and his people to eat. For they said, "The people have become hungry and tired and thirsty in the desert."

15:13–15 Belatedly, David learned from an unnamed messenger[137] that a coup was underway and "the hearts of the men of Israel [were] with Absalom" (v. 13). The "men of Israel" likely referred to the nation's armed forces (cf. Judg 7:23; 9:55; 20:11,17,20; 1 Sam 7:11; 14:24). Immediately the king recognized the gravity of the situation and realized he was facing a crisis unlike any other he had faced. Thanks to Absalom's popular support, as well as his success in taking most of David's administration hostage, David was unable to mount a credible response. Now for the first time in the biblical account David, the

---

[137]Fokkelman suggests that the messenger was an individual sympathetic to David who just happened to observe Absalom's army approaching Jerusalem (*King David,* 177).

brilliant military leader, ordered those under his command to "flee" (v. 14). Without an immediate departure from Jerusalem, the king feared that they would perish. His analysis of the situation probably was correct.

David's servants who had been in Jerusalem when news of the coup reached the king remained steadfast in their support for him. Trusting David implicitly, they indicated they were "ready to do whatever . . . the king chooses" (v. 15).

15:16–18 Affirmed by this endorsement, David hastily organized these loyal followers in an effort to accomplish two all-important objectives: preserve the life of the king and key members of the royal family and administration and make provisions for the maintenance of the City of David in the king's absence.

The first objective was accomplished by having David, "with his entire household following him" (v. 16), make a hasty eastward departure from Jerusalem. Though at that moment David was not sure exactly where he was going (cf. v. 20), he had the group set out in the opposite direction from Hebron to increase the distance between themselves and those who were seeking the king's life. David led the group out of Jerusalem to "a place some distance away" (v. 17),[138] at which point he stopped to organize the group more effectively for military action. At that staging area the king had "all his men," including "all the Kerethites and Pelethites, and all six hundred Gittites who had accompanied him from Gath" (v. 18), march past him. The effect of this maneuver was no doubt to increase the level of protection that would be afforded David and the other members of the royal household during their movement down the road.

The second objective was accomplished by establishing a small group of expendable, nonmilitary personnel who would manage the royal residence in Jerusalem. This group was not responsible for the defense of Israel's capital, only its basic continuance. Lest there be any doubt that David did not wish any fighting to take place around the heavily fortified and almost invincible city, David ordered women—"ten concubines" (v. 16) from his harem—to be in charge of the city. Jerusalem was to be a city of peace (cf. Ps 122:6–9), so only individuals excluded from active participation in military conflict would be permitted to preserve David's interests in the city.

15:19–22 While reorganizing his military forces outside Jerusalem, David seems to have had some second thoughts about the makeup and size of the forces that would accompany him. Apparently he had some serious questions about the loyalty of the Philistine forces led by "Ittai the Gittite" (v. 19). After all, the Philistines previously had waged war against David (cf. 5:17–25; 8:12); their political leaders probably would have rewarded Ittai

---

[138] The MT suggests that the spot was "the [most] distant house" (בֵּית הַמֶּרְחָק), apparently the last residence within the city walls.

gladly if he betrayed and killed David.

David was certainly aware that foreign forces sometimes switched loyalties in the heat of battle (cf. 1 Sam 14:21); he himself had once been sent away from a military confrontation for fear that he would do the same (cf. 1 Sam 29:4–7). Knowing that such a change in loyalties would only compound his woes, David ordered Ittai and his forces to "go back and stay with King Absalom." It seems strange that David would use the title "king" with reference to Absalom; perhaps, as Gordon suggests, it was a test.[139] If Ittai obeyed the king's command, he would go with the king's blessing.

However, Ittai confounded David by rejecting the king's command. Instead, he bound himself with a loyalty oath sworn on the lives of both Yahweh and David. In a commitment rivaling that of Ruth toward Naomi (cf. Ruth 1:16–17), Ittai indicated that "wherever my lord the king may be, whether it means life or death, there will your servant be" (v. 21). Taking the Philistine general at his word, David reversed his decision and ordered Ittai to "march on" (v. 22) with his own forces "and the families that were with him."

15:23 David was a king without a capital city, but he was not without supportive citizens: "the whole countryside wept aloud as all" David's retinue "passed by." Moving down the hill east of Jerusalem, the group "crossed the Kidron Valley" and then "moved on toward the desert" in the direction of Jericho.[140]

15:24–26 A major portion of David's support at this time came from the religious community. David had consistently provided support for Levites in the past (1 Sam 22:20–23) and had given them a position of prominence in the royal city and his own administration (cf. 6:12–18; 8:17). Now in his own hour of need "Zadok was there" (v. 24), accompanied by "all the Levites, who were with him."

In the hastily arranged royal flight from Jerusalem the Levites were "carrying the ark of the covenant of God." David previously had been responsible for the entrance of the ark into Jerusalem (6:1–18). He apparently had undertaken this act because of the belief that he was fulfilling a Torah prophecy (cf. Deut 12:5): the Lord had chosen Jerusalem as the place where he would cause his name to rest (cf. 1 Kgs 8:29; 11:36; 2 Kgs 23:27).

Yet now it seemed as if David would be responsible for the departure of the ark—God's very throne—from the home the Lord had chosen for himself. David deemed this utterly unacceptable, for it would mean the undoing of a

[139] Gordon, *I and II Samuel*, 273.

[140] McCarter (*II Samuel*, 361) and Anderson (*2 Samuel*, 198) accept the Lucianic recension of the LXX's reading for this phrase that mentions "Olive Way/the way of the wild olive tree in the wilderness." To arrive at this translation, it appears that the syntactically difficult אֵת (the usually untranslated particle marking a verb's object) was read as זַיִת ("olive"). Such a reading does eliminate the grammatical tensions in the verse while at the same time producing a credible reading.

sacred Torah promise-fulfillment. Accordingly, the king ordered Zadok to "take the ark of God back into the city" (v. 25). Zadok and the Levites apparently had carried the ark of the covenant in exile in order to buttress David's claim to the throne: David's possession of the ark would demonstrate that he alone possessed the divine favor necessary to rule Israel fitly. David, however, rejected this line of reasoning: the ark would not be used as a talisman or as a means of coercing the Lord to favor David. If the king "found favor in the LORD's eyes," then the Lord would bring him back and let him "see it and his dwelling place again." If the Lord were not pleased with David, then "let him do to me whatever seems good to him" (v. 26). This response lays bare David's heart for God and models a degree of submission to God's will appropriate for all leaders of God's people.

As David and his group of supporters were leaving Jerusalem, Abiathar "offered sacrifices" (v. 24).[141] These sacrifices probably were the usual morning offerings (cf. Num 28:2–4), though they could have been a special offering made to seek the Lord's favor in the matter of David's flight.

15:27–29 Besides ordering the return of the ark of the covenant, David ordered Zadok, whom David also recognized as "a seer,"[142] to "go back to the city in peace, with your son Ahimaaz and Jonathan son of Abiathar." Since these three men were Kohathite priests in Aaron's family line (cf. 1 Chr 6:2–8; 24:6), and therefore charged with caring for the ark of the covenant (cf. Num 4:4–6), it was fitting that they go wherever the ark went.

But David had a second reason for requiring these priests to return to Jerusalem: they would serve as spies, secretly providing David with vital intelligence regarding Absalom's plans and movements. As David planned it, he and his entourage would "wait at the fords in the desert" (v. 28) near Jericho for information regarding Absalom's strategy. "Zadok and Abiathar" agreed to the plan and returned with the ark.

15:30 Ascending out the Kidron Valley—a location that later played a significant role in the life of David's descendant Jesus (cf. John 18:1)—David and his entourage "continued up the Mount of Olives" (v. 30) as they moved eastward toward the Jordan River. David made no attempt to hide his distress from his subjects. Covering the head[143] and going about barefoot were both consid-

---

[141] Keil and Delitzsch understand the verb וַיַּעַל to mean "came up," not "offered sacrifices," noting that the verb never has the latter meaning unless accompanied by the noun עוֹלָה "or unless the context points directly to sacrifices" (*II Samuel*, 421). However, the presence of an Aaronic priest and the ark are sufficient context to permit the NIV's translation decision.

[142] Zadok thus becomes the second levitical prophet of 1, 2 Samuel, taking his place beside Samuel. This identification of many of the most important personages as prophets in the Former Prophets' presentation of the history obviously is in keeping with one of the purposes of this section of the Hebrew Bible.

[143] The NEB translates חָפוּי as "bare-headed."

ered expressions of grief and despair in ancient Israelite society (cf. Jer 14:3–4; Mic 1:8). Out of sympathy for their king, those accompanying David followed his example.

15:31–32 Compounding David's woes was the news that Ahithophel, David's most valued counselor, was "among the conspirators with Absalom" (v. 31). Knowing that he himself was powerless to deny Absalom the benefits of Ahithophel's wisdom, David offered a desperate plea to the Lord.

The very next recorded event following David's prayer concerning Ahithophel was the king's encounter with "Hushai the Arkite" (v. 32), who was awaiting David at an ancient worship site "at the summit" of the Mount of Olives. This narrative juxtaposition of David's prayer with the appearance of Hushai is no accident: it is the writer's demonstration that the Lord was answering David's prayers even in exile. The Lord's love for David was steadfast; as in David's earlier years (cf. 1 Sam 18:12,14,28; 2 Sam 5:10), so now also the Lord was with David.

Hushai was obviously in sympathy with David and symbolically identified with the king's plight by appearing before him with "his robe torn and dust on his head" (cf. 1 Sam 4:12; 2 Sam 1:2).

15:33–37 David deeply appreciated the support of his wise friend, yet he realized that Hushai's counsel was an asset best utilized away from the king's presence. Knowing that each person who joined his entourage only added to the logistical problems of providing sufficient food, water, shelter, and protection, David forthrightly told Hushai that "if you go with me, you will only be a burden to me" (v. 33). Perhaps, as Gordon suggests, Hushai's age—and therefore reduced capacity to travel quickly—was also a factor.[144]

Ironically, however, if Hushai were to "return to the city" (v. 34) and declare his allegiance to Absalom, he might be of great value to David's cause. Having been a leading member of David's administration (cf. 1 Chr 27:33),[145] he was likely to be treated as a valued asset in Absalom's fledgling government. And if Hushai did succeed in gaining Absalom's confidence, then he would be in a position to "help by frustrating Ahithophel's advice."

Hushai would not be the only mole in Jerusalem; joining him in the subterfuge would be "Zadok and Abiathar" (v. 35). However, there was a crucial difference between the role that Hushai would play and that which the others carried out. While all three of these men would reside in Jerusalem with Absalom, only Hushai would have a presence "in the king's palace"; the priestly obligations of the others would keep them away from the king most of the time. Thus it would be up to Hushai to learn—and, hopefully, influence—the new government's strategies regarding David. Once Hushai acquired this

---

[144] Cf. Gordon, *I and II Samuel,* 275–76.

[145] Cf. J. A. Thompson, *1, 2 Chronicles,* NAC (Nashville: Broadman & Holman, 1994), 188.

coveted information, he would then be responsible to tell Zadok and Abiathar anything of strategic value he might hear. In turn, their sons would be given this information and would act as couriers in relaying it to David.

Hushai accepted David's plan, though doing so involved a high degree of risk; if his true intentions were discovered, he would have been summarily executed. Hushai's willingness to put himself at risk for David's sake reveals the depth of commitment he had toward his king.

According to the writer, David escaped from the forces of Absalom by the narrowest of margins. After Hushai left David and made the one-mile walk back to the royal city—a journey of no more than half an hour—"Absalom was entering the city" (v. 37). At that vulnerable moment, David and his followers were separated from Absalom's forces by only one hill. Through his portrayal of this tenuous escape the narrator reaffirms the thesis that the Lord was with David, and he provides additional hope that the Lord would yet bring a good end to the present evil circumstances.

16:1–4 Traveling eastward "a short distance beyond the summit" (v. 1) of the Mount of Olives, David encountered "Ziba, the steward of Mephibosheth." The meeting was not accidental; "Ziba was waiting to meet" David and had brought two valuable gifts: animals for transportation and food to sustain the group for at least a short while. The "string of donkeys saddled" (v. 1) were "for the king's household to ride on" (v. 2); no doubt they would have been used by the women, children, and elderly in the group. Ziba's generous provision was intended to nourish and "refresh those who become exhausted in the desert" (v. 2). The absence of meat in the gift was deliberate, since prepared flesh would quickly have spoiled, and live animals would have greatly impeded the group's flight.

David reacted to Ziba with two responses—suspicion and gratitude. David's suspicion was expressed in the form of two questions: "Why have you brought these?" and "Where is your master's grandson?"[146] The household of Saul was the very group that had worked for seven years following Saul's death to prevent David's rule over all Israel; for them now to assist David during this great crisis must have been almost inconceivable to the king.

More puzzling still was the fact that Mephibosheth did not accompany the gift. After all, he was the only member of the Saulide family who was likely to be supportive of David at this time. Ziba's explanation of Mephibosheth's absence seemed credible to the king: he was "staying in Jerusalem, because he thinks, 'Today the house of Israel will give me back my grandfather's kingdom'" (v. 3). Guided by Ziba's words—which may or may not have been truthful (cf. comments at 19:26–27)—in interpreting the evidence at hand, David

---

[146] The NASB translates the phrase בֶּן־אֲדֹנֶיךָ inconsistently in 2 Sam; here it is "your master's son"; in 9:9 it is "your master's grandson."

made a snap decision to disinherit the son of Jonathan: "all that belonged to Mephibosheth" (v. 4) would be given to Ziba, the only member of Saul's household who showed up to help David during this crisis. As in other situations following God's pronouncement of judgment on David, the king is shown in a less favorable light. Later he would waver and modify this pronouncement (cf. 19:29).

Ziba accepted the king's offer with humility and goodwill, expressing a wish to "find favor in" the eyes of "the king."

16:5–8 David's darkest suspicions regarding Saul's family were confirmed as the royal procession "approached Bahurim" (v. 5), a nearby Benjamite village (cf. 19:16; 1 Kgs 2:8). There Shimei, a relative of Saul, assaulted David's group both verbally and physically. The throwing of stones involved symbolically carrying out a Torah-style execution (cf. Lev 20:2,27; 24:14,16; Num 15:35; Deut 13:10; 21:21; 22:21,24) of them. Shimei did this in spite of the fact that David could have responded instantly with deadly force to eliminate this threat to his life.

Shimei's charge against David was that he was a "man of blood"—that is, a murderer—and a "man of Belial" [NIV, "scoundrel"; cf. 1 Sam 25:25; 30:22; 2 Sam 20:1], that is, a man of base moral character.[147]

Shimei's reasons behind his defiant actions and words toward David were both theological and personal. According to Shimei, David's present troubles were actually from the Lord, brought as judgment for sins David committed against Shimei's relatives. Shimei's reference to Saulide blood that David shed probably is an allusion to David's role in the Gibeonite killing of seven Saulides (cf. 21:5–9). Alternatively, it could be based on some misguided belief, either the assumption that David had fought with the Philistines against Israel on the day Saul and three of his sons died or perhaps the belief that David had commissioned Ish-Bosheth's death.[148] From Shimei's perspective, the Lord had "handed the kingdom over to" Absalom, with the result that David had "come to ruin."

16:9–12 Shimei's words were deeply troubling to many of David's followers, especially "Abishai son of Zeruiah" (v. 9), another of David's nephews who served as a general (cf. 23:18; 1 Chr 11:20). When Abishai heard these

---

[147] Shimei's charge that David was a "man of blood" should not be taken as an echo of Yahweh's comment that David had "shed much blood" (1 Chr 22:8). Shimei used the phrase to charge David with murderous misbehavior; Yahweh referred to David's bloodshed in alluding to "David's warfare and many victories that enabled Solomon and the nation to have the peace in which they could build the temple." Cf. Thompson, *1, 2 Chronicles*, 165.

[148] J. C. VanderKam asserts that the charges that David did play a leading role in the destruction of the house of Saul are true ("Davidic Complicity in the Deaths of Abner and Eshbaal: A Historical and Redactional Study," *JBL* 99 [1980]: 521–39). This position runs counter to the biblical writer's thematic intentions as expressed in the canonical text and for that reason can be dismissed by those who accept the trustworthiness of the biblical record.

harsh words spoken in anger against the king, he wondered aloud why "this dead dog" should be allowed to "curse my lord the king." He also offered to "go over" to Shimei "and cut off his head"—the second time he had asked David for permission to kill a Saulide (cf. 1 Sam 26:8). From Abishai's perspective, Shimei deserved to die because he had cursed the ruler of the Lord's people (cf. Exod 22:28).

Distancing himself from Abishai's position,[149] however, David refused to let Abishai execute judgment against Shimei. As in the previous situation involving a threat against a Saulide, David used a theological reason to prohibit Abishai from carrying out his deadly desires (cf. 1 Sam 26:9–11). In this case David reasoned that the Lord might have actually ordered Shimei to "curse David" (v. 10). If it was indeed true that "the LORD has told him to" (v. 11), it would be for David's ultimate benefit; for then the Lord would see David's "distress" and compensatorily repay him "with good for the cursing" (v. 12; cf. Deut 23:5).

David's central concerns dealt not with Shimei but Absalom. As the king reminded "Abishai and all his officials" (v. 11), the present crisis was fomented by Absalom, "my son who is of my own flesh." By comparison, the Saulides were an inconsequential threat. David was already aware of the resentment held against him by many in Saul's clan, and he had learned to cope with it.

16:13–14 Undaunted by Shimei's persistent show of hatred, "David and his men continued along the road." Slowly they wound their way down the twenty-mile path that descended some 3,700 feet to the Jordan River and came to "their destination" (v. 14) near the ford. The entire group was "exhausted" both physically and emotionally, but at this relatively safe location they "refreshed" themselves.

16:15–19 At this point the account reconnects with a narrative thread left dangling at 15:37, presenting events that occurred while the events described in 16:1–14 were taking place.[150] Thus, Absalom arrived in Jerusalem even as David and his entourage were making their way to the Jordan. Prominent among those arriving to set up the new government in Jerusalem was Ahithophel.

---

[149] The literal rendering of the NIV's "What do you and I have in common?" is "What to me and to you?" The rhetorical question, used elsewhere by David (cf. 19:22 [Hb. v. 23], implicitly disavows a linkage between the speaker and his addressee.

[150] Temporal overlay between 16:15–19 and 16:1–14 is suggested through two text-based clues: first is the obvious semantic connection between 15:37 and 16:15; second is the clause construction in 16:15. Instead of reporting Absalom's arrival in Jerusalem with the expected *wayyiqtol* verb form וַיָּבֹא, the clause is initiated by a *waw*-plus-subject compound noun-phrase followed by a *qatal*-verb form בָּא. Previously published research suggests that clauses of this variety regularly convey "eventive simultaneous alternative" information. Cf. R. D. Bergen, "Varieties and Functions of *Waw*-plus-subject-plus-perfect-verb Sentence Constructions in the Narrative Framework of the Pentateuch," Ph.D. diss., Southwestern Baptist Theological Seminary (Ann Arbor: University Microfilms, 1986).

As Hushai, David's advisor and loyal servant ("friend"), found himself in Absalom's presence, he began carrying out one of the most successful acts of deceit and subterfuge recorded in Israelite history. The greatness of Hushai's performance can only be appreciated as one understands that Hushai was a master of double entendre.

Hushai's subversive ambivalence begins with his first words spoken in Absalom's presence: "Long live the king!" Did these words refer to Absalom, as the social context would indicate, or were they in fact a wish that the king-in-exile be granted life? The careful reader suspects the latter.

Absalom himself was certainly surprised by the apparently warm reception he received from Hushai, for he had expected Hushai to follow David into exile. This naturally caused him to raise questions about the depth of Hushai's "loyalty" (Hb., ḥesed; NIV, "love") to David, the "friend" in whose court he had served for so many years.

Unfazed by Absalom's probing questions, Hushai continued his masterful expressions of ambiguity: "the one chosen by the LORD, by these people, and by all the men of Israel—his I will be, and I will remain with him" (v. 18). Though Hushai never mentioned Absalom's name, in his vanity the upstart king believed these words referred to him. However, for the biblical narrator they were covert affirmations of loyalty to David—whereas the writer repeatedly affirmed that the Lord chose David (cf. 1 Sam 16:1,12; 2 Sam 6:21), no such literary representation of Absalom is given. Furthermore, the men of Israel had previously chosen David as their king (cf. 5:1–3); they were following Absalom only because he had stolen their hearts from their first loyalty (cf. 15:6). Thus, for Hushai to declare his loyalty to an unnamed individual chosen by the Lord and Israel was to take his stand with David.

Even Hushai's declaration that he would serve Absalom "just as I served your father" (v. 19) can be viewed as a silent affirmation of loyalty to David. How had Hushai served David? as David's loyal friend (cf. 1 Chr 27:33); so now as David's loyal friend he would "serve" Absalom. Hushai's semantic subtleties were totally missed by Absalom, and so the sage was fatefully welcomed into his inner council.

16:20–23 Absalom had succeeded in gaining control of both the throne and the royal citadel in an impressive bloodless coup. Now strengthening his grip on both became the central issue for his fledgling administration to deal with. For guidance in this all-important task Absalom sought the advice of Ahithophel.

Ahithophel's plan was brazen, simple, and almost sure to succeed. The plan would accomplish at least two things. First of all, by exercising privileges reserved only for Israel's king, Absalom would unambiguously demonstrate his claim to Israel's throne. At the same time, his outrageous act would energize those participating in the coup: by modeling a flamboyant rejection of King

David, others would be emboldened to become "a stench in" David's "nostrils" as well.

For Ahithophel personally, the scheme must have seemed like a particularly satisfying application of the Torah's *lex talionis* ("eye for eye, tooth for tooth . . .," cf. Exod 21:24; Lev 24:20; Deut 19:21). David had had unlawful sexual relations with Ahithophel's granddaughter at the royal palace in Jerusalem, though she was married to another; so now, unlawful sexual relations with David's harem would take place at the same palace—only in this case the retributive act would be ten times greater than the original offense, and in public!

The plan seemed good to Absalom. Accordingly, his attendants "pitched a tent for Absalom on the roof" (v. 22) of the royal residence—the very location in which David had committed adultery in his heart with Ahithophel's relative (cf. 11:2)[151]—and there Absalom "lay with his father's concubines in the sight of all Israel."

Absalom followed Ahithophel's advice because of Ahithophel's reputation for wisdom. For all its apparent advantages, however, there was a flaw in Ahithophel's proposal to Absalom that insured its ultimate failure: the plan required the performance of a deed strictly forbidden in the Torah. When Absalom had sexual relations with the members of his father's harem, he committed a crime so heinous that the Torah mandated the death penalty for the man who did it (cf. Lev 20:11). Absalom might escape David's hand of judgment, but he could never escape the Lord's: divine justice would ultimately prevail, and the Lord would bring Absalom's aspirations crashing down to an inglorious end.

The fact that Ahithophel seriously proposed such a foolhardy plan can be taken as evidence that the Lord had indeed responded to David's plea to turn Ahithophel's counsel into foolishness (15:31). It stands as one more piece of evidence that the Lord was with David during his hour of crisis. It is also a fulfillment, however, of the Lord's judgment on David in 2 Sam 12:11–12.

17:1–4 Absalom had unambiguously claimed Israel's throne for himself. Now the most pressing task became that of eliminating David, the only credible threat to Absalom's newfound power. This second objective was more challenging than the first, for David was a man of incredible military skill and resourcefulness. No enemy had ever succeeded in capturing or killing David, in spite of repeated efforts. Nevertheless, Ahithophel had devised a plan that maximized the potential for success in this undertaking.

As in his previous plan, Ahithophel's counsel for a military strategy against David was bold, simple, and likely to succeed. It incorporated three hallmarks

---

[151] Youngblood suggests David had actually committed the adulterous act with Bathsheba on the roof ("1, 2 Samuel," 1007).

of classic military strategy: use of overwhelming force, the element of surprise, and a narrowly focused objective.

The first aspect of Ahithophel's plan was the use of overwhelming force: Absalom should assemble a force of "twelve thousand men" (v. 1). David's forces probably consisted of no more than two thousand men and perhaps were considerably fewer in number than that (cf. 15:18). Thus, Absalom would conservatively have at least five times as many men on the battlefield as David. The advantages of having such lopsided numerical superiority were considerable: first, it meant that Absalom's forces could sustain greater casualties than David's and still prevail. Second, it provided Absalom's forces with a great psychological advantage because David's forces would likely be struck "with terror" (v. 2) when they saw the size of the enemy arrayed against them. Third, overwhelming numbers of troops increased the likelihood that "all the people with" David "will flee," choosing not to fight at all instead of going against such great numbers.

The second key aspect of Ahithophel's strategy was the element of surprise. Although military maneuvers normally were limited to daylight hours, Ahithophel counseled Absalom to strike immediately—"tonight" (v. 1). By doing so, they could overtake David's forces while they were still "weary and weak" (v. 2) from the hasty, disorganized flight from Jerusalem. Attacking David's forces during this moment of extreme vulnerability virtually assured success for Absalom's larger military force.

Finally, Ahithophel's plan contained a narrowly defined purpose. The sole objective of the entire maneuver was to kill one man, David. After that one objective was achieved, then "all the people"—mostly innocent victims affected by the coup because of their connection with David—could be returned to Israel "unharmed" and spared the anguish of having to live as refugees. Ahithophel's plan was brilliant, and Absalom seemed ready to act on it almost immediately.

17:5–10 In an act that would have momentous implications for Absalom and his government, however, the new king decided to consult Hushai before proceeding. On the surface Absalom's request seemed reasonable: Ahithophel and Hushai had both provided David with valuable advice, and now David's son wished to determine the best possible plan of action (cf. Prov 11:14; 15:22; 24:6). Accordingly, he invited Hushai to critique Ahithophel's proposal. If Hushai disagreed with Ahithophel, he was to offer an alternative.

Hushai's words spoken in response to Absalom's invitation are perhaps the most significant ones uttered by a counselor in the history of united Israel's monarchy. The speech is masterful in its construction and powerful in its effect: it simultaneously discredits Ahithophel, undermines Absalom's confidence, magnifies the king's worst fears, and buys David precious time to escape and regroup. In the end it lays the foundation for David's return to Jerusalem.

Hushai's first goal in his reply to the king was to debunk Ahithophel's sage counsel. Having given the general opinion that it was "not good" (v. 7), he proceeded to repudiate with conviction the essential presuppositions on which Ahithophel's plan rested. Hushai implicitly accused Ahithophel of misjudging David and the armed forces accompanying him: these men were not "weary and weak" (17:2)—they were "fighters, and as fierce as a wild bear robbed of her cubs" (v. 8).

Hushai also faulted Ahithophel's belief that the element of surprise could be used against David. Since David was "an experienced fighter," he practiced battlefield techniques that essentially eliminated the possibility of being caught off guard. For instance, David did "not spend the night with the troops"; instead, he might hide "in a cave" (cf. 1 Sam 22:1; 24:3; 2 Sam 23:13)—and there were many of them around the north end of the Dead Sea (v. 9).

Of course, this also meant that Ahithophel's suggestion that the military objective be limited to killing only David was flawed. In their vain search for David, Absalom's forces might easily blunder into a trap David had set for them, thus permitting David's forces to attack first. If that happened, then the entire psychological advantage Ahithophel's plan counted on would swing over to David's side. False reports spread by panicky soldiers would get out, indicating that "there has been a slaughter among the troops who follow Absalom." When that happened, "even the bravest soldier, whose heart is like the heart of a lion, will melt with fear" (v. 10). Absalom would lose control of his military forces, and the coup would fail.

17:11–14 As an alternative to Ahithophel's proposal, Hushai offered a much more massive plan. Instead of using a relatively small strike force such as Ahithophel's plan called for, the king should muster "all Israel, from Dan to Beersheba," creating a force "as numerous as the sand on the seashore." Instead of trying to kill only David, all David's forces should be pursued until not "any of his men will be left alive" (v. 12). Furthermore, since the attack would be delayed, the geographic scope must be widened: Absalom's forces would thus be free to attack David "wherever he may be found." Instead of a single, swift raid on David such as Ahithophel envisioned, Hushai envisioned a protracted struggle that might even involve besieging a city. In the case of a siege, however—even a protracted one—Absalom's forces would ultimately prevail.

After hearing Hushai's ponderous, heavy-handed proposal, "Absalom and all the men of Israel" (v. 15) miraculously concluded that it was superior to Ahithophel's. Absalom's decision was indeed the result of divine intervention, for Yahweh "had commanded [Hb., ṣiwwâ; NIV, "determined"] to frustrate the good advice of Ahithophel in order to bring disaster on Absalom" (v. 14; cf. Job 5:12; Prov 21:30; Isa 8:10; 29:14; 1 Cor 1:19).[152] The Lord's action was pre-

---

[152] Gordon suggests that a miraculous dimension exists in this event, even though "the 'Succession Narrative' does not deal in miracles and supernatural events in the manner of, say, the book of Joshua" (*I and II Samuel*, 279).

dictable, for by rebelling against his father Absalom had committed a sin unto death (cf. Lev 20:11). The Lord, the judge of all the earth, would enforce his laws, and no human could succeed in deflecting the divine purposes. Even the greatest possible assemblage of wisdom, political power, and military might could not derail the performance of God's will.

17:15–16 By frustrating Ahithophel's counsel, Hushai had accomplished the first mandate Israel's king-in-exile had given him (15:34).[153] To fulfill his royal mission, however, Hushai had to perform one more task—convey to David the intimate details of Absalom's plan of action.

Without hesitation, Hushai sought out "Zadok and Abiathar" (v. 15), David's Aaronic priests, and told them what both he and "Ahithophel" had "advised Absalom and the elders of Israel to do." Accompanying this information was an urgent plan of action.

Hushai's strategy for David was based on the assumption that Absalom might yet be persuaded to follow Ahithophel's plan. If an attack force was actually sent out against David at sunset, then the king and his followers would have to move from their present location immediately.

17:17–20 In order to convey this vital information to David without arousing suspicion, Zadok and Abiathar entrusted the message to "a servant girl" (v. 17), who was to pass the information outside the city to the priests' sons "Jonathan and Ahimaaz." Jonathan and Ahimaaz were hiding out "at En Rogel," the site of a spring or well in the Kidron Valley less than a quarter of a mile from Jerusalem. Apparently the servant girl used the chore of fetching water as a pretext for going to meet the priests' sons there.

Unfortunately, "a young man saw" (v. 18) Jonathan and Ahimaaz at En Rogel as they were receiving the information from the servant girl and immediately returned to Jerusalem "and told Absalom." Jonathan and Ahimaaz realized that both their lives and their mission were now gravely threatened, and so "the two of them left quickly and went to the house of a man in Bahurim," just over a mile south of Jerusalem. This unnamed citizen of Bahurim was a supporter of David's cause and must have been at least moderately wealthy, for he had a house with a courtyard and a private well. Acting without hesitation to save Jonathan's and Ahimaaz's lives, he permitted them to hide in his well. Then, in order to conceal the existence of their well, his wife covered it and "scattered grain over it."

Later that same day the woman was questioned about the whereabouts of "Ahimaaz and Jonathan." Implicitly admitting she had encountered David's allies, she nevertheless indicated that they were not on the premises. Instead,

---

[153] Oddly, Anderson asserts that "even if Hushai's plan was part of the original narrative, it was *not* accepted by Absalom" (*2 Samuel*, 213). This statement is clearly at odds with the affirmations of the canonical text.

they had "crossed over the reservoir of the water [NIV, "brook"]," suggesting the men had gone south. The omission of any mention of the woman's husband during this encounter suggests that he had deliberately stayed away to avoid the appearance of any irregularity at the house.

Both the man and the woman deliberately misled the would-be assassins of Jonathan and Ahimaaz, yet the writer does not fault the couple for this action. As in previous instances where deceptions were employed to save innocent human life (cf. 1 Sam 19:13–17; 20:6,28–29), neither the letter nor spirit of the Torah were violated (cf. n. at 1 Sam 20:5). To the contrary, the writer implies that when confronted with the horns of this ethical dilemma, the couple chose the least undesirable alternative. As a result, David and his entire entourage escaped Absalom's forces.

17:21–22 Jonathan and Ahimaaz finally arrived at David's camp. Their advice was designed to prepare David and his group for the worst-case scenario, that of an imminent predawn lightning raid of the type suggested by Ahithophel (cf. 17:1–3).

David and his group had spent the entire day making a headlong twenty-mile journey from Jerusalem to the Jordan River. They were exhausted and would have relished a peaceful night's rest. But on this night, "David and all the people with him" (v. 22) denied themselves sleep in order to attempt a dangerous trek through rushing waters of the Jordan in almost total darkness. In spite of the inherent perils, "by daybreak no one was left who had not crossed the Jordan." The Lord's hand of protection and blessing had once again wrapped itself around David.

17:23 As night fell on Jerusalem and the troops were still with the king in the city, Ahithophel realized that his military counsel had been snubbed and that Absalom had lost the only good opportunity he would ever have to destroy David. Along with this, he realized that his own hope of retaining the preeminent position of influence and honor among the counselors in the royal court had also disappeared.

More than that, Ahithophel knew that when David returned to Jerusalem—and return he surely would—he himself would be executed as a traitor. Therefore after careful thought Israel's wisest man made the decision to end his own life.[154]

Ahithophel's decision to control the circumstances of his own death was a calculated one. The writer makes no explicit judgments concerning its moral rightness or wrongness; but this is not surprising, for the text was not written

---

[154] Anderson, who assumes that literary considerations caused the facts of history to be subordinated in the present narrative, rejects the historicity of the canonical account of Ahithophel's death and asserts that "it seems more plausible to assume that he took his life at some later stage, perhaps after the battle in the Forest of Ephraim" (*2 Samuel*, 216). Such a position presupposes more than is justifiable from the text.

as a treatise on the ethics of suicide.

Nevertheless, the detailed description of Ahithophel's death, preceded as it is by the emphasis on his precocious wisdom (cf. 15:31; 16:23), does enhance the writer's critique of human wisdom. Earlier, the counsel of the wise man Shimeah (cf. 13:3–5) was shown to bring humiliation to the royal family and death to an heir of the king; here an even wiser man's wisdom had led to an inglorious and premature death that deprived one of Israel's best families of its most honored member. Without descending to the level of the explicit, the writer conveys the truth that human wisdom untempered by divine revelation produces results that are neither desirable nor productive.

In this entire event the writer has taken great care to describe how King Absalom determined his course of action—like the kings of other nations, he sought the advice of wise men. In so doing he created a strong contrast with his father. At every crux in his life, David sought the word of the Lord, either through an Aaronic priest (1 Sam 23:1–6; 2 Sam 5:19,23) or a prophet (7:3–17). Absalom's pursuit of and compliance with human counsel brought about the hasty end of his regime. David's pursuit of and obedience to divine revelation brought him only success and dynastic blessings. By providing contrasting narrative portraits of these two Davidic kings, the author writes a prescription for the success of all future leaders in Israel: seek the word of the Lord through its authorized mediators[155] and obey it.

17:24–26 Now in exile east of the Jordan, "David went to Mahanaim" (v. 24), the walled city by the Jabbok River from which Ish-Bosheth had previously governed Israel. At this point David's life presages the profound tragedy of sixth-century B.C. Judah. They, too, would be driven into exile eastward from the Promised Land, with their Davidic king forced to live in the capital city of an enemy (cf. 2 Kgs 24:15).

Once Absalom had mustered his massive array of troops, he too "crossed the Jordan with all the men of Israel." Absalom's forces were under the command of Amasa (v. 25), David's nephew and a cousin to David's general Joab. Amasa's father was "Ithra [NIV, "Jether"; cf. 1 Chr 2:17], an Israelite [Ishmaelite? cf. 1 Chr 2:17]." This massive force camped north of Mahanaim "in the land of Gilead" (v. 26). This region included the city of Jabesh Gilead, the city that had expressed such great appreciation for the Saulide dynasty earlier (cf. 1 Sam 31:11–13). Their toleration of the anti-Davidic forces in their region suggests that they, too, were working for David's defeat, in spite of his previous efforts to win their support (cf. 2:4–7).

17:27–29 Though many Israelites east of the Jordan supported the revolt against David, the king had his key supporters in the area as well. Each of the

---

[155] This section thus forms a complement to the narrative of 1 Sam 28:6–19, which functions in part to discourage the pursuit of divine guidance through unauthorized means.

individuals mentioned here was wealthy and perhaps owed the preservation of their wealth to David's successful military campaigns in and around the region of Rabbah (cf. 8:2,12; 10:6–19). Furthermore, Makir may have been appreciative of David's loyal support for Mephibosheth, an individual for whom he himself had previously provided (cf. 9:4).[156]

Collectively, these three individuals provided an impressive supply of matériel to meet the practical needs of David's government-in-exile. No doubt the group had left such items as bedding and pottery behind in Jerusalem, due to the impracticality of transporting them. But now that the group was settling down in Mahanaim, such provisions were needed. Equipped with these mundane but necessary items the royal party could reestablish some reasonable sense of domestic life.

Shobi, Makir, and Barzillai also provided David's group with a generous supply of foodstuffs. This almost-prodigal provision in David's behalf must have seemed akin to the Lord's provision of manna in the wilderness wanderings of earlier Israelites. Perhaps this gift of food was the inspiration for David's immortal psalmodic expression: "You prepare a table before me in the presence of my enemies" (Ps 23:5).

(10) David's Forces Quell Absalom's Revolt (18:1–19:8)

[1]David mustered the men who were with him and appointed over them commanders of thousands and commanders of hundreds. [2]David sent the troops out— a third under the command of Joab, a third under Joab's brother Abishai son of Zeruiah, and a third under Ittai the Gittite. The king told the troops, "I myself will surely march out with you."

[3]But the men said, "You must not go out; if we are forced to flee, they won't care about us. Even if half of us die, they won't care; but you are worth ten thousand of us. It would be better now for you to give us support from the city."

[4]The king answered, "I will do whatever seems best to you."

So the king stood beside the gate while all the men marched out in units of hundreds and of thousands. [5]The king commanded Joab, Abishai and Ittai, "Be gentle with the young man Absalom for my sake." And all the troops heard the king giving orders concerning Absalom to each of the commanders.

[6]The army marched into the field to fight Israel, and the battle took place in the forest of Ephraim. [7]There the army of Israel was defeated by David's men, and the casualties that day were great—twenty thousand men. [8]The battle spread out over the whole countryside, and the forest claimed more lives that day than the sword.

[9]Now Absalom happened to meet David's men. He was riding his mule, and as the mule went under the thick branches of a large oak, Absalom's head got caught in the tree. He was left hanging in midair, while the mule he was riding

---

[156] In agreement with this speculation, cf. Payne, *I and II Samuel*, 242.

kept on going.

¹⁰When one of the men saw this, he told Joab, "I just saw Absalom hanging in an oak tree."

¹¹Joab said to the man who had told him this, "What! You saw him? Why didn't you strike him to the ground right there? Then I would have had to give you ten shekels of silver and a warrior's belt."

¹²But the man replied, "Even if a thousand shekels were weighed out into my hands, I would not lift my hand against the king's son. In our hearing the king commanded you and Abishai and Ittai, 'Protect the young man Absalom for my sake.' ¹³And if I had put my life in jeopardy—and nothing is hidden from the king—you would have kept your distance from me."

¹⁴Joab said, "I'm not going to wait like this for you." So he took three javelins in his hand and plunged them into Absalom's heart while Absalom was still alive in the oak tree. ¹⁵And ten of Joab's armor-bearers surrounded Absalom, struck him and killed him.

¹⁶Then Joab sounded the trumpet, and the troops stopped pursuing Israel, for Joab halted them. ¹⁷They took Absalom, threw him into a big pit in the forest and piled up a large heap of rocks over him. Meanwhile, all the Israelites fled to their homes.

¹⁸During his lifetime Absalom had taken a pillar and erected it in the King's Valley as a monument to himself, for he thought, "I have no son to carry on the memory of my name." He named the pillar after himself, and it is called Absalom's Monument to this day.

¹⁹Now Ahimaaz son of Zadok said, "Let me run and take the news to the king that the LORD has delivered him from the hand of his enemies."

²⁰"You are not the one to take the news today," Joab told him. "You may take the news another time, but you must not do so today, because the king's son is dead."

²¹Then Joab said to a Cushite, "Go, tell the king what you have seen." The Cushite bowed down before Joab and ran off.

²²Ahimaaz son of Zadok again said to Joab, "Come what may, please let me run behind the Cushite."

But Joab replied, "My son, why do you want to go? You don't have any news that will bring you a reward."

²³He said, "Come what may, I want to run."

So Joab said, "Run!" Then Ahimaaz ran by way of the plain and outran the Cushite.

²⁴While David was sitting between the inner and outer gates, the watchman went up to the roof of the gateway by the wall. As he looked out, he saw a man running alone. ²⁵The watchman called out to the king and reported it.

The king said, "If he is alone, he must have good news." And the man came closer and closer.

²⁶Then the watchman saw another man running, and he called down to the gatekeeper, "Look, another man running alone!"

The king said, "He must be bringing good news, too."

²⁷The watchman said, "It seems to me that the first one runs like Ahimaaz son

of Zadok."

"He's a good man," the king said. "He comes with good news."

[28]Then Ahimaaz called out to the king, "All is well!" He bowed down before the king with his face to the ground and said, "Praise be to the LORD your God! He has delivered up the men who lifted their hands against my lord the king."

[29]The king asked, "Is the young man Absalom safe?"

Ahimaaz answered, "I saw great confusion just as Joab was about to send the king's servant and me, your servant, but I don't know what it was."

[30]The king said, "Stand aside and wait here." So he stepped aside and stood there.

[31]Then the Cushite arrived and said, "My lord the king, hear the good news! The LORD has delivered you today from all who rose up against you."

[32]The king asked the Cushite, "Is the young man Absalom safe?"

The Cushite replied, "May the enemies of my lord the king and all who rise up to harm you be like that young man."

[33]The king was shaken. He went up to the room over the gateway and wept. As he went, he said: "O my son Absalom! My son, my son Absalom! If only I had died instead of you—O Absalom, my son, my son!"

[1]Joab was told, "The king is weeping and mourning for Absalom." [2]And for the whole army the victory that day was turned into mourning, because on that day the troops heard it said, "The king is grieving for his son." [3]The men stole into the city that day as men steal in who are ashamed when they flee from battle. [4]The king covered his face and cried aloud, "O my son Absalom! O Absalom, my son, my son!"

[5]Then Joab went into the house to the king and said, "Today you have humiliated all your men, who have just saved your life and the lives of your sons and daughters and the lives of your wives and concubines. [6]You love those who hate you and hate those who love you. You have made it clear today that the commanders and their men mean nothing to you. I see that you would be pleased if Absalom were alive today and all of us were dead. [7]Now go out and encourage your men. I swear by the LORD that if you don't go out, not a man will be left with you by nightfall. This will be worse for you than all the calamities that have come upon you from your youth till now."

[8]So the king got up and took his seat in the gateway. When the men were told, "The king is sitting in the gateway," they all came before him.

Meanwhile, the Israelites had fled to their homes.

18:1–3 As life stabilized for David in Mahanaim, he was able to exercise his administrative and military skills to respond to Absalom's challenge. His first priority was that of organizing a military force that could mount a credible attack on Absalom's troops. David knew the advantages inherent in striking first—being able to choose the time and site of the conflict—and so he acted quickly.

Accordingly, David organized a five-tiered army. At the lowest level were the basic troops; just above them David appointed "commanders of hundreds" and over them "commanders of thousands" (v. 1). Over these lower- and intermediate-level officers David appointed three commanding officers, each with equal authority: Joab, Joab's brother Abishai (v. 2), and Ittai the Gittite. At the highest level of authority was David himself.

As the supreme commanding officer, David fully intended to "march out" with his troops. However, the soldiers rejected this aspect of David's plan as far too risky. As the men told the king, David could best provide "support" for his troops "from the city" (v. 3). Then if the attack faltered, heavy casualties were sustained, and David's men were "forced to flee" (v. 3), the cause would go on. Even if they sustained as much as fifty-percent casualty rates, David would still "have ten thousand" more soldiers like them who could continue the struggle.[157]

18:4–5 David recognized the wisdom of the men's advice. In an uncharacteristic display of royal deference, the king agreed to "do whatever seems best" to (v. 4) his administrative inferiors. Passively the king reviewed his army as they proceeded to engage the enemy.

Though David was to remain in Mahanaim, he exercised his prerogative as supreme commander by ordering his troop commanders to "be gentle with the young man Absalom" (v. 5). The order was not issued in the privacy of the royal residence but publicly so that "all the troops heard" what David said.

18:6–8 The conflict took place a few miles northwest of Mahanaim "in the forest of Ephraim." By choosing a forest as the battlefield, David hoped to minimize the value of Absalom's numerical advantage. The strategy paid off handsomely. Under the capable leadership of Joab, Abishai, and Ittai, David's men fought well in the forest.

One reason for David's success was that his three commanders fragmented the opposition. By deploying their separate units in different areas, they spread Absalom's troops "over the whole countryside" (v. 8), thus preventing them from making a united stand. David's forces also used the terrain to maximum advantage.

18:9–10 During the course of the battle on that day, "Absalom began crying out in the presence of David's men" (v. 9: NIV, "happened to meet David's

---

[157] The NIV's rendering of v. 3b, "Even if half of us die, they won't care; but you are worth ten thousand of us," is at variance with the MT, being based mainly on the Lucianic and Vatican recensions of the LXX as well as the Latin Vulgate. A translation of the MT's reading is as follows: "Even if half of us die, they won't care; for now there are ten thousand like us." Though more obscure, the traditional Hebrew reading suggests that even in the event of a battlefield rout, David would have ten thousand troops he could still use to mount a further attack against Absalom. The MT's rendering implies that large numbers of citizens had joined David's side in the protracted conflict and thus that the Absalom-David conflict had become a bona fide society-wide civil war.

men") in the forest.[158] The reason for the commotion was most remarkable: while riding through the forest "under the thick branches of a large oak, Absalom's head got caught in the tree," probably because his hair (cf. 14:26) had become entangled in the branches. In an effort to avoid having his scalp torn off, he grabbed onto the tree limb and began calling out for help. In the meantime, "the mule he was riding kept on going," with the result that he was left dangling helplessly "between the sky and the earth" [NIV, "in midair"]. Hearing the commotion, "one of the men" (v. 10) in service to David saw the incredible spectacle and immediately reported it to Joab.

The words used by the soldier to report Absalom's condition are of great theological and thematic significance: "Absalom was hanging [Hb., *tālûy*] in an oak tree." The word translated "hanging" here is used only once in the Torah (Deut 21:23) to declare that "anyone who is *hung [tālûy]* on a tree is under God's curse." Absalom had rebelled against divine law by rebelling against his father (cf. Exod 20:12; Deut 5:16; 21:18–21) and sleeping with members of David's harem (Lev 20:11). Absalom had the massive armies of Israel fighting to protect him, and he was personally equipped with a fast means of escape not afforded other soldiers—a mule. Nevertheless, in spite of these seemingly insurmountable advantages, Absalom could not escape God's judgment. The Lord had declared in the Torah that one who dishonored his father was cursed (Deut 27:16) and likewise that one who slept with his father's wife was cursed (Deut 27:20)—Absalom, of course, had done both. Although no army had been able to catch Absalom and punish him, God himself had sent a curse against him that simultaneously caught and punished the rebel. The fearful judgments of the Torah had proven credible: the Lord had upheld his law.

18:11–13 When Joab learned of Absalom's predicament and that the king's son was still alive, he became angry. Through Joab's own words the narrator also reveals that David's nephew/general himself was a rebel against the king. Although David had ordered his commanders to be gentle with Absalom (v. 5), Joab had promised a reward of "ten shekels of silver [approx. four ounces] and a warrior's belt" to anyone who killed the king's son—a reward that could only have come from one determined to disobey the king in this matter. Apparently Joab had decided that the only way to end the civil war was to kill Absalom.

In spite of the reward Joab had posted, the soldier refused to "lift [his] hand against the king's son" (v. 12) even if it were multiplied a hundred times, for

---

[158] The admittedly difficult phrase וַיִּקְרָא ... לִפְנֵי has been dealt with variously: the LXX, "And Absalom went to meet the servants of David"; McCarter: "Absalom was far ahead of the servants of David" (*II Samuel*, 396, 401); Anderson: "Absalom . . . found himself confronted by David's men" (*2 Samuel*, 218). My proposal has the advantage of providing a reasonable circumstance leading to Absalom's discovery (his shouting), while using the most commonly attested semantic domain of קָרָא ("cry out").

his respect for David's order prevailed. Besides, when David discovered who had done it—"and nothing is hidden from the king" (v. 13)—his life would be "in jeopardy." The soldier could not trust Joab to cover for him in the matter; anyone who would betray his king would surely betray a nameless underling.

18:14–15 Joab, irritated and unfazed by the soldier's warnings, impatiently left the underling behind and went in pursuit of Absalom. For the encounter he took "three javelins in his hand" (v. 14) and a contingent of "ten . . . armor-bearers" (v. 15). The group arrived at the oak tree and found the king's son exactly as the soldier had described. Without hesitation Joab took the lead in resolving the matter, thrusting all three javelins "into Absalom's heart." The armor-bearers followed the lead of their commander and likewise "struck" Absalom "and killed him."

18:16–17 Now that Absalom was dead, the uprising was dead. Accordingly, "Joab sounded" the notes "on the shophar" [NIV, "trumpet"], signifying cessation of military activity. In this matter Joab had followed Ahithophel's logic (cf. 17:2–3), believing that the only one who had to be destroyed was the rival to the throne.

In accordance with Torah requirements (cf. Deut 21:23), the rebellious son's mangled corpse was removed from the tree before nightfall. His body was then buried in a contemptuous manner by being thrown "into a big pit in the forest" (v. 17) and covered with a large heap of rocks. This form of burial denied Absalom the honor of being laid to rest in the family tomb. The act was also laden with symbolic value: first, it caused Absalom to be excluded from the Promised Land, since the burial site was east of the Jordan River. Absalom's rebellion had caused King David to remain outside the Promised Land for a time; now the rebellion would cause King Absalom to remain outside the Promised Land forever. Second, it identified Absalom with Achan (cf. Josh 7:26), an Israelite whose earlier rebellion against the Lord's word had brought trouble to Israel; third, it identified him with the Canaanite king of Ai (cf. Josh 8:29), implying that King Absalom, like this previous king, was an enemy to the Lord's people. Finally, it fulfilled the Torah's demand that a rebellious son be stoned (Deut 21:21).

Word spread quickly among Absalom's troops that their king was dead. Since their hopes for Absalom perished with his death, they had no reason to continue the struggle against David. Accordingly, "all the Israelites" who had supported Absalom "fled to their homes" while David's forces were preoccupied with the task of disposing of Absalom.

18:18 Ironically, even as a monument of stone memorialized Absalom's sterile kingship, so also "a monument" (v. 18) of stone memorialized his sterile fatherhood. The former was made by David's loyalists following the death of David's son; the latter was constructed by Absalom himself following the death of his three sons (cf. 14:27). "In the King's Valley," probably located just outside the city walls of Jerusalem, Absalom had "taken a pillar, . . . erected it," and "named" it "after himself."[159]

18:19–23 Soon after Absalom died and Joab had declared an end to the hostilities, "Ahimaaz son of Zadok" (v. 19) requested permission to carry the battle news to the king. Ahimaaz's previous efforts as a messenger had allowed David to flee safely into exile (17:17–22); now the young man wished to deliver the welcome news that the king could safely return from exile.

However, Joab refused to grant Ahimaaz permission to carry the news of Absalom's death back to David. The refusal was not based on a lack of confidence in Ahimaaz's ability—in fact, he would gladly let him "take the news another time" (v. 20). Instead, it was based on Joab's memories of David's treatment of previous messengers who had announced the deaths of David's adversaries. David killed those who had brought news of both Saul's and Ish-Bosheth's deaths (cf. 1:4–16; 4:8–12), and Joab feared he would do the same to Ahimaaz.

To avoid risking the life of Ahimaaz, who was valued as a loyal servant and an Aaronic priest, Joab sent a non-Israelite—"a Cushite" (v. 21), who perhaps was Joab's slave—to "go tell the king." As a foreigner, the Cushite was most likely unaware of David's past history and probably felt honored to have been chosen to share the news of a battlefield victory with the king. Accordingly, he "bowed down before Joab and ran off."

Ahimaaz, more determined than ever to deliver the momentous news to David, approached Joab a second time with his request. He fully intended to be the first to arrive in Mahanaim, yet he only asked Joab for permission to "run behind the Cushite." Joab was bewildered by Ahimaaz's enthusiasm for the task and reminded the priest that he was not bearing "any news that will bring . . . a reward." Undaunted, Ahimaaz restated his desire "to run" (v. 23) to the king "come what may." Seeing that Ahimaaz would not be dissuaded and believing that he would arrive only after David had expended his emotions against the Cushite, Joab gave him leave.

Once on his way, Ahimaaz made his journey to Mahanaim "by way of the plain"—that is, by running over the relatively flat terrain paralleling the Jordan River—instead of climbing up and down over the rugged forested hills as the Cushite was doing. This less arduous path, though longer, permitted Ahimaaz to arrive at Mahanaim before "the Cushite."

18:24–27 Meanwhile, David was anxiously awaiting word on the out-

---

[159] S. B. Frost suggests that Absalom's monument represented an attempt to preserve his glory or memory after his death ("The Memorial of the Childless Man: A Study in Hebrew Thought on Immortality," *Int* 26 [1972]: 437–50). The stone monument popularly known as "Absalom's Monument," located today in the Kidron Valley just outside historic Jerusalem, is not that remembrance; it is actually an architectural feature constructed in the first century A.D., about a thousand years after the time of Absalom.

come of the battle. Assisting him in his vigil was a "watchman." By standing atop the fortified entrance of the city set on a hill, the watchman had a commanding view of all roads in the region.

In the distance the watchman "saw a man running alone" toward the city and "reported it" (v. 25) to David. The king, himself a veteran of countless battles, instantly interpreted this observation for what it was—evidence of a victory for his forces. After all, if his forces had been defeated in battle, they would have made a headlong retreat to Mahanaim in massive numbers.

During the anxious moments when the runner was coming "closer and closer," "another man running alone" (v. 26) was also spotted. This observation, combined with the conclusion that the first man "runs like Ahimaaz son of Zadok" (v. 27), merely confirmed David's theory and added to his expectations of hearing "good news."

18:28–33 Soon Ahimaaz reached Mahanaim's city gate. But even before he was properly situated in front of the king, Ahimaaz provided David with a one-word summary of the battle's outcome: "Peace" (v. 28; NIV, "All is well"). After he arrived and appropriately "bowed down before the king with his face to the ground," he praised the Lord and confirmed that God had "delivered up the men who lifted their hands against . . . the king."

This news simultaneously brought relief and concern to David. Ignoring the good aspects of the news in hopes of relieving his worst fears, the king plied Ahimaaz with the only question that mattered to him: "Is the young man Absalom safe?" (v. 29). Ahimaaz took Joab's previous warnings (cf. vv. 20,22) to heart and discreetly avoided telling David the truth. Although he knew the king's son was dead (v. 20), he deceptively revealed only that he had observed "great confusion" but did not "know what it was."

Ahimaaz's failure to give David a definitive answer only added to the king's anxiety. With growing concern, the king ordered the young priest to "stand aside and wait" until "the Cushite arrived" (v. 31) and could be interrogated. The Cushite confirmed Ahimaaz's report of "the good news" that the Lord had delivered David "from all who rose up against" him. The only good news that the king wanted to hear, however, was that "the young man Absalom" was "safe" (v. 32).

Tactfully the Cushite revealed the truth concerning Absalom's condition. He did so without ever directly stating that Absalom had died—much less that he had been executed by David's highest-ranking military officer. Instead, it was stated in the form of a gentle wish that "all who rise up to harm" David "be like that young man."

The delicate words smashed into the king's consciousness like a sledge hammer, and he "began to tremble violently" (v. 33 [19:1, MT[160]]; NIV, "was

---

[160] The MT begins chap. 19 with this verse. Chapter 19 is forty-four verses long, with the result that the English and Hebrew versifications do not again coincide until 20:1.

shaken"). Seeking isolation from others, David immediately "went up to the room over the gateway," weeping and crying out to his dead son as he went. In this location—ironically situated "between the sky and the earth" (v. 9), the same position in which Absalom had died—David declared to his beloved son his wish to have "died instead of" him.

19:1–4 As Joab made his way back to Mahanaim, he received a report that the king was overcome with grief (v. 1; [19:2, MT]). This information quickly spread among Joab's troops returning from their defeat of Absalom's rebels, with the result that their enthusiasm was soon depleted. Rather than the usual music and dancing (cf. Exod 15:1,20–21; Judg 5:1; 11:34; 1 Sam 18:6–7), they "stole into the city that day as men steal in who are ashamed when they flee from battle" (v. 3). As the men passed through the city gate, they looked up into David's apartment and saw that the reports were true: the king had "covered his face" (v. 4) and was crying out for his "son Absalom."

19:5–8 David's general Joab also saw the king dressed as a mourner and heard the wailing lament as he entered the city. David's highly public actions so incensed Joab that he immediately charged into the king's presence and began to rebuke him. Laying aside all formalities, Joab informed David with strong language that through his unseemly behavior he had "humiliated all" the men who had just saved his life and the lives of all his family (except Absalom, whom Joab neglected to mention). By yearning after a dead enemy, David also "made it clear" that he "would be pleased if Absalom were alive today and all of" his own troops "were dead" (v. 6). David was acting as though his loyal fighters—those who had risked their lives for the deposed king—meant "nothing to" him and that he hated "those who love" him. His reactions conveyed ingratitude and contempt for the very group of people whose support he needed most.

Not only was David's behavior wrong, but it also was foolish. The king had deeply offended his troops, and if he failed to act immediately, "not a man" would "be left with" him "by nightfall" (v. 7). In an effort to help David undo the damage he was doing to his own cause, Joab dispensed with normal courtly speech and tersely ordered the king to "arise, go out, and speak to the heart of [NIV, "encourage"] your men." If he failed to do this, a situation could arise that would likely "be worse for" David "than all the calamities" he had experienced from his "youth till now."

Joab's decisive actions both toward Absalom and David saved David's kingship. The king submitted to Joab's orders and descended from the chamber over the gate. There "in the gateway" (v. 8) area, the center of public and commercial life in any walled city, David "took his seat." As he sat there in silence, "all" his troops "came before him." As Gordon notes, "the act represents a return to normality."[161]

---

[161] Gordon, *I and II Samuel*, 288.

While David's loyal forces stood with their king, the other "Israelites fled [NIV, "had fled"] to their homes" (v. 8).

(11) David Returns to Jerusalem (19:9–43)

⁹Throughout the tribes of Israel, the people were all arguing with each other, saying, "The king delivered us from the hand of our enemies; he is the one who rescued us from the hand of the Philistines. But now he has fled the country because of Absalom; ¹⁰and Absalom, whom we anointed to rule over us, has died in battle. So why do you say nothing about bringing the king back?"

¹¹King David sent this message to Zadok and Abiathar, the priests: "Ask the elders of Judah, 'Why should you be the last to bring the king back to his palace, since what is being said throughout Israel has reached the king at his quarters? ¹²You are my brothers, my own flesh and blood. So why should you be the last to bring back the king?' ¹³And say to Amasa, 'Are you not my own flesh and blood? May God deal with me, be it ever so severely, if from now on you are not the commander of my army in place of Joab.'"

¹⁴He won over the hearts of all the men of Judah as though they were one man. They sent word to the king, "Return, you and all your men." ¹⁵Then the king returned and went as far as the Jordan.

Now the men of Judah had come to Gilgal to go out and meet the king and bring him across the Jordan. ¹⁶Shimei son of Gera, the Benjamite from Bahurim, hurried down with the men of Judah to meet King David. ¹⁷With him were a thousand Benjamites, along with Ziba, the steward of Saul's household, and his fifteen sons and twenty servants. They rushed to the Jordan, where the king was. ¹⁸They crossed at the ford to take the king's household over and to do whatever he wished.

When Shimei son of Gera crossed the Jordan, he fell prostrate before the king ¹⁹and said to him, "May my lord not hold me guilty. Do not remember how your servant did wrong on the day my lord the king left Jerusalem. May the king put it out of his mind. ²⁰For I your servant know that I have sinned, but today I have come here as the first of the whole house of Joseph to come down and meet my lord the king."

²¹Then Abishai son of Zeruiah said, "Shouldn't Shimei be put to death for this? He cursed the Lord's anointed."

²²David replied, "What do you and I have in common, you sons of Zeruiah? This day you have become my adversaries! Should anyone be put to death in Israel today? Do I not know that today I am king over Israel?" ²³So the king said to Shimei, "You shall not die." And the king promised him on oath.

²⁴Mephibosheth, Saul's grandson, also went down to meet the king. He had not taken care of his feet or trimmed his mustache or washed his clothes from the day the king left until the day he returned safely. ²⁵When he came from Jerusalem to meet the king, the king asked him, "Why didn't you go with me, Mephibosheth?"

²⁶He said, "My lord the king, since I your servant am lame, I said, 'I will have my donkey saddled and will ride on it, so I can go with the king.' But Ziba my servant betrayed me. ²⁷And he has slandered your servant to my lord the king. My lord the king is like an angel of God; so do whatever pleases you. ²⁸All my

grandfather's descendants deserved nothing but death from my lord the king, but you gave your servant a place among those who sat at your table. So what right do I have to make any more appeals to the king?"

²⁹The king said to him, "Why say more? I order you and Ziba to divide the fields."

³⁰Mephibosheth said to the king, "Let him take everything, now that my lord the king has arrived home safely."

³¹Barzillai the Gileadite also came down from Rogelim to cross the Jordan with the king and to send him on his way from there. ³²Now Barzillai was a very old man, eighty years of age. He had provided for the king during his stay in Mahanaim, for he was a very wealthy man. ³³The king said to Barzillai, "Cross over with me and stay with me in Jerusalem, and I will provide for you."

³⁴But Barzillai answered the king, "How many more years will I live, that I should go up to Jerusalem with the king? ³⁵I am now eighty years old. Can I tell the difference between what is good and what is not? Can your servant taste what he eats and drinks? Can I still hear the voices of men and women singers? Why should your servant be an added burden to my lord the king? ³⁶Your servant will cross over the Jordan with the king for a short distance, but why should the king reward me in this way? ³⁷Let your servant return, that I may die in my own town near the tomb of my father and mother. But here is your servant Kimham. Let him cross over with my lord the king. Do for him whatever pleases you."

³⁸The king said, "Kimham shall cross over with me, and I will do for him whatever pleases you. And anything you desire from me I will do for you."

³⁹So all the people crossed the Jordan, and then the king crossed over. The king kissed Barzillai and gave him his blessing, and Barzillai returned to his home.

⁴⁰When the king crossed over to Gilgal, Kimham crossed with him. All the troops of Judah and half the troops of Israel had taken the king over.

⁴¹Soon all the men of Israel were coming to the king and saying to him, "Why did our brothers, the men of Judah, steal the king away and bring him and his household across the Jordan, together with all his men?"

⁴²All the men of Judah answered the men of Israel, "We did this because the king is closely related to us. Why are you angry about it? Have we eaten any of the king's provisions? Have we taken anything for ourselves?"

⁴³Then the men of Israel answered the men of Judah, "We have ten shares in the king; and besides, we have a greater claim on David than you have. So why do you treat us with contempt? Were we not the first to speak of bringing back our king?"

But the men of Judah responded even more harshly than the men of Israel.

19:9–10 After Absalom's troops crossed the Jordan River and returned to their clans with news of Absalom's defeat and death, debates began raging about the nation's future, especially about whether to realign themselves with David. In the course of their discussions the indecisive Israelites were reminded that previously David had fulfilled marvelously the nation's expectations for a king (cf. 1 Sam 8:20). Israel needed a king, and now that Absalom was dead, whom they had anointed as king,[162] they had no realistic alternative but that of "bringing the king back." This Israel implicitly decided to do. The separate treatment of Israel's and Judah's response to David continues the sense developed elsewhere in Joshua–2 Kings (cf. Josh 11:21; 1 Sam 11:8; 17:52; 18:16; 2 Sam 2:10; 3:10; 5:5; 11:11; 12:8) that a deep traditional schism existed between Judah and the rest of Israel.

19:11–15 Now that the rest of Israel had recommitted themselves to David, it was time to bring Judah, which had apparently lent strong support to Absalom,[163] back into the king's camp. For this all-important task David did not sit passively on the sidelines hoping that his own tribe would reaffirm their support for him; instead, he took steps to acquire their acceptance.

David's first step in the process was to send a "message to Zadok and Abiathar" (v. 11), two of his key non-Judahite supporters in Jerusalem, asking them to lobby his support among "the elders of Judah." These highly respected priests were to use two elements in their persuasive efforts: first, they were to inform Judah's elders that the other tribes of Israel had already thrown their support behind David. Second, they were to appeal to the leaders' sense of solidarity with one of their own—David was one of their "brothers" (v. 12). Thus in spite of the previous support for Absalom, it was fitting that they should be among the first "to bring back the king."

David's second major step was to enlist the services of Amasa, a key member of Absalom's now-defunct regime. David directed Zadok and Abiathar to offer his nephew Amasa the position of "commander of [his] army in place of Joab" (v. 13). Putting Amasa in this coveted leadership role would build bridges with those who had served under Amasa while fighting against David, and it also would punish Joab for his insubordination in the matter of killing Absalom.

As in every previous struggle in David's life, his strategy proved remarkably successful. He soon received the coveted response inviting him and his entourage to "return" to the royal city of Jerusalem. The Lord's hand of blessing, so evident in David's earlier years, had now cleared the way for his return from exile.

Now that David's reason for remaining in Mahanaim had evaporated, the king and his loyal servants left the capital-in-exile and made their way down the southwesterly path "as far as the Jordan" (v. 15). Taking the lead in bringing David back into the Promised Land were the Judahites.

---

[162] Anderson suggests that the Israelites' decision to anoint Absalom king "may imply that David had ceased to be king of Judah and Israel" (*2 Samuel,* 236). This would explain why a formal action was necessary to restore David to his previous position.

[163] David apparently had been alienated from key factions among the Judahites for the entirety of his public career. Calebites, especially the Ziphites (1 Sam 23:19; 26:1) and Nabal (1 Sam 25:10–11), all members of the tribe of Judah, previously had expressed either active or passive resistance to David's efforts.

19:16–20 David's victory and return meant high anxiety for those who had openly opposed him, and none had been more vocal in their disdain for David than Shimei. Having made a special effort to curse David earlier (cf. 16:5–13), Shimei was now among the very first to welcome him back and to seek his forgiveness and favor.

Shimei was not the only non-Judahite at the Jordan as the king returned: "with him were a thousand Benjamites" (v. 17), including two especially prominent members of that tribe—"Ziba, the steward of Saul's household" and Mephibosheth, the only living direct descendant of the Benjamite royal family (cf. v. 24). Ziba had received a great favor from David not long before (cf. 16:4) and was no doubt anxious to retain the king's approval.

The sizable welcoming party—apparently numbering in the thousands—did not wait for David to cross to them but went across to help him (v. 18). The crossing site was located approximately four miles east of Gilgal and was the same one used by the Israelites under Joshua when entering the Promised Land (cf. Josh 3:16–17).

Making his way to the front of the thousands who passed through the Jordan River to meet David was "Shimei son of Gera." Probably still wet and disheveled from the crossing, Shimei immediately "fell prostrate before the king" and began pleading for forgiveness and mercy. He admitted he had been wrong and that through his mistreatment of David he had "sinned" (v. 20). Yet now the Benjamite was penitent for his sin. In a bold appeal for mercy, Shimei asked David to "put" the unseemly incident "out of his mind" and "not hold" him "guilty" (v. 19) for these acts.

19:21–23 Before David could respond to Shimei's petition, his impetuous general Abishai (cf. 1 Sam 26:8; 2 Sam 16:9) reminded the king that the one bowing before him had "cursed the LORD's anointed" (v. 21) and thus violated the Torah (cf. Exod 22:28). For this serious offense Abishai reasoned he "should be put to death"—even though the Torah did not explicitly mandate such a penalty.

Without disputing that Shimei had committed a capital crime, David refused to darken his day of triumphant return with the execution of a fellow Israelite. Distancing himself from the advice of the "sons of Zeruiah" (v. 22), whom he considered "adversaries" (Hb. *śāṭān*) in this matter (cf. also 1 Sam 26:8–9; 2 Sam 3:29; 16:10),[164] David magnanimously decreed "on oath" (v. 23) that Shimei would "not die" for his crime against the throne. Shimei admittedly deserved to die, and he would yet be punished (cf. 1 Kgs 2:8–9), but on another day and for another reason (cf. 1 Kgs 2:36–46).

---

[164] P. L. Day puts forth the position that David called Abishai a שָׂטָן because he was acting on David's behalf as a legal accuser ("Abishai the *śāṭān* in 2 Samuel 19:17–24," *CBQ* 49 [1987]: 543–47). In view of David's previous rebukes of Abishai and his brother Joab, I reject this conclusion.

19:24-30 The third Benjamite with whom David dealt directly on this day was "Mephibosheth, Saul's grandson" (v. 24). Like the others, Mephibosheth had taken the initiative to make the twenty-mile trek from the Jerusalem area "to meet the king" at the ford of the Jordan. However, Mephibosheth must have made proportionately more effort than the others, since he was lame in both feet (cf. 4:4).

Mephibosheth's appearance during his audience with the king also was considerably more unflattering: "he had not taken care of his feet[165] or trimmed his mustache or washed his clothes from the day the king left" Jerusalem until that day. Such inattention to details of personal health and hygiene made Mephibosheth look as if he had been profoundly mourning for a considerable period of time—he certainly did not look like a pretender to the throne who had been actively attempting to take back his grandfather's kingdom (cf. 16:3). It also signified that Mephibosheth had deliberately identified himself as ceremonially unclean (cf. Lev 13:45) during David's absence.

David was mystified. For weeks or months he had believed Mephibosheth was party to the revolt: Ziba's testimony (16:3) and Mephibosheth's conspicuous absence from the group fleeing Jerusalem had both reinforced this idea in the king's mind. But now Mephibosheth's presence before him and his physical condition testified otherwise. Determined to resolve this critical matter directly, David asked Jonathan's son "why" (v. 25) he did not accompany the king to Mahanaim.

Mephibosheth's answer was surprising yet plausible. His response was also given in a manner that showed extreme deference to David. Never daring to use the king's personal name, he referred to David five times as "my lord the king" (vv. 26,27 [2x], 28,30) and to himself on three occasions as "your slave" (NIV, "servant"; vv. 26,27,28). Mephibosheth declared that he had been "betrayed" (v. 26) by Ziba, who prevented him from gaining access to a "donkey" so that he could "go with the king." Furthermore, Ziba had "slandered" (v. 27) Mephibosheth, spreading lies about him and his true intentions.

Finally, Mephibosheth placed his fate fully in the hands of the king; comparing David to "an angel of God,"[166] he trusted David's handling of this matter would be from God. Humbly Mephibosheth noted that David had already given him far more than he deserved: as one of Saul's descendants he "deserved nothing but death" (v. 28), but David had given him the opposite of

---

[165] The LXX suggests that Mephibosheth's lack of footcare was his failure to trim his toenails.

[166] The phrase מַלְאַךְ הָאֱלֹהִים, "an angel [or "messenger"] of the [true] God" was perhaps an epithet used with Israelite royalty. It denied any attribution of deity to the ruler while at the same time expressing that a king's function was to do the bidding of the deity. It also served as an implied compliment, suggesting one who possessed great power and insight, though all of it was derived from his connection with the deity. Achish's use of a similar phrase, מַלְאַךְ אֱלֹהִים (2 Sam 14:17), omits the definite article and thus seems to possess different semantic implications.

what he deserved. Therefore he would make no "more appeals to the king."

David was now in a quandary. On the one hand, Ziba had provided him with invaluable assistance during a time of great need and had given convincing testimony regarding Mephibosheth's betrayal. On the other hand, Mephibosheth had provided direct physical evidence and credible oral testimony to the effect that he had always been loyal to David. Neither claim regarding Mephibosheth could be refuted beyond reasonable doubt with the evidence at hand.[167]

David had previously given Saul's estate to Ziba for two reasons: to reward him for invaluable support provided during David's flight from Jerusalem and to punish Mephibosheth for his supposed betrayal. Now that Mephibosheth had apparently exonerated himself, David removed the punishment he had inflicted on Jonathan's son.

David decreed a compromise that permitted Ziba to retain a reward for his service to the crown and yet permitted the king to keep faith with commitments made to Jonathan many years before (cf. 1 Sam 18:3; 20:42; 23:18). This judgment in Mephibosheth's favor may also reflect David's appreciation for the assistance he had received from Makir (17:27), who had previously provided refuge for Mephibosheth (9:4–5). Mephibosheth "and Ziba" (v. 29) were "to divide the fields" that had once made up Saul's estate. In a return to his role as supreme judge in Israel, David had successfully divided the "child" with the sword of justice (cf. 1 Kgs 3:25–27).[168]

With characteristic deference, Mephibosheth subordinated any expression of pleasure in the favorable outcome of David's judgment to that of his relief that David "the king has arrived home safely" (v. 30).

19:31–33 The last person David dealt with before leaving his land of exile was "Barzillai the Gileadite" (v. 31). The wealthy and aged patriarch was significant because he "had provided" critical material support "for the king during his stay in Mahanaim" (cf. 16:27–29). The octogenarian had now come from Rogelim, a site perhaps fifty miles northeast of the ford, to welcome David back to the throne.

David was impressed with Barzillai's generosity and his considerable efforts to witness the king's return to power. In an attempt to repay him and create a sort of symmetry in their relationship, the king invited Barzillai to Jerus-

[167] Nevertheless, most commentators conclude that Ziba had lied to gain the king's favor. Cf. Payne, *I and II Samuel,* 234.
[168] Far from condemning David for his decision here, the narrator implicitly commends his decision. Though this reading contradicts that of Baldwin (*1 and 2 Samuel,* 277), it seems the more reasonable and provides a nice complement to Solomon's later verdict regarding a dispute involving two women (1 Kgs 3:16–28)—David's judgment shows what can be successfully divided; Solomon's shows what cannot. McCarter's position is similar; he believes the king divides the estate because "David is persuaded of Meribaal's [= Mephibosheth's] sincerity but still moved by Ziba's recent service" (*II Samuel,* 422).

alem so that he might care for the old man the rest of his life.

19:34–40 Barzillai, while not unappreciative of the king's offer, found it unappealing. After all, he was "eighty years old" (v. 35) and had nothing significant to gain by moving to Jerusalem. Due to deteriorating health Barzillai could no longer experience the pleasures attendant with life in the royal court. Besides, he would no longer be the most important person in his city; instead, by living in Jerusalem Barzillai would just become "an added burden to . . . the king," the royal slaves, and the nation's taxpayers. In addition, he would be isolated from the persons and sights that had meant so much to him throughout his life.

At his advanced stage in life, Barzillai was far more interested in a dignified death than a dynamic life. Instead of desiring to live in the most important urban center in Israel next to the royal palace, he desired to live in a rural village "near the tomb of [his] father and mother" (v. 37).

If King David wished to bestow a favor in Barzillai's behalf, then it should rest on "Kimham," apparently one of Barzillai's relatives. Accordingly, David decreed that "Kimham shall cross over" with him (v. 38) and that he would receive all the benefits that would have been accorded Barzillai.

Evidence in a later text (Jer 41:17) indicates that David fulfilled his word. The existence of a site near Bethlehem named Geruth Kimham (= "the hospitality of/accorded to Kimham") suggests that an estate in Judah was given to Barzillai's designated recipient. But Barzillai himself would not be forgotten by the king: "anything" he might "desire from" David would be done for him.

This last major issue having been settled, the crossing of the Jordan finally took place. The group made their way four miles eastward "to Gilgal" (v. 39). At that traditional Israelite encampment site, David took one last opportunity to express his gratitude to Barzillai. Using the traditional Semitic expression of respect and acceptance, David "kissed Barzillai and gave him his blessing." Then "Barzillai returned to his home," while Kimham remained to begin a new life at the royal court.

19:41–43 The emotion-charged occasion of David's return to the territory west of the Jordan River caused an old and ugly dynamic in Israelite society to come into play, the conflict between Judah and the rest of Israel (cf. Josh 11:21; 1 Sam 11:8; 17:52; 18:16; 2 Sam 2:10; 3:10; 11:11; 12:8). Even before David could make his way back to Jerusalem, the men of Israel demanded an explanation of why he had permitted Judah to "steal the king away." Apparently by having all the Judahite soldiers—but only half the Israelite soldiers—participate in the act of transporting the royal household across the Jordan, David had shown contempt—albeit unintentionally—for the very people who had made his all-Israelite kingship possible (cf. 5:1–2).

Without waiting for the surprised king to respond to the allegations, the men of Judah came to the king's defense. Their status as next-of-kin entitled them to a position of privilege, but they had not abused it. They had not, for example, "eaten any of the king's provisions," nor had they "taken anything for" themselves.

But if Judah claimed kinship, the rest of Israel could claim numbers as their justification for "a greater claim on David" (v. 43). After all, the Israelites had "ten shares[169] in the king." Furthermore, the northern tribes had the claim of priority on David since they were "the first to speak of bringing" David back (cf. vv. 9–10).

The northern tribes accused the Judahites of two serious violations of divine law: kidnapping David at the Jordan, a capital offense in the Torah (cf. Exod 21:16; Deut 24:7), and cursing (Hb. *qālal*; NIV, "treat with contempt") the Lord's covenant people (cf. Gen 12:3). Of course, the Judahites did not take kindly to these trumped-up charges and "responded even more harshly than the men of Israel." David's return had not meant the disappearance of disharmony in Israel. Nathan's prophetic sword of judgment (cf. 12:10) was now in David's nation, not just his household.

(12) Sheba Revolts Unsuccessfully against David (20:1–22)

[1]Now a troublemaker named Sheba son of Bicri, a Benjamite, happened to be there. He sounded the trumpet and shouted,

"We have no share in David,
　no part in Jesse's son!
Every man to his tent, O Israel!"

[2]So all the men of Israel deserted David to follow Sheba son of Bicri. But the men of Judah stayed by their king all the way from the Jordan to Jerusalem.

[3]When David returned to his palace in Jerusalem, he took the ten concubines he had left to take care of the palace and put them in a house under guard. He provided for them, but did not lie with them. They were kept in confinement till the day of their death, living as widows.

[4]Then the king said to Amasa, "Summon the men of Judah to come to me within three days, and be here yourself." [5]But when Amasa went to summon Judah, he took longer than the time the king had set for him.

[6]David said to Abishai, "Now Sheba son of Bicri will do us more harm than Absalom did. Take your master's men and pursue him, or he will find fortified cities and escape from us." [7]So Joab's men and the Kerethites and Pelethites and all the mighty warriors went out under the command of Abishai. They marched out from Jerusalem to pursue Sheba son of Bicri.

[8]While they were at the great rock in Gibeon, Amasa came to meet them. Joab was wearing his military tunic, and strapped over it at his waist was a belt with a dagger in its sheath. As he stepped forward, it dropped out of its sheath.

---

[169] The number "ten" is obtained by omitting the Levites, who had no connected territorial inheritance, and by treating Ephraim and Manasseh—the Joseph tribes—as one.

⁹Joab said to Amasa, "How are you, my brother?" Then Joab took Amasa by the beard with his right hand to kiss him. ¹⁰Amasa was not on his guard against the dagger in Joab's hand, and Joab plunged it into his belly, and his intestines spilled out on the ground. Without being stabbed again, Amasa died. Then Joab and his brother Abishai pursued Sheba son of Bicri.

¹¹One of Joab's men stood beside Amasa and said, "Whoever favors Joab, and whoever is for David, let him follow Joab!" ¹²Amasa lay wallowing in his blood in the middle of the road, and the man saw that all the troops came to a halt there. When he realized that everyone who came up to Amasa stopped, he dragged him from the road into a field and threw a garment over him. ¹³After Amasa had been removed from the road, all the men went on with Joab to pursue Sheba son of Bicri.

¹⁴Sheba passed through all the tribes of Israel to Abel Beth Maacah and through the entire region of the Berites, who gathered together and followed him. ¹⁵All the troops with Joab came and besieged Sheba in Abel Beth Maacah. They built a siege ramp up to the city, and it stood against the outer fortifications. While they were battering the wall to bring it down, ¹⁶a wise woman called from the city, "Listen! Listen! Tell Joab to come here so I can speak to him." ¹⁷He went toward her, and she asked, "Are you Joab?"

"I am," he answered.

She said, "Listen to what your servant has to say."

"I'm listening," he said.

¹⁸She continued, "Long ago they used to say, 'Get your answer at Abel,' and that settled it. ¹⁹We are the peaceful and faithful in Israel. You are trying to destroy a city that is a mother in Israel. Why do you want to swallow up the LORD's inheritance?"

²⁰"Far be it from me!" Joab replied, "Far be it from me to swallow up or destroy! ²¹That is not the case. A man named Sheba son of Bicri, from the hill country of Ephraim, has lifted up his hand against the king, against David. Hand over this one man, and I'll withdraw from the city."

The woman said to Joab, "His head will be thrown to you from the wall."

²²Then the woman went to all the people with her wise advice, and they cut off the head of Sheba son of Bicri and threw it to Joab. So he sounded the trumpet, and his men dispersed from the city, each returning to his home. And Joab went back to the king in Jerusalem.

20:1–2 The bitter feelings aroused in the confrontation between the Judahites and their northern neighbors at Gilgal served as kindling for a second fire of rebellion against David. "A troublemaker named Sheba" (v. 1) was the match that ignited it all.

After the emotional shoving match with Judah, the northern tribes were in no mood to remain with David; and having supported Absalom—a Judahite—in an unsuccessful bid, they were in no mood to remain with the Judahites. Sheba, who may have been a high-ranking Israelite military officer, captured the sentiments of the northerners when he "sounded the trumpet" in retreat "and shouted, 'We have no share in David, no part in Jesse's son.'"

In order to protect David from a possible assault by hostile Israelite forces, the Judahites accompanied him "all the way from the Jordan to Jerusalem." The dynamics of this confrontation were fundamentally different from the one with Absalom. In the Absalom rebellion even many Judahites had aligned themselves against David. The present revolt was in many respects a replay of the conflict between David and Ish-Bosheth (cf. 2:8–4:6); it involved non-Judahites under the leadership of a Benjamite rejecting David as their king.

20:3–5 First on David's list of priorities when he returned to his palace was taking care of "the ten concubines he had left" behind in the royal city when Absalom initiated his revolt (15:16). These women had been raped by a rival king (16:22); they were deeply humiliated, abused, and in need of special attention. Accordingly, David "put them in a house under guard" for protection and "provided for them." Nevertheless, because of their previous sexual contact with his son, he prudently decided not to "lie with them" (cf. Lev 18:15), causing them instead to live "till the day of their death . . .as widows." David's earlier decision to indulge in forbidden sexual activity (11:4) now was responsible for his inability to enjoy legitimate pleasures on a larger scale. Furthermore, by damaging one woman's life (Bathsheba), David now ended up damaging the lives of the ten concubines.

Now that the household issues of immediate concern were taken care of, David had two larger issues to deal with: reunifying the Judahites and putting down the revolt led by Sheba. In an effort to take care of both issues at once, David asked Absalom's former commanding general to lead the king's forces against the non-Judahite rebels.

David understood the importance of attacking Sheba quickly, before the revolt could effectively organize and spread—after all, it had been Absalom's delay in attacking his father (cf. 17:11–14) that permitted David to triumph. Thus, when Amasa "took longer than the time the king had set for him" (v. 5), David knew he had to mount an attack without Amasa's assistance.

20:6–7 Accordingly, David appointed Amasa's cousin Abishai (cf. 1 Chr 2:16–17) to pursue Sheba. The fact that Joab was not appointed, though he had previously served as David's top general (cf. 8:16), suggests he had been demoted as a result of his treatment of Absalom (cf. 18:14). The military resources at Abishai's disposal were meager. Instead of having a massive militia composed of all able-bodied Judahite males, he had perhaps only a few hundred men. David hoped that their lack of numbers would be compensated for by their quick response.

20:8–10 The troops headed northwest into Benjamite territory and soon arrived at Gibeon some seven miles away. There "Amasa came to meet them."

Amasa's appearance aroused a powerful and highly negative response from

"Joab" (v. 8), who was among the troops under his brother Abishai's command. Dressed for battle in a "military tunic" and having "a belt with a dagger in its sheath" strapped around his waist, Joab stepped forward to confront his relative. As he did so, his dagger "dropped out of its sheath." Joab picked it up inconspicuously with his left—that is, his defensive—hand and strode forward as if to greet Amasa in a customary manner, with an inquiry into his welfare and a kiss of respect. The act of grabbing Amasa's "beard with his right hand" (v. 9) prior to the kiss is unattested elsewhere in the Bible but may not have been unusual; using the right hand in this manner would have signaled a lack of hostile intent, since weapons were normally carried and used by that hand.[170]

Amasa was completely oblivious to Joab's hostile intent, and thus without resistance "Joab plunged" the dagger into Amasa's belly, with the result that he died immediately.

Joab's behavior was understandable for at least two reasons: first, he had just finished fighting a bloody war against troops commanded by Amasa, and Joab probably considered Amasa guilty of treason against the crown; second, Amasa had just been chosen to take over the prestigious job from which Joab was fired (cf. 19:14). It may have been understandable, but it was not forgivable. David would later allude to Amasa's blood that "stained the belt around [Joab's] waist and the sandals on his feet" (1 Kgs 2:5) as testimony of the crime and the need for Joab's violent death.

Amasa, David's chosen commander for Israel's troops, was now dead. Though Joab had been deposed, he once again reassumed a leading role over Israel's troops as he "and his brother Abishai pursued Sheba son of Bicri."

20:11–13 Joab certainly had his share of supporters among David's troops. One of them, an unnamed soldier, urged all who supported "Joab and . . . David" to "follow Joab." This appeal was technically treasonous, since David had relieved Joab of his command. Undeterred by this fact, however, the man continued his efforts to bring the troops into line behind Joab. Thus, when he saw the army stopping at the spot where David's recently appointed commander "lay wallowing in his blood," Joab's supporter removed and covered the gory sight. This action freed up the troops to focus on pursuing Sheba.

Significantly, the narrator makes no further mention of Amasa in relating the events of Sheba's rebellion. The clear implication is that Joab had indeed usurped the position of supreme commander of Judahite forces.

20:14–17 David's strategy of an early attack against Sheba proved successful. The northern tribes failed to organize an effective army and were

---

[170] Use of a weapon in the left hand was unusual enough to warrant comment by the narrator elsewhere. Cf. Judg 3:21; 20:16. For further discussion of Joab's use of deception in Amasa's death, cf. E. A. Neiderhiser, "2 Samuel 20:8–10: A Note for a Commentary," *JETS* 24 (1981): 209–10.

forced to flee northward just ahead of the Judahites. In their retreat they "passed through all the tribes of Israel" to a point almost thirty miles north of the Sea of Galilee.[171] Sheba and the troops accompanying him entered Abel [Tel Abil], which apparently was located in the region of the Berites.[172]

Following a time-tested tactic for conquering a walled city, Joab directed his troops to build "a siege ramp" (v. 15) of packed earth leading "up to the city" wall so that the troops could more easily breach or even climb over the city's defenses. The breaching process was carried out in combination with the use of a battering ram, which could crush or displace the stones in the outer wall or perhaps destroy the city gate.

As this task went forward, the sound of the relentless pounding against the city's main defense must have terrified the inhabitants. In order to divert a tragedy of massive proportions for the city, an unnamed "wise woman" attempted to intervene.

20:18–22 Perhaps somewhat wary of the woman's intentions (cf. Judg 9:52–54; 2 Sam 11:21), Joab "went toward her" (v. 17). After the woman determined that she was speaking to the officer in charge of the siege—and thus the one person who could bring it to an end quickly—she asked him to "listen to what [his] handmaid [NIV, "servant"] has to say." Joab consented to listen to her.

What followed was an impassioned plea both for her city and herself. The wise woman began by providing Joab with a historical and cultural lesson about the city he was now besieging: Abel had for a long time enjoyed a reputation as a place where people could make inquiries—by inference, inquiries into God's will[173]—and get their answers. The woman herself was a "peaceful and trustworthy Israelite" (v. 19; NIV, "we are the peaceful and faithful in Israel"). Yet through the siege Joab was "trying to put a city and a mother to death [NIV, "destroy a city that is a mother"] in Israel." She closed her emotional appeal with a haunting question: "Why do you want to swallow up the LORD's inheritance?"

Joab passionately denied that he intended "to swallow up or destroy" (v. 20) either the city or the woman—his only objective was the elimination of the treasonous Sheba. If this objective could be reached without a protracted and

---

[171] Abel (and) Beth Maacah was perhaps a twin city composed of a walled settlement, Abel, and an unwalled settlement, Beth Maacah. Cf. E. C. B. McLaurin, "Qrt-'ablm,' *PEQ* 110 (1978): 113–14.

[172] The NRSV and RSV emend the MT here to read "Bichrites." The emendation is interesting but unconvincing, since it lacks any serious textual support.

[173] The NIV phrase "get your answer" is derived from a verbal cluster composed of two *piel* verbs: an infinitive absolute and an imperfect form of שׁאל. The *piel* of this verb means "to inquire." Implicitly, one would make an inquiry of a divinely sanctioned judge/šōpēṭ (cf. Exod 18:16; Judg 4:5) or a prophet (cf. 1 Sam 9:6) or Levite (cf. Deut 17:8–19).

deadly siege, then so much the better. Abel's fate was in its own hands: if the inhabitants of the city would "hand over this one man," the city could be saved.

Taking Joab at his word, the woman advised "all the people." Though the wording of her advice is not contained in the biblical text, its substance is revealed by the people's actions. Sheba's severed head provided Joab with convincing proof that his military objective had been met: the war was over. True to his word, Joab "sounded the trumpet," calling David's troops to suspend their hostile actions, and they returned home.

As in previous situations throughout the history of Israel (cf. Judg 4:17–21; 9:52–54; 1 Sam 25:14–35), a woman's daring initiative was responsible for the resolution of a significant crisis.

(13) Aside: David's Key Administrative Officials (20:23–26)

[23]Joab was over Israel's entire army; Benaiah son of Jehoiada was over the Kerethites and Pelethites; [24]Adoniram was in charge of forced labor; Jehoshaphat son of Ahilud was recorder; [25]Sheva was secretary; Zadok and Abiathar were priests; [26]and Ira the Jairite was David's priest.

20:23–26   For the second time in the narrator's account of David's reign over Israel, a listing of key administrative officials is provided (cf. also 8:15–18). This list probably presents the key offices and personnel from a point near the end of David's tenure as king.

Joab's reinstatement as army commander (cf. 8:15) had not been David's wish (cf. 19:13), but due to the untimely death of Amasa (20:9)—as well, no doubt, as Joab's indisputable military successes—he was granted permission to retain this post during David's lifetime (but cf. 1 Kgs 2:5–6,28–34). In the case of Joab, David chose to delay, but not eliminate, the just penalty for the murders he had committed (cf. 3:27; 20:8); Joab would not "go down to the grave in peace" (1 Kgs 2:6,34), in spite of his powerful position in David's cabinet.

"Benaiah son of Jehoiada" continued to have command of "the Kerethites and Pelethites," apparently a group of foreign soldiers who functioned as royal bodyguards (cf. 8:18; 15:18). Following Joab's death, Benaiah would be appointed Israel's supreme military commander (cf. 1 Kgs 2:35).

Adoram, called Adoniram in the NIV (cf. 1 Kgs 4:6; 5:14), "was in charge of forced labor" (v. 24). At a later point in time Adoram/Adoniram would be responsible for more than 180,000 men who served as the primary labor force for Solomon's building projects (cf. 1 Kgs 9:15–19). According to 1 Kgs 9:20, only descendants of unexterminated pre-Israelite populations of the Promised Land—Hittites, Perizzites, and Jebusites—were included among the ranks of the forced laborers.

While David formalized the practice of using certain non-Israelites for the benefit of Israelite culture by establishing an administrative position charged with overseeing work, he did not initiate it; instead, he was following a precedent stretching back to the time of Joshua (cf. Josh 9:27; 16:10; 17:13; Judg 1:28,30,33,35).[174] Since this position was not mentioned in the previous list of Davidic administrators, it probably was added only later during David's tenure as king.

"Jehoshaphat son of Ahilud was recorder," serving as an archivist and chronicler of David's administration and of the king's discharge of God's will. He was assisted in the task by "Sheva," who "was secretary" (v. 25). Apparently Sheva replaced Seraiah, who had held the position previously (cf. 8:17).

Zadok and Abiathar continued to oversee the official worship center in Jerusalem (cf. 15:29). They had been with David from the beginning of his reign and were still active when Solomon assumed the throne (cf. 1 Kgs 1:7–8).

Assisting David in the task of carrying out religious obligations within the royal household was "Ira the Jairite" (v. 26), an otherwise unknown priest. In the first list of David's administrators, his sons were listed as priests (cf. 8:18). Their omission in the present list suggests that David reduced the significance of their priestly role during the course of his reign; Hertzberg suggests that Ira had assumed the duties previously assigned to David's sons.[175]

---

[174] Brueggemann is clearly in error when he claims that "we may note especially that in verse 24 we have the first mention of 'forced labor,' an abusive practice" which "suggests that the old tribal vision of covenantal power has considerably eroded under David" (*First and Second Samuel*, 332). These practices extend all the way back to Joshua and the earliest days of Israel's conquest of the Promised Land.

[175] Hertzberg, *I and II Samuel*, 375

V. ASIDE: ILLUSTRATIONS OF DAVID'S ROLES IN HIS
   RELATIONSHIP WITH THE LORD (21:1–24:25)
   1. David Ends a Divinely Sent Famine (21:1–14)
   2. Loyal and Heroic Soldiers of David—I (21:15–22)
   3. David Utters a Hymn of Praise to the Lord (22:1–51)
      (1) Praise for the Lord (22:1–4)
      (2) The Lord's Deliverance of David—I (22:5–20)
      (3) Reasons for David's Deliverance (22:21–29)
      (4) The Lord's Deliverance of David—II (22:30–46)
      (5) Praise for the Lord (22:47–50)
      (6) Postscript: The Lord's Enduring Support for the House of
          David (22:51)
   4. David Utters His Last Oracle (23:1–7)
   5. Loyal and Heroic Soldiers of David—II (23:8–39)
   6. David Stops a Divinely Sent Plague (24:1–25)

V. ASIDE: ILLUSTRATIONS OF DAVID'S ROLES IN HIS RELATIONSHIP WITH THE LORD (21:1–24:25)

The final four chapters contain a carefully arranged set of six accounts and lists that are chronologically detached from the previous narratives. Although they all relate to David's life in some way, they are collected from different periods in his career.[1] At least one section may relate events from days prior to his kingship (23:9–17; cf. 18:13–17); at least one is apparently from a period in David's life chronicled in 1 Kings (23:1–7; cf. 1 Kgs 2:1–10). Because of the evident organization of the materials as well as their lack of strong association with the previous narrative, these chapters are often termed an "appendix"[2] or "epilogue."[3] Because I believe 1 Samuel–2 Kings is a literary unity, I prefer to think of this section as an "aside."

---

[1] Contra C. F. Keil and F. Delitzsch, who assume the events recorded here occurred "after the suppression of the rebellion headed by Sheba" (*II Samuel,* trans. J. A. Martin [Grand Rapids: Eerdmans, n.d.], 458).

[2] H. W. Hertzberg, *I and II Samuel,* OTL (Philadelphia: Westminster, 1964), 380; cf. B. F. Philbeck, "1–2 Samuel," BBC, ed. C. J. Allen (Nashville: Broadman, 1970), 136; R. Gordon, *I and II Samuel* (Grand Rapids: Zondervan, 1986), 298; and A. A. Anderson, *2 Samuel,* WBC (Waco: Word, 1989), 248.

[3] J. G. Baldwin, *1 and 2 Samuel,* TOTC (Leicester: InterVarsity, 1988), 282; cf. R. F. Youngblood, "1, 2 Samuel," EBC (Grand Rapids: Zondervan, 1992), 1050.

As has been commonly observed by post-WWII commentary writers,[4] the six distinct units of material in this section have been arranged into three chiastic pairs (*A B C C′ B′ A′*). All three pairs focus on David's relationship with the Lord: *A* (21:1–14) and *A′* (24:1–25) portray David acting effectively in leadership roles the Lord assigned him—as royal judge and royal priest, respectively; *B* (21:15–22) and *B′* (23:8–39) reflect aspects of David's role as the leader of the Lord's earthly forces, with *C* (22:1–51) and *C′* (23:1–7) giving poetic voice to David's words of faith in the Lord. As the chiastic structure implies, David's career began, was centered in, and ended with his relationship with the Lord. Thus, these final chapters offer a significant theological portrayal of the public roles and private reflections of Israel's consummate citizen.

David plays two disparate roles effectively in the outer pair of the chiastic structure. As a proper royal judge he settles a difficult dispute between the former dynastic house and the citizens of a group whose sacred treaty rights had been violated. As a royal priest David intercedes in behalf of a nation that had aroused the Lord's anger, successfully curtailing the full expression of the divine wrath.

The second pair of literary units in this section centers on David's relationship with loyal and heroic soldiers—what they did (21:15–22) and how David honored them (23:8–39). This dyad taps into David's role as one who zealously fought the battles of the Lord. David was a man of unmatched battlefield success (cf. 1 Kgs 5:3; 1 Chr 22:8–10) who was used mightily by the Lord to deliver Israel from their enemies; yet in a very real sense, David's success was the success of the troops under his command. From beginning to end David's career and calling were inseparably bound to his troops. Thus it was appropriate that his soldiers—not his wives or children—be memorialized in this section.

The core of David's legacy to the world was his intense, intimate relationship with the Lord, especially as it came to expression in the medium of poetry. Built into his life was the desire to carry out the Lord's will at every turn, a desire that was matched by his experience of the Lord's help in every crisis.

Taken as a whole, the so-called aside to 1, 2 Samuel serves as a fitting symbol of and tribute to the career of Israel's most celebrated king.[5] Being placed where it is, the aside serves the useful function of permitting the comparison of David with Israel to be satisfyingly complete; his story ends where the story of Israel must have ended at the time of 1, 2 Samuel's composition (see Introduction), with the return to a ravished Jerusalem and the

---

[4] Cf. P. K. McCarter, Jr., *II Samuel,* AB (New York: Doubleday, 1984), 18–19; Anderson, *2 Samuel,* 248; Youngblood, "1, 2 Samuel," 1051; Gordon, *I and II Samuel,* 298; and Baldwin, *I and 2 Samuel,* 282–83.

[5] W. Brueggemann's suggestion that these chapters were meant to counterbalance the events of 2 Sam 5–8, which led to a social structure that went beyond the Lord's plan for Israel, is interesting but unconvincing ("2 Sam 21–24: An Appendix of Deconstruction?" *CBQ* 50 [1988]: 383–97).

need to deal with resistant troublemakers in the land.[6]

1. David Ends a Divinely Sent Famine (21:1–14)

[1]During the reign of David, there was a famine for three successive years; so David sought the face of the LORD. The LORD said, "It is on account of Saul and his blood-stained house; it is because he put the Gibeonites to death."
[2]The king summoned the Gibeonites and spoke to them. (Now the Gibeonites were not a part of Israel but were survivors of the Amorites; the Israelites had sworn to [spare] them, but Saul in his zeal for Israel and Judah had tried to annihilate them.) [3]David asked the Gibeonites, "What shall I do for you? How shall I make amends so that you will bless the LORD's inheritance?"
[4]The Gibeonites answered him, "We have no right to demand silver or gold from Saul or his family, nor do we have the right to put anyone in Israel to death."

"What do you want me to do for you?" David asked.
[5]They answered the king, "As for the man who destroyed us and plotted against us so that we have been decimated and have no place anywhere in Israel, [6]let seven of his male descendants be given to us to be killed and exposed before the LORD at Gibeah of Saul—the LORD's chosen one."

So the king said, "I will give them to you."
[7]The king spared Mephibosheth son of Jonathan, the son of Saul, because of the oath before the LORD between David and Jonathan son of Saul. [8]But the king took Armoni and Mephibosheth, the two sons of Aiah's daughter Rizpah, whom she had borne to Saul, together with the five sons of Saul's daughter Merab, whom she had borne to Adriel son of Barzillai the Meholathite. [9]He handed them over to the Gibeonites, who killed and exposed them on a hill before the LORD. All seven of them fell together; they were put to death during the first days of the harvest, just as the barley harvest was beginning.
[10]Rizpah daughter of Aiah took sackcloth and spread it out for herself on a rock. From the beginning of the harvest till the rain poured down from the heavens on the bodies, she did not let the birds of the air touch them by day or the wild animals by night. [11]When David was told what Aiah's daughter Rizpah, Saul's concubine, had done, [12]he went and took the bones of Saul and his son Jonathan from the citizens of Jabesh Gilead. (They had taken them secretly from the public square at Beth Shan, where the Philistines had hung them after they struck Saul down on Gilboa.) [13]David brought the bones of Saul and his son Jonathan from there, and the bones of those who had been killed and exposed were gathered up.
[14]They buried the bones of Saul and his son Jonathan in the tomb of Saul's father Kish, at Zela in Benjamin, and did everything the king commanded. After that, God answered prayer in behalf of the land.

---

[6] H. P. Smith suggests that the reason the material in 21:1–14 was not mentioned earlier is "because he had enough unfavourable features without it" (*The Books of Samuel*, ICC [Edinburgh: T & T Clark, n.d.], 374). This presumptive position fails to see an adequate purpose in the final chapters of 2 Samuel. Likewise, B. F. Philbeck concludes that "the incidents which follow are in random order" ("1–2 Samuel," 136). This position cannot be sustained in light of the evident chiastic structure of the material in chaps. 21–24.

21:1–3 No indication is given here about when during David's reign this famine occurred. It probably was after Mephibosheth had come under David's protection in Jerusalem (cf. 9:1–13) and before Absalom's rebellion (cf. 16:7–8).[7] Because of Palestine's almost total dependence on rainfall and dew for crop moisture, poor harvests were not uncommon and were not automatically considered a sign of divine displeasure. However, when crops failed for three successive years, David rightly concluded that Israel had offended the Lord and was experiencing a judgmental Torah curse (cf. Lev 26:20; Deut 28:18).

Accordingly, "David sought the face of the LORD," perhaps with the assistance of Ira the Jairite (cf. 20:26) or a priest who wore the revelatory ephod (cf. 1 Sam 23:9; 30:7). The Lord revealed to the king that "Saul and his blood-stained house" were responsible for this disaster that had come upon Israel.

The specific crime that Saul had committed was heinous: the slaughter of the Gibeonites,[8] thus violating a centuries-old nonaggression treaty established before the Lord between Israel and these non-Israelite "survivors of the Amorites" (v. 2; cf. Josh 9:15–18; Ps 15:4). On the one hand, Saul's reason for doing so was commendable—he had "zeal for Israel and Judah," apparently to give them total control of the Promised Land. On the other hand, it was despicable because it put nationalism ahead of zeal for the Lord, the kingdom of Israel ahead of the kingdom of God.

Now that the Lord had revealed the cause of the curse, David met with the Gibeonites to determine a means of turning it aside. Though they were Israel's virtual slaves (cf. Josh 9:27), David placed himself at the Gibeonites' mercy by asking what he could do "to atone [from *kāpar;* NIV, "make amends"] so that they [NIV, "you"] will bless the LORD's inheritance" (v. 3). David's request subtly referenced the Abrahamic blessing (cf. Gen 12:3): the king could not bring a blessing to the Gibeonites; but as the Gibeonites' attitude toward Israel changed to one of blessing, the Lord himself would bless the Gibeonites.[9]

21:4–9 At first the Gibeonites refused to make any requests—much less demands—of the king. As members of a servile alien subculture in Israel, they had "no right to demand" material compensation ("silver or gold"; v. 4) from

---

[7] So also A. F. Kirkpatrick, *The Second Book of Samuel,* CBC (Cambridge: University Press, 1903), 192.

[8] W. Brueggemann notes that "there is no hint anywhere in the Saul narrative that Saul conducted such a slaughter" and concludes that "there never was such a report" (*First and Second Samuel,* IBC [Louisville: John Knox, 1990], 336). He concludes that "the narrative intends to be ironic" and "intends to show that David is indeed a ruthless opportunist who has found a way to eliminate the Saulide threat." This interpretation is a mischievous one, clearly rejecting the Scripture's intended meaning; namely, that the Gibeonites—not David—had initiated the proposal to kill members of Saul's household (cf. 21:5–6). This position is tenable only if one rejects the assumption that the testimony of Scripture is necessarily trustworthy.

[9] Youngblood suggests that David's request of the Gibeonites was for them to pray that God will bless David's people" ("1, 2 Samuel," 1053).

Israel's former dynastic family. They also had no "right to put anyone in Israel to death." No doubt the Israelites had limited the power of Gibeonite courts so that they could not carry out a death penalty, much as the Romans did to the Jewish courts following their subjugation of Palestine hundreds of years later (cf. John 19:6–10).

Although the Gibeonites had not initially given David a specific proposal for atonement, they did have one in mind. When the king repeated his request, the Gibeonites shared it with him. Compensation was not to come in the form of money or land, but in a manner prescribed by the Torah. In cases involving the unsanctioned taking of human life, the Torah called for retribution-in-kind (cf. Exod 21:23; Lev 24:21; Deut 19:21), even though the case might involve aliens (cf. Lev 24:22). Thus the Gibeonites requested that justice be served by executing seven of Saul's descendants. It is probable that the request for seven deaths carried symbolic value. Since Saul likely had been responsible for far more than seven Gibeonite deaths, blind justice might have required equal numbers of Saulides' deaths. Mercifully, however, only a limited, symbolic retribution was requested. Saul had murdered most of the Gibeonites in their hometown, so now the house of Saul would be decimated in his hometown. Perhaps also in an attempt to create symmetry between Saul's act and that of the Gibeonites, the request was also made that the corpses be left unburied "before the LORD."

As D. F. Payne notes, the situation described here "is strange and repellent."[10] Nevertheless, after evaluating the Gibeonites' proposal, David approved it. The proposal was consistent with the Torah's stern rules regarding the unsanctioned taking of human life, and so David "handed" (v. 9) seven of Saul's male descendants "over to the Gibeonites." Because David took responsibility for this virtual elimination of the house of Saul, it is not surprising that Benjamites were among David's least supportive followers in the latter portion of his reign (cf. 16:5–14; 20:1–2).[11] It also is not surprising that many modern biblical scholars have accused David of ordering the deaths based on ulterior motives, specifically the desire to eradicate the house of Saul.[12]

Now that David had decreed that seven Saulides must die, he was faced with the disturbing task of choosing whom to include among that number. To carry this out, David would have to do essentially the impossible—keep faith with an oath of loyalty and protection to the house of Saul (cf. 1 Sam 18:3; 20:42; 23:18; 24:21–22) and satisfy the legitimate demands of the Gibeonites. In this deadly balancing act "the king spared Mephibosheth son of Jonathan, the son

[10] D. F. Payne, *I and II Samuel*, DSB (Philadelphia: Westminster, 1982), 259.

[11] David's willingness to believe that Mephibosheth was plotting to recover the crown for himself may also be attributed to the king's awareness of intensely hostile feelings the Benjamites had toward him (cf. 16:3–4).

[12] Cf. Brueggemann: "The oracle that links the famine to the failure of Saul serves primarily to give David warrant for his violence against the house of Saul" (*First and Second Samuel*, 337). Also McCarter, *II Samuel*, 446.

of Saul" (v. 7). Having done this, he fulfilled the terms of "the oath before the LORD" that he had made with "Jonathan son of Saul."

From the pool of those who remained, the king chose the two sons of Saul's concubine, Rizpah. Because of their status as a concubine's offspring, they probably were ineligible for consideration as heirs to Saul's throne. If this is so, then it probably was this inferior status that doomed them.

A textual problem raises questions regarding the remaining five individuals. The remaining males were selected from the offspring of one of Saul's daughters, either "Michal"—so the MT—or "Merab," as a few ancient manuscripts and versions suggest. The NIV, attempting to harmonize biblical passages as much as possible, states that David delivered up "five sons of Saul's daughter Merab, whom she had borne to Adriel son of Barzillai the Meholathite" (cf. 1 Sam 18:19).[13] This choice takes into account the biblical claim that Michal had no children (cf. 6:23) and that no mention is made of a husband for her named Adriel. If Michal was in fact the mother of these sons, then she must have had two other husbands besides David, for she was also previously married to Paltiel son of Laish (cf. 1 Sam 25:44; 2 Sam 3:15); also, 6:23 must be taken to mean that Michal produced no offspring by David.

The Gibeonites ritually "killed and exposed" Saul's male relatives "on a hill before the LORD" (v. 9). The form of killing is not mentioned in the passage; proposals include crucifixion, dismemberment, and dropping the men from a height.[14] The killings took place on a single day "during the first days of the harvest, just as the barley harvest was beginning"—that is, in the month of Nisan (March-April), at the beginning of the religious year. The fact that this taking of life occurred "before the LORD" suggests that it was carried out with due consideration of the Lord's will and was religious in nature. The fact that the corpses were left "exposed" indicates that they were considered to be the objects of divine displeasure (cf. Ps 53:5; Ezek 6:5).

21:10–14   Rizpah represents perhaps the supreme expression of maternal loyalty in the Bible. Death had taken her two sons from her, but through her selfless efforts she made sure it would not also rob them of their dignity. Thanks to her efforts, her sons and relatives were given the honor of a mourned death. Her sackcloth bed provided for her a spartan abode in which to grieve among the corpses. Furthermore, until the Lord lifted the curse that had eventuated the death of her loved ones through the sending of drought-concluding rains,[15] she

---

[13] J. J. von Glück suggests that the preferable alternative is to substitute the name Phaltiel for Adriel, since David would have desired to kill all sons of Michal because they would have represented potential claimants to David's throne ("Merab or Michal," *ZAW* 77 [1965]: 72–81).

[14] McCarter concludes the Saulides were crucified (cf. *II Samuel*, 432, 436).

[15] Disagreement exists about which rains might have been meant here. Youngblood ("1, 2 Samuel," 1055), Gordon (*I and II Samuel*, 301) and McCarter (*II Samuel*, 442) suggest they were unseasonable late-spring or summer rains; Kirkpatrick (*Samuel*, 376) believes it is impossible to determine when the rains came, though they could have been the late (October) rains.

protected the corpses from being dishonored by birds and wild animals. By vigilantly seeing to it that none of the bones were stolen or destroyed, Rizpah preserved the possibility of a dignified and proper burial for her sons and relatives.

When David learned of Rizpah's vigil, he chose to reward her efforts and at the same time create a lasting memorial to honor Israel's first dynastic family. The king ordered that "the bones of those who had been killed and exposed" (v. 13) be gathered up and taken to an appropriate burial site. Then David had "the bones of Saul and his son Jonathan" (v. 12)—and no doubt the bones of Abinadab and Malki-Shua as well—exhumed from a burial site under a tamarisk tree at Jabesh Gilead (cf. 1 Sam 31:13) and brought back across the Jordan River into the Promised Land. The text's special emphasis on the bones of Saul and Jonathan is no doubt because they were the two most prestigious individuals being honored in the reburial and because the biblical writer wished to emphasize David's loving loyalty to his father-in-law and best friend, a loyalty that extended beyond death.

The site selected by David for memorializing the house of Saul was "Zela in Benjamin" (v. 14; cf. Josh 18:28), an unidentified spot a few miles north of Jerusalem. The location was appropriate, for it permitted Saul and his descendants to be buried "in the tomb of [his] father Kish."

2. Loyal and Heroic Soldiers of David—I (21:15–22)

[15]Once again there was a battle between the Philistines and Israel. David went down with his men to fight against the Philistines, and he became exhausted. [16]And Ishbi-Benob, one of the descendants of Rapha, whose bronze spearhead weighed three hundred shekels and who was armed with a new [sword], said he would kill David. [17]But Abishai son of Zeruiah came to David's rescue; he struck the Philistine down and killed him. Then David's men swore to him, saying, "Never again will you go out with us to battle, so that the lamp of Israel will not be extinguished."

[18]In the course of time, there was another battle with the Philistines, at Gob. At that time Sibbecai the Hushathite killed Saph, one of the descendants of Rapha.

[19]In another battle with the Philistines at Gob, Elhanan son of Jaare-Oregim the Bethlehemite killed Goliath the Gittite, who had a spear with a shaft like a weaver's rod.

[20]In still another battle, which took place at Gath, there was a huge man with six fingers on each hand and six toes on each foot—twenty-four in all. He also was descended from Rapha. [21]When he taunted Israel, Jonathan son of Shimeah, David's brother, killed him.

[22]These four were descendants of Rapha in Gath, and they fell at the hands of David and his men.

The Philistines were Israel's most foreboding foreign threat during David's lifetime. They had been the primary focus of Israel's military efforts since the days of Samson, and individuals who helped Israel defeat them were lionized.

The four Israelite heroes mentioned in this section were particularly noteworthy because they defeated four "of the descendants of the Rapha" (v. 16).

The events recorded here cannot be correlated with previous narrative
accounts. It is likely that they occurred earlier, rather than later, in David's
career—probably prior to the Bathsheba affair (cf. comments at 11:1). A. F.
Kirkpatrick speculates that the material for this section came from "some
'golden book of deeds' recording the exploits of David and his warriors."[16]

21:15–17 Of the four accounts of heroic actions David's men took, clearly
the most significant was the one mentioned first. On this occasion, rather than
directing his troops from a distance, David placed himself in the midst of the
fray.

When the Philistines became aware that Israel's king was on the battlefield,
they doubtless focused their efforts on eliminating him. As a result David
"became exhausted" but was unable to retreat from the conflict. As David
wilted, "Ishbi-Benob" (v. 16) moved forward to kill him.

Ishbi-Benob was a particularly formidable foe. First of all, he was one of the
descendants of the Rapha (the Hebrew has the definite article). The significance
and meaning of this description is unknown and contested. The KJV translates
the Hebrew *hārāpâ* as "the giant"; the NRSV, as "the giants," understanding the
singular noun collectively. Perhaps taking a cue from 1 Chr 20:6,8, where the
word is spelled *hārāpā*, they seem to connect the word with Deut 2:11 and Josh
17:15, a decision accepted by Youngblood.[17] By omitting the definite article
from the translation and treating the noun as a name, the NIV breaks this linkage. McCarter, following recent scholarly speculation, translates it as "the
votaries of Rapha," suggesting that Ishbi-Benob and the other three Philistines
mentioned here were members of an elite military unit devoted to a pagan
god.[18] Second, Ishbi-Benob possessed remarkable weaponry. His "bronze
spearhead weighed three hundred shekels"—about 7.5 pounds. The Hebrew
term for "spearhead," *qayin*, occurs as a noun with this meaning only here;
however, it is also the name of Cain, the first murderer (cf. Gen 4:8). Furthermore, he "was armed with" an unnamed "new" weapon; the NIV, following
some ancient versions, has speculated that it was a sword.

Before Ishbi-Benob could complete his objective, however, "Abishai son of
Zeruiah" (v. 17)—whom David would later entrust to quell the rebellion by
Sheba (cf. 20:6)—killed him. After Abishai helped David and the battle was
over, the king was confronted by his loyal troops. They established a rule that
David, referred to here as "the lamp of Israel," would "never again" go out with
his troops "to battle." The laudatory title "lamp of Israel" is used in the Bible

---

[16] Kirkpatrick, *The Second Book of Samuel,* 196.

[17] Cf. Youngblood, "1, 2 Samuel," 1059.

[18] Cf. McCarter, *II Samuel,* 449; also, C. E. L'Heureux, "The הָרָפָא יְלִידֵי—A Cultic Association of Warriors," *BASOR* 221 (1976): 83–85.

only here; it suggests that David's leadership was as valuable to the nation as a steady light source would be on a dark night. David apparently followed this rule, for in the narratives extending from 2 Samuel 11–20 he always assigned the leadership of his troops to others: Joab (11:1; 18:2), Abishai (18:2; 20:6), Ittai (18:2), and Amasa (20:4).

21:18–22 For killing Saph, another descendant of the Rapha known elsewhere as Sippai (cf. 1 Chr 20:4), David appears to have rewarded Sibbecai, one of David's mighty men (cf. 1 Chr 11:29), by making him the commander of a division of twenty-four thousand men (cf. 1 Chr 27:11). Both Saph and Goliath were killed "at Gob," a so-far unidentified site but perhaps the same as Gezer (cf. 1 Chr 20:4).

For obvious reasons v. 19 is easily the most controversial verse in this entire section—its declaration that "Elhanan son of Jaare-Oregim the Bethlehemite killed Goliath the Gittite" appears to contradict the affirmations of 1 Sam 17:50,57; 18:6. Scholars have dealt with v. 19 in three ways: they either treat it as a true contradiction present in the original manuscripts,[19] a true contradiction introduced by a careless copyist in pre-Christian times,[20] or as only a seeming contradiction that can be removed in interpretation.[21] The traditional Jewish explanation resolves the difficulty by asserting that "Elhanan" was an alternate name for David; others have expanded this concept, suggesting that "Elhanan" was David's original name and that "David" was his regnal name, that is, the name given him when he became king.[22] No explanation acceptable to all scholars can be given to resolve the tension between 1 Sam 17 and this verse. The suggestion that best harmonizes 1 Chr 20:5 with 2 Sam 21:19 suggests that the present verse was corrupted during the copying process. For that reason it may be the most satisfying proposed solution.

The following table summarizes the explanations given:

View	Explanation
True contradiction, present in the original manuscript of 1, 2 Samuel	Proof of conflated sources; accurate document is 2 Sam 21:19; 1 Sam 17:50 attached to David late in time for hero worship

---

[19] Cf. J. M. Miller and J. H. Hayes, *A History of Ancient Israel and Judah* (Philadelphia: Westminster, 1986), 153.

[20] Cf. Archer, *Survey of Old Testament Introduction,* 292. Other scholars who express an opinion on this option almost universally conclude that the Chronicler purposely changed the reading he encountered in 2 Sam 21:19 in order to resolve the problem. Cf. Anderson (*2 Samuel,* 255) and Gordon (*I and II Samuel,* 303).

[21] Cf. Baldwin, *1 and 2 Samuel,* 286.

[22] Cf. A. M. Honeyman, "The Evidence for Regnal Names among the Hebrews," *JBL* 67 (1948): 23–24.

View	Explanation
True contradiction, introduced by a careless pre-Christian-era copyist	1 Chr 20:5 preserves accurate text of 1 Sam 21:19's original reading
Seeming contradiction	Various possible explanations: 1. "Elhanan" an alternate name for David 2. "Goliath" a title, not a personal name 3. Two fighters from Gath named Goliath

The Philistine defeated by Elhanan "had a spear with a shaft like a weaver's rod." This statement may be either a reference to the unusually large size of Goliath's weapon or to its construction—that it had a loop of cord attached to it (cf. discussion at 1 Sam 17:7).[23] Goliath, like the other Philistines mentioned in this passage, was one of "the Rapha."

The fourth Philistine was killed in "another battle, which took place at Gath" (v. 20), in the heart of Philistine territory. At that location David's nephew "Jonathan son of Shimea" (v. 21) slew "a huge man with six fingers on each hand and six toes on each foot" (v. 20). This individual, who had the unusual condition known as hexadigitation, was killed when "he taunted Israel." He too was one of the descendants of the Rapha.

3. David Utters a Hymn of Praise to the Lord (22:1–51)

At the center of the biblical writer's appendix are the words of David himself—words spoken here in praise to the Lord.[24] Among David's words, none are marked as more significant in the appendix than those in this section. Besides being the longest quotation attributed to David (365 words in Hebrew) and displaying the richest variety of vocabulary, the section is cast in a formal structure, a classic example of Hebrew poetry. The psalm is closely related to Psalm 18—which is itself the longest of the psalms specifically attributed to David[25]—though it differs from the psalmodic work in its function and in subtle language features.[26] Differences between Psalm 18 and the present section

---

[23] Cf. Y. Yadin, "Goliath's Javelin," *PEQ* 86 (1955): 58–69; and L. Krinetzki, "Ein Beitrag zur Stilanalyse der Goliathperikope (1 Sam 17,1–18,5)," *Bib* 54 (1973): 187–236.

[24] Many modern scholars reject David's role in the composition of these materials (cf. Anderson, *2 Samuel,* 262–63). But such skepticism about the plain statements of Scripture is unwarranted.

[25] Due to the differences in these closely related compositions, Psalm 18—excluding the introductory, nonquotative materials—contains 376 words in the MT. The second-longest explicitly Davidic psalm is Psalm 37, which contains 297 words.

[26] For analysis of similarities/differences between 1 Samuel 22 and Psalm 18, cf. F. M. Cross, Jr., and D. N. Freedman, "A Royal Song of Thanksgiving: II Samuel 22 = Psalm 18," *JBL* 72 (1953): 15–34. An older comparative study is in Kirkpatrick, *The Second Book of Samuel,* 235–36.

can be accounted for by their differing functions; whereas Psalm 18 was intended for hymnic use in public worship, 2 Sam 22:1–51 was intended to reveal the religious core of Israel's most revered king. In its general shape it usually is classified as an individual thanksgiving psalm and is recognized as "one of the oldest major poems in the OT,"[27] dating to the tenth century B.C.

On the semantic level the psalm is constructed as a symmetrical chiasmus consisting of five units of thought, with a one-verse postscript. It can be analyzed as follows:

a   Praise for the Lord (vv. 1–4)
  b   The Lord's deliverance of David (vv. 5–20)
    c   Reasons for David's deliverance (vv. 21–29)
  b′ The Lord's deliverance of David (vv. 30–46)
a′ Praise for the Lord (vv. 47–50)
d   Postscript: the Lord's enduring support for the house of David (v. 51)

Since the main body of the psalm has an odd number of units, there is a natural focus on the central component, which contains the material of primary thematic significance.[28] If this is so, then this psalm can be seen as a restatement of a central thesis of the Torah—obedience to the Lord results in life and blessing. The message of the psalm may thus be summarized as follows: Because David scrupulously obeyed the Lord, the Lord rewarded him by responding to his pleas, delivering him during times of trouble and exalting him. For this the Lord is to be praised. This unit of material therefore "is a theological commentary on the history of David."[29]

(1) Praise for the Lord (22:1–4)

[1]David sang to the LORD the words of this song when the LORD delivered him from the hand of all his enemies and from the hand of Saul. [2]He said:
"The LORD is my rock, my fortress and my deliverer;
[3]my God is my rock, in whom I take refuge,
my shield and the horn of my salvation.
He is my stronghold, my refuge and my savior—
from violent men you save me.
[4]I call to the LORD, who is worthy of praise,
and I am saved from my enemies.

22:1 The narrator's introduction to this psalm suggests it was composed

---

[27] Youngblood, "1, 2 Samuel," 1064.

[28] For further discussion of the structural significance of chiastic structures, cf. L. F. Bliese, "Structural and Metrical Parameters in Hebrew Poetry," unpublished paper (Dallas: Seminar on Discourse Linguistics and Biblical Hebrew, June 1993): "Metrical chiasmus points to the peak in the center."

[29] Hertzberg, *I and II Samuel,* 393.

after David had been king in Israel for several years. The separation of Saul from the category of David's enemies is consistent with the author's portrayal of David elsewhere as a loyal servant and supporter of the house of Saul.

The introduction to the psalm found here differs from the one preceding Psalm 18 in that it contains no musical directions. Whereas the rendition in the Book of Psalms states it is "for the director of music" (Ps 18, preface), such a notation is absent in the present text. The difference demonstrates how the same piece of literature might be employed for different purposes in Israelite religious life: in one case it was intended as an aid for public worship, to be sung by an individual or group as part of a public religious service; here, however, it is used to showcase the pious core of David's being.

22:2–4   Using language replete with metaphors, David began his psalm with eight praise-filled descriptions of the Lord: the Lord is "my rock" (v. 2), "my fortress," "my deliverer," "my shield" (v. 3), "the horn of my salvation," "my stronghold," "my refuge," and "my savior." All of the images conjured up by Israel's king reflect his perception that the Lord is a strong and benevolent protector. Each of the eight descriptions is highly personal: the Lord is not just a source of salvation for the world in general. The extensive use of the first-person personal pronoun suffix is significant: for David, the Lord is a very personal helper, a living resource whose interventions in the king's life have consistently spelled the difference between life and death. David did not deny that the Lord is a Savior for others as well, but he wrote this psalm to affirm that the Lord was indeed his deliverer.

Seven of the initial images present the Lord as a defensive refuge in which David finds unfailing protection from all of life's threats. One of them portrays the Lord as one who actively moves against David's enemies: the Lord is not only a passive "rock," but he also is an aggressive "horn of . . . salvation"—a metaphorical comparison to a bull's dangerous horns (cf. Exod 21:28–32)—whose intervention saves the king "from violent men."

For the warrior David, a man who had been constantly threatened by enemies (v. 1) on and off the battlefield, the Lord's shelter and shield were treasured provisions he never took for granted. Unfailingly, when he called "to the LORD, who is worthy of praise" (v. 4), David was "saved from [his] enemies."

(2) The Lord's Deliverance of David—I (22:5–20)

> ⁵"The waves of death swirled about me;
>   the torrents of destruction overwhelmed me.
> ⁶The cords of the grave coiled around me;
>   the snares of death confronted me.
> ⁷In my distress I called to the LORD;
>   I called out to my God.
> From his temple he heard my voice;

my cry came to his ears.

⁸"The earth trembled and quaked,
the foundations of the heavens shook;
they trembled because he was angry.
⁹Smoke rose from his nostrils;
consuming fire came from his mouth,
burning coals blazed out of it.
¹⁰He parted the heavens and came down;
dark clouds were under his feet.
¹¹He mounted the cherubim and flew;
he soared on the wings of the wind.
¹²He made darkness his canopy around him—
the dark rain clouds of the sky.
¹³Out of the brightness of his presence
bolts of lightning blazed forth.
¹⁴The LORD thundered from heaven;
the voice of the Most High resounded.
¹⁵He shot arrows and scattered [the enemies],
bolts of lightning and routed them.
¹⁶The valleys of the sea were exposed
and the foundations of the earth laid bare
at the rebuke of the LORD,
at the blast of breath from his nostrils.

¹⁷"He reached down from on high and took hold of me;
he drew me out of deep waters.
¹⁸He rescued me from my powerful enemy,
from my foes, who were too strong for me.
¹⁹They confronted me in the day of my disaster,
but the LORD was my support.
²⁰He brought me out into a spacious place;
he rescued me because he delighted in me.

22:5–7 Using a vivid nautical metaphor, Israel's master poet described the threats to his life as "waves of death" (v. 5) that "swirled around" him. The image must have been particularly effective to the original Israelite audience, since both the Mediterranean (cf. Jonah 1:4–15) and Red Seas[30] were to them mysterious and foreboding and deadly regions of their world. Throughout the entire history of Israel, the nation made only occasional and often disastrous attempts to ply the seas.

---

[30] On only two occasions in the Bible were the Israelites mentioned as becoming involved in commercial activity on the high seas, during the reigns of Solomon (cf. 1 Kgs 9:26; 10:22) and Jehoshaphat (cf. 1 Kgs 22:48). Solomon's ships were manned by Phoenician sailors (1 Kgs 9:27); in the second instance, the ships were wrecked before they ever set sail (1 Kgs 22:48).

In the parallel line (v. 5) David described the threats to his life as "streams of Belial" (NIV, "currents of destruction") that "overwhelmed" him. The use of the term *bĕliyya'al* (lit., "without worth") to describe the threats to his life assures the reader that the threat to David is dangerous people, not dangerous waters. Within the recorded life of David he confronted *bĕliyya'al* people on three occasions: when dealing with Nabal (1 Sam 25:17,25), Sheba (2 Sam 20:1), and some of his disgruntled soldiers (1 Sam 30:22). In each instance he overcame their threats with the Lord's help.

Graphically David continued his poetic description of the threats against him, calling them "ropes of Sheol" (v. 6; NIV, "cords of the grave")—the realm of the dead—that "coiled around" him. "The snares of death" confronted him. A tactical misstep at any turn in David's career would have spelled death.

Through the use of yet another emphatic chiastic structure,[31] David revealed the secret that enabled him to cope with the stresses threatening to overwhelm him: he "called out to the LORD" (v. 7) his God, an action Brueggemann terms "Israel's most elemental act of faith."[32] Though the Lord was in "his temple" (Hb., *hêkāl*)—perhaps a reference to the Lord's dwelling place in heaven or the earthly worship site where the ark of the covenant resided—David's cry nevertheless "came to his ears," and "he heard" the king's voice. The Lord's ability to respond to David was not limited by physical distance: David did not need the ark of the covenant on the battlefield (cf. 1 Sam 4:3–4) for the Lord to be near to rescue—he could bring God's saving presence into any crisis by reaching out to him in faith.

22:8–11 The Lord's overwhelming response to David's desperate plea is magnified in these verses. God metaphorically moved mountains to respond to the king's petition: "the earth trembled and quaked, the foundations of the mountains [NIV, "heavens"] shook" (v. 8). Though there is no account in the biblical text of an earthquake occurring during David's lifetime, the Lord certainly rearranged the political landscape of Canaan to carry out the divine plan through David.

In vv. 9–11 David depicted a striking contrast between his own frailty and the Lord's strength. David's cry was one of terrified weakness and vulnerability; the Lord's response was one of terrifying, cataclysmic power. Weak, invisible sound waves had come from David's mouth as he called out for help: "consuming fire came from [the Lord's] mouth—burning coals blazed out of it" (v. 9). David was earthbound and on his way to Sheol; the Lord was in heaven with "dark clouds . . . under his feet"—nevertheless "he parted the heavens and came down" (v. 10). David was sinking beneath the

---

[31] "I cried to Yahweh, even to my God I cried"—an *A B B´ A´* chiasmus.

[32] Brueggemann, *First and Second Samuel,* 340.

waves of death (v. 5; cf. Jonah 2:5 [Hb. v. 6]); the Lord "appeared [NIV, "soared"][33] on the wings of the wind" (v. 11) as he "mounted the cherub [NIV, "cherubim"] and flew."

22:12–16 Powerful meteorological images not unlike those found in Canaanite hymns[34] abound in these verses. Each of them portrays the Lord as a being whose power and presence are vastly superior to all things human. Even his "temporary dwellings" (Hb., *sukkôt;* NIV, "canopy") are vastly beyond those used by humans: his are darkness and rain clouds (v. 12); the *sukkôt* used by humans were made of sticks and fronds.

In vv. 13–16 David extended the metaphor of the Lord the raincloud-dweller. Poetically picturing the internal lightning of a cumulonimbus cloud as the awesome presence of the Lord, the inter-cloud and cloud-to-ground "bolts of lightning" (v. 14) that "blazed forth" were divine "arrows" (v. 15) that "scattered" and "routed" the enemies. The thunder attendant with the awesome display of lightning was poetically expressed as "the voice of the Most High" (v. 14). The powerful gusts of wind associated with a violent storm were brought into the metaphor as "the blast of breath from [the Lord's] nostrils" (v. 16).

Life and breath were closely related in Israelite thought;[35] thus when the Lord's breath was portrayed as exposing "the valleys of the sea" and laying bare "the foundations of the earth"—things infinitely beyond the power of any human's capacity—David was simultaneously affirming that the Lord's life force was vastly superior to that of humanity.

22:17–20 David's high and powerful God is also depicted as a caring and saving God. When David was sinking in "deep waters" (v. 17), the Lord "reached down from on high, . . . took hold of" him, and "drew [him] out."

The narrator never portrayed David's life as being threatened by water, but figuratively David's life was often gravely imperiled by "foes who were too strong" (v. 18) for him. Nevertheless, without fail the Lord "rescued" David from every "powerful enemy."

---

[33] Following the Syr. and Vg, the NIV assumes the original reading was אֵרָא and not the MT's יֵרֶא. The NIV has demonstrated a distinct tendency to emend the Hebrew text of this chapter in order to harmonize it with Psalm 18. Although this practice may be justified, it effectively eliminates the possibility that this version of the poem was intended to serve a different function from the one in Psalms, and therefore chose to use a different reading. Unlike Ps 18, this rendition of David's work was not "for the director of music" (preface to Ps 18 [Hb. v. 1]). The differing readings may be due to this subtle but important change in cultural context.

[34] In Ugaritic literature Baal is sometimes termed "Rider of the Clouds"; cf. *The Ancient Near East, vol. 1: An Anthology of Texts and Pictures,* ed. J. B. Pritchard (Princeton: Princeton University Press, 1958), 100. D. F. Payne points out that "Israel's God was no less strong than other storm-gods; . . . But he was far more than just a storm-god" (*I and II Samuel,* DSB [Philadelphia: Westminster, 1982], 266).

[35] Note that the term נֶפֶשׁ can be translated as "breath" (cf. Job 41:21) or "life" (cf. Gen 9:5).

David shifted the domain of poetic imagery in v. 19 from the sea to the meadow by drawing from his own pastoral background. In this verse he poetically described the Lord as being "a staff" (v. 19; NIV, "support") to him. The term employed here—*miš'ān*—refers to the large stick with a bowed top used by shepherds to pull sheep out of danger or off a wrong path. By using this metaphor David affirmed that the Lord acted in his behalf as a protective deliverer—a good Shepherd (cf. Ps 23:1,4) "in the day of . . . disaster." As the divine Staff intervened in David's life to snatch him from disaster, the Lord "brought [David] out into a spacious place" (v. 20).

(3) Reasons for David's Deliverance (22:21–29)

²¹"The LORD has dealt with me according to my righteousness;
　according to the cleanness of my hands he has rewarded me.
²²For I have kept the ways of the LORD;
　I have not done evil by turning from my God.
²³All his laws are before me;
　I have not turned away from his decrees.
²⁴I have been blameless before him
　and have kept myself from sin.
²⁵The LORD has rewarded me according to my righteousness,
　according to my cleanness in his sight.

²⁶"To the faithful you show yourself faithful,
　to the blameless you show yourself blameless,
²⁷to the pure you show yourself pure,
　but to the crooked you show yourself shrewd.
²⁸You save the humble,
　but your eyes are on the haughty to bring them low.
²⁹You are my lamp, O LORD;
　the LORD turns my darkness into light.

22:21–25 With these verses David moved the poem forward from discussing what the Lord had done on his behalf to the issue of why the Lord did it. This subject is of central concern in the poem, since it suggests how others can come to know the Lord's blessing as well—a matter of great interest to all worshipers of the Lord. David indicated that his success resulted from scrupulous obedience to the Lord's law: by implication, others who wish to experience God's blessing must do the same. David's personal appraisal of his conduct does not necessarily overlook the fact that he had also sinned grievously (cf. 11:27; 12:9). To be accepted as accurate, however, one must assume that David's actions against Uriah and Bathsheba were uncharacteristic (cf. 1 Kgs 11:4; 14:8; 15:3,11; 16:2; 18:3; 22:2) and thoroughly repented of (cf. 12:13; Ps 51:1–12[Hb. 3–14]).

To provide additional emphasis to this material, the poet employs a tightly knit eight-element chiastic structure. This sophisticated literary device increases the organizational complexity as well as the aesthetic interest of this region of the poem and thus makes these verses more memorable to readers. The following chart illustrates the balance of semantic elements within vv. 21–25:

Chiastic Element	Subject	Text
A	the Lord	The LORD has dealt with me according to my righteousness; according to the cleanness of my hands he has rewarded me (v. 21).
B	David	For I have kept the ways of the LORD (v. 22);
C	David	I have not done evil by turning from my God (v. 22).
D	the Lord's law	All his laws are before me (v. 23);
D'	David	I have not turned away from his decrees (v. 23).
C'	David	I have been blameless before him (v. 24)
B'	David	and have kept myself from sin (v. 24).
A'	the Lord	The LORD has rewarded me according to my righteousness, according to my cleanness in his sight (v. 25).

David begins and ends this unit by giving ultimate credit for his success in life to "the LORD" (vv. 21,25). The Lord was the source of his success, but that success was not accidental. As the center of the chiasmus suggests, it was based on David's diligence in keeping the Torah: he had kept "all" the Lord's "laws" before him, refusing to turn "away from his decrees" (v. 23). In accordance with the promises of the Torah (cf. Lev 26:1–13; Deut 28:1–14) the Lord "rewarded" (vv. 21,25) him for the proper moral choices he had made in life, for David had "kept the ways of the LORD" (v. 22). He had not "done evil" but had "kept [him]self from sin" (v. 24), maintaining "cleanness in his sight" (v. 25). To avoid creating a conflict with Pauline theology (cf. Gal 3:10–11), we must assume that genuine God-centered faith was the wellspring of David's scrupulous attention to the law and his personal conduct. David received his reward from God because he had a faith-based righteousness that produced actions consistent with it (cf. Jas 2:17).

22:26–28 Having revealed why he had experienced the Lord's blessing, David here makes six observations about God's treatment of various types of individuals. The statements in this section were addressed to the Lord but were clearly intended to instruct the reader in virtue.

David suggests four virtues that please the Lord: faithfulness, moral blamelessness, purity, and humility—the list is suggestive of God-honoring behavior, but not exhaustive. To one who possesses faithfulness (Hb., *ḥāsîd*)—that is, a commitment-based love for God and people—God demonstrates himself to be "faithful" (v. 26). To one who is a "morally blameless champion" (Hb., *gibbôr tāmîm*; NIV, "the blameless") God shows himself "blameless"—one who acts with unmixed benevolence. To the morally "refined" (v. 27; Hb., *bārar;* NIV, "pure") God conducts himself in a "refined" (NIV, "pure") manner. To "the humble" (v. 28; Hb., *ʿānî*), the Lord brings salvation. Though different in structure and function from its New Testament counterpart, David's list of virtues with attendant blessings foreshadows Jesus' Beatitudes (cf. esp. Matt 5:3,7–8).

The Lord does not treat all people alike—to do so would demonstrate a moral indifference that is not found in the biblical view of God. While the virtuous find God to be a source of life and help, the wicked experience God's wrath. Those who are "crooked" (v. 27; Hb., *ʿiqqēš*) find that the Lord is "tortuous" (NIV, "shrewd"). Those who are "haughty" (v. 28; Hb., *rwm*), exalting themselves at the expense of God and others, ultimately find that the Lord brings "them low."

In a world of darkness, unlit by opportunity and hope, David found the Lord to be his "lamp" (v. 29)—the one who turned his "darkness to light."

(4) The Lord's Deliverance of David—II (22:30–46)

[30]With your help I can advance against a troop;
  with my God I can scale a wall.
[31]"As for God, his way is perfect;
  the word of the LORD is flawless.
 He is a shield
  for all who take refuge in him.
[32]For who is God besides the LORD?
  And who is the Rock except our God?
[33]It is God who arms me with strength
  and makes my way perfect.
[34]He makes my feet like the feet of a deer;
  he enables me to stand on the heights.
[35]He trains my hands for battle;
  my arms can bend a bow of bronze.
[36]You give me your shield of victory;
  you stoop down to make me great.
[37]You broaden the path beneath me,
  so that my ankles do not turn.

[38]"I pursued my enemies and crushed them;
  I did not turn back till they were destroyed.

³⁹I crushed them completely, and they could not rise;
     they fell beneath my feet.
⁴⁰You armed me with strength for battle;
     you made my adversaries bow at my feet.
⁴¹You made my enemies turn their backs in flight,
     and I destroyed my foes.
⁴²They cried for help, but there was no one to save them—
     to the LORD, but he did not answer.
⁴³I beat them as fine as the dust of the earth;
     I pounded and trampled them like mud in the streets.

⁴⁴"You have delivered me from the attacks of my people;
     you have preserved me as the head of nations.
 People I did not know are subject to me,
⁴⁵and foreigners come cringing to me;
     as soon as the'y hear me, they obey me.
⁴⁶They all lose heart;
     they come trembling from their strongholds.

22:30 The blaze of the Lord within him enabled (cf. v. 29) David to burst forth beyond his own limitations: because of the Lord's "help" (v. 30) David could "run through a barrier" (NIV, "advance against a troop") and "scale a wall."

22:31–33 These three verses appear to make up a single semantic unit. Both vv. 31 and 33 begin with the same word—*hāʾēl*—and both contain the phrase *tāmîm darkô*.³⁶ This suggests that this unit was constructed chiastically, magnifying the Lord, whose way, word, and protection are perfect.

"The God" (v. 31; NIV, "God")—that is, the one true God—had provided a pathway of life for David. The king had walked in that "way" and found it to be "perfect." In the poetic context of a synonymously parallel distich, the divine "path" to which David referred should be understood as the "smelted" (NIV, "flawless")—that is, devoid of all impurity—"word of the LORD." The Lord's word, both as it was written in the Law and spoken through the prophets, had invariably guided David to safety and success. Through the gracious provision of insight and help the Lord had been David's "shield" and "refuge."

The Lord was David's only source of divine help because there was no other "God besides the LORD" (v. 32). Every other external hope was a sham; only "our God"—the God of Israel—was "the Rock" capable of shielding David from the terrors and troubles of life.

In v. 33 David continued and extended the reference to the Lord as a refuge; in this case he notes that the one true God is a "mountain stronghold" (v. 33; compare with v. 32). But the Lord is more than just a defense; he is also

---

³⁶ One must accept the *ketiv* reading of v. 33 to find the parallel: the *qere* reads דַּרְכִּי instead of דַּרְכּוֹ.

"power."[37] He is also the one whose "way" was "perfect"—that is, consistently trustworthy.

22:34–35 By walking on the Lord's path David found that God made his "feet like the feet of a deer" (v. 34), a metaphor expressing inner stability, strength, and adeptness at handling life's struggles. This image may have been borrowed by Habakkuk at a later point in time (cf. Hab 3:19). David's diligent adherence to the ways of the Lord transformed him, making the end result of his life something more than could be explained through natural processes. The Lord's paths led the man of faith to great prominence and domination in the wildernesses of life—God enabled him "to stand on the heights."

Every part of David's life was transformed by his walk on the Lord's path. Reflective of this fact is the confession that the Lord trained David's "hands for battle" (v. 35). So effective was the Lord's transformation of David that his "arms can bend a bow of bronze"—an astonishing feat for anyone. Since bows were made of wood and not bronze in Israel, the description is likely to be taken figuratively and, as such, yet another poetic depiction of the Lord's power to make an otherwise ordinary life extraordinary.

22:36–37 In vv. 34–35 David confessed that the Lord was the true source of his exceptional personal abilities. In these verses he confessed that the Lord was also the source of unparalleled external assets. God also provided his anointed with a divine "shield of victory" (v. 36; Hb., *māgēn*), thus affording David protection from all threats that might be hurled against him. The Lord's gracious gift complemented the ones David had received from Jonathan (cf. 1 Sam 18:4), thus granting him an invincibility denied the previous dynastic family (cf. 1:21).

David had previously noted that though the Lord resided in heaven, he had come down to help David (v. 10). Here David picks up that theme again to note with wonder that the Lord had humbled himself (NIV, "stooped down") to make David "great." God debased himself to exalt David! In God's action toward David we see a foreshadowing of the work of Christ (cf. Phil 2:6–8).

A further external blessing that came from the Lord was the provision of a broad "path beneath" (v. 37) David "so that [his] ankles do not turn." The sovereign God who controls every facet of life granted his faithful follower circumstances that permitted him to stand and move confidently against all of life's foes.

22:38–39 David did not idly accept these divinely wrought gifts and cir-

---

[37] In an attempt to reshape v. 33 to conform to the reading of Ps 18:32 as well as the Dead Sea Scrolls, Vulgate, and Syriac, the NIV has completely changed the reading of the first portion of this verse. Their suggestion, "It is God who trains my hands for battle," is significantly different from the MT's reading: "The [one true] God my mountain stronghold is power." I prefer the MT's reading for two reasons: first, because of the principle of lectio difficilior; and second, because it is more semantically consistent with v. 32.

cumstances—he used them vigorously. With a holy zeal David "pursued [his] enemies and crushed them"; he "did not turn back till they were destroyed" (v. 38). As the Lord's agent of judgment he "crushed" the enemy "completely," leaving them collapsed beneath his feet, unable to rise.

22:40–43 David's unbridled victory celebration continues in these verses. He unabashedly recounts his triumphs over his foes and marvels over the international prominence given him as a result of his conquests. Overarching his celebration of success, however, is the recognition that the Lord—not any talent or ability naturally present within David himself—is the reason for his unparalleled success.

In an intimate, confessional section of the psalm, David here meditatively confesses to the Lord that he is simultaneously the source of David's prowess and the reason for his enemies' defeats. It was the Lord who "armed" the king "with strength for battle" (v. 40); it was the Lord also who caused his enemies to "turn their backs in flight" (v. 41) and ultimately "bow at [David's] feet" (v. 40).

Because of the Lord's help, David "destroyed [his] foes" (v. 41). But the Lord's provision of assistance was selective; when David's adversaries—perhaps Israelites in this case (cf. 18:2–7; 20:15–22)—cried out to the Lord for help, "he did not answer" (v. 42). As a result, David "beat them as fine as the dust of the earth; [he] pounded and trampled them like mud in the streets" (v. 43).

22:44–46 By the time David penned this psalm, he had faced and overcome both Israelite and non-Israelite opposition. The Lord "delivered" David "from the attacks of my people" (v. 44), whether they came from a family member (i.e., Absalom) or from someone of another Israelite tribe (i.e., Sheba the Benjamite). These assaults, coming as they did from family members and fellow countrymen, were perhaps the most difficult of all to endure.

Throughout David's battles with foreign adversaries the Lord had "preserved" him, so that the son of Jesse maintained his position as "the head of nations," including Moab, Edom, Ammon, Damascus, and various other Aramean city-states (cf. 8:2,6,14; 10:19; 12:29–31). So successful was David in his military encounters with foreigners that even "peoples" he "did not know" became "subject to" him. Apparently, some foes would "lose heart" (v. 46) and come "trembling from their strongholds" (v. 46) before David could mount a full-scale assault on their position. These subjugated foreigners would "come cringing to" (v. 45) Israel's king and would servilely "obey" whatever command he might issue.

(5) Praise for the Lord (22:47–50)

47"The LORD lives! Praise be to my Rock!
    Exalted be God, the Rock, my Savior!

⁴⁸He is the God who avenges me,
     who puts the nations under me,
⁴⁹   who sets me free from my enemies.
You exalted me above my foes;
     from violent men you rescued me.
⁵⁰Therefore I will praise you, O LORD, among the nations;
     I will sing praises to your name.

22:47–50   While David marveled at the incredible social power he possessed, he was careful to contextualize it. David's victory was in a larger sense the Lord's victory; if David reigned over neighboring peoples, it was because the Lord reigned supreme over all peoples. Therefore it was fitting that, after describing his own enviable success, he should bring the psalm to a climactic end with the brightest sustained praise of the Lord found in the composition.

References to the Lord as the Rock, the declaration that God "avenges" (lit., "gives vengeance to") David's enemies and the statement that "the Lord lives" link this latter portion of David's last song with the latter portion of the song of Moses, especially Deut 32:31–43. The similarity in vocabulary and themes suggests that the writer consciously attempted to produce an echo and a parallel between the final song of Moses and the final song of David.

David begins the crescendo of praise by declaring the first and greatest reason for celebration: "the LORD lives!" (v. 47). But the good news does not end with this most profound reality: the Lord is also on David's side! The Lord is praiseworthy because he is "the Rock" (cf. Deut 32:30–31)—that is, a protector and "Savior." Furthermore, the Lord is to be praised because he acted on the basis of moral considerations: in keeping with Torah promises (cf. Deut 32:35), he "avenges" (v. 48) David for the wrongs done to him and has "put the nations under" David's control.

The Lord was also to be praised because he was David's source of true freedom: God "causes [him] to go forth" (v. 49; NIV, "sets me free"), liberating him "from violent men." As if all this were not enough, the Lord was also the one who set David "above [his] foes."

In view of all the Lord is and has done, David exuberantly commits himself to the task of proclaiming the greatness of God to all, even those outside the covenant community. The king himself "will sing praises to" the Lord's name "among the nations" (v. 50).

(6) Postscript: The Lord's Enduring Support for the House of David (22:51)

⁵¹He gives his king great victories;
     he shows unfailing kindness to his anointed,
     to David and his descendants forever."

Undergirding David's ministry was the certain knowledge that he was the

Lord's "anointed" (Hb., *māšiaḥ*; v. 51; cf. 1 Sam 16:13)—one chosen by the Lord to be "king," formally set apart and empowered for divine service. His ministry was sustained by God's "unfailing kindness" (Hb., *ḥesed*), that is, a commitment on God's part to fulfill every promise he had made to David. The Lord's transforming acts of grace and "unfailing kindness" had given this one-time shepherd from the rural regions of Judah a higher and deeper purpose in life—David would use his considerable gifts to make the Lord known throughout the world.

Among the most prized of the Lord's promises to David was that "his descendants" would sit on Israel's throne "forever" (cf. 7:11–16). David's conviction that future generations of his descendants would follow in his footsteps as the Lord's designated leader over Israel must have caused him to act with a certain sense of sobriety: his actions would be models for good or ill as long as Israel had a king.[38]

A notable similarity exists between the final verse of Hannah's song (1 Sam 2:10) and the final verse of David's song. Both speak of the Lord assisting "his king" and "his anointed" and mention these two nouns in the same order. At the same time, there is a notable difference—David names himself and his descendants as being the Lord's kings, whereas Hannah made no such mention. The resulting effect of the apparently intentional contrast between the two verses is the affirmation that the house of David was in fact the fulfillment of Hannah's prophetic word.

4. David Utters His Last Oracle (23:1–7)[39]

¹These are the last words of David:
"The oracle of David son of Jesse,
    the oracle of the man exalted by the Most High,
the man anointed by the God of Jacob,
    Israel's singer of songs:

²"The Spirit of the LORD spoke through me;
    his word was on my tongue.
³The God of Israel spoke,

---

[38] Cf. 1 Kgs 3:14; 9:4; 11:6,33,38; 14:8; 15:3,5,11; 2 Kgs 14:3; 16:2; 18:3; 22:2.

[39] For detailed studies that view this section as a well-structured unity and propose some textual emendations, cf. H. N. Richardson, "The Last Words of David: Some Notes on II Samuel 23:1–7," *JBL* 90 (1971): 257–66; and G. Del Olmo Lete, "David's Farewell Oracle (2 Samuel XXIII:1–7): A Literary Analysis," *VT* 34 (1984): 414–37. G. A. Rendsburg suggests on the basis of six features of nonnormative Hebrew present in these verses that they were either edited or composed by someone from the northeastern portions of Israel ("The Northern Origin of 'The Last Words of David' [2 Sam 23,1–7]," *Bib* 69 [1988]: 113–21); R. J. Tournay is inclined to date the work in the period of Malachi ("Les 'dernières parôles de David, II Samuel XXIII,1–7," *RB* 88 [1981]: 481–504). H. P. Smith asserts that this section is "a comparatively late production" of non-Davidic origin (*Samuel*, 381). Smith's and Tournay's position can be accepted only if one assumes that v. 1 is inaccurate, an assumption I am unwilling to make.

the Rock of Israel said to me:
'When one rules over men in righteousness,
    when he rules in the fear of God,
⁴he is like the light of morning at sunrise
    on a cloudless morning,
like the brightness after rain
    that brings the grass from the earth.'

⁵"Is not my house right with God?
    Has he not made with me an everlasting covenant,
    arranged and secured in every part?
Will he not bring to fruition my salvation
    and grant me my every desire?
⁶But evil men are all to be cast aside like thorns,
    which are not gathered with the hand.
⁷Whoever touches thorns
    uses a tool of iron or the shaft of a spear;
    they are burned up where they lie."

David's prophetic oracle presents the ideal of a righteous king guided by the fear of the Lord. Such a king brings life and blessing to his nation but judgment and death to all who would threaten it. At the same time the oracle affirms that David's dynasty alone is certified by the Lord to be Israel's righteous kings.

The *Targum of Jonathan* interpreted this section as a prophecy of the coming Messiah.[40] Jesus also seems to have understood this passage as messianic; his comparison of himself to "light" (John 8:12; 9:5; cf. v. 4) and his prophetic parable comparing the wicked to weeds to be burned (Matt 13:30,40; cf. v. 7) suggests that he was drawing upon images derived from this passage.[41]

23:1–2 Though called "the last words of David" (v. 1), this "oracle" (Hb., *nēʾum*) is not the last of the words attributed to David in 2 Samuel (cf. 23:15; 24:2,10,14,17,21,24). This rather obvious fact reminds us that the writer was more than an editor concerned only with chronological details. He was in fact a true author, deliberately arranging and shaping the materials at his disposal to convey the intended themes as effectively as possible.

The present section is clearly one of the highlighted passages in 2 Samuel, being given prominence in at least three ways. First, it—along with 22:1–51—was placed at the core of the aside's chiastic structure: it thus functioned as part of the thematic centerpiece of this portion of 1, 2 Samuel. Second, it was designated an "oracle," a special speech-act category reserved for

---

[40] For a readily available English translation of the *Targum of Jonathan* relating to this passage, cf. Kirkpatrick, *The Second Book of Samuel,* 237.

[41] Baldwin also connects this passage with Jesus, though less directly: "When Jesus went about proclaiming 'the kingdom of God is at hand' (Mk. 1:15), David's aspirations were at last to be realized; the very name 'Jesus' spoke of salvation (Mt. 1:21)" (*1 and 2 Samuel,* 292).

prophetic utterances of unusual significance.[42] Finally, it was memorialized as the final utterance of "the man exalted by the Most High" who became Israel's greatest king.

In the introductory verse David is designated in several different ways. First, he is contextualized according to his genealogy: he was the "son of Jesse." This first credential would seem to be an insignificant one, since Jesse himself played no recorded role in Israel's history. However, it did mark David as a true Israelite—and in fact a Judahite—and thus as one who fulfilled the requirements established in the Torah for proper kingship (cf. Gen 49:10; Deut 17:15).

Whatever limitations may have been imposed on David by his background were overcome by the next two realities: David also was "the man exalted by the Most High" and "the man anointed by the God of Jacob." This divine intervention in the life of Jesse's son meant first of all that David fulfilled the other remaining Torah qualification for kingship, since only one who had been chosen by the Lord could serve in this capacity (cf. Deut 17:15). Additionally, David's selection by the God who was above all meant that he could be lifted above any human limitation. David's anointing by the God of Jacob implicitly connected David's career with Jacob's—Jacob was used of God to found a nation; David, to found the royal family that ruled Jacob's nation.

Finally, David was defined by the opinions of others: he was "the beloved of Israel's songs" (NIV, "Israel's singer of songs"):[43] David was an admired hero, memorialized in popular Israelite songs mostly lost to us today (but cf. 1 Sam 18:7; 21:11; Pss 78:70–72; 89:3–37).

But in addition to all these other appellations, David was a prophet (cf. Acts 2:30). Thus David has now been portrayed throughout the books of Samuel as king, priest, and prophet. In these roles David foreshadows the work of his greatest descendant, Jesus Christ. Throughout the New Testament Jesus is likewise depicted as a king (John 18:37; 19:21), priest (Heb 3:1; 4:14–5:10; 7:21–8:6), and prophet (Luke 1:76; 4:24; 13:33; 24:19; Acts 3:22). Since David, the first member of Israel's royal messianic line, functioned in these three roles, it seems appropriate that Jesus the Messiah should not only be depicted by the

---

[42] V. Parunak concludes that the formulaic saying "oracle of the LORD" creates "a highly local highlighting of a clause or phrase that merits the recipient's special attention. It sets off the clause or phrase with which it is associated from the context, as though it were printed in italics or bold-face type" ("Some Discourse Functions of Prophetic Quotation Formulas," in *Biblical Hebrew and Discourse Linguistics* [Dallas: SIL, 1994], 511). We can conjecture that a section called an "oracle of David," Israel's greatest king, is an equally highlighted section of text.

[43] The phrase יִשְׂרָאֵל זְמִרוֹת נְעִים has been translated variously. Other options include: "Israel's beloved singer" (NIV footnote); "the sweet psalmist of Israel" (NKJV); "the favorite of the Strong One of Israel" (NRSV); and "the darling of the stronghold of Israel" (McCarter, *II Samuel*, 476). McCarter's and the NRSV's translations require both a repointing of זְמִרוֹת to זִמְרַת and the assignment of a conjectural definition ("strong [one]"/ "stronghold") to the term. The NIV's and NKJV's translations assume that David is the beloved composer, not *topic*, of the songs of Israel. Both relationships accurately depict the link that exists between David and Israel's music.

New Testament writers as inheriting these roles but superseding David's accomplishments in them. He did not choose this role but accepted it when "the Spirit of the LORD spoke through" (v. 2) him. David's role was essentially passive in this event. When he spoke, it was the Lord's "word"—not his own—that was on his "tongue" (cf. 2 Pet 1:21). As in the case of at least one other Old Testament prophet (cf. 1 Kgs 13:21–22), David's status as a prophet did not prevent him from receiving prophetic messages from other prophets (cf. 1 Sam 22:5; 2 Sam 7:5–17; 12:11–14; 24:12–13,18).

23:3–4 In these verses the Lord reveals the two primary demands of the ideal king and then characterizes the reign of a king who meets these ideals. First of all, the king who pleases the Lord must rule over men "in righteousness" (v. 3): one who exercises authority over others must use that authority in a manner consistent with the Lord's teachings. Second, a proper king must rule "in the fear of God." Only one who is under God's authority is fit to be an authority over others.

A king who fulfills these two fundamental requirements is a great blessing to his subjects. "He is like the light of the morning at sunrise on a cloudless morning" (v. 4). The comparison suggests that a ruler who rules according to the Lord's guidelines ushers in a new period of opportunity, growth, and blessing for his people.

Furthermore, a righteous king is "like the brightness after rain that brings the grass from the earth." For well-watered seedlings to fulfill their potential, they must have bright sunlight; similarly, strong, righteous leaders help create an environment in which the people under their care can fulfill their potential.

23:5 God's blessing on David was evident: the blessings indicated that his "house" was "with God" (NIV, "right with God"). Though other families also had known the blessing of being with God, David's was given something from the Lord others did not receive, for with David the Lord had "made . . . an everlasting covenant" of kingship (cf. 7:11–16), "arranged and secured in every part." Because of the trustworthy word of the Lord, David was confident that he who had begun a good work would carry it to completion (cf. Phil 1:6). The Lord would "bring to fruition" David's salvation and grant him his "every desire."

David's use of the term "salvation" probably was primarily in the material sense, that is, with reference to victory over enemies and hostile circumstances; however, a spiritual dimension cannot be discounted (cf. Ps 27). To the extent that David's heart was attuned to God's will, David could expect God to grant him his "every desire" (cf. 7:2–16). As P. E. Satterthwaite notes, this verse portrays "David as he should always have been, not as he always was" (cf. David's sinful desire toward Bathsheba; 11:4).[44]

---

[44] P. E. Satterthwaite, "David in the Books of Samuel: A Messianic Expectation?" in *The Lord's Anointed: Interpretation of Old Testament Messianic Texts,* ed. P. E. Satterthwaite, R. S. Hess, and G. J. Wenham (Carlisle: Paternoster, 1995).

23:6–7   Even as the Lord could be counted on to bring blessing to the house of David, so David could be counted on to bring the blessing of justice to his land. As a righteous king David would see to it that "evil men" would be "cast aside like thorns" (v. 6).

In a brilliant oracle-ending analogy, David likened the fate of the evil in his realm to the fate of weeds in a farmer's field: both would be killed with "a tool of iron or the shaft of a spear" (v. 7) and be "burned up where they lie." The king's righteous zeal would purge evil from his realm, through the use of deadly force where necessary.

5. Loyal and Heroic Soldiers of David—II (23:8–39)

[8]These are the names of David's mighty men:

Josheb-Basshebeth, a Tahkemonite, was chief of the Three; he raised his spear against eight hundred men, whom he killed in one encounter.

[9]Next to him was Eleazar son of Dodai the Ahohite. As one of the three mighty men, he was with David when they taunted the Philistines gathered [at Pas Dammim] for battle. Then the men of Israel retreated, [10]but he stood his ground and struck down the Philistines till his hand grew tired and froze to the sword. The LORD brought about a great victory that day. The troops returned to Eleazar, but only to strip the dead.

[11]Next to him was Shammah son of Agee the Hararite. When the Philistines banded together at a place where there was a field full of lentils, Israel's troops fled from them. [12]But Shammah took his stand in the middle of the field. He defended it and struck the Philistines down, and the LORD brought about a great victory.

[13]During harvest time, three of the thirty chief men came down to David at the cave of Adullam, while a band of Philistines was encamped in the Valley of Rephaim. [14]At that time David was in the stronghold, and the Philistine garrison was at Bethlehem. [15]David longed for water and said, "Oh, that someone would get me a drink of water from the well near the gate of Bethlehem!" [16]So the three mighty men broke through the Philistine lines, drew water from the well near the gate of Bethlehem and carried it back to David. But he refused to drink it; instead, he poured it out before the LORD. [17]"Far be it from me, O LORD, to do this!" he said. "Is it not the blood of men who went at the risk of their lives?" And David would not drink it.

Such were the exploits of the three mighty men.

[18]Abishai the brother of Joab son of Zeruiah was chief of the Three. He raised his spear against three hundred men, whom he killed, and so he became as famous as the Three. [19]Was he not held in greater honor than the Three? He became their commander, even though he was not included among them.

[20]Benaiah son of Jehoiada was a valiant fighter from Kabzeel, who performed great exploits. He struck down two of Moab's best men. He also went down into a pit on a snowy day and killed a lion. [21]And he struck down a huge Egyptian. Although the Egyptian had a spear in his hand, Benaiah went against him with a club. He snatched the spear from the Egyptian's hand and killed him with his own spear. [22]Such were the exploits of Benaiah son of Jehoiada; he too was as famous

as the three mighty men. ²³He was held in greater honor than any of the Thirty, but he was not included among the Three. And David put him in charge of his bodyguard.

²⁴Among the Thirty were:
   Asahel the brother of Joab,
   Elhanan son of Dodo from Bethlehem,
   ²⁵Shammah the Harodite,
   Elika the Harodite,
   ²⁶Helez the Paltite,
   Ira son of Ikkesh from Tekoa,
   ²⁷Abiezer from Anathoth,
   Mebunnai the Hushathite,
   ²⁸Zalmon the Ahohite,
   Maharai the Netophathite,
   ²⁹Heled son of Baanah the Netophathite,
   Ithai son of Ribai from Gibeah in Benjamin,
   ³⁰Benaiah the Pirathonite,
   Hiddai from the ravines of Gaash,
   ³¹Abi-Albon the Arbathite,
   Azmaveth the Barhumite,
   ³²Eliahba the Shaalbonite,
   the sons of Jashen,
   Jonathan ³³son of Shammah the Hararite,
   Ahiam son of Sharar the Hararite,
   ³⁴Eliphelet son of Ahasbai the Maacathite,
   Eliam son of Ahithophel the Gilonite,
   ³⁵Hezro the Carmelite,
   Paarai the Arbite,
   ³⁶Igal son of Nathan from Zobah,
   the son of Hagri,
   ³⁷Zelek the Ammonite,
   Naharai the Beerothite, the armor-bearer of Joab son of Zeruiah,
   ³⁸Ira the Ithrite,
   Gareb the Ithrite
   ³⁹and Uriah the Hittite.
   There were thirty-seven in all.

David's unparalleled success was the result not only of his relationship with the Lord, but also of his valiant soldiers' efforts. In this rather extended section some thirty-six[45] individuals are singled out by name for their brave deeds and/or positions in David's administration. The list appears to be cumulative, since it includes the names of at least two individuals who died during different but relatively early periods in David's administration. Alternatively, it may have

---

[45] The text of the NIV lists only thirty-four names. The number thirty-six is derivable from a reading of the MT. For a fuller treatment of the issue, cf. the footnote at 23:24.

come from "a time relatively early in his reign over all Israel."[46]

23:8–12　First in the list of "David's mighty men" was "Josheb-Basshebeth, a Tahkemonite" (v. 8), who was made "chief of the Three." This position was not mentioned elsewhere in 1, 2 Samuel but obviously was prestigious—undoubtedly Josheb-Basshebeth reported directly to David. He earned this position with the amazing battlefield feat of raising "his spear against eight hundred men,[47] whom he killed in one encounter." Josheb-Basshebeth also may have been known as "Adino the Eznite" and as Jashobeam (cf. 1 Chr 11:11).

The second most-honored individual in his administration was "Eleazar son of Dodai the Ahohite" (v. 9). This individual had accompanied "David when they taunted the Philistines gathered . . . for battle," apparently at Pas Dammim/Ephes Dammim (cf. 1 Chr 11:13; 1 Sam 17:1). In a remarkable show of courage and strength, Eleazar "stood his ground and struck down the Philistines" (v. 10), even though the remainder of David's forces retreated from the Philistines during the battle. Eleazar was so intense and unrelenting in his attack that he ceased only when "his hand grew tired and froze to the sword," that is, after muscle cramps temporarily disabled him. The writer attributed Eleazar's extraordinary efforts ultimately to the Lord, who "brought about a great victory that day." Through this one soldier the Philistines were vanquished; all that remained for the other soldiers was "to strip the dead" (cf. 1 Sam 31:8), a practice that provided booty for the victorious soldiers—perhaps in lieu of other payment.

The writer's acknowledgment of a union between human skill and divine enablement affirms and extends the theology of war present in the previous chapter (cf. 22:35,38). Yahweh the Warrior trained, strengthened, and gave victory on the battlefield to his anointed David, but he did not limit this treatment to David. Other soldiers of the covenant, such as Eleazar, could also experience this divine blessing.

The third member of the Three was "Shammah son of Agee the Hararite" (v. 11). Like Eleazar, he distinguished himself through a courageous one-man stand against the Philistines, putting his life at risk to defend the Promised Land.

Shammah's willingness to die for the sake of the land may properly be understood as a defense of the Israelite faith. According to the Torah, the Lord owned the Promised Land (cf. Lev 25:23; Deut 32:43) and Israelites were its tenants and caretakers; thus to defend the land was to take a stand in behalf of the Lord. Through his valor Shammah was expressing a deep level of faith in Torah promises regarding Israel's right to the land (cf. Gen 12:7; 13:15; 17:8;

---

[46] Youngblood, "1, 2 Samuel," 1087.

[47] 1 Chr 11:11 states that Jashobeam the Tahkemonite, apparently the Chronicler's name for Josheb-Basshebeth the Hacmonite, killed three hundred men. Assuming that both names refer to the same person, the existence of a copyist's error becomes evident. However, it is impossible at this point to determine whether the reading in Samuel or Chronicles preserves the accurate figure.

26:3; 28:13; Exod 33:1; Num 32:11; Deut 1:8; 6:10; 30:20).

The Lord honored Shammah's faith, with the result that Shammah "struck the Philistines down." Though Shammah's sword slew the enemy, in actuality it was the Lord who "brought about a great victory."

23:13–17 During one of David's more difficult encounters with the Philistines—perhaps one from his premonarchical period (cf. 1 Sam 22:1) or, possibly, in the early stages of his reign in Jerusalem (cf. 5:17)—David and a few men were confined to "the cave of Adullam" (v. 13). Their escape was blocked by "a band of Philistines . . . encamped in the Valley of Rephaim." In a move apparently designed to taunt David and motivate him to venture forth from "the stronghold" (v. 13), the Philistines stationed an occupying force "at Bethlehem," David's hometown.

Being trapped in the cave that had no natural water supply, David became thirsty. He openly expressed a desire, perhaps nothing more than a wish—certainly not a command—for someone to fetch him "a drink of water from the cistern near the gate of Bethlehem" (v. 15), more than twelve miles away.

Living up to their reputation for fearless faith—or arrogant courage—"the three mighty men" (v. 16) left David in the care of "three of the thirty chief men" (v. 13) and set out to fulfill their leader's wishes. Somehow they "broke through the Philistine lines," entered the occupied city of Bethlehem, "drew water from the well near the gate," and safely "carried it back to David"—a journey of at least twenty-five miles.

David was overwhelmed by the act of devotion and bravery performed by these three men. Knowing what was involved in their acquisition of the liquid, David did something that initially appears to be absurd or insulting: he "refused to drink it." The gift of water acquired at such great peril represented something so precious that David considered himself unworthy to drink it. In fact, because of "the risk" (v. 17) that the Three took, the Bethlehem waters symbolized "the blood of men who" had literally faced death. Accordingly, David "poured it out before the LORD," giving it there in the cave as an offering to the Lord. This act finds a rough parallel in the unnamed woman's extravagant decanting of perfume on Jesus' body (cf. Mark 14:3–9 and parallels).

23:18–19 An individual who was "held in greater honor than the Three" (v. 19) was "Abishai the brother of Joab son of Zeruiah" (v. 18), David's nephew. Abishai's prestige was based on his heroic exploits on the battlefield. His most outstanding accomplishment was against an unnamed enemy, when he "raised his spear against three hundred men," all of "whom he killed." Elsewhere in Scripture he is credited with numerous other daring and brilliant military activities: he accompanied David on a stealthy foray into Saul's camp (cf. 1 Sam 26:6–12), commanded most of David's forces on an Ammonite campaign (cf. 10:10), led one-third of David's troops against Absalom's rebels (cf. 18:2), was given command of David's troops in quelling Sheba's revolt (cf. 20:6), and killed eighteen thousand Edomites in the Valley of Salt (cf. 1 Chr 18:12). For these reasons he was appointed "commander" (v. 19) of the Three, "even though he was not included among them."

23:20–23 A man of similar military aptitude was "Benaiah son of Jehoiada" (v. 20), the son of a levitical priest (cf. 1 Chr 27:5) from the southern Judahite city of "Kabzeel" (cf. Josh 15:21). A unique display of courage on his part—one to which David could somewhat relate (cf. 1 Sam 17:34–36)—involved going "down into a cistern [NIV, "pit"] on a snowy day" and killing "a lion"; apparently this wild animal had accidentally fallen into an underground tank used for collecting and storing drinking water.

Benaiah's encounters with Israel's enemies included confronting and killing "two of Moab's best men" and striking "down a huge Egyptian" (v. 21). The contest with the Egyptian was particularly memorable, since Benaiah was armed with only "a club" while his massive opponent possessed "a spear in his hand." Since no canonical accounts describe an encounter between Israel and Egypt during David's administration, it is possible the Egyptian was a mercenary soldier fighting with another of Israel's enemies.

Though Benaiah "was not included among the Three" (v. 23), he was "as famous as" they were and "held in greater honor than any of the Thirty." No doubt because of Benaiah's skill and bravery, but perhaps also because of his priestly devotion to the Lord, David "put him in charge of his bodyguard"—the Kerethites and Pelethites (cf. 8:18). David's decision to use a Levite as leader of those most directly responsible for his personal safety is a measure of the degree of cooperation that existed between the king and the priesthood at that time (contrast with Saul, 1 Sam 22:9–19).

23:24–39 At least thirty-one individuals are mentioned in the section that lists "the Thirty"[48] (v. 24)—the actual count depends on how one treats issues present in vv. 32–33.[49] The list begins and ends with individuals known to have

---

[48] N. Na'aman ("The List of David's Officers šālîšîm]," VT 38 [1988]: 71–79) suggests that the term "Thirty" (שָׁלִשִׁים), found in vv. 8,13,19,23–24, should be repointed שְׁלִישִׁם. Such a modification, it is argued, would eliminate most of the semantic and translational issues that are naturally a part of this section.

[49] The MT seems to list thirty-four names, omitting the word בֶּן, from the beginning of v. 33. This omission, and the versification strategy of the passage, suggests that "Jonathan" (v. 32) and "Shammah" (v. 33) were two separate individuals. The number thirty-four is also based on the assumption that "the sons of Jashen" (v. 32) refers to two individuals. If the number "thirty-seven" mentioned in v. 39 refers to the total number of individuals inducted into the Thirty, then the sons of Jashen would have numbered five; alternatively, Joab may be considered as the thirty-seventh individual. Cf. Baldwin, *1 and 2 Samuel*, 294. The NIV appears to have concluded that thirty-seven refers to all David's men listed in chap. 23; thus it lists twenty-nine men by name in vv. 24–39 and seems to assume that the "sons of Jashen" and "the son of Hagri" refer to a total of three people. With these manipulations and assumptions, exactly thirty-seven persons are listed. McCarter assumes the number "thirty" of v. 24 was to control the list of vv. 24–39. Thus he translates the section to have exactly thirty persons (*II Samuel*, 488–89), with the result that fewer than thirty-seven persons are mentioned in the chapter. After discussing options, he concludes that "it is futile to guess" the meaning of the number (*II Samuel*, 499). For further discussion, cf. Youngblood, "1, 2 Samuel," 1091. Any option that takes seriously the numbers thirty and thirty-seven should be given due consideration. Without further evidence no final conclusion is possible in this matter.

died on the battlefield—"Asahel the brother of Joab" (cf. 2:23) and "Uriah the Hittite" (v. 39; cf. 11:17). This suggests that the persons actually designated as the Thirty at any given time varied throughout David's administration.

Asahel's presence on the list, even though he died before David became king of all Israel, indicates that David had organized this special squadron very early in his public career, perhaps even while a fugitive from Saul in the desert.

A study of the cities of origin for these individuals suggests that the majority of the Thirty—perhaps all but twelve[50]—were Judahites. This is not surprising, considering David's own tribal affiliation and the tensions that existed between Judah and the other tribes. Of the non-Judahite Israelites among the Thirty, at least three came from the tribe of Benjamin—"Abiezer from Anathoth" (v. 27), "Ithai son of Ribai from Gibeah in Benjamin" (v. 29), and "Naharai the Beerothite" (v. 37). Two others may have come from Manasseh—"Shammah the Harodite" and "Elika the Harodite" (v. 25), and another two from Ephraim— "Benaiah the Pirathonite" and "Hiddai from the ravines of Gaash" (v. 30). "Eliphelet son of Ahasbai the Maacathite" (v. 34) may have come from the tribal territory of Dan (cf. 20:14). "The son of the Gadite" (v. 36; NIV, "the son of Hagri") may have come from the tribe of Gad.

Three of the non-Judahites—"Igal son of Nathan from Zobah" (v. 36), "Zelek the Ammonite" (v. 37), and "Uriah the Hittite" (v. 39) apparently were foreigners. If "Eliphelet son of Ahasbai" (v. 34) was not a Danite, then he must have come from the city-state of Maacah. If David founded the Thirty during his fugitive period, then it is possible that some of these individuals—perhaps the foreigners—were runaway slaves or debtors (cf. 1 Sam 22:2).

The issue of the ethnic and tribal composition of the Thirty is made more complex by the fact that at least three of the cities—Barhum (v. 31), Shaalbon (v. 32), and Harar (vv. 33–34)—are not mentioned elsewhere in the Old Testament. Complicating the picture still further is the fact that more than one "Carmel" (v. 35) is mentioned in the Bible, one within Judah (cf. Josh 15:55) and the other in Manasseh (cf. 1 Kgs 18:19)—and, as mentioned earlier, more than one Maacah (cf. 10:8; 20:14).

What is the practical value of having this list in Scripture? It demonstrates David's willingness to reward those under his command when they performed their tasks with excellence. Thus it reflects David's great skill in relationships and suggests a model to be emulated by godly leaders of all generations.

6. David Stops a Divinely Sent Plague (24:1–25)

[1]Again the anger of the LORD burned against Israel, and he incited David against them, saying, "Go and take a census of Israel and Judah."

---

[50] Shammah, Elika, Abiezer, Ithai son of Ribai, Benaiah, Hiddai, Eliphelet, Igal son of Nathan, and Zelek, Naharai, Uriah, and the son of the Gadite.

²So the king said to Joab and the army commanders with him, "Go throughout the tribes of Israel from Dan to Beersheba and enroll the fighting men, so that I may know how many there are."

³But Joab replied to the king, "May the LORD your God multiply the troops a hundred times over, and may the eyes of my lord the king see it. But why does my lord the king want to do such a thing?"

⁴The king's word, however, overruled Joab and the army commanders; so they left the presence of the king to enroll the fighting men of Israel.

⁵After crossing the Jordan, they camped near Aroer, south of the town in the gorge, and then went through Gad and on to Jazer. ⁶They went to Gilead and the region of Tahtim Hodshi, and on to Dan Jaan and around toward Sidon. ⁷Then they went toward the fortress of Tyre and all the towns of the Hivites and Canaanites. Finally, they went on to Beersheba in the Negev of Judah.

⁸After they had gone through the entire land, they came back to Jerusalem at the end of nine months and twenty days.

⁹Joab reported the number of the fighting men to the king: In Israel there were eight hundred thousand able-bodied men who could handle a sword, and in Judah five hundred thousand.

¹⁰David was conscience-stricken after he had counted the fighting men, and he said to the LORD, "I have sinned greatly in what I have done. Now, O LORD, I beg you, take away the guilt of your servant. I have done a very foolish thing."

¹¹Before David got up the next morning, the word of the LORD had come to Gad the prophet, David's seer: ¹²"Go and tell David, 'This is what the LORD says: I am giving you three options. Choose one of them for me to carry out against you.'"

¹³So Gad went to David and said to him, "Shall there come upon you three years of famine in your land? Or three months of fleeing from your enemies while they pursue you? Or three days of plague in your land? Now then, think it over and decide how I should answer the one who sent me."

¹⁴David said to Gad, "I am in deep distress. Let us fall into the hands of the LORD, for his mercy is great; but do not let me fall into the hands of men."

¹⁵So the LORD sent a plague on Israel from that morning until the end of the time designated, and seventy thousand of the people from Dan to Beersheba died. ¹⁶When the angel stretched out his hand to destroy Jerusalem, the LORD was grieved because of the calamity and said to the angel who was afflicting the people, "Enough! Withdraw your hand." The angel of the LORD was then at the threshing floor of Araunah the Jebusite.

¹⁷When David saw the angel who was striking down the people, he said to the LORD, "I am the one who has sinned and done wrong. These are but sheep. What have they done? Let your hand fall upon me and my family."

¹⁸On that day Gad went to David and said to him, "Go up and build an altar to the LORD on the threshing floor of Araunah the Jebusite." ¹⁹So David went up, as the LORD had commanded through Gad. ²⁰When Araunah looked and saw the king and his men coming toward him, he went out and bowed down before the king with his face to the ground.

²¹Araunah said, "Why has my lord the king come to his servant?"

"To buy your threshing floor," David answered, "so I can build an altar to the LORD, that the plague on the people may be stopped."

²²Araunah said to David, "Let my lord the king take whatever pleases him and offer it up. Here are oxen for the burnt offering, and here are threshing sledges and ox yokes for the wood. ²³O king, Araunah gives all this to the king." Araunah also said to him, "May the LORD your God accept you."

²⁴But the king replied to Araunah, "No, I insist on paying you for it. I will not sacrifice to the LORD my God burnt offerings that cost me nothing."

So David bought the threshing floor and the oxen and paid fifty shekels of silver for them. ²⁵David built an altar to the LORD there and sacrificed burnt offerings and fellowship offerings. Then the LORD answered prayer in behalf of the land, and the plague on Israel was stopped.

This chapter serves as the counterpart to 21:1–14 within the chiastic structure of the Samuel aside. In both sections David is portrayed as the person responsible for halting disasters brought about by the foolish actions of Israelite kings.[51] In both cases it is David's pursuit of the Lord's will—David acting as the man after the Lord's heart—that saves the nation. By this the author demonstrates the necessity of having leaders obedient and sensitive to the Lord.

This concluding chapter also serves as a fitting climax to 1, 2 Samuel, for it simultaneously links David with the best of Israel's past and the glory of their future. By sacrificing burnt offerings provided for him in the very area where Abraham had once done the same (cf. Gen 22:13; cf. 1 Chr 3:1), David's life and ministry become identified with the greatest of the Torah patriarchs. By acting as an intercessor to bring a divinely sent plague to a halt, as Aaron once did (Num 16:47–49), he assumes the status of a priest and thus foreshadows the priestly actions of Jesus, the ultimate Davidic priest. By acquiring the site of the Lord's temple for Israel, David also lays the groundwork for the most celebrated material aspect of Israelite religion.

24:1–4 "Again" (v. 1), that is, sometime after the events of 21:1–14, "the anger of the LORD burned against Israel." The reason for the Lord's wrath is not stated, but as on previous occasions,[52] it must have stemmed from Israel's violation of some aspect of the Torah.

In order to bring judgment against Israel, the Lord "incited David" to "take a census of Israel and Judah." The writer's attribution of the action to the Lord is not contradictory to 1 Chr 21:1; it reflects his understanding that Yahweh is

---

[51] McCarter likewise understands that here "David was presented not as a king who had brought grief to the people but, on the contrary, as a king who saved them from grief" (*II Samuel,* 518).

[52] E.g., Saul's sin against the Gibeonites (21:2). In that instance Saul had violated the Torah's requirements regarding oath taking (cf. Num 30:2). Numerous examples are presented in the Torah depicting the Lord bringing terrible judgment against people for sins committed: e.g., Adam and Eve (Gen 3:14–24); humanity in the days of Noah (Gen 6:13); and rebellious Israelites in the desert (Num 16:46).

Lord of the universe, exercising dominion over all powers and authorities, whether in heaven or on earth (cf. Ps 97:9; Eph 1:20). From this position of utmost strength the Lord apportions power to lesser beings to be used in enforcing the moral aspects of the created order. The Bible teaches that God empowers even destructive beings—whether superhuman (cf. 1 Kgs 22:19–23; 2 Thess 2:11) or human (cf. Judg 1:14; Hab 1:6; Acts 4:28)—in limited ways to bring judgment and, ultimately, redemption. In the present case the Lord used both superhuman and human beings to enforce the moral order, enabling Satan to entice David to act foolishly so as to bring judgment on Israel.

The fact that the Lord oversees the entire judgment process is ultimately a comfort to humanity. It means that no malevolent action can occur that is not subject to God's oversight and divinely imposed limitations. It also means that nothing can occur in the universe that God cannot ultimately use for good (cf. Gen 50:20; Acts 2:36; Rom 8:28).

David obeyed the judgment-inciting command and ordered "Joab and the army commanders with him" (v. 2) to "go throughout all the tribes of Israel from Dan to Beersheba" and take a military census. The Torah permitted such censuses but warned that a plague would result if they were not conducted properly (cf. Exod 30:12). Since the Lord explicitly permitted censuses to be taken and even ordered their undertaking in the Torah (cf. Num 1:2; 4:2,22; 26:2), David's sin does not seem to lie in the mere fact that he conducted one.

What then created the problem in this census? It was either David's motivation for the census or the manner in which it was carried out.[53] Perhaps it was undertaken for purposes of self-aggrandizement[54]—David may have wanted to "know how many" Israelite males above the age of twenty there were in Israel in order to be able to boast more accurately. Alternatively, it may be that David did not require all enrolled males to pay the half-shekel ransom required by the Torah (cf. Exod 30:13–16), an oversight guaranteed to bring a plague against Israel.[55] Speaking in favor of this second option is the fact that on a previous occasion, David had failed to enforce Torah regulations for an otherwise permissible action—transporting the ark of the covenant—with disastrous actions (cf. 6:7).

"Joab" (v. 3) was clearly troubled by the king's order and openly questioned

---

[53] Brueggemann suggests a third alternative: "The census ordered by David (which the Lord instigates) is a sin" (*First and Second Samuel*, 351). This position, however, ignores the plain statements of the Torah (Exod 30:12).

[54] Cf. Keil and Delitzsch: "The true kernel of David's sin was to be found, no doubt, in self-exaltation, inasmuch as he sought for the strength and glory of his kingdom in the number of the people and their readiness for war" (*II Samuel*, 502). Gordon accepts this position as well (*I and II Samuel*, 316) as do D. M. Gunn and D. N. Fewell, who suggest the census contained "the potential for military aggrandizement at the expense of trust in the power of YHWH" (*Narrative in the Hebrew Bible* [Oxford: Oxford University Press, 1993], 126).

[55] So Josephus (*Ant.* 7.13.1), McCarter (*II Samuel*, 514), Hertzberg (*I and II Samuel*, 411–12).

it when it came. While expressing the wish that the Lord might "multiply the troops a hundred times over" during David's lifetime, Joab was convinced—perhaps based on the Torah warning (Exod 30:12)—that ascertaining the number of Israelite soldiers would automatically endanger them.

In spite of Joab's public misgivings about the project, "the king's word . . . overruled Joab and the army commanders" (v. 4). Thus David's leading officers set about the daunting task "to enroll the fighting men of Israel."

24:5–8 The census takers made a lengthy counterclockwise loop through all Israelite-controlled territories on both sides of the Jordan River to complete their assignment. The men departed from Jerusalem and went eastward, "crossing the Jordan" (v. 5). They then proceeded to the southern extremity of Israelite possessions east of the Jordan, camping some fourteen miles east of the Dead Sea "near Aroer" (modern 'Ara`ir). After gathering their data in that region, "they went" northward through territories allotted to "Gad and on to Jazer," at the border of Ammon. Continuing their northward trek, "they went to Gilead and the region of Tahtim Hodshi" (v. 6),[56] apparently the territory northeast of the Sea of Galilee. From there they went twenty-five or more miles north of the Sea of Galilee "on to Dan Jaan"[57] and then curved westward "toward Sidon" at the northern extreme of Israelite territory. From there they headed southwest to the Mediterranean coast, going "toward the fortress of Tyre" (v. 7). In this region allotted to Asher there were many unconquered towns (cf. Judg 1:31–32) still inhabited by "the Hivites and Canaanites."

Joab and the officers then made their way through the heartlands of the Promised Land moving southward "on to Beersheba in the Negev of Judah," the largest city in the southern regions of Israel. Finally, the census-takers closed the geographical loop by going some forty miles northward "back to Jerusalem" (v. 8).

The information-gathering phase of the census had taken "nine months and twenty days," or 285 days.[58] Since it involved Israel's top military officers, it was likely initiated toward the end of a military campaign season and concluded in the spring, "the time when kings go off to war" (11:1).

24:9–10 In contrast to the census totals of the Torah (cf. Num 2:32; 26:51), the numbers given here appear to have been rounded. Perhaps Joab

---

[56] The NRSV translates the phrase "the region of Tahtim Hodshi" (אֶל אֶרֶץ תַּחְתִּים חָדְשִׁי) as "Kadesh in the land of the Hittites." To do this they followed an ancient textual reconstruction (אֶל אֶרֶץ הַחִתִּים קָדֵשָׁה) first appearing in the Lucianic recension of the LXX. Following P. W. Skehan ("Joab's Census: How Far North [2 Sm 24,6]? *CBQ* 31 [1969]: 42–49); McCarter (*II Samuel*, 502, 504–5) prefers "the region beneath Hermon."

[57] The NRSV follows the LXX in omitting the word "Jaan"; Aharoni and Avi-Yonah (*Macmillan Bible Atlas,* 69) apparently modify the text to translate Jaan as "Ijon."

[58] The reckoning assumes that each "month" was actually 29.5 days in length, the equivalent of one cycle of the moon.

deliberately presented inexact figures to David in hopes of averting a divine judgment against the king and nation. Alternatively, the accurate numbers may have been lost from history (cf. 1 Chr 27:24), with the result that the figures recorded here are approximations handed down to the writer through oral tradition. The census figures in the parallel account of 1 Chr 21:5 are higher—1.1 million for Israel and 470,000 for Judah, a fact that can perhaps be accounted for by understanding the Chronicler's largest figure as including individuals of Judah and the rest of Israel;[59] other differences in the numbers may be related in part to the apparent tendency of 1, 2 Samuel's author to round numbers.

Apart from the tensions that exist between the census figures in Samuel and those in Chronicles, modern biblical commentators almost universally reject the validity of the numbers on the grounds that they are too large.[60] The usual means of adjusting the number downward is to interpret the Hebrew term *ʾelep,* normally rendered "thousand," as a clan-based "military unit" of uncertain number—thus Israel had a total of thirteen hundred military units. While intellectually appealing to minds influenced by modern Western cultural thought, this explanation is unsatisfying since it requires the reader to conclude that Israel's population had shrunk significantly since the days of Moses, when the clearly literal census figure for Israelite fighters was 603,550 (cf. Exod 38:26; Num 2:32).[61]

After David received the reckoning, his "heart struck him" (v. 10; NIV, "was conscience-stricken"). He recognized that the census as he conducted it was in violation of the Lord's will. Wisely, David took responsibility for his transgression and confessed that he had "sinned greatly in what" he had done (cf. Ps 32:1–5). Employing a verb that can denote morally deficient activity (Hb., *sākal;* cf. 1 Sam 13:13), he admitted that in taking the census he had "done a very foolish thing."

24:11–14 The Lord, the Judge of all the earth and Chief Enforcer of Torah judgments (cf. Exod 30:12), heard David's confession and responded "before David got up the next morning" (v. 11). Though David was himself a prophet (cf. Matt 22:43; Mark 12:36; Acts 1:16; 2:30; 4:25; Heb 4:7), the Lord chose not to reveal his word directly to David. Instead, "the word of the LORD" came

---

[59] For a discussion of the differences between the census counts in Samuel and Chronicles, cf. J. A. Thompson, *1, 2 Chronicles,* NAC (Nashville: Broadman & Holman, 1994), 161, n. 54.

[60] Cf. Youngblood ("1, 2 Samuel," 1099), Gordon (*I and II Samuel,* 319, 93); McCarter (*II Samuel,* 510); and Baldwin (*1 and 2 Samuel,* 296). A twentieth-century exception to this is Kirkpatrick, *The Second Book of Samuel,* 226–27.

[61] That census figures given in the Torah must be taken literally is clear from Exod 38:25–26, where it is stated that 100 talents and 1,775 shekels of silver were collected in a census of the adult males eligible for military service. Since each male contributed a half-shekel and each talent consisted of 3,000 shekels, the resulting census count must have been 603,550—a number confirmed in Exod 38:26 and Num 2:32.

"to Gad the prophet, David's seer."

The Lord ordered Gad, David's trusted prophetic advisor since the preregnal days (cf. 1 Sam 22:5), to inform the king that the Lord was giving him "three options" (v. 12) for divine judgment. Each of the three alternatives carried the threat of great disruption and death for Israel, though the length and means of judgment varied considerably. God could use the forces of weather to bring "seven [NIV, "three"][62] years of famine" (v. 13)—he had used a similar form of judgment to punish Saul's sin (cf. 21:1). Alternatively, the Lord could use human instrumentality to bring about "three months of fleeing from your enemies while they pursue you." Finally, the Lord could act apart from famine and sword to bring a third apocalyptic horseman, "three days of plague" (v. 13).

Hearing the gruesome alternatives, David "was in deep distress" (v. 15). Yet he chose to fall back on a timeless principle: trust God to do the right thing (cf. Gen 18:25). He knew from experience that the Lord would be more merciful than any of his enemies, and the king preferred the wounds of a friend (cf. Ps 141:5; Prov 27:6)—especially a divine one—to those of an enemy. David knew from both the Torah (cf. Exod 34:6) and personal experience that the Lord's "mercies are numerous" (NIV, "mercy is great"). After all, he had deserved to die for sins committed against Uriah and Bathsheba; yet the Lord had mercifully commuted his death sentence. Thus David chose a form of punishment that did not require a human intermediary, one that was incidentally the shortest.

24:15–17 Beginning that very morning, "the LORD sent a plague on Israel" (v. 15). Unrelentingly for a period of three days—"until the end of the time designated"—the Lord's divine surrogate, "the angel of the LORD" (v. 16), inflicted the plague on Israel's citizens.[63] In the process "seventy thousand of the people from Dan to Beersheba died."[64]

---

[62] The NIV's decision to employ "three" here is consistent with its tendency to harmonize Scripture whenever possible, even at the expense of long-standing Masoretic traditions. In 1 Chr 21:12 the duration of the famine is listed as "three years"; this number is present in the LXX readings of 2 Sam 24:13 as well. Arguing in favor of the seven-year famine is the fact that all famines—outside of the one mentioned in 21:1—for which a specific length of duration is given, lasted seven years (cf. Gen 41:26,54; 45:6,11; 2 Kgs 8:1–3). This agreement exists for some now inexplicable reason—outside the possible use of numeric symbolism. The three-year figure in 21:1 may have been intended as a subtle expression of David's effective leadership—i.e., because of David's effective leadership the famine lasted less than half as long as would have been expected otherwise. The LXX's and Chronicler's use of "three" here appears to be a well-intended attempt to harmonize the three figures in v. 13.

[63] This is the only narrative passage in the OT where the angel of Yahweh is recorded as bringing an act of judgment against people of the covenant; however, the angel of Yahweh did unsheath his sword against Balaam (Num 22:31) and kill 185,000 Assyrians (2 Kgs 19:35; Isa 37:36). Normally he acts as a benevolent intercessor (Gen 16:7–11; 22:11; 1 Kgs 19:5–6) and messenger (Gen 22:15–18; Judg 2:1–3; 6:11–12; 13:3–21; 2 Kgs 1:3–15).

[64] Youngblood suggests that only "fighting men" died. Disavowing the traditional rendering of אֶלֶף, he also suggests that "seventy military units" were lost to Israel as a result of the plague ("1, 2 Samuel," 1100).

Even more destruction would doubtless have occurred were it not for the Lord's mercy; for "when the angel stretched out his hand to destroy Jerusalem," the Lord ordered him to "withdraw" it.[65] Once again David is seen to have understood the Lord correctly: so real was the Lord's mercy that he was unwilling to pursue the killing further and "was grieved because of the calamity."[66] Perhaps the Lord's mercy had been aroused by David's courageous faith. The king reminded the Lord that it was David himself who had sinned. Therefore, it was most fitting that the Lord's "hand fall upon" David and his family, not on the "sheep"—that is, Israel's citizens.

24:18–23   On that climactic concluding day of the plague, David received instructions from the Lord through the prophet Gad to build an altar on the site where the plague had stopped. The Lord had once ordered Jacob, the founder of the nation of Israel, to build an altar (Gen 35:1); now God ordered David, the founder of the nation of Israel's worship center at Jerusalem, to do the same. The threshing floor, apparently situated at the crest of the plateau on which Jerusalem was resting, would later become the site of the Lord's temple (cf. 1 Chr 22:1).[67]

Obediently, David did "just as the Lord had commanded" (v. 19). The phrase "as the Lord had commanded" is employed fifty-three times in the Torah[68] but only once in all of the Former Prophets. Not surprisingly, perhaps, the majority of the Torah occurrences relate to the establishment of Israelite religion, especially the construction and erection of the tabernacle. The employment of the phrase here thus links David's action with the formation of Israelite worship and suggests an extension of that tradition. This connection is made explicit in 1 Chr 21:29–22:1.

No doubt one reason David came to Araunah—and not vice versa—was that Araunah was prohibited from entering the king's palace (cf. discussion at 5:8), but that did not explain to Araunah why a meeting of the two of them was necessary at all.

David resolved the issue by explaining his intention to purchase Araunah's property for worship. Perhaps Araunah knew that a previous divine judgment against Israel ended with the killing of seven people (cf. 21:6–9). If so, he probably was quite content to give "the king whatever pleases him" (v. 22), includ-

---

[65] Payne asserts that David saw the angel only "in a vision" (*I and II Samuel,* 274). This conclusion cannot be drawn solely on the basis of the facts presented in the text.

[66] Cf. discussion of "grieved" (נחם) at 1 Sam 15:11,29.

[67] K. Rupprecht argues that the site was previously the location of a Jebusite worship site ("Die Zuverlässigkeit der Überlieferung von Salomos Tempelgründung," *ZAW* 89 [1977]: 205–14). The text neither confirms nor denies this possibility.

[68] Exod 7:6,10,20; 12:28,50; 16:34; 34:4; 39:1,5,7,21,26,29,31,43; 40:19,21,23,25 27,29,32; Lev 8:4,9,13,17,21,29; 9:7,10; 10:15; 16:34; 24:23; Num 1:19; 2:33; 3:42,51; 8:3,22; 15:36; 17:11 [Hb., 17:26]; 20:27; 26:4; 27:11,22; 31:7,31,41,47; 36:10; Deut 1:19; 5:32; 34:9.

ing the land, the animals, and even the wood for the fire—as long as he did not have to give up his own life or the lives of any family members. Along with the material aspects, Araunah also offered the king the prayerful wish that "the LORD your God" might "accept you" (v. 23).

24:24–25 Although Araunah's offer probably was sincere, David knew that compensation for land, animals, and goods was a moral necessity in human society (cf. Gen 23:7–16). Thus, he insisted on paying Araunah a fair price for his possessions. Furthermore, David understood the religious imperative of true sacrifice. For him, religion that cost nothing was worth nothing, either to God or humanity. The price David paid for the field was the established value of a large field dedicated to the Lord for one Jubilee cycle (cf. Lev 27:16).

Whether David actually made the offerings himself or had Aaronic priests carry out the task is not clear—presumably it was Aaronic priests (cf. 2 Chr 26:16–21). However, since the king assumed responsibility for the expenses and oversaw the activities, he was credited with them.

In purchasing the land from Araunah and then utilizing it for sacrifice to the Lord, David was apparently following Torah guidelines regarding the dedication of land to the Lord (cf. Lev 27:20–21). When he did this, the land became permanently holy and was set aside in perpetuity for priestly use, a situation completely consistent with the site's subsequent use for the temple of the Lord.

Because of David's decisive and costly actions, "the LORD answered prayer in behalf of the land and the plague on Israel was stopped." In making these sacrifices for his people, David foreshadowed the actions of Jesus, the ultimate son of David, who also gave sacrificially on a hill near Jerusalem for his people so that an even more tragic plague might be stopped. David's climactic sacrifice involved the use of wood and blood on a hill outside the city; so did Jesus' sacrifice. David's sacrifice stopped a physical plague that had taken the lives of many Israelites; by Jesus' wounds the new Israel likewise has "been healed" (1 Pet 2:24) because "he himself bore our sins in his body" (1 Pet 2:24).

Selected Bibliography

Commentaries

Ackroyd, P. R. *The First Book of Samuel.* CBC. Cambridge: University Press, 1971.

Anderson, A. A. *2 Samuel.* WBC. Dallas: Word, 1989.

Baldwin, J. G. *1 and 2 Samuel.* TOTC. Downers Grove: InterVarsity, 1988.

Brueggemann, W. *First and Second Samuel.* IBC. Louisville: John Knox, 1990.

Gordon, R. P. *I and II Samuel.* Grand Rapids: Zondervan, 1986.

Hertzberg, H. W. *I and II Samuel.* OTL. Translated by J. S. Bowden. Philadelphia: Westminster, 1964.

Keil, C. F., and F. Delitzsch. *Biblical Commentary on the Books of Samuel.* Grand Rapids: Eerdmans, 1956.

Kirkpatrick, A. F. *The First Book of Samuel.* CBSC. Cambridge: University Press, 1880.

———. *The Second Book of Samuel.* CBSC. Cambridge: University Press, 1891.

Klein, R. W. *1 Samuel.* WBC. Waco: Word, 1983.

Mauchline, J. *1 and 2 Samuel.* NCB. London: Marshall, Morgan & Scott, 1971.

McCarter, P. K., Jr. *I Samuel: A New Translation with Introduction, Notes and Commentary.* AB. Garden City: Doubleday, 1980.

———. *II Samuel: A New Translation with Introduction, Notes and Commentary.* AB. Garden City: Doubleday, 1984.

McKane, W. *I and II Samuel.* Torch Bible Commentaries. London: SCM, 1963.

Philbeck, B. F., Jr. "Commentary on 1 and 2 Samuel." In BBC. Vol. 3. Edited by C. J. Allen. Nashville: Broadman, 1970.

Smith, H. P. *A Critical and Exegetical Commentary on the Books of Samuel.* ICC. Edinburgh: T & T Clark, 1904.

Vos, H. F. *1, 2 Samuel.* Bible Study Commentary. Grand Rapids: Zondervan, 1983.

Youngblood, R. F. "1, 2 Samuel." In EBC. Vol. 3. Edited by F. E. Gaebelein. Grand Rapids: Zondervan, 1992.

General Works

Aharoni, Y., and M. Avi-Yonah. *The Macmillan Bible Atlas.* Rev. ed. New York: Macmillan, 1977.

Ahlström, G. *The History of Ancient Palestine.* Edited by D. Edelman. Minneapolis: Fortress, 1993.

Archer, G. *A Survey of Old Testament Introduction.* Rev. ed. Chicago: Moody, 1974.

Blaiklock, E. M. and R. K. Harrison, eds. *The New International Dictionary of Biblical Archaeology.* Grand Rapids: Zondervan, 1983.

Bright, J. *A History of Israel.* 3d ed. Philadelphia: Westminster, 1981.

Cate, R. L. *An Introduction to the Historical Books of the Old Testament.* Broadman & Holman, 1994.

de Vaux, R. *Ancient Israel.* 2d ed. 2 vols. Translated by J. McHugh. New York: McGraw-Hill, 1965.

Hill, A. E., and J. H. Walton. *A Survey of the Old Testament.* Grand Rapids: Zondervan, 1991.

Howard, D. M., Jr. *An Introduction to the Old Testament Historical Books.* Chicago: Moody, 1993.

Kenyon, K. M. *The Bible and Recent Archaeology.* Rev. ed. Atlanta: John Knox, 1987.

LaSor, W. S., D. A. Hubbard, and F. W. Bush. *Old Testament Survey: The Message, Form, and Background of the Old Testament.* Grand Rapids: Eerdmans, 1982.

Long, V. P. *The Art of Biblical History.* Grand Rapids: Zondervan, 1994.

Mazar, A. *Archaeology of the Land of the Bible: 10,000–586* B.C.E. New York: Doubleday, 1990.

Miller, J. M., and J. H. Hayes, *A History of Ancient Israel and Judah.* Philadelphia: Westminster, 1986.

Pritchard, J. B., ed. *The Ancient Near East in Pictures Relating to the Old Testament.* 3d ed. Princeton, N.J.: Princeton University Press, 1969.

————, ed. *Ancient Near Eastern Texts Relating to the Old Testament.* 3d ed. Princeton, N. J.: Princeton University Press, 1969.

Waltke, B. K., and O'Connor, M. *An Introduction to Biblical Hebrew Syntax.* Winona Lake: Eisenbrauns, 1990.

Wiseman, D. J., ed. *Peoples of Old Testament Times.* Oxford: Oxford University Press, 1973.

Yadin, Y. *The Art of Biblical Warfare.* New York: McGraw Hill, 1963.

Special Studies

Alter, R. *The Art of Biblical Narrative.* London: George Allen & Unwin, 1981.

Birch, B. C. *The Rise of the Israelite Monarchy: The Growth and Development of I Samuel 7–15.* Missoula, Mont.: Scholars Press, 1976.

Brooke, A. E., N. McLean, and H. Thackeray, eds. *The Old Testament in Greek. Vol II, Part I: I and II Samuel.* Cambridge: University Press, 1927.

Campbell, A. F. *The Ark Narrative (1 Sam 4–6; 2 Sam 6): A Form-critical and*

Traditio-historical Study. Missoula, Mont.: Scholars Press, 1975.

Crockett, W. D. *A Harmony of the Books of Samuel, Kings, and Chronicles.* Grand Rapids: Baker, 1956.

Cross, F. M. *Canaanite Myth and Hebrew Epic.* Cambridge: Harvard University Press, 1973.

Dothan, T. *The Philistines and Their Material Culture.* New Haven/London: Yale University, 1982.

Driver, S. R. *Notes on the Hebrew Text and Topography of the Books of Samuel.* Reprint ed. Winona Lake: Alpha, 1983.

Eslinger, L. M. *Kingship of God in Crisis: A Close Reading of 1 Samuel 1–12.* Sheffield: Almond, 1985.

Fokkelman, J. P. *Narrative Art and Poetry in the Books of Samuel: A Full Interpretation Based on Stylistic and Structural Analysis.* Vol. 1: King David (II Sam 9–20 and I Kings 1–2). Assen: Van Gorcum, 1981.

———. *Narrative Art and Poetry in the Books of Samuel: A Full Interpretation Based on Stylistic and Structural Analysis.* Vol. 2: The Crossing Fates (I Sam 13–31 and II Sam 1). Assen: Van Gorcum, 1986.

Garsiel, M. *The First Book of Samuel: A Literary Study of Comparative Structures, Analogies and Parallels.* Ramat Gan: Revivim, 1983.

Gnuse, R. K. *The Dream Theophany of Samuel: Its Structure in Relation to Ancient Near Eastern Dreams and Its Theological Significance.* Lanham: University Press of America, 1984.

Gros Louis, K. R. R., ed. *Literary Interpretations of Biblical Narratives.* Vol. II. Nashville: Abingdon, 1982.

Gunn, D. M. *The Fate of King Saul.* Sheffield: JSOT, 1980.

———. *The Story of King David.* Sheffield: JSOT, 1982.

Gunn, D. M. and D. N. Fewell. *Narrative in the Hebrew Bible.* Oxford: University Press, 1993.

Halpern, B. *The Constitution of the Monarchy in Israel.* Chico, Cal.: Scholars Press, 1981.

Ishida. T. *Studies in the Period of David and Solomon.* Winona Lake: Eisenbrauns, 1983.

Jobling, D. *The Sense of Biblical Narrative: Three Structural Analyses in the Old Testament (I Samuel 13–31, Numbers 11–12, I Kings 17–18).* Sheffield: JSOT, 1978.

———. *The Reign and Rejection of King Saul.* Atlanta: Scholars Press, 1989.

Miscall, P. *1 Samuel: A Literary Reading.* Bloomington: Indiana University Press, 1986.

———. *The Workings of Old Testament Narrative.* Chico: Scholars, 1983.

Pisano, S. *Additions or Omissions in the Books of Samuel.* Göttingen: Vandenhoeck & Ruprecht, 1984.

Polzin, R. *Samuel and the Deuteronomist.* New York: Harper & Row, 1989.

Rost, L. *The Succession to the Throne of Israel of David.* Translated by M. D. Rutter and D. M. Gunn. Sheffield: Almond, 1982.

Shiloh, Y. *Excavations at the City of David 1978–1982.* Qedem Monograph. Jerusalem: Hebrew University, 1984.

Sternberg, M. *The Poetics of Biblical Narrative.* Bloomington: Indiana University Press, 1985.

Stuart, D. *Studies in Early Hebrew Meter.* HSM 13. Missoula, Mont.: Scholars Press, 1976.

Ulrich, E. *The Qumran Text of Samuel and Josephus.* Missoula, Mont.: Scholars Press, 1978.

Whybray, R. N. *The Succession Narrative: A Study of II Samuel 9–20; I Kings 1 and 2.* Naperville, Ill.: Alec R. Allenson, 1968.

Yadin, Y., ed. *Jerusalem Revealed: Archaeology in the Holy City 1968–1974.* New Haven: Yale University Press, 1976.

Selected Articles

Armerding, C. E. "Were David's Sons Really Priests?" In *Current Issues in Biblical and Patristic Interpretation: Studies in Honor of Merrill C. Tenney.* Edited by G. F. Hawthorne. 75–86. Grand Rapids: Eerdmans, 1975.

Arnold, B. "The Amalekite's Report of Saul's Death: Political Intrigue or Incompatible Sources?" *JETS* 32 (1989): 289–98.

Bergen, R. D. "Evil Spirits and Eccentric Grammar: A Study of the Relationship between Text and Meaning in Hebrew Narrative." In *Biblical Hebrew and Discourse Linguistics.* Edited by R. D. Bergen. 320–35. Dallas: SIL, 1994.

Brueggemann, W. "I Samuel 1: A Sense of Beginning." *ZAW* 102 (1990): 33–48.

Culpepper, R. A. "Narrative Criticism as a Tool for Proclamation: 1 Samuel 13." *RevExp* 84 (1987): 33–40.

DeVries, S. J. "David's Victory over the Philistines as Saga and as Legend." *JBL* 92 (1973): 23–36.

Dumbrell, W. J. "The Davidic Covenant." *RTR* 39 (1980): 40–47.

———. "The Content and Significance of the Books of Samuel: Their Place and Purpose within the Former Prophets." *JETS* 33 (1990): 49–62.

Eslinger, L. "Viewpoints and Points of View in 1 Samuel 8–12." *JSOT* 26 (1983): 61–76.

Figart, T. "Saul, the Spiritist, and Samuel." *GTJ* 11 (1970): 13–29.

Garsiel, M. "The Story of David and Bathsheba: A Different Approach." *CBQ* 55 (1993): 244–62.

Gordon, R. "David's Rise and Saul's Demise: Narrative Analogy in 1 Sam 24–26." *TynBul* 31 (1980): 37–64.

Greenhow, S. "Did Samuel Sin?" *GTJ* 11 (1970): 34–40.

Howard, D. M., Jr. "The Transfer of Power from Saul to David in 1 Sam 16:13–14." *JETS* 32 (1989): 473–83.

Kidner, D. "Old Testament Perspectives on War." *EvQ* 57 (1985): 99–113.

Kleven, T. "Hebrew Style in 2 Samuel 6." *JETS* 35 (1992): 299–314.

Lawton, R. "Saul, Jonathan and the 'Son of Jesse.'" *JSOT* 58 (1993): 35–46.

Lemche, N. P. "David's Rise." *JSOT* 10 (1978): 2–25.

Martin, J. "Studies in 1 and 2 Samuel, Part 1—The Structure of 1 and 2 Samuel." *BibSac* 141 (1984): 28–42.

———. "Studies in 1 and 2 Samuel, Part 2: The Literary Quality of 1 and 2 Samuel." *BibSac* 141 (1984): 131–45.

———. "Studies in 1 and 2 Samuel, Part 3: The Text of Samuel." *BibSac* 141 (1984): 209–22.

McCarter, P. K., Jr. "The Apology of David." *JBL* 99 (1980): 489–504.

McCarthy, D. J. "II Samuel 7 and the Structure of the Deuteronomic History." *JBL* 84 (1965): 131–38.

Neiderhiser, E. A. "2 Samuel 20:8–10: A Note for a Commentary." *JETS* 24 (1981): 209–10.

Satterthwaite, P. E. "David in the Books of Samuel: A Messianic Expectation?" In *The Lord's Anointed: Interpretation of Old Testament Messsianic Texts,* 41–65. Edited by P. E. Satterthwaite, R. S. Hess, and G. J. Wenham. Carlisle: Paternoster, 1995.

Smothers, T. G. "Historical Criticism as a Tool for Proclamation." *RevExp* 84 (1987): 23–32.

Tov, E. "The David and Goliath Saga." *BibRev* 2 (1986): 34–41.

Wenham, G. J. "Were David's Sons Priests?" *ZAW* 87 (1975): 79–82.

Willis, J. T. "An Anti-Elide Narrative Tradition from a Prophetic Circle at the Ramah Sanctuary." *JBL* 90 (1970): 288–308.

———. "The Function of Comprehensive Anticipatory Redactional Joints in I Samuel 16–18." *ZAW* 85 (1973): 294–314.

———. "The Song of Hannah and Psalm 113." *CBQ* 35 (1973): 139–54.

Selected Subject Index

Person Index

Selected Scripture Index